I0815919

Lee Besieged

GRANT'S SECOND PETERSBURG OFFENSIVE,

JUNE 18–JULY 1, 1864

JOHN HORN

SB
Savas Beatie
California

First edition, first printing

ISBN-13: 978-1-61121-738-4 (hardcover)
ISBN-13: 978-1-61121-739-1 (ebook)

Names: Horn, John, 1951- author.
Title: Lee besieged : Grant's Second Petersburg Offensive, June 18-July 1, 1864 / by John Horn.
Other titles: Grant's second Petersburg offensive, June 18-July 1, 1864
Description: El Dorado Hills, CA : Savas Beatie LLC, 2025. | Includes bibliographical references and index. | Summary: "The nine-month siege of Petersburg was the longest continuous operation of the Civil War. Large-scale Union "offensives"-grand maneuvers that triggered some of the large-scale battles-broke the monotony of siege warfare. This is tactical battle action at is finest. Horn's explanation for the context and consequences of every decision is grounded in hundreds of primary sources and supported by 40 original maps. This is the first full-length book to put Grant's second effort into its proper perspective-not only in the context of Petersburg's siege and the Civil War, but in the context of warfare's history"-- Provided by publisher.
Identifiers: LCCN 2024056369 | ISBN 9781611217384 (hardcover) | ISBN 9781611217391 (ebook)
Subjects: LCSH: Petersburg (Va.)--History--Siege, 1864-1865. | Grant, Ulysses S. (Ulysses Simpson), 1822-1885--Military leadership.
Classification: LCC E476.93 .H677 2025 | DDC 973.7/37--dc23/eng/20250111
LC record available at https://lccn.loc.gov/2024056369

Savas Beatie
989 Governor Drive, Suite 102
El Dorado Hills, CA 95762
916-941-6896 / sales@savasbeatie.com / www.savasbeatie.com

Printed and bound in the United Kingdom

In memory of my parents, John and Ann Horn

"A general who fears failure should never take the field,
for fear in itself is the foundation of failure."

J. F. C. Fuller, *The Generalship of Ulysses S. Grant*

TABLE OF CONTENTS

LIST OF MAPS

LIST OF MAPS (continued)

LIST OF ILLUSTRATIONS

LIST OF ILLUSTRATIONS (continued)

LIST OF ABBREVIATIONS

ADAH	Alabama Department of Archives and History
ACWM	American Civil War Museum
AHEC	United States Army Heritage and Education Center
B&L	*Battles and Leaders of the Civil War*
CSR	Compiled Service Record
CV	*Confederate Veteran*
FNBP	Fredericksburg and Spotsylvania National Battlefield Park
GDAH	Georgia Department of Archives and History
GNBP	Gettysburg National Battlefield Park
LOC	Library of Congress
LV	Library of Virginia
MHSM	*Papers of the Military Historical Society of Massachusetts*
NA	National Archives
RG	Record Group
SHC	Southern Historical Collection
SHSP	*Southern Historical Society Papers*
VHS	Vermont Historical Society
VMHC	Virginia Museum of History and Culture

Acknowledgments

I AM particularly grateful for help from my publisher, Theodore Savas, Esq., for persuading me to expand this book beyond the battle of Jerusalem Plank Road to include the Wilson-Kautz Raid because together they prove far more dramatic than separately; to the late Richard J. Sommers, who helped define the scope of the book; to Hampton Newsome, Esq., for reading my first draft and making very helpful observations and suggestions; to Bryce A. Suderow, with his general knowledge of the Petersburg siege and his excellent research; to Hal Jespersen, who patiently drew the 40 maps for the book; to the late Donald Richard Lauter, with his knowledge of the Jerusalem Plank Road battlefield and Winslow Homer; to Alfred C. Young, III, for sharing his knowledge of Confederate casualties; to Greg Eanes, for his helpful book on the Wilson-Kautz Raid; to Dr. David Faris Cross, for his helpful book on the ordeal of the Vermont Brigade on June 23, 1864; to Wilson Greene, for sharing his research into June 22, 1864, and for his reading and correcting of my final draft; to Gerry Netherland of the Petersburg Battlefield Foundation, for his reading and criticism of the final draft; to Sean Chick, who read and commented on the manuscript; to George Fickett, also of the Petersburg Battlefield Foundation, who conducted me on a tour of the Jerusalem Plank Road and Reams Station battlefields; to Keith Poulter, editor of *North & South Magazine*, for his reading and criticism of my final draft; to editor David Snyder, who added significantly to the value of my text with criticism and suggestions; to Lee Meredith, for indexing my third book in a row; and, last but not least, to production manager Veronica Kane, for her skillful placement of maps and images.

Criticism usually helps more than praise.

I am also grateful for the help of my law office staff, the staff at Savas Beatie, the staffs at Petersburg, Fredericksburg, and Richmond National Battlefield parks, the staff at Eastern Carolina University, Bruce Allardice, Denise Arcure, Rachel Ariel, Elizabeth Dunn, Valerie Gillispie, Brooke Guthrie, Roger Pena, Cristian Perez, and Neal Z. Shipe of the David M. Rubinstein Rare Book and Manuscript Library at Duke University, Todd Berkoff, David L. Bright, M. Chris Bryan, Thomas Burgess, Jacqui Celecia of the University of North Carolina at Charlotte, Ronald S. Coddington, Kate Collins, Sierra Dixon of the Connecticut Historical Society, Nancy Dupree at the Alabama Department of Archives and History, Greg Eanes, Bobby Edwards, Jim Epperson, Diane Fishburn, Victoria Garnett, Digital Collections Assistant at the Library of Virginia, Hope Ketcham Geeting, James A. Goecker, Matthew E. Guillen of the Virginia Historical Society, my brother Charles Horn, my son John M. Horn, Nigel Lambert, Marlea D. Leljedal of the United States Army Heritage and Education Center, David Lowe, William Marvel, Sharon MacDonald, Patricia A. Millican of the Rome-Floyd (GA) County Library, Allen Ottens, Ralph Peters, Nathan Provost, Dennis Rasbach, Kevin Ray at the William Stanley Hoole Special Collections Library at the University of Alabama, Chamisa Redmond at the Library of Congress Duplication Services, Julia Steele, DeWitt Stone, Terri Stout-Stevens, Marjorie J. Strong, Assistant Librarian at the Vermont Historical Society, Noah Andre Trudeau, Matthew Turi of the Southern Historical Society at the University of North Carolina at Chapel Hill, Ashley Webb of the History Museum of Western Virginia, David White, Kerrie Cotten Williams, Head of Reference and Reader Services, Manuscript Division, Library of Congress, Lamar Williams, Kerri Cotton Williams of the Library of Congress, and Scott Williams, GIS Analyst, Chesterfield County Environmental Engineering.

Introduction

WHEN LT. GEN. Ulysses S. Grant's first offensive against Petersburg ended in failure to take the city, he did not fear to fail again but launched a series of initiatives that within 48 hours began his second offensive against Petersburg. Capturing the city would practically force his opponent, Gen. Robert E. Lee, to abandon Richmond, the Confederate capital, and might well end the Civil War before the critical November presidential election.

Grant ordered a cavalry raid against the railroads supplying Petersburg and Richmond. He summoned his heavy artillery to interdict Petersburg's bridges. He directed the establishment of a bridgehead on the north bank of James River that would allow him to shift from threatening Petersburg to menacing Richmond. He attempted to invest Petersburg from the Appomattox River below the city to the Appomattox above. His soldiers took the initiative themselves as a regiment of miners determined to tunnel under an enemy salient facing them and blow it up.

Grant's foes launched their own initiatives. They tried to drive the United States Navy from Trent's Reach in James River. They repeatedly counterattacked Grant's advancing infantry and attempted to recapture the ground lost to him during his first offensive. They laid a trap for his cavalry raiders, trying to capture them. The Secessionists strained to repair as quickly as possible the damage the raiders caused to the railroads supplying Petersburg and Richmond.

This book describes the progress of Grant's initiatives during his second offensive, the response of the Southerners to those initiatives, and the progress of the Rebels' own initiatives. Some initiatives set the parameters for the siege of Petersburg—one of the longest and bloodiest in the history of the western hemisphere. Others ended in disaster. Which initiatives of either side most influenced the siege will spring some surprises.

This book provides the most detailed account yet of the campaign of 1864 in southeastern Virginia from the end of Grant's first offensive against Petersburg on June 18 until July 1, the termination of his second—the farthest flung and one of the longest and most dramatic of his nine offensives against the city between June 15, 1864, and April 2, 1865. The text draws on eyewitness accounts of participants on both sides, statistically analyzes the offensive's results, assesses the significance of the battles, and measures the effectiveness of the officers and men of both sides. The battle of Jerusalem Plank Road, the Wilson-Kautz Raid, and the relationship between the two form the book's heart. Each side had some of its best laid plans go awry.

Chapter One

"We Will Try to Gain Advantages Without Assaulting Fortifications"

EVEN BEFORE Grant's first offensive against Petersburg ended, he began planning another and launched it while the wounded from the first were still suffering and dying on the battlefield. Having failed to storm Petersburg, he would now lay siege to the city.

* * *

By the spring of 1864, the American Civil War was entering its fourth year. The combatants knew that the 1864 campaign would decide the fate of the United States of America. Either the Federals would make enough progress to persuade Northern voters to re-elect President Abraham Lincoln, a Republican who would continue to pursue victory, or those voters would probably elect a Democrat running on a peace platform that would doom the Union.[1]

Lincoln summoned from the west his best general, then Major General Grant, captor of Fort Donelson, victor of Shiloh, captor of Vicksburg, and savior of Chattanooga. The president promoted Grant to lieutenant general so that he would outrank all other active Northern generals, and put him in charge of the armies of the United States in the hope that he would produce a victory on the national scale as he had in the war's western theater.

Grant took command fresh from his experience as commander in the west, where in November 1863 he had led Federal forces to the relief of Chattanooga.

1 Abraham Lincoln, "Blind Memorandum," Aug. 23, 1864, Abraham Lincoln Papers, Manuscript Division, LOC, Washington, D.C.

He had seen how, after the Federal Army of the Cumberland captured Chattanooga from the Confederate Army of Tennessee, the Secessionists employed their interior lines to reinforce their Army of Tennessee from their Army of Northern Virginia because the latter army was under insufficient pressure from its foe, the Union's Army of the Potomac. The reinforced Army of Tennessee had then defeated the Army of the Cumberland at Chickamauga and besieged it in Chattanooga until Grant's forces came to its rescue.

The general-in-chief determined that a disaster such as Chickamauga must not reoccur. He decided that the armies of the United States would no longer act "separately and independently of each other, giving the enemy opportunities of depleting one command, not pressed, to reinforce another more actively engaged." He planned "to concentrate all the force possible against the Confederate armies in the field" and accordingly "arranged for a simultaneous movement all along the line."[2]

His troops would prevent incursions into the northern states as effectively by advancing as by remaining still and, Grant wrote, "would compel the enemy to keep detachments to hold them back, or else lay his own territory open to invasion."

This feature appealed to Lincoln.

"Oh, yes! I see that," the president declared. "As we say out West, if a man can't skin he must hold a leg while someone else skins."[3]

Grant directed the Army of the James under Maj. Gen. Benjamin F. Butler to land on the south side of James River and operate against Richmond. The general-in-chief would remain with the Army of the Potomac to move across the Rapidan River against the Army of Northern Virginia. He intended for an army group under Maj. Gen. William Tecumseh Sherman to advance toward Atlanta and break up the Army of Tennessee. A pair of smaller columns would also attack. One, under Maj. Gen. Franz Sigel, would march up the Shenandoah Valley and cut the Virginia Central Railroad. The other, led by Brig. Gen. George Crook, would strike from West Virginia and sever the Virginia & Tennessee Railroad. Sigel's and Crook's columns would then unite and attack the vital Southern supply center of Lynchburg, Virginia. Grant hoped that Maj. Gen. Nathaniel P. Banks would complete as soon as possible his expedition already in progress against Shreveport, Louisiana, return to Sherman men borrowed from that general, leave small forces to hold the Mississippi and Rio Grande Rivers, and advance against the Confederate port of Mobile, Alabama.

2 Ulysses S. Grant, *Personal Memoirs of U. S. Grant*, 2 vols. (New York, 1886), 2:129–130.

3 Ibid., 143.

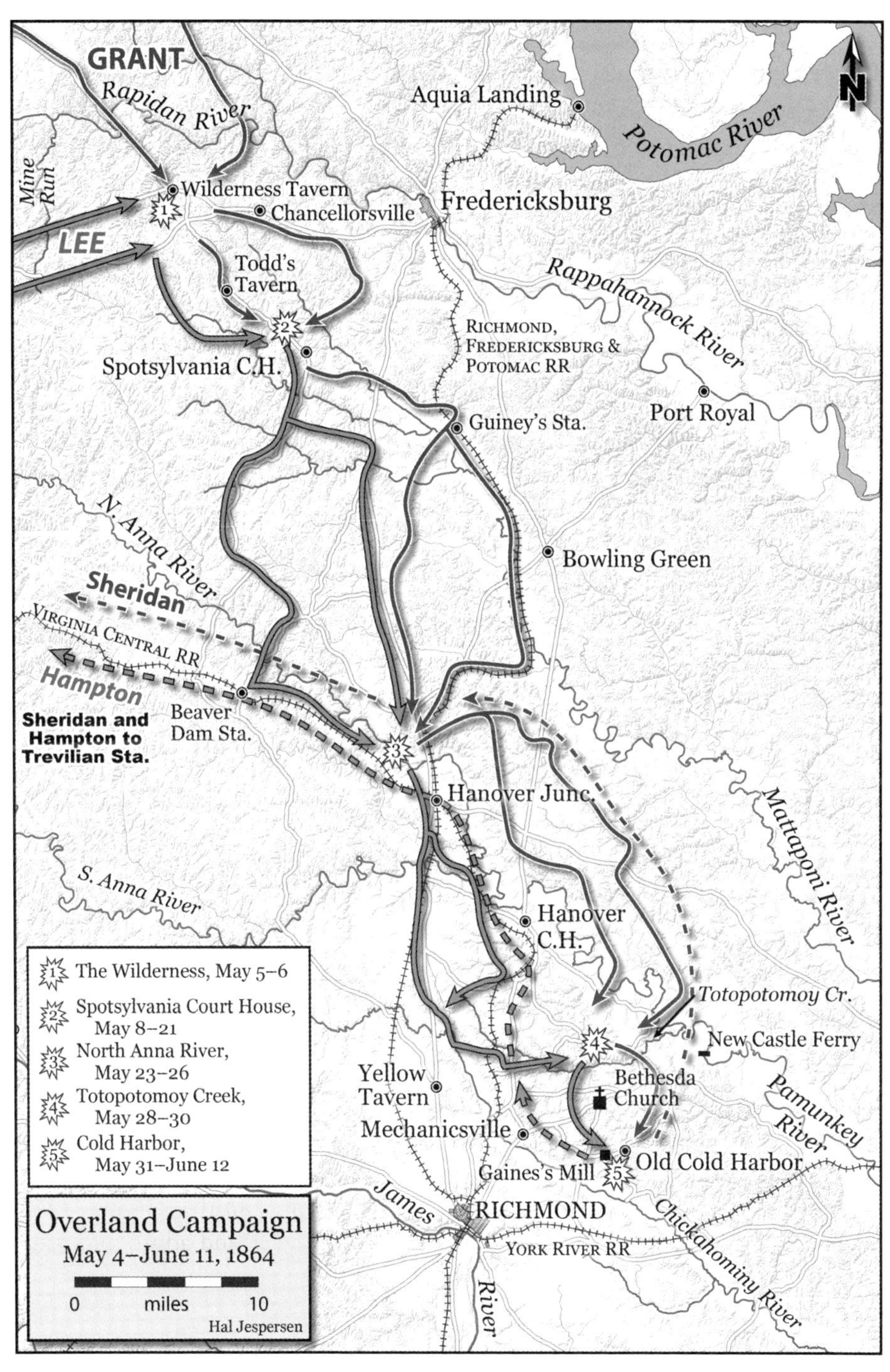
GRANT
Rapidan River
Mine Run
LEE
Aquia Landing
Potomac River
N
Wilderness Tavern
Chancellorsville
Fredericksburg
Todd's Tavern
Rappahannock River
Spotsylvania C.H.
Richmond, Fredericksburg & Potomac RR
Guiney's Sta.
Port Royal
N. Anna River
Bowling Green
Sheridan
Virginia Central RR
Hampton
Beaver Dam Sta.
Sheridan and Hampton to Trevilian Sta.
Hanover Junc.
Mattaponi River
S. Anna River
Hanover C.H.
Totopotomoy Cr.
New Castle Ferry
Bethesda Church
Pamunkey River
Yellow Tavern
Mechanicsville
Old Cold Harbor
Gaines's Mill
James River
RICHMOND
York River RR
Chickahominy River
1 The Wilderness, May 5–6
2 Spotsylvania Court House, May 8–21
3 North Anna River, May 23–26
4 Totopotomoy Creek, May 28–30
5 Cold Harbor, May 31–June 12
Overland Campaign
May 4–June 11, 1864
0 miles 10
Hal Jespersen

The campaign commenced in early May. It did not go according to plan. The Secessionists nearly captured Banks's army and a supporting fleet. Crook's column from West Virginia cut the Virginia & Tennessee but by May 11 began withdrawing on exaggerated reports of gathering opposition. Sigel's force, advancing by way of the Shenandoah Valley, met with defeat at New Market on May 15. Butler failed to take Richmond and by May 20 found himself largely confined to City Point and Bermuda Hundred on the James. Grant and Sherman made substantial progress but did not destroy their respective opposing enemy armies. The general-in-chief reached Cold Harbor, 15 miles from Richmond, about June 1 after fighting bloody battles in the Wilderness and at Spotsylvania Court House but failed to drive the Army of Northern Virginia into the Richmond defenses. Sherman captured Allatoona, more than halfway to Atlanta from his starting point, around June 4.

By that time, some of the other Northern columns were getting a second wind. Sigel's force, now under the command of Maj. Gen. David "Black Dave" Hunter, won a battle at Piedmont on June 5, and severed the Virginia Central at Staunton. Reinforced by Crook and almost 10,000 more men from West Virginia, Hunter headed for Lynchburg by way of Lexington. Butler found a way out of Bermuda Hundred by crossing the Appomattox River on June 9, but his attempt to seize a lightly defended Petersburg failed. Grant decided to cross James River and capture Petersburg, cutting Richmond's connections with the Deep South. To distract Lee, the general-in-chief sent two cavalry divisions under Maj. Gen. Philip Sheridan on June 7 to rip up the Virginia Central northwest of Richmond and possibly link up with Hunter at Lynchburg. Hunter's advance toward Lynchburg pressured Lee on June 12 into ordering Early's Corps to the Shenandoah Valley to destroy Black Dave, then march down the Valley and threaten Washington and Baltimore. Lee hoped such a move would compel Grant "either to weaken himself so much for their protection as to afford us an opportunity to attack him, or that he might be induced to attack us."[4] On the same day, Grant began heading for the James.

Grant's crossing of the James began on June 14 and at first proceeded flawlessly, but the drive on Petersburg broke down. Two army corps arrived at the city's eastern edge on June 15, but only one of them attacked the small Southern garrison, and not until evening. The attackers did not capture the city but only some of its eastern fortifications. Petersburg's fortifications, constructed from 1862 until early 1864 and called the Dimmock Line after Capt. Charles H. Dimmock,

4 United States War Department, *The War of the Rebellion: A Compilation of the Official Records of the Union and Confederate Armies* (*OR*) (Washington, D.C.: U.S. Government Printing Office, 1880–1901), 128 vols., Series I (all will be from Series I unless otherwise specified), vol. 37, pt. 1, p. 346 (*OR* 37, 1:346).

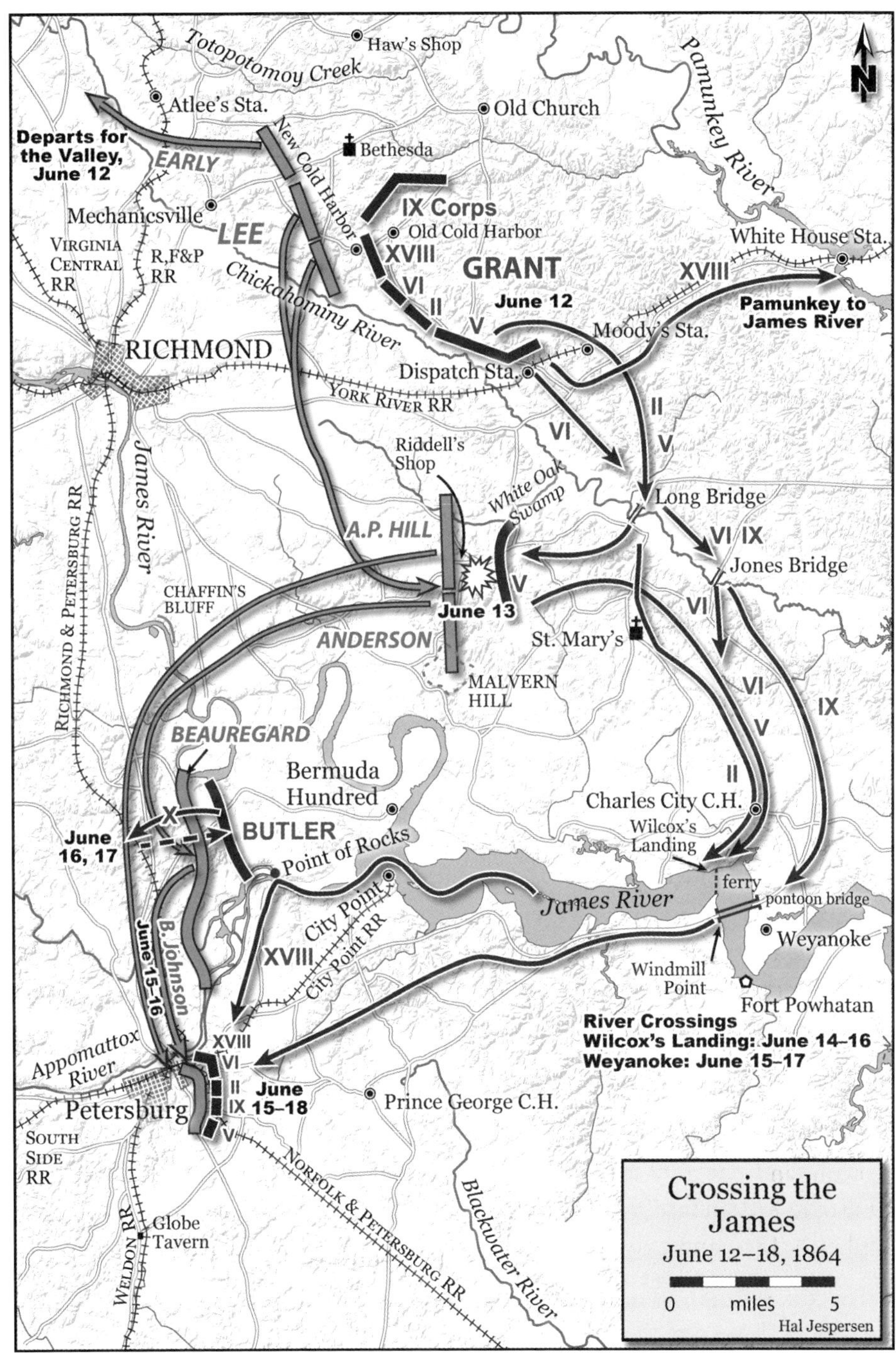
Totopotomoy Creek
Haw's Shop
Pamunkey River
Atlee's Sta.
Old Church
Departs for the Valley, June 12
EARLY
New Cold Harbor
Bethesda
IX Corps
Mechanicsville
LEE
Old Cold Harbor
White House Sta.
Virginia Central RR
R,F&P RR
Chickahominy River
XVIII
VI
II
V
GRANT
June 12
Pamunkey to James River
Moody's Sta.
RICHMOND
Dispatch Sta.
York River RR
Riddell's Shop
White Oak Swamp
Long Bridge
Jones Bridge
James River
Richmond & Petersburg RR
A.P. HILL
June 13
Chaffin's Bluff
ANDERSON
St. Mary's
Malvern Hill
IX
BEAUREGARD
Bermuda Hundred
Charles City C.H.
BUTLER
Wilcox's Landing
June 16, 17
Point of Rocks
ferry
pontoon bridge
City Point
City Point RR
Weyanoke
June 15–16
B. Johnson
Windmill Point
Fort Powhatan
River Crossings
Wilcox's Landing: June 14–16
Weyanoke: June 15–17
Appomattox River
Petersburg
June 15–18
Prince George C.H.
South Side RR
Norfolk & Petersburg RR
Blackwater River
Globe Tavern
Weldon RR
Crossing the James
June 12–18, 1864
0 miles 5
Hal Jespersen

the engineer who had overseen the line's construction, ringed Petersburg for about 10 miles from the Appomattox below the city to the Appomattox above.

Southern reinforcements began arriving at Petersburg that night. To defend the city better, the Confederates pulled out of the Howlett Line holding Butler's troops in Bermuda Hundred, and Butler advanced on June 16 to seize the Richmond & Petersburg Railroad. Assaults that day captured more of Petersburg's eastern fortifications, but not enough to break into the city. Meanwhile the Secessionists from the Howlett Line reinforced the city's defenders. Yet another assault on the morning of June 17 pierced the next Confederate line east of Petersburg. By this time the Army of Northern Virginia was marching toward Petersburg and drove Butler's troops off the Richmond & Petersburg, back into Bermuda Hundred. The Southerners at Petersburg largely plugged the hole in their line by day's end.

The Federals began shelling Petersburg on the night of June 17–18, terrorizing many of the city's inhabitants. "It was a lovely moonlight night, and I had just gone to bed after listening to a band belonging to some brigade encamped across the river, when I heard the sound of heavy firing, and by and bye a shell flew with a whiz over the house and exploded near by," remembered Mrs. Charles E. Waddell, who lived on Bollingbrook Street in the heart of the city. "My heart sank within me!" Praying for the shells to spare her, Mrs. Waddell lay listening to the gunfire and shell bursts until nearly 1:00 a.m. on June 18, when a shell exploded so near that its flash lit her face and a fragment struck her back porch. This terrified her sister, who insisted on going to a neighbor's basement for safety. "Oh, what sad weary hours were those as we lay listening to the fearful sounds that seemed to threaten us every moment with destruction," Mrs. Waddell recalled.[5]

An exodus of Petersburgers began. Mrs. Waddell packed her mother and sister off to Raleigh, North Carolina, in the morning. She felt compelled to remain in Petersburg until she could learn the fate of her husband, Capt. Charles E. Waddell, who served with Lee's army in the Petersburg City Guard, Company A of the 12th Virginia Infantry, called "the Petersburg Regiment" because six of its ten companies hailed from the city.[6] The exodus included people from all walks of life.

5 David Macrae, *The Americans at Home: Pen-and-Ink Sketches of American Men, Manners and Institutions*, 2 vols. (Edinburgh, 1870), 1:170. Macrae identified the author of the diary quoted as "the wife of a captain in Lee's army." Ibid., 167. Macrae also calls her "Mrs. W----." Ibid., 174. The diary quoted is essentially the same as the Mrs. Charles E. Waddell Diary, June 17–19, Papers of Miss Georgia Hicks, Collection of the United Daughters of the Confederacy, North Carolina Division, North Carolina Department of Archives and History, Raleigh, NC.

6 John Horn, *The Petersburg Regiment in the Civil War: A History of the 12th Virginia Infantry from John Brown's Hanging to Appomattox, 1859–1865* (El Dorado Hills, CA, 2019), 16.

"We left Petersburg when de shellin' commenced an' went to Pamplin in box cars, getting out of de way," remembered Fannie Berry, a slave in 1864.[7]

The Army of Northern Virginia began arriving at Petersburg on the morning of June 18 and was reinforcing the troops in the city's defenses as Grant's forces launched a series of increasingly disjointed and unsuccessful frontal attacks. That afternoon, during the Union assaults, the usually audacious Lee declined to strike the vulnerable Federal left despite the urging of Gen. G. T. "Gus" Beauregard, whom Lee succeeded as the principal defender of Petersburg. Lee explained that his men would need rest after their long march from north of the James, and that the best policy lay in remaining on the defensive.[8]

While Grant prepared to authorize an end to four days of bloody assaults on Petersburg, he was already thinking of other ways to capture the city. "If this assault does not carry, we will try to gain advantages without assaulting fortifications," he wrote to Maj. Gen. George Gordon Meade, the West Pointer in command of the Army of the Potomac.[9]

Shortly afterward, the general-in-chief spoke to Col. Horace Porter, a governor's son who served as one of Grant's aides. "Lee's whole army has now arrived, and the topography of the country about Petersburg has been well taken advantage of by the enemy in the location of strong works," the general-in-chief told Porter. "I will make no more assaults on that portion of the line, but will give the men a rest, and then look to extensions to our left, with a view to destroying Lee's communications on the south and confining him to a close siege."[10]

At 10:00 p.m., as Grant sat in his tent at City Point near the confluence of the James and the Appomattox, he accepted that his first offensive against Petersburg

7 "Interview of Mrs. Fannie Berry, Ex-slave 861 E. Bank Street—Petersburg, Virginia, Feb. 26, 1937," 6, in *Slave Narratives, A Folk History of Slavery in the United States From Interviews with Former Slaves: Typewritten Records Prepared by the Federal Writers Project 1936–1938, Assembled by the Library of Congress Project, Works Projects Administration for the District of Columbia Sponsored by the Library of Congress* (Washington, D.C., 1941). Pamplin City straddles the border between Appomattox and Prince Edward counties. appomattoxcountyva.gov. Retrieved Jan. 30, 2024.

8 G. T. Beauregard, "Four Days of Battle at Petersburg," in Robert Underwood Johnson and Clarence Clough Buel, eds., *Battles and Leaders of the Civil War* (*B&L*), 4 vols. (New York, 1884, 1888), 4:544; G. T. Beauregard, "The Battle of Petersburg, Part II," in *North American Review* 145, no. 372 (Nov. 1887), 514–515. Colonel Alfred Roman, aide-de-camp and inspector general to Beauregard, gives a different account involving a more favorable initial reception of Beauregard's idea followed by a rejection because of the obstacles posed by Second Swamp, about six miles south of Petersburg, and the cuts of the Norfolk & Petersburg Railroad. Alfred Roman, *The Military Operations of General Beauregard in the War Between the States 1861 to 1865 with a Brief Personal Sketch and a Narrative of His Services in the War with Mexico 1846–1848*, 2 vols. (New York, 1884), 2:254.

9 *OR* 40, 2:156.

10 Horace Porter, *Campaigning with Grant* (New York, 1906), 210.

had failed. The Cockade City—known as such because of cockades in the hats of a company of soldiers from Petersburg defending Ohio's Fort Meigs during the War of 1812—had withstood the Federal onslaught.

The general-in-chief reacted characteristically. He neither sought scapegoats nor made excuses. He brushed aside his own blunders and those of his subordinates and made his current position the jumping off point for his next effort.

"I am perfectly satisfied that all has been done that could be done, and that the assaults to-day were called for by all the appearances and information that could be obtained," Grant wrote to Meade. "Now we will rest the men and use the spade for their protection until a new vein can be struck." The general-in-chief had more than one new vein in mind. In his next sentence, he revealed one of them, writing, "As soon as Wilson's cavalry is rested we must try and cut the enemy's line of communication."[11]

Grant was referring to Brig. Gen. James H. Wilson's cavalry division of the Army of the Potomac, the only one of that army's three cavalry divisions present outside Petersburg. A West Pointer hailing from Illinois, Wilson had served with distinction on Grant's staff during the Vicksburg campaign. Wilson's cavalry division was pitching camp near Mount Sinai Church on the Blackwater River, southeast of Prince George Court House. The division's horsemen had worn themselves out screening the Army of the Potomac during its crossing of James River.

By partially investing Petersburg for about three miles from the Appomattox on the north to the vicinity of Jerusalem Plank Road on the southwest, Grant was already laying siege to the city. At the same time as he decided to launch Wilson's cavalry division against the enemy's lines of communication, the general-in-chief began laying the foundation to extend his infantry's left westward to sever the roads and railroads running southward and westward from Petersburg, further confining Lee.[12]

Grant directed the taking of defensive measures in case the United States Navy failed to contain the Confederate warships on James River despite the recent sinking of obstacles in Trent's Reach. "In view of a temporary blockade of the river being possible, I think it advisable that supplies in depot should be kept up to full twenty days', besides ten days in wagons and haversacks," he informed Meade.[13] A siege could not succeed without adequate supplies.

11 *OR* 40, 2:157. Grant showed remarkable charity toward the commander of the Army of the Potomac, given that Beauregard thought Meade by extending his left to Jerusalem Plank Road could easily have flanked the Confederates out of Petersburg. Letter, G. T. Beauregard to C. M. Wilcox, June 9, 1874, *MHSM* 5:117–123.

12 Porter, *Campaigning with Grant*, 210.

13 *OR* 40, 2:157.

The depot at City Point—where the Appomattox River flowed into the James—was already growing by leaps and bounds. That day personnel of the United States Military Railroad Construction Corps were rebuilding the City Point Railroad, which ran from City Point to Petersburg, as well as constructing wharves and buildings for the use of Grant's army group in unloading and storing supplies.

The general-in-chief's headquarters at City Point consisted of a few tents for his entourage and himself. Those with Grant at the time included Sylvanus Cadwallader, a Wisconsin reporter who had belonged to the general-in-chief's retinue since late 1862. "My own tent was under the umbrageous branches of a large mulberry tree which afforded protection from the blistering sunshine, until it had to be removed to conform to the general camp arrangement," the scribe recalled.[14] Headquarters took the form of a parallelogram, with the two ends and the north side packed with tents and the south side open. The west end stretched to a bluff overlooking the confluence of the Appomattox and the James. The cavalry escort camp lay behind Grant's headquarters and reached nearly to the bank of the James. Infantry on fatigue duty camped east of headquarters.

Tents, shanties, mess halls, and sutlers soon covered the plateau east of the infantry camp. "The place was beautiful for situation, easily policed and drained," remembered Cadwallader. "The landing on the James below the mouth of the Appomattox . . . presented a scene of indescribable bustle and activity."[15] Vessels and transports which had followed the army with supplies had covered the James since June 17. As the ships unloaded horses, mules, wagons, caissons, limber chests, cannons, railroad trains, rations, clothing, shoes, rifles, ammunition, and every other form of ordnance, warehouses rose and parks expanded to contain their cargoes. City Point would soon grow into one of the largest ports on the continent. Like Sherman, Grant had served as a supply officer earlier in his career.

With the transports came crowds of curious civilians. "They swarmed around the wharves, filled up the narrow avenues at the landing between the six-mule teams which stood there by the acre, plunged frantically across the road in front of your horse wherever you rode, plied everybody with ridiculous questions about 'the military situation,' invaded the privacy of every tent, stood around every mess-table till invited to eat unless driven away, and wandered around at nearly all hours," recalled the newspaperman. They stood in rows just outside the guard-line of headquarters, gawking at Grant and his staff and importuning anyone who

14 Benjamin P. Thomas, ed., *Three Years with Grant as Recalled by War Correspondent Sylvanus Cadwallader* (New York, 1961), 230.

15 Ibid., 230–231.

ventured out of headquarters with questions about the celebrities. "For several days headquarters resembled a menagerie," Cadwallader remembered.[16]

An immense general hospital, amounting to a city in itself, grew near City Point. Hundreds of clean, white hospital tents, with their flaps turned up on account of the warm weather, covered many acres and could hold thousands of patients. The tents stood in regular blocks with broad, clean streets. Fragrant green pine boughs ornamented some of the tents to keep off the hot sun, others with their ends laid all one way carpeted the floors and streets. "After coming from the front one wished he might have a 'flesher,' if for nothing more than to get a change of diet from hard-tack, pork and fresh meat to nice food furnished by the medical department and the goodies from the sanitary commission," recalled Pvt. James Madison Aubery, regimental clerk of the 36th Wisconsin.[17]

In the same missive to Meade of 10:00 p.m. on June 18 in which Grant called for a cavalry raid and directed the taking of defensive supply measures, the general-in-chief alluded to his determination to seize a bridgehead on the north bank of James River. The bridgehead he sought would extend Grant's right across the James and would allow him to communicate rapidly with all parts of his command as he distracted the Confederates by threatening their left. "If nothing occurs to prevent I shall be absent to-morrow from 10 a.m. to about 3 p.m. up the river near the naval fleet," he wrote.[18]

Meade, the commander of the Army of the Potomac and a former civil engineer, anticipated a siege of Petersburg. At 10:00 p.m. on June 18 he informed the general-in-chief that the Army of the Potomac's siege train remained at Washington. It consisted of 40 rifled siege guns, either 4.5-inch siege rifles or 30-pounder Parrott rifles, 10 10-inch mortars, 28 8-inch mortars, 20 Coehorn mortars, six 100-pounder Parrott rifles and the necessary mortar wagons, battery wagons, forges, carriages, platforms, ammunition and miscellaneous articles loaded aboard about a dozen schooners each of around 200 tons' burden. "I think it proper to advise you of this fact, as in case you contemplated using them it would take some time to procure them," Meade wrote to Grant.[19]

* * *

16 Ibid., 231.

17 James M. Aubery, *The Thirty-Sixth Wisconsin Volunteer Infantry, 1st Brigade, 2d Division, 2d Army Corps: An Authentic Record of the Regiment from Its Organization to Its Muster Out* (Milwaukee, 1900), 93.

18 *OR* 40, 2:157.

19 Ibid., 158.

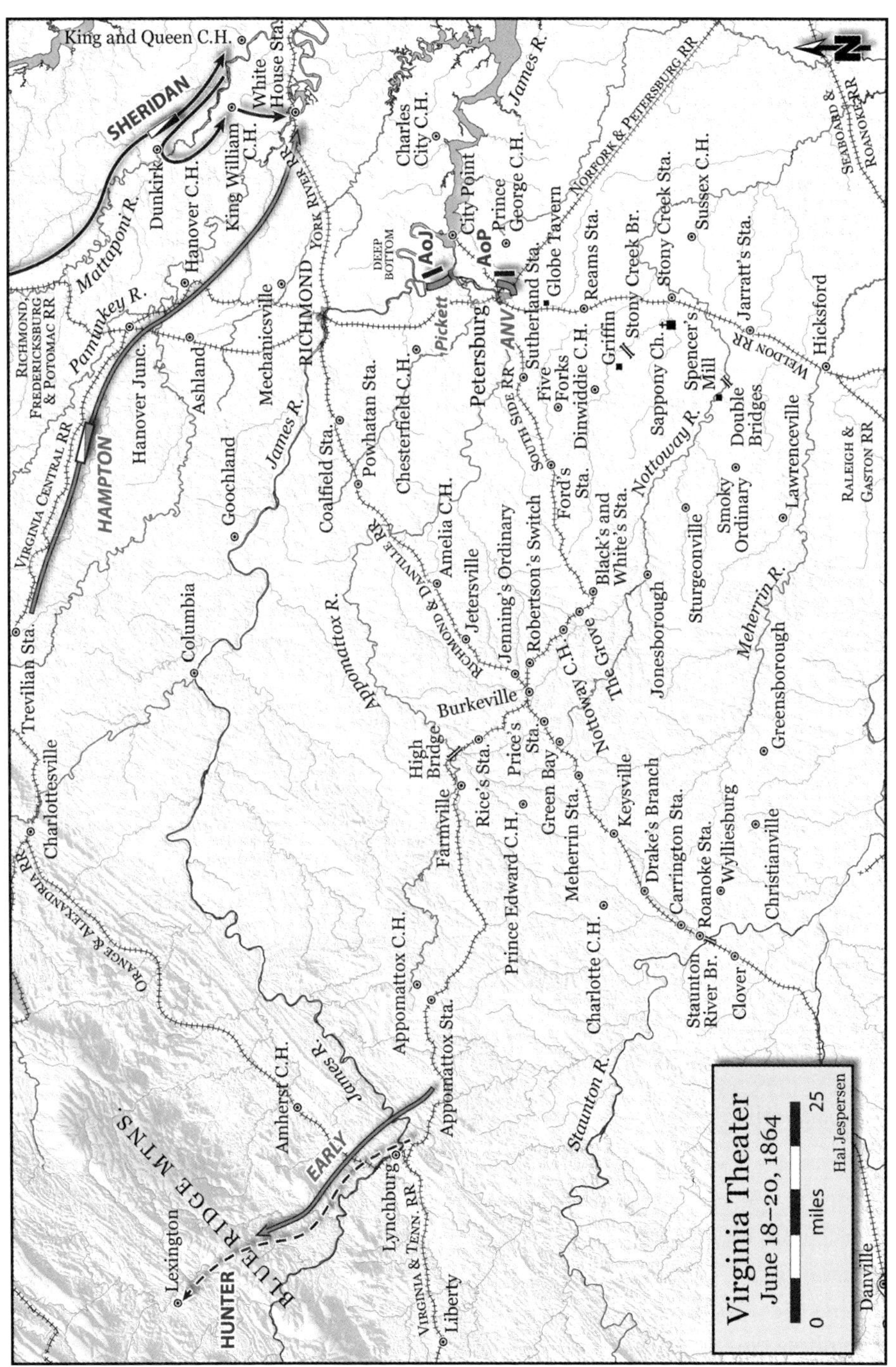
Virginia Theater
June 18–20, 1864
0
miles
25
Hal Jespersen
SHERIDAN
HAMPTON
EARLY
HUNTER
AoJ
AoP
ANV
Pickett
DEEP BOTTOM
RICHMOND
Petersburg
King and Queen C.H.
White House Sta.
King William C.H.
Dunkirk
Hanover C.H.
Hanover Junc.
Ashland
Mechanicsville
Goochland
Columbia
Trevilian Sta.
Charlottesville
Lexington
Lynchburg
Liberty
Amherst C.H.
Appomattox C.H.
Appomattox Sta.
Farmville
High Bridge
Rice's Sta.
Burkeville
Price's Sta.
Prince Edward C.H.
Green Bay
Meherrin Sta.
Keysville
Drake's Branch
Carrington Sta.
Roanoke Sta.
Wylliesburg
Staunton River Br.
Clover
Charlotte C.H.
Christianville
Greensborough
Danville
Nottoway C.H.
The Grove
Jonesborough
Black's and White's Sta.
Robertson's Switch
Jenning's Ordinary
Jetersville
Amelia C.H.
Chesterfield C.H.
Powhatan Sta.
Coalfield Sta.
Ford's Sta.
Five Forks
Dinwiddie C.H.
Sutherland Sta.
Globe Tavern
Reams Sta.
Griffin
Stony Creek Br.
Stony Creek Sta.
Sappony Ch.
Spencer's Mill
Double Bridges
Smoky Ordinary
Sturgeonville
Lawrenceville
Jarratt's Sta.
Sussex C.H.
Hicksford
Prince George C.H.
City Point
Charles City C.H.
BLUE RIDGE MTNS.
James R.
Appomattox R.
Nottoway R.
Meherrin R.
Staunton R.
Mattaponi R.
Pamunkey R.
RICHMOND, FREDERICKSBURG & POTOMAC RR
VIRGINIA CENTRAL RR
ORANGE & ALEXANDRIA RR
VIRGINIA & TENN. RR
RICHMOND & DANVILLE RR
SOUTH SIDE RR
WELDON RR
NORFOLK & PETERSBURG RR
SEABOARD & ROANOKE RR
RALEIGH & GASTON RR
YORK RIVER RR
N

Sheridan's raid succeeded in diverting Lee's attention from the James crossing and drew off most of the Virginian's cavalry, but accomplished little else. Defeated by Maj. Gen. Wade Hampton at Trevilian Station on June 11 and 12 in Louisa County, Sheridan's horse soldiers were limping back toward White House Landing near the mouth of Pamunkey River encumbered by wounded, prisoners, dismounted men, a long wagon train and contrabands who had joined the column. Hampton's cavalrymen hung about the flanks of Little Phil's column, capturing stragglers and killing those who were plundering civilians.

With the way to Lynchburg kept clear by Hampton's Trevilian Station victory, Early's Corps began arriving at Lynchburg on June 17. On June 18 Hunter, short on supplies and thinking his forces outnumbered, retreated westward pursued by the Confederate Army of the Valley—Early's Corps joined by local troops.

* * *

Lee, now pitching his tent at the Violet Bank estate on Dunn's Hill in present day Colonial Heights north of the Appomattox, fully grasped that Grant had targeted Richmond's communications with the Deep South. On June 19 the Southern chieftain gloomily assessed his chances of maintaining his lines of communication with the rest of the Confederacy. In a letter to President Jefferson Davis, the Virginian despaired of defending the Petersburg and Weldon Railroad, which ran from Petersburg to near Weldon, North Carolina, where it connected with the port of Wilmington, North Carolina and points south. "The enemy's left now rests on the Jerusalem [plank] road, and I fear it would be impossible to arrest a sudden attack aimed at a distant point," he wrote. "In addition, the enemy's cavalry, in spite of all our efforts, can burn the bridges over the Nottoway and its branches, [and] the Meherrin." Lee considered the South Side Rail Road, running from the Cockade City to Lynchburg, where it connected with the Virginia & Tennessee, "very much exposed" as well.

In Lee's eyes, the Confederates could depend only on the Richmond & Danville Railroad, which ran southwestwardly from Richmond through Danville, Virginia and connected with the Deep South. "Every effort should be made to secure that road sufficient rolling stock by transferring that of other roads, and to accumulate supplies of all kinds in Richmond in anticipation of temporary interruptions," he declared. He urged Davis to give "every aid" to the railroads to enable them to restore traffic as soon as possible after the Unionists broke them. "Duplicate timbers for all the bridges should be prepared in safe places to be used in an emergency, and every other arrangement made to keep the roads in running order," wrote the Southern army group commander.[20]

James A. Seddon, Davis's secretary of war, would soon respond to Lee. Seddon appreciated Lee's concern for the Danville railway but doubted its ability to supply the Richmond-Petersburg area alone. The secretary of war thought Lee must defend all the area's rail communications for several weeks longer until the local wheat crop, which would sustain the Richmond-Petersburg area for several months, ripened.

The Confederates would need to take precautions to protect their railroads soon. Grant had the Weldon, the South Side, and the Danville railroads in his mind's gunsights.

* * *

At 10:00 a.m. on June 19, while most of the Federal forces outside Petersburg rested, Grant ordered forward his siege train. He then proceeded by steamer to choose the site for a bridgehead on the north bank of the James. "Went with General [Grant] & [General] Butler & one or two others up James river to see site for crossing & bridgehead on [the] other side," recorded Lt. Col. Cyrus B. Comstock, one of Grant's aides. "Deep Bottom selected, not as being easily defended but as covering the other side of the river as well."[21] At Deep Bottom, after running northwardly along the west side of a pencil-like peninsula called Jones Neck that stuck out from the south bank, the James made a 180-degree turn at the foot of a bluff on the north bank and ran southwardly along Jones Neck's east side. The approximately 80-foot depth of the river at the foot of the bluff gave the place its name.

After selecting the spot for the bridgehead, the party proceeded to USS *Malvern*, a big, fast steamer and the flagship of Acting Rear Adm. Samuel P. Lee, commander of the North Atlantic Blockading Squadron. Grant and Butler consulted with Admiral Lee about dealing with Confederate threats to the Federal forces' principal line of communication—the James.

The admiral, a Virginian and third cousin of the Confederate general, had served in the Navy since 1825. Known as a troublesome officer, Admiral Lee had

20 Douglas Southall Freeman, ed., *Lee's Dispatches: Unpublished Letters of General Robert E. Lee, C.S.A., to Jefferson Davis and the War Department of the Confederate States of America 1862–65* (Baton Rouge, 1994), 252–253. The Petersburg and Weldon Railroad was officially known as the Petersburg Railroad. A. Wilson Greene, *A Campaign of Giants: The Battle for Petersburg*, 3 vols. projected (Chapel Hill, NC, 2018), 1:7. It was sometimes called "the Petersburg and Weldon Railroad" but usually just "the Weldon railroad." *OR* 40, 2:274–275, 678, 689.

21 Merlin E. Sumner, comp., *The Diary of Cyrus B. Comstock* (Dayton, OH, 1987), 274–275.

engaged in several duels, and even killed a man on a Mississippi steamboat. Before taking charge of the North Atlantic Blockading Squadron, he had seen action in the Mexican War, at Charleston, at New Orleans, and at Vicksburg. When asked why he remained loyal to the Union, the admiral said, "When I find the word Virginia in my commission I will join the Confederacy."[22] His hold on his position was growing shaky because Secretary of the Navy Gideon Welles was losing confidence in him. Admiral Lee frequently sought instructions from Welles, who preferred subordinates who exercised their own discretion.

Grant and his companions next went aboard and inspected USS *Onondaga*, the biggest of the monitors that protected the James from incursions by the Confederate ironclads upriver. The Union fleet on the James included four monitors. Three—USS *Canonicus*, USS *Saugus* and USS *Tecumseh*—had single turrets armed with two fifteen-inch Dahlgren guns. These Dahlgrens could fire a 350-pound shell up to 2,100 yards at an elevation of seven degrees. The fourth monitor, *Onondaga*, had two turrets, each of them armed with a 15-inch smoothbore Dahlgren gun and a 150-pounder (eight-inch) Parrott rifle. The Parrott could fire its shell 8,000 yards when elevated 35 degrees.

"Then to horse & rode along Butler's line to Appomattox [river] where we took a steamer back," remembered Comstock.[23] Grant still had to inspect Butler's lines. The general-in-chief and his entourage began their ride at the northern end of Butler's line near Trent's Reach, a stretch of the James that ran along the southeastern side of Farrar's Island, a miscategorized peninsula formed by a big loop of the river. The ride of Grant's party took it along the line of fortifications across the mouth of Bermuda Hundred to Point of Rocks at the southern terminus of the works.

The journey brought the group past the headquarters of the Army of Potomac's VI Corps, two divisions of which Grant had loaned to Butler, who had scarcely employed them during the assaults on Petersburg. "They halted, and Grant took special delight in exhibiting a fine looking horse he had recently procured," recalled Pvt. George Prowell of the 87th Pennsylvania. "He dismounted and his noble looking animal was admired by a number of officers."[24]

22 Adolph A. Hoehling, *Thunder at Hampton Roads: The U.S.S. Monitor—Its Battle with the Merrimack and Its Recent Discovery* (Boston, 1993), 6.

23 Sumner, *Diary of Cyrus B. Comstock*, 275.

24 George R. Prowell, *History of the Eighty-Seventh Regiment, Pennsylvania Volunteers, Prepared from Official Records, Diaries, and Other Authentic Sources of Information* (York, PA, 1903), 164.

Butler did not make as favorable an impression. "It was my first sight of Butler," remembered 1st Lt. Lemuel Abijah Abbott of the 10th Vermont. "His beauty won't kill him."[25]

The ride also took the cavalcade past the 142nd Ohio, a regiment of 100-days men. Private Charles O. Poland of the 142nd's Company B thought that Grant "looks exactly like his photograph."[26]

By the time the general-in-chief and his staffers boarded the steamer back, Grant had communicated to Butler the decision to throw a brigade across the James the following night "from Jones Point to Deep Bottom, to fortify and hold that point, connecting the two shores by a pontoon bridge."[27] Butler decided to put in charge of the operation Brig. Gen. Godfrey Weitzel, an engineer and Butler's acting chief of staff.

During the ride, Grant inquired of Butler where Mrs. Grant and Grant's two sons might lodge at Fort Monroe. The politically savvy Butler invited Grant's family to stay at the fort with Mrs. Butler in Butler's permanent quarters. Butler informed his wife, "if you do all that your knowledge of the world, tact, and genius will enable you to do, then you will do a thousand times more in captivating the woman than I could possibly do with the husband."[28]

The commander of the Army of the James had good reason to draw upon his wife's tact. "Navy hate Butler cordially—& no wonder," Comstock recalled.[29] In the absence of a unified command, the divergent interests of the army and navy increased the friction between them. Oblivious to the difficulty of navigating—under enemy fire—the shallow, narrow, meandering, obstructed, and torpedo-strewn channels of the James, ignorant of the disadvantage at which ships engaged land batteries, the cockeyed general had made himself obnoxious to the tars by pushing Admiral Lee to use his gunboats to cover the flanks of the Army of the James. Admiral Lee wanted Butler to clear the riverbanks of enemy artillery so that the navy could sweep for torpedoes. Butler urged Lee to protect himself from a sortie by the Confederate ironclads by sinking obstructions in the James.

Lee feared that if he did so, others would assume that he lacked the nerve to fight the Secessionist fleet. He and his sailors did not think Butler and the army

25 Lemuel Abijah Abbott, *Personal Recollections and Civil War Diary* (Burlington, 1908), 85.

26 Charles O. Poland Diary, June 19, 1864, Special Collections, Virginia Polytechnic Institute and State University, Blacksburg, VA.

27 *OR* 40, 2:209.

28 Jessie Ames Marshall, *Private and Official Correspondence of Gen. Benjamin F. Butler during the Period of the Civil War*, 5 vols. (Norwood, MA, 1917), 4:417.

29 Sumner, ed., *Diary of Cyrus B. Comstock*, 275.

were doing their fair share. The Confederate navy had to be kept in check lest it sortie and cut Grant's supply line, which ran up James River to City Point. The Federals dreaded this to the point that on June 15 they had, according to the *New York Herald*, "performed an act that . . . has called an honorable blush to the cheek of every officer in [the] fleet."[30] Under Grant's orders, they had sunk five ships in Trent's Reach, barring themselves from a foray up the James to Richmond as effectively as a sortie of the Secessionist ships against City Point. The Lincoln administration considered the chance of capturing Richmond by a thrust up the tortuous, treacherous James under the guns of bastions such as Fort Drewry remote enough that giving it up to secure City Point seemed a good bargain.

* * *

That morning an obscene charade began over a truce to bury the dead and retrieve the wounded. Meade proposed an armistice, which would not amount to an admission of defeat by Grant. That the commander of the Army of the Potomac proposed it indicates that he considered the general-in-chief, who had remained back at City Point throughout the assaults on Petersburg, absent. Otherwise, Meade knew very well that any communication by flag of truce would have to come from Grant—the Confederates did not consider the victor of Gettysburg in command in the general-in-chief's presence.

The assignment to carry the armistice proposal to Beauregard fell to Lt. Col. Theodore Lyman III, an 1855 graduate of Harvard who had become the archivist on Meade's staff, "as the man having good clothes," Lyman recalled. Accompanied by a bugler "with a German-silver key-bugle" and "a tall sergeant, in Sunday best, with Gen. Seth Williams's new damask tablecloth, on an appropriate staff," Lyman proceeded on his mission "furnished with a large letter."[31] At 7:00 p.m., Lyman received a rejection from Beauregard, who implicitly considered Grant present and insisted that he admit defeat as a prerequisite to a truce because practically all the dead and wounded between the lines were Northerners. Besides, the prevailing west wind carried the stench from the decomposing dead away from Petersburg and toward the Unionists.

30 Craig L. Symonds, *Lincoln and His Admirals* (Oxford, UK, 2008), 320; *Official Records of the Union and Confederate Navies in the War of the Rebellion* (*ORN*), 30 vols., Series I (All references will be to Series I unless otherwise noted), 10:149. For a discussion of the risk to reward ratio of leaving the James unobstructed, see David D. Porter, *The Naval History of the Civil War* (New York, 1886), 475–477.

31 George R. Agassiz, ed., *Meade's Headquarters, 1863–1865: Letters of Colonel Theodore Lyman from the Wilderness to Appomattox* (Boston, 1922), 171. Williams was serving as Grant's inspector general. Ezra J. Warner, *General in Blue: Lives of the Union Commanders* (Baton Rouge, 1988), 562–563.

Theodore Lyman III
Digital Commonwealth, Massachusetts Collection Online

The commander of the Army of the Potomac did not renew his request for a truce, telling the general-in-chief, "I have reason to believe there are but few wounded not brought off," which was only true because so many of those wounded on June 18 had already died.[32] The political repercussions of an admission of defeat by Grant outweighed soldiers' lives.

Lyman returned with Beauregard's negative response sometime after 7:00 p.m. The Harvard-educated naturalist failed to understand the significance of the exchange. Attributing Beauregard's refusal to "his mean Creole blood," Lyman wrote in his journal that, "Lee does not do such things."[33] In fact, Lee had done the same thing in the protracted negotiations that failed to produce a truce at Cold Harbor until most of the Northern wounded between the lines there had expired—he had insisted that Grant admit defeat prior to the Republican National Convention in Baltimore, where Lincoln would be nominated for reelection. The difference between the negotiations at Cold Harbor and at Petersburg lay in that at the Cockade City, the Federals gave up negotiating rather than admit defeat.

* * *

While Grant and his party selected a spot for a bridgehead on the north bank of the James, the army group's staff at City Point scurried about to comply with his order to meet the possibility of a temporary blockade of the river. "Everything progressing finely here; wharves are being built for the accommodation of all the departments; issues of all necessary stores have been made," wrote Brig. Gen. Rufus Ingalls, Chief Quartermaster of the Army of the Potomac and the general-in-chief's classmate at West Point. "Since yesterday morning over 800 wagons were

32 *OR* 40, 2:210–211.

33 Agassiz, ed., *Meade's Headquarters*, 173.

loaded."[34] Ingalls had transports ready for the wounded and upon inspection had found the wagon trains well-parked.

Upon Grant's return to City Point, he began issuing orders for the seizure of a bridgehead across the James the following night. At 6:15 p.m., he informed Meade of the plan for the bridgehead and directed the Army of the Potomac's commander to turn over to Butler as many pontoons and as much bridging material as the operation would require. Five minutes later, Grant instructed Butler that a brigade of not less than 2,000 men on the following night must "seize, hold, and fortify the most commanding and defensible ground that can be found . . . and so near the river that, with the protection of the gun-boats and their own strength, they can always get back to Bermuda Hundred if attacked by superior numbers."[35] The general-in-chief wanted left in the bridge a passage for vessels, with the means at hand to close the gap whenever the army needed to use the structure.

At 10:00 p.m., Butler designated Brig. Gen. Robert S. Foster, a Hoosier who had enlisted as a private, to lead the forces making the crossing. Under Col. Harris M. Plaisted of the 11th Maine, a lawyer, Foster's brigade would cross the James with 100 rounds of ammunition and two days' rations per man. The brigade consisted of the 10th Connecticut, the 11th Maine, the 24th Massachusetts, the "New England Guard Regiment," and the 100th New York, the "Buffalo Board of Trade Regiment." The commander of the Army of the James directed Brig. Gen. William T. H. Brooks, the acting corps commander, to reinforce the brigade until it numbered 2,000 men and ordered that Brooks keep Foster and his command from any duty the following day to preserve the brigade's strength. To bring it up to 2,000 soldiers, Brooks chose from Howell's brigade the 39th Illinois, known as the "Yates Phalanx" because of the strings pulled by Governor Richard Yates of Illinois to find the regiment a place in Federal service after Illinois had filled its initial quota of troops, and the 85th Pennsylvania.

Brooks also received instructions to detail 1,800 100-days' men the following evening for work under Weitzel's direction. The 130th, 132nd, 134th, and 142nd Ohio drew this assignment with orders to leave behind their knapsacks and blankets but take their arms, their canteens, two days' rations in their haversacks, and 60 rounds of ammunition per man. "We was called into line and marched to Butlers head quarters and was ordered to get two days rations and be ready to march at four o'clock in the morning," recorded Private Poland. "I don't know where we will go but it [is] the general opinion that we are going to fight."[36]

34 *OR* 40, 2:211.

35 Ibid., 222.

36 Poland Diary, June 20, 1864.

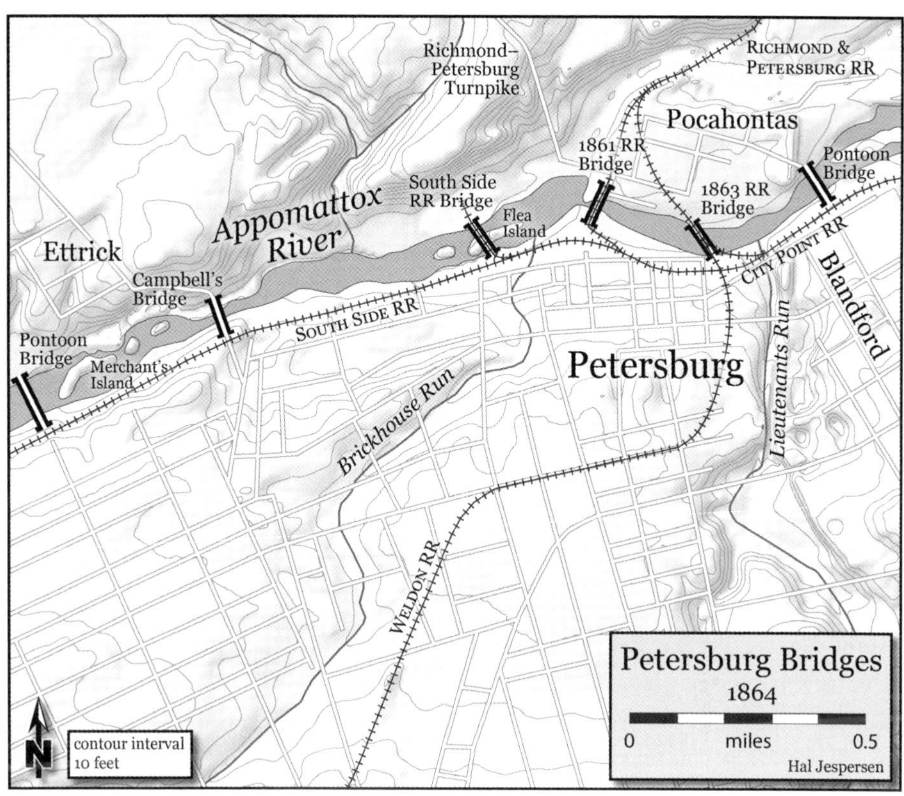

Later that night, Weitzel requested the delivery at Bermuda Hundred the following day at 8:00 a.m. of 35 bateaux, 100 pontoniers, two days' rations, and everything else necessary for a bridge 700 feet long. "At this point," remembered Weitzel, "James River is but 575 feet wide at high water."[37] Brigadier General Henry W. Benham of the Army of the Potomac's Engineer Brigade hastened to comply with Weitzel's request.

* * *

At 10:40 p.m., unable to wait for the arrival of his siege train, Grant began scrounging siege guns from Butler. The general-in-chief wanted some 30-pounder Parrott rifles to bring under fire Petersburg's railroad bridges over the Appomattox. By 8:25 a.m. on June 20, Butler had found two 30-pounder rifles that he could spare from his lines on Bermuda Hundred, another in the works at City Point, and a 4.5-inch siege rifle farther downriver at Fort Powhatan; he inquired of Grant which to send.

37 *OR* 40, 1:677.

Gunners considered the 30-pounder Parrott very accurate and reliable. The gun tended to break elevating screws, but artillerists liked it anyway—the 30-pounder functioned just as well with the broken screws removed. The gun could throw a 30-pound shell four miles. Fire from 30-pounder Parrotts would require passengers to debark short of the railroad bridges, scramble aboard horse-drawn omnibuses or proceed on foot, cross the river by a safer means farther west, and re-embark on the cars on the other side of town. The passengers would need at least an additional hour to cross. When it came to freight, the Confederates would have to "break bulk"—unload it from the cars, put it on wagons, cross by a bridge or ferry farther west, cart it through town, and then reload it on another train. This would require much more time and labor.

* * *

On the morning of June 20, Hunter appeared to have no chance of joining Sheridan at White House Landing, and Little Phil could not make another raid on the Virginia Central or join Hunter in the Shenandoah. At Meade's suggestion, Grant directed the breakup of the depot at White House Landing upon Sheridan's departure from that place, with the Veteran Reserves going to Washington and the remainder of the garrison proceeding with Little Phil to City Point.

Hampton began massing his forces to attack the Federal supply base at White House Landing. He requested that a brigade of infantry and two batteries be sent via the York River Railroad to Meadow Bridge, or that he be given all the cavalry on the Chickahominy—Gary's brigade of the Department of Richmond. Hampton's command lacked forage and many of his horses had broken down. With the approaches to White House Landing guarded by a brigade of infantry and Federal gunboats, Hampton made no attack except with artillery from a crest almost a mile away. The Federals easily withstood the shelling. Sheridan's main force arrived at the landing in the evening followed by his lengthy column. That night Hampton again begged for a brigade of infantry, with which he believed he could take White House Landing and the big wagon train gathering there. He also needed artillery horses, because his own were worn out.

* * *

That same morning, Brig. Gen. Marsena R. Patrick, the Army of the Potomac's Provost Marshal, hanged William Johnson, a deserter from the 23rd United States Colored Troops, who had under an assumed name joined the quartermaster department as a teamster. Near Cold Harbor, Johnson had tried to rape a local white woman. A court-martial sentenced him to death by hanging. Patrick, a West Pointer and veteran of the Seminole and Mexican wars who had served as a railroad executive and college president, intended to make the execution a spectacle.

He had the gallows built on Jordan house hill in full view of the Confederates to show them that the Federals would not tolerate mistreatment of Southern women. The Secessionists failed to appreciate the gesture and shelled the gallows. "So that I had to form the troops below the crest & leave as few exposed as possible," Patrick remembered.[38]

The hanging therefore failed to provide the entertainment expected. Private Charles H. Peterson of Company A from the 12th New Jersey, who was working in the division hospital, went to see the hanging with a pair of friends and recalled, "We made an about face, and came back, did not get to see the dark hanged after all."[39]

Several days earlier, while lying in the trenches, Sgt. Maj. George F. Polley of the 10th Massachusetts had carved with his knife upon a wooden headboard the words, "Serg.-Major George F. Polley, 10th Mass. Vols.; Killed June ___, 1864," telling his colonel, "I guess I'll leave the day blank."[40] Relieved on June 19 as the enlistments of its men expired, the 10th encamped behind Jordan's hill on the way home. Polley figured his premonition had proved wrong and split up the headboard to cook his coffee. On the morning of the 20th a shell from a Confederate 20-pounder Parrott rifle north of the Appomattox overshot the gallows and proved his premonition right by striking him in the breast and tearing his body to pieces.

The death of Polley, who had become a regimental favorite through his gallantry and fearlessness, cast gloom over his regiment's homeward trip, commenced the next day. "[M]ore died by shells than by the rope!" recalled Lyman of Johnson's hanging.[41]

* * *

While Johnson and Polley perished, Grant got a pair of siege guns. Early that morning, Company I of the 1st Connecticut Heavy Artillery Regiment received

38 David S. Sparks, ed., *Inside Lincoln's Army: The Diary of Marsena Rudolph Patrick, Provost Marshal General, Army of the Potomac* (New York, 1964), 386.

39 Charles H. Peterson Diary, June 20, Charles H. Peterson Pocket Diary Collection, Digital Collections, Oviatt Library, California State University Northridge, Northridge, CA.

40 Joseph Keith Newell, ed., *"Ours." Annals of the Tenth Regiment, Massachusetts Volunteers, in the Rebellion* (Springfield, MA, 1875), 281, 337.

41 David Lowe, ed., *Meade's Army: The Private Notebooks of Lt. Col. Theodore Lyman* (Kent, OH, 2007), 217.

orders from Butler to limber up its two 30-pounder Parrott rifles and proceed to the south side of the Appomattox at 10:00 a.m., "which we did very cheerfully as it was whispered around that our destination was Petersburg or near it," Company I's Sgt. Charles W. Smith wrote a few days later to his sweetheart.[42] As Company I rolled southward, Grant expanded the mission of the borrowed siege guns. He hoped not only to destroy the railroad bridges, but "possibly silence the enemy's guns on the north side of the Appomattox" which were enfilading the Federal lines south of the river—the same guns that killed Polley[43]

Company I arrived at its destination around two miles northeast of Petersburg, about dark. The artillerists unlimbered in Battery No. 5, a former Secessionist fort captured on the first day of Grant's assaults on the city. The railroad bridge they had come to shell stood about 3,500 yards west of Battery No. 5. The Cockade City lay in plain sight before the gunners. "We could easily burn the city in a few hours, but it doesn't seem to be Gen Grants plan to burn the place if he can take it without," wrote Smith, who started to kid his sweetheart, "and it does seem most to bad to burn it for it is said to be the handsomest city in the Southern States and is also the home of the handsomest girls of the South." His kidding continued. "Now Emma aint it too bad just think of it here we are within two miles of the prettiest girls in the Southern States and there is a short and level road that connects our Fort with the City (just a pleasant walk you know in the evening)," Smith wrote, "yet they wount let us go and see the girls (aint that to bad?) but we shall soon have the place I hope and then it wount be for the rebels to say whether we shall call on the ladies present."[44]

* * *

During the early afternoon, Weitzel made what Butler termed "a careful reconnaissance of the position at Deep Bottom." The site posed a difficult problem. "The best position would bring the bridge under close artillery fire from commanding positions, and the work itself would be under this fire," Butler informed Grant. Confederate fortifications on New Market Heights commanded the place Weitzel wanted to seize, as well as the bridge. New Market Heights loomed about a mile northeast of the position and around two miles northeast of the bridge. Weitzel requested Comstock's assistance in solving the problem, but

42 Letter, Charles W. Smith to "Dear Emma," June 24, 1864, Lewis Leigh Collection Book 37: 41–65, AHEC, Carlisle Barracks, PA.

43 *OR* 40, 2:233.

44 Smith to "Dear Emma," June 24, 1864.

Comstock and Brig. Gen. John G. Barnard, chief engineer of the United States Army, proved unavailable. Grant suggested that Weitzel "give the problem the best solution he can, and after occupying the north bank of the river we can occupy also the ground commanding the fortifications and bridge, or can make any change that may be necessary."[45]

At 4:30 p.m., Butler ordered Foster to muster his command at Brooks's headquarters at 6:00 p.m. The commander of the Army of the James postponed the arrival of the 1,800 100-days' men at Brooks's headquarters until 5 a.m. Butler directed Brooks to have at his headquarters at 6 a.m. for duty with Foster a four-gun battery of two rifles and two smoothbores with full complements of ammunition and two days' rations.

Weitzel meanwhile indicated to 1st Lt. Peter S. Michie, Butler's acting chief engineer, the fortifications envisioned and directed him to see to the details. Butler informed Foster that his soldiers would cross the James under the direction of the engineers, who would begin construction of a pontoon bridge behind the foot soldiers as soon as they had crossed. The commander of the Army of the James wanted Foster, after crossing, to entrench his men immediately along the line that Weitzel or Michie would indicate. The engineers would furnish entrenching tools. After Foster's men dug in, working parties would arrive to complete and strengthen the earthworks and prepare them for the reception of artillery. "You are to hold your position as long as possible and at all hazards till the bridge is completed," Butler emphasized.[46]

By 5:55 p.m., the orders flowing down through the chain of command had designated the two sections of light artillery that would cross in support of Foster's foot soldiers the following morning. The smoothbore section would come from the 5th Battery, New Jersey Light Artillery, the rifled section from the 1st Battery, Connecticut Light Artillery. The guns would not withdraw from the Bermuda Hundred entrenchments until 5:00 a.m., leaving them only an hour to arrive at X Corps' headquarters.

An enemy picket post manned by troopers of the 24th Virginia Cavalry stood watch within 300 or 400 yards of the spot Weitzel had picked for his troops to land. He had to exercise great caution in assembling his forces and material to prevent the Rebel videttes from giving the alarm. That meant his forces could not approach the James until after dark.

Late that afternoon, Plaisted's brigade broke camp and in light marching order tramped down in heat and clouds of dust from the Bermuda Hundred front to

45 *OR* 40, 2:257.

46 Ibid., 262.

Jones's landing, some three miles from camp. The soldiers wondered where they were going, "some said to make an attack & charge the rebel trenches in front, others to go on a secret expedition," recalled Cpl. Samuel H. Root, a Boston clerk in Company D of the 24th Massachusetts.[47]

The two regiments from Howell's brigade followed. "The men were congratulating themselves that they would have a good night's rest, as the enemy was quiet in front, when they received orders to get ready for an expedition," remembered commissary Sgt. John B. Bell in the 85th Pennsylvania.[48]

"So farewell to the poor comfort of camp," recalled Pvt. Valentine C. Randolph of the 39th Illinois. "We are ready for the fiery ordeal through which we are to pass."[49] Randolph had studied classics at Dickinson College in Carlisle, Pennsylvania, and at Illinois College, and he had suffered wounds on the wrist and lip on June 1 and 2.

"Wool picking somewhere but the boys are ready," remembered Pvt. Anthony Gaveston Taylor of the 39th's Company A, a farm boy from Will County rated a veteran because he had reenlisted in January 1864.[50] The two regiments from Howell's brigade bivouacked at Jones Neck.

Just after dark, the army group's engineers brought the pontoon boats to the James near Bermuda Hundred's commissary wharf, a mile and a half above Deep Bottom. Benham exceeded himself—he delivered not 35 bateaux, but 36. The engineers silently unloaded the boats and placed them in the river. Divided into details, infantrymen from Plaisted's brigade carried the planks and string pieces for the bridge and positioned them in the boats. Plaisted's brigade then boarded 40 men to the boat and pushed off into the current by 10:10 p.m. Less than 30 minutes later, 1,200 soldiers had quietly landed at the foot of Deep Bottom's wooded bluff. They then turned the boats over to the pontoniers for the bridge.

The brigade skirmish line advanced. Private Hiram T. Peck of the 10th Connecticut recalled "a good moon lighted our way."[51] The skirmishers surged up the bluff and seized the pits from which by day Confederate snipers harassed

47 Samuel H. Root Memoir, 11, Samuel H. Root Papers, Civil War Miscellaneous Collection, AHEC.

48 Luther S. Dickey, *History of the Eighty-fifth Pennsylvania Volunteer Infantry, 1861–1865, Comprising an Authentic Narrative of Casey's Division at the Battle of Seven Pines* (New York, 1915), 339.

49 David R. Roe, *A Civil War Soldier's Diary, Valentine C. Randolph, 39th Illinois Regiment*, (DeKalb, IL, 2006), 222.

50 Bambi Rae Brown, *Haystacks of Limbs, The Siege of Petersburg, Virginia—1864–1865: The Civil War Diary of Anthony Gaveston Taylor, 39th Illinois Regiment—Company A—Volunteer Veteran Infantry* (Parker, CO, 2017), 39.

51 Hiram T. Peck, *Army Journal: A Private Record of Life in the Federal Service during the Great Rebellion* (New Haven, CT, 1874), 214.

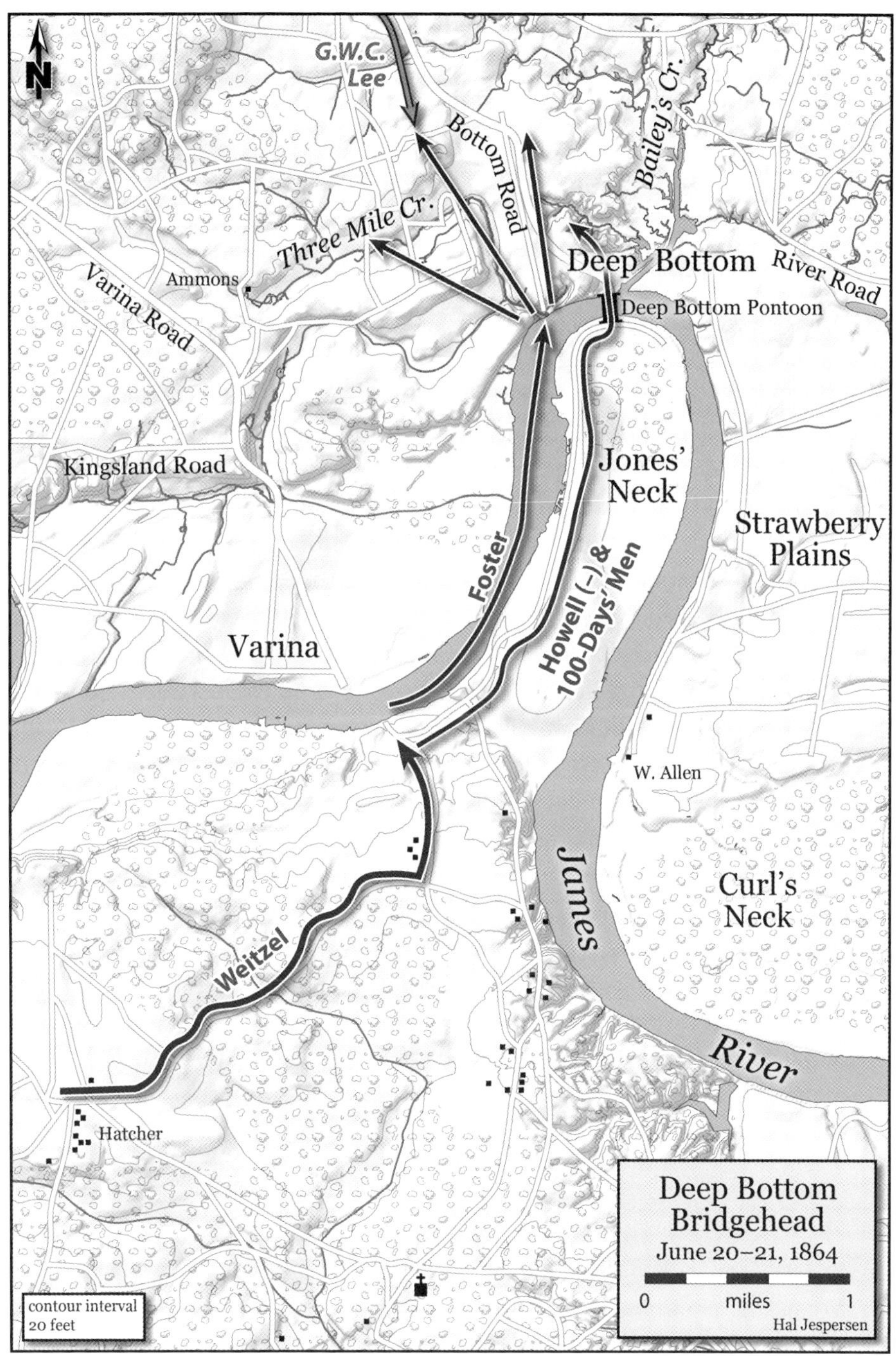
G.W.C. Lee
Bottom Road
Bailey's Cr.
Three Mile Cr.
Deep Bottom
River Road
Ammons
Varina Road
Deep Bottom Pontoon
Kingsland Road
Jones' Neck
Strawberry Plains
Foster
Howell (–) & 100-Days' Men
Varina
W. Allen
James River
Curl's Neck
Weitzel
Hatcher
Deep Bottom Bridgehead
June 20–21, 1864
0 miles 1
Hal Jespersen
contour interval 20 feet

passing Union ships. The pickets of the 24th Virginia Cavalry quickly withdrew through the darkness.

Ordinary soil would have allowed the earthworks to progress rapidly, but the dirt only permitted throwing up a simple defensive line. "The ground was most unfavorable for excavation and embankments," remembered Weitzel. "It was a hard, white soil, breaking into small lumps on every application of the pick, and of such a character that the ravines formed were narrow, deep, and steep."[52]

At first the digging required an extraordinary proportion of picks to shovels—one pick to every shovel. By 11:00 p.m., 500 men were working with shovels, 200 with picks, and 200 with axes, while a regiment stood picket in advance of all. "One regt. took the picks, one shovels, one axes, & the other stood to arms to look out for advance of the rebels," Root wrote to his wife.[53]

First Lieutenant George H. Stowits, commander of Company A in the 100th New York, recalled that "the axes of the Eleventh Maine were ringing in echoes through the woods, and the shovel was busily employed."[54] A well-wooded bluff when seized, by morning Deep Bottom was nearly bare.

Foster established his picket line against no resistance by 1:15 a.m. on June 21. The engineers completed the bridge, roads, and approaches before daybreak. No enemy except cavalry pickets had yet appeared in Foster's front. The 39th Illinois and the 85th Pennsylvania crossed the river between 8:00 a.m. and 10:00 a.m. Heavy details from the 85th went to work fortifying the northern end of the pontoon bridge while other soldiers relaxed. "Our regiment stacked arms and lay in the shade till evening," recalled Private Randolph, who perceived a bright side to service at Deep Bottom. "Wheat was ripe enough to harvest and oats were in the milk," he recalled. "Fruit of various kinds is plentiful."[55] The 24th Massachusetts, ordered to support the picket line, lay all day in the hot sun but had the opportunity to forage. The Bay Staters found superlative cherries and an abundance of delicious mulberries.

Weitzel called upon the 1,800 100-days' men to take over the fatigue labor. After a march of five or six miles, the 100-days' men arrived around the same time

52 *OR* 40, 1:677.

53 Letter, Samuel H. Root to Wife, June 25, 1864, Samuel H. Root Papers.

54 George H. Stowits, *History of the One Hundredth Regiment of New York State Volunteers, Being a Record of Its Services from Its Muster in to Its Muster Out; its Muster in Roll, Roll of Commissions, Recruits Furnished Through the Board of Trade of the City of Buffalo, and Short Sketches of Deceased and Surviving Officers* (Buffalo, 1870), 272.

55 Roe, ed., *A Civil War Soldier's Diary*, 222.

as the soldiers from Howell's brigade. The 100-days' men, basically militia, posed a serious problem.

An ill-considered idea had summoned them into service. The Federal authorities called them up to relieve troops with longer terms of service and allow the longer termed men to participate in a spring campaign expected to subdue the Confederacy quickly. The Southerners had not cooperated and no end appeared in sight for the war. The 100-days' troops belonged far in the rear, out of harm's way. Through some oversight they found themselves in a combat zone. Any casualties they suffered might well result in a political firestorm.

Sergeant John Harrod, a 100-days' man in the 132nd Ohio, described the delicate handling the 100-days troops received:

> We have never been put in an engagement yet nor do I think we will. We are kept very close to those that do fight but we have never been asked to fire a gun yet. We have been several times close enough to fight, but as soon as it was discovered we were moved back out of danger and the old soldiers done the fighting and let us go to our quarters. There has never been a time that I considered we were in much danger.[56]

Now, with the Rebels nearby, the 100-days' men expected an attack. "So we will have to fight or swim," noted Private Poland."[57]

* * *

As the Federals at Deep Bottom were digging in that morning, the Rebels were launching an operation of their own. The Secessionists had an unpleasant surprise planned for the ships of the Northern fleet on Trent's and Varina Reaches of James River on June 21.

Preparations for the Southern operation had begun after an incident on June 19, when the three ironclads of the James River Squadron—CSS *Virginia II*, CSS *Richmond*, and CSS *Fredericksburg*—and three wooden gunboats dropped down the James from their moorage at Chaffin's Bluff. They anchored at 2:00 p.m. in the shelter of Howlett's Bluff, on the right bank of the James above Howlett's farm, which lay above Farrar's Island. Their sailors could see the top of the Federal army-navy signal tower at Trent's Reach, and their ships could be seen from the tower, but the Confederate tars could not see the Northern monitors that had entered

56 Jim Leeke, ed., *A Hundred Days to Richmond: Ohio's "Hundred Days" Men in the Civil War* (Bloomington, IN, 1999), 95.

57 Poland Diary, June 19, 1864.

Trent's Reach. Scarcity of ammunition prevented the Southerners from trying to destroy the tower.

The Union monitors opened on the Secessionist ironclads, employing indirect fire with the assistance of spotters atop the signal tower. As *Richmond*'s commander, Lt. William H. Parker, sat reading in an armchair on the shield of his ship, a shell fired from one of the monitors "exploded just at the river bank and scattered the pieces about the forward deck of the *Virginia*, wounding three men," recalled Parker, a New York native and former commandant of the Confederate States Naval Academy. "While we were wondering at this, another shell came and exploded just after it had passed over us, and again another." Unable to return fire, the Rebel rams weighed anchor and returned to Chaffin's Bluff. "The authorities in Richmond now became very anxious that the navy should make some demonstration on the river in order to relieve the great pressure on the army," Parker remembered.[58]

On the morning of June 20, Maj. Gen. George E. Pickett, commander of the Bermuda Hundred lines, and Capt. John K. Mitchell, the unsuccessful naval commander at New Orleans now in charge of the James River Squadron, agreed on the specifics of a combined army-navy operation. Brigadier General George Washington Custis Lee, the eldest son of the Army of Northern Virginia's commander, would that afternoon with his Department of Richmond brigade of Local Defense Troops, 1,450 strong but mainly government clerks and laborers, drive in any Union pickets on the James's north bank between Aiken's and Dutch Gap and on Farrar's Island. This would allow the ironclads and gunboats under Mitchell's command to drop down the James at night and anchor between Cox's Ferry and Cox's Landing just above Dutch Gap without being observed. Colonel Thomas H. Carter that evening would plant his two battalions of Army of Northern Virginia field batteries in pits on the elevated slope between Aiken's and Cox's Landing, near the Signal Tower.

The Confederates intended to unmask four heavy guns at Battery Dantzler on Howlett's Bluff, at the north end of the Bermuda Hundred line. They aimed to surprise and destroy the Federal ships on station in Trent's and Varina Reaches. Before Grant's opening assaults on Petersburg, the Rebels had begun building emplacements for six guns in Battery Dantzler and filled four of the emplacements with artillery as big as a 10-inch Columbiad and an 8-inch rifle. The Southerners abandoned the battery along with the rest of the Howlett Line on June 15, burying the guns. Upon reoccupying the Howlett Line, they dug up the guns and began restoring the battery. It lay behind a screen of trees, which soldiers would cut down on the night of June 20, leaving the guns covered with brush.

58 William Harwar Parker, *Recollections of a Naval Officer* (New York, 1883), 337.

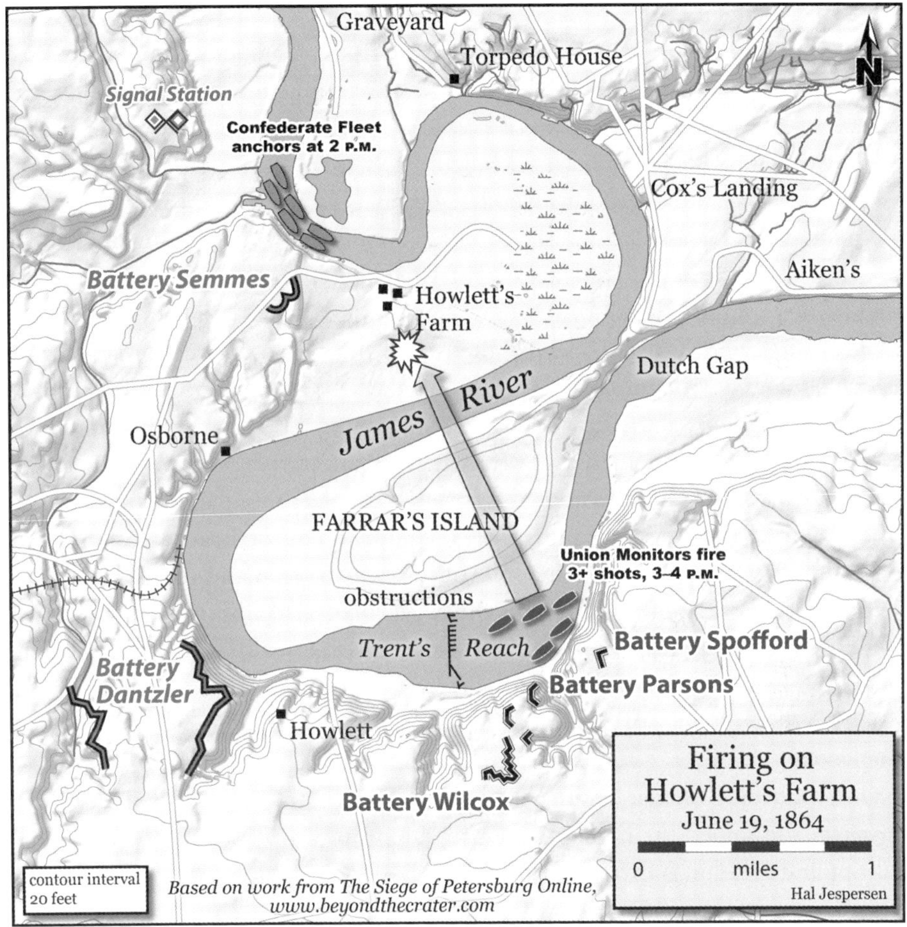

Battery Dantzler would open fire at noon on June 21. Its guns would focus on the Union vessels in Trent's Reach. The ironclads and gunboats under Mitchell's command above Dutch Gap would begin shooting indirectly over the intervening trees at the Federal vessels in Trent's and Varina Reaches when Battery Dantzler opened. A signal officer from each Southern vessel would position himself to direct this fire. Carter's field batteries would fire upon the Unionist wooden vessels below Aiken's in Varina Reach.

Some segments of the plan went smoothly. The Confederate infantry and field artillery moved in stifling heat and dust from Chaffin's Bluff to New Market Heights. There Custis Lee established his headquarters at the Drill Room, an assembly point for local guards at the junction of New Market and Turner Roads. Despite losing many stragglers, he put his soldiers to work throwing up earthworks four miles long to connect Chaffin's Bluff with New Market Heights.

Other elements of the plan encountered problems. On June 20, a Union army lookout observed the Rebel ironclads taking on sand in bags. His report alerted the Federal navy that the Secessionists were preparing for action. As the Confederate ironclads got underway, *Richmond* parted her wheel-chain, which fouled her rudder, disabling her. *Virginia II* anchored below Cox's Landing, *Fredericksburg* at Cox's Ferry, and the Secessionist wooden gunboats took station nearby.

Not Battery Dantzler but the monitor *Tecumseh* opened the fight at about 10:30 a.m. on June 21, after discovering that the Confederates had during the night felled the trees north of the Howlett barn, exposing the new line of works there covered with brush. *Tecumseh* fired from below the obstructions in Trent's Reach, at a range of approximately 2,000 yards. The Southerners did not remove the brush and unmask Battery Dantzler until around 11:30 a.m., when monitors *Saugus* and *Canonicus* entered the fray at the summons of Cmdr. Tunis A. M. Craven of *Tecumseh*. Only at noon did Battery Dantzler's four guns begin shooting. Then, remembered Acting Ensign John W. Grattan on the Federal flagship *Malvern* behind the monitors, "four white puffs of smoke were seen and the whistling and screaming of heavy solid shot told us the engagement had commenced."[59]

Not until about 12:30 p.m. did the Secessionist ships and Carter's field artillery open fire. "Shot & shell fell within a few feet of our vessel and bursted over our heads," recorded Grattan, who knew that a single well-aimed shot would annihilate the wooden *Malvern*.[60] The double-turreted monitor *Onondaga* went into action against Battery Dantzler around 12:45 p.m., when the wooden gunboat USS *Agawam* also joined the fight and split the fire from her 9-inch smoothbores and 100-pound (6.4-inch) Parrott rifles between Battery Dantzler and the Confederate vessels, aiming her forward guns at the former and her aft guns at the latter. At 1:30 p.m., amid this storm of steel, Commander Craven coolly ceased fire and allowed his crew to rest and eat lunch before resuming shooting at 2:00 p.m.

Agawam, after hitting neither Battery Dantzler nor the Southern ships, ceased fire about 2:30 p.m. Aboard *Malvern*, Grattan noted, "[at] 3.15 [p.m.] a shell from the rebel iron clad struck within ten feet of the ship and threw mud over our deck in great quantity." The monitors bombarded Battery Dantzler until late in the afternoon, dismounting a gun with *Tecumseh*'s last shot. *Tecumseh* "sent five XV-inch shell in rapid succession into the battery, and destroyed a platform, throwing the earth and timber in every direction," recalled Grattan. Battery Dantzler and the Secessionist vessels were still firing at 6:00 p.m. "The fight still continues nearly

59 Robert J. Schneller, Jr., ed., *Under the Blue Pennant, or Notes of a Naval Officer 1863–1865, by John W. Grattan, Acting Ensign, United States Navy* (New York, 1999), 108.

60 Ibid., 109.

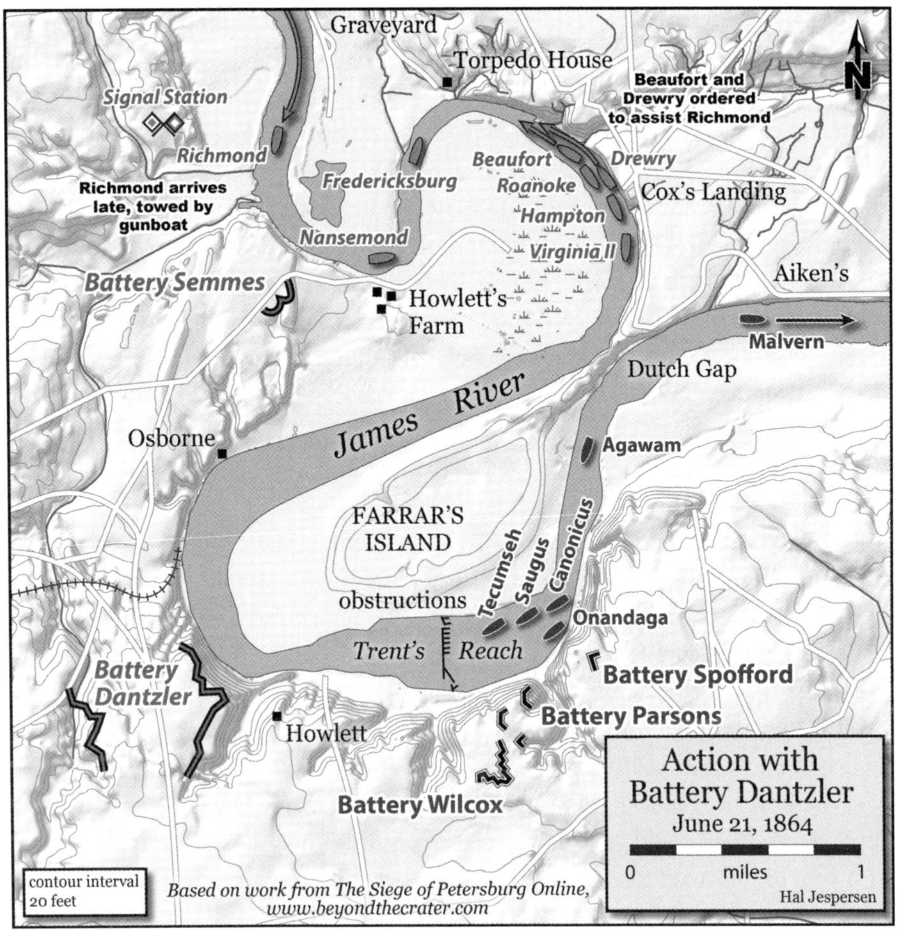

100 shot & shell have been fired nearly a dozen have fell within 20 yards of the ship," recorded Grattan aboard *Malvern*. "One burst right ahead and threw some fragments on deck."[61] The Rebel missiles from the battery and the Confederate ships drove *Agawam*—the sole Union wooden vessel in Trent's Reach—below Aiken's, where *Agawam* with *Malvern* took ineffective fire from Carter's field batteries and Custis Lee's field guns on New Market Heights.

The Confederate batteries and ships kept shooting until sunset. The exchange caused some disruption in the Deep Bottom bridgehead. "Shot and shell were flying lively in our camp," Commissary Sgt. Charles A. Hotchkiss of the 1st Connecticut Light Artillery wrote in his diary. "We make shelter by piling up bales of hay. The pow-wow between the enemy and our gunboats and batteries was kept

61 Ibid., 108–109; John W. Grattan Diary, June 21, 1864, John W. Grattan Papers, LOC.

up all day. I couldn't cook or do much or keep covered and take a look at the fight of the big guns."[62]

Overall, the naval affair caused little damage. The ten-inch columbiad in Battery Dantzler inflicted minor damage on the deck of *Saugus*, while an eight-inch rifle slightly damaged *Canonicus*'s deck. Battery Dantzler required re-masking that night and remained out of action two or three days because of the damage caused by *Tecumseh*. "The whole affair . . . was a *fiasco*," remembered Lieutenant Parker. The Confederate sailors knew their guns could not hurt the monitors at long range, their ironclads could not stand up to the 15-inch Dahlgrens of the monitors at short range, and the only hope of sinking the monitors lay in a suicidal dash by wooden gunboats armed with spar torpedoes through the obstructions in Trent's Reach under the fire of Federal land batteries. "The fact is we were wrong in yielding to the clamor of the army to 'do something,'" Parker recalled.[63]

Parker proved too pessimistic. Battery Dantzler largely drove the U.S. Navy out of Trent's Reach. Wooden vessels could not remain there under the crossfire of the battery at the upper end of the reach and the Confederate ironclads dropping down from Chaffin's Bluff to Dutch Gap at the upper end of Farrar's Island. The Union monitors could not maintain a protracted fire on the battery because of the short life of their guns, the endurance of their men, and their supplies of ammunition and fuel. Admiral Lee wanted Butler to place batteries of heavy guns at the lower end of Trent's Reach to keep Battery Dantzler in subjection. "This would allow the ironclads to drop around the point, withdrawing a few hundred yards, where they could keep their hatches off in hot weather, whence they could in a few minutes return and engage the rebel ironclads, should they appear in the upper part of the reach or interfere with the obstructions," wrote Lee. "Our naval resources would thus be reserved for their ironclads and not exhausted on their earthworks."[64] Though Butler complied with the admiral's wishes, stalemate prevailed on the James for months to come.

* * *

While the naval battle raged, Custis Lee and his superior—Lt. Gen. Richard S. Ewell, commander of the Department of Richmond—determined what to do about the Federal bridgehead at Deep Bottom.

62 Herbert W. Beecher, *History of the First Light Battery Connecticut Volunteers, 1861–1865, Personal Records and Reminiscences, the Story of the Battery from Its Organization to the Present Time*, 2 vols. (New York, 1906), 2:496–497.

63 Parker, *Recollections of a Naval Officer*, 338.

64 *ORN* 10:184.

By 2:00 p.m., Custis Lee's father had ordered Cooke's North Carolina Brigade and Davis's brigade to proceed from the left of the Howlett Line to New Market Heights. Around the same time, Foster's cavalry—the 1st New York Mounted Rifles—drove pickets from the 24th Virginia Cavalry back toward Kingsland Road and New Market. The New York horsemen captured the Grover house, about a mile from the pontoon bridge. The house belonged to a talkative New Jersey matron, who kept the rumor mill grinding. "She was very communicative and it was easy to see that her sympathies were with the Union cause," remembered Cpl. Henry W. Beecher of the 1st Connecticut Light Artillery, who had lived in Virginia for thirteen years before the war. "General Foster did not place very much reliance on Mrs. Grover's report, believing that she was over-sensitive and anxious."[65] The Mounted Rifles drove back the enemy's cavalry pickets toward New Market and the Kingsland Road and developed Custis Lee's Local Defense Troops advancing in skirmish formation on Foster's front. Across the James at 3:20 p.m., Bell's brigade prepared to move to Foster's aid if necessary.

By 5:40 p.m., Foster's cavalry pickets covered Kingsland Road from Four-Mile Creek to Three-Mile Creek, a rivulet that provided little protection. Custis Lee's troops held their ground on the opposite side of the road. Foster stationed his infantry pickets behind his horsemen to cover the distance between Kingsland Road and James River. At 6:00 p.m., the 24th Massachusetts tramped to the riverbank and bivouacked, amused at the sight of troops adjusting their steps to the sway of the pontoon bridge. Seven companies of the 85th Pennsylvania replaced the 24th on picket duty. Commissary Sergeant Bell remembered that he "brought a ration of whiskey to the men, with other rations, but was not permitted to take it to the picket-line."[66]

The 100-days' men continued digging that evening but disliked their working conditions. "We only get half rations and work night & day," complained Private Poland.[67]

Around this time the 60th Alabama and Smith's battery arrived at New Market Heights after hurrying westward from Bottom's Bridge on the Chickahominy River, twelve miles away. "The march this day, on account of the heat and dust, was exceedingly fatigueing and unpleasant," remembered Sgt. Maj. Llewellyn Adolphus Shaver of the 60th. The Alabamians began throwing up earthworks.[68]

65 Beecher, *First Light Battery Connecticut Volunteers*, 2:498.

66 Dickey, *Eighty-fifth Regiment Pennsylvania Volunteer Infantry*, 339.

67 Poland Diary, June 22, 1864.

68 Lewellyn A. Shaver, *A History of the Sixtieth Alabama Regiment: Gracie's Alabama Brigade* (Montgomery, AL, 1867), 55.

The two infantry brigades from Maj. Gen. Henry Heth's division plodded out of the Howlett Line at sunset. Corporal Joseph Mullen Jr. of Company F, the Perquimans Beauregards in the 27th North Carolina, noted, "The weather was warm and the roads were very dusty, consequently, it was very disagreeable marching!"[69]

* * *

Meade preferred Sheridan to cross the James by the pontoon at Deep Bottom, but the chance of that seemed remote to the Army of the Potomac's commander, who wrote at 9:00 a.m. on June 21, "I don't think Sheridan will have much chance of getting to the Deep Bottom bridge in the face of Hampton unless he is able to give him a severe and serious defeat."[70] Meade trusted that Sheridan would keep Hampton occupied even though Little Phil would probably have to cross by ferryboat about 10 miles downstream from Deep Bottom at Douthat's landing. The victor of Gettysburg overlooked the extra miles and slower crossing that would leave the South Carolinian free to turn his attention to Wilson's raiders.

Events developed that day the way Meade expected. After breaking up the depot at White House Landing and packing the Veteran Reserves off to Washington, Sheridan proceeded westward toward Deep Bottom with the remainder of the garrison. Hampton halted Little Phil's westward progress near Tunstall's Station. The South Carolinian that evening made his headquarters at Bottom's Bridge. There his forces barred the most direct road to Deep Bottom and shunted Sheridan onto a route through Charles City Court House and then past Harrison's Landing and Malvern Hill, making the crossing by pontoon at Deep Bottom impracticable.

* * *

On June 21, the day after arriving at Battery 5, Company I engaged in an artillery duel with the Rebels near Petersburg for three or four hours. The Nutmeggers suffered no casualties.

If Sergeant Smith had told the Southerners that, "it doesn't seem to be Gen Grants plan to burn the place," they would have thought Smith was joking. As soon as Company I's thirty-pounder Parrotts opened, the bombardment of Petersburg intensified.

"The fire at first seemed chiefly directed toward the Old Market, presumably on account of the South Side Rail Road depot, which was situated there, and about which troops would naturally be collected," recalled Dr. John H. Claiborne, who

69 Joseph Mullen Jr. Diary, June 22, 1864, VHS.

70 *OR* 40, 2:232, 255, 267.

had begun the war as a private in the Petersburg Riflemen, Company E of the 12th Virginia.[71] Dr. Claiborne had quickly become the 12th's surgeon, and as of 1864 he had left the Petersburg Regiment to take charge of all the military hospitals in the Cockade City.

Around the time that Company I's thirty-pounder Parrotts commenced firing, General Lee directed Dr. Claiborne to remove the sick and wounded as well as the stores and furnishings of the hospitals to the cars of the South Side Rail Road. Dr. Claiborne promptly began evacuating his approximately 3,000 patients. "To remove this number with the limited means of transportation at hand was no small job," he recalled.[72]

The bombardment altered traffic patterns in Petersburg. Trains from Richmond stopped at a deep cut about a mile north of the city because the train could not safely approach nearer. Pocahontas Bridge, the railroad bridge, and an army pontoon bridge all lay under the fire of the Federal guns. Railroad passengers from the north could enter the city on foot by way of the railroad bridge so long as they did not attract attention, or they could play it safe and detour west to Ettrick, where they might cross safely on Campbell's Bridge. The Union gunners soon figured out the train schedules and shelled the vicinity of the depots around arrivals and departures.

The appearance of the city became depressing. "The streets were almost deserted, and the destructive work of the shells was visible on every hand," recalled John A. Wise, a cadet from Virginia Military Institute and the son of Brig. Gen. Henry A. Wise, a former governor of Virginia. "Here a chimney was knocked off; here a handsome residence was deserted, with great rents in its walls, and the windows shattered by explosion; here stood a church tower mutilated, the churchyard filled with new-made graves."[73] Occasionally, on the sidewalks and pavements, one could find a corpse.

* * *

At midnight, Heth's Mississippians and North Carolinians crossed the James on the Chaffin's Bluff pontoon bridge and encamped at 2:00 a.m. on June 22 at Chaffin's Bluff. Before daybreak and without breakfast, Heth's infantry hurried

71 John Herbert Claiborne, *Seventy-Five Years in Old Virginia: With Some Account of the Life of the Author and Some History of the People Amongst Whom His Lot was Cast—Their Character, Their Condition and Their Conduct Before the War, During the War and After the War* (New York, 1904), 204–205.

72 Ibid., 206.

73 John S. Wise, *The End of an Era* (Boston, 1899), 316.

down New Market Road to New Market Heights. There 500 heavy artillerymen from the command of Lt. Col. John C. Pemberton, the unfortunate former commander of Vicksburg, had supplemented the 60th Alabama. Upon Heth's arrival, he assumed command of the Confederate forces opposite Foster. Heth's defensive line stretched north on New Market Road from New Market Heights to the McCoull House, whence the line extended westward almost to Aiken's farm near Chaffin's Bluff.

Those of Foster's men not on picket duty were laying out camp. They now had a three-sided fortification with a road running up through the steep ravine of Four Mile Creek to convey artillery to the top of the Deep Bottom bluff. The line resembled an L with its angle up, the short leg stretching southeast, and the long leg running to the southwest roughly parallel to Kingsland Road. Foster sent off 600 of his 100-days' men for rations while the remainder of the 100-days' men rested.

The two brigades of Heth's division, with Davis's brigade on the left and Cooke's brigade on the right, formed line along the Kingsland Road facing the river and threw forward skirmishers. Advancing about three quarters of a mile, the skirmishers met the Federal cavalry videttes. The Southern pickets "charged to run them in but saw very formidable works near the river," remembered Private Mullen.[74] Discovering the 1st New York Mounted Rifles trying to flank them, the Confederate skirmishers fell back. Their battle lines immediately advanced to their support, and the 48th North Carolina of Cooke's brigade drove Foster's pickets out of the Grover house. Heth stationed about 40 Tarheels in the house.

Around 2:00 p.m., Brooks visited Foster and suggested that he retake the Grover house, hold it with a company of infantry, and advance his picket line to a crest close behind the house. Foster assigned the task to Col. George B. Dandy of the 100th New York. Dandy supplied the regiment's Company K. Stowits, who had commanded Company K for most of the year, accompanied his former troops at Dandy's request.

Foster drew up a regiment of 100-days' men confronting the Grover house—a risky procedure considering the possible political consequences of casualties among the 100-days' men. A sergeant and a few picked skirmishers from Company K sneaked through the woods to the left to deceive the North Carolinians at the house about the strength of the Federal thrust. Stowits and the rest of Company K slipped out to the right until the New Yorkers faced the house across a field of knee-high corn. "At a double quick, amid a shower of balls, while the crack of rifles in the woods told us that our skirmishers were at work, we pushed on and reached

74 Joseph Mullen Jr. Diary, June 22, 1864, VHS.

the fence at the right flank of the house, without firing a shot and with the loss of only one man . . . shot in the foot," remembered Stowits.[75]

The skirmish line assisted Company K. "At the same time our picket line was advanced and fired on the rebels," recalled Private Randolph of the 39th Illinois. "Each one of the pickets took a shovel and when he reached the place designated, which was the crest of a hill, dug a pit for his protection."[76]

The North Carolinians in the Grover house retreated. Stowits remembered, "the firing of our men in the woods, and the strong front of a full regiment of one hundred days men drawn up in line at the spot where we started, and our quick dash to gain the fence, completely frightened the 'Johnnies,' and the Grover House was ours."[77]

The 100-days' men came in for fulsome praise from the veterans. "We have ever felt respect for that regiment from Ohio of one hundred days men," recalled Stowits. "The sight of that large regiment, sent to dig and not to fight, surprised and frightened the rebels, and saved Co. 'K' from destruction."[78] Foster sent all but 600 of the 100-days' men back to Bermuda Hundred shortly afterward. The 600 remained at work on the redoubt on the bluff below Four Mile Creek.

Foster established his picket line along the brow of the rise in front of New Market Heights, overlooking the Grover house and the Rebel front line, with the right and left of the picket line refused. The Grover house constituted the most advanced post on the Federal picket line at Deep Bottom, in easy range of the Confederate artillery on New Market Heights. Foster left two companies at the Grover house and posted the pickets on the left in view of a point of woods, fearing a flank movement. Secessionist infantry was digging in at the Ruffin house 400 yards away, and it seemed that Rebels would try to retake the Grover house.

A prisoner from Cooke's brigade reported Confederate reinforcements on the way. Foster added this report to the evidence of the other Secessionist forces facing him. He became concerned about a possible Confederate counterattack that night and requested naval fire support. Two gunboats were supporting the bridgehead, USS *Hunchback* above the pontoon and USS *Mendota* below. The gunboats began lobbing their huge shells inland. The bridgehead's pickets had hardly taken position before a stray Parrott shell struck a few rods from Company K at the Grover house.

75 Stowits, *One Hundredth New York*, 273.

76 Roe, *A Civil War Soldier's Diary*, 222.

77 Stowits, *One Hundredth New York*, 273.

78 Ibid., 275.

The shell "ploughed up the soft soil, which knocked over the man on post, nearly covering him with dirt, and passed on, exploding in the woods beyond," recalled Lieutenant Stowits.

Soldiers of Company K said to the picket, a German, "Are you hurt?"

He replied, "No."[79]

Stowits soon perceived the picket's shock and demoralization. Company K furnished a replacement for him. The next shot passed over the New Yorkers' heads and burst among the Southerners. The gunboats having found the range, Company K felt no further anxiety.

The gunboats drove the Secessionist foot soldiers away from Foster's picket line and made the Rebels very chary of an advance. "The enemy opened on us from one of their land batteries and also from their gun boats which lasted until some time in the night, several of the shells from the gun boats burst over our regiment but fortunately doing no damage," 2nd Lt. Thomas J. Strayhorn of the Orange Guards remembered.[80]

The Confederate field batteries could not effectively reply. "Colonel Carter could find no position from which he could accomplish anything" with his two battalions of field guns, recalled General Heth.[81] Sergeant Major Shaver described the unequal contest between the Secessionist field batteries and the Union gunboats:

> The shell fired from these boats were of almost incredible size—each one was a magazine in itself. On striking the earth, they created an excavation from six to ten feet in diameter and from four to five feet in depth, sufficiently capacious for the burial place of a platoon of men. As one passed high over head, it sounded very much like a flock of wild geese, and, on exploding near at hand, the whizzing and buzzing of the fragments reminded one of the noise made by the spindles of a cotton-factory in full blast. The land-batteries could hold no hand with these young earthquakes; they were soon rudely boxed out of breath and countenance, and made a narrow escape from being entombed alive.[82]

79 Ibid.

80 Henry McGilbert Wagstaff, ed., "Letters of Thomas Jackson Strayhorn," *North Carolina Historical Review* 13 (1936): 320.

81 *OR* 51, 2:1026.

82 Shaver, *A History of the Sixtieth Alabama Regiment*, 55–56.

Under the circumstances, Heth thought it inadvisable to attack the fortifications. Even if he could capture the Federal earthworks, he recalled, "I could not have held the position on account of the gun-boats."[83]

Around 5:00 p.m., Heth's men withdrew about a mile towards Chaffin's Bluff, filed into thick woods in a bottom to their left, and deployed pickets two steps apart. "When we are not deployed we are in two ranks close together, and when we are deployed we are five steps apart in one rank," Pvt. Samuel P. Lockhart of the 27th North Carolina's Company G, the Orange Guards, wrote. "But to make a reliable strong skirmish line, [Brig.] General [John R.] Cooke only deploys us two steps apart." Neither the woods nor the bottom provided the North Carolinians with much respite from the Union navy. Lockhart admitted that the big shells "mortally scare us some times."[84]

Some of Heth's men considered the enemy's reliance on the gunboats unsporting. "The yankees take care not to come out from their gunboats," wrote 1st Lt. Joseph J. Hoyle of Company F, the South Mountain Rangers, in the 55th North Carolina of Davis's brigade. "Occasionally they give us some shells from their boats, but do us no damage."[85]

Darkness provided little relief for the Confederates. In charge of Davis brigade's skirmish line, Lt. Col. James A. Blair of the 2nd Mississippi, wounded at Second Manassas and Sharpsburg, recorded, "During the night the Gun Boats kept up a continuous fire, throwing the largest shell I ever saw."[86]

Other things made the surroundings unpleasant for the Southerners. "At this place we had no battle, except with flies," recalled Capt. William Henry Harrison Lawhon in the 48th North Carolina. "I never saw so many flies in all my life."[87]

* * *

"Dig, watch and chop were the orders day and night," recalled Stowits. "The fatigue of the regiment was excessive." But the move from the Bermuda Hundred front to Deep Bottom in many respects profited Plaisted's brigade. "We had the best of spring water bubbling from the earth, making small streams, and in

83 *OR* 51, 2:1026.

84 Letter, Samuel P. Lockhart to Sister Ellen Lockhart, June 24, 1864, Samuel P. Lockhart Papers, Hugh Conway Browning Papers, Duke University, Durham, NC.

85 Jeffrey M. Girvan, *The 55th North Carolina in the Civil War, A History and Roster* (Jefferson, NC, 2006), 119; Joseph J. Hoyle to Wife, June 24, 1864, Joseph J. Hoyle Papers, Duke University.

86 James A. Blair Diary, June 22, 1864, James A. Blair Papers, GDAH, Atlanta, GA.

87 Walter Clark, ed., *Histories of the Several Regiments and Battalions from North Carolina in the Great War 1861–'65 ("North Carolina Regiments")*, 5 vols. (Goldsborough, NC, 1901), 3:121.

quantity to supply many brigades," remembered Stowits. Much of the picket line occupied the woods, "a welcome shade during the very warm days," he recalled.[88]

Of the fine buildings overlooking the James, only big chimneys remained. Sailors had burned the houses after the destruction of a Union gunboat the previous month. On shore and from the pontoon bridge, Foster's men had unequaled facilities for bathing, which they happily improved. Some soldiers from the 24th Massachusetts ran down rabbits, but the black servant of the 24th's colonel drowned while swimming in the James. Corporal Root wrote home, "Soldiers in bathing, find the bottom a clay soft substance & into it the negro servant sank & was drowned."[89]

That evening some drummer boys were digging at the edge of the ravine near the pontoon landing among the chimneys of the burned mansions. "They were hunting for fish worms," recorded Private Poland of the 142nd Ohio.[90] The spade of a lad from the 10th Connecticut struck a big pot. His excitement got the better of him, and instead of keeping the pot and its contents to himself, he blurted out his astonishment. Men from the 1st Connecticut Light Battery and 100th New York rushed to join him and help him unearth the jar. Taking off the cover, they found the jar nearly full of gold and silver coins. Those who unearthed and opened the jar divided its contents among themselves according to who could grab the most the quickest, with older men muscling out the drummer boys. Estimates of the loot ranged from 500 to 6,000 dollars.

"Like the rush of gold seekers to Cape Nome or the Klondyke, the soldiers lost no time in going to the river side and digging for treasure," Corporal Beecher of the 1st Connecticut Light Artillery remembered. "They sifted the sand, they searched under stones and tree roots, looked in the crotches of the tree branches, and spent all their leisure time in the vain search for the treasure, vain, because that jar was the only treasure found."[91]

Men plunged their shovels into every auspicious-looking mound or plot of fresh earth. Some even opened an apparent grave in case "the earth might be thus purposely shaped into a mound in order to disarm suspicion and render it less liable of being disturbed," recalled Private Peck of the 10th Connecticut. "The coffin was broken into, and a fellow of greater credulity than was really called for under the

88 Stowits, *One Hundredth New York*, 275–276.

89 Root to Wife, June 25, 1864.

90 Poland Diary, June 22, 1864.

91 Beecher, *First Light Battery Connecticut Volunteers*, 2:500.

circumstances explored the same with his hand but did not succeed in bringing anything to light except a few stained rags in which the body was buried."[92]

* * *

Long before Grant had finished laying the foundation for the siege of Petersburg, he had set out to extend his investment of the Cockade City from Jerusalem Plank Road to the Appomattox above the city and had launched his cavalry on a raid against Lee's railroads. When the drummer boys found their pot of gold at Deep Bottom, the main operations of the general-in-chief's second offensive against Petersburg were already well under way Southside.

No pot of gold awaited Grant's soldiers there.

92 Peck, *Army Journal*, 216.

Chapter Two

"Extend to the Left . . . by Rapid Movement, and with as Heavy Force as Possible"

PLANNING FOR the main operations of Grant's second offensive at Petersburg—the infantry's investment of the city from Jerusalem Plank Road to the Appomattox above the city and the cavalry raid on the railroads running southward from Richmond—began in earnest on the morning of June 20.

Thick fog shrouded the Southside that morning. Before 8:45 a.m., Meade learned that he now faced infantry from two divisions of Hill's Corps and two divisions of Anderson's Corps from the Army of Northern Virginia, as well as two divisions of Beauregard's Department of North Carolina and Southern Virginia. Within 15 minutes, the commander of the Army of the Potomac decided to redeploy his forces to put II Corps into reserve while V, VI, and IX Corps held the front line. He directed two divisions of VI Corps and the three White divisions of IX Corps to relieve II Corps after dark in order that II Corps might "be held in rear of the left center at some point easily accessible from all parts of the position now held by the army, and from the crossing of the Blackwater," a stream flowing eastward into Albemarle Sound.[1] The left center of the Army of the Potomac lay behind the right of V Corps, the left of which stretched about a mile beyond the Norfolk & Petersburg Railroad and almost to Jerusalem Plank Road, where it hung unprotected. From a position behind the right of V Corps, II Corps could serve several purposes. It could meet a Confederate attack against the left of V Corps, defend against a Rebel assault on the army's rear, or extend the army's left.

1 *OR* 40, 238, 250–251. Local parlance denominated a stream such as the Blackwater a "swamp." surrycountyvahistory.org. Retrieved Jan. 30, 2024.

Meade's decision to put II Corps in reserve made sense if he intended II Corps to remain in reserve long enough to afford the corps rest, because it had suffered more casualties than any of his other corps in the initial assaults on Petersburg. Putting II Corps in reserve made little sense if he intended to use the troops again soon. Ricketts's division of VI Corps already stood in reserve and VI Corps' other two divisions, in the line at the time, could join Rickett's division in reserve more easily than they could relieve II Corps. In the initial assaults on Petersburg, II Corps had suffered almost 20 times as many casualties as VI Corps.[2]

By 10:00 a.m. Maj. Gen. David Bell Birney, the Alabama-born Philadelphia lawyer in command of II Corps that day, who had suffered wounds at Gettysburg and Spotsylvania, directed some of his artillery to open slowly, "firing in the direction of the town and bridge." At 10:30 a.m., Meade in a humanitarian vein, wired Birney, "Unless there is some military object other than mere annoyance to the enemy, I would prefer not shelling the town." Birney replied, "Shelling the town seems to require the enemy to cease firing. . . . The enemy commenced the artillery firing on us." That satisfied Meade. His chief of staff, Maj. Gen. Andrew Atkinson Humphreys, an engineer and former division commander, replied on Meade's behalf, "Shelling the town to stop the firing of the enemy's batteries is a legitimate military operation, and may be resorted to whenever necessary."[3]

Meanwhile, pursuant to Meade's orders, the staffs of II and V Corps examined the ground for the new camp of II Corps. "The only good camping ground is in the vicinity of the Avery house," Lt. Col. Charles H. Morgan, chief of staff of II Corps, reported to Birney. "We would be between the main turnpike to Norfolk and the Norfolk railroad." Birney replied, "That ground will suit."[4]

Major General Ambrose E. Burnside, the commander of IX Corps on the right of V Corps, no sooner heard of the plan than he raised an alarm about his corps' inability to man its portion of II Corps' line without its Fourth Division, which consisted of African-American troops and was known as the "Colored Division." That division was slated to join Butler's forces north of the Appomattox. To appease Burnside, a former commander of the Army of the Potomac who had waived rank to serve under Meade, the latter rescinded the order transferring the Colored Division to Butler.

2 Ibid., 1:222, 228 (6,624 II Corps casualties in June 1864 minus the approximately 2,407 casualties of June 21–23 or about 4,217, and 893 VI Corps casualties in June 1864 minus around 651 casualties of June 21–23, or about 242); see Table 3: Casualties at Jerusalem Plank Road, June 21–24, 1864, *infra.*

3 *OR* 40, 2:238–239.

4 Ibid., 240–241.

That morning Grant instructed Meade, "As soon as Wilson's cavalry is rested they should make a raid upon the enemy's railroads." The general-in-chief wanted Wilson's division to cross the Weldon Railroad "as near Petersburg as possible," strike the South Side railway first, and afterward hit the Richmond & Danville to do "all the damage possible." Grant hoped that destroying the railroads would force Lee to abandon Petersburg and Richmond for want of supplies. With Wilson would ride out 30 volunteers from the Iron Brigade "equipped and ready . . . to destroy distant railroad bridges." They would accompany Wilson "until the proper time for cutting loose."[5] Grant expected them to return by way of New Berne on North Carolina's coast.

Meade prepared his cavalry for the raid contemplated by Grant but urged that they await the return of Sheridan from his unsuccessful attempt to link up with Hunter in the Shenandoah Valley. The victor of Gettysburg feared that as Little Phil crossed to the Southside, Hampton would disengage from Sheridan and pounce on Wilson's raiders. Meade thought that if Sheridan ventured up the south bank of the James with Wilson, that would "make his force such that it could not be stopped."[6] The commander of the Army of the Potomac ignored that Hampton had just stopped Little Phil at Trevilian Station and would follow if not precede him Southside, where the South Carolinian could expect reinforcement by the Southside Rebel cavalrymen facing Wilson.

Grant declined to wait for Sheridan's return with his tired troopers.

* * *

On the afternoon of June 20, Wilson declared that he could not prepare adequately for his raid before daylight on June 22. He selected for the raid about 3,100 cavalrymen from his own division, designating most of the 3rd New Jersey Cavalry, a smaller part of the 22nd New York Cavalry, and most of the 18th Pennsylvania Cavalry with about 1,146 men to remain with the Army of the Potomac.[7] His cavalry division would bring two brigades on the raid. The

5 Ibid., 232, 234. See also Jim Epperson, "A secret sidebar to the Wilson-Kautz Raid," petersburgsiege.org. Retrieved Feb. 13, 2023.

6 *OR* 40, 2:232. Wilson agreed with Meade. James Harrison Wilson, *Under the Old Flag: Recollections of Military Operations in the War for the Union, the Spanish War, the Boxer Rebellion, etc.*, vol. 1 (New York, 1912), 457; James Harrison Wilson, *The Life of John A. Rawlins: Lawyer, Assistant Adjutant-General, Chief of Staff, Major General of Volunteers, and Secretary of War* (New York, 1916), 258–259.

7 Wilson recalled detaching only the 18th Pennsylvania Cavalry and part of the 3rd New Jersey Cavalry. Wilson, *Under the Old Flag*, 1:458. Part of the 22nd New York Cavalry was detached as well. *OR* 40, 1:228. Attached to the portion of the 22nd New York Cavalry that Wilson took with him was a group of 69 horsemen from Gregg's cavalry division. Noble D. Preston, *History of the Tenth Regiment*

1st Connecticut Cavalry, 2nd New York "Harris Light" Cavalry and 5th New York Cavalry, and the 2nd Ohio Cavalry formed McIntosh's brigade. The 1st New Hampshire Cavalry, 8th New York "Rochester Regiment" Cavalry, 22nd New York "Rochester Cavalry," 1st Vermont Cavalry, and the right wing (Companies A–F) of the 3rd Indiana Cavalry formed Chapman's brigade.

Wilson considered the 2nd New York and 1st Vermont of his division good regiments and the 5th New York Cavalry "as good as any cavalry regiment in the Army of the Potomac." The rest of the division he thought "all entirely inexperienced; they were greener than grass."[8] To make matters worse, their Smith's carbines had rubber cartridges that sealed the gases in the breach and were hard to remove.

The horse artillery attached to Wilson's division consisted of two batteries, Battery K, 1st United States Artillery, and Battery C–E, 4th United States Artillery. A detachment of the 3rd New Jersey Cavalry remained with Wilson as his provost guard, and a detachment of the 8th Illinois cavalry as his escort.

The need to leave detachments from the 3rd New Jersey Cavalry, 22nd New York Cavalry, and 18th Pennsylvania Cavalry for various details led Wilson to seek reinforcement by at least a brigade of cavalry from the Army of the James. Grant instructed Butler to send Wilson all the cavalry that the Army of the James could spare. Butler directed four regiments of the Army of the James's cavalry division under Brig. Gen. August V. Kautz to report to Wilson at Prince George Court House with two pieces of artillery. A native of Germany who had grown up in Ohio, Kautz had served in the Mexican War and had graduated from West Point. In 1863 he led the 2nd Ohio Cavalry in pursuit of Confederate Brig. Gen. John H. Morgan and his raiders, and later worked with Wilson at the Cavalry Bureau.

Kautz's division numbered 2,414 horsemen.[9] His first brigade consisted of the "Van Alen Cavalry," the 3rd New York Cavalry, and the "Cameron Dragoons"—the 5th Pennsylvania Cavalry. His second brigade included the 1st District of Columbia Cavalry and the 11th Pennsylvania Cavalry, known as "Harlan's Light Cavalry." Wilson considered Kautz's troopers some of the "wildest

of Cavalry New York State Volunteers, August, 1861, to August, 1865 (New York, 1892), 604; Warren W. Irish, "How 80 of the 10th N. J. [sic] Cav. Came to be with Gen. Wilson on His Raid in June, 1864," in *National Tribune* (Washington, D.C.), Feb. 1, 1900, p. 3, cols. 5–6. Part of the 3rd New Jersey Cavalry served as Wilson's provost guard on the raid while part of the 8th Illinois Cavalry served as his escort. Ibid., 232.

8 James H. Wilson, "The Cavalry of the Army of the Potomac," *MHSM*, 13:77–78.

9 *OR* 40, 1:750.

rag-tag and bob-tail cavalry I ever saw." The Illinoisan also thought Kautz's division "poorly organized."[10]

Butler retained only the 1st Battalion, 4th Massachusetts Cavalry, and the 1st New York Mounted Rifles from Kautz's division. Horse artillery accompanying Kautz's division consisted of four guns in Battery B, 1st United States Artillery. The division also brought with it four mountain howitzers.

The orders to prepare for a raid inspired a lighthearted attitude in Wilson's division. First Sergeant John P. Matthews of Company E in the 3rd Indiana wrote, "the change of base which General Grant has now assumed opened up new fields for us cavalry, in which there were several railroads for us to inspect and put into [dis]repair and [in]convenience of our confederate brethren."[11]

The orders also caused excitement in Kautz's division in its encampment on Bermuda Hundred. "Nearly all night was spent adjusting our equipments and packing up for a move, we knew not where," recalled Cpl. Wilbur F. Lunt of Company I in the 1st District of Columbia Cavalry of Spears's brigade. "Many of us did not sleep at all, but as we used to do, as boys, the night before the Fourth of July, we kept awake so that we might be the first on hand in the morning."[12]

* * *

After Meade made his suggestions about the proposed cavalry raid, he and Grant agreed to a person-to-person conference to discuss the future operations of their army group's infantry. The commander of the Army of the Potomac, on the way to meet the general-in-chief, paused for a talk with Maj. Gen. Gouverneur Kemble Warren, an engineer wounded at Gettysburg and the commander of V Corps. The talk, in Warren's tent, turned into a shouting match in front of other officers present.

Warren had thrice failed, according to Meade, "to yield his judgment so as to promptly execute orders, where these orders should happen not to receive his sanction or be in accordance with his views." Warren had first displayed this trait on November 30 of the previous year during the Mine Run campaign. In command of II Corps during Maj. Gen. Winfield Scott Hancock's convalescence from a Gettysburg wound, Warren had called off an attack that he had proposed. On May 12, 1864, in command of V Corps at Spotsylvania, despite peremptory

10 Wilson, "The Cavalry of the Army of the Potomac," *MHSM*, 13:60; Wilson, *Under the Old Flag*, 1:454; Wilson, *The Life of John A. Rawlins*, 258–259.

11 James A. Goecker, *Hoosier Spies and Horse Marines: A History of the Third Indiana Cavalry, East Wing* (Jefferson, NC, 2023), 130, 238.

12 Edward P. Tobie, *History of the First Maine Cavalry, 1861–1865* (Boston, 1887), 338.

orders, he had delayed attacking in support of the troops who had overrun the Mule Shoe until Grant had authorized Meade to relieve Warren. On June 18 at Petersburg, Warren once again had delayed executing peremptory orders to attack. During their argument on June 20, Meade thought Warren forgot "the respect due to me as his superior officer."[13]

Grant and Meade met at City Point after noon on June 20. Apprised of Meade's dissatisfaction with the V Corps commander, Grant once again authorized Meade to relieve Warren. Grant and Meade then determined to invest Petersburg from the Army of the Potomac's left near Jerusalem Plank Road to the Appomattox above the city. This would entail an extension of the Federal left by about seven miles along the outside of the remainder of the Dimmock Line, cutting the roads and railroads connecting the Cockade City with the south and west—particularly the Weldon and South Side railroads. Grant and Meade intended that this, like the cavalry raid, would force Lee to abandon Petersburg and Richmond, but unlike the raid would force him to fight in the open field.

The original plan called for the commander of the Army of the Potomac to put II Corps into reserve and afterward on V Corps' left. Then he would draw back VI Corps into reserve while XVIII Corps of Butler's army took its place in the trenches. Afterward VI Corps would go into position on the left of II Corps. Next Meade would withdraw IX Corps, while all of X Corps that Butler could spare from his strong Bermuda Hundred fortifications would take the place of IX Corps in the line. IX Corps, when available, would deploy on the left of VI Corps. The troops would fortify as they went, cutting first the Weldon Railroad and then the South Side railway, destroying them as far from Petersburg as possible. Fortifying would allow the ten divisions from II, VI, and IX corps, 52,279 effectives, to stretch the approximately seven miles from the left of V Corps just east of Jerusalem Plank Road to the Appomattox above Petersburg. "[T]hen if necessary [the] Army of the Potomac may take ten days' rations and move upon the Danville road, leaving its base of supplies here to be guarded by its fortifications and the forces of General Butler," Assistant Secretary of War Charles A. Dana reported to his boss, Secretary of War Edwin M. Stanton, at 5:00 p.m.[14]

13 John G. Selby, *Meade: The Price of Command, 1863–1865* (Kent, OH, 2008), 224–226.

14 *OR* 40, 1:25–26. Grant had invested about eight miles of fortifications at Vicksburg in May 1863. Donald L. Miller, *Vicksburg: Grant's Campaign that Broke the Confederacy* (New York, 2019), 420. Grant accomplished this with about 50,490 soldiers present for duty. *OR* 24, 3:371–372. Infantry effectives equaled around 93 percent of present for duty. Thomas L. Livermore, *Numbers and Losses in the Civil War in America, 1861–65* (Boston, 1900), 67–70. Grant thus invested Vicksburg with roughly 46,955 effectives or about 5,869 per mile. Ibid.

At Petersburg, Grant's forces at Petersburg outnumbered Lee's by about two to one at this time. See Table 1: Federal Strength, June 30, 1864, and Table 2: Confederate Strength, June 1864, *infra*. II Corps

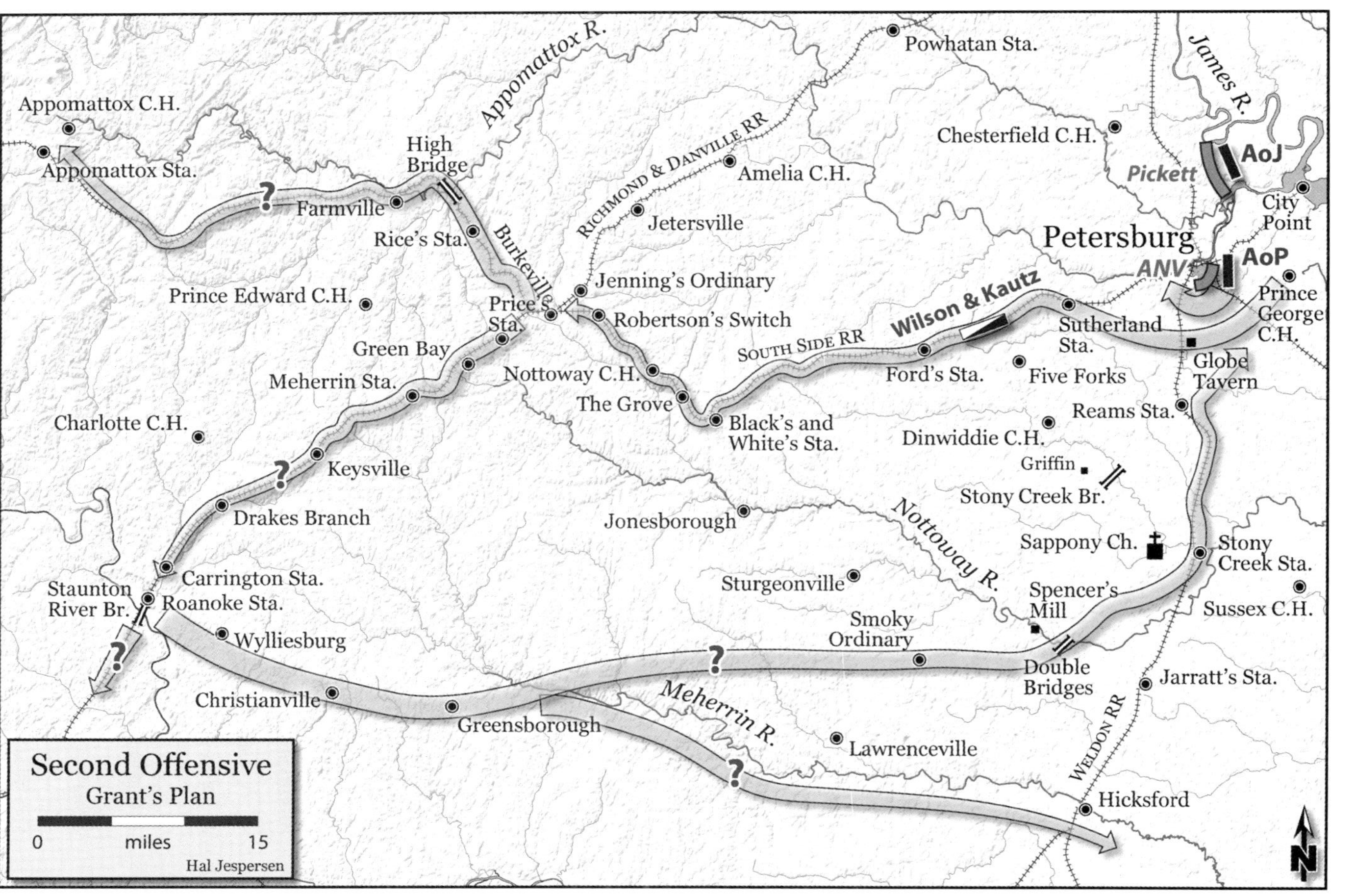
Second Offensive
Grant's Plan
0
miles
15
Hal Jespersen
Appomattox C.H.
Appomattox Sta.
Farmville
High Bridge
Appomattox R.
Rice's Sta.
Burkeville
Prince Edward C.H.
Price's Sta.
Green Bay
Meherrin Sta.
Charlotte C.H.
Keysville
Drakes Branch
Carrington Sta.
Staunton River Br.
Roanoke Sta.
Wylliesburg
Christianville
Greensborough
Powhatan Sta.
RICHMOND & DANVILLE RR
Amelia C.H.
Jetersville
Jenning's Ordinary
Robertson's Switch
Nottoway C.H.
The Grove
Black's and White's Sta.
SOUTH SIDE RR
Wilson & Kautz
Ford's Sta.
Jonesborough
Sturgeonville
Nottoway R.
Smoky Ordinary
Meherrin R.
Lawrenceville
Chesterfield C.H.
Pickett
James R.
AoJ
City Point
Petersburg
ANV
AoP
Prince George C.H.
Sutherland Sta.
Globe Tavern
Five Forks
Reams Sta.
Dinwiddie C.H.
Griffin
Stony Creek Br.
Sappony Ch.
Spencer's Mill
Stony Creek Sta.
Sussex C.H.
Double Bridges
Jarratt's Sta.
WELDON RR
Hicksford
N

When Meade returned to his headquarters in a house east of Petersburg, he mulled over relieving Warren and learned that Grant had decided at 5:40 p.m. to direct Butler to extend his lines to relieve the two VI Corps divisions in Butler's line by noon on June 21. The two VI Corps divisions, with Ricketts's division already in reserve, would give Meade "another army corps foot-loose" to begin the extension of the Federal left. At 6:30 p.m. Meade responded, "Then, when the Sixth is relieved, as you propose, I will move both corps, Second and Sixth, to the left and endeavor to stretch to the Appomattox." Until IX Corps strengthened its line, it would remain unavailable. Grant wanted Meade to "extend to the left . . . by rapid movement, and with as heavy force as possible."[15]

Meade's idea of moving both corps, an improvement on the original plan of moving II Corps first and then VI Corps, would satisfy Grant's desire for a movement with as heavy a force as possible, but Meade must have soon suspected that moving II and VI corps together was unlikely. That evening his chief of staff Humphreys wrote, "It is probable that [VI Corps] will not be relieved before tomorrow night."[16]

* * *

The relief of II Corps began, as planned, that night of June 20 while Butler's troops established the Deep Bottom bridgehead. II Corps' troops tramped a few miles back to the Avery house in their left rear and encamped on the house's

---

had 21,190 officers and men present for duty and thus 19,706 effectives on June 20, 1864. *OR* 40, 2:277. VI Corps had 18,311 officers and men present for duty and thus 17,029 effectives on June 30, 1864. Ibid., 542. Adding losses of 651 effectives from June 21 through June 23 gives VI Corps 17,680 effectives on June 30, 1864. (For the losses of VI Corps from June 21 through June 23, see this chapter, n. 86, Chapter Six, n. 59, and Chapter Seven, n. 57, *infra*. Adding losses to the next end-of-month tally to determine strength prior to a battle, while logical, is not infallible because of the tendency of detached soldiers to return to their unit after it suffered a disaster. Johnson Hagood, *Memoirs of the War of Secession from the Original Manuscripts of Johnson Hagood* (Columbia, SC, 1910), 299–300.) IX Corps had 16,014 officers and men present for duty and hence 14,893 effectives on June 30, 1864. *OR* 40, 2:542. A force of 52,279 effectives in II, VI and IX Corps on June 20, 1864, would have yielded 7,469 effectives for each of the seven miles they had to cover. *OR* 40, 1:25-26, 2:277, 542.

Furthermore, the initial plan called for seizing and fortifying the projected contravallation a section at a time rather than trying to take and hold all the ground at once. Ibid., 1:26. Even II Corps alone could have covered the first section, extending about three miles from Jerusalem Plank Road to the Weldon Railroad, with its 19,706 effectives providing 6,568 effectives per mile. Ibid., 1:25–26, 2:277.

By "Danville road," the Richmond & Danville Railroad is meant. Those familiar with railroads often refer to them as roads. The "Milwaukee Road," for example, was the Chicago, Milwaukee, St. Paul, and Pacific Railroad. american-rails.com. Retrieved Nov. 13, 2024.

15 Ibid., 233.

16 Ibid., 245.

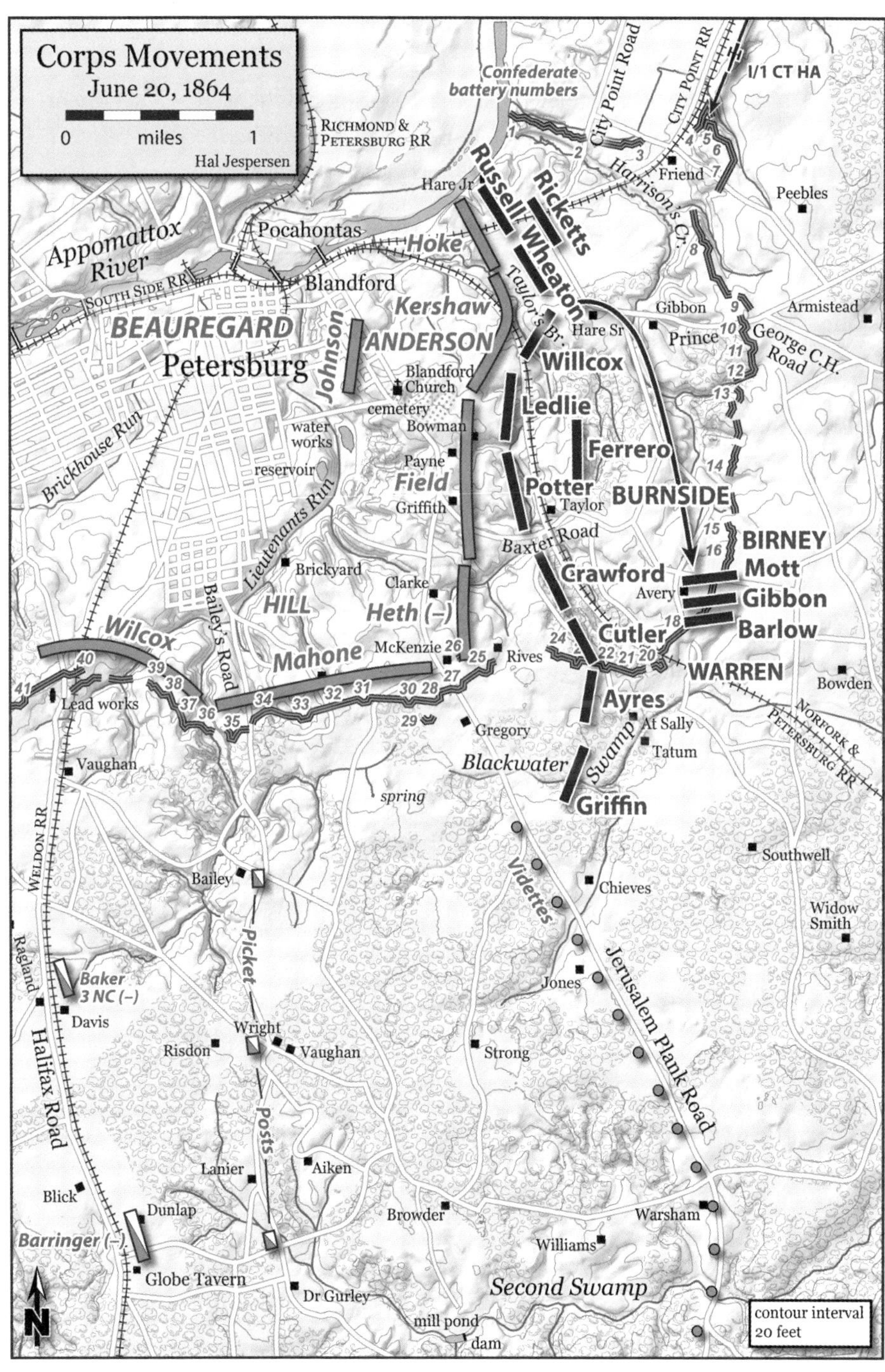
Corps Movements
June 20, 1864
0 miles 1
Hal Jespersen
Confederate battery numbers
I/1 CT HA
Richmond & Petersburg RR
City Point Road
City Point RR
Appomattox River
South Side RR
Pocahontas
Blandford
Hoke
Kershaw
BEAUREGARD
ANDERSON
Johnson
Petersburg
Russell
Ricketts
Wheaton
Harrison's Cr.
Taylor's Br.
Hare Jr
Friend
Peebles
Gibbon
Armistead
Hare Sr
Prince
George C.H. Road
Willcox
Ledlie
Ferrero
Blandford Church
cemetery
Bowman
water works
reservoir
Payne
Field
Griffith
Potter
Taylor
BURNSIDE
Brickhouse Run
Lieutenants Run
Baxter Road
BIRNEY
Mott
Gibbon
Barlow
Crawford
Avery
Cutler
WARREN
Brickyard
Clarke
HILL
Heth (–)
Wilcox
Bailey's Road
Mahone
McKenzie
Rives
Bowden
Norfolk & Petersburg RR
Ayres
At Sally
Tatum
Lead works
Gregory
Vaughan
Blackwater
Swamp
spring
Griffin
Weldon RR
Southwell
Bailey
Videttes
Chieves
Widow Smith
Picket
Posts
Ragland
Baker 3 NC (–)
Davis
Jones
Jerusalem Plank Road
Wright
Risdon
Vaughan
Strong
Halifax Road
Lanier
Aiken
Blick
Dunlap
Browder
Warsham
Barringer (–)
Williams
Globe Tavern
Dr Gurley
Second Swamp
mill pond
dam
contour interval 20 feet
N

plowed fields. Many men hoped for a long respite from battle during which they might recuperate.

A soldier in the 57th New York, the National Guard Rifle Regiment, in MacDougall's New York Brigade of Barlow's division, described his reaction on going into reserve. "We felt like veterans whose wars were over and henceforth we would rest from bloodshed, for a season at least, far from the din of musketry and the unceasing pop, pop of the pickets, that through the livelong day and night kept up a Fourth-of-July racket in dead earnest," the soldier told 1st Lt. Gilbert Frederick of the 57th's Company C. Congratulating themselves on the "good time" awaiting them, the 57th's troops "stopped to camp and actually laid out company streets, and lay down to sleep and pleasant dreams."[17]

Other soldiers felt similarly. "I recall that a rumor, which veteran soldiers will recognize as of familiar sound, spread through the ranks of the regiment that the corps was now to be held in reserve, to rest and recruit after its months of arduous and wasting service," noted 1st Lt. Thomas J. Hastings, a former machinist commanding Company D in the 15th Massachusetts of Pierce's brigade in Gibbon's division.[18]

Capt. Edwin B. Houghton of the 17th Maine, wounded at Chancellorsville and Spotsylvania, shared Hastings's impression. "Having been continually in the front for so long a period, it was supposed that we were sent to the rear for a temporary rest," Houghton recalled.[19]

But for other II Corps veterans, the word "reserve" left a bitter taste in the mouth. These troops expected neither rest, nor recruiting, nor a good time. Their experience at Gettysburg had made them cynical. There a member of II Corps' Irish Brigade, informed that his division would remain in reserve, scoffed: "In resarve," he said. "Yis, resarved fur the hivy foightin."[20] His remark became proverbial in II Corps, which at Gettysburg had not remained in reserve for long and had done some very heavy fighting.

Lieutenant Frederick typified those who took the reserve designation with a grain of salt. "Reserve, did I say?" he wrote of II Corps' reserve experience. "Yes! A reserve which gave rise to the name, 'Hancock's Cavalry;' a reserve that seldom

17 Gilbert Frederick, *The Story of a Regiment, Being a Record of the Military Services of the Fifty-Seventh New York State Volunteer Infantry in the War of the Rebellion, 1861–1865* (Chicago, 1895), 251–252.

18 Andrew E. Ford, *The Story of the Fifteenth Regiment Massachusetts Volunteer Infantry in the Civil War, 1861–1864* (Clinton, MA, 1898), 333.

19 Edwin B. Houghton, *The Campaigns of the Seventeenth Maine* (Portland, ME, 1866), 207.

20 Francis A. Walker, *History of the Second Army Corps in the Army of the Potomac* (New York, 1886), 543; St. Clair A. Mulholland, *The Story of the 116th Regiment Pennsylvania Volunteers in the War of the Rebellion, the Record of a Gallant Command* (Philadelphia, 1903), 271.

stayed in one place long enough to get rested from its last tramp to and from the extreme end of the line; a reserve that was in nearly every fight . . . reserved for surprises, for heavy marching and for the support of every charge."[21]

Orders to move out on the morning of June 21 therefore did not surprise the skeptical. Sergeant Edward H. Wade of Company F of the 14th Connecticut tumbled to his predicament quickly. "We were told to put up our tents, as we might stay there a week or more," he remembered. "So, of course, we went to work next morning and had just got our streets nearly laid out when orders came to pack up, and at ten o'clock we started in the direction of the Weldon railroad. It was the hottest day of the season and we nearly suffocated in the dust."[22]

The gullible took longer to shed their illusions. Lieutenant Frederick's anonymous comrade in the 57th New York described how hopes sank as June 21 progressed. This soldier's tentmate slept late. "He could afford to take one good sleep now for weren't we relieved?" commented the anonymous soldier. Just as his tentmate rose and prepared to eat, "an exceedingly mean-looking officer, a mounted Aid, brought orders to move at once, as they usually did when we were comfortably fixed," the soldier recalled. "And so vanished that camp, and before Abe could say grace he saw the last of breakfast and was on the march again." For a while the "dusty road winding through green fields and pine forests far away to the rear" allowed the men to console themselves that they were going to "a new and pleasant district" on the Blackwater, untouched by war. "But presently we began to turn to the front and then we understood that we were going to another attack," recollected the soldier.[23]

One man had no wish for rest. "General Hancock's wound is in such a condition that the doctor finds it necessary to insist upon his keeping as quiet as possible this hot weather, in order to save his life, but he has a hard time in carrying out his wishes, as the General is so restless and anxious to be in his saddle and on the front line with the boys," remembered 2nd Lt. George Augustus Armes, who had originally enlisted as a private in Company B of the 16th West Virginia Infantry. Wounded at Fairfax Court House in May 1861, he had made his way from the Invalid Corps to the staff of II Corps. "We all do our best to keep him posted on every movement and everything of importance."[24] Hancock, a West Pointer and Mexican War veteran wounded at Churubusco, Fredericksburg, Chancellorsville,

21 Frederick, *Fifty-Seventh New York State Volunteer Infantry*, 250.

22 Charles D. Page, *History of the Fourteenth Regiment, Connecticut Vol. Infantry* (Meriden, CT, 1906), 288.

23 Frederick, *Fifty-Seventh New York State Volunteer Infantry*, 252.

24 George A. Armes, *Ups and Downs of an Army Officer* (Washington, D.C., 1900), 204.

and Gettysburg, had commanded II Corps since before Gettysburg. On the night of June 17–18, his Gettysburg wound reopened and forced him to relinquish command of II Corps to Birney, the senior division commander. Command of Birney's division shifted to Maj. Gen. Gershom Mott, wounded at Second Manassas and Chancellorsville.

* * *

At 5:10 a.m. on June 21 Birney notified Meade of II Corps' readiness to proceed. At 7:15 a.m. Meade began to implement the plan to invest Petersburg from his army's left to the Appomattox above the city. He instructed V Corps to extend its left to Jerusalem Plank Road and directed Birney to take position on the left of V Corps, stretch as far left as practicable toward the Weldon Railroad, and keep as close to the Confederate works as possible. Meade, abandoning his idea of moving II and VI Corps together, intended to send VI Corps to take post on Birney's left that night, hopefully stretching to the Appomattox above Petersburg.

Miles's brigade of Barlow's division led II Corps' march southward from the Avery house at 8:00 a.m. Divisions that had belonged to II Corps prior to the March 23, 1864, consolidation of the corps with the former III Corps wore as their insignia a club or clover, with a different color for each division. Barlow's division wore a red club. Inadvertently left on the fog-shrouded picket line until five that morning, Pvt. William Horton of the 26th Michigan in Miles's brigade of the Red Club Division began the hike with little sleep. "We come up with the regt about 8 o'clock," he recorded. "We eat our Breakfast and lay Down for a little rest. We are routed up and ordered to march."[25]

At 8:45 a.m., Meade assigned the two companies of the 1st Massachusetts Cavalry in the provost guard to assist Birney in reconnoitering. By 9:00 a.m., Barlow's and Gibbon's divisions had both departed the Avery house. Gibbon's division, which wore a white club, departed the Avery house next. "Everyone is talking of home, for we have but a matter of days to wear the blue uniform that we have worn so long," 1st Lt. Thomas Francis Galwey in the 8th Ohio of Smyth's brigade, the Gibraltar Brigade, wrote before the White Club Division's departure. "We discuss what we will do. Some of the younger ones will go back to school." Galwey thought he might join them. "If I ever recover the hearing in my ear, I may accept General Carroll's offer to get me an appointment for the Military Academy

25 William M. Horton, William M. Horton Diary, June 21, 1864, civilwardigital.com. Retrieved Feb. 11, 2023.

at West Point," noted Galwey. "I have found that although it is bloodthirsty the science of arms is all-absorbing."[26]

The trek took place on what seemed the hottest day of the season. "The weather is exceedingly hot and the dust intolerable," Cpl. Daniel Bond of the 1st Minnesota Battalion in Pierce's brigade recorded after the fog had burned off. "Our sufferings are such as no citizen would believe could be born."[27]

Mott's division, the consolidation of the former III Corps, left the Avery house last, at 9:00 a.m., wearing III Corps' old diamond insignia instead of II Corps' clubs by special dispensation.[28] At 10:00 a.m., as the men of the Diamond Division crossed the Norfolk & Petersburg, Birney ordered Mott to dispatch the 2nd United States Sharpshooters to lead the column of Barlow's division.

At the same time Lieutenant Colonel Lyman fell in with the men of Mott's division. Meade had sent Lyman to accompany II Corps and report on its progress. "The road was narrow and full of troops, and led by several clearings where young corn was growing—small, it seemed to me for the season," Lyman recalled.[29]

The column marched through a gently undulating landscape of fields and woods, parched by the sun and affording little opportunity for the employment of artillery. "The weather is very hot, and we cannot procure anything to drink but warm, muddy water, made so by men, mules and horses all rushing into it," Armes remembered. "Canteens and tin cups by the hundreds can be seen by the side of a mule's or horse's front or hind leg or nose in the water, and other men hurrying out of their way, so as to dip their caps in and drink, as if the water was from a nice cool spring."[30] During the march, three soldiers in the 11th New Jersey captured a big turkey. They took turns carrying it, hoping to get a chance to cook the bird.

Meanwhile, the relief of VI Corps met with delay, as had seemed probable the previous night. At 9:10 a.m., Meade instructed VI Corps to move to the assistance of II Corps as soon as relieved by XVIII Corps. At 9:30 a.m., Maj. Gen. Horatio Wright, a West Pointer and engineer in command of VI Corps, notified Meade of the impracticability of relieving its two divisions in the trenches. Fire from the Confederate batteries across the Appomattox would make that impossible until

26 Thomas Francis Galwey, *The Valiant Hours, Narrative of "Captain Brevet," an Irish-American in the Army of the Potomac* (Harrisburg, PA, 2011), 234–235. Galwey refers to Brig. Gen. Samuel S. Carroll, a former commander of the 8th Ohio who lost his left arm at Spotsylvania. Ezra Warner, *Generals in Blue: Lives of the Union Commanders* (Baton Rouge, 1964), 73.

27 Daniel Bond Diary and Memoir, June 21, 1864, 231, Newberry Library, Chicago, IL.

28 *OR* 40, 1:391; John Horn, "The Army of the Potomac's proud III Corps fell victim to intra-army politics," *America's Civil War* (July 1993), 20.

29 Lowe, ed., *Meade's Army*, 218.

30 Armes, *Ups and Downs of an Army Officer*, 105.

dark. The two VI Corps divisions in the trenches would remain unavailable before midday on June 22 at the earliest.

Wright prepared to dispatch Ricketts's division to Birney's assistance. At 11:45 a.m. Meade gave Wright permission to keep his entire corps in place until dark even though under the circumstances Grant's instruction to move "with as heavy force as possible" meant moving with Ricketts's division.[31] The commander of the Army of the Potomac apparently expected II Corps to require no assistance on its drive toward the Weldon Railroad—even though so far during the Virginia Campaign of 1864 the Confederates had resisted practically every Federal attempt to get around their right.

* * *

As II Corps moved out to extend the investment of Petersburg, Federal cavalry gathered for its raid on southern Virginia's railroads. Departing Bermuda Hundred at daybreak, Kautz's division reached Mount Sinai Church in Prince George County about 9:00 a.m. There Kautz found a troubling situation, writing, "Wilson, I find, is not much liked in his command."[32]

This opinion rested on the resentment of Wilson that Kautz noticed among the men of his old command, the 2nd Ohio Cavalry, such as 2nd Lt. Luman H. Tenny of the 2nd Ohio Cavalry. They had served in the more informal western theater before their reassignment to Wilson's division that spring and they chafed under Wilson's insistence on strict adherence to army protocols. "It seemed good to shake his hand and talk with him once more," Tenney recorded of his former commander. "Hope that we can be transferred to his command."[33] Tenney's comrades shared his hope, along with his dislike for Wilson. That dislike would spread to Kautz's division during the raid as the two generals clashed over how the raid should progress.

Preparations for the raid continued. "Drew rations for three days," noted German-born Phillip Koempel, promoted sergeant the previous day in Company B, the Bridgeport Rifles, of the 1st Connecticut Cavalry. "Marching order for a ten-day raid."[34]

31 *OR* 40, 2:233, 281.

32 Janet B. Hewett, et al., eds., *Supplement to the Official Records of the Union and Confederate Armies*, 100 vols. (Wilmington, NC, 1994–2001), 7:239.

33 Frances Andrews Tenney, ed., *War Diary of Luman Harris Tenney, 1861–1865* (Cleveland, 1914), 120.

34 Phillip Koempel, *Phil Koempel's Diary, 1861–1865* (n.p., 1923), 11.

First Sergeant Horace Knights Ide of the 1st Vermont got ready for a long raid, writing, "Some four or five of us messed together, and receiving a lot of beans (some four or five quarts), concluded to save them till we could get a good chance to cook them."[35] Ide, captured at Gordonsville in 1862, had suffered a wound at Bucklands in 1863.

Shortly after Kautz joined Wilson, Meade gave the Illinoisan his orders. The commander of the Army of the Potomac directed Wilson to move at 2:00 a.m. the next day, destroy the junction of the Richmond & Danville and South Side railroads at Burkeville, wreck as much of those railways as possible—including High Bridge on the South Side railway and Staunton River Bridge on the Richmond & Danville—and join with Hunter near Lynchburg if practicable.

* * *

While the infantry marched and the cavalry got marching orders, the plan to invest Petersburg from the army's left to the Appomattox above the city evolved. At 10:00 a.m., Grant suggested having V and IX corps hold a threatening attitude and prepare to advance and occupy the Confederate line opposite them the moment the Rebels weakened it in response to the move of II and VI Corps west of the plank road. "When you get there in force I do not see how the enemy can hold his present line," the general-in-chief wrote to Meade. "You certainly will have it in reverse."[36] Enfilading the Rebel line with artillery fire looked practicable to Grant from the map as marked by Lieutenant Colonel Comstock and Brigadier General Barnard, but Grant left it to Meade to determine whether the topography permitted. The suggestion puzzled Meade, who asked Grant to send Barnard and Comstock to explain Grant's views.

Grant assured Meade at 11:30 a.m. that Barnard was on the way, then suggested another possibility—shifting reserves from V and IX Corps west of Jerusalem Plank Road. "I do not know that the threatening attitude recommended for the troops left to hold the ground already ours will be so advisable as to hold our front with a thin line, and form as large reserves from each corps as possible, ready to move to the front or to the left to support the troops moving in that direction as circumstances may require."[37] Such reserves had not yet become available for the purposes Grant envisioned. V Corps required Griffin's division, which had withdrawn into reserve

35 Elliott W. Hoffman, *History of the First Vermont Cavalry Volunteers in the War of the Great Rebellion* (Baltimore, 2000), 183.

36 *OR* 40, 2:268.

37 Ibid., 268–269.

the previous night, to lead the corps' own advance to Jerusalem Plank Road. IX Corps had not yet strengthened its lines enough to release its reserves.

* * *

Around noon, President Lincoln arrived at City Point on a white side-wheel steamer, the USS *Baltimore*, to pay his first visit to Grant's army group. The president's entourage included his son Tad, Assistant Secretary of the Navy Gustavus V. Fox, and the proprietor of the Willard Hotel. Lincoln had simply jumped aboard the ship the previous day and cruised down. Soon after arrival at City Point, the president flirted with misadventure on the way to see Grant.

"About one o'clock p.m., a long, gaunt bony man with a queer admixture of the comical and the doleful in his countenance that reminded one of a professional undertaker cracking a dry joke, undertook to reach the general's tent by scrambling through a hedge and coming in alone," recalled Cadwallader. "He was stopped by a hostler and told to 'keep out of here.'" The man who looked like an undertaker responded that he thought the general would allow him to enter.

"No sanitary folks allowed inside," declared the guard, referring to personnel of the US Sanitary Commission.

The man who looked like an undertaker identified himself as "Abraham Lincoln, President of the United States, seeking an interview with Gen. Grant!" remembered Cadwallader.

Saluting, the guard allowed the president to pass.

Lincoln stepped under the large fly in front of Grant's tent.[38]

Major General George B. McClellan, one of Grant's predecessors as general-in-chief and Lincoln's expected opponent in the election of the coming November, had in 1861 snubbed Lincoln by refusing to see him under far less stressful circumstances.

The idea of such a reception never occurred to Grant, who rose and shook hands with the president cordially. Lincoln announced to Grant, "I don't expect I can do much good, and in fact I'm afraid I may do some harm but I'll put myself under your orders and if you find me doing anything wrong just send me right away."[39] Though seasick, the Railsplitter declined a recommended glass of champagne. "I have seen too many fellows seasick ashore from drinking that very stuff," the president said.[40]

38 Thomas, ed., *Three Years with Grant*, 231–232.

39 Greene, *A Campaign of Giants*, 1:228.

40 Porter, *Campaigning with Grant*, 217.

Grant introduced to Lincoln such members of the general-in-chief's staff as were present and unacquainted. A lunch was soon served where Honest Abe entertained Grant and his staff with jokes and stories. "He seldom indulged even in a smile until he reached the climax of a humorous narration; then he joined heartily with the listeners in the laugh which followed," Colonel Porter recollected. "He usually sat on a low camp-chair, and wound his legs around each other as if in an effort to get them out of the way, and with his long arms he accompanied what he said with all sorts of odd gestures."[41] In the severe heat, the lunch lasted well into the afternoon.

* * *

About noon on June 21, Barlow's division reached a wide road—Jerusalem Plank Road—at right angles to the division's march route about six miles south of Petersburg. To the left lay a big cornfield and a large white wooden house with several dependencies, deserted by the Williams family. The Williamses had fled to Petersburg taking their furniture but leaving some slaves, some cows, and, most importantly to Lyman, some ice.

At the plank road, the Red Club Division encountered solitary videttes from the 3rd North Carolina Cavalry of Barringer's North Carolina Cavalry Brigade. The videttes had advanced about a mile east of the picket line of the 3rd's picket line, which lay about a mile east of the regiment's picket post. The picket post stood about a mile east of the 3rd's body encamped near the Davis house, on the railway at the junction of the Halifax and Vaughan roads about five miles south of Petersburg. The rest of Barringer's brigade tented by the railroad near Globe Tavern, over a mile south of the 3rd. Dearing's cavalry brigade of the Department of North Carolina and Southern Virginia, horsemen temporarily assigned to W. H. F. Lee's division, picketed the railroad still farther south, to the vicinity of Reams Station, about 12 miles south of the Cockade City. Both Confederate brigades had orders to drive off any raiding party attempting to damage the railway.

After arriving at Jerusalem Plank Road, Birney sent Barlow's division westward as if to extend II Corps to the Weldon Railroad and then close up to the Dimmock Line. Instead, the corps commander decided to hold back Gibbon's and Mott's divisions near the Williams house to await developments. If Barlow's division could not reach the Weldon Railroad, II Corps might have to close up to the Dimmock Line near the plank road and then extend to the tracks.

41 Ibid., 220.

Barlow's division crossed the plank road and slowly advanced along the lane beyond the Williams farm, throwing up rifle pits during pauses. Captain Benjamin Williams Crowninshield's two-company detachment of the 1st Massachusetts Cavalry led, supported by Miles's brigade. Crowninshield, a former captain of Harvard College's crew team, had served as the Army of the Potomac's provost marshal in 1863.

"The firing began to grow very lively as soon as we reached the Jerusalem plank road, where we were obliged to halt, and feel our way slowly, and fortify as we advanced," remembered Armes.[42] Barlow's division groped its way along a lane that led westward from the plank road. Wounded began to come back from the Unionist front, some walking and others on stretchers.

Companies H and K of the 116th Pennsylvania skirmished on the flank of Barlow's column. "I shot at a reb cavalry man I thought I had killed him, I went down and found the Johnnie gone, but I found where he had been the most beautiful double barreled shot gun I ever seen," noted 1st Sgt. Samuel A. Clear of Company K. "I kept it a while and then I had to lay it down in the woods and leave it lay. I would have given fifty dollars to of had it sent home."[43]

On the Browder farm, about halfway across the approximately three miles separating Jerusalem Plank Road from the Weldon Railroad, Barlow's division encountered the 3rd North Carolina Cavalry's picket line. Firing increased. The Red Club Division reached a fork in the lane and took the track leading northwestward past the Aiken farm, about a mile east of the railway, toward the 3rd's picket post on the Risdon farm. Brigadier General Francis Channing Barlow rode with Miles's brigade. A Harvard educated New York lawyer wounded at Antietam and Gettysburg, Barlow liked to wear a red flannel shirt and carry a saber with which to swat skulkers. His wife Arabella, ten years older than he, worked as an army nurse at the City Point hospital where she was contracting a fever which would kill her the following month. New York diarist George Templeton Strong had written years earlier that she was "certainly the most brilliant, cultivated, easy graceful, effective talker of womankind, and has read, thought and observed much and well."[44]

By 12:55 p.m., Gibbon's and Mott's divisions were massing at the Williams farm though Barlow expected Gibbon's division to follow closely behind the Red

42 Armes, *Ups and Downs of an Army Officer*, 104.

43 W. Springer Menge and J. August Shimrak, *The Civil War Notebook of Daniel Chisholm: A Chronicle of Daily Life in the Union Army, 1864–1865* (New York, 1989), 24–25.

44 Alan Nevins and Milton Halsey Thomas, eds., *The Diary of George Templeton Strong*, 4 vols. (New York, 1952), 2:217.

Francis Channing Barlow

Library of Congress

Club Division. Gibbon's and Mott's divisions could still support Barlow's division if it ran into trouble, but they could also proceed directly to the left of V Corps if that proved preferable. During a halt at about 1:10 p.m., a contraband informed Barlow that his division had arrived within two and a half miles of the railway. "The cavalry report the enemy in force and have had a little firing," reported Barlow. "It is nothing."[45] The Red Club commander had Brig. Gen. Nelson A. Miles, a former crockery clerk wounded at Chancellorsville where he earned a Medal of Honor, deploy as skirmishers the 61st New York, the Clinton Guards, to the right of the lane, and the 81st Pennsylvania to the lane's left.

* * *

Alerts from the 3rd North Carolina Cavalry's videttes went to the regiment's picket posts and from there to the 3rd's commander at his camp near the Davis house. He brought the body of his regiment up near the picket post at the east end of the Risdon farm preparatory to the arrival of the Federals on the track they had taken. He also dispatched a courier to his brigade's headquarters at Globe Tavern to apprise his superior of the 3rd's need for support.

Brigadier General Rufus C. Barringer led the North Carolina Cavalry Brigade of W. H. F. Lee's division. An attorney who had read law with his brother after graduating from the University of North Carolina at Chapel Hill, Barringer had suffered wounds at Brandy Station and Bristow Station and was known as "Aunt Nancy."[46] Captain John Marion Galloway of the 5th North Carolina Cavalry of Barringer's brigade considered Barringer, "Brave enough, but of a prudent,

45 *OR* 40, 2:275–276.

46 Clark, ed., *North Carolina Regiments*, 4:88.

methodical, cautious temperament."[47] Another Tarheel trooper thought Barringer old and slow but a good officer.[48]

The brigadier and his staff "had mounted and were only waiting for the Bugle to sound, the signal to march, when a courier dashed up at breathless speed from Col. John A. Baker, who, with his regiment, the 3rd, was on picket duty about three miles away, reporting that he was being hard pressed by the enemy and was in dire need of quick re-enforcements," recalled 1st Lt. Fred C. Foard, recently appointed aide-de-camp to Barringer.[49] Aunt Nancy hurriedly formed his line. "We were wholly without support, but the thick undergrowth and other surroundings favored a vigorous resistance in a dismounted fight," Foard recollected.[50]

Barringer prepared an ambush for the advancing Federals. He had McGregor's battery, the 2nd Stuart Light Horse Artillery, unlimber at a high yet screened spot near the Davis house. The brigadier kept the 5th North Carolina Cavalry in reserve behind the guns. He dismounted the 1st North Carolina Cavalry and 2nd North Carolina Cavalry and formed two heavy skirmish lines. The men of the 2nd formed the first line, concealed in the undergrowth on the eastern border of the Davis farm, about a quarter mile behind the 3rd's picket post on the Risdon farm and around a mile from the railroad. The 2nd's troopers received instructions not to fire until the Federals came within 100 yards of them. Then these Tarheels would fire a single volley and withdraw to the trees a short distance to the rear, where they would join the 1st North Carolina Cavalry in a second line and make a stand on the lane that led to the railway. When the Federals reached that defile in the timber, the four three-inch rifles of McGregor's battery would open fire. Barringer dispatched Foard to Baker to apprise him of the plan.

* * *

The men of the 2nd United States Sharpshooters were still hustling from Mott's division at the rear of Birney's column to Barlow's division at its head. The marksmen had started off almost at the double quick. As they hurried along, they

47 Ibid., 3:538.

48 Letter, M. P. Person to Sally, June 9, 1864, Presley Carter Person Papers, Duke University.

49 Fred C. Foard Memoir, 5, Fred C. Foard Papers, North Carolina Department of Archives and History, Raleigh, NC. While the 3rd North Carolina encamped little more than a mile from the camp of the rest of Barringer's brigade as the crow flies, about three miles separated the brigade's camp from the picket post of the 3rd on the Risdon farm by way of the Weldon Railroad and the Davis farm. Donald Richard Lauter, Unpublished Records of Artifacts Recovered from the Battlefields of Southeastern Virginia, Disputanta, VA.

50 Clark, ed., *North Carolina Regiments*, 1:431.

left behind 1st Sgt. Wyman S. White of Company F, one of the regiment's New Hampshire companies.

Infantrymen were marching abreast of the sharpshooters on the other side of a high fence in the slightly rolling fields, interspersed with woods, streams, and swamps. White had lost his rifle's tompion, a wooden plug designed to keep water out of the rifle barrel. As he hastened along, he noticed an infantryman's tompion just hanging in the muzzle of his rifle. "I called Captain [Samuel F.] Murry's attention to it and told him that when the [tompion] dropped, I was going to get it," remembered White. "I climbed over the high fence and had just gotten over when the coveted [tompion] hit a fence stake and fell to the ground." Picking up the tompion, White walked along the fence hoping to find a place with the boards down so that he could get back onto the road without climbing over the fence again.

White found such a place near a fork in the road. He discovered that his regiment had outmarched him and gotten out of sight. He could not tell which road his comrades had taken. "I took the right hand road for it led more towards the enemy's lines and I heard firing in that direction," White remembered. "I knew General Barlow had borrowed our regiment to do skirmishing where he was intending to attack the enemy." White hurried on intending to overtake his regiment, passing infantrymen who were forming a line at right angles to the road. Expecting to find his unit deployed in a skirmish line, he followed the road until he reached a curve. Two or three hundred feet ahead, he saw a Rebel picket post. "There were three of them around a small fire right in the road and they were doing some cooking for there was no other use of a fire that hot June day," he recalled. "They did not see me at all."

White turned and put as much distance as he could between the Southerners and himself. "The firing became quite brisk at that time," he remembered.[51]

* * *

Before 2:00 p.m., "what was left of the Regt . . . were placed in the advance, as advance guard," recalled Pvt. William B. Greene, a former student in New Hampshire in the 2nd United States Sharpshooters' Company G. "The men were nearly played out with fast marching but no rest was granted them."[52] Barlow

51 Russell C. White, ed., *The Civil War Diary of Wyman S. White, First Sergeant of Company F, 2nd United States Sharpshooter Regiment, 1861–1865* (Baltimore, 1993), 265–266. White called the tompion a "tomkin." Ibid., 265.

52 William H. Hastings, ed., *Letters from a Sharpshooter: The Civil War Letters of William B. Greene, Co. G, Berdan's Sharpshooters* (Belleville, WI, 1993), 226–227.

employed the sharpshooters, known as Green Coats because of their uniforms, to replace the cavalry, which he considered generally useless. He deployed MacDougall's brigade to the left of the lane and Miles's brigade to the right.

The landscape the sharpshooters negotiated, remembered 1st Lt. Charles A. Stevens of Company G from Wisconsin, "was covered with deep woods, tangled brush, creeks and swamps, making the movement tedious and unsatisfactory."[53] The marksmen quickly pushed back the 3rd North Carolina Cavalry from its picket post at the east end of the Risdon farm. The 3rd retreated to the line of the 2nd North Carolina Cavalry.

Around 2:00 p.m. the sharpshooters arrived near the border of the Davis farm. Lieutenant Colonel Homer R. Stoughton, a Vermonter and former railroad man wounded at Po River that May, had just rejoined the 2nd United States Sharpshooters and assumed its command that morning. Stoughton "was marching along in his shirt sleeves singing I haven't got long to stay etc.," Greene recalled. Dismounted troopers of the 2nd North Carolina Cavalry in Barringer's first skirmish line along with fugitives from the 3rd poured a volley into the Green Coats. Stoughton reacted immediately. "When the volley came in he sung out to the boys to go over the fence and give it to them," Greene remembered. "Over the boys went and pitched into them & drove them in to their entrenchments near by."[54] Stoughton sought support from Col. Clinton F. MacDougall, a former banker whose brigade had taken the place of Miles's brigade in the van of Barlow's division. MacDougall's regiment, the 111th New York, led the brigade. The Vermonter told the New Yorker that the Rebels outnumbered the sharpshooters.

"Go on," replied MacDougall, unable to see the Tarheels because they had withdrawn, "there is nothing in your front."[55]

The Red Club commander considered his brush with the dismounted enemy cavalry "quite a skirmish." The contraband with Barlow's column informed the division commander that he had arrived two miles from the railroad. This accurately described the distance ahead on the lane Barlow was taking, which approached the railroad diagonally, but the tracks lay closer as the crow flew. Barlow, believing his division isolated, slowed his advance and sought orders from his corps commander. "It is for you to decide whether it is safe for us to advance so as to separate this division farther from the rest of the corps," Barlow at 2:10 p.m. wrote to Birney, who had established his headquarters at the Williams house. "We

53 Charles A. Stevens, *Berdan's United States Sharpshooters in the Army of the Potomac, 1861–1865* (St. Paul, MN, 1892), 463.

54 Hastings, ed., *Letters from a Sharpshooter*, 226.

55 Stevens, *Berdan's United States Sharpshooters*, 464.

cannot both advance and keep up connection with the rest of the corps. Is General Gibbon close behind me, as I understood he was to be?"[56]

Barlow's message to Birney illuminated the problems now faced by the Federal high command in its attempt to sever the Weldon and Southside railroads and invest Petersburg to the Appomattox above the city. Meade was pushing piecemeal into unfamiliar territory with roughly half the troops contemplated by the Federal plan. Because of the distance involved as the roads ran rather than as the crow flew, Birney could not connect with both the Weldon Railroad and V Corps and Barlow could not both advance and connect with the rest of II Corps. The only force otherwise available to extend Birney's line or assist Barlow—Ricketts's division of VI Corps—remained in reserve near the trenches which the other divisions of its corps occupied.

Stoughton resumed his advance.

* * *

Meade, who had been querying II Corps about progress since 11:30 a.m. without getting a response, became impatient. Shortly after 1:00 p.m. he rode out toward the Williams house by way of V Corps headquarters at the Chieves house. Around 1:30 p.m., he found Griffin's division massed behind its skirmishers there rather than at Jerusalem Plank Road. Meade got into a tiff with the division's commander, Brig. Gen. Charles F. Griffin, a former artillerist whom Lyman described as "always kindly to his inferiors; gruff and fault-finding to his superiors." Meade asked Griffin if his orders were not to form a continuous line of battle. Griffin replied that he could form line at any time.

"Those were not your orders, sir!" replied Meade.

"Shall I change the disposition?" Griffin asked gruffly.

"No, sir," said Army of the Potomac's leader severely. "I give you no orders; you may get those from your corps commander."[57]

At 2:30 p.m. Meade complained to Griffin's corps commander that Griffin's division had not yet advanced to Jerusalem Plank Road. A directive from Warren at 3:00 p.m. got Griffin's division moving toward the plank road, but the division advanced through Crawford's division of V Corps, causing confusion in the ranks and a kerfuffle between the division commanders. Once past Crawford's division, Sweitzer's brigade of Griffin's division deployed the left wing of the 91st Pennsylvania as skirmishers backed up by the balance of their regiment and the

56 *OR* 40, 2:276.

57 Lowe, ed., *Meade's Army*, 218.

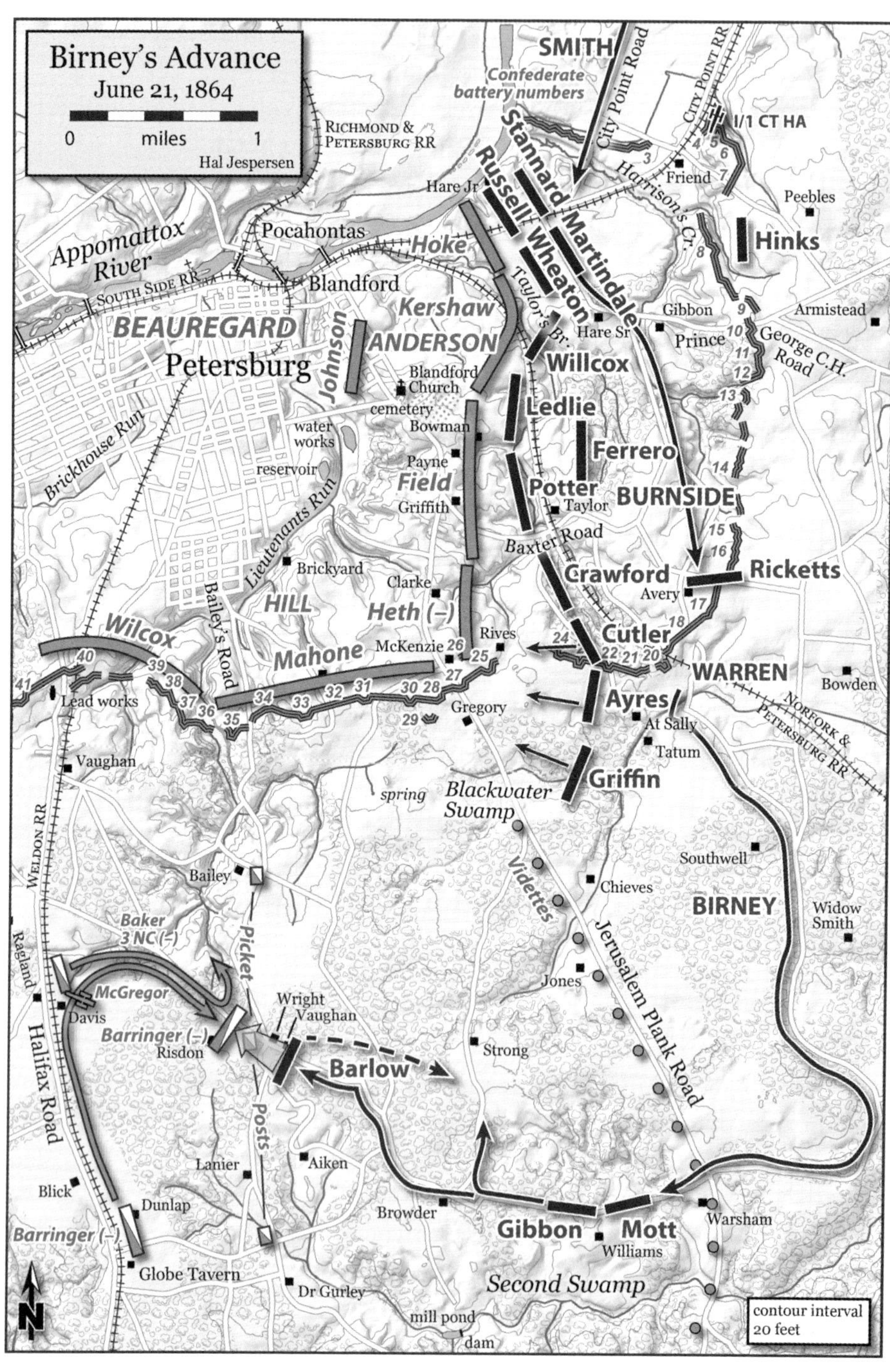
Birney's Advance
June 21, 1864
0 miles 1
Hal Jespersen
SMITH
Confederate battery numbers
City Point Road
City Point RR
I/1 CT HA
Richmond & Petersburg RR
Stannard
Russell
Martindale
Wheaton
Harrison's Cr.
Friend
Peebles
Hinks
Hare Jr
Appomattox River
Pocahontas
Hoke
South Side RR
Blandford
Kershaw
Taylor's Br.
Gibbon
Armistead
BEAUREGARD
Johnson
ANDERSON
Hare Sr
Prince
George C.H. Road
Petersburg
Blandford Church
Willcox
cemetery
Ledlie
Bowman
water works
Ferrero
Brickhouse Run
Payne
reservoir
Field
Potter
BURNSIDE
Griffith
Taylor
Lieutenants Run
Baxter Road
Brickyard
Crawford
Ricketts
Clarke
Avery
Bailey's Road
HILL
Heth (–)
Wilcox
Rives
Mahone
McKenzie
Cutler
WARREN
Bowden
Lead works
Ayres
Norfolk & Petersburg RR
Gregory
At Sally
Tatum
Vaughan
Griffin
spring
Blackwater Swamp
Weldon RR
Southwell
Bailey
Videttes
Chieves
BIRNEY
Widow Smith
Baker 3 NC (–)
Picket
Jerusalem Plank Road
Ragland
McGregor
Jones
Davis
Wright
Vaughan
Barringer (–)
Risdon
Strong
Barlow
Halifax Road
Posts
Lanier
Aiken
Blick
Dunlap
Browder
Warsham
Gibbon
Mott
Williams
Barringer (–)
Globe Tavern
Dr Gurley
Second Swamp
mill pond
dam
contour interval 20 feet
N

62nd Pennsylvania. The 91st's skirmishers, with their left on Jerusalem Plank Road and their right adjacent to Ayres's division of V Corps, pushed their Rebel counterparts back from the site of the future Fort Sedgwick, also known as Fort Hell, then dug in along with the rest of Sweitzer's brigade. At least seven skirmishers from the 91st suffered wounds, two of them mortal.[58]

* * *

Meade reached the Williams house about the same time as the carrier of Barlow's 2:10 p.m. message to Birney. Considering the ambush Barlow had endured, the difficulties encountered by Russell's and Wheaton's divisions extricating themselves from the trenches, and the unforeseen distance between Jerusalem Plank Road and the Weldon Railroad, Meade lowered his sights. He authorized Birney to terminate Barlow's reconnaissance toward the railway, swing all three divisions of II Corps into position on the left of V Corps, get as close as possible to the foe's fortifications, and extend leftward as far as practicable. This could be no farther than the Weldon Railroad even if II Corps stretched westward in a single line. The army commander countermanded part of his earlier order to Wright and instructed him to reinforce II Corps with Ricketts's division, which began preparing to move out from its bivouac about 3:00 p.m.

Birney ordered Barlow to withdraw and directed Gibbon's and Mott's divisions to move up beside V Corps. Barlow would have to wait to join them until Ricketts's division arrived to take the place of the Red Club Division. Meade, apprised by a staffer of the president's visit, headed back northward to pay his respects to Lincoln.

* * *

As the bearer of Barlow's 2:10 p.m. message headed for the Williams house, Stoughton's marksmen moved slowly ahead. At 3:00 p.m. while Meade and Birney adjusted their plans, the sharpshooters struck the second line of Barringer's skirmishers. The Secessionists—the 1st North Carolina Cavalry and the fugitives from the 2nd and 3rd—loosed another volley. Fire from the dismounted Tarheels at short range cut down many Green Coats. "The Federal officers dashed bravely forward and called upon their troops to follow," remembered Pvt. Paul B. Means

58 Samuel P. Bates, *History of Pennsylvania Volunteers, 1861–5, Prepared in Compliance with Acts of the Legislature*, 5 vols. (Harrisburg, 1869–1871), 3:192; "The 91st Pennsylvania Volunteer Infantry," freepages.rootsweb.com/~pa91/military/cc46.html#19, retrieved Nov. 18, 2023.

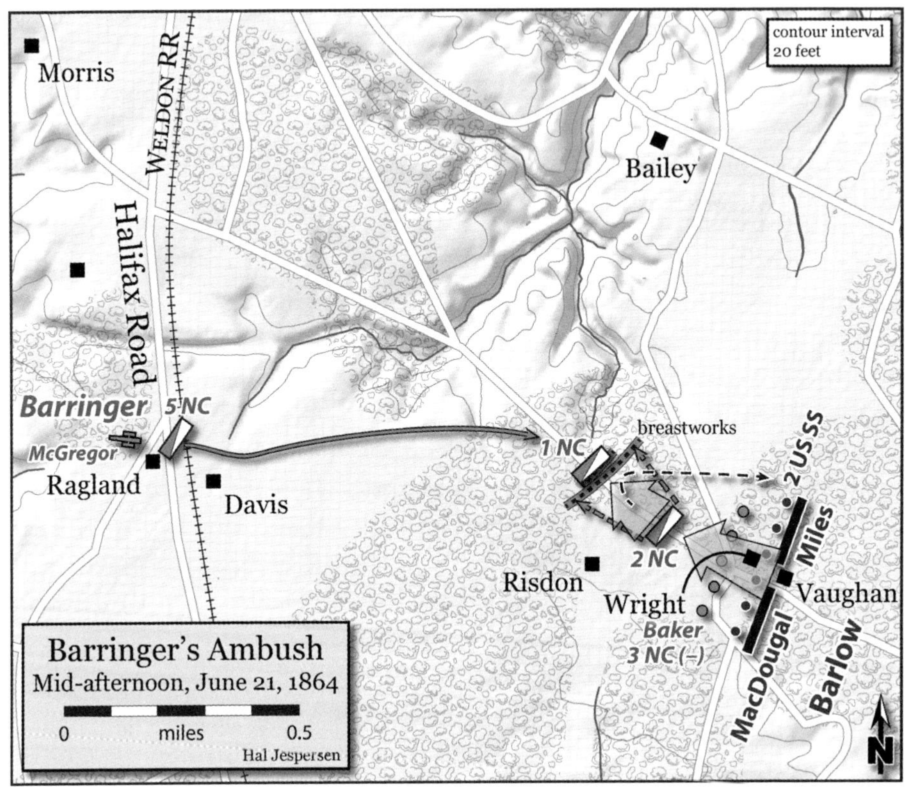

of the 5th North Carolina Cavalry's Company F. "But volley after volley thinned their ranks and they broke and fled."[59]

Captain McGregor's guns opened. Shells burst over the Red Club men behind Stoughton's troops. In the 57th New York of MacDougall's brigade, one projectile killed three men and a second killed one and wounded others. The 61st New York of Miles's brigade took a severe shelling.

Led by Baker and Foard, the Tarheels counterattacked. The Green Coats continued their flight. "Our boys met them but it was a dear old meet for they came right up near enough to use the bayonet," Greene remembered. Soon Companies A and B of the sharpshooters reported themselves in danger of capture because the Rebels were overlapping their line. Stoughton directed his men to break for the rear on their respective flanks. "Some of the boys run & in fact, most all of them," recalled Greene.[60]

59 Clark, ed., *North Carolina Regiments*, 3:610.

60 Hastings, ed., *Letters from a Sharpshooter*, 226.

The North Carolinians surged back across the Risdon farm and seized many prisoners from the Green Coats, including Stoughton. He remembered, "I heard what I supposed was support coming on my left and rear, and in attempting to adjust and join the line, fell into the hands of the 2d N.C. cavalry, dismounted."[61]

At least one other Federal field officer met the same fate. "The ground over which we . . . fought was wooded with dense undergrowth, the opposing lines were very close together, not more than 15 or 20 yards apart," recalled Foard. "Captain Henry Coleman of the 1st Regiment perceiving a field Officer mounted and close up to his line, dashed throught both skirmish lines, seizing his bridal rein and with the muzzle of his pistol against the Officer's body, brought him in to our lines a prisoner," recalled Foard.[62]

Rallying quickly near the captured picket post, the Union sharpshooters charged again. On the lane's left, Colonel MacDougall led his New Yorkers in support of the Green Coats and had his horse shot from under him. Private Sydney B. Rice in the 126th New York recalled that, "a withering fire of musketry was pinned on the head of our column but we drove them back."[63]

On the lane's right, Miles's brigade advanced. Some of the men in the 2nd United States Sharpshooters' Company B, a mostly Michigan unit, captured Foard and Baker, a Harvard educated lawyer, near the Risdon barn in front of the 5th New Hampshire of Miles's brigade. The pair had gotten too far ahead of their troops. "In the surging of the battle back and forth, I suddenly found myself entirely surrounded by the enemy and was taken prisoner just at the close of the battle," Foard recalled.[64]

At this point the order from Birney to withdraw reached Barlow, who halted his advance within a mile of the railroad while the Confederate cavalry pulled back to the west side of the tracks near the Davis house. Unfortunately for the Federals, at no time that afternoon did the smoke, rattling, or whistle of any train alert them to how closely they had come to their objective. Either might have spurred Barlow and Birney onward.

The Red Club commander retreated by a more northerly route than he had taken on the way out and threw up another line of pits northwest of the Browder

61 Stevens, *Berdan's United States Sharpshooters*, 464.

62 Foard Memoir, 5. The memoir has "throught"; as elsewhere, I kept the original spelling.

63 Wayne Mahood, *"Written in Blood," A History of the 126th New York Infantry in the Civil War* (Hightstown, NJ, 1997), 286, 502.

64 Foard Memoir, 6; Clark, ed., *North Carolina Regiments*, 2:779. The 5th New Hampshire claimed to have captured Baker and Foard while they were sleeping in a barn. William Child, *A History Of The Fifth Regiment New Hampshire Volunteers in the American Civil War 1861–62*, 2 vols. (Bristol, NH, 1893), 1:262–263.

farm. Barlow's division had lost at least 30 killed, wounded, and missing.[65] The North Carolinians had suffered five killed, 23 wounded, one wounded and captured, and six missing for a total of 35.[66]

First Sergeant White found his regiment. "I was soon on the left hand road and came into an open field and there found my regiment, or what was left of it," he recalled. "I was lucky enough to escape being in the frazzle of a skirmish, all through the picking up of the lost_[tompion]. I was pleased for I could have been of no use if I had been there and I might have been either killed, wounded or captured. As it was, I was spared to fight another day."[67]

* * *

During the planning of the offensive, it had not occurred to Grant and Meade that the departure of Wilson and Kautz on June 22 would probably clear most of the Confederate cavalry Southside from the path of II and VI corps. When Sheridan had taken his entire corps of three cavalry divisions on his Richmond raid of early May, Lee had dispatched three brigades in pursuit. When Little Phil had gone on his Trevilian Raid with two cavalry divisions, the Southern chieftain had sent two of his own cavalry divisions after the Federal horsemen. It stood to reason that when Wilson and Kautz departed on their raid, Lee would likely send a substantial portion of his Southside cavalry in pursuit of the raiders and—since Lee's cavalry

65 Birney reported 20 killed and wounded. *OR* 40, 2:276. Ten prisoners captured by Confederate cavalry on June 21 reached the provost marshal's office in Petersburg that night. "More Prisoners Brought In," *Petersburg Daily Express*, June 22, 1864. Another Southern newspaper reported the capture of two officers and 10 or 12 privates. "The News from Petersburg," *Daily Richmond Examiner*, June 23, 1864, p. 2 col. 4. One source claimed the Federals left 38 dead on the field and 15 prisoners. D. B. R., "Barringer's N. C. Cavalry Brigade," *The Daily Confederate* (Raleigh, NC), Feb. 22, 1865, p. 2, cols. 3–5. Other Tarheels claimed more than 20 prisoners and more than 100 dead and wounded, with 40 corpses left on the field. Clark, ed., *North Carolina Regiments*, 1:432, 3:610. An estimate of the losses in MacDougall's brigade was "about fifty men" (Lewis H. Clark, *Military History of Wayne County, N.Y.: The County in the Civil War* (Syracuse, NY, 1883), 579); the 111th New York lost three wounded, three missing (Martin W. Husk, *The 111th New York Volunteer Infantry, A Civil War History* (Jefferson, NC, 2009), 145); the 125th New York reported a loss of six men (*OR* 40, 1:352). In Miles's brigade, the 61st New York lost "several men." Ibid., 342.

66 CSRs show that Barringer's brigade lost three killed, four mortally wounded, 22 wounded (one of whom died), one wounded and captured (who died), and five otherwise captured. Alfred C. Young III, "Confederate Casualties during June 1864 at Petersburg," Private Collection of Alfred C. Young III, PA. Barringer's brigade reported three killed, 15 wounded, nine captured. D. B. R., "Barringer's N. C. Cavalry Brigade." The 2nd North Carolina Cavalry lost two killed or mortally wounded, two wounded, and two captured. Roger H. Harrell, *The 2nd North Carolina Cavalry* (Jefferson, NC, 2004), 295. Because Confederate casualties were typically undercounted, I have usually relied on the higher number shown by the CSRs. Alfred C. Young III, *Lee's Army During the Overland Campaign, A Numerical Study* (Baton Rouge, 2013), 19.

67 White, ed., *The Civil War Diary of Wyman S. White*, 266.

Rufus Clay Barringer

Library of Congress

Southside patrolled his extreme right—out of the path of the Federal infantry. Neither Grant nor Meade ever imagined that a brigade of Southern cavalry would defeat one of the hardest-fighting divisions in the Union army.

The attempt to extend the investment of Petersburg to the Appomattox above the city had begun inauspiciously for the Federals. Without Barringer's repulse of Barlow, the Northerners would have reached the Weldon Railroad on June 21. Now the parried Unionist thrust had alerted the Southerners about the danger to their right. Subsequent attempts to turn the Rebel right would encounter more resistance.

Barlow's friend Winslow Homer accompanied the Red Club Division that day, sketching as he went. After the war, Homer drew upon that day's drawings to paint Barlow confronting a trio of prisoners. The painting, *Prisoners from the Front*, established Homer's reputation when exhibited in 1866. In the painting, Homer had Barlow assume a heroic pose akin to that of Washington crossing the Delaware River in a famous 1851 painting by another artist. The defiant attitude of one of the prisoners provides Homer's only clue that the prisoners' side had defeated Barlow. After crossing the Delaware, Washington won the ensuing battle.

* * *

Birney led his troops toward the left of V Corps. Gibbon's division advanced westward from the Williams farm to the Browder farm and made a right turn on to a track that ran northward past the Strong house. Part of Bryan's *ad hoc* cavalry brigade—most of the 3rd New Jersey Cavalry, a detachment from the 22nd New York Cavalry, and a detachment from the 18th Pennsylvania Cavalry—led the way.

As the skirmishers of Bryan's brigade closed with the Confederate lines a short distance west of Jerusalem Plank Road, things began to get hot for men on the left of Mahone's division. Harris's Mississippi Brigade manned the Dimmock Line near the plank road. A skirmish line of Magnolia State men that included

Prisoners from the Front (1866) by Winslow Homer. *The Metropolitan Museum of Art, New York, NY*

Company K of the 16th Mississippi—the Wilkinson Rifles—hurried through a pasture, deployed on a crest about half a mile in front of the fortifications, and lay down. Part of Bryan's brigade, spread very thinly along the left of Birney's troops, appeared on the ridge opposite the Mississippians. An officer among the horsemen began using a field glass. Company K received orders to fire and find the range. Soon saddles began to empty, and horses started to fall. The enemy horsemen "fell back in haste leaving some dead horses to mark the spot," remembered Pvt. David E. Holt of Company K. "A large white horse was among the number, and he was a landmark for many days."

The Northern cavalrymen soon dismounted. A sharpshooter among them hid in a drain behind an apple tree and made it hot for Holt's company. Opposite the marksman stood German-born Pvt. Theodore Foltz, wounded at Cross Keys in 1862, not much of a shot and no match for the Yankee. Company K's first lieutenant told Foltz to go to the rear, lie down, and let men who could shoot better handle the enemy sharpshooter.

Foltz, angry about the joshing he constantly took from his comrades about his poor marksmanship, disobeyed. He stood up to shoot. The lieutenant ordered Foltz to lie down, and his comrades yelled at him to comply. "He shot, but instantly fell over with a bullet through the center of his forehead," Holt remembered.

Foltz's comrades determined to avenge him. "We got a glimpse of the Yank at our end of the line and soon saw him roll over into the drain," recalled Holt.

Company K's survivors started digging rifle pits with their bayonets. They scooped out the loose dirt with their frying pans. Soon they had enough dirt in front of them to stop a bullet. "This became our permanent skirmish line, although the battle line was nearly a half mile behind," Holt recalled.[68]

Late that afternoon the White Club Division passed the Jones house and deployed on Jerusalem Plank Road a few rods north of where the lane entered the plank road from the southwest at an angle of approximately 25 degrees. The division's main body began entrenching along the lane and the plank road. A skirmish line deployed and pushed through woods into plain view of the Confederates in the Dimmock Line. The Federals soon began losing men to Rebel sharpshooters in the Gregory house, west of the plank road and several hundred yards north of the Unionists. Birney established corps headquarters just in front of the Jones house, west of the plank road and around two miles south of the Dimmock Line. Major General John Gibbon, a West Point graduate and the former commander of the Iron Brigade, set up his division's headquarters behind the Jones house.

"Am in a very hard place," remembered 1st Sgt. Joseph Fitch Murphey of the 20th Massachusetts, a former grocery clerk from Nantucket wounded at Fredericksburg.[69] Murphey's regiment—called the Harvard Regiment because so many Harvard men marched in its ranks—occupied a timbered rise on the right of the brigade. The 20th's left extended across an open field into another wood. In the front line, Murphey faced fire from Southern sharpshooters in the Dimmock Line and in Battery 29, which stood out just west of Jerusalem Plank Road.

The artillery of II Corps advanced by way of the plank road. Facing Battery 27 and east of the plank road, Battery B, 1st New Jersey Light Artillery, unlimbered at the edge of the woods behind a hill south of a little stream meandering toward Blackwater Swamp. A gap remained along the plank road between the right of Gibbon's division and the left of Griffin's division farther north, but Federal artillery controlled the gap.

* * *

Mott's division followed Gibbon's division up the lane from the Browder farm. The Diamond Division formed line with its right near the Jones house. The rear echelon occupied the clearing around the house. "We stopped at a large farm house where there was a fine garden and lots of cherries," remembered Musician

68 Mahone's division and the cavalry attached to II Corps each lost at least one on June 21. Thomas D. Cockrell and Michael B. Ballard, eds., *A Mississippi Rebel in the Army of Northern Virginia: The Civil War Memoirs of Private David Holt* (Baton Rouge, 1995), 281–282. Bryan's brigade reported no casualties from June 15 to June 30, 1864, which is hard to believe. *OR* 40, 1:228.

69 Richard F. Miller and Robert F. Mooney, eds., *The Civil War: The Nantucket Experience, Including the Memoirs of Josiah Fitch Murphey* (Nantucket, 1994), 110.

3rd Class John L. Ryno, who had originally enlisted in the 126th New York in Barlow's division but was currently serving in the hospital of Mott's division.[70]

The frontline soldiers lacked the benefit of clearings. "It took a long time to get located, as the trees were very dense and there was a great deal of underbrush to dispose of," recalled Pvt. John West Haley of the 17th Maine.[71] The 70th New York, the 1st Excelsior Regiment in Brewster's brigade, tramped to the rear for the mustering out of the soldiers whose enlistments had expired. Orders consolidated the rest of the 70th with the 86th New York of Madill's brigade.

Pursuant to Birney's authorization, Barlow withdrew his division from the hastily dug pits northwest of the Browder house. Part of Crowninshield's cavalry covered the retreat. As Barlow's division withdrew, Maj. Gen. William Henry Fitzhugh "Rooney" Lee, another of General Lee's sons, another Harvard man and Barringer's division commander, came to Barringer's support with the balance of Dearing's brigade, recently assigned to Rooney Lee's division. While at Harvard, Lee had become friends with Crowninshield. In 1863, Lee had been captured while convalescing from a Brandy Station wound. Crowninshield, as the Army of the Potomac's provost marshal at that time, had held custody of Lee until his exchange. During Lee's captivity, he declined as a matter of principle many of the kindnesses offered in the spirit of friendship by Crowninshield.

Baker accepted every kindness that Barlow offered him. The two had "instantly recognized each other as former friends and college mates at Harvard," recalled Foard. "Gen'l Barlow, who was very civil and kind, told Col. Baker, who was mounted when taken, to retain his horse for the time and to follow around with his staff until they should go into bivouac for the night, when he would be glad to have a good talk with him about old times." Perceiving Foard's exhaustion from his exertions on foot in the dense undergrowth, Baker obtained Barlow's permission to take up Foard behind him. Foard remembered whispering to Baker, "that the Federal troops were being withdrawn and that in the confusion of retreat we could easily make a dash and a few hundred yards would bring us back into our own lines, and that the way in which the Federal troops were converging, but little firing could be done at us without their firing into each other." Baker thought that the privilege of retaining his horse extended to him by Barlow amounted to a parole which would render any attempt to escape dishonorable. "No doubt, the correct view for a man of honor to take," Foard acknowledged.[72]

70 John L. Ryno Diary, June 21, 1864, Interlaken Historical Society, Interlaken, NY.

71 Ruth L. Silliker, ed., *The Rebel Yell and the Yankee Hurrah: The Civil War Journal of a Maine Volunteer* (Camden, ME, 1985), 175.

72 Fred C. Foard, "In a military work by Marshal Marmont," Fred C. Foard Papers, 2–3.

Lyman rode west from the Williams house to meet his friend and fellow Harvard alumnus Barlow. A little beyond the Browder house, Lyman spotted Barlow at the head of his column, wearing his checked shirt and as usual lolling about on his horse.

"Hullo! See here!" Barlow shouted to Lyman. "I've caught a Cambridge man."

A stout, handsome man, mounted on a fine white horse and "daintily dressed," Baker wore "a fanciful sort of helmet of gray felt," remembered Lyman. "His effect was spoiled by Barlow's quaint device of mounting a most scaly looking Adjutant, *en croupe*, behind him!" recalled Lyman.[73]

In the rear, the configuration of the captives inspired amusement. "The Confederate colonel, clothed in the finest of Confederate gray, was mounted upon a beautiful, well caparisoned white horse, and one of his staff was securely mounted behind," remembered Maj. William Child, the 5th New Hampshire's surgeon. "Both Unionists and Confederates, captors and captives, were laughing, though the cheeks of the Confederates were blushing with shame and chagrin."[74]

Hospital orderlies laid the wounded in the shade in the Williams yard. "There . . . lay one of our sharpshooters desperately shot through the lungs, and dying fast," Lyman noted. "He was breathing, with the characteristic quick, sobbing expiration, and in a feeble, wandering voice, asked for more morphine."

The attendant said, "We have just given you some."

"Yes," replied the sharpshooter, "but it don't do no good!"

Lyman commented in his journal, "Nothing could do *him* good."[75]

* * *

Ricketts's division got under way by about 4:20 p.m. and was crossing the Norfolk & Petersburg and turning south on Jerusalem Plank Road around 4:40 p.m. The Red Club Division fell back to a line extending southeastward from the Strong house to the Williams Road and began to entrench again. By 5:10 p.m.,

73 Lowe, ed., *Meade's Army*, 218–219.

74 Child, *Fifth Regiment New Hampshire Volunteers*, 1:262–263. Of Baker's white mare, Barlow recalled, "He wanted to give it to me, but I refused." Barlow described the mare as "fine (for the Army)" and declared that he would buy her. Christian G. Samito, ed., *Fear Was Not in Him, The Civil War Letters of Major General Francis C. Barlow, U.S.A.* (New York, 2004), 203–204. The members of II Corps' staff all wanted Baker's "beautiful white thoroughbred horse," but none could use her and "we decided that as General Barlow had done most of the work he should have the horse," Armes recalled. Armes, *Ups and Downs of an Army Officer*, 104. The splendid creature would become very fond of Barlow and followed him around camp begging for the lumps of sugar that the general kept in his pocket as treats for the horse. Mulholland, *116th Regiment Pennsylvania Volunteers*, 278.

75 Lowe, ed., *Meade's Army*, 219.

Barlow's pioneers were cutting a road through the woods to go into position on Mott's left. Crowninshield's cavalry picketed the left of Barlow's division from the Williams Road to Second Swamp. At 6:00 p.m., Miles's brigade was relieved and marched to the rear.[76]

From the left of Gibbon's division, Birney observed to the west a division-strength column of Rebels tramping southward along the railroad. This spelled trouble for the Federals.

* * *

The luncheon for Lincoln broke up around 4:00 p.m. The president wanted to ride to the front. Grant and three members of his staff rode out with Lincoln to inspect the soldiers. The general-in-chief gave his big bay "Cincinnati" to the president. Grant rode his black pony, "Jeff Davis." Lincoln wore a high black silk hat, black trousers, and a black frockcoat. On the way the party stopped at VI Corps headquarters, where the president hobnobbed with Meade and his staff before proceeding. "By the time [Lincoln] had reached the troops he was completely covered with dust, and the black color of his clothes had changed to Confederate gray," remembered Porter. "As he had no straps, his trousers gradually worked up above his ankles, and gave him the appearance of a country farmer riding into town wearing his Sunday clothes."[77]

Despite the president's appearance, the troops cheered him enthusiastically. Some greeted him familiarly as "Uncle Abe." Others addressed the president as "Old Abe." A few men knew him personally, and when he recognized one, he practiced retail politics—an election was coming, and Lincoln needed every vote he could get. "One cavalry private had known him in Illinois," Cadwallader recalled. "Mr. Lincoln shook him by the hand, as an old familiar acquaintance, to the infinite admiration of all bystanders."

A particularly warm reception awaited the president among United States Colored Troops. "They were lounging by the roadside, and when they approached they came rushing by hundreds," remembered Cadwallader.

"Hurrah for the Liberator!" they shouted. "Hurrah for the President!"[78]

As Lincoln rode through their ranks, he tipped his hat and bowed to the black soldiers. "They crowded around him and fondled his horse," Porter recalled. "Some of them kissed his hands, while others ran off crying in triumph to their

76 *OR* 40, 1:342.

77 Porter, *Campaigning with Grant*, 218.

78 Thomas, ed., *Three Years with Grant*, 233.

comrades that they had touched his clothes."[79] Tears came to the president's eyes and his voice became choked with emotion as he thanked and congratulated the African American troops.

The party broke up after a 9:00 p.m. tea with the understanding that Grant and his staff would accompany Lincoln's party up the James to visit Butler, the Bermuda Hundred lines, and Admiral Lee on his flagship. The president and his entourage adjourned for the night to their staterooms on *Baltimore*. Lincoln did not ask about Grant's plans and stated that he did not want to know them.

* * *

Late that afternoon infantrymen from Wilcox's division arrived at the Davis farm from their position in the Dimmock Line between the Weldon Railroad and Lieutenants Run. The corps commander, Lt. Gen. Ambrose Powell "Little Powell" Hill, a West Point graduate and Seminole War veteran wounded at Chancellorsville, had ordered them out around 3:00 p.m. to check the thrust of the enemy toward the Weldon Railroad reported by Barringer. Hill directed Mahone's division of his corps to move out of its position in the Dimmock Line east of Wilcox's division and co-operate with it in any attack it should make. Such an attack would uncover the front of Mahone's division, which occupied the Dimmock Line between Lieutenants Run and Rives's Salient, where Kirkland's and Fry's brigades of Heth's division held the trenches and cannon of Richardson's battalion occupied the artillery emplacements. If Barlow's division had reached and attempted to hold the Weldon Railroad, it might well have faced annihilation at the hands of Wilcox's and Mahone's divisions.

The march of Wilcox's division, still called the Light Division because it consisted of four of the six brigades that had constituted the Light Division under Hill, took it southward along the Weldon Railroad's tracks. At the Davis farm, the foot soldiers of Wilcox's division found Barringer's cavalry on the west side of the railway. McGregor's guns were still shelling the woods supposedly inhabited by the Federals east of the Davis field.

Major General Cadmus M. Wilcox, a West Point graduate and Mexican War veteran, put McGowan's South Carolina Brigade and Thomas's Georgia Brigade of the Light Division in line at the western edge of the field. The infantrymen started throwing together breastworks. Then Wilcox directed his troops to march southeastward by the flank across the field into the woods. The division, led by the Georgia and South Carolina brigades, with skirmishers in advance, entered the trees.

79 Porter, *Campaigning with Grant*, 220.

The men followed the lane along which Barlow's division and Barringer's brigade had fought. "A few dead were seen along the road, they were part infantry and part cavalry," Wilcox recalled, observing the results of the earlier struggle.[80] In front of Wilcox's men, Crowninshield's troopers slowly retired toward the Browder farm.

Second Lieutenant James Fitz James Caldwell of the 1st South Carolina was marching behind the skirmish line. "Just after sunset, when our wonder at not striking the enemy was at its height, we heard a sharp volley of musketry in front, which sent a pretty good shower of balls whizzing over our heads," he remembered. Across a little opening to the left of the lane, Thomas's Georgia Brigade was advancing in line of battle. "The skirmishers in front cheered and fired freely, and the battle seemed to be right at hand," Caldwell recalled. The South Carolinians pressed into the woods ahead, driving Crowninshield's cavalry pickets back to the Williams farm. The firing grew more rapid as Barlow's infantry became involved. McGowan's brigade lay down in the lane. "The balls of the enemy came over us by spells, sometimes quite thickly," Caldwell remembered, "but they were very high."[81]

Opposite the Rebels, the Northerners lay down as well. London-born Cpl. Frederic E. Lockley of the 7th New York heavies, prone behind breastworks under fire from Wilcox's men, recorded in a letter home, "Our division commander—Genl. Barlow—a very young man, appears to me to be rash; the way in which he uses up men is fearful."[82]

The outburst of firing alarmed Hancock. "General Hancock became so excited that he rushed out of his room in the Jones house, and wanted his horse brought up, so as to go to the front line, where the fighting was taking place, but Drs. Dougherty and Smart made him return to his bed with the greatest difficulty," recalled Armes. "I am afraid some thing will happen to the Corps," Hancock kept saying.[83] He always wanted to accompany his men into action.

The South Carolinians lay still till dark, less than half a mile from Jerusalem Plank Road. Mahone's division, too distant to cooperate, remained in the Dimmock Line. With the Weldon Railroad apparently safe, Wilcox halted his division and led it back to its position beside Mahone's division, arriving before midnight.

* * *

80 Cadmus M. Wilcox, Wilcox Report, "Petersburg," 1, Lee Headquarters Papers, VMHC, Richmond, VA.

81 Caldwell, *History of a Brigade of South Carolinians*, 163–164.

82 John E. Pomfret and Fred Lockley, "Letters of Fred Lockley, Union Soldier 1864–65," *Huntington Library Quarterly* 16, no. 1 (Nov. 1952): 81–82.

83 Armes, *Ups and Downs of an Army Officer*, 104.

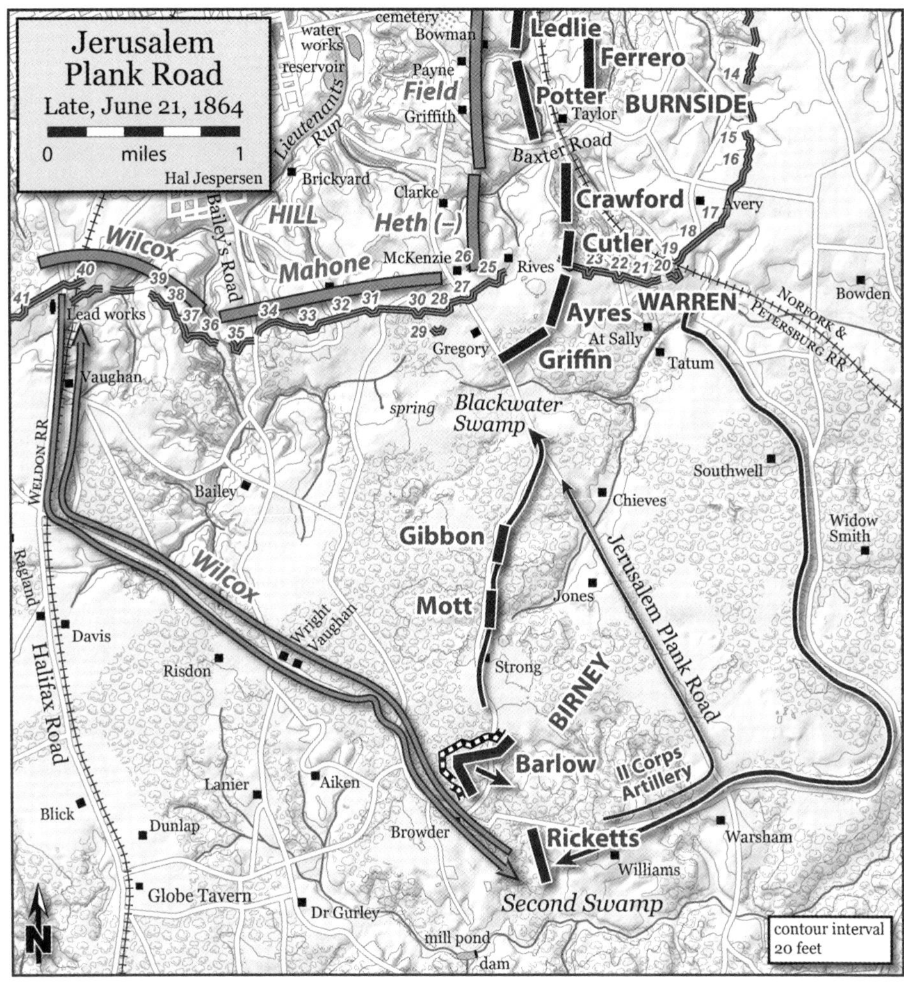

Wilcox's thrust toward Jerusalem Plank Road prevented Barlow's division from getting into position on the left of Mott's division. About dark, Ricketts's division started reaching the Williams house. Around 9:00 p.m., Truex's brigade of Ricketts's division moved out on the road past the Williams house and thrashed forward in the thick underbrush of the woods to deploy to the left of Barlow's division though a gap remained between the two. Truex's brigade "immediately began to throw up earthworks, with bayonets and tin cups," remembered Private Prowell. "It was tedious business. . . . The soil was loose and sandy."[84]

84 Prowell, *Eighty-Seventh Regiment, Pennsylvania Volunteers*, 164–165; Norbert A. Kuntz, ed., "A Brookfield Soldier's Report: The Civil War Recollections of Edwin C. Hall," *Vermont History* 57, no. 4 (Fall 1989): 211.

The 10th Vermont of Truex's brigade advanced about 80 rods and used wooden spades to build earthworks. "Our boys went to a spring to get water and a Johnny came up and asked where is the Regiment," recalled 1st Sgt. Walter Graham of the 10th's Company E. "[O]ur boys told him up here, said he 'it is my mistake, but I will go with you boys' so they brought him in, we went to sleep at 2 o'clock in the morning."[85] The lost Confederate probably came from Wilcox's division, which lost seven that evening, including at least one missing.[86]

To relieve the cavalry, the 87th Pennsylvania deployed 125 skirmishers who struggled still farther forward in darkness that permitted the men to see only a short distance ahead. Corporal Christian List of the 87th's Company K went only a few yards past the picket line's front. "Hello!" said a Confederate. "Yank, come with us." List marched into captivity.[87] This part of the picket line and the opposing Confederate sentinels then both fell back.

Despite the deployment of Truex's brigade, Barlow could not comply with orders to join the rest of II Corps until a staff officer arrived who would point out the new position on Mott's left described by a previous staff officer. Barlow was not connected with Ricketts's right and the new position precluded such a connection because of the distance involved. "In the dark woods it is impossible to form unless conducted by some one who knows the ground," Barlow wrote around 9:00 p.m.[88] About an hour later, when Keifer's brigade of Ricketts's division joined Truex's brigade and began building breastworks near the Williams house, Birney thought it imprudent to swing Barlow's division forward until the rest of VI Corps arrived. VI Corps' other two divisions were just starting their trek toward the Chieves house, a short distance east of Jerusalem Plank Road and around a mile south of the Confederate fortifications—many miles short of their destination on the left of II Corps. Relief had begun for Wheaton's and Russell's divisions around 8:00 p.m. It did not arrive for the Vermont Brigade of Wheaton's division until at least 11:00 p.m.

85 Graham Diary, June 21, 1864.

86 Lane's brigade lost three wounded; Thomas's brigade, two wounded, one (in the 35th Georgia) missing. Young, "Confederate Casualties in June 1864 at Petersburg." McGowan's brigade lost one on June 21, 1864. Caldwell, *History of a Brigade of South Carolinians*, 166. The missing Georgian may have fallen into the hands of the 106th New York instead of the 10th Vermont; both belonged to Truex's brigade. Abiel T. LaForge Diary, June 23, 1864, Abiel T. LaForge Letters and Diaries, Alleghany County Historical Society, Andover, NY.

87 Prowell, *Eighty-Seventh Regiment Pennsylvania Volunteers*, 165.

88 *OR* 40, 2:276–277; Arthur McClellan Diary and Notebook, June 21, 1864, Series 5, Diaries, 1846–1884, George Brinton McClellan Papers, LOC.

* * *

At nightfall the brigades of Gibbon's division sent forward their pioneers and detachments of their infantry regiments around 500 yards to erect breastworks closer to the Dimmock Line. The work took place under enemy fire. The skirmishers covering this line advanced to within 200 yards of the entrenched Confederate picket line, and within 110 yards of the foremost Southern pickets. Gibbon's pickets dug shallow pits for themselves. The pickets of the 15th Massachusetts scraped out shallow pits in "the black, peaty muck" near the densely thicketed branch that snaked its way eastward through the Federal picket line and main line toward Blackwater Swamp.[89]

Sergeant Joseph E. Hodgkins had just received a promotion to orderly sergeant—first sergeant—of the 19th Massachusetts' Company K, which put him in charge of the company because its only officer had command of the right flank of the regiment. Hodgkins and his company went out on the skirmish line that night. "Commenced throwing up works, first by piling up rails and then throwing the dirt over them," he wrote in his diary. "As I was piling up the rails in front of me I was hit in the knee by a ball which passed through a rotten rail which I had just put up, but the force of the ball being broken not much harm ensued, only a tingling sensation in my knee."[90]

Some of the pioneers cut a road to a winding wood lane and built lunettes for the 12th Battery, New York Light Artillery on the Federal skirmish line about a quarter mile west of the plank road in the edge of a piece of woods. The 1st Minnesota Battalion picketed in front of the immediate right of the battery's lunettes. "I was on Vidette all night and many bullets struck in front of the little pit where I was laying," noted Corporal Bond.[91] Battery B, 1st New Jersey Light Artillery, built works on the brow of the hill that had sheltered the gunners during daylight.

Around 11:00 p.m., Mott's division advanced over a road cut through the woods and deployed in a single line on the left of Gibbon's division in the rear line of the earthworks Gibbon's troops had dug. "We are eternally grateful for their hard labor in throwing up those works," Private Haley remembered. "An attack is expected at every moment, so we are kept under arms and ordered to stay awake."[92] General Mott rode forward to the left of Gibbon's front line.

89 Ford, *Fifteenth Massachusetts Volunteer Infantry*, 333.

90 Kenneth C. Turino, ed., *The Civil War Diary of Lt. J. E. Hodgkins, August 1862 to July 1865* (Camden, ME, 1994), 95–96.

91 Daniel Bond Diary and Memoir, June 21, 1864, 232. Bond, who was not mounted, was strictly speaking a sentinel rather than a vidette. merriam-webster.com. Retrieved Jan. 30, 2024.

92 Silliker, ed., *Rebel Yell and Yankee Hurrah*, 175.

Birney's staffers pointed out to Mott where he should deploy two brigades in the morning—extending westward from Gibbon's left and facing northward toward the Dimmock Line, leaving the two brigades in Mott's rear line in reserve.

II Corps stood deployed in a long line in very unfamiliar territory close to the enemy. At II Corps headquarters, Armes thought the corps seemed on the eve of a great battle, but its soldiers looked too tired to do more than hold their ground if that. "General Birney seems extra wide-awake this evening, doing all he can to prepare for the worst," Armes remembered.[93]

Around the hospital of Mott's division, Musician 3rd Class Ryno foraged. "I dug a mess of potatoes by moonlight and would have got a lot of peas and cherries but the guard came around and chased us out."[94]

* * *

That evening Meade wrote a lengthy letter to Brig. Gen. John A. Rawlins, the Galena lawyer who served as Grant's chief of staff, in which the commander of the Army of the Potomac explained why he was asking for Warren's relief. Meade never sent the letter because, as he later explained to Warren, "It is my earnest desire to have harmony and cooperation with my subordinate officers, but I cannot always yield my judgment to theirs."[95] The commander of the Army of the Potomac was deceiving himself; as his attempt to extend the Federal left proceeded, he would again yield his judgment to a subordinate with similarly unpleasant consequences.

Meade also wrote a letter to his wife that evening, which he did send. "Mr. Lincoln honored the army with his presence this afternoon, and was so gracious as to say he had seen you in Philadelphia," the general graciously noted.[96] He appreciated the president's kindness. Their relations had been glacial since the previous year's Gettysburg campaign, when Meade had disappointed Lincoln by making little effort to destroy Lee's army as it returned to Virginia.

* * *

Wilson proved unable to keep his promise to Meade to have all supplies ready by noon. Some of Kautz's troopers did not receive their horse equipment until 9:00 p.m. "The different parts of saddle were in different boxes, and so unacquainted

93 Armes, *Ups and Downs of an Army Officer*, 105.

94 Ryno Diary, June 21, 1864.

95 Selby, *Meade: The Price of Command*, 226.

96 George Meade, ed., *The Life and Letters of George Gordon Meade*, 2 vols. (New York, 1913), 2:206.

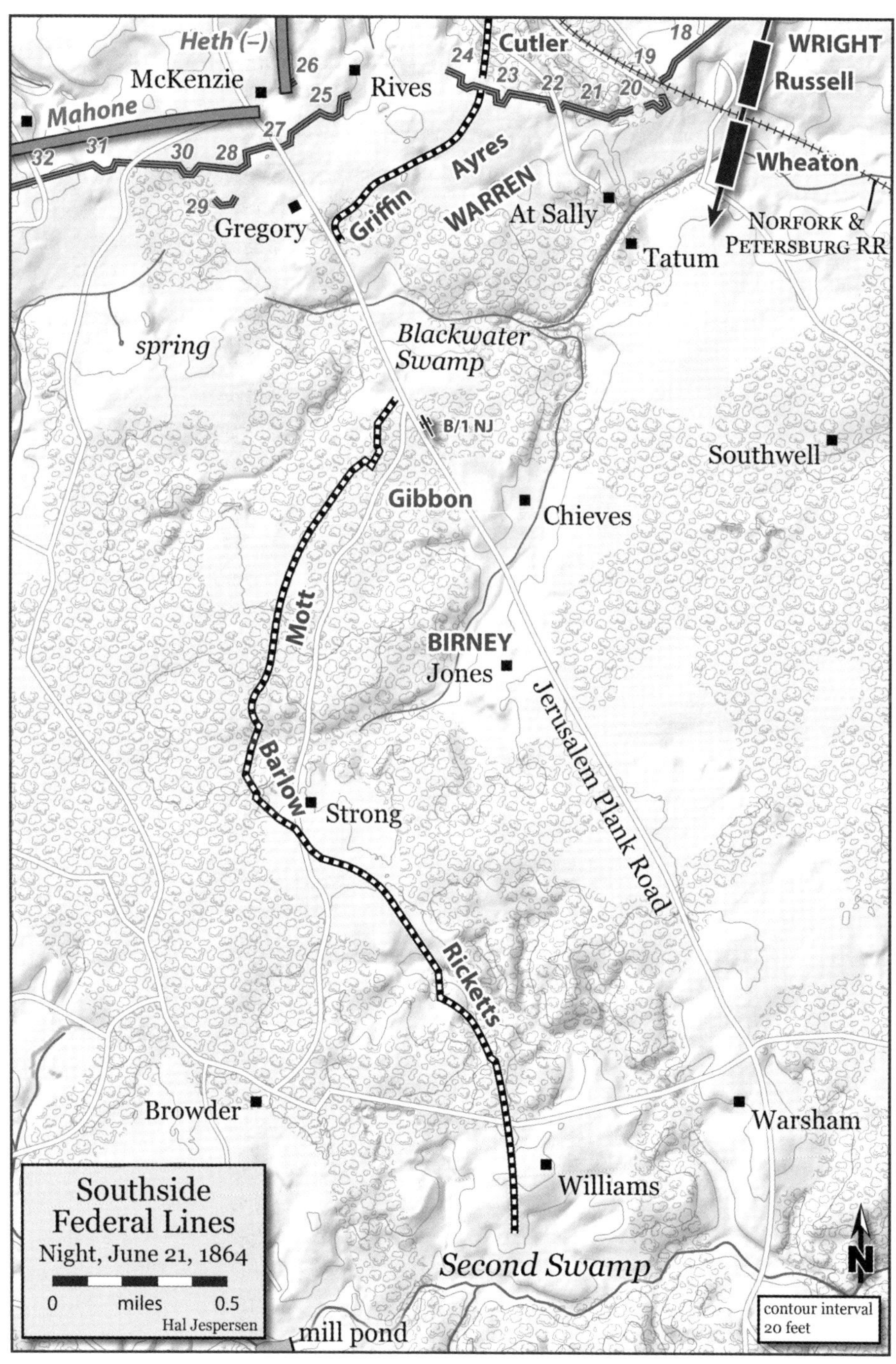
Heth (–)
McKenzie
Mahone
Rives
Cutler
WRIGHT
Russell
Wheaton
Griffin
Ayres
WARREN
Gregory
At Sally
Tatum
NORFORK & PETERSBURG RR
spring
Blackwater Swamp
B/1 NJ
Southwell
Gibbon
Chieves
Mott
BIRNEY
Jones
Jerusalem Plank Road
Barlow
Strong
Ricketts
Browder
Warsham
Williams
Second Swamp
mill pond
Southside Federal Lines
Night, June 21, 1864
0 miles 0.5
Hal Jespersen
contour interval 20 feet
N

were the men with the horse gear, that many of them were unable to adjust the various parts without assistance," remembered Chaplain Samuel H. Merrill of the 1st District of Columbia Cavalry, principally composed of men recruited in Maine. "Nor was this strange. Before their enlistment they had no occasion to learn, and subsequently, no opportunity, and yet, three hours later, they started on the celebrated Wilson's raid."[97]

Some of Wilson's and Kautz's men remained awake until midnight. "Up last night till midnight issuing oats, etc., and drawing clothing," recalled Lieutenant Tenney.[98] Midnight ended the slumber of others. "We were routed out at midnight and got into line," remembered First Sergeant Ide of the 1st Vermont Cavalry.[99]

At 6:00 p.m., Wilson shared his plans with Meade. They conformed to Grant's suggestion that the cavalryman begin with Sutherland Station on the South Side Rail Road, work his way west to Burkeville, and from there head toward Danville, Greenesborough, and ultimately Georgia or the North Carolina coast, depending on the circumstances.[100] In case Wilson could not cross Staunton River and had to return to the Army of the Potomac, he anticipated no trouble from Hampton if Sheridan looked after the South Carolinian, but—concerned about how the raiders could return safely—he wanted to know if the infantry would extend to the Weldon Railroad.[101]

At 8:30 p.m., Meade's chief of staff Humphreys painted a very rosy picture for Wilson. Humphreys assured the cavalryman through Capt. Edward W. Whitaker, a member of the 1st Connecticut Cavalry on Wilson's staff, that the Illinoisan could expect Sheridan to occupy Hampton and that Grant's infantry would extend to the Weldon Railroad by the following morning and the South Side Rail Road by the evening following that.[102] Meade's chief of staff conveyed these assurances even though he had known since at least 9:00 a.m. that Sheridan probably could not cross the James at Deep Bottom, which would limit his ability to occupy

97 Samuel H. Merrill, *The Campaigns of the First Maine and the First District of Columbia Cavalry* (Portland, ME, 1866), 261. See also Tobie, *First Maine Cavalry*, 333. Much of the 1st Maine served in the 1st District of Columbia Cavalry, principally recruited in Maine. Ibid., 319.

98 Tenney, ed., *War Diary of Luman Harris Tenney*, 121.

99 Hoffman, *First Vermont Cavalry Volunteers*, 185.

100 *OR* 40, 1:620, 2:286; Wilson, "The Cavalry of the Army of the Potomac," *MHSM*, 13:62.

101 Ibid., 60; *OR* 40, 1:620.

102 Ibid., 2:286; Andrew A. Humphreys, *The Virginia Campaign of '64 and '65: The Army of the Potomac and the Army of the James* (New York, 1883), 236n; Robert B. Angelovich, *Riding for Uncle Samuel: The Civil War History of the 1st Connecticut Cavalry Volunteers* (Chicago, 2014), 427.

Andrew Atkinson Humphreys
Library of Congress

Hampton.[103] Humphreys had also known by at least 5:30 p.m. that Meade's infantry had failed to reach the Weldon Railroad that day.[104]

If Wilson decided to return to the Army of the Potomac instead of proceeding to Georgia or New Berne, he would expect to find the rosy scenario depicted by Humphreys.[105]

103 *OR* 40, 2:267.

104 Ibid., 275.

105 Wilson, *Under the Old Flag*, 1:458, 492, 495–496, 502, 518, 520; Wilson, "The Cavalry of the Army of the Potomac," *MHSM*, 13:60–61, 64; Wilson, *The Life of John A. Rawlins*, 259; Angelovich, *Riding for Uncle Samuel*, 427.

Chapter Three

"It Is an Easy Matter for a Mouse to Reach the Cheese in a Trap"

AT ABOUT 2:00 a.m. on June 22, Wilson's and Kautz's divisions set out on their raid against the Weldon, South Side, and Danville railroads. "While the moon was yet bright in the heavens, and all was quiet, save the stir of the horses and the occasional braying of a mule, the notes of the bugle and the orders of the orderly sergeant roused us from our slumbers, and after feeding and watering our horses and getting a hasty breakfast, 'Boots and saddles!' was sounded, and away we started for the enemy's country," recalled Corporal Lunt in the 1st District of Columbia Cavalry.[1]

The men carried five days' rations in their haversacks "and two days' feed in bags made for the occasion," recalled Pvt. James Barrett, a New Hampshire-born mechanic serving as bugler of Company G in the 1st Vermont Cavalry.[2] Soldiers in questionable condition pushed themselves to keep up out of loyalty to their comrades. "I started sick . . . but could not bear to be left behind," remembered Capt. Rowland M. Hall, a Harvard graduate and New York attorney commanding Company E of the 3rd New York Cavalry. "I shall die in the harness, I believe."[3]

1 Tobie, *First Maine Cavalry*, 338.

2 Donald H. Wickman, comp., *Letters to Vermont from Her Civil War Soldier Correspondents to the Home Press*, 2 vols. (Bennington, VT, 1998), 2:176.

3 Rowland M. Hall and Edward G. Longacre, "'Would to God that War Was Rendered Impossible': Letters of Rowland M. Hall, April–July 1864," *The Virginia Magazine of History and Biography* 89, no. 4 (Oct. 1981): 460.

Wilson put Kautz's division in the advance because Kautz had acquired some knowledge of the countryside on two raids he conducted during May's Bermuda Hundred Campaign. The 11th Pennsylvania Cavalry of Spear's brigade led the way.

Bringing up the rear, Wilson's division got off to a bad start. "A standing rule in the division required that the leading brigade commander, with his head of column, should start exactly on time, and if he did not, no matter for what reason, the next brigade commander should take the road at the minute and have it for the day," remembered Wilson.[4] Around an hour before starting time, Col. John B. McIntosh, a native of Florida, a naval veteran of the Mexican War, and the brother of a Confederate general killed at Pea Ridge in 1862, asked that his brigade, the division's first, might delay its departure long enough to issue clothing just received. Wilson denied permission, but when he mounted up and pounded past with Spear's brigade at the head of the column, he found McIntosh issuing clothing. The Illinoisan severely chastised McIntosh, assuring him that ordinarily he would have found himself relieved of command and sent to the rear under arrest. Colonel George H. Chapman, another Mexican War naval veteran, immediately took the lead in the division with his brigade as day broke.

The horsemen headed through Prince George Court House, across the Norfolk & Petersburg, and then southward, "principally through by-paths, and unfrequented ways, to avoid any force of the enemy," recalled Chaplain Louis Napoleon Boudrye of the 5th New York Cavalry, who had been captured two days after Gettysburg and spent several months in Richmond's Libby Prison before his exchange.[5] The 11th Pennsylvania Cavalry and Company E of the 1st District of Columbia Cavalry encountered Confederate videttes at Jerusalem Plank Road around daylight and advanced as skirmishers. The bluecoats captured a few Southerners and put the rest to flight.

Kautz learned from the captives that Rooney Lee's division of horsemen lay encamped at Globe Tavern six miles south of Petersburg and blocked the direct route to Sutherland Station. Though Grant wanted the raiders to cross the Weldon Railroad as close to Petersburg as possible, Kautz decided to turn south, then west. This "was the initial success of the raid, for it enabled us to get inside the enemy's line and to accomplish the object of the expedition," Kautz remembered.

4 Wilson, *Under the Old Flag*, 1:459.

5 Louis N. Boudrye, *History Records of the Fifth New York Cavalry, First Ira Harris Guard: Its Organization, Marches, Raids, Scouts, Engagements, and General Services during the Rebellion of 1861–1865, with Observations of the Author by the Way, Giving Sketches of the Armies of the Potomac and Shenandoah. Also, Interesting Accounts of Prison Life and of the Secret Service* (Albany, NY, 1865), 144.

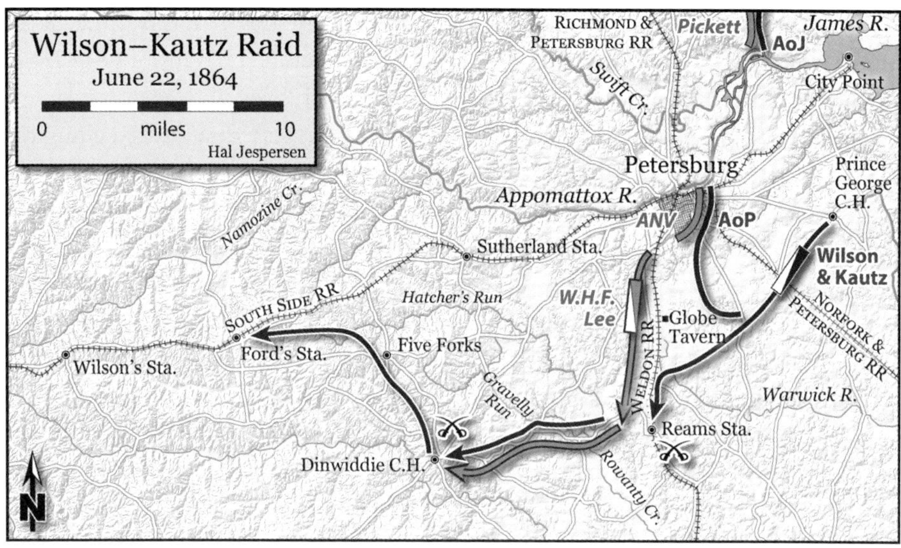

"A (significant) battle might and probably would, have caused our immediate return."[6] The mission lay in wrecking railroads, not fighting.

Kautz's horse soldiers first pursued the Rebels to Reams Station, a pleasant village with its fruit trees in flower about 12 miles south of Petersburg. The Federals reached Reams before 7:00 a.m. and encountered more butternuts. "The rebel guard of one hundred militia fled without resistance," remembered 1st Sgt. George F. Cruikshank of Company A, which hailed from Iowa, in the 11th Pennsylvania Cavalry.[7] Kautz destroyed the depot, some track, and 13 dirt cars, then turned westward on the Depot Road toward Dinwiddie Court House.

When Wilson's men followed through Reams Station at about 10:30 a.m., the 2nd Ohio Cavalry and 8th New York Cavalry drew the task of ripping up the Weldon Railroad's rails. Wilson's division destroyed all the buildings at the station, the telegraph wire, a locomotive, and about half a dozen freight cars. Tearing up the track for about a mile, the Northerners built fires and laid the rails across the flames. At nearby Dutch Crossroads, they burned a big sawmill.

Discipline was already breaking down. Some men of the 2nd Ohio Cavalry tried to carry off a ham from the burning commissary stores at Reams Station. A near-sighted member of Wilson's staff posted by a gate to prevent looting ordered them to drop the meat. "Here's the man that's got the ham," a Buckeye taunted the

6 August V. Kautz, "Operations South of the James River," in Johnson and Buel, eds., *B&L*, 4:535.

7 Greg Eanes, *Destroy the Junction: The Wilson-Kautz Raid and the Battle for the Staunton River Bridge* (Lynchburg, VA, 1999), 7; John L. Roper, et al., *History of the Eleventh Pennsylvania Volunteer Cavalry, together with a complete roster of the regiment and regimental officers* (Philadelphia, 1902), 23, 194.

officer. "It is on the other side of the saddle."[8] His comrades kept this up until the staffer rode off and complained to the 2nd's officers about the want of respect but he received no sympathy.

Horses, mules, bacon, wine, and other articles of value disappeared along the route of the Federal horsemen. They needed an enormous number of horses and seized every steed available. Battery K, with many surplus animals, had as many as 230 horses. Many contrabands along the way were liberated or freed themselves.

Rooney Lee quickly gathered his forces to pursue the raiders. Barringer left the 3rd North Carolina Cavalry to picket the railroad. With the balance of his brigade, about 1,200 strong, he began attacking the rear of Wilson's column at Reams Station by 11:00 a.m.[9]

The Illinoisan deployed the 1st Vermont Cavalry to fend off Barringer's attacks. "They attacked our rear at the station, but not very forcibly," recalled First Sergeant Ide.[10] Rooney Lee's artillery shelled the Vermonters as they left the burning station, harried by the 5th North Carolina Cavalry. Brigadier General James Griffin Dearing Jr., who had studied at West Point, and the roughly 800 men of his brigade, followed Barringer.[11]

Because of the presence of Rebels at Reams Station, the raiders would not have with them any of the special tools Federal engineers had devised to twist heated iron rails and render them useless unless re-rolled at a mill, of which the Confederacy had few. The ship carrying a supply of these implements to Grant's army group ran aground in the Pamunkey and did not arrive before Wilson set out on his raid. Meade sent a detachment of cavalry to follow Wilson and deliver the tools, but when its men got to Reams Station, they found the Confederates between them and the Illinoisan, and they turned back. Wilson's troopers would have to twist rails the old-fashioned way to do sufficient damage to the T-rails and U-rails of the Weldon and South Side railways—by heating them and bending them around trees. The strap rail of the Richmond & Danville would require substantially less effort.

8 Isaac Gause, *Four Years with Five Armies: Army of the Frontier, Army of the Potomac, Army of the Missouri, Army of the Ohio, Army of the Shenandoah* (New York, 1908), 276.

9 Clark, ed., *North Carolina Regiments*, 1:434. Not including Dearing's brigade, W. H. F. Lee's division had 190 officers and 2,677 men present for duty on June 30, 1864. *OR* 40, 2:707. If Barringer pursued Wilson with three regiments totaling 1,200 present for duty, it is logical to estimate that the 3rd North Carolina Cavalry, which he left behind, numbered about 400 present for duty and that his brigade had around 1,600 present for duty. Ibid.

10 Hoffman, *First Vermont Cavalry Volunteers*, 185.

11 "Grant," "Defeat of Wilson's Raiders." *Macon Daily Telegraph*, July 14, 1864, p. 2 col. 4–5, in Hewett, et al., eds., *Supplement to the Official Records*, 7:313.

A running skirmish between Vermonters and Tarheels followed beyond Reams Station. "The weather was exceedingly hot and it was terribly dusty," remembered Maj. William H. H. Cowles of the 1st North Carolina Cavalry. "In close column it was almost impossible to breathe or see for the dust, so we were forced to march in column of twos, and with long intervals between the regiments."[12]

The sun blazed on Confederate and Federal alike. "By-and-by the sun rose in the heavens and the heat became intense," Lunt recalled. "The roads were dusty, and the way a most weary one to me."[13]

Accompanied by Wilson, the 1st Vermont Cavalry continued as rear guard west of Rowanty Creek. "We faced to the rear, and after waiting about half an hour were attacked by the enemy," remembered Ide. "While we were skirmishing sharply there came out of the woods and between our lines, a colored man and woman nearly frightened out of their wits, and we had hard work to make them move off to the right and get out of range." Soon the Vermonters fell back, just as a Confederate gun unlimbered and hurled some shells their way, without effect.

After going through a farmyard a short distance farther, the 1st Vermont Cavalry again faced to the rear. Some of Rooney Lee's Confederates came up and skirmished while others tried to flank the Vermonters. Six companies of the 1st kept the Rebels back from the main Federal column for a long time. "When one company retired, the other one would be at the side, or across, the road a short distance to the rear, and would stand facing to the front till the companies in the rear were posted, and thus they each retire successively from front to rear, and at no time did the Rebels dare charge us although pressing close," remembered Ide.[14]

Kautz's cavalry reached Dinwiddie Court House at 1:00 p.m., then spent around an hour and a half destroying county records, liberating prisoners, and stealing chickens. Afterward, Kautz's troopers headed northwestward toward Five Forks. As they departed, they captured Rev. Dr. Theodorick Pryor, a chaplain in the Confederate States Army, while he rode southwestward on Boydton Plank Road to visit a sick relative in Brunswick County. Kautz's men passed Pryor on to Wilson, who invited Pryor to lunch. Pryor declined, instead demanding that the Illinoisan parole him. This request Wilson denied.

To Pryor, Wilson seemed "a fine looking man, about thirty years of age, of pleasant countenance, and most urbane manners." Wilson, Pryor recalled, "was very jauntily dressed in black velvet pants, polished high top boots, a neat fitting

12 Clark, ed., *North Carolina Regiments*, 1:468.

13 Tobie, *First Maine Cavalry*, 338.

14 Hoffman, *First Vermont Cavalry Volunteers*, 185.

jacket, and wore an elegantly trimmed cap." The Illinoisan and his staff halted briefly at Gravelly Run north of Dinwiddie Court House and let their horses drink.

At 3:00 p.m., Barringer attacked Wilson's rear guard within two miles of the courthouse. Wilson and Pryor were passing through Five Forks in Kautz's wake when a courier rode up with the news of the clash. "General Wilson received the communication with much apparent nonchalance, and coolly inquired if only cavalry showed themselves," remembered Pryor. "Upon being informed that no other branch of the service was seen, he smiled derisively, and rode on, with the remark that he did not regard the Confederate cavalry in the least."[15] Wilson turned Pryor over to the provost marshal's guard.

Chapman ordered the 1st Vermont Cavalry reinforced with the 22nd New York Cavalry. The New Yorkers formed on both sides of the road facing to the rear and allowed the Vermonters to pass through their ranks before firing on the North Carolinian pursuers. "Our regiment was in front, and as we fell back slowly the rebels were piled in the roads and woods close together, and were not aware of our movement until a sharp, stinging volley from hundreds of carbines halted them in confusion," recollected Barrett. "But they were sullen and determined, even as were our boys, and for forty minutes a thick shower of bullets whisteled through that golden wheat field, and cracked through the thick pulpy oak leaves of the wood where a short time before the mockingbird sung his varied tunes."[16]

The Federals pushed back the Confederates a short distance, then withdrew through the courthouse village of about 15 homes and rejoined Wilson's column. "The badly wounded had to be abandoned, because the ambulances were too far in the advance to be reached in time," recalled Pvt. R. Alfred Allen, a hospital steward in the 22nd.[17]

Kautz's van reached the South Side Rail Road between Sutherland and Ford's Stations about 4:00 p.m. The 11th Pennsylvania turned westward and arrived at Ford's Station about 5:30 p.m. The engine of a train of cars standing at the station fired up and escaped toward Burkeville, carrying information about the approach of the Northerners.

The evening passenger train was chugging in from the west. The station agent caught sight of the Yankees and gave the alarm. The engineer reversed his engine and escaped. A member of the 11th Pennsylvania Cavalry shot the agent in the arm. The agent found himself confined in a hog pen while a contraband to whom he had entrusted his watch and cash absconded with the Federals.

15 Eanes, *Destroy the Junction*, 12.

16 Wickman, comp., *Letters to Vermont*, 2:177.

17 R. Alfred Allen Diary, June 22, 1864, R. Alfred Allen Papers, Duke University.

James H. Wilson
National Archives

The South Side Rail Road's mail train was also puffing in from the west. A Dinwiddie man hailed the train and informed the crew and passengers of the presence of Federals at Ford's Station. The train backed about three miles and sent forward a crank car to reconnoiter, but it did not return. Then four men advanced on foot to scout, but they also failed to return. The train backed to Burkeville, where a member of the 59th Virginia aboard wired this information to Gen. Braxton Bragg, who was serving in Richmond as President Davis's military advisor.

A freight train and another passenger train did not prove as fortunate. "We captured two trains of cars and two engines, which were destroyed, as well as a good portion of the track," wrote Kautz, whose men in Spear's brigade after supper burned the depot, water tanks, wood piles, and storehouses containing tobacco and other merchandise.[18] West's brigade of Kautz's division damaged miles of track and destroyed a sawmill that prepared lumber for the railroad.

The Federals captured several slaves of the Griffin farm who were chopping wood south of Ford's Station. The Griffin farm lay about six miles southeast of Dinwiddie Court House and around a mile from the Stage Road. The raiders encountered these African Americans very unexpectedly. One, Chamberlain Nelson, decided to make the Federals think he was glad to see them. Pleased, they gave him a mule to ride while forcing the others to walk. During a halt, Nelson obtained permission to water the mule at a branch they had just passed. He intended to ride into the bushes and escape with the mule as soon as the column resumed moving. When the bugle sounded for resumption of progress, he could not prevent the mule from returning toward the command a short distance ahead. Thinking that it would be better to lose the mule than be recaptured, he dismounted, turned the animal loose and, slipping into the bushes, escaped. Five of his other comrades soon escaped as well.

18 Hewett et al., eds., *Supplement to the Official Records*, 7:239.

The troops of Wilson's division reached the South Side Rail Road about the same time as Kautz's men reached Ford's Station. Wilson's men began ripping up the ties, rails, culverts and bridges. "Destroyed several miles of track, tearing up much and burning fence rails on the rest," remembered Lieutenant Tenney in McIntosh's brigade. "Don't think this did much good."[19] The South Side line consisted principally of T-rails that required hard work to destroy—tearing up the rails, heating them over burning ties, and twisting them around trees. The Federal horsemen ignored the roadbed, which required even more work to wreck.

Farther back in the column, weariness set in. "The horses became much jaded before reaching Ford's Depot, and the teamsters several times informed the captain of the guard that they would be forced to stop, their horses then having the 'thumps,' and being rarely able to put one foot in front of the other," recalled Reverend Pryor. "The Captain told them that stopping was out of the question, and they must apply the whip freely."[20]

At the rear of the column, the 1st Vermont Cavalry and 22nd New York Cavalry continued skirmishing with Barringer's van. Three miles west of Dinwiddie Court House, the Rebs rushed the Federals, "charging and yelling in their peculiar fiendish way," recollected Barrett. "They followed us until after dark when our men fell back in such a way as to receive them with volleys every few rods, so they concluded to let the Yankees alone."[21]

Moments of quiet during the running fight allowed for contemplation of the surroundings. "Saw the widest spreading oak by the roadside 3 or 4 miles west of Dinwiddie C. H. I ever saw," recalled Allen. "I think it covered a surface at least 60 ft perhaps 75 would be nearer in diameter."[22]

The wagons of Wilson's division reached Ford's Station around 9:00 p.m. The raiders seized 80 or 90 sacks of county salt, and Wilson's guard pitched its tents south of the railway. The captain of the guard went in search of fodder for the horses. Reverend Pryor abandoned his favorite mare and groped through the darkness, the thickets and the swamps, to freedom.

Kautz's men continued their work of destruction around Ford's Station until midnight and afterward rested briefly. The 1st Vermont Cavalry and 22nd New York Cavalry of Chapman's brigade arrived around then. Just one day into his

19 Tenney, ed., *War Diary of Luman Harris Tenney*, 120.

20 Eanes, *Destroy the Junction*, 12.

21 Wickman, comp., *Letters to Vermont*, 2:177.

22 Allen Diary, June 25, 1864.

raid, Wilson had already lost at least 72 troopers to Barringer's pursuing North Carolinians.[23] Barringer's brigade lost seven.[24]

While the depot, wood piles, and two engines with trains of cars blazed at Ford's Station, Wilson ordered Kautz to move out for Burkeville at 1:00 a.m. Like Kautz's troopers, Wilson's horse soldiers got little sleep. "The engines, having been set on fire by means of rails and boards piled around them, made the night hideous with their unearthly shrieks, which continued for several hours, disturbing the rest, which, weary and sleepy, we sought in vain to enjoy," recalled Chaplain Boudrye.[25]

A few miles northeast of Dinwiddie Court House, at Boydton Plank Road's crossing of Hatchers Run, lay the Burgess farm inhabited by transplanted New Yorkers. The raiders did not disturb the farm as they passed to its south and west. Over the next few days, many other farmers would be unable to say the same.

* * *

By 2:00 p.m. on June 22, General Lee knew that enemy cavalry was moving through Dinwiddie County inquiring about the road to Burkeville and High Bridge on the South Side Rail Road. He asked Secretary of War James A. Seddon to have Brig. Gen. James Lawson Kemper, the commander of the Virginia State Reserves, immediately collect all the reserves possible at the most critical points threatened. Badly wounded at Gettysburg, Kemper that afternoon and evening activated Farinholt's Battalion Virginia Reserves at Staunton River Bridge, a covered structure about 600 feet long with a tin roof and weatherboard sides on the Richmond & Danville. Kemper also activated Averell's Battalion of Southside Virginia Reserves, including the Amelia, Lunenburg, Nottoway, and Powhatan Reserve Companies. The Amelia and Powhatan men mustered at High Bridge with

23 The 1st Vermont Cavalry had four wounded (one mortally). Vermont, Adjutant General, *Revised Roster of Vermont Volunteers and Lists of Vermonters Who Served in the Army and Navy of the United States During the War of the Rebellion, 1861–66* (Montpelier, VT, 1892), 213, 236, 262. The 22nd New York Cavalry lost one killed, four wounded, and 61 missing. RG 94, Records of the Adjutant General's Office, Entry 652, Regimental Cavalry List Civil War (1861–1865), Box 39: New York Cavalry Regiments; Entry 653, Box 30: 3 Cav Div, Army of the Potomac, NA. The 1st Connecticut Cavalry lost one wounded and missing (mistakenly listed for June 21). Connecticut, Adjutants-General, *Record of Service of Connecticut Men in the Army and Navy of the United States in the War of the Rebellion* (Hartford, CT, 1889), 64. The 1st New Hampshire Cavalry lost one captured. New Hampshire, Adjutant General, *Report of the Adjutant General of the State of New Hampshire for the Year Ending May 20, 1865*, 2 vols. (Concord, NH, 1865), 2:570.

24 The 1st North Carolina Cavalry of Barringer's brigade had one killed, five wounded, and one missing according to CSRs. Young, "Confederate Casualties during June 1864 at Petersburg."

25 Boudrye, *Fifth New York Cavalry*, 145.

the 13th Virginia Reserves Battalion, while the Nottoway and Lunenburg reserves joined Farinholt's Battalion at Staunton River Bridge.

The president of the Richmond & Danville implored Seddon for protection. At Burkeville, 300 men, many of them convalescent wounded, and a couple of guns could offer little resistance. At Flat Creek, the railroad lay unguarded. Two hundred ninety-six men and six guns garrisoned the Richmond & Danville's Staunton River Bridge, but its earthworks remained incomplete. "There are no troops except the army under General Lee and the reserves," said Bragg. "They are all ordered out."[26]

This included the walking wounded in the hospitals of the areas threatened by Wilson and Kautz. "I was a convalescent wounded soldier in the hospital at Farmville and they called in all soldiers who could stand a week's service to go help protect the High Bridge and the [South Side] Railroad," remembered Cpl. Charles Champe Taliaferro of the 6th Virginia Cavalry's Company F. "A good many of our soldiers volunteered, I being one of them."[27]

Captain Benjamin Lyons Farinholt of the 53rd Virginia's Company E had commanded six companies of the Local Reserves at the bridge for about 40 days and was organizing and drilling them while improving the bridge's defenses. Wounded and captured at Gettysburg, he had escaped from Johnson's Island in Lake Erie but was still convalescing. At 10:00 p.m. on June 22, he received a telegram from General Beauregard warning that a large body of Union horsemen was heading in the direction of the bridge, and directing Farinholt "to make every possible preparation immediately," the captain remembered.[28] He sent off orderlies by the midnight trains with circulars urging the citizens of Halifax, Charlotte, and Mecklenburg counties to assemble for the bridge's defense, and ordering all companies of the Local Reserves to report to the bridge immediately.

* * *

26 *OR* 40, 2:682.

27 Eanes, *Destroy the Junction*, 26. Taliaferro termed the railway, "the Norfolk & Western Railroad," a successor of the South Side Rail Road. Ibid. Eanes has Taliaferro belonging to the 9th Virginia Cavalry. Ibid. Another source suggests the 4th Virginia Cavalry. "Charles C. Taliaferro," The Civil War, Search for Soldiers, nps.gov. Retrieved Sept. 4, 2023. Yet another source has him in the 6th Virginia Cavalry at this point in the war, as does his tombstone. findagrave.com/memorial/9905991/charles_champe-taliaferro. Retrieved Feb. 22, 2024.

28 B. L. Farinholt, "The Staunton River Fight," in *SHSP* XIX (1891), 202. Farinholt's report says he received warning June 23. *OR* 40, 1:764.

Despite the detour through Reams Station on June 22, the raiders had accomplished everything that could reasonably be expected of cavalrymen for the first day of the raid. Things did not go as smoothly the following day.

When Wilson's column had passed through Dinwiddie Court House on the afternoon of June 22, the time came for the bridge breakers to cut loose. They rode southwest on Boydton Plank Road. That evening, they reached Red Oak in Virginia's Brunswick County. There they captured Capt. George D. White of the 3rd Virginia Cavalry's Company A, the Boydton Cavalry. White was on furlough to recover from a Gettysburg wound. The bridge breakers wanted to bring White along but lacked a spare horse. They offered to parole White, but White indicated he would not accept a parole. The Federals left White behind and continued on their way.

On the morning of June 23, White gathered a half dozen neighbors and pursued the bridge breakers. The pursuers could see the tracks of the enemy in the mud.

"We shall soon be upon them," White told his followers. "When we come in sight, my order will be to charge, go through them and await further orders."

Daylight came. White, at the head of the little column, wheeled and dashed up to his men.

"We've got 'em," he said. "We've got 'em."

The Unionists were eating breakfast in the yard of a farmhouse 200 yards from the road, with their arms stacked and their horses feeding. Clumps of bushes stood on either side of the big gate in front of the house. White stationed his men in these thickets, three on one side, three on the other.

Tying a white handkerchief to his sword, he galloped down upon the bluecoats. They immediately sprang to their feet. Their leader stepped forward.

"What does this mean?" he said.

"It means your unconditional surrender," said White.

"Well, give me a few moments to consider. We are in a strange country and do not know what your force is and I am not willing to sacrifice my men needlessly. I will leave the question with them."

The Federals voted to fight.

"Bear in mind the responsibility is on you," White said.

He wheeled his horse and started to return to his men.

The leader of the bridge builders called out.

"On further consideration, I deem it my duty to surrender," he said.

"Lay off your side arms, fall into line, forward march," ordered White.

When the Northerners passed through the big gate, a single soldier and five civilians stepped forward leveling old shotguns and rusty pistols, mortifying the Yanks.

"We'll fight them without arms," said one of the Northerners.[29]

White called out orders to call up non-existent reinforcements. This ruse subdued the Federals and he led them into captivity.

* * *

Kautz's division led the way again on June 23, departing the vicinity of Ford's Station around 2:00 a.m. The 11th Pennsylvania Cavalry again formed the van in the cool, dew-laden pre-dawn air, passing Wilson's Station about 4:00 a.m. Kautz's troopers left destruction of the track between Wilson's Station and the vicinity of Burkeville for Wilson's men.

After sunrise the heat grew intense. In the drought, the horses kicked up stifling clouds of dust. At 6:30 a.m., Kautz's men burned three cotton gins near the town of Black's and White's, then named after two taverns and now known as Blackstone. There they destroyed one car and a water tank. They halted at Nottoway Court House at 10:30 a.m., torching the station and a large warehouse filled with cotton. Afterward, Kautz's column took the road paralleling the railroad to Burkeville. His troops reached Burkeville at 3:00 p.m.

"I remember calling at some negro quarters adjoining a fine old mansion which had been deserted by its proprietor, and there informing the negroes that we were Yankees coming to set them free," remembered Lunt. "Some of these colored people were almost white, and I shall never forget their eagerness, coupled with a doubt, which their countenances expressed. They could not believe that a day so long hoped for, and delayed, had at last arrived."[30]

At Burkeville the walking wounded and security detachment at the three hotels and empty stores used as Confederate hospitals offered token resistance, then withdrew to the woods. The inhabitants of the hospitals unable to move inspired pity. Some lay on the floor of the screenless buildings. Others lay on cots in the shade of the trees. Flies swarmed around these unfortunates. The local doctor in charge could not tend to them all. Some of the Federals tried to help the ailing Southerners, but several died nonetheless.

The Unionists cut rail and telegraph service between Richmond and the Deep South. Spear's brigade destroyed the tanks, turnouts, turntables, trestles, ties, tracks, depot buildings, storehouses, and a train of cars loaded with cotton and furniture. Alerted by the trains coming back from Ford's Station the previous night, the

29 Eanes, *Destroy the Junction*, 15–16; Epperson, "A secret sidebar to the Wilson-Kautz Raid," petersburgsiege.org.

30 Tobie, *First Maine Cavalry*, 338.

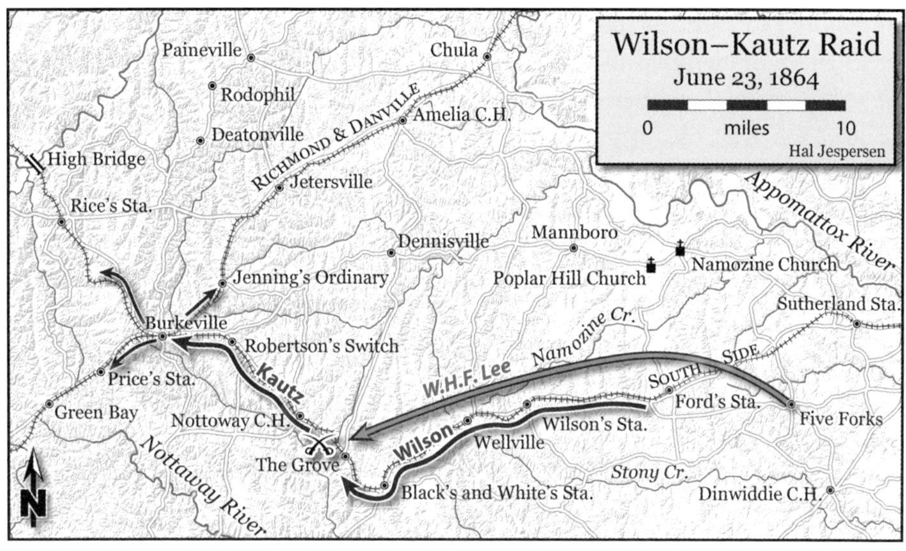

Confederates had emptied the storehouses. Kautz's men wrecked the Richmond & Danville for about four miles to the northeast, to Jennings's Ordinary, and a couple of miles southwestward toward Price's Station. They ripped up the South Side Rail Road as far as Robertson's Switch, now known as Crewe, about six miles east of Burkeville, and three or four miles toward Rice's Station, which stood around ten miles west of Burkeville and only three miles east of High Bridge. Destruction went on well into the night. After dark the scene became hellish, with burning track visible for miles, men carrying fuel to feed the fires, and iron rails glowing red and twisted into bizarre shapes.

Kautz's division exhausted its forage. The troops had to graze their horses in the fields and pastures. By midnight, the men required rest. "I felt . . . so tired and lame and sore that I was obliged to creep on hands and knees while I held the halter of my horse, as he grazed," remembered Lunt.[31]

* * *

Wilson's division followed Kautz's horsemen westward from Ford's Station, tearing up the South Side Rail Road's tracks along the way. Wilson's troops did not have time to dig up the roadbed, the best way to destroy a railroad. Some units pulled up the track, built fires with the ties, heated the iron rails and bent them out of shape on trees and fence posts. Other outfits slacked off a little, just starting fires, dropping the rails on the fires and letting the rails bend themselves. Still

31 Ibid.

other units did even less, just laying a few fence rails or pieces of wood along the tracks and igniting them to burn the ties in the frequently vain hope of warping the rails to make them useless. Thousands of cords of dry wood lay piled along the roadbed and available for this purpose. "One regiment after another was detailed to perform this labor, and such was the wisdom of the arrangement, that the main column was not impeded in its progress, while the work was going on," Chaplain Boudrye recalled.[32] Wilson's division thus wrecked in various degrees the South Side Rail Road from the vicinity of Ford's Station to Black's and White's.

As on the previous day, the Yankees did not limit their depredations to the tracks. A couple miles west of Ford's Station stood the White Oak United Methodist Church, with its grounds in use as a wayside hospital for Confederate wounded. Wilson's men burned the church, three big hospital wards, and a cook house. At Wilson's Station, they burned the Rebel barracks. At Black's and White's, they burned three warehouses loaded with government cotton and tobacco, as well as 150 loose cotton bales. Wilson, who had kept his own division back to hold off Rooney Lee's pursuers and enable Kautz's troops to wreck the railroads around Burkeville completely, assessed the damage Kautz's men had done to the T-rails of the South Side line as those horse soldiers passed through the same area earlier. He thought "one or two" of Kautz's "impatient colonels, under the burning sun, did not do their work as well as they should have done."[33]

Around 10:00 a.m., Wilson's division halted at Black's and White's. By that time, troopers were beginning to suffer from sunstroke. Wilson's men made coffee, ate lunch, groomed their horses, or rested. Afterward, they continued demolishing the South Side Rail Road. Rooney Lee's pursuit inhibited the Federals. "We had no time to do a right job," remembered Sgt. Roger Hannaford of Company M in the 2nd Ohio Cavalry. "So we would turn the road, iron and ties altogether, this is easy enough once you get started."[34]

The division's troopers never touched the stretch of rails between Nottoway Court House and Robertson's Switch. Intentionally given bad directions by a local civilian, Wilson led his men westward on the Hungarytown Road. After crossing the Little Nottoway River, the Illinoisan caught on to the ruse. He turned his column westward and took The Grove Road back toward the main road to Burkeville. The bluecoats struck the South Side railway at The Grove, also called Oak Grove. There Wilson found that the Confederate horsemen he despised had interposed between Kautz's division and his own.

32 Boudrye, *Fifth New York Cavalry*, 145.

33 Wilson, *Under the Old Flag*, 1:461.

34 Stephen Z. Starr, *The Union Cavalry in the Civil War*, 3 vols. (Baton Rouge, 1985), 2:182.

* * *

After four or five hours of rest, Rooney Lee's troopers resumed their pursuit of the Northerners from south of the charred remains of Ford's Station, now with Dearing's brigade in the lead. "Fired with a spirit of revenge at the signs of these burning ruins, and the tales of woe the frightened ladies eagerly poured into their ears, our men were eager to overtake the 'robbers' and put an end to some of them, and if possible all," recalled a soldier who styled himself "Grant" and accompanied the 62nd Georgia Cavalry of Dearing's brigade.[35] With the Rebels also rode a former brigadier general, Pvt. Roger A. Pryor, Reverend Pryor's son. So inept as a general that General Lee had stripped Roger of troops, Roger had resigned and rejoined the army as a scout. He had grown up in the area through which Rooney Lee's horsemen were passing and knew all the short cuts.

As Rooney Lee's division headed west on Cox Road, which had followed the railroad so far, the column reached Hardy's Fork, where Cox Road and the railway diverged to the south toward Black's and White's before resuming a northwesterly course toward Burkeville near The Grove. Private Pryor advised Rooney Lee to depart from Cox Road to the right along the lane that would take them straight to The Grove without a detour toward Black's and White's. This saved Lee two miles and allowed him to block Wilson's Federals at The Grove.

The two sides collided at the crossing of the railroad tracks near Nottoway Court House. The bluecoats of Chapman's brigade reached the roadbed first. They found it an excellent breastwork. The railroad cut in their front, about four feet deep and around 800 feet long, enabling them to defy any charge the Confederates could make, though the Southerners held higher ground. Wilson picketed his right all the way south to the Little Nottoway.

His superlative defensive position did him little good. He bore the onus of trying to break through the Secessionists or side-stepping them to reunite with Kautz. The former course would at least tie up the Rebels while Kautz completed the destruction of Burkeville. The latter, if Wilson's division got lost again, might result in the Southerners defeating and annihilating his command in detail. Wilson elected to fight, but the struggle began with the butternuts attacking his formidable position.

The 7th Confederate States Cavalry of Dearing's brigade led the Confederates down the lane toward the railroad. Arriving in the woods north of the railway and west of the lane, the 7th's men dismounted and deployed, then advanced. They faced Chapman's brigade in the long curve of the railroad cut running almost

35 Hewett, et al., eds., *Supplement to the Official Records*, 7:311.

at right angles to the lane. Dearing's troopers approached on the inside of the curve. Chapman's men waited on the curve's outside. The ends of Chapman's line stretched "around the right and left of our line, giving them the advantage, not only of the railroad cut and the deep ditch on top of the banks on each side, but an enfilading fire also," recalled "Grant," whose 62nd Georgia Cavalry was advancing at the double-quick. Colonel Joel R. Griffin of the 62nd sent his three North Carolina companies into the open field on the left of the lane and his other eight, seven from Georgia and one from Virginia, into the timber on the right of the 7th. Taliaferro's mounted party of troops from the Farmville hospital, having crossed High Bridge and bypassed Burkeville to the north, fought its way past the pickets on Wilson's left to The Grove on the right of the 7th. "As each regiment was brought forward and placed in position, the firing along the lines increased," remembered "Grant." The four Napoleons of Graham's battery of horse artillery, the Petersburg Light Artillery, unlimbered in the open field left of the lane, within 400 yards of Chapman's troops. The Secessionist gunners immediately unleashed on Chapman's men a storm of shot, shell, and cannister.

"As soon as all was ready, a charge was ordered and under the protecting fire of our battery, which was very effectual, our troops advanced, sending up such a 'yell' as only Southerns can, drove the Yankees out of the railroad cut, away from their fence rail breastworks, and held the position for some minutes, but being enfiladed by the enemy's fire from the left and about to be flanked on our right, we fell back some twenty-five yards in rear of the railroad," recalled "Grant." Chapman's troopers counterattacked, and Dearing's men poured hot lead into them. "The firing was now at its height, and the mingled roar of the musketry, and heavy lumbering of the artillery, seemed to rend the whole heavens," remembered "Grant." Outnumbered by more than two to one, Dearing's soldiers could not prevent Chapman's men from reoccupying the railroad cut.

The firing slackened and for about 15 minutes "Grant" could hear only a few straggling shots. "Suddenly," he recalled, "(as if mutually enraged at the sound of these desultory shots) each party fired volley after volley into the other and the report of the musketry swelled into a long, loud and prolonged roar." Dearing's men again attempted to drive Chapman's troopers out of the railroad cut. "The word being passed along the lines, a loud huzza was given and away they went, driving the enemy before them and out of the cut," remembered "Grant."[36]

Chapman's soldiers counterattacked Dearing's line three times. Dearing's men repulsed the Federals each time. Then Chapman massed troops on his right to concentrate his next assault. This onslaught drove back the three North Carolina

36 Ibid., 311–313.

William Henry Fitzhugh "Rooney" Lee
National Archives

companies of the 62nd Georgia Cavalry on Dearing's left. As those companies crumbled, the 2nd North Carolina Cavalry of Barringer's brigade charged straight down the lane leading to the railroad and supported the right flank of the three Tarheel companies, which had fallen back to the woods and continued to offer resistance. McGregor's battery of rifled guns unlimbered near the Napoleons of Graham's battery. In response to a courier with a message from Rooney Lee to come up as quickly as possible, the 1st North Carolina Cavalry broke into a gallop and formed from twos into fours. The courier passed the short wagon train of Barringer's brigade and dashed up to the 5th North Carolina Cavalry.

"Open ranks; forward, gallop, march," came the order.

Private Means of the 5th remembered, "And past those wagons the [5th] went in a rushing pace right after the [1st]."[37]

The 1st reached the field as the left of Dearing's brigade buckled. Rooney Lee sat his horse beside the road with "the expression upon his face of a brave man hard pressed," Major Cowles of the 1st recalled.

"Save the guns!" said Lee. "Save the guns!"

"We'll do it, General," Cowles said.

Cowles turned to his regiment.

"Prepare to fight on foot," he commanded. "Dismount; front into line; double-quick, march!"[38]

In the open field, the collapse of Dearing's left flank left Graham's and McGregor's batteries unsupported. Chapman's men surged toward the guns, which the 1st Vermont Cavalry tried to seize from the artillerists. The gunners of McGregor's battery prepared to fight hand to hand with the Vermonters. One section of Graham's battery limbered up and escaped. Federal fire forced the gunners to abandon the other section, though its teams got away. "The enemy fired

37 Clark, ed., *North Carolina Regiments*, 3:613.

38 Ibid., 1:468.

too high, and their bullets went mostly over our heads," remembered Sgt. George W. Shreve of McGregor's battery. "We were on the higher ground."[39]

Barringer's 1st North Carolina Cavalry on the left and 5th North Carolina Cavalry on the right dismounted and charged. "The blue coated fellows had begun to think they were to have it all their own way; one of them fell right at the mouth of the cannon," recalled Cowles. "I think he was knocked on the head by one of McGregor's gunners with a rammer."[40] The 1st Vermont Cavalry captured some of the guns but the arrival of Barringer's brigade evened the odds. Each side had about 2,000 men engaged.

The 1st North Carolina Cavalry threatened the right flank of Chapman's troopers now defending the guns. Captain Galloway of the 5th North Carolina Cavalry and a volunteer advanced through the wood to the left of the open field and reconnoitered the unprotected left flank of Chapman's brigade in the railroad cut. Each received a bullet in the hat brim as they retired. Galloway explained to Major Cowles of the 1st North Carolina Cavalry the vulnerability of Chapman's left. Cowles sent a squad to cross the railway. The men of the 2nd North Carolina Cavalry wheeled and faced left with a few companies of the 5th, firing into the left rear of Chapman's soldiers. Colonel Griffin of the 62nd Georgia Cavalry detached all but two of his companies and dispatched them to Dearing's left.

Facing possible envelopment, the 1st Vermont Cavalry could neither drag away nor spike the guns of Graham's battery. With the rest of Chapman's men, the Vermonters retreated to the railroad cut. The 1st North Carolina Cavalry took possession of the guns half an hour after their abandonment. "[I]f we had had a hundred men mounted to have charged, the Rebel battery would have been ours and the day won," remembered Ide in the 1st Vermont Cavalry. "But our general was not equal to the occasion, and the enemy receiving reinforcements, drove us back to near the starting point."[41]

After the 1st North Carolina Cavalry's relief, Rooney Lee thanked its officers and men profusely for their conduct. Captain McGregor rushed forward and seized Cowles's hand. "Henceforth those guns," McGregor said, pointing to his battery, "belong to the First North Carolina Cavalry; you saved them today, and they are yours."

39 Robert J. Trout, ed., *Memoirs of the Stuart Light Artillery Battalion: Volume 2, Breathed's and McGregor's Batteries* (Knoxville, 2010), 305.

40 Clark, ed., *North Carolina Regiments*, 1:468–469.

41 Hoffman, *First Vermont Cavalry Volunteers*, 186.

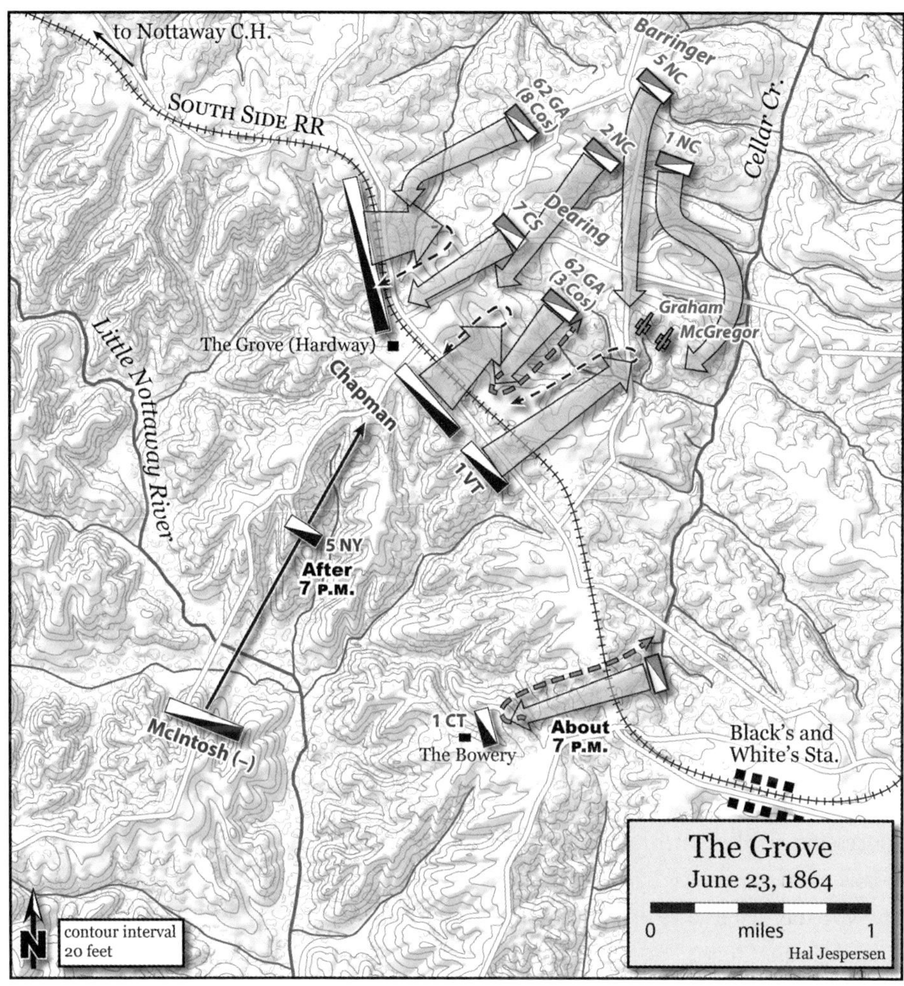

The fight then stalemated, but the fire remained hot. "Their bullets swept the small growth from the crest of the ridge, and good sized saplings and small trees were almost cut down by them," Cowles recollected.[42]

The 1st Connecticut Cavalry of McIntosh's brigade thwarted a mounted Confederate attempt to outflank Wilson near the Bowery plantation on his right just before dark, around 7:00 p.m. "My horse was killed under me and I was thrown into the air and badly bruised," recalled Taliaferro, whose band had made its way

42 Clark, ed., *North Carolina Regiments*, 1:469.

around the main battle and managed to get into this attack. "I was unconscious for a while and lay there in front of my horse for several hours."[43]

Shortly afterward, Wilson reinforced Chapman with the 5th New York Cavalry from McIntosh's brigade, but the stalemate continued. "Towards night the enemy used their battery freely, throwing shell, cannister, and solid shot, cutting off the tops of the trees, but not doing much damage as our led horses were back out of range," recalled Ide.[44] Waiting to hear what Kautz had accomplished at Burkeville, Wilson did not want to press the issue at The Grove. Skirmishing and sniping continued until midnight.

Wilson considered this fight "one of the most determined cavalry engagements in which this division has participated."[45] Corporal John D. Timmerman of Company L, 3rd New York Cavalry viewed the matter more pessimistically and thought the column "was split up and Wilson got whipped and had to make back tracks."[46]

The Confederates realized what a difficult struggle they had survived. "General Lee says it was the hardest cavalry fight of the war," remembered "Grant" in the 62nd Georgia Cavalry of Dearing's brigade. "It had been a warm day and our men suffered much from heat and thirst, but more from hunger than all else—as General Dearing had sent our wagons back to Petersburg, fearing their capture, and our men were compelled to do without a morsel of food."[47] A local woman recalled, "Trees at the 'Oak Grove' had cannon balls in them from this fight."[48]

Once again, Barringer had distinguished himself. Dearing's brigade would "always remember with pride and pleasure the timely aid of [Barringer's] Brigade in this conflict, for we had fully as much as we desired to handle," recollected 2nd Lt. W. F. Parker in one of the 62nd's North Carolina companies.

After the fight, Parker remembered, "General Dearing remarked if 'Aunt Nancy' (Gen. Barringer) had not got there just at the time he did, that he would have had a much harder time, for, said he, they outnumbered us three to one."[49]

Dearing exaggerated the odds, though not by much—Chapman's brigade outnumbered Dearing's brigade by about two and a half to one, but the arrival of

43 Eanes, *Destroy the Junction*, 41.

44 Hoffman, *First Vermont Cavalry Volunteers*, 186.

45 *OR* 40, 1:626.

46 Eanes, *Destroy the Junction*, 50.

47 Hewett et al., eds., *Supplement to the Official Records*, 7:313.

48 Eanes, *Destroy the Junction*, 47.

49 Clark, ed., *North Carolina Regiments*, 4:88.

Barringer's brigade made the odds even until reinforcement by the 5th New York Cavalry of McIntosh's brigade gave the Federals a slight edge.

Rooney Lee had suffered about 96 killed, wounded, and missing, principally in the 62nd Georgia Cavalry.[50] Wilson lost at least 71 killed, wounded, and captured, mostly in the 1st Vermont Cavalry and the 8th New York Cavalry of Chapman's brigade.[51]

* * *

50 CSRs indicate that in Dearing's brigade the 7th Confederate Cavalry had four killed, five wounded, and 13 missing; the 62nd Georgia Cavalry lost six killed, one mortally wounded, and 33 otherwise wounded; and the 4th North Carolina Cavalry had one wounded and one missing. Young, "Confederate Casualties during June 1864 at Petersburg." According to "Grant," 41 of the 64 casualties in Dearing's brigade were in the 62nd Georgia. Hewett, et al., eds., *Supplement to the Official Records*, 7:313. W. A. Hopson, "Sixty-Second Georgia Regiment of Cavalry," *Macon Daily Telegraph*, July 15, 1864, p. 1, col. 2 lists six killed or mortally wounded, 30 otherwise wounded, and one captured but escaped as the 62nd's casualties. CSRs indicate that in Barringer's brigade, the 1st North Carolina Cavalry lost one killed and three wounded; the 2nd North Carolina Cavalry had two killed, three mortally wounded, and three otherwise wounded; and the 5th North Carolina Cavalry lost one killed, seven wounded and five missing, a loss of 25. Young, "Confederate Casualties during June 1864 at Petersburg." Another source reports that the 2nd North Carolina Cavalry of Barringer's brigade lost five killed or mortally wounded and one wounded. Harrell, *The 2nd North Carolina Cavalry*, 304–305.

Graham's battery lost three killed and three wounded, McGregor's battery one wounded. Robert J. Trout, *Galloping Thunder: The Stuart Horse Artillery Battalion* (Mechanicsburg, PA, 2002), 545–546. CSRs report that Graham's battery had one killed, one mortally wounded, and two otherwise wounded, McGregor's battery one wounded. Young, "Confederate Casualties during June 1864 at Petersburg."

51 In Chapman's brigade, the 1st Vermont Cavalry lost three killed, two mortally wounded, 12 otherwise wounded, six wounded and captured, and two captured. Vermont, Adjutant General, *Revised Roster of Vermont Volunteers*, 227–261, *passim*. According to Ide, the 1st Vermont Cavalry lost seven killed or mortally wounded at The Grove on June 23, 1864. Hoffman, *First Vermont Cavalry Volunteers*, 292. The 8th New York Cavalry had four killed, eight wounded, eight wounded and captured, and six missing. RG 94, Entry 652, Box 38, NA. The 1st New Hampshire Cavalry lost six wounded, one missing. New Hampshire, Adjutant General, *Report of the Adjutant General of the State of New Hampshire*, 2:568–72, *passim*. The 3rd Indiana Cavalry lost six wounded. Goecker, *Hoosier Spies and Horse Marines*, 190–256, *passim*. Corporal Samuel J. V. B. Gilpin of the 3rd's Company E thought Chapman's brigade suffered 90 killed and wounded at The Grove. Samuel J. V. B. Gilpin Diary, June 23, 1864, E. N. Gilpin Papers, LOC. Gilpin wrote his accounts of June 21 through July 1 on July 1. Ibid., June 21–July 1, 1864. In McIntosh's brigade the 1st Connecticut Cavalry had two captured. Angelovich, *Riding for Uncle Samuel*, 437. The 5th New York Cavalry lost one wounded and three missing. RG 94, Entry 652, Box 38, NA. Wilson's provost guard, a detachment of the 3rd New Jersey Cavalry, had one missing. RG 94, Entry 653, Box 30, NA.

Dyer reports Federal losses at The Grove as 16 killed, 52 wounded, and 34 missing. Frederick H. Dyer, *A Compendium of the War of the Rebellion: Compiled and Arranged from Official Records of the Federal and Confederate Armies Reports of the Adjutant Generals of the Several States, the Army Registers and Other Reliable Documents and Sources* (Des Moines, 1908), 947. Dearing wrote that the Confederates captured "about thirty" at The Grove. James Dearing to Wife, June 24, 1864, James Dearing Letters, Dearing Family Papers, VMHC.

Unable to break through the Confederates at The Grove, in part because he had to keep almost half his division back to protect escape routes, Wilson put aside for the time being the idea of destroying High Bridge and uniting with Hunter. The destruction of High Bridge, the third most important of the raid's objectives, would have hobbled the transportation of supplies and troops from Lynchburg to Lee's army. For that reason alone, The Grove fight amounted to a Southern victory. The action also prevented Wilson from arriving at Staunton River Bridge the next day. The Illinoisan would have to use that day to reunite with Kautz at Meherrin Station on the Richmond & Danville, a decision which Captain Whitaker of Wilson's staff communicated to Kautz on the night of The Grove fight.

Kautz had destroyed the raid's primary objective—Burkeville, making it impossible for Rebels from the Valley or from the Deep South to debark from trains near the Petersburg battlefield as Confederate reinforcements had at Chickamauga the previous autumn. Wilson and Kautz had also accomplished the fourth most important goal of their raid—cutting the Weldon Railroad to prevent reinforcements from the Deep South from stepping out of the cars almost behind the backs of Federal infantry investing the Cockade City. Now Wilson focused on destroying Staunton River Bridge, the second most important of his objectives, which would add to the delay of reinforcements and supplies reaching Petersburg and Richmond. He still entertained the possibility of destroying High Bridge, his third most important goal, but not until he had destroyed Staunton River Bridge.[52]

* * *

That day at Staunton River Bridge, Captain Farinholt had his entire battalion working. On the southwestern side of Staunton River, where hills rose from the water's edge, they labored on entrenchments, an artillery emplacement, and a fort. In the level bottom on the river's northeastern bank, they scraped out rifle pits. The artillery emplacement, about 100 yards above the Richmond & Danville, held two iron six-pounders. Farinholt gave command of these guns to Capt. John W. Lewis, who found that their ammunition included only solid shot and cannister. "We at once covered the works with green bushes," Lewis recalled.[53]

Two smoothbore twelve-pounders, a three-inch rifle, and an iron six-pounder armed the fort below the railroad. Farinholt put Capt. William C. Marshall of the Fauquier (Stribling) Artillery in charge of these guns. Marshall had been in Halifax recovering from a wound when he received word that every sick and

52 James Harrison Wilson Diary, June 24, 1864, Delaware Public Archives, Dover, DE.

53 Hewett, et al., eds, *Supplement to the Official Records*, 7:269.

wounded soldier who could report must do so at once to Staunton River Bridge. First Lieutenant Robert L. Ragland of Wright's Company in the Halifax Artillery commanded an eight-man crew on one of the 12-pounders at the fort. Ragland's gun crew included Pvt. James D. Gilliam of Company D in the 38th Battalion, Virginia Light Artillery, a sixteen-year-old who recalled that he "handled the sponge and staff and rammed the charge home."[54] Range stakes posted in the fields approaching the bridge gave the Confederate gunners more accurate range estimates for their loads.

* * *

President Davis continued to take steps to protect the Confederate railroads from the Federal raiders. At Raleigh, Lt. Gen. Theophilus Holmes received orders to collect all available reserves and proceed to Weldon to cover the line to Petersburg.

With five comrades Chamberlain Nelson covered the 20 miles back to the Griffin farm that day. Unneeded on the farm, they were sent to work on the dam of the farm's mill, still called Spencer's Mill after a previous owner, in Greensville County on the Nottoway River near the Double Bridges.

* * *

West's brigade of Kautz's division resumed its destruction of the Richmond & Danville at 4:00 a.m. on June 24. The flimsy constitution of the track aided the Federals. The track, called strap rail, consisted of strap iron an inch and a half deep by three wide, resembling heavy wagon tire, firmly secured to wooden supports two inches deep by four inches in width and at least four inches embedded in large, heavy ties. Tearing up such tracks took only half the time ordinary rails required. West's brigade reached Price's Station halfway between Burkeville and Green Bay, then halted, burned the station, and sent out parties to wreck the track and its accompanying installations northeast of the station. The brigade also torched three sawmills, necessary for lumber to replace the wood destroyed.

The troopers of Spear's brigade, reaching Price's Station at 7:30 a.m. while West's brigade was still working, demolished the railway for two miles southwest of the station. Spear's troopers then marched to Meherrin Station, arriving at 9:00 a.m. They also pillaged the countryside as they went. "If their haversacks were sometimes empty, and they were fain to gnaw the raw corn, which the horses did eat, their appetites were all the more clamourous when they came within reach of food," Chaplain Merrill of the 1st District of Columbia Cavalry recalled. "At

54 Eanes, *Destroy the Junction*, 58.

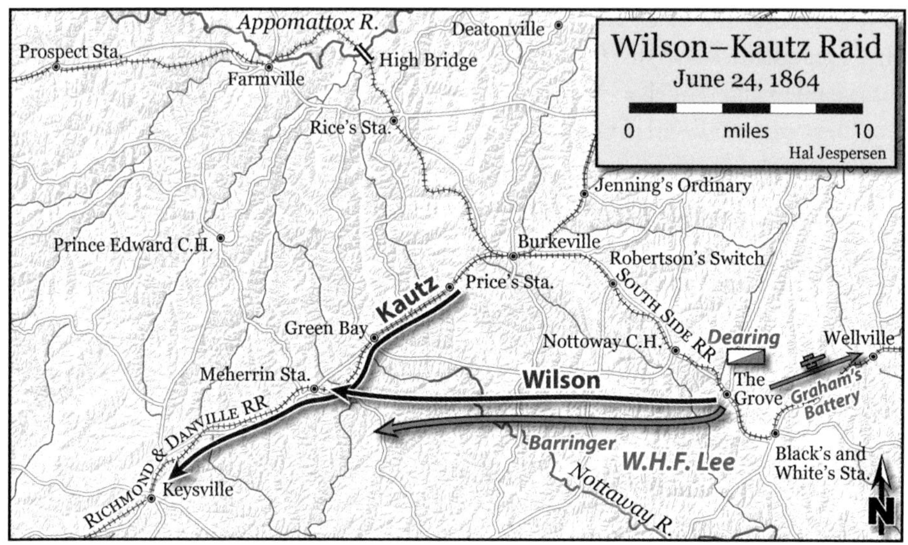

such times, bread, and meat, and butter, and milk, and eggs, and cream, in a word, whatever the smokehouse or spring-house, or the field or garden, or stall or pasture of a rebel contained, which was capable of being readily converted into good food, was remorselessly appropriated without waiting for either commissary or quartermaster process."[55]

Second Lieutenant Leander M. Comins, a Maine man in the 1st District of Columbia's Company G, shed still more light on this matter, writing, "It costs us much less to live when on a raid as we take every thing eatable we can find without money or price."[56]

The raiders did not limit their confiscations to food and horseflesh but would take anything they needed. Contrabands suffered as well as Confederates. "I would get asleep while riding in the night and the boughs of the trees would take off my hat and the next minute it would be in the center of the column and trampled in the dirt where I could not get it without halting the whole column," Comins recalled. "The next morning the first citizen or negro with a good hat had to hand over, or the first house would be looked through for the same article."[57]

After burning Meherrin Station, Spear's soldiers destroyed the railroad down to Keysville, which they reached at 1:30 p.m. Kautz made his headquarters in the

55 Merrill, *First Maine and First District of Columbia Cavalry*, 264.

56 Letter, L. M. Comins to "My dear wife," July 6, 1864, Leander M. Comins Letters, Private Collection of Diane Fishburn, Meadow Vista, CA.

57 Letter, L. M. Comins to "My dear wife," July 13, 1864, Leander M. Comins Letters.

Keysville Hotel. His men burned among other things the depot and other railroad buildings, the harness store, the Masonic Hall, and a smokehouse. Work parties again went out to wreck the tracks.

Company I of the 1st District of Columbia Cavalry picketed a crossroad. "We made our headquarters in the house of Mr. Foster, whose wife, although she had been born in Ohio, appeared to be a very ardent sympathizer with the Confederates, and to be extremely anxious to obtain all the information possible as to the number of our force and the object of our raid, but I fear that the information that she obtained was far from accurate, and she herself seemed to doubt our veracity," recalled Lunt. "Nevertheless, we were here bountifully supplied with ripe cherries and a good supper, and about midnight a family of negro slaves prepared a turkey supper for us, which was a very welcome change from hardtack and pork."[58]

* * *

That morning Mrs. Mary Purnell Dupuy Watkins learned at her Prince Edward County home, Oldham, that the Yankees had reached Meherrin Station. She dispatched a slave to care for her house and horses while she buried in some weeds jewelry, other valuables, and her husband's papers. The slave reached Oldham "just in time to find the house full of Yankees and all of our horses and mules and a good many of the negroes in their possession," Mrs. Watkins recalled. The bluecoats left only a pair of colts. The Federals ordered a neighbor's slaves to stop plowing and come along with them. The Unionists burst into the Watkins house, kicking out a panel to one of the doors, and searched for gold, silver, and papers. "They injured the two top drawers to the bookcase very much cutting and hacking them with their sabres. . . . [T]hey did not break open or injure in any way the bookcases where your law books were. . . . They tried the door to my china closet but concluded not to force it," Mrs. Watkins wrote to her husband, Capt. Richard Henry Watkins of the 3rd Virginia Cavalry's Company K, the Prince Edward Dragoons, a lawyer as well as a farmer.

The raiders took with them six of the Watkins's slaves, mounting them on horses. "I do not think the negroes were entirely to blame for going. . . . [T]hey were ordered . . . to throw down their hoes, cut the horses from the plows and follow them," Mrs. Watkins recalled. The Northerners took all the plow gear but did not touch the corn. "I never believed one half of what I had read about the Yankees before, but now I think there is nothing too mean for them to do, at least these Raiders," Mrs. Watkins remembered. One of her neighbors had to put up

58 Tobie, *First Maine Cavalry*, 339.

with the Yankees the entire day. Another, recalled Mrs. Watkins, "ran away from home whereupon the wretches took all of her and her childrens . . . clothes, ripped up all of her beds, broke up her earthenware and furniture, even destroyed her kitchen furniture, brought in negroe women and made them dress up in [her] clothes . . . and then shot two of their broken down horses in her porch leaving them dead with their heads in her door."[59]

* * *

At 3:00 a.m., Wilson withdrew from The Grove and its environs. "They were fleeing so fast they did not have time to bury their dead," a local man recalled about the Unionists. "The Confederates and the darkies took all their clothes and weapons."[60] Wilson's horsemen took the Hungarytown Road southwestward and halted at Concord Church in Hungarytown. They resumed their progress at 9:00 a.m., laying waste to the countryside. The bluecoats stripped the local farms of slaves, declaring them free, and plundered houses of furniture, silver plate, and other valuables. The Northerners burned hundreds of bales of cotton. The 22nd New York Cavalry of Chapman's brigade incinerated a large quantity of tobacco. The 2nd Ohio Cavalry of McIntosh's brigade, which acted as the column's rear guard, torched two or three small tobacco barns full of the weed.

Another segment of the 2nd impressed horses. Ridden hard and starting to give out, the raiders' mounts required replacing. "Horses playing out fast," noted Sergeant Koempel in the 1st Connecticut Cavalry.[61]

The raiders had orders to shoot their horses lest the Southerners nurse them back to health for their own use. "We shot an average of one horse every quarter mile," recalled Quartermaster Sergeant Hannaford of the 2nd Ohio Cavalry.[62] Eventually, to save bullets, the Yankees began slashing the throats of the unfortunate beasts. With the Federals having stolen all the fresh horses available, their Confederate pursuers had to make do on the horses with which they started. As a result, the Secessionist pursuit waned.

The country easily furnished the Federals' needs out of its bounty. Captain Hall of the 3rd New York Cavalry in Wilson's division called the land "the best

59 Jeff Toalson, ed., *Send Me a Pair of Old Boots & Kiss My Little Girls: The Civil War Letters of Richard and Mary Watkins, 1861–1865* (New York, 2009), 294–295, 298.

60 Eanes, *Destroy the Junction*, 50.

61 Koempel, *Phil Koempel's Diary*, June 23, 1864, 11.

62 Eanes, *Destroy the Junction*, 45–46.

I ever saw in Virginia, out of the Shenandoah Valley."[63] Others agreed. "Hams, bacon, corn, wheat and flour we would find at almost every house," remembered Pvt. John H. Powers of the 1st Vermont Cavalry's Company D, who also rode with Wilson's division. "It was not at all unusual to find corn enough to feed the horses of the whole command."[64]

Company E of the 2nd Ohio Cavalry received orders to report to its former commander, General Kautz, who ordered the company's soldiers to notify another regiment of a change in Wilson's plans. On their way, they "saw a few home guards and a small squad of Confederate cavalry, but they gave us the road and no trouble," recalled Company E's Sgt. Isaac Gause.[65] Delivering the message, Company E encamped, fed, made coffee, and rejoined its command.

The Confederates did not interfere with the progress of the raiders. "[T]he Johnnies had last night quite as much as they wished to digest for one day . . . for although they still followed us, yet it was at a respectful distance," remembered Hannaford.[66] The 1st Connecticut Cavalry of McIntosh's brigade in the column's van joined Kautz's men at Meherrin Station at noon.

At the same time, the 1st Vermont Cavalry of Chapman's brigade halted at Concord Church in Lunenburg County. Word arrived that a comrade mortally wounded at The Grove had died, "and that they were agoing to take his body out of the ambulance and leave it," recalled Ide. "Orders were sent back to have it brought up to the church, and three of us, with the pioneers, were left to bury him, as the column moved on."[67] With no time to make a coffin, they wrapped their comrade in a blanket and buried him near the church. Taking a board from the church's desk, they cut his name and regiment on it and set it at his grave's head.

Wilson's rear guard reached Meherrin Station at 5:00 p.m. "The road bed was wrapt in smoke as far as the eye could reach . . . and the few inhabitants visible were dejected and despairing, and although now cringing, their dislike towards us could not be entirely hid," Hannaford recalled.[68]

Upon arriving, Wilson's soldiers pitched in on the demolition of the Richmond & Danville. The men of each regiment received a certain stretch of track to burn. The railroad's straps of iron atop wooden rails and ties burned easily in the hot,

63 Hall and Longacre, "Would to God that War Was Rendered Impossible," 460.

64 J. H. P., "Vermont Cavalry," *Windsor* (VT) *Park*, July 16, 1864.

65 Gause, *Four Years in Five Armies*, 278–279.

66 Eanes, *Destroy the Junction*, 44–45.

67 Hoffman, *First Vermont Cavalry Volunteers*, 187.

68 Eanes, *Destroy the Junction*, 45.

dry conditions. Dropping a few fence rails or pieces of wood along the tracks and lighting them did more damage than on the South Side railway. On the Richmond & Danville the fire burned not only the ties but the wooden portion of the strap rails, warping the iron to make it useless. As usual, the Federals ignored the roadbed, which required real work to wreck.

When finished, the troops would march forward through fire and smoke under the broiling sun a mile or a mile and a half until they came to the front again and had another stretch allotted to them. This proved too much for many of the horse soldiers. "A great part of the way we could find no water, and many of the boys began to give out," Hannaford remembered. "At last, what with the intense heat and fatigue, railroad burning, except under the most favorable circumstances, was abandoned, and we marched along just as we saw proper, every man for himself." Corporal Samuel J. B. V. Gilpin of the 3rd Indiana Cavalry's Company E summarized the day's oppressive heat simply as, "HOT."[69]

The burning of some buildings met with disapproval. "While tearing up the track at this point a Masonic temple was fired by some men of the command and burned down, to the great indignation of the mass of our troops," recalled 2nd Lt. Thomas Ward of Battery K.[70]

Though the troopers of Wilson's and Kautz's divisions remained tasked with railroad wrecking until late that night, they did not tear up the railway as thoroughly as on the previous day. They destroyed "the road at intervals to Meherrin Station and from there to Keysville almost entirely," Kautz recorded.[71]

Many more slaves emancipated themselves and were following the column, even joining in the railroad-wrecking. In the middle of the night, a slave escaped his bondage, walked into the picket post of the 1st District of Columbia Cavalry's Company I and spoke to the sergeant in charge about some wagons containing provisions hidden in woods an indeterminate distance away. The sergeant ordered Lunt to take two men and bring in the wagons. "Experienced soldiers would have been more careful, but, ignorant of danger, away we went, following our dusky guide through the gray of the morning, across fields and pastures and through woods, until at length, in a secluded spot, under the thick [foliage] of lofty trees, just at daybreak, we found several wagons laden with trunks and furniture, and one small cart filled with bacon and corn meal, and an old roan horse tied to a tree near by," remembered Lunt. The soldiers seized the provisions and allowed their

69 Ibid., 46; Gilpin Diary, June 24, 1864.

70 William L. Haskin, *The History of the First Regiment of Artillery: From Organization in 1821 to January 1, 1876* (Portland, ME, 1879), 561.

71 Hewett, et al., eds, *Supplement to the Official Records*, 7:239.

guide to do as he pleased with the other items. Afterward, the troopers made him their driver. He hitched the roan to the cart containing the bacon and meal and they all headed back to the picket post. "The bacon and ham we were glad to eat raw, although portions of it presented a very animated spectacle," Lunt recalled.[72]

* * *

Rooney Lee did not think the Northerners had damaged the railroads very materially. He expected Wilson and Kautz to unite near Staunton River Bridge and return by way of Stony Creek Station, damaging the Weldon Railroad as much as possible. Lee's men and animals had become so exhausted that they had to rest. He spent the morning reorganizing his forces. "I shall send back some of my artillery, as I am out of ammunition and am delayed here this morning for the want of rations for the men, but am resting and grazing my horses and will push on this afternoon," he reported.[73] Some of the troopers had their horses reshod. Graham's battery returned to Petersburg.

With Dearing's wagons sent back to Petersburg early during the pursuit of the raiders, his men had not eaten in two days of 100-degree temperatures and they could not possibly keep up with Barringer's troopers, whose number had dwindled to about 1,000.[74]

The two brigades had to separate. "Dearing was to move on the enemy's left flank, while my three regiments were to follow the enemy's line of march directly to the Staunton River bridge," recalled Barringer. "This was the most important structure on General Robert E. Lee's whole line of communication for supplying his army."[75]

Taliaferro still lay stunned beside his dead horse that morning. After the Federals withdrew, members of the Epes family, "those good citizens—God Bless 'em—soon came out to see the wounded and the dying—they were anxious to take me but I told them I was not wounded, was only hurt, from the fall," he recalled. "They insisted on moving me but I told them no, just to give me a drink of water to take those who needed it more than I did."[76] Late that evening, they took him to the Epes house, bathed him and fed him. He returned to the hospital in Farmville next morning.

72 Tobie, *First Maine Cavalry*, 340.

73 *OR* 51, 1:272.

74 Harrell, *The 2nd North Carolina Cavalry*, 304.

75 Clark, *North Carolina Regiments*, 1:433.

76 Eanes, *Destroy the Junction*, 46–47.

* * *

Small groups of soldiers and civilians began gathering at Staunton River Bridge in response to Farinholt's call for assistance. Some came on foot. John Powell, who ran the John Powell Academy in Halifax, led his entire school out of the classroom and marched toward the bridge, as did other schoolmasters. Captain William D. Hurt was drilling Company D of the 1st Virginia Reserves, the Halifax company, when Farinholt's summons came; the company ceased instruction and hiked to the bridge. Local Reserves from Pittsylvania County and some from Amelia County joined the others mobilizing at the bridge.

Horses brought others. Colonel Thomas S. Flournoy of the militia and Capt. Paul Edmonds, home on leave, rode in with about 150 citizens and furloughed soldiers. Farinholt posted most of these horsemen at the fords around two miles above and below the bridge to prevent the Federals from crossing and attacking the fortifications from the rear. Flournoy's group guarded the eastern ford, Edmonds's band the western. Other horsemen picketed the hills north of Roanoke Station. Patrick Henry's granddaughter, Mrs. William Clark of Banister Lodge, hauled her harp up to the bridge in a wagon and entertained the troops.

Colonel Eaton Coleman of the 12th North Carolina had been convalescing from a life-threatening head wound 25 miles away in Halifax County. When Farinholt's summons reached Coleman, he was starting to improve. He insisted upon traveling to the bridge even though his doctor said the trip alone could kill Coleman and begged him to remain quietly in bed. With cold bandages around his head, Coleman ordered a bed made up in the family carriage and had a slave drive him to the bridge.

Trains carried most of the reinforcements to the bridge. Another company of the Virginia Local Defense troops, ordnance personnel from the leather shops at Clarkesville in nearby Mecklenburg County, arrived by rail. Two infantry companies from Danville rode the 55 miles from that city along with every soldier in the city's hospitals who could shoulder a rifle. Men from the Corps of Engineers pitched in and took over the construction of the bridge's Halifax defenses from Farinholt. The railroad carried to the bridge 125 disabled soldiers working at the Danville arsenal. The cars hauled in 59 men awaiting transportation in Danville, who volunteered to serve under a Lieutenant Colonel Jackson, a veteran from North Carolina suffering from a leg wound. This group included Sgt. Theophilus F. Meece of Company K, the Polk County Flying Artillery, in the 5th Texas, who was returning to active duty from parole, and Pvt. John T. Eason, a member of Company I, the Pettus Rifles, in the 17th Mississippi, who had stopped in Danville on his way back from furlough.

After dark, Capt. James E. Riddick of Richmond's 1st Regiment 2nd Class Volunteer Militia arrived on the Danville train with two other officers, half a dozen non-coms, and 53 privates—soldiers between the ages of 45 and 55. With them came 50 foreigners in Richmond's 2nd Regiment Virginia State Reserves required to perform military duty because they had voted in the Confederacy. Captain James A. Hoyt of South Carolina's 1st Palmetto Sharpshooters rode in by rail in command of citizen volunteers from South Boston and Scottsburg.

Farinholt held a council of war. Two or three gray headed ministers reported that they had brought their schoolboys armed with shotguns and squirrel rifles to save the bridge. Captain Marshall advised Farinholt to put the boys on the north side of the river, where they could not retreat. Farinholt, convinced that the destruction of the bridge would render Richmond untenable, agreed. The ministers protested because of the age of the boys. Farinholt asked if they had not come to save the bridge and he insisted that the boys hold the advanced positions. "This seemed fearfully cruel," Marshall remembered.[77] The boys and the ministers went into the hills north of the river with the militia from Richmond. Coleman and Hoyt then positioned the rest of the infantry on the south side and Marshall went back to the artillery.

* * *

Wilson's men got a big head start in the race against Rooney Lee's troopers for Staunton River Bridge on June 25. The 5th Pennsylvania Cavalry of West's brigade led Kautz's division out of Keysville at 4:00 a.m. These troops stopped only to destroy the railroad and nearly every sawmill on the line, as well as tobacco houses and corn cribs with their contents. The Keystoners spared the grist mills at the request of the slaves. Reaching Drake's Branch Station about 9:00 a.m., the Pennsylvanians halted for two hours and burned all the depot buildings and works. West's brigade then advanced and demolished Mossingford and Carrington's stations and Carrington's Mill on Little Roanoke Creek.

"Papa's losses were extremely heavy," wrote Margaret Watkins, who lived at "Do Well," the plantation of her father, William M. Watkins, near Mossingford. "He sent off his negroes and horses, but unfortunately the overseer did not take them far enough, and 22 negroes and 16 horses were captured and carried away." The Federals did not find Do Well's meat nor more than 20 barrels of corn. "We had sent away all our valuable clothing, bed and table linen, blankets, plate, etc., etc., so these were saved," she recalled. "But our house was robbed of many things

77 Ibid., 59.

that were very valuable to us." The Watkins house lost all its sugar, butter, and flour as well as much of its lard and tinware, and many of its fowls, bags, pillowcases, and towels. "They broke the locks to the storerooms before I could hand them the keys; had all the negro women on the place cooking for them all day; at least for six hours and a half, which was the time the Yankee army took to pass our gate, and they were marching in a close line all the time," Margaret recollected. It seemed as if more than 1,000 Federals had descended upon the place. "The house, yard, garden, orchard, negro cabins, kitchen, just swarmed with them the whole day," she remembered. "I was cursed at several times, but with this exception I received no indignity and they were generally respectful."[78]

The trains and artillery followed Kautz's division. Wilson's division, now under McIntosh, brought up the rear. The bluecoats reached and destroyed Roanoke Station about 2:00 p.m. This made a total of about 15 miles of track they had wrecked on the Richmond & Danville. Because of the nature of the strap rails, the combustibility of the pine ties, the heat and dryness, and the kindling afforded by the adjoining fences, the destruction was unusually thorough for a cavalry raid. South of Roanoke Station, they met the motley force of Confederate reserves, active duty soldiers, schoolboys, and convalescents defending Staunton River bridge.

* * *

The raid continued to take its toll on mounts, and Unionist parties charged with impressing fresh horseflesh ranged far and wide on the flanks of the main column. "Many horses 'played out' by the way," recalled Chaplain Boudrye. "They were invariably shot, and replaced by horses and mules captured in the country. Scouting parties and flankers are constantly replenishing the column with installments of fresh, fat animals, which the people have not the time or adroitness to hide from the swift moving Yankees."[79]

Tenney led a detail of 20 men away from the 2nd Ohio Cavalry into a larger force that left the column in search of horses and mules because of all the men dismounted by the heat of the previous day. Tenney and his troopers rode through "a very rich and beautiful country," he remembered. "Never saw more splendid crops."[80] The horsemen went to Charlotte Court House, where they remained for three or four hours. Some of the group's soldiers broke open stores, released two

78 Ibid., 83. Margaret was writing to her brother Joel Watkins in Florida and it is unclear what if any relationship she had to Richard and Mary Watkins of Oldham. Ibid., 82–83, 126n.

79 Boudrye, *Fifth New York Cavalry*, 146–147.

80 Tenney, ed., *War Diary of Luman Harris Tenney*, 121.

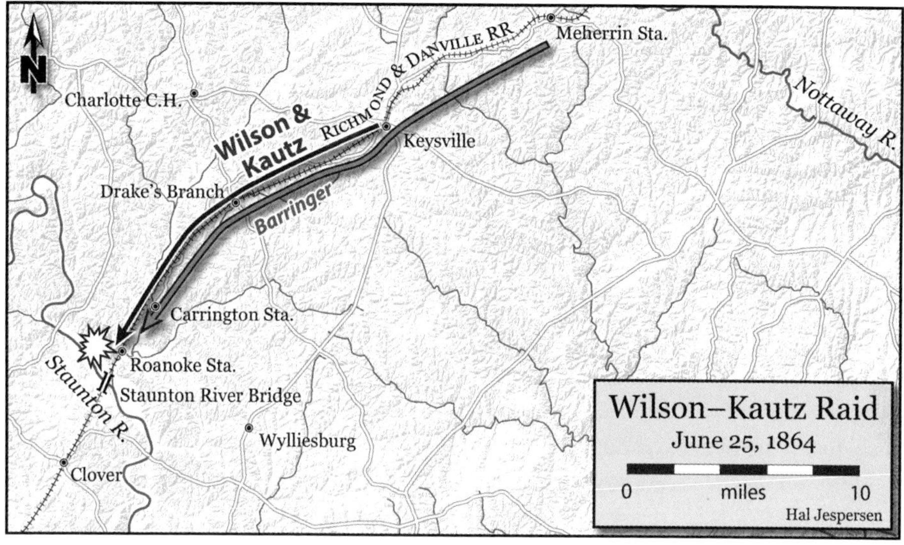

civil prisoners, stole horses, destroyed furniture, cracked iron safes, and robbed civilians of money, watches, and jewelry. The cavalrymen rejoined Wilson's column near Mossingford with about 25 horses and mules.

After breakfast around 7:00 a.m., Gause received orders "to take two men, leave the main road, take all the horses we could find to replace the artillery horses that had given out, and join the column at Clover," he remembered. Clover stood about three miles southwest of the Staunton River Bridge. Two privates of Gause's company volunteered to accompany him. They left the main road at once, six miles from Roanoke, and took the direct road to Clover, but they "were soon in close proximity to the advance of the enemy's cavalry," Gause recalled. "We passed ourselves for W. H. F. Lee's scouts, and by that means were enabled to get information freely." They learned where the locals had hidden their valuables. The three Buckeyes also ate and drank of the best. "We learned where the stock was and it was freely offered, but as we were sailing under a false flag we knew we would be detected before we could get them, as the home guards were near by," remembered Gause.

He and his comrades decided to try another place about 10 miles distant, thinking they would have a better chance at horse hunting there, but on the way it became apparent "that there was something wrong, for the original plan was not being carried out," recalled Gause.[81] According to the intelligence the Buckeyes gathered, the Confederates still seemed to be occupying both Roanoke Station and

81 Gause, *Four Years in Five Armies*, 279–281.

Clover. Abandoning the horse hunt, Gause and his companions entered a village and chased out a few Local Reserves. Late in the afternoon the three Buckeyes learned of some horses nearby, but the time had come to rejoin Wilson's column. About a mile beyond the edge of the village, they met the van of the 5th New York Cavalry, reported, retired to a house, and ate supper.

* * *

By 10:00 a.m. on June 25, Farinholt had gathered 642 civilians and militia along with around 150 horsemen and a leavening of about 150 regulars, for a total of approximately 938. He remembered the bulk of his force as "a heterogenous mass . . . the rawest kind of recruits, from fourteen to twenty and from fifty to sixty-five years of age, whom I was as rapidly as possible instructing in the duties of a soldier when they were not working with pick and spade on the fortifications."[82]

The old ministers, their schoolboys, the 59 regulars in transit, and the Richmond militia in the earthworks northeast of the bridge numbered about 250. These works formed a semi-circle with the ends anchored on the river and the railroad tracks going through the middle. Farinholt directed these troops to crouch down concealed "to reserve fire upon the enemy's approach until they could aim with deadly precision and at close range."[83] He put Colonel Coleman in charge of this portion of the field and gave him around 200 additional men to command on the river's southwest bank.

On his own initiative, Coleman had the men on the northeast side continue to improve the fortifications, crossing heavy timbers at the mouth of the bridge in the shape of an "A" to give 20 of their number loopholes through which to fire. Coleman directed those improving the earthworks to throw the dirt down the bank toward the river to conceal the works. His men dug with "canteens, a spade or two, sticks and whatever they could lay their hands on," recalled Sgt. Paul C. McPhail of the Engineer Corps, the son of a nearby farmer.[84]

Coleman thus prudently strengthened the portion of the position that Farinholt already considered impregnable. "Farinholt never would believe that the enemy would attack him from the front, and thereby expose themselves to the fire

82 B. L. Farinholt, "The gallant defense of Staunton river Bridge. From Richmond, Va., Times-dispatch, Aug. 1, 1909," in *SHSP* XXXVII (1909), 323–324.

83 B. L. Farinholt, "The Staunton River Fight," *SHSP* XIX (1891), 203.

84 Paul C. McPhail, "The Battle of Staunton River Bridge, As Seen by Paul C. McPhail, Sergeant of Engineer Troops, C.S.A., Who Participated in the Engagement," *Richmond Times-Dispatch*, Sept. 19, 1909, p. 26, cols. 2–3.

of his artillery, for almost a mile across the plain between the station and the river, but Coleman insisted," remembered Hurt.[85]

Lieutenant Colonel Jackson, serving on the same side of the river as Coleman, assumed command of the 59 regulars in transit and made a speech to the militia about the importance of defending the bridge. More importantly, Jackson "very wisely," remembered Eason, removed all means of retreat such as small boats to the other side of the river.[86]

Farinholt remembered of the disposition of his forces southwest of the river, "I had abandoned all idea of retreat and intended that it was to be victory, death or imprisonment."[87] Below the bridge, three or four companies from Pittsylvania and Danville occupied a ditch facing down the river between the fort and the river. Men from Halifax County held a ditch running parallel with the railroad between the fort and the tracks. Four-cornered rail pens filled with dirt protected the ends of the ditch. The Drakes Branch Home Guard manned a ditch near the riverbank covering the gun position just west of the bridge.

William Clarke, one of the elderly civilians who had come to the defense of the bridge, put the predicament of the defenders another way as he watched Farinholt deploy his command. "We are between the devil and the deep sea," Clarke said.[88]

That afternoon, Coleman, Hoyt, Marshall, and some troops reconnoitered by train engine, traveling a short distance northeast of the bridge. They saw the main column of Federals moving toward them from Mossingford Station.

* * *

West of the railroad and north of Roanoke Station stood Mulberry Hill of the McPhail farm, a house on a downward slope toward Staunton River. East of the tracks lay the Bruce farm. Little Roanoke Creek began west of the railway, crossed beneath a railroad trestle, and emptied into Staunton River east of the bridge. The main wagon road ran down the slope and past the McPhail home to Roanoke Station, where the creek flowed southeastward. At the station, the wagon road came to a T-intersection, with one road going west to Clark's Ferry; the other, headed eastward over Little Roanoke Creek by a wooden bridge, followed Staunton River

85 William D. Hurt to T. M. R. Talcott, Aug. 11, 1909, *Richmond Times-Dispatch*, Sept. 19, 1909, p. 26, col. 2.

86 J. T. Eason, "The Battle Of Staunton River Bridge, VA.," *CV* 2 (1894): 19.

87 Farinholt, "The Staunton River Fight," *SHSP* 19:203.

88 Ibid.

southeastward for a short distance, and then turned eastward towards Wyliesville and Christiansburg. The Simms farm stretched south of Staunton River bridge.

Between Roanoke Station and Staunton River bridge lay several hundred yards of lowlands, with a wheat field east of the rails and a grass field to the west. A rail trestle extended a short distance north of the bridge through the lowlands, which had a series of ditches, mounds, and underbrush that made them difficult to cross on foot. A final ditch crossed a stretch of boggy, muddy ground about 75 yards from the bridge. "The bluff on the opposite side of the river was lined with earth works, and bristled with cannon, both above and below the bridge, whilst a strong line of skirmishers had been thrown across the bridge and deployed along the shore," remembered Chaplain Merrill of the 1st District of Columbia Cavalry.[89]

The Federals suspected that the works were well-manned. "At nearly every house that we had passed for the last two days, when we asked the Darkeys where the Old Man was, they always replied that he had taken his gun and gone to defend the bridge," recalled First Sergeant Ide of the 1st Vermont Cavalry.[90]

Kautz, assigned by Wilson to burn the bridge, reconnoitered and "did not consider it practicable as it was fortified on both sides of the [Staunton] river."[91] Wilson nonetheless ordered Kautz to attack.

The Yanks began deploying for an assault on Staunton River Bridge about 3:45 p.m. Kautz's division led, with West's brigade on the western side of the Richmond & Danville and Spear's brigade on the eastern side. McIntosh's brigade remained in reserve at the McPhail farm on Little Roanoke Creek, protecting the road to Christiansburg around 18 miles eastward. Near the farm the 1st Connecticut Cavalry met the only Union sympathizers encountered on the raid, an old man and his wife who would draw water from their well and fill a washing tub which the old man would wheel to his gate in a barrow for the Union soldiers to fill their canteens. "They can only burn my house down and kill us," said the old man. "They have been persecuting us since the war began." A sheet took the place of the stars and stripes on his flagpole.[92]

Chapman's brigade stood rear guard near Mossingford Station. Batteries B, K, and C-E unlimbered on the slope leading down from the McPhail farm to Roanoke Station, about three quarters of a mile from Staunton River Bridge. Just as the Unionist artillery opened fire, 2nd Lt. Thomas W. Lindsay of the 49th North

89 Merrill, *First Maine and First District of Columbia Cavalry*, 266.

90 Hoffman, *First Vermont Cavalry Volunteers*, 187.

91 Eanes, *Destroy the Junction*, 63.

92 "An Account of Wilson's Expedition," *Hartford Courant*, July 12, 1864, p. 2, col. 4.

Carolina's Company K, a convalescent, arrived from Danville with a company of 84 furloughed soldiers and deployed behind the works southwest of the river.[93]

An artillery duel began that lasted for around 90 minutes as Kautz's men formed to attack. When Marshall in the fort below the bridge saw the approaching bluecoats, his heart went out to the boys in the trenches north and east of the river. "I opened fire at once with the four guns and did all the harm I could," he recalled. "I tried to make them think we had a large force in front."[94]

His gunners aimed primarily at the dismounted Federal cavalry. "We first noticed the cut just above the depot to be full of Yankees," remembered Gilliam. "Ragland gave the order to load, and we dropped a shell right plumb into this cut densely packed with Yanks. The cut quickly emptied."[95]

Hitting the Unionist guns seemed hopeless to Gilliam. "The enemy's pieces were on top of the hills, in plain view, but the foot of the hill was the utmost limit to which we could throw a ball," recalled Gilliam.[96]

The Unionists pelted the Secessionists with shot and shell. "The shells striking the thin roof of the bridge made a fearful racket, scaring some of the small boys into weeping," remembered Eason.[97]

A few steps behind the fort, as Sergeant McPhail was delivering a message to Farinholt, a shower of shells came over and one burst in front of them, hiding them in dust and smoke.

"Dar now, Old Farinholt done killed," someone said.[98]

When the smoke and dust cleared away, Farinholt stood unperturbed, while McPhail was gesticulating wildly.

Federal projectiles killed "Dr. Sutphin, whose head was shot off at the rail pen in the ditch parallel to the railroad, [and] Rev. Mr. Burke, whose head was shot off by solid shot directly under the abutment of the bridge on the Charlotte side," recalled Gilliam.[99]

At the bridge, remembered Lewis, "Jack Carter, who was a farmer and lived near Mount Carmel, was killed by a shell."[100]

93 Hewett, et al., eds., *Supplement to the Official Records*, 7:268.

94 Eanes, *Destroy the Junction*, 64.

95 Ibid., 67.

96 Ibid., 63–64.

97 Eason, "The Battle Of Staunton River Bridge, VA," *CV* 2:19.

98 Eanes, *Destroy the Junction*, 65.

99 Ibid., 85.

100 Farinholt, "The Staunton River Fight," *SHSP* 19:57.

Benjamin Lyons Farinholt

Library of Virginia

In the ditch just above the bridge on the Halifax side, where the greybeards of the Drakes Branch Home Guards hunkered, a voice arose.

"Let us pray," said Rev. W. T. Gilliam.[101]

While the gunners dueled, Old Farinholt employed deception. "I designedly had the empty trains frequently run back and forth between our defenses and Clover depot, while the enemy were approaching and deploying, our men being instructed to huzza on the arrival of every train," he remembered.[102]

This tactic convinced Mrs. McPhail at the McPhail farm, where Wilson had his headquarters, that the Confederate garrison in the fortifications around the bridge numbered 10,000 and was rapidly being reinforced. Wilson questioned her very carefully. Deep in Secessionist territory and uncertain of the strength of the opposing and pursuing Rebel forces, the Illinoisan could not entirely discount Mrs. McPhail's claims. He did not dare order McIntosh's and Chapman's brigades out of reserve.

"We were as much deceived as was Wilson," remembered Confederate Scout J. B. Faulkner, stationed on the Charlotte side of the river on a high hill that permitted him to see the river valley from the bridge to his mill, five miles below.[103]

During the artillery duel, Kautz's division made minimal preparations for the attack. "General Kautz gave the duty of destroying the bridge to his two Brigade commanders without (as I learn from one of his staff officers) forming *any plan himself*," recalled Hall. Between 5:30 p.m. and 6:00 p.m., Kautz's men advanced. To the railroad's right, West's brigade marched down the deep ravine from McPhail's farm to the river road in column of four and filed into line on the edge of the flats.

101 Eanes, *Destroy the Junction*, 65.

102 Farinholt, "The Staunton River Fight," *SHSP* 19:205.

103 J. B. Faulkner, "Farinholt's Ruse Deceived Enemy," *Richmond Times-Dispatch*, Oct. 17, 1909, p. 41, cols. 5–6.

A detail carried light combustible material to fire the bridge. "Of course the only hope now was to *charge the bridge*, on the two flanks at a run, but instead of this, a skirmish line was sent out and opened fire," remembered Hall. At the double-quick, with loud hurrahs, the 5th Pennsylvania Cavalry advanced with one of its squadrons deployed as skirmishers while the 3rd New York Cavalry remained to the left and rear in reserve. Secessionist guns in the pits above the bridge opened on the line of West's brigade with shell and cannister when its troopers came within 150 yards of the bridge. Charges of grape "flew like a flight of noisy birds close over us," recollected Hall.[104]

"When we opened up on them with canister they were thrown into great confusion at once," recalled Lewis, the Confederate artillerist."[105] The Federals recovered and came on fifty yards farther.

The veterans among the Rebel infantry poured a sharp fire upon the Unionists from the trenches on the Charlotte side of the river and on the Halifax side above the guns. "We reserved our fire until in close musket range, and then poured volley after volley, repulsing their first attack with ease," recalled Eason. "This greatly encouraged some of the militia, who had refused to fight."[106]

Now the militia opened with their muskets, squirrel rifles, and shotguns. The infantry below Lewis's guns did not fire a shot. "It was the prettiest fight I ever saw," Lewis remembered. "We did not have one man hurt, though several of us had holes through our clothing."[107]

The foot soldiers below Lewis's guns included Sergeant Meece. When a ball from a sharpshooter hit the earth in front of Meece and knocked the dirt against him, he recalled that the ball then "passed between my arm and my body, cutting the sleeve and body of my coat."[108]

Spear's brigade formed at the depot on the left of the railroad. Under fire from the fort below the bridge, Col. Samuel P. Spear gave the order to dismount and prepare to fight on foot. Three squadrons of his command deployed as skirmishers. The 1st District of Columbia Cavalry formed in line by companies under the shelter of a bluff. "For many of the men this was the first time they had received such orders knowing that it meant business," Lunt recalled.[109] These green troops

104 Hall and Longacre, "Would to God that War Was Rendered Impossible," 460–461.

105 Farinholt, "The Staunton River Fight," *SHSP* 19:56.

106 Eason, "The Battle Of Staunton River, VA," *CV* 2:19.

107 Farinholt, "The Staunton River Fight," *SHSP* 19:56.

108 Mamie Yeary, *Reminiscences of the Boys in Gray 1861–1865*, 2 vols. (Dallas, TX, 1912), 2:511.

109 Tobie, *First Maine Cavalry*, 337–344.

carried one of the most formidable small arms of the war, the 16-shot Henry rifle. Behind them, the 11th Pennsylvania Cavalry went into action with a limited number of carbines, inferior when received and since become almost useless, along with defective ammunition. Spear instructed the men without carbines to use their pistols.

The 1st District of Columbia Cavalry advanced, 550 strong. As Spear's troopers got into range, crossing deep, dry ditches fringed with thick hedges of blackberry bushes that disordered their ranks, the guns of the fort switched to cannister, which wounded several men before they could open fire. The range stakes posted in the fields approaching the bridge made the Secessionist guns deadly to the assaulting Unionists. "We pounded it into them for all they were worth, but on they came, as pretty and straight a line as was ever seen on dress parade," Gilliam recalled.[110]

The Rebels on the Charlotte side were taking friendly fire in the form of pieces of grapeshot and cannister aimed too low from the fort's cannons. "I sent Private Fenton of the Maryland Artillery, with a message to the commandant on the other side," recalled Hoyt. "He went across the bridge under the enemy's guns to stop the firing of our own artillery, and I watched his red cap with a great deal of interest as he emerged from the bridge and ascended the hill to the fort."[111] Fenton fell, hit in the leg by friendly grapeshot. By this time, Hoyt's men and the other butternuts on the Charlotte side had opened on Spear's men with small arms, wounding still more bluecoats before they could open fire.

The Southerners "suddenly stood up and took a long breath in that peculiar way," remembered Sgt. Jefferson L. Coburn of Company A in the 1st District of Columbia Cavalry, then fired a volley which did not stop the Unionists.[112] Captain Andrew M. Chase and his Company H, the closest of the 1st to the railroad, rushed forward to reach and burn the bridge.

"On they came, nearer, close, until they were shot off the railroad embankment within ten steps of the mouth of the bridge," remembered Gilliam. The 1st's wounded included Chase. "So close did they get before breaking, that some of them ran clear into our lines and were captured," Gilliam recalled."[113] The rest of the 1st's men dove into a slimy ditch that paralleled the river a little more than 100 yards ahead.

110 Eanes, *Destroy the Junction*, 67.

111 Ibid., 73.

112 Jeff L. Coburn, "An Episode of the Wilson Raid: City Point to Roanoke, Va., June 21–30, 1864," *Maine Bugle*, (July 1895), 196.

113 Eanes, *Destroy the Junction*, 68.

* * *

After the failure of the first Federal rush on the bridge, Old Farinholt reinforced his front line. "I immediately threw across company after company of reinforcements, notwithstanding the enemy were shelling the bridge furiously and a strong line of sharpshooters directing their line on it, the difficulty of crossing being increased by not having been able to procure plank to floor it, and the only mode of crossing being upon the ties," he recalled. "I had in this manner crossed over in all 500, and placed them in position, when the enemy's skirmishers, having fallen in with their line of battle, and the whole line arriving within close range of my rifle pits (which I had almost entirely manned) were scattered before a withering fire from my infantry which was totally unexpected."[114]

Bullets riddled the weatherboarded sides of the bridge, while shot and shell rent its roof. As Hurt led his company across, a minie ball struck his belt buckle and glanced off into his side, knocking him off the bridge and onto the riverbank before he picked himself up and rejoined his men. Captain Riddick and five members of the Richmond Reserves suffered wounds crossing the bridge, one proving mortal. The Drakes Branch Home Guards also crossed. Some soldiers refused to negotiate the bridge and Farinholt directed Lieutenant Lindsay to reinforce Coleman. Lindsay's company advanced at the double-quick, lost two men wounded, and deployed to the right of the bridge with a company of Halifax reserves under Capt. William R. Branch on the left and Riddick's company on the right.

Ten minutes after the failure of the first Federal assault on the railroad bridge, "a beardless young staff officer crept along the lee side of the ditch and [parted] the long grasses," recalled Coburn. The staffer ordered the 1st District of Columbia Cavalry to take the bridge. "Just then the boys let loose their repeaters and the responding minie bees from over the river made it exceedingly waspish among the grasses above our ditch and we were suddenly reinforced by a pair of gay shoulder straps from the leeward, and there is no mistake about it, the young officer's face did have an ugly look upon it as he found himself stuck fast half knee deep in mud," Coburn remembered.[115]

Captain Charles C. Chase and several men of his Company L pressed onward toward the bridge. "Crawling cautiously alongside of the embankment, they reached a point where they were obliged to expose themselves, and scarcely one of the whole squad escaped uninjured, Capt. Chase being seriously wounded,"

114 *OR* 40, 1:764.

115 Coburn, "An Episode of the Wilson Raid," 197.

recollected Lunt.[116] Branch's, Lindsay's, and Riddick's companies broke up one Unionist thrust after another.

The Northerners advanced again west of the railroad as well. Under cover of one of the trestles, Col. Robert M. West "formed an assaulting party and directed it up the embankment in the hope that by a quick move we might obtain possession of the main bridge sufficiently long to fire it," he recalled. "The men tried repeatedly to gain a foothold on the railroad, and to advance along the sides of the embankment, but could not."[117]

From the Rebel position down by the water's edge, across the stream, the Secessionists swept the sides and track with a devastating fire. "It was not pleasant . . . to be in the furrow of a wheat field and see the bullets cut the stalks over your head and body," remembered Hall.[118]

East of the tracks, the 11th Pennsylvania Cavalry replaced the 1st District of Columbia Cavalry in the front line as that unit withdrew to replenish its quickly expended ammunition—a weakness of their 16-shooters. The Keystoners deployed in the dry bed of Little Roanoke Creek with a trestle on their right. Lieutenant Colonel George Stetzel took cover under the trestle.

"Isn't the Colonel going to form the men in line for a charge on the bridge?" asked Pvt. Nelson W. Ward of Company M.

"Forward, men, forward!" ordered Capt. Gerard Reynolds of Ward's company.

From under the trestle, Stetzel directed Reynolds to shift to the right, toward the tracks.

Pierced by a Confederate bullet, Reynolds fell dead.

With their captain dead and the regiment's commander skulking, the men wavered under the fire of the Southerners.

"What are we to do?" one of Ward's comrades asked.

"Follow me, boys," said Ward.

Swinging his carbine over his head, he led a charge against the bridge until the Rebels had shot down all but one of his companions. The two started back toward the dry creek bed.

"On the way I found the dead body of my captain, and stopping, I knelt down to secure his money, watch, revolver and spur," Ward remembered. "Although repeatedly urged by comrades across the railway and further back on the line, I remained fully twenty minutes at his side, endeavoring to procure assistance to

116 Tobie, *First Maine Cavalry*, 341.

117 *OR* 40, 1:734.

118 Hall and Longacre, "Would to God that War Was Rendered Impossible," 460.

carry the corpse off the field, but I waited and begged in vain, and finally had to retreat to the main force without the body of our brave, beloved captain."[119]

Rebel bullets hit Ward in his boot heel and pierced his blouse during his vigil beside the captain's corpse. He received a Medal of Honor for his exploit.

* * *

The Northerners on both sides of the railway kept up the skirmishing after nightfall, trying to reach the bridge in the darkness, but the exertions of the last four days, the extraordinary heat, and the strength of their foe's position all tended to discourage the men. The 5th Pennsylvania Cavalry and 3rd New York Cavalry crawled back on their bellies to the Federal guns, infuriating Kautz, who had sanctioned no such withdrawal. Kautz ordered Hall to take up the former position. "I told him, that I thought we could not go so far down, that the enemy had only permitted us to come so close, for the purpose of slaughtering us, but that I would do the best I could," Hall remembered.[120] His best did not capture the bridge but satisfied Kautz.

"Our failure to carry the bridge was owing to the extreme heat and the exhaustion of the men, who have had little rest or sleep and had little to eat," recorded Kautz.[121] When Kautz reported his inability to take the bridge, Wilson responded angrily, "Can't take it . . . hell . . . I've got a Squadron that can," noted Corporal Timmerman of Kautz's division.[122] Kautz requested the squadron. Wilson dispatched from his own division two officers and 75 men from the 1st Connecticut Cavalry, including Sergeant Koempel.

"Ordered to dash for the bridge at night, set it on fire," Koempel recalled. "Was countermanded."[123]

* * *

During the Federal attacks on Staunton River Bridge, Barringer's North Carolina Brigade arrived and began pressing Chapman's brigade. Rooney Lee accompanied the Tarheels, who had left behind McGregor's battery for want of ammunition. A skirmish began near Mossingford.

119 Eanes, *Destroy the Junction*, 78–79.

120 Hall and Longacre, "Would to God that War Was Rendered Impossible," 461.

121 Hewett, et al., eds., *Supplement to the Official Records*, 7:240.

122 Eanes, *Destroy the Junction*, 72.

123 Koempel, *Phil Koempel's Diary*, June 25, 1864, 11.

Margaret Watkins could not stand the thought that the Yankees would camp at Do Well that night. She was talking to one of them when firing commenced between Barringer's butternuts and Chapman's bluecoats.

"Oh! What's that?" she asked.

"The d--- rebels," the Federal said.

He immediately mounted and fled.

"Hurrah for the rebels," she shouted, screaming to the Yankees that she hoped they would be shot before they could leave her yard.

Before the Federals exited the outer gate, a dozen North Carolinians surrounded her asking for information about the foe. "They were covered with dust and dirt, but I told them they were splendid and glorious and I don't know what other foolishness I said, for I was nearly crazy with excitement and anxiety," she remembered.[124] The Tarheels ordered her into the cellar just as two shells from Wilson's guns burst on her lawn.

Barringer's brigade, now fewer than 1,000 in number, drove the pickets of Chapman's brigade over Little Roanoke Creek at Carrington's Mill. This forced Wilson's wagon train to shift southward and take refuge behind McIntosh's brigade on the road to Wyliesburg. The Confederates at the bridge heard Lee's firing on the Federal rear guard, "and we felt assured that we had won," recalled Eason in the earthworks on the north side of the river.[125]

The Union gunners of Battery K, protecting the Federal rear, did not find their plight as pleasant as it seemed to the Confederates in the fort below the bridge. A few weeks earlier, the Northern batteries had exchanged four rifles for two rifles and two smoothbores, and now the exchange made their task more difficult because of the smoothbores' limited range. A lucky Rebel shot reduced the battery's guns and manpower. "One gun was hit on the right trunnion by a percussion shell, as the gunner, Cpl. [Edward P.] McNamara, was sighting the piece," recalled Lieutenant Ward. "The shell exploded, carrying away a portion of the gunner's head, knocking down four other cannoniers, and permanently disabling the piece."[126]

Barringer's North Carolinians, lacking the strength to drive Chapman's brigade farther, withdrew at dark and fell back to the Watkins plantation. "The fight did not last very long, and we went to bed quietly that night with Confederate Cavalry sleeping around us," Margaret Watkins wrote to her brother. "I tell you t'was a glorious change!"[127]

124 Eanes, *Destroy the Junction*, 83.

125 Farinholt, "The Staunton River Fight," *CV* 2:19.

126 Haskin, *First Regiment of Artillery*, 205, 561.

127 Eanes, *Destroy the Junction*, 83.

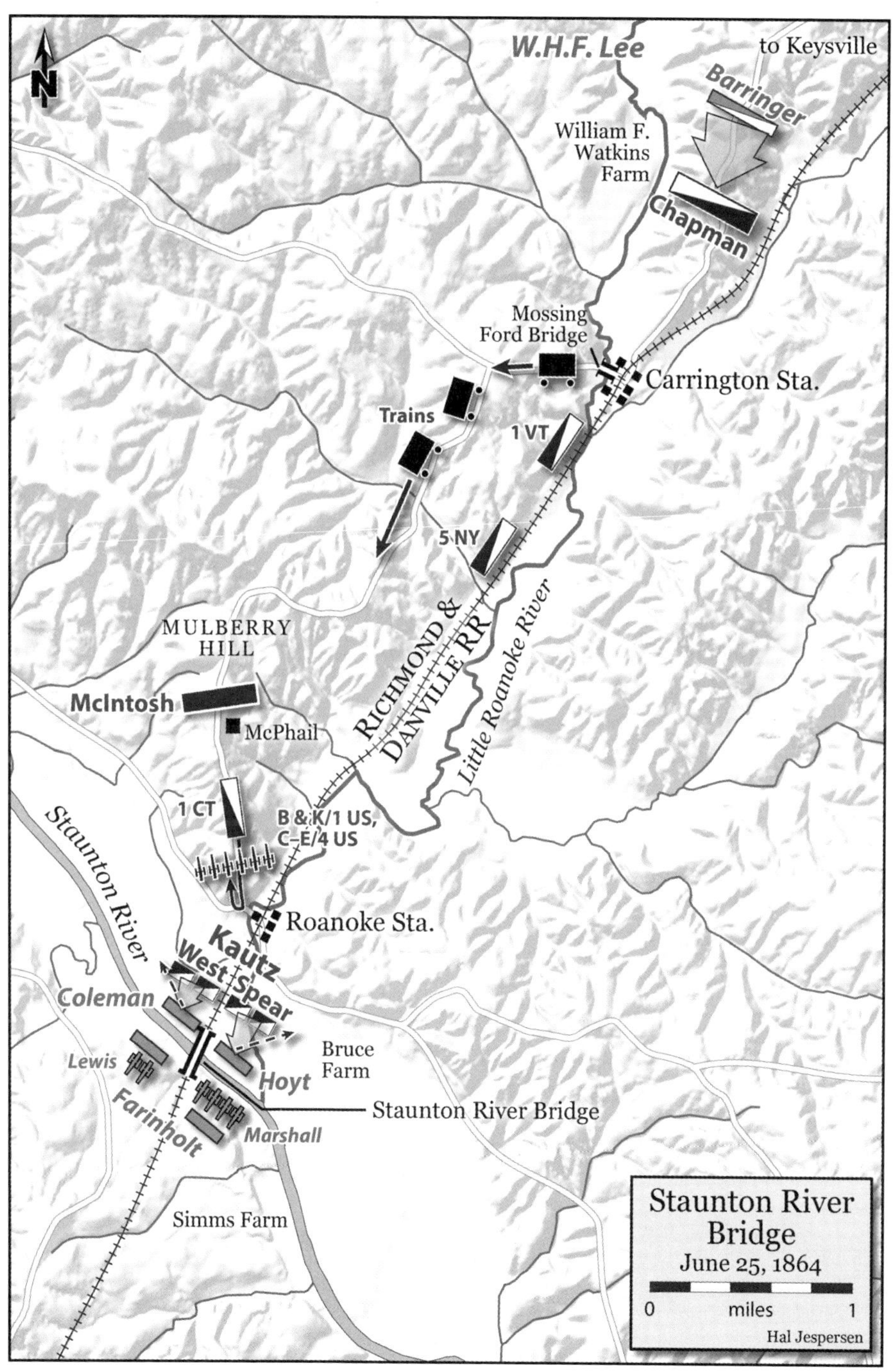
W.H.F. Lee
to Keysville
Barringer
William F. Watkins Farm
Chapman
Mossing Ford Bridge
Carrington Sta.
Trains
1 VT
5 NY
RICHMOND & DANVILLE RR
Little Roanoke River
MULBERRY HILL
McIntosh
McPhail
1 CT
B & K/1 US, C–E/4 US
Staunton River
Roanoke Sta.
Kautz
West
Spear
Coleman
Lewis
Hoyt
Bruce Farm
Farinholt
Marshall
Staunton River Bridge
Simms Farm
Staunton River Bridge
June 25, 1864
0 miles 1
Hal Jespersen

* * *

The railroad bridge seemed unassailable. It barred the way to Sherman. Wilson's men were passing out from the heat. In his rear lurked Barringer, who barred the way to High Bridge and Hunter. The Illinoisan gave up trying to carry Old Farinholt's defenses, abandoned any idea of reaching High Bridge, Hunter, Sherman, or the North Carolina coast, and decided to return to the Federal lines at Petersburg.

The scout Faulkner thought Wilson ought to have turned Staunton River Bridge. To Faulkner, the Federal failed to reconnoiter thoroughly. Faulkner considered the fords below the bridge "easily passable." Wilson could "have gone down the river, either to Elliott's Falls or to the mill and ferry," believed the scout. Wilson "could then have crossed without the least difficulty or resistance, and could have gained the rear of Farinholt's men," thought Faulkner. "It would then have been easy to burn the bridge and march on to Danville."[128]

The Rebels lost 47 killed and wounded.[129] The wounded included Colonel Coleman, who took a bullet in the right knee just before the battle's end, remained with his men for another hour to see if the Federals would attack again, and then departed in his carriage for his residence.

The Federals lost at least 104 killed, wounded, and missing.[130] The fight left a bitter taste in the mouth for some raiders, such as Hannaford, who considered the

128 Faulkner, "Farinholt's Ruse Deceived Enemy." Kautz disagreed, thinking that the Confederates "would have been able to reinforce the garrison by the direct road across the bridge before we could make the crossing and attack." August V. Kautz, "Wilson Raid: An Expedition to Destroy the Petersburg & Lynchburg and the Richmond & Danville Railroads," in *National Tribune*, June 8, 1899, p. 1, cols. 5–7.

129 Eight were killed and 39 wounded, according to Lindsay. Hewett, et al., eds., *Supplement to the Official Records*, 7:268. Farinholt reported 10 killed, 24 wounded. *OR* 40, 1:765.

130 Kautz underestimated his casualties at about 60 troopers, including a large proportion of officers. Ibid., 731. He lost at least 95.

In West's brigade, the 3rd New York Cavalry had two killed and seven wounded. Ibid., 736. The 5th Pennsylvania Cavalry lost seven killed and 17 wounded. Ibid. In Spear's brigade, the 1st District of Columbia Cavalry had four killed, 22 wounded, and 30 missing. Ibid., 742. The 11th Pennsylvania Cavalry lost three killed and three wounded. Bates, *History of Pennsylvania Volunteers, 1861–5*, 3:910–952, *passim*. In McIntosh's brigade of Wilson's division, the 5th New York Cavalry's had three men captured. RG 94, Entry 652, Box 38. The 1st Connecticut Cavalry lost one captured. Angelovich, *Riding for Uncle Samuel*, 437. The 2nd Ohio Cavalry had one man captured. Roster Commission, *Official Roster of the Soldiers of the State of Ohio in the War of the Rebellion, 1861–1866*, 12 vols. (Cincinnati, 1891), 11:58. In Chapman's brigade, the 1st New Hampshire Cavalry had one wounded and one missing. Adjutant General, *Report of the Adjutant General of the State of New Hampshire*, 2:571, 573. The 22nd New York Cavalry lost one wounded. RG 94, Entry 652, Box 39, NA. Battery K had one wounded. Haskin, *First Regiment of Artillery*, 561; *OR* 40, 1:733.

second attack a fool's errand after the first had failed. "Many a brave mans life was uselessly lost here," he wrote.[131]

Though bullets had riddled its sides while shot and shell had torn its roof, the bridge remained capable of bearing trains, its timbers uninjured. The destruction of Burkeville, a short stretch of the Weldon Railroad's tracks, intermittent sections of the South Side railway, and substantial lengths of the Richmond & Danville accomplished Wilson's mission, but the survival of High Bridge and Staunton River Bridge spared the Rebels major delays in the restoration of their rail network.

* * *

"It is an easy matter for a mouse to reach the cheese in a trap, but another matter for him to eat the cheese and walk out again," recalled Old Po'keepsie of the 2nd Ohio Cavalry's Company G.[132]

Wilson had reached the cheese. Now, without having had the satisfaction of eating it, he had to figure a way out of the vise in which Rooney Lee and Old Farinholt held the Unionist command. "I not only had to choose my route and bring off my wounded, but make my way rapidly toward our army through the forest and small farms which covered the intervening country," he remembered. "It was, of course, almost impossible to return by the road I had come on, and, looking over my maps, I concluded that my best chances lay due east through Wyliesville, Christianville, and Greensborough, toward Jarratt's Station on the Petersburg and Weldon Railroad."[133]

The Federals rested, fed, and cared for their horses and around 200 wounded in ambulances and confiscated carriages, then began their retreat. "Our position, from the peculiar topography of the site, was rather dangerous, and in order to extricate the command it became necessary to move it by night by a road crossing the railroad running to the southeast along the foot of the bluffs and within 500 to 600 yards of the enemy's guns," Wilson recalled. "The march was therefore begun about midnight, McIntosh in advance, followed by the trains and Chapman's brigade, Kautz's division covering the movement."[134]

The column crossed the railroad at Roanoke Station. The Unionists spread hay on the rails to muffle the sound. Farther on, they passed within 400 yards of the

131 Eanes, *Destroy the Junction*, 86.

132 Old Po'keepsie, "From the 2nd Ohio Cavalry," *Painesville* (OH) *Telegraph*, July 14, 1864, p. 2, cols. 4–5.

133 Wilson, *Under the Old Flag*, 1:464.

134 *OR* 40, 1:627.

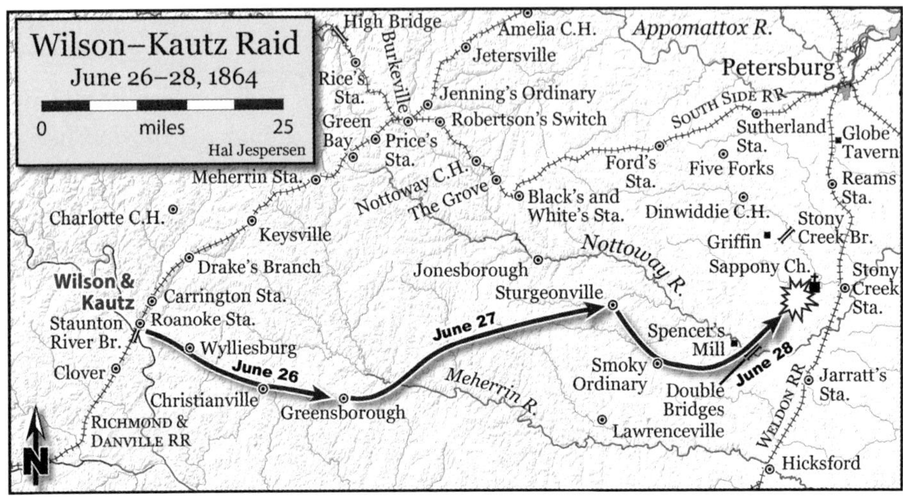

Confederate lines, with only the river separating them. "Not a whisper scarcely was heard, everybody seemed not only to hold his coffee pot and frying pans to prevent their . . . jingling, but his breath even," remembered Hannaford in McIntosh's brigade.[135] Most of the men slept in the saddle.

The column moved slowly. At dawn Farinholt's guns opened fire on Spear's brigade as it crossed Little Roanoke Creek. "I was one of those who remained on the field all night, and I distinctly remember the flash of the cannon, and seeing the black speck of the approaching shells, which passed over us and exploded a short distance in our rear," recalled Lunt.[136]

The Confederate fire forced some bluecoats to veer off the road into the woods, briefly increasing the difficulty of their withdrawal. "Rebs threw some 20 shells at the column while passing but our batteries soon put a stop to that," noted Timmerman in West's brigade.[137]

Barringer's tired troopers cautiously advanced and occupied the Unionist positions. "They delayed us by a long range cannonade until they could get away, which they did, leaving only a few broken down horses and unserviceable guns behind them," recalled Captain Galloway.[138]

The Confederates then prepared to pursue. "The North Carolina Cavalry Brigade was much diminished in its effective force by the awful heat, dust and

135 Eanes, *Destroy the Junction*, 80.

136 Tobie, *First Maine Cavalry*, 341.

137 Eanes, *Destroy the Junction*, 84.

138 Clark, ed., *North Carolina Regiments*, 3:539.

marches of the last few days," remembered Private Means of the 5th North Carolina Cavalry.[139]

The officers of each regiment had to cull the best men and horses. "It was more a selection of horses than men," recalled Pvt. George Barnhardt of Company H in the 5th. "Horses able to make rapid and continuous pursuit."[140]

Sending back to Petersburg Dearing's brigade, the artillery, and the disabled men and horses from Barringer's brigade, Rooney Lee renewed the chase with the remnant of the Tarheels. Fewer than 300 had horses capable of pursuit. The 5th furnished more such men than all the other regiments put together, and the 5th North Carolina Cavalry's Company F supplied more men and horses than any other company of the brigade.[141]

The Rebs followed "with all the fury of Deamonds [and] a great number of negres joined us 1000," noted Sgt. Philander Burnham of the 1st Vermont Cavalry's Company I, a farmer with a wife and six children at home.[142] Lead elements of the Northern column reached Wyliesville at daylight on June 26.

Each brigade stopped for two hours. Some soldiers made coffee. Others grabbed such sleep as they could. "We march long and camp late. Four rails, saddle bags and saddle cloth for my bed," wrote 2nd Lt. Uriah N. Parmalee of the 1st Connecticut Cavalry's Company H. "Something of a sleep after all."[143]

The march then resumed. The Rebels at Staunton River Bridge lost sight of the Unionist rear guard around 8:00 a.m. In the terrible heat, the Yanks had to move very slowly, yet fast enough to elude their Secessionist pursuers. "Horses were continually staggering and falling with the heat and the pistols of the Officers were in constant use," recalled Hannaford. "If it had not been that we were continually capturing horses, full one half of the command would have been dismounted; as it was, a number were now footing it."

Some troopers had mercy on their mounts and turned them loose. Others nursed them along. "I had taught my horse, Pet, to drink from my tin cup," remembered First Sergeant Cruikshank. "I would place the cup in his mouth, he would raise his head and swallow the water." Cruikshank filled his canteen as often

139 Ibid., 615.

140 Ibid., 618.

141 D. B. R., "Barringer's N. C. Brigade of Cavalry;" Harrell, *The 2nd North Carolina Cavalry*, 304; Clark, *North Carolina Regiments*, 3:618.

142 Philander Burnham Civil War Diary, 1864, June 25, 1864, VHS.

143 Angelovich, *Riding for Uncle Samuel*, 425.

as possible on Pet's behalf. "I also let him eat corn from my hand as I walked by his side as I occasionally did to rest him."[144]

Wilson's troops began reaching Christiansville around noon and fed from the Confederate government stores on 4,000 bushels of corn collected to pay taxes. The Federals stole horses and mules, killed farm animals, stove in molasses barrels at nearby plantations, and scrounged what they could. Private Elisha Bradley, a former store clerk in the 1st Connecticut Cavalry's Company K, picked up a Richmond newspaper with a headline offering a 500-dollar reward for capture of a raider. He remembered as akin to "grim death" the pursuit of the Rebel horsemen after the fight at Staunton River Bridge. "They were in front and in the rear and they followed like blood hounds on both flanks," he recalled.[145]

Some encounters between the opposing sides proved fatal. "Left my sabre, being all bent up," recorded Koempel. "Got another from a dead rebel."[146]

The march continued eastward toward Greensborough. On this, the hottest day of the raid, the thermometer stood at 105 degrees in the shade at 2:30 p.m. Enough Confederates followed front and rear to hinder the bluecoats from ranging too far and wide. "They could not strike hard, but it was like the blows of enraged birds on the hawk," remembered Means in the 5th North Carolina Cavalry.[147] About 5:00 p.m., the Yankee rear guard, the 1st District of Columbia Cavalry, fended off attacks by small parties of Rebels from Barringer's brigade.

The 1st reached Christiansville in Mecklenburg County around 7:30 p.m., about the time that McIntosh's brigade in the column's van encamped at nearly dry Buckthorn Creek, a short distance southeast of Christiansville. The early arrivals profited from tending to their mounts. All could see that a healthy horse might make the difference between a return to Grant's army and imprisonment at Andersonville. "Many of the horses backs by this time were in terrible condition," recalled Hannaford. "This was the cause of many of the horses giving out." A little before sundown, his 2nd Ohio Cavalry encamped and unsaddled near Buckthorn Creek in Mecklenburg County. "The horses backs were most all washed, and I have no doubt many a horses life was saved by this night's rest and care," Hannaford remembered.[148]

144 Eanes, *Destroy the Junction*, 92.

145 Angelovich, *Riding for Uncle Samuel*, 425.

146 Koempel, *Phil Koempel's Diary*, June 26, 1864, 11.

147 Clark, *North Carolina Regiments*, 3:616.

148 Eanes, *Destroy the Junction*, 92.

Chapman's brigade arrived next. "Nearly every man in our regiment had a servant," First Sergeant Ide of the 1st Vermont recalled. "It was here that [Company D's Capt. William Garrison] Cummings' Darkey 'Ned' went to sleep standing up," Ide remembered.[149]

Kautz's division rode until late that night to catch up with the van of the column at Buckthorn Creek. When the 11th Pennsylvania Cavalry of Spear's brigade reached the camp, "The men dismounted, lay down alongside the road, and were fast asleep almost as soon as they touched the ground," recalled Cruikshank.[150]

The 1st Connecticut Cavalry of McIntosh's brigade drew the unenviable task of riding another 40 miles to seize Saffold's Bridge over the Middle Meherrin River. Burnham recorded that the hot, dry, dusty ride took the regiment through "a distressed country" but that he "had a good nights rest lots of negroes coming in from evry Plantation."[151]

* * *

After four or five hours of repose, Wilson's forces departed Buckthorn Creek on June 27 and passed through Greensborough. The column's head crossed the Meherrin River into Lunenburg County on Saffold's bridge at 10:00 a.m. Around 1,200 contrabands were following the column and their number was growing by the hour. "Such an army almost had they become that Wilson had appointed officers to take charge of the slaves, and now they were marching by fours in column," Hannaford remembered. "Most of them carried a bundle, those that had been marching a day or so carried small ones, those who had just joined us generally carried large ones; some had enormous bundles on their heads."[152]

The column halted for two hours after crossing the Meherrin. "Our scouts reported rebel cavalry coming up on our left, probably with the intention of preventing our crossing Stoney Branch, a small stream with high steep banks, that empties into the Meherrin; but Gen. Wilson evaded them by passing to the right of the main ford," recollected Bugler Barrett. "The rebels after waiting a long time, came down the main road and charged the 8th N.Y.; but the 8th was in position and charged them in turn, driving them in a hurry."[153]

149 Hoffman, *First Vermont Cavalry Volunteers*, 188.

150 Eanes, *Destroy the Junction*, 92–93.

151 Burnham Diary, June 26, 1864.

152 Eanes, *Destroy the Junction*, 94.

153 Wickman, comp., *Letters to Vermont*, 2:179.

From Saffold's bridge, the Unionists rode north and then east to Boydton Plank Road. "Our forces since we had commenced our return from the Roanoke were increasing in numbers but not in strength, as negroes, both male and female from a few days old to those who appeared to lack only a few years of a hundred, were flocking in from around and joining our column," recalled Cpl. William W. Watlington of the 3rd Indiana Cavalry.[154]

Wilson reorganized his column. "[W]e halted, while the Contrabands were all collected together, along with the wagons," remembered Ide.[155] Then the column followed Boydton Plank Road northeastward.

Barringer's dwindling band of Confederate horsemen still harassed Wilson's column. "Rebs hovering around us front and rear fighting and skirmishing all the way," noted Burnham.[156] In Mecklenburg and Lunenberg counties, groups of the raiders robbed citizens of watches, jewelry, silverware, clothing, and cash at gunpoint. The Yankees broke up furniture and burned houses. "No respect is shown to private property," wrote Gilpin. "Every house is Entered by a host of Yankees who take from cellar, garrett, pantry, wardrobe and drawer, everything which they want, and they want everything of value."[157]

Straggling Federals also had to fear irate citizens. One lad met with a fate worse than Andersonville after he fell out of the ranks along the Lunenburg-Brunswick border. He sought the help of a farmer, who instead turned him over to a local magistrate. With another man, the magistrate took the Unionist to some nearby woods, stripped him, tied him to a tree, shot him, and divided his clothing after burying him in a ravine.

In Brunswick County, Captain White and his neighbors employed the same stratagem as they had on the bridge breakers to gobble up a band of seven or eight troopers from the 1st District of Columbia Cavalry. The captain delivered the Yanks to Rev. George T. White's house. "They were very hungry and very humble *and there in the presence of my negro servants*, I fed them and they were marched off as prisoners to Gen. W. H. F. Lee," Reverend White recalled.[158]

154 William Watlington Diary, June 27, 1864, Indiana State Library, Madison, IN. The 3rd Indiana Cavalry may have been the only regiment in the Army of the Potomac in which the troopers owned their horses as Confederate cavalry usually did. Benjamin W. Crowninshield, "Cavalry in Virginia in the War of the Rebellion," *MHSM* 13:5.

155 Hoffman, *First Vermont Cavalry Volunteers*, 188.

156 Burnham Diary, June 27, 1864.

157 Gilpin Diary, June 27, 1864.

158 Eanes, *Destroy the Junction*, 97.

During the day, Wilson dispatched a messenger to Humphreys with an account of the expedition up to this point, but the rider did not get through.[159] Sundown brought a thunderstorm as Kautz's division at the rear of the column was reaching Boydton Plank Road. The rain refreshed all after the day's oppressive heat.

The men of the 11th Pennsylvania Cavalry in the rear guard, though weary from lack of sleep, continued slaughtering exhausted mounts. Farther ahead in the column, about 80 Rebs watched as the 8th New York of Chapman's brigade passed.[160] Chapman's brigade camped at Great Creek. At the head of the column, McIntosh's brigade crossed Sturgeon Creek on an unstable wagon bridge." The bridge collapsed, throwing several men and horses into the swollen creek, where they drowned. McIntosh's brigade pitched camp near Sturgeonville after midnight. The men lay down in a field until daylight, joined throughout the night by later arrivals.

In Richmond, President Davis ordered Holmes reinforced at Weldon with North Carolina's junior infantry reserves.

* * *

Rising at daybreak, Wilson and his men continued limping southeastward through Brunswick County on June 28. Their route took them through Smoky Ordinary toward Greensville County on Poplar Mount Road. "Our ambulance train was filled with wounded and disabled soldiers, while a vast number of vehicles of every description, and contrabands to the number of several thousand, crowded the roads and hindered the column," remembered Col. Edmund M. Pope of the 8th New York Cavalry. "This exodus of negroes was not desired or encouraged, but it could not be prevented by us without the use of more severe measures than the commander would authorize."[161]

This exodus would impair the harvest of the big fields of corn, ripe wheat, and cotton that lined the roads. "[A]s nearly every slave, man and woman, joined our column I fear the whites will have to work or want for bread," Barrett recalled.[162]

Chaplain Boudrye recollected of the contrabands:

159 Wilson, *Under the Old Flag*, 498. For the message sent, see *OR* 40, 2:473.

160 Eanes, *Destroy the Junction*, 95.

161 Edmund M. Pope, "Personal Experience—A Side Light of the Wilson Raid, June 1864" in *Glimpses of the Nation's Struggle: Papers Read before the Minnesota Commandery of the Military Order of the Loyal Legion of the United States, 1897–1897* (St. Paul, 1898), 4:587.

162 Wickman, comp., *Letters to Vermont*, 2:179.

> There was no end of the interesting tales they had to tell, which, at times, excited our admiration, and then incited to tears. To us most of them came destitute of all things, except the *hope of liberty*. This was the circle of all their thoughts. For this the gray-haired slave, bending with the infirmities of many toilsome years, was 'toting' his grandchild on his arm and on his head by turns, along the column. The mother, with her young babe clinging to her breast, traveled through the woods and brush, the heat and dust, hoping for better days. Young men and maidens, with more of the European than the African in their features and complexion, plodded on their way, happy to be among those whom they recognized as their deliverance.[163]

The raid had very nearly worn out the raiders and their steeds. Troopers who had lost their mounts, such as Timmerman, whose horse had been stolen, had to hoof it until they could find or steal another. First Sergeant Henry Whipple Chester of Company H in the 2nd Ohio Cavalry had abandoned his horse when the animal gave out. "I secured for my 'mount' a little mule, so small that I could almost put my feet on the ground, when I was on his back," he recalled. "He was able to carry me and my outfit very well as he was strong."[164]

Brunswick County had at least one pleasant encounter with the Federals. A group of them strayed southward into Lawrenceville, the county seat. Just before the raiders entered town, Edward Randolph Turnbull, the Brunswick County Clerk, took a Masonic apron and spread it on his office's table with the assistance of his son, Robert. Then they withdrew to their house. About 20 minutes later, a Unionist came to the house and returned the apron. "After the raiders left we went back to the office and it looked as if all the records were destroyed, or a great part of them, as the floor of the office was about a foot deep in papers, but upon careful examination we found nothing was injured that was of any value," Robert remembered. "We had a case in the office that was filled with old blanks and they threw these all over the floor; otherwise nothing was injured."[165] The clerk's Masonic brethren had spared the records of Brunswick County, which still go back to the county's creation, unlike those in so many other war-ravaged Virginia counties.

Behind the Federal troopers, Dearing's rested brigade reinforced the remnant of Barringer's brigade. Company F of the 1st North Carolina Cavalry dogged the tracks of the bluecoats while the rest of the two brigades harried the foe's left flank.

163 Boudrye, *Fifth New York Cavalry*, 148.

164 H. W. Chester, *Recollections of the War of the Rebellion: A Story of the 2nd Ohio Volunteer Cavalry, 1861–1865* (Wheaton, IL, 1996) 87–88.

165 Gay Neale, *Brunswick County, Virginia 1720–1975* (Brunswick County, VA, 1975), 175.

Danger loomed ahead of the retreating raiders as well. "The citizens now seemed to be watching for our advance and occasionally a rebel cavalryman would ride on before us, telling all the citizens that Wade Hampton had got things arranged near the Weldon Railroad to capture every one of us, telling them that we were tired and worn out and our horses were unable to go much further," Barrett remembered.[166]

Reaching the Double Bridges on the Stage Road over the Nottoway, Wilson and Kautz conferred about which of three routes to take back to the Army of the Potomac. The shortest ran northeast by north on the Stage and Halifax roads and crossed the Weldon Railroad north of Reams Station. Another proceeded northeastward from the Stage Road on the road to Prince George Court House, which ran past Sappony Church two and a half miles west of Stony Creek Station, then crossed the Weldon Railroad south of Reams Station. The third lay still farther south through Jarratt's Station. On departing from the vicinity of Staunton River Bridge, Wilson had been planning to use this route. Its distance from Petersburg made it the safest route back to the Army of the Potomac, but also the longest. Wilson now abandoned it in favor of one of the two shorter routes to spare those in his column the additional hot, dusty, sleep-deprived miles. He expected that neither of the shorter routes would pose any more danger than the route through Jarratt's Station. Humphreys had assured Wilson that Federal infantry would occupy the Weldon and South Side railroads. Contrabands had informed the Illinoisan that Meade had seized Reams Station.[167]

Kautz would have preferred to proceed to North Carolina, not the Army of the Potomac, but he confined his comments to the two routes remaining under consideration.[168] Based on Wilson's account of Humphreys's representations and reports from the contrabands, Kautz thought the route to the north of Reams Station the better of the two routes.

The route past Stony Creek Station "was not practical, owing to the number of streams and bridges, furnishing opportunities for detention by inferior forces,"

166 Wickman, comp., *Letters to Vermont*, 2:179.

167 Eanes, *Destroy the Junction*, 100. Long afterward, Kautz determined that "the best way of getting through" to the Army of the Potomac would have been by Jarratt's Station. Kautz, "Wilson Raid: An Expedition to Destroy the Petersburg & Lynchburg and the Richmond & Danville Railroads," in *National Tribune*, June 8, 1899, p. 2, col. 1.

168 Second Lieutenant Comins wrote, "Our Gen. Kautz wanted to go out of the Rebelliondom by way of North Carolina." Letter, L. M. Comins to "My dear wife," July 3, 1864, Leander M. Comins Letters.

Kautz believed. "We were in no condition to engage the enemy, and a battle should have been avoided."[169]

Nonetheless it seemed to Kautz that speed would overcome the Stony Creek Station route's deficiency. "I gave my opinion that he could go either way by not delaying," Kautz recalled. "I thought that he could pass at either point by continuous marching."[170]

The raiders had never rested longer than six hours and at this point were at no time stopping longer than four hours. The two generals, addled by lack of sleep, came to a misunderstanding. Wilson decided to return to Grant's army via the road which ran past Stony Creek Station. Kautz thought they would return to Federal lines via Reams Station.

* * *

In the afternoon, the 2nd Ohio Cavalry led the column into Dinwiddie County following the Stage Road over the Nottoway on the Double Bridges. The Buckeyes had been skirmishing with the Confederate pickets for the past six miles and scattered the Rebels before they could burn the bridges. This part of Dinwiddie County "was a wild, poor country, mostly forest, broken here and there by small clearings," Wilson remembered.[171]

The area seemed uninhabited except for slaves. "There was nothing to get in the way of supplies," recalled Sergeant Gause, who observed from the stolen carriage he drove filled with wounded from his company "a lack of confidence that prevailed throughout the whole command."[172]

As the raiders passed the Double Bridges, some of them captured the slaves at Spencer's Mill. "The Yankees dropped down like they came out of the clouds—thousands of them, and called for fire or matches with which to burn the mill," recalled Charles Cross, one of the slaves at the mill. He tried to persuade the Federals not to burn the mill, telling them that the Confederates had taken his farm's crops and that bread for him and his fellow slaves depended on operation of the mill. The Yanks seemed almost convinced to spare the mill until Cross gave them one more reason for not burning the mill, that his master was "an old Union man." This had the opposite effect of what Cross had intended. The Northerners said that his master must be "a d----d hypocrite" and prepared to burn the mill.

169 Roper, et al., *Eleventh Pennsylvania Volunteer Cavalry*, 131.

170 Eanes, *Destroy the Junction*, 100

171 Wilson, *Under the Old Flag*, 1:465.

172 Gause, *Four Years in Five Armies*, 285.

August V. Kautz
Library of Congress

After further appeals from Cross, they spared the structure. Quickly released from captivity, he headed for the Griffin farm.[173]

* * *

All the information Wilson could gather from slaves and captured pickets led him to believe that Hampton's cavalry had not reached the area through which the Illinoisan intended to proceed, and that no more than 1,000 Secessionists barred the way back to Grant's army—a detachment of horsemen cut off from Rooney Lee's division at the beginning of the raid and a battalion of infantry, both posted at Stony Creek Station on the Weldon Railroad. A picket of 50 Rebels stationed at Sappony Church, about 20 miles south of Petersburg, reportedly guarded the junction, two and a half miles west of Stony Creek Station, of the road northeastward to Prince George Court House with the road westward from Stony Creek Station to the Stage Road. "The most diligent inquiry from the negroes and captured pickets gave no information of any other force," recalled Wilson.[174] He turned eastward, to Kautz's surprise, off the Stage Road on to the road to Stony Creek Station.

Under the direction of Wilson's staffer Whitaker, the 3rd Indiana Cavalry of Chapman's brigade galloped forward near dusk toward the Stony Creek Station road's junction with the road to Prince George Court House. Wilson's plan called for the Hoosiers to drive the Rebel pickets back through the junction toward Stony Creek Station, allowing his command to turn on to the road to Prince George Court House and pass as rapidly as possible. Corporal Gilpin of the 3rd considered that "Our Regt was . . . thrown in advance of 1st Brigade <u>to</u> <u>be</u> <u>sacrificed</u>."[175]

173 Griffin, "Life in Dinwiddie County in the vicinity of the opposing armies of the war," 6.

174 *OR* 40, 1:627.

175 Gilpin Diary, June 28, 1864.

Approaching Sappony Church, the 3rd dismounted just before sundown. The Hoosiers attacked the Secessionist pickets—four companies of the Holcombe South Carolina Legion's infantry. The 3rd drove the South Carolinians across a field and orchard, back to the church.

Confederate reinforcements were already on the way in the form of Chambliss's Virginia Brigade. "We had not been at Stony Creek long before our videttes and pickets announced [the enemy's] approach," remembered Sgt. Thomas F. Ruffin of the 13th Virginia Cavalry's Company F. "The bugler immediately sounded to horse, and we were on our way to meet him." The 10th Virginia Cavalry and the 13th crossed Stony Creek and came to the support of the pickets as twilight passed. The "invincible 13th" led the way. "We soon encountered his advanced guard which we drove rapidly back, but rapidly receiving reinforcements, they flanked us pouring an enfilading fire into our ranks, which caused us to fall back until the rest of the brigade came up," recalled Ruffin.[176]

The 9th Virginia Cavalry of Chambliss's brigade followed the 10th and 13th. "On reaching Sappony Church, we could see one regiment on the right and the other on the left of the road half a mile in front, engaged, dismounted, with the enemy, and driving them back," recalled Col. Richard Lee Turburville Beale of the 9th, a lawyer and legislator who had attended Dickinson College in Carlisle, Pennsylvania and graduated from the University of Virginia. "We were directed by our General to push forward, mounted, and we moved down the road at a trot in column of fours." Companies D and E formed the van supported by G and H while C and K veered off to guard a road a mile to the right. Company D charged a dismounted line of Federal troopers in a wood about 200 yards ahead. The squadron came under heavy fire from a small body of pines to its right. Ordered to form a line on the road's right and charge the trees, the company dashed "into the pines and up to a barricade too high to leap, behind which, and partly concealed in a young growth of pines, the enemy was in force," remembered Colonel Beale. "The flashes of rifles (it was now growing dark) revealed the fact that the enemy's line ran far to our right."[177]

The charge drove the Federal advance guard—the 3rd Indiana Cavalry—back on its column west of the church. The 2nd Ohio Cavalry galloped to the assistance of the Hoosiers, dismounted and in the timber stopped the Virginian advance. Brigadier General John Randolph Chambliss, a West Point graduate, then withdrew his 10th Virginia Cavalry and his 13th as well as Company D of his 9th.

176 Daniel T. Balfour, *13th Virginia Cavalry* (Lynchburg, VA, 1986), 35.

177 Richard L. T. Beale, *History of the Ninth Virginia Cavalry, in the War Between the States* (Richmond, VA, 1899), 132–133.

McIntosh dismounted the rest of his brigade and pressed the Confederates back toward Sappony Church. As soon as he reached the open field, he deployed a strong line with, from right to left, the 5th New York Cavalry, the 1st Connecticut Cavalry, the 2nd Ohio Cavalry and, from Chapman's brigade, the 1st Vermont Cavalry. Then McIntosh's line advanced halfway across the field and pushed the Secessionists back into a wood west of the church where they made a determined stand and his men could advance no farther. They erected breastworks made of anything at hand.

The position at Sappony Church favored the defense. "The meeting-house stood upon a narrow tongue or strip of land flanked on either side by a small stream, and the intervening land not over five hundred yards wide, and passable by cavalry only at one or two points," Colonel Beale remembered. The 9th Virginia Cavalry dismounted and occupied the road and ground to the left, between the 10th and 13th. "Seizing upon rails, boards, the stalks of green corn, any and everything we could get hold of, the best barricade we could make was hastily thrown up," he recalled.[178]

Out on the Confederate right, Companies C and K of the 9th prepared their defense. "Our party, after collecting rails, logs and brush, blocked the road to which we had been sent, so as to prevent horses from passing over it, and laid down on our arms to dispute the enemy's passage, should any appear in the night," recollected 1st Lt. George Washington Beale of Company C, Colonel Beale's son.[179]

The 7th Virginia Cavalry of Rosser's Laurel Brigade in Hampton's division arrived and dismounted to fight on foot, reinforcing the 9th on the left of the road and church. "The regiment had barely time to get in position on the left of the road and church, in fact it formed under fire," remembered 2nd Lt. Charles H. Vandiver, commander of the 7th's Company F. "It was then dark, and the bullets and shells went over the heads of the men."[180] The 7th built breastworks of fence rails and any other movable material within reach.

Hampton reinforced the Virginians with Young's brigade of Butler's division. Dismounted, Young's brigade deployed on Chambliss's right in an open corn field. "After firing one volley, we lay flat on the ground," recalled Lt. Col. Joseph F. Waring of the Jeff Davis Legion Cavalry in Young's brigade, a Georgia farmer

178 Ibid., 133.

179 George W. Beale, *A Lieutenant of Cavalry in Lee's Army* (Boston, 1918), 29, 76.

180 Eanes, *Destroy the Junction*, 123; Richard L. Armstrong, *7th Virginia Cavalry* (Lynchburg, VA, 1993), 70.

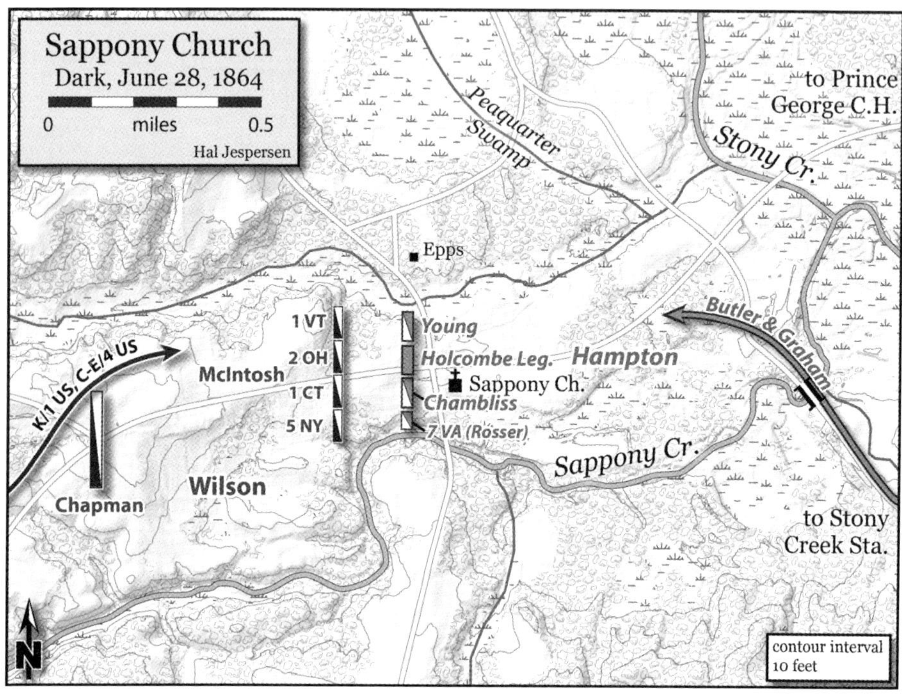

wounded in December 1861 and at Gettysburg.[181] Soon after the Confederates established this line, the remaining six infantry companies of the Holcombe South Carolina Legion—several hundred men—arrived from the bridges over Rowanty Creek and the Nottoway. Hampton posted these foot soldiers in the line's center, between Chambliss's and Young's brigades.

Thus matters stood after dark at Sappony Church on June 28. A week earlier, before the raid began, Humphreys had told Wilson that to ensure the raiders' safe return to the Army of the Potomac, Sheridan would occupy Hampton. Wilson and Kautz learned from the prisoners taken during the evening's struggle that, contrary to Humphreys's assurance, Sheridan had not occupied Hampton.

The two raider generals must have wondered what had gone wrong.

181 Joseph Frederick Waring Diary, June 28, 1864, Joseph Frederick Waring Papers, SHC, University of North Carolina at Chapel Hill, Chapel Hill, NC.

Chapter Four

"Each Corps Must Look Out for Itself"

AS FAR as Wilson and Kautz were concerned, almost everything had gone wrong.

Meade had missed his best chance to cover the Weldon Railroad on June 21 and had lost the element of surprise. He prepared to try again early on June 22 even though Russell's and Wheaton's divisions of VI Corps had not moved into position to advance with II Corps. Birney's troops began the process of extending from the left of V Corps on Jerusalem Plank Road to the right of Ricketts's VI Corps division on the Williams farm just west of the plank road's crossing of Second Swamp.

By 12:50 a.m. on June 22, Barlow had his division in line preparatory to connecting with the right of Ricketts's division. Barlow thought his division would be stretched too thinly, reaching over a mile to connect with the left of Mott's division while Ricketts's division stood compactly in two lines extending just a quarter mile across the Williams Road. To the right of Mott's division, the pioneers and infantry of Gibbon's division finished entrenching at about 3:00 a.m.

Then, in the cool, very foggy air of early dawn, Pierce's and O'Brien's brigades of Gibbon's division, with Pierce's brigade on the right, plodded forward to the line dug during the night. The line faced roughly north by northeast. Smyth's and Blaisdell's brigades remained in the division's rear line, with Blaisdell's brigade on the right near Jerusalem Plank Road and Smyth's brigade along the lane diverging at 25 degrees from the plank road. Battery B, 1st New Jersey Light Artillery maneuvered its cannon into the works its gunners had built on the brow of the hill to the right of the plank road. The 12th New York Battery unlimbered in the lunettes just erected by the pioneers between Pierce's and O'Brien's brigades.

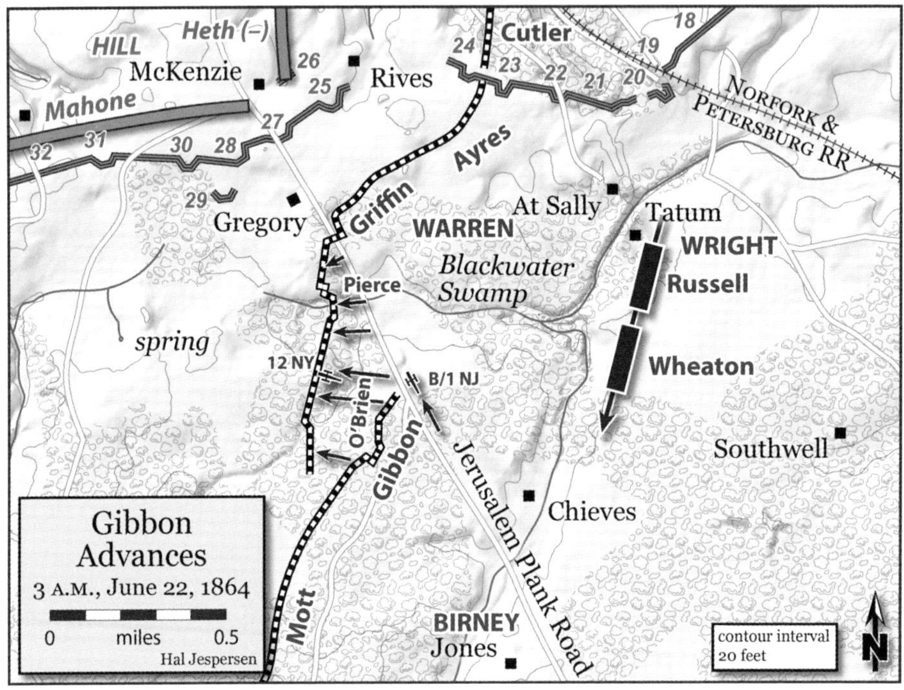

The new position left many of its occupants dissatisfied. The line "was in a swamp, covered with a thicket of undergrowth so dense that even in the light of the morning sun one could scarcely see from flank to flank of our little battalion, numbering now less than a hundred men," remembered Lieutenant Hastings in Pierce's brigade. The enemy's works in the Dimmock Line, on high ground, completely dominated the line of Gibbon's division. "From these works a worrying fire of pickets and sharpshooters was constantly kept up," Hastings recalled.[1] Destructive fire from the Secessionist batteries in the Dimmock Line added to the perils the men of Gibbon's division faced.

The gunners of the 12th New York Battery, next to Pierce's brigade, found their lunettes "very defective in every respect," one of them who styled himself "G" wrote. "We were so near the enemy that we had to dismount our ammunition chests and sink them in the ground and send the horses to the rear."[2] The artillerists set to improving the lunettes.

O'Brien's brigade occupied the new line south of the 12th New York Battery. The brigade included three regiments of the Philadelphia or California Brigade as

1 Ford, *Fifteenth Regiment Massachusetts Volunteer Infantry*, 333.

2 "G." to the Editor of the *Buffalo Express*, June 27, 1864, "The Loss of Capt. McKnight's Battery," dmna.ny.gov. Retrieved Sept. 4, 2023.

well as the 152nd New York and the 184th Pennsylvania. Adjacent to the guns stood the 72nd Pennsylvania, also known as the Third California Regiment or the Philadelphia Fire Zouaves because of all the firemen in its ranks. The 106th Pennsylvania, the Fifth California Regiment, occupied the works to the left of the 72nd. The commander of the 106th, Capt. John R. Breitenbach, who bore the scar of a Gettysburg wound, found the line "very defectively constructed and entirely too limited in extent."[3] The breastworks did not afford his men enough room and exposed them to enemy sharpshooters. The works of the 184th Pennsylvania on his left presented the same problem and diverged from the brigade's line at 45 degrees, leaving a 50-yard gap before the line resumed to the 184th's left, exposing the regiment to a flank fire.

The 152nd New York held the line behind and to the left of the 184th. The 184th's "flanks were exposed, the enemy raking one side of their low earthworks with shell, while the opposite side was exposed to infantry," remembered Pvt. Henry Roback of the 152nd, wounded on June 18.[4] To the left of the 152nd stood the 69th Pennsylvania, the Second California Regiment. Like the artillerists in their midst, the infantrymen of Pierce's and O'Brien's brigades tried to improve their works.

While Gibbon's division of II Corps adjusted to its position, Wheaton's and Russell's divisions of VI Corps struggled to catch up. After getting out of the trenches, the two divisions had commenced what Pvt. James Lorenzo Bowen of Company I in the 37th Massachusetts of Wheaton's division remembered as, "a monotonous night march . . . the column feeling its way slowly to the left."[5]

At 2:00 a.m., the column began crossing the Norfolk & Petersburg.[6] Captain Aldace Freeman Walker, valedictorian of Middlebury College's class of 1862 and commander of a battalion of four companies in the twelve-company 1st Vermont Heavy Artillery of Wheaton's division, wrote about such night marches, "They are very fatiguing, slow at times, then very rapid, blundering along through the woods and byways, across fields, open sometimes, sometimes full of stumps and

3 *OR* 40, 1:376, 386.

4 Henry Roback, comp., *The Veteran Volunteers of Herkimer and Otsego Counties in the War of the Rebellion Being a History of the 152d N. Y. V. with Scenes, Incidents, Etc., Which Occurred in the Ranks, of the 34th N.Y, 97th N.Y., 121st N.Y, 2d N.Y. Heavy Artillery, and 1st and 2d N.Y. Mounted Rifles; also, the Active Part Performed by the Boys in Blue Who Were Associated with the 152d N. Y. V., in Gen. Hancock's Second Army Corps during Grant's Campaign from the Wilderness to the Surrender of Gen. Lee at Appomattox Court House, Va.* (Little Falls, NY, 1888), 103.

5 James L. Bowen, *History of the Thirty-Seventh Regiment Mass. Volunteers in the Civil War of 1861–1865, with a Comprehensive Sketch of the Doings of Massachusetts as a State, and of the Principal Campaigns of the War* (Holyoke, MA, 1884), 343.

6 *OR* 40, 1:497.

underbrush; but on the whole, though sleepy and weary, we endure them better than the heat and dust of noonday."[7]

Bowen, wounded at Gettysburg, recalled, "That being the second night that the regiment had been without sleep, it was difficult to prevent the men from lapsing into insensibility at each of the frequent temporary halts."[8]

Soon Wheaton's and Russell's exhausted divisions reached Jerusalem Plank Road near the Jones house, about a mile and a half south of the Confederate fortifications. Around 3:00 a.m. the divisions began stopping in Birney's rear for breakfast and rest.[9] The 2nd Connecticut Heavy Artillery of Upton's brigade in Russell's division, bivouacked near the Jones house "not much farther from Petersburg than before," recalled the regimental adjutant, 1st Lt. Theodore Freylinghuysen Vaill, wondering, "How can we march so far and yet go so little way?"[10]

* * *

Birney expected Russell's and Wheaton's divisions to take position on his left at daylight. Only then could Barlow advance toward the left of Mott's division by roads cut through the woods and still maintain a connection with VI Corps. At 4:50 a.m., around daylight, pursuant to Meade's directions, Birney ordered Mott to move ahead to a line parallel with the Confederate fortifications and put part of his division into reserve. At that time units of Wheaton's and Russell's divisions were still arriving and bivouacking near the Jones house.[11] Birney directed Barlow to go forward closing in to the right on Mott while conforming to VI Corps' movements. Shortly after 5:00 a.m., II Corps got under way. It had difficulty getting out a skirmish line. The 2nd United States Sharpshooters went forward on picket for Mott's division early and lay quietly at the edge of a wood watching enemy cavalry assemble in an open field preparatory to the pursuit of Wilson's raiders.

Mott began advancing Chaplin's and McAllister's brigades one regiment at a time at least half a mile in some places and more than three quarters of a mile in

7 Letter, Aldace Freeman Walker to "Dear Father," June 23, 1864, Aldace Freeman Walker Papers, VHS.

8 Bowen, *Thirty-Seventh Regiment Mass. Volunteers*, 343.

9 *OR* 40, 1:497, 500; 2:308; Robert S. Westbrook, *History of the 49th Pennsylvania Volunteers: A Correctly Compiled Roll of the Members of the Regiments and Its Marches from 1861 to 1865* (Altoona, PA, 1898), 209; Arthur McClellan Diary and Notebook, June 21–22, 1864. An officer in the 119th Regiment Pennsylvania Volunteers noted that his regiment in Russell's division, "Reached a position just after daylight to the left of Gen. Hancock's Corps." James William Latta Diary, June 22, 1864, James William Latta Papers, LOC.

10 Theodore F. Vaill, *History of the Second Connecticut Volunteer Heavy Artillery, Originally the Nineteenth Connecticut Vols.* (Winsted, CT, 1868), 77.

11 *OR* 40, 1:500.

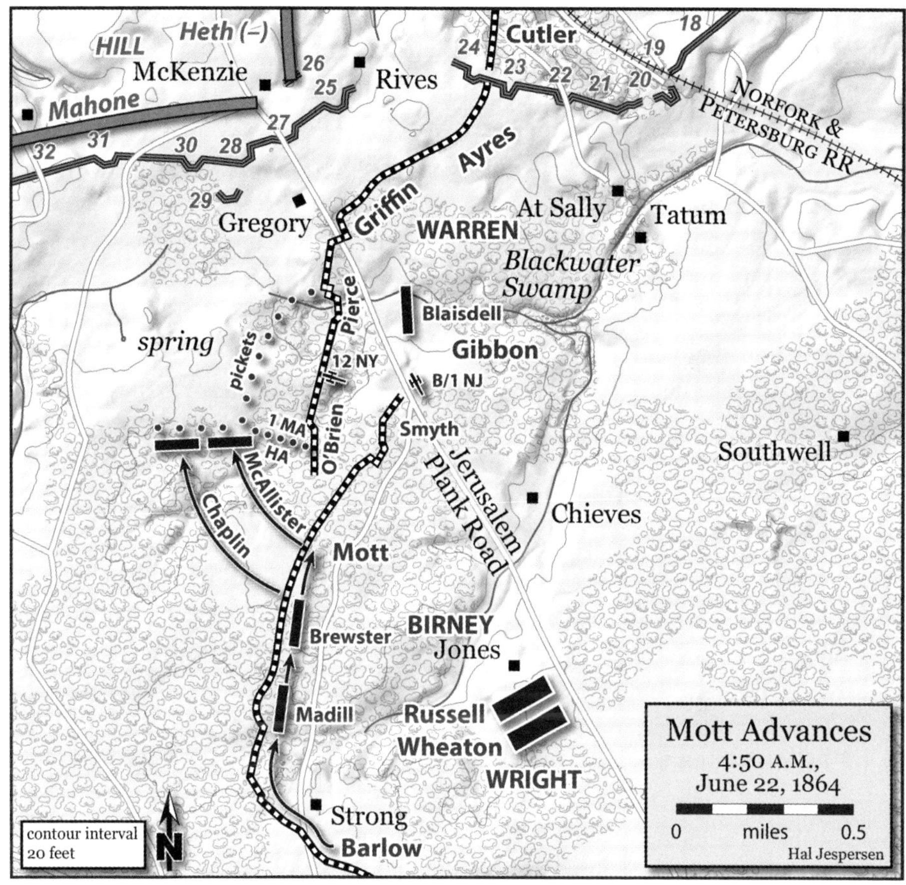

others, with McAllister's brigade on the right. Madill's and Brewster's brigades, with Brewster's brigade on the right, shifted rightward in the second line into the spaces formerly occupied by Chaplin's and McAllister's brigades. "We moved forward across an open space into a belt of heavy woods," remembered Capt. Horace H. Shaw of Company F in the 1st Maine heavies in Chaplin's brigade, wounded at Spotsylvania. "During the early morning we could hear the enemy chopping and digging in our front and not far away."[12] Mott posted his sharpshooters well out to keep the enemy from his frontline troops, who began entrenching as soon as in position.

For the 72nd New York, the Third Excelsior Regiment in Brewster's brigade, this proved a happy day. Orders pulled the regiment out of the line and sent it to

12 Horace H. Shaw, *The First Maine Heavy Artillery, 1862–1865: A History of Its Part and Place in the War for the Union with an Outline of Causes of War and Its Results to Our Country* (Portland, ME, 1903), 131.

the rear. The enlistments of most of its men had expired. They were directed to muster out while the remainder consolidated into three companies which would be attached to the 120th New York, the Ulster Regiment, of Brewster's brigade—but not until the following morning.

The movement of II Corps proceeded very slowly. While Mott's division shifted into two lines, Gibbon's division improved its breastworks under heavy Confederate fire. In Pierce's brigade, the frontline brigade with its right on the plank road, the 36th Wisconsin's Pvt. David Coon had returned to Company A the previous day after a stint in the hospital for swollen legs. "This morning, as I was digging on the breast-work, a bullet struck the bank close by the side of me (there goes another shell) and a few minutes after a bullet struck a man of another regiment about a rod from me, mortally wounding him I think," Coon wrote home. "I have no doubt but it was aimed at me, as I was exposed at work."[13]

After carrying a dispatch to Brig. Gen. Byron Root Pierce, a dentist wounded at Chancellorsville, Gettysburg, Spotsylvania, and on June 18 at Petersburg, First Sergeant Murphey in the 20th Massachusetts, adjacent to and immediately south of the 36th Wisconsin, started going back to his regiment the way he had come.

"Sergeant, you will get hit by a sharpshooter if you return that way," Pierce said.

"No, I guess not," replied Murphey. "I came that way and was not fired at."

When Murphey got about a quarter of the way across an open field, he saw a puff of smoke and a bullet struck the ground near him. Before he could "pop down," two or three more bullets whizzed past. Murphey ran under cover of some bushes. The firing ceased. "I looked at the Genl, and he was watching me," Murphey remembered. "I waived my hand to him and kept under cover until I reached the regiment in the breast works."[14]

Opposite the 1st Minnesota Battalion on the extreme left of Pierce's brigade, the Confederates labored to improve their lines. An opposing battery in the Dimmock Line lacked embrasures permitting cannon to fire westward. "During the entire forenoon we could see the rebels digging away and preparing the fort for firing down our lines," recalled Corporal Bond in the 1st Minnesota adjacent to the right of the 12th New York Battery.[15]

O'Brien's brigade, immediately left of the 12th New York Battery, had an equally difficult time. During the morning, the 152nd New York took a pasting as shells knocked logs off the regiment's breastworks and hit the exposed flank of

13 Letter, David Coon to "My dear Wife and Children," June 22, 1864, David Coon Letters, David Coon Papers, LC.

14 Miller and Mooney, eds., *The Nantucket Experience*, 110.

15 Bond Diary and Memoir, June 22, 1864, 234.

Companies E and B. "[W]e built a short work on the flank, which offered some projection," recalled Roback. "We were kept quite busy replacing the logs as they were knocked off, the shells meanwhile screaming and shrieking overhead, and burying in the ground behind us."[16]

The 69th Pennsylvania occupied the extreme left of O'Brien's brigade and experienced similar problems. "Our lines were pushed out so close to the rebel forts that it was with great difficulty that we were enabled to hold our position long enough to construct earthworks which afforded us sufficient protection to make a vigorous stand and return a spirited fire," recollected Adjt. Anthony W. McDermott of the 69th.[17]

* * *

Russell's and Wheaton's divisions finally had enough light to advance down Jerusalem Plank Road, but their exhausted, famished soldiers required rest and breakfast.[18] Their inability to move made illusory Birney's expectation that they would take position on his left. The skirmish line of Ricketts's VI Corps division, confronted by bewildering woods, impenetrable thickets, forbidding swamps and the pickets of the 3rd North Carolina Cavalry, made no progress and hindered Barlow's advance.

The failure of VI Corps to move forward frustrated the commander of the Army of the Potomac. Around 7:15 a.m., he summoned Captain Crowninshield to army headquarters, which was still at the house east of Petersburg. Meade questioned Crowninshield about the Confederate attack of the previous evening in front of the army's staff and some of its generals. "After being told," Crowninshield recalled, "General Meade refused to believe the report, saying it was impossible Hill's corps should be there; and speaking very disrespectfully of cavalry in general, and this detachment in particular, gave the order to advance his troops towards the Weldon Railroad, on the supposition that nothing was there to interpose."[19]

Before 7:30 a.m. Meade sent Birney an order with a different tenor than the order of 4:50 a.m. The new order instructed Birney to have Barlow swing forward his left while his right closed up with Mott, but only to notify Wright of the movement instead of maintaining contact with VI Corps. At least one of the four

16 Roback, comp., *152d N. Y. V.*, 103.

17 Anthony W. McDermott, *A Brief History of the 69th Regiment Pennsylvania Volunteers from Its Formation until Final Muster Out of the United States Service* (Philadelphia, 1895), 45.

18 *OR* 40, 1:497, 500.

19 Benjamin W. Crowninshield, *A History of the First Regiment of Massachusetts Cavalry Volunteers* (Boston, 1891), 230.

divisions in V Corps had a reserve brigade available to help fill the gap Meade's new order would cause between II and VI Corps, but he did not call upon V Corps for help. IX Corps continued strengthening its earthworks with abatis and Burnside did not yet feel safe allowing his reserves to go to the assistance of II and VI corps.

About 8:00 a.m. the Army of the Potomac's headquarters began moving to a new camp on Jerusalem Plank Road opposite and south of the Jones house. Meade saddled up and accompanied his headquarters on its move as he headed for Birney's headquarters to explain the new order.

* * *

Around the same time as Meade headed for Birney's headquarters, USS *Baltimore* carried Lincoln and his general-in-chief to Bermuda Hundred, where she stopped to take on General Butler. *Baltimore* then resumed her journey up the James and Admiral Lee boarded the vessel from his flagship, *Malvern*. Some of Foster's troops on the riverbank at Deep Bottom had sufficient leisure to spot and cheer the president's ship as the pontoon bridge opened for her to steam upriver that afternoon. Farther upriver the party inspected the double-turreted monitor *Onondaga*, anchored near Crow's Nest just east of where Trent's Reach veered into Varina Reach. After proceeding up the James as far as safety permitted, the party disembarked for a tour of the Bermuda Hundred Lines.

As the president and his subordinates rode along the fortifications, Butler sent word ahead of Lincoln's approach to arrange a warm welcome. The troops in the area, nearly all 100-day men unhappy to serve in harm's way, received the message coldly. Only a few squads of soldiers met Lincoln and they displayed neither enthusiasm nor interest. Captain James M. Nichols, a graduate of Phillips Academy and Williams College, led Company C of the 48th New York, a regiment known as "Perry's Saints" or "The Fighting Parson's Regiment" after the minister who had raised the unit. Nichols had never seen Butler so disconcerted. "As the party neared the point where we stood, an aid was hurriedly sent forward to command the men to cheer, and General Butler, dropping behind the President, endeavored, by frantic gestures and pantomime, to enforce the orders of his aid," recalled Nichols. These tactics failed. The angry, sullen 100-day men responded with hoots of derision as Butler, "rising in his stirrups, shook his fist at them," Nichols remembered.[20]

Other troops politely applauded the president though they held Butler in low esteem. But Lincoln's promise that the fighting would end by the Fourth of July

20 James M. Nichols, *Perry's Saints or The Fighting Parson's Regiment in the War of the Rebellion* (Boston, 1886), 245–246.

met with skepticism. "I wonder if he thought we were all fools," recalled Pvt. Hermon Clarke of D Company in the 117th New York.[21]

The president's party proceeded to the marquee Butler had ordered erected for lunch. Shortly after the meal's end, Lincoln decided to return to Washington immediately. Boarding Butler's vessel, USS *Greyhound*, the president steamed down the James, transferred to the *Baltimore* and after disembarking Grant at City Point, departed. Grant's lack of progress in the spring campaign disappointed Lincoln but the general-in-chief's confidence encouraged the commander-in-chief. After his return to the capital, Lincoln said of Grant that "it may be a long summer's day before he does his work, but . . . he is as sure of doing it as he is of anything in this world."[22]

* * *

Between 9:00 a.m. and 10:00 a.m., Lieutenant Colonel Morgan of II Corps' staff and Barlow discussed the implications of the change in Meade's order of 7:30 a.m. They agreed that it would lead to a gap between Barlow's left and the right of VI Corps—a gap into which the enemy might intrude. Thinking the order a mistake, Morgan rode back to II Corps headquarters to inquire. Meade arrived at Birney's headquarters around 10:00 a.m. The Army of the Potomac's commander explained to II Corps' leader that the order of 7:30 a.m. was not a mistake, then set off to visit Barlow. Morgan and Meade unknowingly passed one another in the woods as Meade headed toward Barlow and Morgan proceeded to Birney.

At II Corps headquarters, Morgan asked Birney if the order of 7:30 a.m. amounted to a mistake. Birney gave Morgan a peremptory order for Barlow to move independently of VI Corps. Around the same time at Barlow's headquarters, Barlow asked Meade whether the order of 7:30 a.m. was an error. "You cannot connect with both," the Army of the Potomac's leader told Barlow. "[K]eep your connection to the right; each corps must look out for itself." By the time Morgan reached Barlow's headquarters with Birney's clarification, Meade had departed. "The movement then progressed without delay," remembered Morgan.[23] Barlow joined Wright near Upton's brigade of Russell's division for a conference. Russell's division was preparing to fill the gap between Barlow's and Ricketts's divisions

21 Harry F. Jackson and Thomas F. O'Donnell, *Back Home in Oneida: Hermon Clarke and his Letters* (Syracuse, NY, 1965), 144.

22 Henry Adams, et al., eds., *Letters of John Hay and Extracts from Diary*, 3 vols. (Washington, D.C., 1908), 1:209.

23 *OR* 40, 1:328.

George Gordon Meade

Library of Congress

as the Red Club Division readied itself to sever its connection with VI Corps and close up to the right with Mott's division.

* * *

About 11:00 a.m., the officers of Wheaton's and Russell's divisions shook their men awake to get moving again.[24] With Wheaton's division in the lead, the column soon headed south on Jerusalem Plank Road. Wheaton's division followed the road to the lane running westward from the Williams house and formed behind Ricketts's division. Edwards's brigade faced south on the plank road after having taken up the planks on the road's bridge over Second Swamp. Farther west, Bidwell's brigade and then Lewis Grant's Vermont Brigade faced southward. Next, Ballier's brigade faced westward toward the Weldon Railroad.

Russell's division followed the plank road south no farther than Ricketts's right flank, then plunged westward into the thickets to plug the gap between Ricketts's division and II Corps. The 2nd Connecticut Heavy Artillery of Upton's brigade reached a square, open field bounded by dense timber. Colonel Ranald Slidell Mackenzie of the 2nd, a West Pointer wounded at Second Bull Run and Gettysburg, dispatched an officer and 20 men to find the left of the II Corps pickets. The detachment found the II Corps sentinels near the Strong house and the 2nd made the connection. "Upton and Russell were both out in the jungle on foot, to see the connection made," recalled Vaill.[25]

To the left of Russell's division, Ricketts's division advanced due west very slowly toward the Aiken house and the railroad. On the left of Truex's brigade, skirmishers of the 87th Pennsylvania went forward, "slowly through woods,

24 Ibid., 500.

25 Vaill, *Second Connecticut Volunteer Heavy Artillery*, 77.

thickets and open fields, feeling their way as they moved along," without seeing the enemy's battle line, Private Prowell recalled. "Occasionally a single man could be seen on a tree-top, a distance ahead, keeping a watch of the movements of the skirmishers."[26]

As Russell's and Ricketts's divisions advanced, Meade learned from Crowninshield that his cavalry detachment was out of ammunition. The commander of the Army of the Potomac demonstrated why Lyman called him "the Great Peppery." Meade "burst out upon" Crowninshield and "told him he was unfit for his command and would see that he was relieved," Lyman recalled. "Poor Ben!"[27]

The Great Peppery arrived about 11:15 a.m. at Upton's brigade of Russell's division, where Wright was still talking to Barlow. Meade was highly agitated about maintaining a cavalry screen on his left flank. Before he departed, he ordered Provost Marshal Patrick to send the rest of the provost guard cavalry—the 3rd Pennsylvania Cavalry and two companies of the 1st Indiana Cavalry—to relieve Crowninshield's men. The Keystoner and Hoosier troopers arrived at the Williams house, now headquarters for VI Corps, around 12:10 p.m.

About the same time, Russell's and Ricketts's divisions encountered Wilcox's division of Confederates. "A heavy skirmish followed, the stray bullets coming spitefully about us," recalled Lyman, whom Meade had tasked with keeping an eye on VI Corps.[28] By about 1:10 p.m. the skirmishers of the Light Division had begun pushing back against Ricketts's division and part of Russell's division.

* * *

Early that morning, before the fog lifted, Hill received reports that the Federals were again advancing toward the Weldon Railroad. Again he instructed Wilcox to prevent the enemy from reaching the tracks. The corps commander pledged that he would catch up with Wilcox and give him additional directives later. As on the day before, Mahone's division had orders from Hill to move out of the trenches and cooperate with Wilcox in any attack he made on the Unionists.

Wilcox's troops departed the Dimmock Line and headed southward along the Weldon Railroad. They tramped down the tracks in column of fours and entered the woods southeast of the Davis house. After the soldiers plodded to the Browder house on the lane that led toward the Williams farm and Jerusalem Plank Road, they turned onto a farm track conducting them to their right, toward Second

26 Prowell, *Eighty-Seventh Regiment, Pennsylvania Volunteers*, 165.

27 Agassiz, ed., *Meade's Headquarters*, 176; Lowe, ed., *Meade's Army*, 221.

28 Ibid.

Ambrose Powell "Little Powell" Hill

National Archives

Swamp. Wilcox wanted them to cross Second Swamp on the dam of the Smith millpond into the Unionist left and rear.[29] His idea proved time-consuming and impracticable. The dam did not provide a crossing and the adjacent morass did not permit fording.

Wilcox led his men back to the lane leading to the Williams farm. The Light Division turned eastward. Thomas's brigade formed line of battle on the left of the lane and McGowan's brigade on the right with their sharpshooter battalions deployed in front of them, all facing eastward. They entered trees and underbrush so tangled that a colonel could not see his entire regiment deployed in line of battle. Skirmishing quickly grew heavy in the thick woods facing McGowan's and Thomas's brigades as they encountered the enemy. On the left of the lane leading to the Williams house, the marksmen of Thomas's brigade drove Yankee skirmishers. On the lane's right the sharpshooters of McGowan's brigade advanced unopposed, supposing that their comrades on the lane's left had only flushed a flock of wild turkeys.

Opposite Wilcox's marksmen, Russell's and Ricketts's divisions of VI Corps were pushing westward from Jerusalem Plank Road, Russell's division on the right and Ricketts's division on the left. The first line of Upton's brigade in Russell's division, which included the 2nd Connecticut heavies, advanced into the timber about 200 yards. A few minutes later the 2nd's pickets engaged in a sharp skirmish with the marksmen of Thomas's brigade resulting in 19 casualties.[30]

As Colonel Mackenzie stretched out his right hand to give an order, a bullet removed the first two fingers, earning him nicknames such as "Three Finger Jack"

29 "The Fighting Around Petersburg—Further Particulars of the Flanking of Hancock's Corps—Movements of the Two Armies," *Daily Richmond Examiner*, June 25, 1864, p. 2, col. 1.

30 The 2nd Connecticut Heavy Artillery had six killed, seven wounded (several mortally), and six missing. Vaill, *Second Connecticut Volunteer Heavy Artillery*, 77.

and "Bad Hand."[31] After some maneuvering incomprehensible to the soldiers, the 2nd returned to the open field, shifted a regiment's length to the right, and advanced again somewhat farther than before "into a wilderness of woods, bushes, brambles and vines, so thick that a man could hardly see his neighbor," remembered Vaill.[32]

Farther south, the battle lines of the 87th Pennsylvania and the 10th Vermont of Truex's brigade went forward in line of battle about a quarter mile and halted. "We had lain here about 20 minutes when we were attacked and our pickets driven in we went to work with our hands, and tin cups and plates to build works when we had some shovels come and we made good works," First Sergeant Graham remembered.[33]

The picket lines of the two regiments, crossing a swamp, swung around to the right with thick timber to the front and left. The skirmishers passed the order "Forward," from man to man in a whisper. The marksmen of McGowan's brigade rose up, charged the skirmishers, and drove them back, cutting off and capturing from the left of the 87th's line a lieutenant and twelve men.[34]

"Had it not been for the bravery of [Lt. Col. John W. Schall], the 87th would have been captured entirely," recalled Pvt. Edwin C. Hall of the 10th Vermont's Company G, who had been wounded at Cold Harbor. "I was on the skirmish line that day and ran till I fainted dead away but came to and finally made our lines in safety," recollected Hall.[35]

McGowan's and Thomas's brigades occupied some of the breastworks constructed by the Federals on the previous night north of the Browder farm. The rest of Wilcox's division deployed on the left of the lane behind Thomas's brigade. Scales's and Lane's brigades formed facing north with Scales's brigade to the east and Lane's brigade to the west.

Ricketts's skirmishers withdrew to their starting point about 2:00 p.m., then advanced again half an hour later until the Johnnies made a stand in the hollow near the Aiken house and began pushing back the Yanks around 2:55 p.m. Fire soon slackened and the bluecoats, awaiting news from II Corps but not hearing a shot, fell back to the position they held in the morning. "Did lie under the

31 Charles M. Robinson III, *Bad Hand: A Biography of General Ranald S. Mackenzie* (Abilene, TX, 2005), 20.

32 Vaill, *Second Connecticut Volunteer Heavy Artillery*, 78.

33 Graham Diary, June 22, 1864.

34 Prowell, *Eighty-Seventh Regiment, Pennsylvania Volunteers*, 165.

35 Kuntz, ed., "A Brookfield Soldier's Report: The Civil War Recollections of Edwin C. Hall," 211–212.

tree and take a doze, putting a branch over my face, to avoid the intense sun," remembered Lyman.[36]

* * *

II Corps frontline troops slowly complied with Meade's directions while the soldiers in the rear adjusted to their new surroundings. "This morning we drew rations of sugar, coffee, hard tack, pork, beans & sour krout," recalled Private Peterson in the hospital of Gibbon's division. "At 10 Oclock A M we moved our Hospital back about 1 ½ miles" to the Chieves house east of the plank road.[37] It took until around 11:00 a.m. for Mott's division to double up and get its front line roughly parallel to the Dimmock Line in prolongation of Gibbon's front line. The men of Mott's division came under fire as hot as that faced by Gibbon's troops but Mott's skirmishers prevented the Rebels from pressuring his front.

About 11:00 a.m. Barlow started bringing up his Fourth Brigade, commanded by Col. John Fraser, wounded at the Wilderness and Spotsylvania, to extend Mott's roughly east-west front line westward. The regiments of Fraser's brigade required more than an hour to inch across the mile through the dense timber between II Corps' rear line and the left of Mott's front line. Arriving, Fraser's troops halted, stacked arms and rested. Barlow's division hospital established itself at a house near Jerusalem Plank Road and a few hundred yards from the Jones farm. "We are nicely situated again, my tent on a beautiful yard that surrounds a fine house and we have plenty of good shade which is a consideration of importance," remembered Surgeon William W. Potter, in charge of the hospital. "In an open, out of door life like this, the difference between good shade and none at all is simply immense." Tapestry carpeted the floors of the house, which had sufficient conveniences. "We used the dining room for our mess, and some of the rooms for the sick officers," Potter recalled.[38]

As Barlow's troops deployed, the officers of the 19th Massachusetts of Pierce's brigade in Gibbon's division strolled to the rear to eat. Their regiment held breastworks at the edge of an open field covered by a crossfire from Battery B, 1st New Jersey Light Artillery and the 12th New York Battery. "Our regiment was so small that we were in single rank and the formation was two companies instead of ten," recalled Capt. John Gregory Bishop Adams, who commanded the

36 Lowe, ed. *Meade's Army*, 221.

37 Peterson Diary, June 22, 1864.

38 John Michael Priest, ed., *One Surgeon's Private War: Doctor William W. Potter of the 57th New York* (Shippensburg, PA, 1996), 109.

left company. After enlisting as a private, Adams earned a Medal of Honor and a promotion to captain at Fredericksburg prior to suffering a Gettysburg wound.

The 19th's commander shared an unsettling experience with his fellow officers.

"I fell asleep a little while ago, and had a queer dream," said Maj. Moncena Dunn, a Maine-born bookkeeper, cutler, and hotel manager wounded at Fredericksburg. "We were lying just as we are here, and the rebels came in our rear and captured the entire regiment."

Dunn's fellow officers reacted with disbelief.

"We laughed at his story, said we guessed we should not go to Richmond that way, and returned to our places in line," remembered Adams. "The firing in our front increased, the batteries doing good service for the rebels."[39]

The Confederate batteries annoyed not only the Federal infantry but the Unionist gunners. "About noon the enemy opened upon our position with four guns from an old fort and redoubts about a thousand yards to our right and front, throwing their shot and bursting their shell in and about our works with most accurate range," recalled the artillerist "G" in the 12th New York Battery. "We were ordered to open upon them, and immediately set our men to altering the embrasures (facing before to the front, as we were informed the enemy would probably open upon us from our immediate front) so as to enable us to return the fire of the enemy."[40]

Fraser's brigade on the left of II Corps' front line had its left flank unprotected. To rectify this situation, Barlow advanced the Irish Brigade between 1:00 p.m. and 2:00 p.m. about a mile and a half from the rear line to begin a return that would run at what he called "nearly a right angle to General Mott's line as a protection to" Fraser's left flank.[41]

Around an hour passed before the Irish Brigade arrived and halted at the top of a ravine. Like Fraser's men, the Irish Brigade stacked arms and rested. "We lay down and we could hear the rebels coming forward," recalled Sergeant Clear of the 116th Pennsylvania.[42]

Barlow, to further protect his left and rear, summoned MacDougall's New York Brigade to prolong the return. The tramp into the trees made the soldiers of the 57th New York in MacDougall's brigade uneasy. "We were taken out to the thick woods where we could hardly see the end of a company, and 'monkeyed around,' as the boys used to say, till we lost our bearings," Pvt. George W. Kelly of

39 John G. B. Adams, *Reminiscences of the Nineteenth Massachusetts Regiment* (Boston, 1890), 102–103.

40 "G." to the Editor of the *Buffalo Express*.

41 *OR* 40, 1:328–329, 360.

42 Menge and Shimrak, *The Civil War Notebook of Daniel Chisholm*, 25.

the 57th's Company C remembered. "When we think of the many struggles our men had with unseen foes in the woods, and the disasters which often followed, it is easy to account for the distrust we felt as we entered such places, and a certain 'backwardness to go forward,'" he recalled.[43] II Corps' most recent sylvan disasters had occurred on May 6 in the Wilderness when the Rebels routed it and the rest of the left wing of Grant's army, and on May 10 west of Spotsylvania Court House when II Corps had for the first time in its history abandoned a gun—though the corps excused this because the piece had become disabled.

MacDougall's New Yorkers advanced around 2:00 p.m. to extend the return to the Irish Brigade's left. The 125th New York, except for its colors, went out on the skirmish line of MacDougall's brigade. The brigade's "main line was in no particular order of battle, nor was it in readiness for action," remembered the 125th's Ezra D. Simons, who had enlisted in the regiment as a private in Company D, risen to become commissary sergeant, and surrendered at Harpers Ferry September 15, 1862, before becoming the 125th's chaplain. "The men were lying along the road."[44]

About the same time, the 12th New York Battery opened on the opposing Confederate artillery. The enemy "replied with a very heavy musketry fire and with a rapid fire from eight guns, bursting their shells over and in our works," recalled "G," the New York gunner.[45] The tempo of skirmishing increased, with the Confederate pickets pushing in the sentinels in front of II Corps, between the two lines of II Corps, and between II and VI Corps.

The 70th New York had lain in the woods in the rear all day. "In the afternoon our names was called and the old Excelsior Boys went home," recalled Pvt. Wilbur H. Proctor of Company G, who had enlisted as a drummer boy. "We all bid them good bye." Consolidated into Company K of the 86th New York, the Steuben Rangers, Proctor marched with it not back to Madill's brigade in the rear line of works but into the forward line.[46]

Farther left and also in the forward line, Lt. Col. John Schoonover of the 11th New Jersey in Chaplin's brigade, as he had several times earlier that day, strolled up a wood road intersecting his regiment's line and leading out to an opening across which Secessionist pickets stood in plain view. On his previous jaunts, he had not drawn fire. This time he drew a volley.

43 Frederick, *Fifty-Seventh New York*, 254.

44 Ezra D. Simons, *A Regimental History: The One Hundred and Twenty-Fifth New York State Volunteers* (New York, 1888), 228.

45 "G." to the Editor of the *Buffalo Express*.

46 Wilbur Huntington Proctor Diary, June 22, 1864, Wilbur Huntington Proctor Papers, LOC.

Schoonover, who had enlisted as a private in the 1st New Jersey, transferred to the 11th as adjutant and suffered two wounds at Gettysburg, another at Spotsylvania, and yet another at Cold Harbor, dodged this day's bullets and hurried back to his regiment. On the way, he met the mail-carrier of Barlow's division ambling forward with a mule and two pouches stuffed with letters. Schoonover explained the situation to the postman. Without a word, the mail-carrier performed an about-face and headed for the rear. Schoonover, after alerting his regiment to the change of affairs, hastened to inform Barlow.

The division commander had just finished reconnoitering between the lines and was washing his feet in a spring a few hundred yards north of the angle formed by his division's return. His staff surrounded him. Schoonover observed that Barlow's division, "which had just got into position, was taking things very coolly, the shade of the forest being very grateful after their hot and dusty march."[47]

The heat oppressed the soldiers. "You must remember it was in the middle of the day, hotter than tophet, the line was in thick woods, and our men had begun to believe that Johnny Reb was never going to attack again," recalled Maj. Henry Lyman Patten, commander of the 20th Massachusetts.[48] Patten, a Harvard student from New Hampshire when he enlisted in the Harvard Regiment in November 1861, had been wounded five times so far during the war.

A special ration did not help matters. "A whiskey ration had been issued most of the officers and many of the soldiers were drunk," recalled Bond, positioned with some recruits. "Capt. Far[w]ell had had whiskey enough in him to make a bare fool of him, for be it know[n] he is a coward and cannot face danger without whiskey." Captain James C. Farwell had previously served as sergeant major of the battalion's predecessor, the 1st Minnesota Regiment, mauled at Gettysburg.

Farwell was hoisting his foot above the breastworks.

"Say Johnny, give us a flesher," he would shout.

Bond considered General Birney inebriated as well.

"Colonel, advance your brigade till you develop something, you haven't developed anything yet," Birney told Irish-born Maj. Timothy O'Brien of the

47 Thomas D. Marbaker, *History of the Eleventh New Jersey Volunteers, from its Organization to Appomattox, to which is Added Experiences of Prison Life and Sketches of Individual Members* (Trenton, NJ, 1898), 199–200; Silliker, ed, *Rebel Yell and Yankee Hurrah*, 175; "The Fighting Around Petersburg—Further Particulars of the Flanking of Hancock's Corps—Movements of the Two Armies," *Daily Richmond Examiner*, June 25, 1864, says, "A Yankee General, who had stopped with several of his aids, at a small spring to procure water, narrowly escaped capture. His Adjutant and two aids were taken."

48 Letter, H. L. Patten to "Dear Col.," July 10, 1864. Association of Officers of the 20th Massachusetts Volunteer Infantry, "Reports, letters & papers appertaining to 20th Mass. Vol. Inf." (Boston, MA: Boston Public Library, 1868), 235. "Tophet" means "hell."

David Bell Birney

Library of Congress

152nd New York in a drunken manner at about 2:00 p.m.

Bond turned to the recruits.

"It is my opinion that brigade will not advance far before it develops something," he remarked.[49]

The brigade indeed did not advance far before it developed something—an increasing degree of Confederate fire. Around the same time, Wright sent a message to Birney warning of a Secessionist intrusion between II and VI corps. Morgan rode out to warn Barlow. Birney returned to his headquarters and had his staff start saddling up for an inspection of his lines.

Shortly before 3:00 p.m., Barlow summoned his reserve, Miles's brigade, from the breastworks west of the Strong house. Miles's brigade advanced, severing II Corps' connection with VI Corps. With around a mile and a half of woods and underbrush to negotiate, the brigade would require at least half an hour to arrive.

Events did not wait for Miles's brigade. Private Charles G. Barth of Company C in the Irish Brigade's 116th Pennsylvania recalled that he had wandered "out to the left and was kneeling by some water filling the company canteens when, zip! went a ball into the water." Barth looked up and saw Rebs fewer than 50 yards away. He made what he called "a blue streak for the regiment."[50]

His comrades quickly rose and formed line. The 116th's commander dispatched 1st Lt. James D. Cope and Sgt. Maj. William J. Burk to the left of the regiment's line to see if the Southerners were flanking the 116th. "In a very short time they returned in hot haste and reported the Confederates marching in column of fours past our left," recalled Capt. Charles Cosslett of Company D.[51]

49 Bond Diary and Memoir, June 22, 1864, 235–236.

50 Mulholland, *116th Regiment Pennsylvania Volunteers*, 276.

51 Ibid., 355.

A few moments later they and the rest of the men in Barlow's return heard the rebel yell's "Ki-yi."[52]

* * *

That morning, after the departure of Wilcox's division from the Dimmock Line, Brig. Gen. William Mahone went out to Battery 29, which still lacked guns. By this time the fog had burned off, and from Battery 29 he saw a Federal line digging in west of Jerusalem Plank Road and conforming itself to the Dimmock Line. Confederate engineers were altering Battery 29's embrasures to allow guns to fire westward from there and enfilade the Unionist line.

General Lee rode up, sat his horse, and looked through his field-glass. The Federal probe of the previous day toward the Weldon Railroad had prodded him into inspecting his right. Finishing his inspection, he put up his field-glass and turned to Mahone.

"General, I don't want the Federals to advance any further in this direction," said Lee.

"General Lee, do I understand that you wish me to drive them back?"

"You understand me correctly, sir."

Saluting Mahone in the most formal manner, Lee rode back toward Petersburg.

"I knew every foot of the ground in and around Petersburg," Mahone recalled.[53]

A graduate of Virginia Military Institute, Mahone had built roads as a civil engineer and then risen to the presidency of the Norfolk & Petersburg Railroad. He began the war as colonel of the 6th Virginia. As a brigadier, he suffered a wound at Second Manassas and impressed Lee as a disciplinarian. On July 2, 1863, at Gettysburg, Mahone created controversy by failing to support his division's advance on Cemetery Ridge promptly. He moved up to division command when Maj. Gen. Richard H. "Fighting Dick" Anderson advanced to command Longstreet's Corps after Lt. Gen. James Longstreet's wounding in the Wilderness on May 6.

Mahone sent scouts southward up a deep ravine that flowed northward into Lieutenants Run near his division's right. The skirmishing that was already going on waxed and waned as the Secessionist pickets probed for weaknesses in the Federal position. By the early afternoon, the scouts confirmed that the Northerners of II Corps did not occupy the ravine but that their left lay nearby. The scouts also reported a battle line—VI Corps—advancing through the woods far to the

52 Gilbert Adams Hays, comp., *Under the Red Patch: Story of the Sixty Third Pennsylvania Volunteers, 1861–1864* (Pittsburgh, 1908), 257.

53 John D. Smith, *The History of the Nineteenth Regiment of Maine Volunteer Infantry, 1862–1865* (Minneapolis, 1909), 210.

William Mahone

National Archives

south and east of the gully. A big gap stretched between the two Yankee formations. The scouts did not detect the rear line of II Corps.

"I formed my plan at once, to push my division down into this gap between the Second and Sixth Corps, and endeavor to get into the rear of the Second Corps," remembered Mahone.[54] At 1:00 p.m. he directed Sanders's, Wright's, and Weisiger's brigades of his division to the rear.

"Everyone instantly commenced surmising where was our probable destination," noted Sgt. John Francis Sale of the Norfolk Juniors, Company H of the 12th Virginia in Weisiger's brigade. Sale, who had been wounded at Malvern Hill in 1862, called Mahone "Old Porte" or "Porte" because he lived as luxuriously as the Sultan of Turkey, even employing a pastry cook.[55] Mahone did not want to arouse Northern suspicions. His soldiers shucked their baggage and pulled out of the Dimmock Line one by one. The men remaining in the Rebel fortifications spread out, filling the places of those who had departed.

Old Porte's plan called for Wilcox's division to break contact with the enemy, hasten northwestwardly by one of the paths known to Mahone, and place itself on the immediate right of the Virginian's own three brigades. In the attack that would follow, Wilcox's division would conform its movements to those of Mahone's troops.[56] As the Virginian's brigades struck the first Federal line's left, Wilcox's division would strike deep into that line's rear.

Mahone conveyed his plan to Hill through Capt. Victor Jean Baptiste Girardey, a French-born, Louisiana-educated Georgian on Mahone's staff. Girardey explained the scheme to Little Powell, who by this time had moved his headquarters out to the Davis house. The extraordinarily conscientious Girardey, hoping to prevent

54 Ibid.

55 John F. Sale Diary, June 22, 1864, John F. Sale Papers, LV.

56 John D. Young, "A Campaign With Sharpshooters," in *The Annals of the War, Written by Leading Participants, North and South* (Philadelphia, 1879), 280.

any misunderstanding about Mahone's plan, proceeded to Wilcox near the Aiken house, around a mile southeast of the Davis house. Girardey explained the plan to Wilcox.

"Captain, I don't know what I was sent here to do," said Wilcox. "General Hill promised to overtake me and give me further instructions."[57]

Shortly before 2:00 p.m., after Girardey departed from the Aiken house, Hill reached Wilcox. The corps commander accurately told Wilcox that Mahone had directions to move out and attack the Union left flank. Then Hill demonstrated that he misunderstood Mahone's plan. Little Powell ordered Scales's and Lane's brigades cross-country northwardly on a course roughly parallel to Jerusalem Plank Road, instructing Col. Thomas Jefferson Simmons, a former attorney then in command of Thomas's brigade, to send a detachment behind Scales's right leaving a man every 40 or 50 yards to facilitate communication with or support of Scales's and Lane's brigades. This northward course would take Scales's and Lane's brigades through swamps and thickets that would slow them severely. It would also bring them into contact with the enemy near the Strong house, which would slow them further. Hill then returned to the Davis house.

Wilcox recognized that Little Powell's version of Mahone's plan differed from Girardey's but naturally elected to follow the corps commander's instructions rather than the captain's directions. Scales's and Lane's brigades soon diverged to the left from the prescribed route as their skirmishers bumped up against the VI Corps line. Because of the dense undergrowth, the advance was very slow. "I communicated several times by means of my staff, with the advancing brigades, they moved under great difficulty through the woods in line, though directed to move promptly," Wilcox remembered.[58] McGowan's and Thomas's brigades remained facing VI Corps and exchanged fire with the bluecoats.

At 2:00 p.m., while Hill conferred with Wilcox, Mahone's column started up the ravine that ran northward into Lieutenants Run, concealed by the ravine's banks until reaching the open field in front of the Bailey house.[59] There, behind a line of sharpshooters, the men of Porte's three brigades formed line of battle. Sanders's

57 Letter, W. Gordon McCabe to William Mahone, July 17, 1872, in William Mahone, "A Reply to a Communication Published by Gen. C. M. Wilcox in the *New Orleans Times*, of January 1st, 1872," Folder 2, William Mahone Papers, LV.

58 Wilcox, Wilcox Report, "Petersburg," 3.

59 The owner, Bailey, leased to one Johnson (sometimes misspelled "Johnston"), and consequently the farm appears under one of the three aforesaid names on contemporary maps. "The Fighting Around Petersburg—Further Particulars of the Flanking of Hancock's Corps—Movements of the Two Armies," *Daily Richmond Examiner*, June 25, 1864. I have employed "Bailey" here to avoid confusion because of the deployment of Bushrod Johnson's division on the farm later. See this chapter, n. 60, *infra*.

Alabama Brigade stood on Mahone's left, facing most of the Irish Brigade. Wright's Georgia Brigade constituted Mahone's right, fronting the left of the Irish Brigade and the right of MacDougall's brigade. Weisiger's Virginia Brigade deployed 400 yards behind the Georgia Brigade.

Elements of Bushrod Johnson's division moved out from reserve behind Field's and Kershaw's divisions into the Dimmock Line east of the Lead Works in support of Mahone's troops. These elements included Wise's Virginia Brigade, Elliott's South Carolina Brigade, and Ransom's North Carolina Brigade minus its 49th North Carolina.[60]

Around 3:00 p.m., Lane's and Scales's brigades were struggling northward. Thomas's and McGowan's brigades were pushing VI Corps eastward toward the Williams farm. Mahone began his advance eastward on the Bailey farm. His skirmishers struck Barlow's pickets in a skirt of woods about 600 yards east of the Bailey house. Driving the enemy sentinels through the timber, the Confederates passed enemy rifle pits. Farther on, the Secessionists encountered the Union breastworks, fully occupied by a line of battle. While Mahone's strike force advanced, the rest of his division's picket line began a series of pushes southward against the bluecoat sentinels north of the forward line of II Corps.

The 1st Maryland Artillery, Dement's battery, left its caissons behind and rumbled forward, halting near the Bailey barn without unlimbering. Federal shells passed over the battery, which the battalion commander accompanied. He and the battery's commander decided to deploy upon a rise on Mahone's far left, facing open country. The battery commander called up his caissons, then sortied. The gunners dashed across a field toward the crest.

60 Hewett, et al., eds., *Supplement to the Official Records*, 7:278; *OR* 40, 1:761; Thomas T. Wiatt, ed., *Rev. William E. Wiatt, The Life and Times of a Confederate Chaplain and Related Family Stories* (Morrisville, NC, 2018), 182. Elliott's brigade also went out to the Dimmock Line. Smith Kitchens Diary, June 22–23, 1864, Winthrop University, Rock Hill, SC; *OR* 40, 2:376; Mickey Beckham, ed., *A Confederate Soldier's Eloquent War: The Complete Diary of Samuel Lowry, Enlistment, Hardship, Battles and Death; Yorkville to Columbia, Charleston to Kiawah, to Manassas, to Petersburg, Finally Borne Home by Servant Henry Avery* (Charleston, SC, 2008), 91. Johnson's Tennessee Brigade and Gracie's Alabama Brigades did not go out to the Bailey farm because Beauregard had ordered them to the north side of the Appomattox on June 19. *OR* 40, 2:668–669, 678; William Henry Harder Memoir, Tennessee State Library and Archives, Nashville, TN, 525. Ransom's Brigade had received orders to relieve Colquitt's brigade of Hoke's division the previous day but after the 49th North Carolina relieved the pickets of Colquitt's brigade, the rest of Ransom's brigade got instructions to support Mahone and went out to the Bailey farm. *OR* 40, 2:678; Clark, *North Carolina Regiments*, 3:367; T. H. Pearce and Selby A. Daniels, eds., *Diary of Captain Henry A. Chambers* (Wilmington, NC, 1983), 205; Washington L. Dunn, Diary of Washington L. Dunn, Company A, 27th Georgia Infantry, June 21, 1864, Confederate Reminiscences and Letters 1861–1865, Volume XVI, Georgia Division United Daughters of the Confederacy, 2001, GDAH; James Carson Elliott, *The Southern Soldier Boy: The Experiences of a Confederate Soldier of the 56th North Carolina Regiment During the American Civil War* (Driffield, UK, 2010), 34.

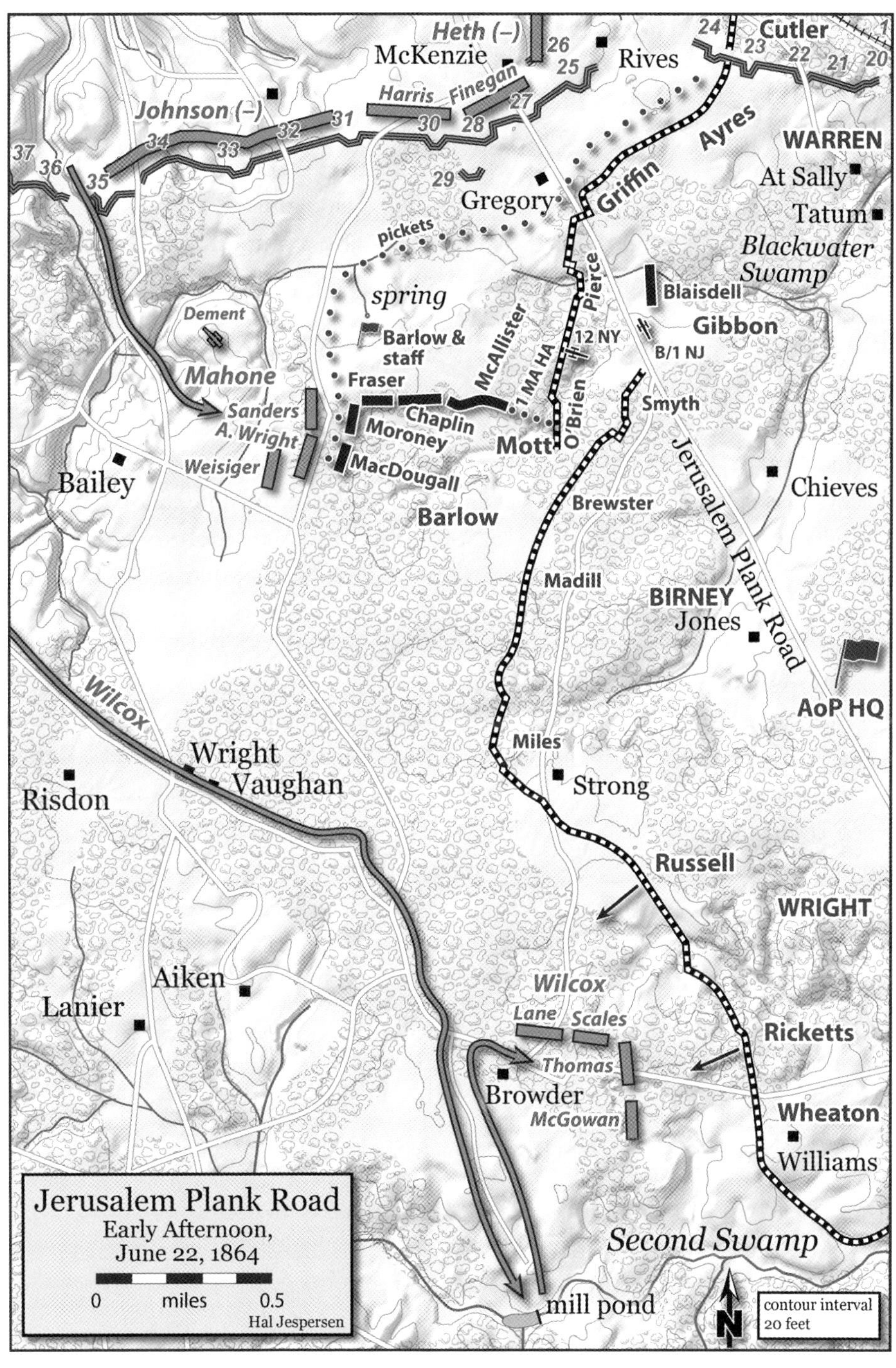

Heth (–)
McKenzie
Rives
Cutler
Johnson (–)
Harris
Finegan
WARREN
At Sally
Tatum
Gregory
Griffin
Ayres
pickets
Blackwater Swamp
spring
Pierce
Blaisdell
Dement
Barlow & staff
McAllister
12 NY
Gibbon
B/1 NJ
Mahone
Fraser
1 MA HA
Sanders
Chaplin
Smyth
A. Wright
Moroney
O'Brien
Mott
Weisiger
MacDougall
Bailey
Chieves
Barlow
Brewster
Jerusalem Plank Road
Madill
BIRNEY
Jones
AoP HQ
Wilcox
Miles
Wright
Vaughan
Risdon
Strong
Russell
WRIGHT
Aiken
Lanier
Wilcox
Lane
Scales
Ricketts
Thomas
Browder
McGowan
Wheaton
Williams
Second Swamp
mill pond
contour interval 20 feet

Jerusalem Plank Road
Early Afternoon,
June 22, 1864
0 miles 0.5
Hal Jespersen

At the foot of the rise, the guns had to cross a small ditch. "As the wheels of my gun struck the ditch bank, one of the horses fell dead, either from heart failure, or stricken by a bullet," remembered Cpl. John W. F. Hatton of Dement's battery. "This caused some delay, and mine was not the first gun to fire on this occasion." The other guns got off a round before Hatton's joined them rapidly throwing solid shot. "Rifle balls and bursting shells and flying solid shot were playing a lively tune around us," Hatton recalled. Dement's battery and the Rebel artillerists in the Dimmock Line blasted the Yankee batteries and the Unionist troops in the woods. The Marylanders unlimbered so close to the Irish Brigade's breastworks that half a dozen of the young gunners from Baltimore and the Eastern Shore suffered wounds. "Our men were falling, and ammunition growing scarce," Hatton remembered. The Ambulance Corps took off the wounded as fast as they fell, and the battery commander dispatched riders to hasten the caissons. At this point, Alabama infantry arrived on the battery's right. "As the infantry charged in with the yell, an officer stationed to the left of my gun gave the word to cease firing," recalled Hatton. "My gun was loaded—I turned the breech-screw with twist thus elevating the muzzle to its highest [angle]—jumped aside and exclaimed 'Fire!'" The last cannonball fired by the battery flew high over the field.[61]

On the right of Dement's battery, the Alabama Brigade pressed through the timber until it reached the open space. Though Mahone had aimed for the gap between II and VI corps, he had not struck it yet. Across the field from the Alabamians stood the Irish Brigade in its breastworks. The Irish Brigade unleashed a terrific fire on the Alabamians. On the Alabama Brigade's left, the 8th Alabama lost three color corporals to the storm of Federal fire.

The 11th Alabama's Brig. Gen. John C. C. Sanders, 24 years old, led the brigade. He had left his studies at the University of Alabama in April 1861 to enlist as a private in the 11th's Company C, the Confederate Guards. About 75 yards from the breastworks, "My horse was struck with a Minnie ball just behind the . . . shoulder and just in front of my leg," he recalled. "She was disabled so that I had to dismount and go on foot."[62] His troops halted and lay down in the face of the fire from the Irish Brigade.

61 J. W. F. Hatton Diary and Memoir, June 20, 1864, LOC, 606. Though mistakenly reported dead in 1862 in W. W. Goldsborough, *The Maryland Line in the Confederate Army, 1861–1865* (Baltimore, 1900), 261), Hatton had to seek a writ of habeas corpus in October 1864 to be released from service on expiration of his enlistment. "Local Matters, Confederate States District Court," *Daily Richmond Dispatch*, Oct. 27, 1864, p. 2, col. 2.

62 Letter, John C. C. Sanders to "Dear Ma," June 28, 1864, Sanders Collection, W. S. Hoole Library, University of Alabama, Tuscaloosa, AL.

Ambrose Ransom "Rans" Wright
Library of Congress

To the right of Sanders's brigade, the Georgia Brigade fared no better at hitting the gap between II and VI corps. The Georgians confronted on their left the Irish Brigade and on their right MacDougall's brigade, which overlapped them. Brigadier General Ambrose Ransom "Rans" Wright, an Augusta, Georgia lawyer and the Georgia Brigade's commander, began on the left of his brigade, with the 48th Georgia. While that regiment formed line of battle, he rode up a small rise with his staff in plain view of the Unionist pickets and not very far from them.

"Shoot them --------- officers," said the Federal skirmishers.[63]

A shower of bullets followed but Wright proceeded down his brigade's line unhurt.

The 48th Georgia formed line on the immediate right of the Alabama Brigade as soon as the regiment came out of the ravine.[64] The 3rd Georgia deployed farther right. "We formed a line on a corner field at the edge of the woods in our front," remembered 2nd Lt. Alfred H. Zachry of the 3rd Georgia's Company H, the Young Guards. The 3rd's battle line advanced as if the men did not expect to meet anything more than a picket line. Riding a gray horse, 1st Lt. John "Josh" Evans led the Young Guards.

"Shoot the man on the gray horse," his men heard a Federal say.

"Josh, they will shoot you," said Girardey, who had returned from his mission to Hill and Wilcox. Girardey had formerly served as adjutant of the Georgia Brigade.

Evans dismounted at once.

63 J. A., "From Wright's Brigade," *Southern Watchman* (Athens, GA), July 20, 1864, p. 4, col. 2. The source has only hyphens but nine hyphens suggests that the word was "Goddamned." For the identity of "J. A.," see Lillian Henderson, *Roster of the Confederate Soldiers of Georgia, 1861–1865*, 5 vols. (Hapeville, GA, 1959–1964), 5:124.

64 W. A. B., "Letter from the 48th Georgia." *Augusta* (GA) *Daily Constitutionalist*, July 20, 1864, beyondthecrater.com. Retrieved June 15, 2024. For the identity of "W. A. B.," see Henderson, *Roster of the Confederate Soldiers of Georgia, 1861–1865*, 5:177.

The 3rd Georgia's men lay down quietly until they could see the bluecoated skirmishers through the brush, then fired and raised the rebel yell. "They went like chaff before a strong wind," recalled Zachry.[65]

The 2nd Georgia Battalion formed line on the 3rd Georgia's right. The 10th Georgia Battalion emerged from the ravine on the 2nd's right along the edge of a thick wood full of Unionist pickets. The 10th's skirmishers immediately engaged these Northerners. Rans Wright, who wore his hair long, busied himself aligning his men. Private Thomas W. Methvin of the 10th's Company E remembered that "all at once a Yankee out in front of us called to some of his men to shoot that 'long-haired man'; he wanted his hat." Hearing this, Wright turned his horse.

"Forward, Third Georgia Brigade!" he ordered.[66]

Wright's Georgians advanced.

The 48th Georgia's Company I, the Wilson Tigers, "with its usual impetuosity, bound[ed] forth with a 'yell' towards the enemy's breastworks," recalled Capt. William A. Bachelor, the company commander, who had enlisted as sergeant major and suffered wounds at Malvern Hill and Gettysburg. Private George L. Blackstone immediately fell, pierced through the lungs by a Minie ball.

"Lieutenant, I am wounded, but go ahead boys," he said before he died.[67]

"We then drove the enemy out of their rifle pits and held them until we got off all our wounded," recalled Pvt. John Anderson of the 48th's Company C, the Georgia Light Guards, farther right than the Tigers.[68]

The Georgia Brigade "with the deafening Southern yell, leaped the fence and dashed into the thick undergrowth leading the advance," remembered 1st Lt. Lawson H. Carter, the 10th Georgia Battalion's adjutant, who had enlisted as a private in its Company C, the Zollicoffer Rifles of Sumter County. "The double line of Yankee skirmishers fled before us as on we pressed, through the dense thicket, making the woods ring with cheers, to the assault on the enemy's breastworks."[69]

Private Methvin recalled, "We had not gone fifty steps before we captured some Yankees."[70]

As the Georgians proceeded, they encountered increasingly heavier fire.

65 Alfred Zachry, "Four Shots for the Cause," *Civil War Times Illustrated* (*CWTI*) XXXIII, no. 5 (Nov./Dec. 1994): 105.

66 T. V. Methvin, "In the Wilderness Campaign," *CV* XXIII (1915): 455.

67 W. A. B., "Letter from the 48th Georgia."

68 J. A., "From Wright's Brigade."

69 L. H. Carter, "For the Daily Telegraph," *Macon Daily Telegraph*, July 9, 1864, p. 2, cols. 3–4.

70 Methvin, "In the Wilderness Campaign," *CV* 23:455.

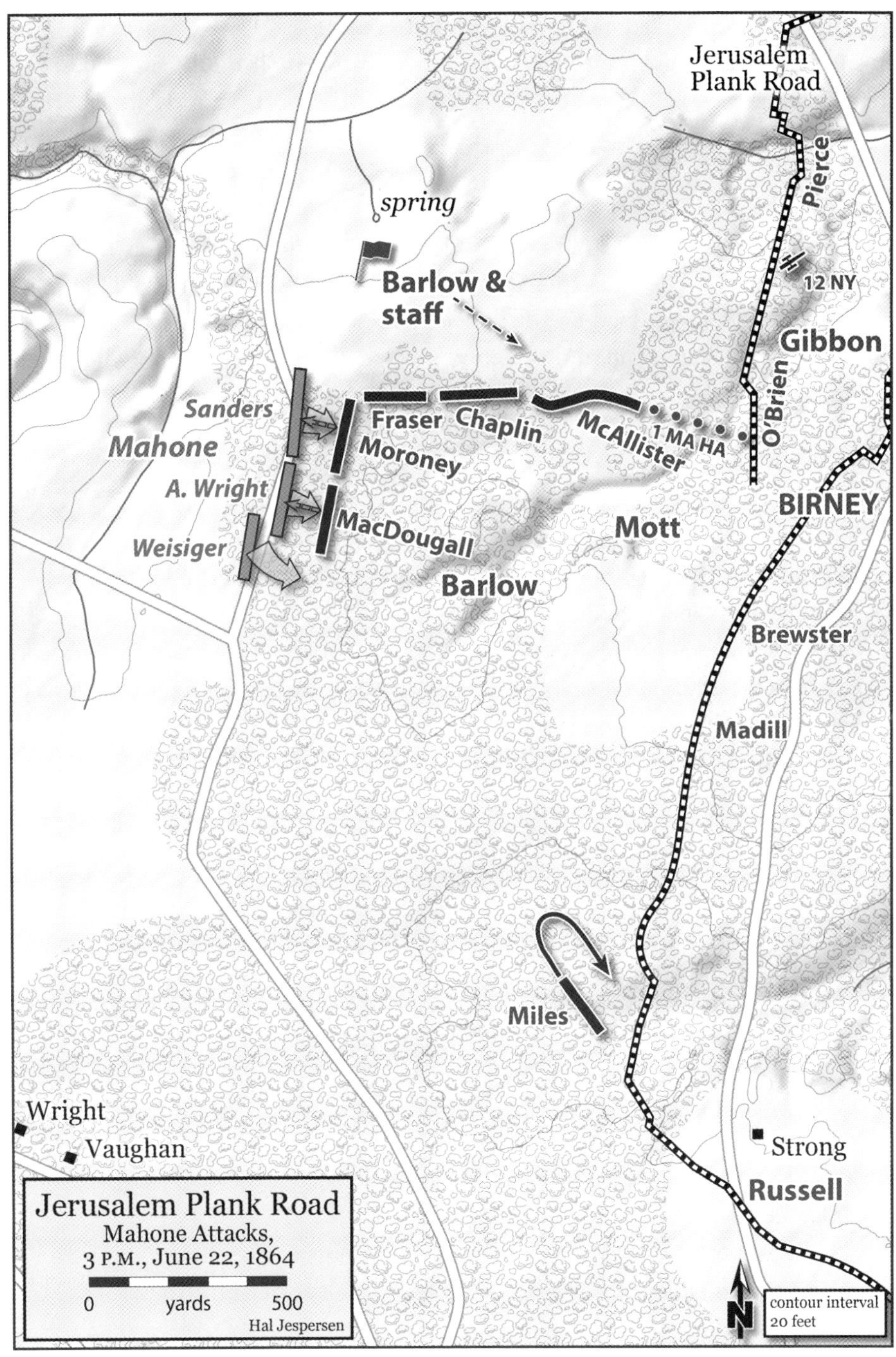

Jerusalem Plank Road
Mahone Attacks,
3 P.M., June 22, 1864
0 yards 500
Hal Jespersen

The left of the Georgia Brigade came out into the same open field as the Alabama Brigade and received the same concentrated fire from the breastworks of the Irish Brigade. The Georgians suffered severely. The 48th charged "under a most galling fire ever endured by men," remembered the 48th's Col. William Gibson, Rans Wright's law partner, wounded at Malvern Hill and wounded and captured at Gettysburg.[71]

"In that open and level old field did [Pvts. Eli Beasley and Thomas J. Sanders of the Wilson Tigers] stand exposed to the missiles of death that were falling thick and fast around them, load and fire their rifles with much deliberation (and no doubt with much effect upon the enemy) until they both fell pierced with Minnie balls, Eli through the heart and T. J. Sanders through the forehead, resulting fatally," recalled Bachelor.[72]

Private James P. Verdery remembered, "T. J. Sanders was shot through the head his brains being knoked out by the ball."[73]

Between the 3rd Georgia and the 10th Battalion, the 2nd Georgia Battalion suffered heavily. To the immediate right of the 2nd, MacDougall's New Yorkers blasted the 10th Georgia Battalion, shooting down Adjutant Carter, the color bearer, a captain, and many others. "All the color guard except one, were wounded," Carter remembered. "An order was here passed down from the right to fall back, and the line was much exposed in falling back to the woods."[74]

The crisis of the battle had arrived.

Mahone and Barlow had crossed swords before. Both had undergone their baptism of fire at Fair Oaks (or, to Southerners, Seven Pines) on June 1, 1862.[75] There Barlow had led the 61st New York and, after Brig. Gen. Oliver O. Howard's wounding, Howard's brigade. The Red Club commander had distinguished himself on that occasion by repulsing Mahone's brigade, which fell back ignominiously.

They would soon find out who would prevail on their second deadly encounter.

71 James M. Folsom, *Heroes and Martyrs of Georgia, Georgia's Record in the Revolution of 1861* (Macon, GA, 1864), 91–92; Russell Brown, "Ambrose Wright, 1826–1872," New Georgia Encyclopedia, georgiaencyclopedia.org, retrieved Sept. 4, 2023.

72 W. A. B., "Letter from the 48th Georgia."

73 Letter, James Paul Verdery to "Dear Father Mother & all," June 25, 1864, Eugene and James Verdery Letters, Duke University.

74 L. H. Carter, "For the Daily Telegraph."

75 That is, as far as land combat was concerned; Mahone had come under naval gunfire on May 15, 1862, at the first battle of Drewry's Bluff. Horn, *The Petersburg Regiment*, 45–47.

Chapter Five

"Run Like the Devil"

IN THEIR park near the Jones house, the II Corps reserve artillerymen had been listening since just after dawn to the sounds of skirmishing in the direction of Petersburg. Skirmishing continued "until about the middle of the afternoon, when the firing increased to rapid volleys, indicating hot work ahead," remembered Cpl. John Davis Billings of the 10th Massachusetts Battery.[1]

The change from picket fire to volleys alarmed Barlow, who was still washing his feet. Abandoning all hope of progressing farther that day and focusing on damage control, he immediately dispatched orders to Miles's brigade to double-quick back to the rear line of Union works and re-establish connection with VI Corps. Then Barlow put on his socks and shoes and galloped toward the rear Federal line. His withdrawal commenced what became known as "Barlow's skedaddle."[2]

Meade too, in his new headquarters across Jerusalem Plank Road from the Jones house, recognized the significance of the change in the sound of the firing. Only now did he remember Grant's idea about the reserves of V and IX corps. The Army of the Potomac's commander at 3:15 p.m. ordered Warren and Burnside to prepare their commands to advance or send a portion to the left.

About the same time, Mahone committed his old brigade, Weisiger's Virginia Brigade. When the two bluecoat brigades in the return stopped the Alabamians and

1 John Davis Billings, *The History of the Tenth Massachusetts Battery of Light Artillery in the War of the Rebellion: formerly of the Third Corps and afterwards of Hancock's Second Corps, Army of the Potomac, 1862–1865* (Boston, 1909), 290.

2 J. W. Muffly, ed., *The Story of Our Regiment, A History of the 148th Pennsylvania Vols.* (Des Moines, 1904), 740.

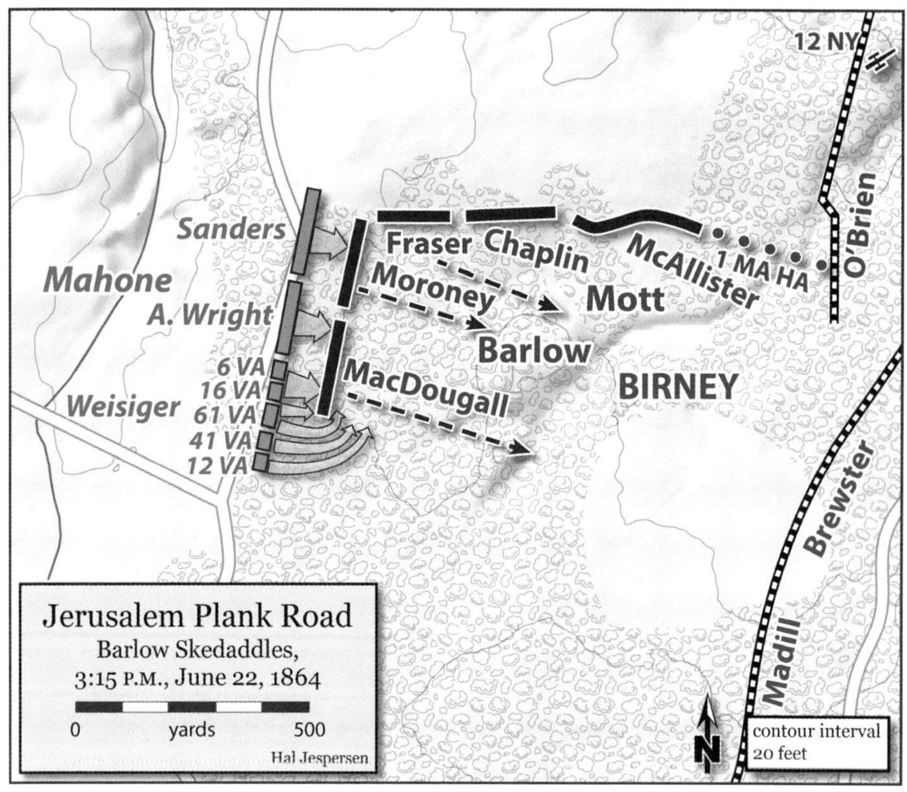

Georgians, Weisiger's brigade had gone only a few steps forward. Porte deployed his old brigade on the Georgia Brigade's right. By the right flank, the Virginians double-quicked into position with the 6th Virginia on the left, then the 16th Virginia, the 61st Virginia, the 41st Virginia, and the 12th Virginia, the Petersburg Regiment, to the right. Union fire wounded a member of the Petersburg New Grays, the 12th Virginia's Company C. The Virginians charged through the underbrush, sweeping aside the Northern skirmish line in front of them. "During this advance I picked up a new spade and took it along, as our pioneer corps was very much in need of such instruments," remembered the 61st's Lt. Col. William H. Stewart, who had suffered wounds at Salem Church, Spotsylvania, and Cold Harbor.[3]

The Virginians on the left of Weisiger's brigade ran into Colonel MacDougall's New Yorkers behind breastworks and received a scorching fire. Acting Major Thaddeus G. Williams, a former farmer in the 6th on the Virginia Brigade's extreme left, received a mortal wound in the charge. "A minnie ball passed through

3 William H. Stewart, *A Pair of Blankets: War-Time History in Letters to the Young People of the South* (Wilmington, NC, 1990), 148.

his head above the right eye," recalled his brother-in-law, Pvt. Walter B. Wellons of Company H, a former mechanic wounded at Second Manassas.[4]

Private William S. Hubbard in Company A, the Marion Rangers, of the 16th Virginia immediately to the 6th's right, remembered encountering "the hottest fire that I ever was in since the war commenced."[5] Private John S. Wills, a former clerk in the 16th's Company C, the Virginia Defenders, who had been captured at Crampton's Gap in 1862, fell with a chest wound and offered Pvt. Phillip Miller of the adjacent 61st's Company D, the Jackson Light Infantry, who was serving in the Ambulance Corps, twelve dollars in gold to take him off the field. Miller declined, telling Mills that his first duty lay to the wounded of the 61st. Miller promised that after he had fulfilled that duty, he would return for Mills, but under no circumstances would he accept Mills's money.

Farther south, other men of the 61st Virginia finally found the gap between the two Union corps, as well as the gap between the two lines of II Corps. Lieutenant Colonel Stewart remembered, "Our regiment, about the colors or center, struck the enemy's newly-made earthworks, and by wheeling the right half of the regiment to the left, we were at once in their front and rear, fighting hand to hand with bayonets, butts of muskets, swords and pistols." Just as the right of the 61st wheeled around the earthworks, a captain of Company A, the Jackson Grays, fell shot through the head near Stewart and died instantly. Stewart's spade came in handy at the earthworks. "I saw a man with his musket to his shoulder, who had not yet realized that we had surrounded them, aiming at one of our men over in front of his works," Stewart recalled. "I ran up and struck him a hard blow on the side of his head, forcing him to drop his rifle and surrender unconditionally."[6] The hand-to-hand fighting lasted only briefly before the bluecoats surrendered and the butternuts held the works.

The whole right half of Weisiger's brigade pivoted on the center of the 61st. "We faced by the left flank & moved down on the enemy and drove them pell mell out of their temporary breastworks made of wood," recalled 1st Lt. James E. Phillips of the 12th Virginia's Company G, the Richmond Grays, on the brigade's extreme right.[7] A master tinner, Phillips had been captured at Crampton's Gap on September 14, 1862. As the Virginians flanked MacDougall's New Yorkers, the Georgians facing MacDougall's front returned to the charge.

4 Letter, W. B. Wellons to Mary Williams, June 23, 1864, 6th Virginia File, FNBP, Fredericksburg, VA.

5 Greene, *A Campaign of Giants*, 1:248.

6 Stewart, *A Pair of Blankets*, 148.

7 James Eldred Phillips, "Sixth Corporal," James Eldred Phillips Papers, VMHC, 58.

Barlow's division "melted away like ice in the sun," 1st Sgt. James Edward "Eddie" Whitehorne of the 12th's Company F, the Huger Grays, recorded.[8] Whitehorne had been wounded at Gettysburg on July 2, 1863. The delays deploying Mott's and Barlow's divisions in the woods had worked against the Federals. If Miles's brigade had arrived to extend the left of Barlow's return, Weisiger's brigade could have been stopped as abruptly as the Alabamians and Georgians. The further progress of the Confederates would then have depended on the arrival of Wilcox's division or the commitment of the elements of Bushrod Johnson's division.

Instead, as Lt. Col. Francis Amasa Walker, the assistant adjutant general of II Corps, later commented, "The whole operation [was] like that of an expert mechanician who touches some critical point with a fine instrument, in exactly the right way, producing an effect seemingly altogether out of proportion to the force exerted."[9]

* * *

MacDougall's New Yorkers crumbled first. "Suddenly from three directions the bullets came cutting savagely about us," recalled Chaplain Simons in the 125th New York. "Such was the unformed state of the line, and so bewildering were the lines of fire that the men did not attempt any defense, but broke at once." Strenuous efforts to rally a line at first seemed successful, but the line started for the rear at the double-quick, instead of toward the Rebels. Many New Yorkers fell into enemy hands by retreating along a road cut through the woods. "The rebel line had crossed it and caught our men in the meshes of their own skill and of our folly," Simon recalled. Others headed southeastward for the second line of Union works. "Any halting on that rapid run was quickly replaced with another turn at the double-quick as the bullets came buzzing and shrieking by," Simons remembered.[10] The 125th's colonel had returned to duty despite a wound received six days earlier and barely escaped capture.

The Confederates flanked the left of the 57th New York of MacDougall's brigade. Private Kelly recollected, "bullets came 'zipping' through the woods—invisible shafts of death from unseen hands." A brief lull followed. Kelly's company learned from the next company's first sergeant and temporary commander that one of that company's men had just been killed. Secessionist bullets flew fast again.

8 Fletcher L. Elmore, Jr., ed., *Diary of J. E. Whitehorne 1st Sergt., Co. "F" 12th Va. Infantry A. P. Hills 3rd Corps A. N. Va.* (Louisville, KY, 1995), 51.

9 Walker, *History of the Second Army Corps*, 546.

10 Simons, *One Hundred and Twenty-Fifth New York State Volunteers*, 229.

The New Yorkers began to shoot back though they could see no Confederates in the hazy woods. "I pulled the trigger, the cap snapped and as I turned to put on another, I saw the line on the left giving way, and the Irish Brigade on the right getting ready to go, for they were rising from the ground," Kelly recalled. "A bullet crushed a sapling in front of me, so I hurriedly primed my gun, aimed at the green space in the direction of the foe, fired and fell back." He realized that he was alone. "The only man to be seen was the dead man on the ground, with a handkerchief over his face," Kelly recollected. "I remember how, in my flight, I hopped over many fat haversacks which had been thrown away."[11]

The 111th New York's men heard a loud Rebel yell from their left. Bullets flew at them from front, left, and rear. Company A's Cpl. Thomas Geer remembered that the "trees were so thick we could not see far and the rebels got us nearly surrounded before we knew it." Troops to the regiment's left broke and bolted for the rear. The 111th took what its men termed "leg bail" and joined the stampede. "I tell you the way we got up and got out of the woods was a caution," Geer recalled. "The rebs tried to halt us. They sayed hold on yanks, we won't hurt you, but we couldn't see it."[12]

MacDougall ordered his brigade to withdraw. "Being largely outnumbered, besides being outflanked—we were obliged to fall back," he remembered. "Immediately [I] announced the retreat with my Brigade, fighting as I fell back to keep the enemy from closing in upon us and capture our whole force."[13]

The 126th New York of MacDougall's brigade kept firing as it retreated but continued losing men as well. The color bearer fell into enemy hands. Another soldier snatched the banner but a ball killed him. Still another member of the color guard collapsed with a bullet in the thigh. The Confederates captured the colors.

Captain Morris Brown Jr. of the 126th's Company A commanded the regiment that day. Though he had recently advised his brother to resign rather than accept a commission, Brown wanted a major's commission. In fact, he had received a lieutenant colonel's commission, but it had followed home the corpse of the regiment's previous lieutenant colonel in his valise, leaving Brown still a captain. With the 126th collapsing, Brown tried to rally the regiment as men fell all around him. As the Secessionists closed in, he fell when a bullet struck him near the right ear and came out near his forehead. A Southern soldier poured water on Brown's wound, but MacDougall thought Brown died instantly.

11 Frederick, *Fifty-Seventh New York*, 254–255.

12 Husk, *The 111th New York Volunteer Infantry*, 146.

13 Mahood, *"Written in Blood,"* 287.

The flight of MacDougall's New Yorkers bared the left of the Irish Brigade farther up the return. As Virginians and Georgians charged into the rear of the Irish Brigade, the Georgians and Alabamians in front of the Irishmen picked themselves up and resumed their advance. The Wilson Tigers of the 48th Georgia, taking careful aim as they fired, pressed on toward the breastworks of the Irish Brigade. There, remembered Captain Bachelor, "for our brief work, we captured many prisoners, and passed over more dead and wounded Yankees than we ever did before on the same space of ground."[14]

General Sanders, one of the first to scale the Federal works, nearly lost his life. "When the Confederates mounted the works most of the enemy cried out 'we surrender'—some, however, were disposed to keep up the fire and a Federal soldier seeing that Genl S. was an officer aimed his gun at his breast only a few feet off," remembered the general's brother, Surgeon William Henry Sanders of the 11th Alabama. "A Federal officer, feeling that it would be a violation of honor, and happening to be within reach, turned away the barrel of the gun."[15]

At first, the skirmish line of the 116th Pennsylvania in the Irish Brigade advanced. "We moved out and met them, and then the woods resounded with the crashing volleys of musketry," recalled Sergeant Clear. "We moved towards them slowly, our boys dropping wounded or killed at every step." Suddenly fire came from the rear, "so we wheeled around and charged through them," Clear remembered. "I reached our works in safety but a great [many] was taken prisoners, wounded and killed," he recalled.[16]

Lieutenant Cope and Sergeant Major Burk rushed back from their reconnaissance and had little time to report before the 116th came under fire from the left flank and rear. Men ran in every direction, some straight into the Southerners. Others slowly began to return fire. Cope and Burk fell into Confederate hands.

After ten minutes, Capt. Richard M. Moroney of the 69th New York State Volunteers, the brigade's commander, ordered the brigade to retire. The 116th departed by the right flank, abandoning its dead and wounded. Still firing, the regiment's able-bodied charged through the Rebels in the rear. The Secessionists surrounded a group that hid in some laurel bushes inhabited by wild hogs. The grunting and squealing drew Confederate fire that hit both hogs and men.

Captain Charles Cosslett of the 116th's Company E, wounded in the Wilderness and at Cold Harbor, fell back with the rest of the front line. "Being

14 W. A. B., "Letter from the 48th Georgia."

15 William Henry Sanders Papers, ADAH, Montgomery, AL.

16 Menge and Shimrak, *Civil War Diary of Daniel Chisholm*, 25.

lame I could not get along very fast and when I got out of the woods and walked over a field I came to a partly constructed breastwork," he recalled. "I crossed over this into another wood with dense brush so thick I could not see through it." There he met around 30 men from different regiments listening to voices coming from behind but unable to see the talkers. "Some thought they were our men who were talking, but others said they were Johnnies," Cosslett remembered. "However, no one seemed inclined to find out the real state of affairs." Finally, Cosslett and a young sergeant in another New York regiment volunteered. They pushed through the undergrowth to an open space where they found a Confederate line of battle a few paces away. The Southerners pointed their rifles at the Federals and told them to surrender.

"It is no use trying to get away; we have been going behind you fellows for two hours," the Rebels said.[17]

Private Allen Landis of the 116th's Company C, whose brother in the same company had fallen by Fredericksburg's stone wall, wrote that the "Rebels . . . had worked around us and were right in our rear, blazing away and cheering like wild men." Taken by surprise, Company C offered little resistance. "You can bet high that there was some 'skedaddling' done about that time," Landis remembered. Many thought it too dangerous to run the gauntlet of Confederate fire and lay down and waited for the butternuts to gobble them up. "I have long since made up my mind that they shall not capture me as long as my legs are able to carry me out of such places," Landis recalled. "I would very frequently get off the right road and run in the exact direction of the rebs, which I would soon find out, and turn my course." Though struck by a bullet in the right leg, it only broke the skin and badly bruised the flesh. Landis kept hoofing it toward the second line of works.[18]

Fired on from three directions, the other regiments of the Irish Brigade fled. "We were attacked in front, on the left flank, and in rear, compelling us to retire in confusion to the works constructed the night previous," remembered Capt. Robert H. Milliken of the 69th New York.[19]

"We were repulsed, being attacked in front, flank, and rear, fell back to our breast-work" recalled Lt. Col. Denis F. Burke of the 88th New York, Mrs. Meagher's Own.[20]

The collapse of the two brigades in the return uncovered the left of Fraser's brigade in its east-west line. The Alabamians and Georgians rolled up Fraser's

17 Mulholland, *116th Regiment Pennsylvania Volunteers*, 356.

18 Letter, Allen Landis to "Dear Father," July 2, 1864, Allen Landis Letters, LOC.

19 *OR* 40, 1:349.

20 Ibid., 351.

brigade while the Virginians swung through the woods between the two Unionist lines and gobbled up prisoners sprinting for the rear.

The 66th New York, the Governor's Guard, had just gone out on the skirmish line. Second Lieutenant Simon Pincus of the 66th's Company G had enlisted as a corporal in the 66th's Company I and suffered wounds at Antietam and Fredericksburg before reenlisting as a veteran. "We had scarcely got deployed when the enemy [flanked] us and got into our rear," he remembered. The captain "then commanding the regiment, ordered every man to take care of himself."[21] The regiment retreated to the second line of Federal works. Wounded, the captain fell into enemy hands. The 66th emerged from its flight with Pincus in command.

The other men of Fraser's brigade lay resting in the dense woods where they had halted and stacked arms a couple hours earlier. Colonel Fraser and his staff formed a group just behind the line. Adjutant Joseph Wendel Muffly of the 148th Pennsylvania, a former student at Dickinson Seminary, had enlisted as a private in its Company B and suffered wounds at Gettysburg and on the Po River. "We soon began to hear a racket on our left, and presently a scattering fire of musketry was heard," Muffly recalled. The volume of fire increased, and the line on the left started melting away. "Now an occasional minie sang by us or cut a twig close by, and then a line of battle of the enemy appeared on the brow of a hill away on the left," remembered Muffly. "They came steadily on, moving right up on our rear, firing rapidly, and our line kept melting away, the men passing rapidly to the rear." The regiment's officers failed to issue orders. No one knew Barlow's whereabouts. "As the enemy approached the left of our brigade, I asked Colonel Fraser what he intended to do," Muffly remembered. "His reply was that his orders were, to remain in position until further orders from the division commander."

Captain James H. Hamlin of the 145th Pennsylvania rode up and saluted Fraser.

"Have you any orders for my regiment?" Hamlin said.

"No, sir; my orders are to remain here," Fraser said. "You can do as you think best."

Hamlin saluted and rode to the front of his regiment.

"Fall in—Take arms—Forward by file right—March," he said.

Hamlin rode off at the head of the 145th, still in regular order, toward the rear line of Federal works. By this time, little remained of Fraser's brigade except its commander and his staff. "I again appealed to the Colonel for orders, but he declined to assume any responsibility, saying, however, that the staff was free to do as we chose," Muffly recalled. "Having no desire for prison life, I said, 'Gentlemen,

21 Ibid., 357.

I think we had better follow the troops,' and with a hasty good-bye we left the Colonel to the courtesies of Mahone's troop."[22]

Muffly remembered that as the Confederates flanked Fraser's brigade, "Corporal Samuel R. Gettig, of Company A, was struck on his knapsack with a minie ball, which, knocking him down and passing through his wardrobe, penetrated his Bible which he had carefully stowed away in the knapsack and buried itself in its sacred pages." Gettig picked himself up and kept heading back toward the second line of Federal works.[23]

Chaos reigned in the timber through which Fraser's men fled. "The Federal troops were willing enough to run, but the difficulty was, they didn't know which way to start," recalled Mahone. "We captured those who hesitated and those who could not run as fast as my men."[24]

Second Lieutenant John H. Harpster of the 148th Pennsylvania's Company G was serving as an ambulance officer. He had suffered a wound at Gettysburg. Orders sent him to the front when the heavy firing began. Riding along a road, he encountered a Rebel force that had taken some of his regiment's men prisoner. Among the captives he recognized Company G's Pvt. Brice David Brisbin, also wounded at Gettysburg. Harpster feared that Brisbin might give him away, but Brisbin kept his mouth shut. Harpster's garb of corduroy trousers without a blouse led the Secessionist officer in charge to believe Harpster a fellow Confederate. The officer asked Harpster which way to take the prisoners. Anxious to get away, Harpster directed the Johnnies into a byway and turned to go back the way he had come. Suddenly he rode into another body of enemy troops. Ordering the officer in charge of them to clear the road because a battery was following him, Harpster put spurs to his sorrel and escaped. Brisbin continued on his way toward Richmond.[25]

The 53rd Pennsylvania also belonged to Fraser's brigade. When the enemy opened fire on the 53rd from the left and rear, "We sprang to our guns were ordered to about face and marched back to the right of where we came in in order to pass the Rebs and reach the line we left," recalled Company G's Cpl. Leavitt W. Cushing, a farmer from Potter County wounded at Fredericksburg and Gettysburg. Forming the 53rd into a battle wedge, its commander directed fire to the left and right. The regiment fought its way through the butternuts and back to the second line of the corps near Jerusalem Plank Road. "The brush and small timber were so

22 Muffly, ed., *148th Pennsylvania*, 274–275.

23 Ibid., 157. "He still retains the book with the missile embedded therein and has unbounded confidence in the Bible as a life preserver, here and hereafter," Muffly recalled. Ibid.

24 Smith, *Nineteenth Regiment of Maine Volunteer Infantry*, 210.

25 Muffly, ed., *148th Pennsylvania*, 718–719.

thick it was impossible to keep in line, and were soon entirely broken up, and every man got back the best way he could," remembered Cushing.[26]

Riding out to convey Horatio Wright's warning to Barlow, Lieutenant Colonel Morgan encountered Barlow's men skedaddling. By the time that Birney and the rest of his staff had all mounted for their inspection of the lines, they heard a tremendous firing in front. "[General Birney] ordered me to ride out as fast as I could and ascertain the cause," recalled Lieutenant Armes.[27]

While the three forward brigades of Barlow's division disintegrated, Miles's brigade countermarched to the works built the previous night that the brigade had just left. "[W]e advance to the front about 5 ½ rods for the purpose of coming up but in double quick time [back] to the breast works our pickets are coming in + the rebs come nearly up to works but not in range of our guns," recorded Private Horton.[28]

Second Lieutenant George Gove, wounded at Fair Oaks, belonged to Company K of the 5th New Hampshire. The 5th had undergone its baptism of fire at Fair Oaks opposite the 12th and 41st Virginia. Gove recalled, "we were doublequicked back into the rifle pits we had left."[29] Miles deployed the 28th Massachusetts as skirmishers. Fugitives from the forward Federal line disordered the rear line, too far back in the thick timber to provide support or flank the flanking Secessionists. For the next two hours, Confederates who had lost their way in the woods would stumble into conflict with Miles's brigade and the fugitives gathering around it.

After putting to flight Barlow's division, the Rebels flanked the first line of Mott's division. They rolled up Mott's division "like a sheet of paper," Whitehorne noted.[30]

The Secessionists crashed into the left flank of Mott's unsuspecting soldiers, who like Fraser's brigade occupied an east-west line. Mott recalled, "The first intimation of an attack was the troops of the First Division coming in on the left flank *en masse*."[31]

The Southerners first struck the left of Chaplin's brigade. The brigade "had made but little progress" entrenching "when a heavy fire was opened upon my left on the position occupied by the First Division of this corps, occasionally a

26 L. W. Cushing, "Some Experiences of the Civil War," paintedhills.org. Retrieved Feb. 11, 2023.

27 Armes, *Ups and Downs of an Army Officer*, 105.

28 Horton Diary, June 22, 1864.

29 Letter, George S. Gove to "Dear Sister," June 23, 1864, George S. Gove Letters, Milne Special Collections and Archives, University of New Hampshire, Durham, NH.

30 Elmore, ed., *Diary of J. E. Whitehorne*, 51.

31 *OR* 40, 1:388.

Gershom Mott
Library of Congress

few shots coming from the rear," remembered Canadian-born Col. Daniel Chaplin of the 1st Maine heavies, a former clerk for a firm of ships chandlers. In minutes crowds of men from Barlow's division passed the rear of Chaplin's line reporting the enemy behind them. "My command was immediately formed and prepared for an attack, when the enemy poured a volley of musketry directly in rear of my line," Chaplin recalled. "The command was immediately faced about, but the troops coming from our left in great disorder carried my command with them."[32]

Captain Thomas C. Thompson of the 7th New Jersey's Company A led his regiment that day. The 7th held the extreme left of Chaplin's brigade, with Fraser's brigade of Barlow's division on its left and the 16th Massachusetts on its right. While Thompson's troops entrenched, Barlow's division collapsed and fled past the Jerseymen. Soon afterward, "I was informed by several of my officers that there were no troops upon my right, and finding that to remain was certain capture, I ordered my command to fall back," Thompson remembered. "Following along the line of earth-works, I halted and rallied a portion of my command, but finding the confusion so great that a stand would be useless I again ordered a retreat." In the confusion, the national colors, two officers, and around 40 enlisted men went missing.[33] The national colors fell into the hands of the 6th Virginia.

"This was a case of run or be gobbled," remembered Captain Shaw of the 1st Maine heavies in Chaplin's brigade. "Look out for yourselves," shouted first the staff officers, then the regimental and company officers. "Make a stand in the old line." All who heard these orders obeyed them immediately.

Some exhibited rare speed on the way back to the rear line. "During our sudden start the tattered remains of the flag presented to our Regiment by the ladies of Bangor was left sticking in the partly constructed breastworks at our right," recalled Cpl. Charles J. House of the 1st Maine's Company E, wounded in

32 Ibid., 414.

33 Ibid., 418.

the head and right ear on June 18. He remembered, "This was rescued by one of our own officers then doing staff duty."[34]

The 5th New Jersey's men held the line to the right of the Mainers and quickly joined the rout. "[T]he enemy suddenly appeared on our left flank, causing the troops on our left to become panic-stricken, and in the general stampede that followed the whole line fell back to the breast-works," remembered Capt. Thomas C. Godfrey of the 5th. "Every effort was made to stay the flying troops, but all efforts proved utterly futile and of no effect."[35]

The Johnnies gobbled the three soldiers of the 11th New Jersey who were still holding the turkey they had captured.

At least 900 yards to the rear in the second line of Mott's division stood Madill's brigade, in position to outflank the flanking Confederates. "We were surprised to see our front lines falling back in great disorder, with but very little fighting, and no apparent cause," Captain Houghton in the brigade's 17th Maine recalled. "Indeed there was so little fighting, that we were at a loss to understand the meaning of the panic. . . . We formed promptly behind the second line of works, and prepared to meet the enemy."[36]

Fugitives from II Corps' brigades in the first line began reaching Madill's brigade. "When we found them coming, we did wonders trying to urge them to stand fast," remembered Private Haley in the 17th Maine. "We soon became alarmed, for words of encouragement didn't seem to check them, so we added copious threats to punch them with the bayonet if they didn't turn about and check the Rebs." Haley's comrades feared that they might have to stop the Southerners by themselves if the fugitives would not stand fast.[37] The butternuts attacked Madill's brigade by advancing a section of artillery to the edge of the woods in front of that brigade and shelling the bluecoats. Private Proctor made it safely back to Madill's brigade from the forward line through a hail of shot and shell.

Behind Madill's brigade, at the artillery park near the Jones house, the gunners began to stir. "Orders soon came to harness and be ready to move without delay, which, under the circumstances, we obeyed with our accustomed alacrity," recollected Corporal Billings in the 10th Massachusetts Battery, "for the firing

34 Shaw, *First Maine Heavy Artillery*, 131.

35 *OR* 40, 1:416.

36 Houghton, *Seventeenth Maine*, 208; see also John D. Bloodgood, *Personal Reminiscences of the War* (New York, 1893), 287 ("Being in the rear line, our regiment [the 141st Pennsylvania of Madill's brigade] was not engaged in this affair, but lost one man killed and one man captured on the picket line."). Mott's reserve brigades did not leave the rear line in the morning. Ibid.

37 Silliker, ed, *Rebel Yell and Yankee Hurrah*, 175.

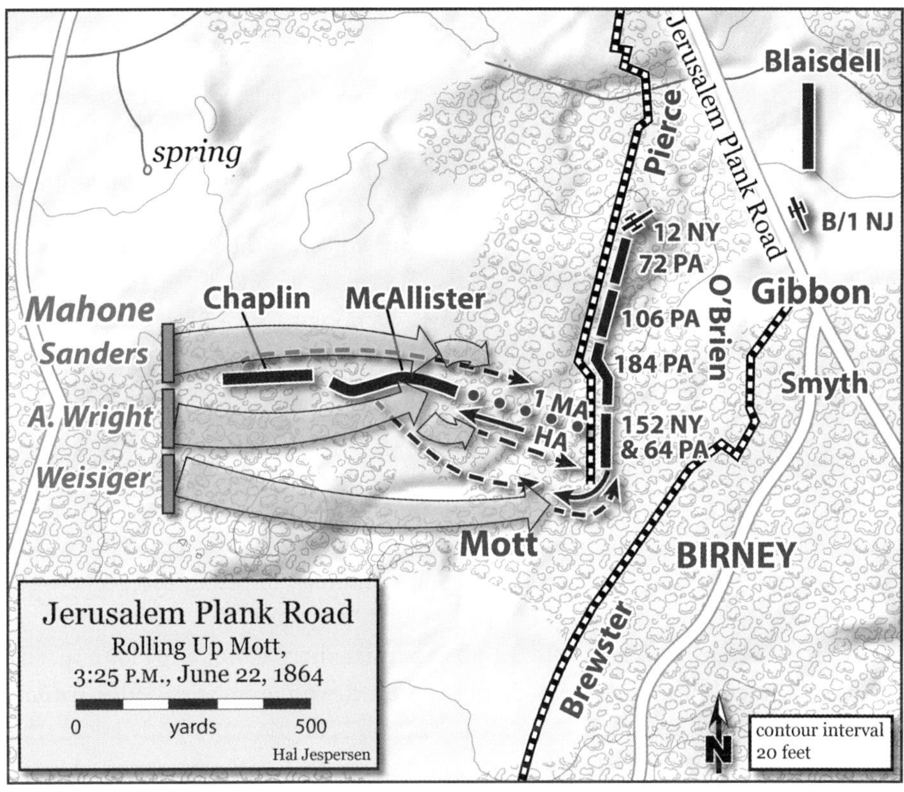

drew nearer and the road was bustling with couriers dashing to the rear, and other appearances indicating that all was not right."[38]

To the right of Chaplin's brigade in the front line of Mott's division stood McAllister's brigade. That brigade's left regiments formed nearly at right angles to the rest of the brigade, exposing their left flank to the enemy in the Dimmock Line. The brigade's right had initially deployed on a knoll which exposed it to murderous fire from the Confederates that forced it to withdraw and dig in behind the elevation. The brigade's commander, the 11th New Jersey's Col. Robert McAllister, wounded at Gettysburg, connected the brigade's right with O'Brien's brigade of Gibbon's division by throwing out the 1st Massachusetts Heavy Artillery, which entrenched behind a crest.

The 5th Michigan included consolidated soldiers of the 3rd Michigan and picketed the front of McAllister's brigade. These sentinels had noticed a movement of the enemy toward their left, then heavy picket firing in that direction. "My first intimation of the disaster and of the giving way of the picket-line on my left was

38 Billings, *History of the Tenth Massachusetts Battery*, 290.

the appearance of the pickets from my left passing to the rear of my line, closely pursued by the enemy," remembered Capt. Daniel S. Root of the 3rd, wounded at Second Bull Run. Root, the commander of Company A of the consolidated 5th, led the entire regiment that day. "To prevent capture I immediately withdrew my picket-line and retired to the rifle-pits occupied by the First Massachusetts Heavy Artillery."[39]

The 5th Michigan in its flight lost one of its colors to the 41st Virginia. "The old 41st covered itself with glory by dashing in between two lines of Yankee breastworks," remembered 1st Lt. Charles E. Denoon of the 41st's Company C, the McRae Rifles. "This was done by the flank and at the right time, which caused the first line of Yankees to break in confusion."[40]

On picket with the 5th Michigan stood companies A, F, and I of the 1st United States Sharpshooters. By this time the Confederate cavalry in the open field in front of the pickets had long since taken off after Wilson's and Kautz's divisions and "some of the men went to sleep, some went to hunting 'grey backs,'" recalled Private Greene of the 2nd United States Sharpshooters, meaning that some were picking lice.[41]

A sergeant from the 1st's United States Sharpshooters' Company I led a special detail of 10 men through the woods to suppress the fire of a Secessionist battery annoying the Federal line. The detail found four cannon 400 yards away. The sharpshooters quieted the battery but did not notice the Rebel infantry enveloping them from behind. Completely surrounded but determined not to surrender, they charged into the scattered Southerners. Six of the 11 broke through and returned to their regiment. Company A's Pvt. Frederick Zeller of Zurich, Switzerland was among the five captured. The Johnnies took "all the prisoners' money and everything else of value," Zeller recalled.[42]

Out on the skirmish line, Greene recalled hearing someone speak from behind him.

"Now we have got you yanks so come in & we won't fire," the voice said.

The 2nd United States Sharpshooters' Green Coats realized that the Southerners had nearly surrounded them and it was every man for himself. "So I jumped to the rear as most of those in the center of the Regt. did & through a shower bullets we made good our escape," Greene remembered. "But about twenty on both flanks of

39 *OR* 40, 1:401.

40 Richard T. Couture, ed., Charlie's Letters: *The Correspondence of Charles E. DeNoon* (Collingswood, NJ, 1982), 97.

41 Hastings, ed., *Letters from a Sharpshooter*, 228.

42 Heinz K. Meier, *Memoirs of a Swiss Officer in the American Civil War* (Bern, Switzerland, 1972), 170.

the Regt. were captured & taken to the enemy's lines." Greene and his companions fell back toward the rear line of breastworks.[43]

Colonel McAllister heard heavy firing to the left and supposed it arose from Barlow advancing his line. The firing quickly came nearer. McAllister called his men to attention. "Very soon a retreating mass of the First Division came running along in my rear, with the rebels on their flank and rear," McAllister remembered. "I could not fire on account of our men." The Confederates "poured in" on his flank as well as on his left after Chaplin's brigade had fled.[44]

"Stand men!" shouted McAllister when his brigade's line broke. "Rally 'round the flag, men!"

Soon he found the line irreparably broken and that to remain meant certain annihilation or capture. He could do nothing but fall back toward a continuance of the second line.

"Run, boys, run," he sang out. "Run like the devil."

McAllister then proved that he could run as fleetly as any soldier under his command.[45]

The 105th Pennsylvania, the Wildcat Regiment, had orders to erect breastworks at the edge of the woods near the enemy's line. While the men tore down fences and built works with the rails, "whiz! bang!" came a storm of bullets from the wrong direction. The Rebels had gotten in their rear and almost captured the regiment entire.[46]

The 57th Pennsylvania had just finished throwing up works and was sitting down to rest.

"Oh, God, there comes the rebs," cried Pvt. Josiah N. Smith of Company B.

Private William H. Sallada of Company B, who like Smith had enlisted March 15, 1864, rose to look around and saw his comrades all running. He supposed they were going to get their arms, stacked a short distance to the rear. "The bullets were flying so fast that I crowded up close to the breastworks; on looking around again, I found the boys had all left and the rebels coming up in our rear, and mowing the thick underbrush with their bullets like they would with a scythe, and yelling like demons to us to surrender," he remembered. "My first thought was I would have

43 Hastings, ed., *Letters from a Sharpshooter*, 228.

44 *OR* 40, 1:412.

45 David H. King, et al., *History of the Ninety-Third Regiment, New York Volunteer Infantry, 1861–1865* (Milwaukee, 1895), 100n.

46 Kate M. Scott, *History of the One Hundred and Fifth Regiment of Pennsylvania Volunteers: A Complete History of the Organization, Marches, Battles, Toils, and Dangers Participated in by the Regiment, from the Beginning to the Close of the War, 1861–1865* (Philadelphia, 1877), 113.

to surrender; my second thought flashed upon me NEVER." He picked up his haversack and struck for the timber, which proved very swampy. "I came to a brush fence having a small pathway on either side of which stood a large tree," recalled Sallada. "Just as I passed the tree a rebel came running along the opposite side of the fence, and came around the tree from one side just as I came from the other." As surprised as the Pennsylvanian, the Southerner called on Sallada to surrender but Sallada kept running. "The Johnny, vexed at my lack of courtesy, stuck out his gun and fired at me without taking aim, being so very close I suppose he thought it would be impossible to miss me, but he did; at every step I expected to be shot," Sallada recalled. "This was the only time I relinquished the idea I had always entertained of returning home safe."[47]

The 63rd Pennsylvania had stacked arms. Pickets reported heavy bodies of the enemy moving toward the regiment's left. An aide rode along the line and one of the 63rd's captains asked the aide what was happening.

The aide shrugged his shoulders.

"I do schmell von tam pig rat," he said.

Spurring his horse, he galloped away.

The assault of the Secessionists on the 63rd's left while howling "their infernal 'Ki-yi'" came as a complete surprise.[48] The Pennsylvanians were expecting a frontal attack, of which their pickets would notify them. Striking Company B on the 63rd's extreme left, the Johnnies rolled up the line until Company B became mixed up with the color company in the regiment's center. The right gave way. It became every man for himself as the Keystoners dashed down the road they had marched up that morning.

A stack of cordwood several feet high stretched along the right side of the road for several hundred yards—the byproduct of cutting the road through the woods. A creek with banks about three feet high ran along the road's left side. Several companies veered off to the right and escaped. Company B ran the gauntlet. Captain Robert A. Nesbit and a comrade were sprinting down the road between the cordwood and the branch. A line of slouched hats rose from the other side of the cordwood.

"Halt! You Yankee _____ _____ _____," shouted the wearers of the slouched hats.[49]

47 William H. Sallada, *Silver Sheaves, Gathered through Clouds and Sunshine* (Des Moines, 1879), 99–100.

48 Hays, *Under the Red Patch*, 257. The aide was German. Ibid.

49 Ibid., 258.

Nesbit leaped into the branch without pausing to think. His companion hesitated. The next instant Nesbit's companion fell, riddled by bullets. Nesbit escaped as the balls passed over his head.

After outflanking Barlow's return, the Confederates did not encounter serious resistance until they reached the 1st Massachusetts heavies on the extreme right of McAllister's brigade. Some of the fugitives from the other regiments of McAllister's brigade and from Chaplin's brigade rallied on the heavies. These Yanks briefly held off the enemy in front until they took a volley from the left and had to retreat. Many had sacrificed their freedom by rallying. "Here is where the most of the prisoners taken from my command were captured, they remaining in the intrenchments until the enemy were upon them and escape was impossible," Chaplin remembered.[50]

First Sergeant Nathan P. Cutler of Company D in the 1st Massachusetts heavies recollected that the 1st left "in pretty good order" after the regiment's colors had gone. "It was hard going to the rear," he remembered. "There was a perfect storm of bullets and a great many were wounded and killed, some taken prisoner."[51]

More than half a mile southeast of McAllister's brigade stood Brewster's brigade, which included the remnants of the old Excelsior Brigade. Positioned like the troops in Madill's brigade to outflank the flanking Confederates, the men of Brewster's brigade puzzled over the spectacle in front of them until the time for action had passed. Colonel William R. Brewster, captured during the Peninsula Campaign, merely deployed his old regiment, the 73rd New York, the Fourth Excelsior Regiment, also known as the Second Fire Zouaves because so many firemen had enlisted in it, in skirmish order to hold the enemy in check until he could reestablish his picket line. Some fugitives from the front line, upon reaching Brewster's brigade, repulsed Mahone's troops. "[O]ur men when they got near our breastworks they turned round and gave the Rebels fits when they went back on a run," recollected Cpl. Jacob Lyons of the 120th New York, an immigrant from England who made cigars in New York City. "We took some prisoners."[52]

Aggravating the confusion caused by the resistance at the right of McAllister's brigade, one of the Secessionist batteries in the Dimmock Line brought the advancing Southern foot soldiers under fire and further disordered them. Mahone turned to one of his couriers, Pvt. James Hamilton Blakemore, a native

50 *OR* 40, 1:414.

51 Alfred Seelye Roe and Charles Nutt, *History of the First Regiment of Artillery Massachusetts Volunteers, Formerly the Fourteenth Regiment of Infantry, 1861–1865* (Boston, 1917), 183.

52 Jacob Lyons Diary, June 22, 1864, SHC, Wilson Library, University of North Carolina at Chapel Hill, Chapel Hill, NC.

of Tennessee on detached duty from the 12th Virginia's Petersburg Riflemen. Blakemore galloped to the Dimmock Line and delivered the order for the battery to cease fire. Mahone's troops regrouped as Wilcox's two northbound brigades brushed aside VI Corps pickets in the swamps and chaparral between the Browder farm and II Corps. Porte could hear the skirmishing between Wilcox's men and the Unionists. It was around this time that the sharpshooters of Thomas's brigade, following the withdrawing VI Corps soldiers, charged the breastworks west of the Williams farmhouse and met a fierce fire which surprised and repulsed them.

When Blakemore returned from the Dimmock Line, Mahone directed the courier to find Wilcox with the following message: "I am driving the enemy back upon his main works. If you will promptly bear down with your command in the direction of my firing we can sweep everything before us."[53] Porte told Blakemore to guide himself by the sound of Wilcox's skirmishing. Blakemore on his way spotted Northerners advancing toward Mahone's right.

Mahone dispatched his chief of staff, Maj. Thomas Sumter Mills, into the timber with the same message as Blakemore carried. Suspecting that the Yanks might have another line behind their first, Porte cautioned Mills to take care and not go too far. A "herculean seven footer" from South Carolina known as "the kid glove major" and inherited as assistant adjutant general from the previous commander of the division, Mills bore the scars of wounds from Santa Rosa Island and Seven Pines.[54] He drafted Lieutenant Zachry and some other Georgians, including Pvts. Joseph C. Anderson and Thomas J. Hincey, to escort him to the flank. Mills, on horseback, led the way through brush where they could only see a few feet ahead. Hincey walked beside Mills's horse, followed by Anderson and then Zachry.

Suddenly, Anderson pushed Zachry back.

"We are right among the Yanks," said Anderson.

"Surrender," said the Federals.

"In a few feet we were out of sight, Joe and I," Zachry recalled. "The others were captured."[55]

The others fell into the hands of the 26th Michigan of Miles's brigade in the rear line of II Corps.

53 Letter, J. H. Blakemore to William Mahone, n.d., in Mahone, "A Reply to a Communication Published by Gen. C. M. Wilcox in the *New Orleans Times*, of January 1st, 1872."

54 "Capture of Confederate Officers," *Evening Star* (Washington, D.C.), June 25, 1864, p. 2, col. 1; "Thomas Sumter Mills," findagrave.com, retrieved Feb. 11, 2023. In combat situations, at least two messengers were usually sent separately as on Aug. 19, 1864, at the battle of Globe Tavern. Horn, *The Battles for the Weldon Railroad, August 1864*, 163.

55 Zachry, "Four Shots for the Cause."

Reorganized, Mahone's three brigades prepared to resume their onslaught. Ahead lay Gibbon's division "in a strong line of fortifications, supported by four pieces of artillery," Bachelor remembered.[56] Ordered forward again, the Secessionists again charged. Mahone's men hit the extreme left of O'Brien's brigade.

Major O'Brien, wounded in the Wilderness, remembered that while his command had fended off pushes by the Confederates in front, the Secessionists forced their way through Mott's division to the left. The enemy occupied the abandoned works of the 1st Massachusetts heavies and opened what O'Brien recalled as "a galling fire" on his brigade.[57] The 69th Pennsylvania on the brigade's far left and the adjacent 152nd New York filed to the left oblique and fired in that direction. This change of position exposed the right of the 69th and the 152nd to the Rebels previously in front of those regiments.[58] O'Brien recalled that his brigade "began falling back from the left in some disorder" as he headed toward his right attempting to save the 12th New York Battery.[59]

Adjutant McDermott of the 69th Pennsylvania recalled that the Johnnies emerged from woods on the left front into the open field directly ahead. The Rebels wore dark uniforms and formed line of battle facing the 69th while the regiment's soldiers mistook them for Federals. "Their true character was not discovered until a battery of artillery dashed to their front, unlimbered and opened fire, they being so close that the range of their guns was point blank, and their shot and shell struck into our works plowing deep furrows and almost smothering us from the dense dust created by the destructive missiles hurled against us," remembered McDermott. The Pennsylvanians returned fire. They "poured bullets so thick and fast into the rebel ranks, that they would have been obliged to retire, were it not for a fact of a force of the enemy getting round upon our rear demanding our surrender," he recalled. The Keystoners declined to lay down their arms but fell back by the right flank a short distance from the works. This was, recollected McDermott, "a very difficult undertaking as we were subject to an artillery and infantry fire from our front, and the guns from a fort on our right front . . . while the rebels who were pouring down upon our rear also maintained a vigorous fire." The 69th had no choice other than to retire.[60]

56 W. A. B., "Letter from the 48th Georgia."

57 *OR* 40, 1:376.

58 "To March to the Oblique," drillpad.net. Retrieved Aug. 14, 2023.

59 *OR* 40, 1:376.

60 McDermott, *69th Regiment Pennsylvania Volunteers*, 45.

Captain Charles H. Banes of the 72nd Pennsylvania, the assistant adjutant general of O'Brien's brigade, observed the fate of the 69th Pennsylvania. "[T]he Sixty-Ninth was . . . fortunate in retaining its flag," Banes recalled. "The officers and men who escaped capture did so at the risk of their lives, by retreating along the front of the enemy, which they had faced during the entire day."[61]

The Rebel skirmish line distracted the bluecoats by pushing down from the Dimmock Line. Private Roback of the 152nd New York recollected, "The noise and confusion in our front drowned the music on the left." Three officers of the 152nd "occupied the skirmish line with a detail from the regiment and brigade," remembered Roback. "There being no salvation for them in that position they were gobbled up."

Then came the turn of the 152nd's main body as the Johnnies pressed through the woods and struck the regiment's left. A sergeant of Company H fired at a Secessionist color bearer. As O'Brien passed, he ordered Company H "to fall back; but the confusion was so great, with the shot and shell, and the rebel horde closing around, with furious and exultant yells, that few heard the order," recalled Roback. "Everyone acted independently, and used their own judgment and legs in getting away, a few running into the ranks of the enemy amid the blinding smoke, and were captured." Company H's commander and 20 more men formed around the colors and started fighting their way back to the rear line of works.

The Confederates in front then routed the 184th Pennsylvania. The regiment remained about 500 feet in front of and at right angles to the 152nd New York. "Their flanks were exposed, the enemy raking one side of their low earthworks with shell, while the opposite side was exposed to infantry," Roback remembered. "However, they held their position and did not retire until forced from the field by superior numbers."[62]

The turn of the 106th Pennsylvania on the right of the 184th came next. "I saw amidst a dense dust and smoke troops running out from our line and toward the enemy firing," Captain Breitenbach recalled. "Supposing these troops to be our left regiments driving the enemy, I gave the order to cease firing." He feared shooting at his own men. "Before this order could be fully obeyed or heard on account of the noise of the fire, and the excitement and enthusiasm of the men, Capt. [Edward B.] Whitaker, commanding Seventy-second Regiment, being division officer of the day, quickly came from the left, and throwing up his sword in hand called out that the whole left had given away; that we were flanked, and that

61 Charles H. Banes, *History of the Sixty-Ninth, Seventy-First, Seventh-Second, and One Hundred and Sixth Pennsylvania Volunteers* (Philadelphia, 1876), 285.

62 Roback, comp., *152d N. Y. V.*, 104.

the enemy was in our immediate rear, and ordered all to fall back," Breitenbach remembered. "I now saw that the enemy was in my rear, and that instead of our left driving the enemy, he was driving our men into his lines." The enemy fire from the rear became heavy and casualties mounted. Breitenbach's little regiment could accomplish nothing under the circumstances and he could see no support at hand. "It was too late," he recalled. "Before this order could be obeyed nearly the whole regiment, still in the trenches and firing, were captured with the colors in the hands of the color-sergeant." Breitenbach escaped with about 40 muskets.[63]

The men in the 106th's line experienced the Rebel attack much as described by their commander.

Corporal Joseph R. C. Ward of the 106th's Company I, a former drummer boy, remembered fugitives from Mott's division pouring past him.

"Fall back," they called out, "you are flanked."

Before the 106th's men grasped the meaning of the warning from Mott's troops, an enemy column appeared behind the Pennsylvanians with a demand to surrender. The soldiers of the 106th had not changed front before almost all of them found themselves prisoners. Several Confederates sprang for the regiment's colors. Seeing there was no chance to escape with them, the acting color sergeant and another soldier tore them from the staff and tried to hide them under their shirts. The Secessionists spotted this. "Immediately a scuffle began for the possession of them," recalled Ward. "Two or three other members of the Regiment rushed to their assistance, and together they tore the colors to pieces before the Rebs had time to get possession of them, hid the pieces, and the staff was broken in two by others and thrown over the works."

A Georgia major approached Capt. Lynford D. C. Tyler of Company K, mistaking him for the commander of the 106th. "Colonel, I thank you for your sword," the Georgian said. Tyler surrendered his sword and gave the order to cease fire. The Georgian then directed Tyler and his men to the rear.[64] The 11th Alabama captured the other flag of the 106th.

O'Brien reached the 72nd Pennsylvania as it repulsed a Confederate push on its front. He remained with the 72nd until it started taking fire from its left and rear and then fell back with the regiment. The adjutant of the 72nd, with its color sergeant, brought away the regimental colors. Such officers and men who escaped captivity retreated along the front of the enemy.

63 *OR* 40, 1:387.

64 Joseph R. C. Ward, *History of the One Hundred and Sixth Regiment Pennsylvania Volunteers, 2d Brigade, 2d Division, 2d Corps, 1861–1865* (Philadelphia, 1906), 270–271.

About 500 yards behind O'Brien's brigade stood Blaisdell's brigade, which included the Corcoran or Irish Legion as well as the 8th New York Heavy Artillery. Blaisdell's brigade seemed oblivious to the struggle going on ahead in the dense timber. Smyth's brigade, in the rear line of works about the same distance back to the southeast, equally failed to react.

Mahone's troops pressed northeastward toward the 12th New York Battery. "We kept going until we reached the third line of their breastworks, where their cannons were planted, and they shelled us in a hurry," remembered Private Methvin of the 10th Georgia Battalion. "It seemed that we would all be killed, but we rallied and charged and captured the works and a four-gun battery."[65]

Unionist fire played among the 48th Georgia's Wilson Tigers, nicking among others Private Verdery, who according to Bachelor "manifested great coolness and deliberation under a most deadly fire."[66] Verdery downplayed the matter, recalling, "I was struck by minie ball a glancing blow in the side which bruised me a little."[67]

To the right of the 72nd Pennsylvania in O'Brien's brigade, Capt. George F. McKnight's four 3-inch rifles in the 12th New York Battery belched fire against the Confederate artillery to the north in the Dimmock Line. Blue-coated infantrymen came running in from the left. "We are flanked on the left," they cried. "The left has broken."[68]

McKnight kept firing canister and case-shot without fuse until everyone to the left gave way and ran off through the woods, leaving the battery's left unprotected. The 1st Minnesota, on the right of the battery, broke when the left gave way. The Confederates came down the works from the left and divided to sweep around the only gun that could fire in their direction. Planting their colors on the gun's lunette, the Johnnies ordered the gunners to surrender. The 1st Minnesota rallied, fired one volley, then fell back in confusion.

Corporal W. D. Robinson and the other members of the work party from the 4th New York Heavy Artillery's Company C were still hanging around McKnight's battery when the adjacent infantry stood up and fired. "We thought it was time to leave just then, and started at a 2.40 gait for the woods, running part of the way through them," recalled Robinson. "We had not been there more than ten seconds

65 Methvin, "In the Wilderness Campaign," *CV* 23:455.

66 W. A. B., "Letter from the 48th Georgia."

67 Verdery to "Dear Father Mother & all," June 25, 1864.

68 *OR* 40, 1:436.

when we discovered the infantry we had just left running back."[69] The heavies hastened their departure.

"Up to this time none of my men had left their posts, nor did they do so until ordered by myself and officers," McKnight remembered. "The order was given to fix prolonges, but the enemy poured into the works in such overwhelming numbers that it was apparent that further exertions to save the guns were useless, and my men fell back to the winding road running through the woods." First Lieutenants George K. Dauchy and William S. Bull tried to persuade the infantry to return and help draw off the guns. "What few infantry remained in the road near the battery at this time were willing and desirous to return and help retake the guns, but not enough could be rallied at any one time to make an effective advance," recalled McKnight. "During this time my chief of caissons, Second Lieut. H. D. Brower, whom I had dispatched to the rear a few moments before, now came up and gallantly assisted Lieutenants Dauchy and Bull in endeavoring to rally the infantry."

Two soldiers from the 106th Pennsylvania were retreating to the right along the breastworks, still firing. Reaching the 12th New York Battery, they found its first sergeant and about six artillerists close by the pieces. The first sergeant asked the two Keystoners to help work the two left guns, and the two complied. While the guns fired once more, a lieutenant of the 1st Minnesota rallied a few men and returned with McKnight and some of the gunners who were falling back and tried to save the piece on the right. "At this juncture the enemy poured in a heavy volley, killing my first sergeant and several men who were endeavoring to pull off the piece, and at the same time calling upon us to surrender," McKnight remembered. "I then ordered the men near me to fall back, the enemy at this time occupying my entire position."[70] The two Pennsylvanians, before retreating, spiked with the rammers of their muskets the guns they had helped man.

A sergeant and a corporal of Company A, 10th Georgia Battalion, were the first to reach two of McKnight's pieces and a private from the 10th's Company B took two flags. Though wounded, Private Verdery of the 48th Georgia "after reaching the works bounded over and overtook some fleeing bluecoats and brought them in prisoners," recalled Bachelor.[71] Securing the battery, the Confederates turned the guns on the Federals and shelled the woods, then continued sweeping up the line of Gibbon's division.

69 Hyland C. Kirk, *Heavy Guns and Light: A History of the 4th New York Heavy Artillery* (New York, 1890), 315. The meaning of "two-forty" is a speed of a mile in two minutes and forty seconds.

70 *OR* 40, 1:436–437.

71 W. A. B., "Letter from the 48th Georgia."

John Gibbon
Library of Congress

The Secessionist onslaught now fell upon Pierce's brigade. "The first intimation I had of the assault of the enemy was firing far to the left," remembered Pierce. "I heard the musketry on the left, and in a very short time the road leading to McKnight's battery was filled with troops from the Third Division in a disorganized state, coming to the rear."[72] Pierce ordered them to organize behind Blaisdell's brigade near the second line of works.

Following Mott's division streamed the fugitives of O'Brien's brigade. Pierce tried in vain to stop them in the woods. A quarter mile behind the front line, the fugitives ran into and confounded Gibbon and his staff, who were eating dinner and had heard no fighting. Captain A. Henry Embler of Gibbon's staff formed most of the fugitives behind Blaisdell's brigade near the second line. Next came the officers and men of McKnight's battery, reporting their guns captured. Pierce ordered to the rear the horses of Battery B, 1st New Jersey Light Artillery.

When bullets began flying down the left flank of the 1st Minnesota Battalion to the right of McKnight's battery, Captain Farwell sprang to his feet.

"Boys they are flanking us!" he cried.

Without issuing orders he then fled, followed by most of the battalion's recruits and old soldiers.

Corporal Bond had seen his old regiment stop similar stampedes. He heard a call for help from McKnight, who was trying to bring off his guns. Bond called to nearby Cpl. Charles A. E. Berdan, a former student wounded at Fredericksburg and Bristoe Station, and to Pvt. Peter Berg, an illiterate Swedish immigrant. The three returned to their pit and fired a few shots. Bullets still flew from the left, but no enemy had yet appeared.

"I believe we can hold the works yet," Bond said to Berdan.

"I don't know about that," Berdan replied, speaking as if he saw something outside Bond's field of vision.

72 *OR* 40, 1:369.

Bond was loading his musket.

"We can hold them or go to Richmond," he said.

"I'll die before I'll be taken prisoner," said Berdan, taking to his heels as he spoke.

When Bond finished loading, he looked up, found Berdan gone and saw Confederate flags on the artillery emplacement a few steps to his left. He fired and started to run but Secessionists surrounded him.

"Throw down that gun!" came one order.

Bond obeyed.

"Get over the breast works here you damned son of a bitch," came another.

Again, Bond obeyed.

"Thus was I sure enough bound for Richmond, though I never expected to go there when I made that reply to Berdan," Bond recorded. Berg joined Bond in captivity.[73]

Some Minnesotans fought at close quarters. Second Lieutenant Charles C. Parker of Company A used his revolver to shoot a Confederate who had the muzzle of his musket against Parker's throat.

On the right of the 1st Minnesota, Capt. Joseph W. Spaulding commanding the 19th Maine discovered the troops on his left falling back. "It was impossible to change front in that position, as the enemy in our old front would have an enfilading fire of artillery and infantry on our line," Spaulding remembered. "The regiment held its position until the enemy were close upon its left flank and rear, when it was compelled to retire, losing heavily in killed, wounded, and prisoners."[74]

Corporal John Day Smith of the 19th's Company F, a member of the regiment's color guard, recollected, "The first thing the Nineteenth knew of the approaching catastrophe was the giving way of the Second Brigade and First Minnesota Battalion on our immediate left—the men of which did not run directly to the rear, but ran more lengthwise toward the right and in the rear of our Regiment, closely pursued by the exultant foe." When the 19th's men faced the Johnnies charging from left to right behind them, Mott's and O'Brien's disorganized, fleeing troops filled the ground behind McKnight's battery. The gunners stood by their pieces until the enemy closed in on them from front and rear, demanding their surrender. The Mainers quickly withdrew into the trees and halted across an old wood road. "Three times during that afternoon the man bearing the colors was shot dead in his tracks, but another man would immediately catch the flag and bear it to the front," recalled Smith. "Not once did the old flag touch the ground."[75] The Secessionists

73 Bond Diary and Memoir, June 22, 1864, 237–238.

74 *OR* 40, 1:372.

75 Smith, *Nineteenth Regiment of Maine Volunteer Infantry*, 207.

killed, wounded, or captured all six members of the 19th's color guard, shooting Smith in the face and leaving him for dead.

Next in line came the 19th Massachusetts. "We heard loud talking and cheering on our left and the fighting ceased," Captain Adams remembered. "The woods were so thick we could not see through them, but knowing something was up, I went to the right of the line and reported to Major Dunn."

Adams, while returning to his place, met Pvt. Billy Smith of Company F.

"Come with me," said Smith. "If you go farther you are sure to be captured."

While Adams and Smith spoke, Lt. Col. I. Harris Hooper of the 15th Massachusetts passed them on his way to the rear.

"The colonel had *been there* and escaped through the tunnel at Libby," Adams realized. "He did not propose to go again."[76]

Adams told Smith to flee, but that he himself must return to his company.

The first that some men of the 19th knew of the foe's presence, they heard the order, "Forward 14th Alabama!"[77] Then came a stern command for them to throw down their guns and get over the breastworks and into the enemy lines. Confederate muskets leveled at them lent authority to the order.

Adams, still on his way back to the 19th, met two rebels who ordered him to surrender, but he declined. "I saw my men standing up and the rebels as thick as mosquitoes," he recalled. A major of a Georgia regiment demanded Adams's sword, which Adams presented to the Georgian. The Rebels took Adams to the right. He saw Capt. Lysander J. Hume, the commander of the regiment's right company, standing on the works looking left.

"They have us, Hume," shouted Adams.

Hume immediately stamped his sword into the dirt and broke the scabbard against a tree.

"There is the second one the cusses haven't got," he said.[78] Prostrated by heat after the battle of Savage Station on June 29, 1862, Hume had fallen into enemy hands during the retreat to Glendale.

The 19th's color bearer, Irish-born Sgt. Michael Scannell of Company A, wounded at Gettysburg, was hiding in a pit behind the line with the colors and another member of the color guard. Suddenly Secessionists surrounded them.

"You damned Yank, give me that flag!" demanded a Confederate.

76 Adams, *Nineteenth Massachusetts*, 103.

77 Miller and Mooney, eds., *The Nantucket Experience*, 111.

78 Adams, *Nineteenth Massachusetts*, 103.

"Well, it's twenty years since I came to this country, and you're the first man who ever called me a Yankee," said Scannell. "Take the flag for the compliment."[79]

The 19th Massachusetts lost both of its colors, one to the 11th Alabama and the other to the 2nd Georgia Battalion.

The butternuts drove the captives from the 19th Massachusetts to the rear, taking their hats, belts, and other property despite their protests. "I had just received that morning a little hat, weighing only an ounce, from home and had just placed it on my head when I was taken," remembered First Sergeant Hodgkins. "A big rebel grabbed it and threw me his old one—a very heavy one, so I got no comfort from my new cap from home."[80]

A rebel officer demanded Adams's belt.

"Don't give it to him, Jack," said Hume. "Private property is to be respected, and all he has a right to claim is your sword."

The Rebel turned on Hume and with a revolver and a volley of oaths extorted Hume's belt. "I gave him mine without more argument," recalled Adams.[81]

Ill for some time, Lt. Col. Ansel D. Wass of the 19th, wounded at Glendale, Gettysburg, and Bristoe Station, rode up to within view in an ambulance just in time to see the enemy gobble up his regiment. Stricken with sunstroke after Savage Station, he had never fully recovered his reason. Wass and about 30 members of the 19th escaped, mostly rank and file, clerks, quartermasters, cooks, and sick. The captives included Major Dunn.

Next to the 19th Massachusetts stood the 42nd New York, the Tammany Regiment, and then came the 82nd New York, the Second New York State Militia. Confederates surrounded the 42nd and 82nd, both of which surrendered almost entirely. Pierce reported, "Officers and men who escaped informed me that the first they knew of the close proximity of the enemy [he] was in their rear in force, ordering them to surrender, which they did, colors and all."[82] The 11th Alabama captured a color of the 42nd New York.

The Rebels then reached the 15th Massachusetts. "Our eyes were strained to the front for the onslaught of the foe with whom the expected struggle was to come," Lieutenant Hastings recalled. "But suddenly, without warning, except the discredited reports of a few men straggling in from the left, a considerable force

79 Ibid., 105.

80 Turino, ed., *Civil War Diary of Lt. J. E. Hodgkins*, 96–97.

81 Adams, *Nineteenth Massachusetts*, 104.

82 *OR* 40, 1:371.

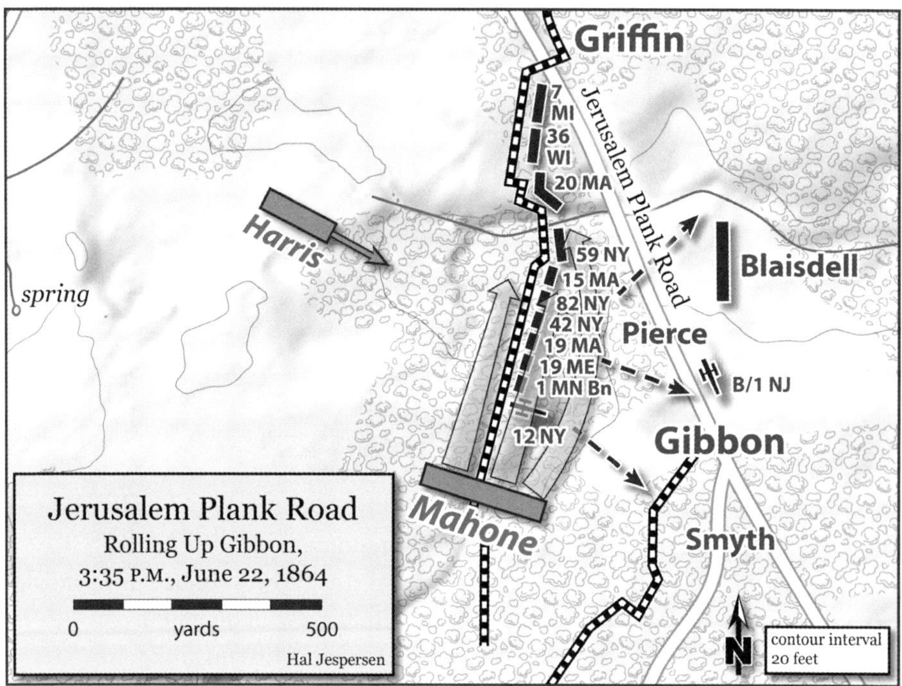

of the enemy appeared in our rear."[83] With Confederates in front, on flank and in rear, surrender became inevitable. The color-bearer, hoping to save the colors, hid them in a ditch. After the surrender he crept back, intending to retrieve the colors and escape with them to the rear. Members of the 3rd Georgia detected him and asked what he was looking for. He told them he was searching for a blanket. The Georgians hustled him to the rear with the rest of his captured comrades and afterward found the flag. Six on the right of the 15th, including Hooper, escaped.

The next regiment to the right, the 59th New York, the Union Guards, also surrendered almost entirely. The Secessionists suddenly appeared in the regiment's rear, demanding its surrender. The 59th yielded colors and all.

To the 59th's right stood the 20th Massachusetts, behind the branch draining into Blackwater Swamp across the plank road. The Harvard Regiment had half its men in the forward line of works and the other half out on the skirmish line. Private Murphey and his comrades heard some sharp firing in the woods to their left and wondered what it meant, but it lasted only a few minutes. "Immediately on looking over the breastworks I saw a large body of troops of our men on the move towards the rebel line," Murphey recalled. "I immediately got ready to move thinking that our troops had gained a point and we should have to follow it up but

83 Hastings, *Fifteenth Regiment Massachusetts Volunteer Infantry*, 334.

"Head quarters near Jerusalem 'pike', A. of P." (June 23, 1864) Alfred R. Waud. *Library of Congress*

we soon found out that the rebs had captured a large number of our men and were marching them into the rebel lines, prisoners."[84]

II Corps headquarters in front of the Jones house came under fire. "During the attack the enemy was at one time very close to corps headquarters, and their bullets struck among our tents," remembered Birney's senior aide-de-camp, Maj. William G. Mitchell, a civil engineer who had originally enlisted as a private in the 25th Pennsylvania. "They also sent a great many round shot through our camp, one of them cutting a canteen from the side of a mounted orderly of Doctor Dougherty, medical director of the corps." Bullets and shells threatened Meade at his headquarters across Jerusalem Plank Road.[85] Stray minies whizzed and shot bounded among the wounded and dying at the hospital of Gibbon's division near the Chieves house, farther east. The Rebels seemed about to break the Federal grip on the plank road.

As the butternuts swept up the line from the left, Major Patten of the 20th Massachusetts apprehended the situation from the advancing noise and changed his regiment's front to the left, the south, at a turn in the breastworks. On the Harvard Regiment's right, the 36th Wisconsin changed directions by the left flank

84 Miller and Mooney, eds., *The Nantucket Experience*, 111.

85 *OR* 40, 1:319.

and also presented a front to the Johnnies. The extreme right regiment of Pierce's brigade, the 7th Michigan, remained facing northwestwardly.

By this time, under the weight of captives, the Confederate attack was bogging down in the thick undergrowth of the little branch cutting through the Federal front and rear lines toward Blackwater Swamp. Mahone remembered, "Here I found that my [three] brigades had been severely depleted in carrying off prisoners, and, after a hurried reconnaissance which disclosed that the Federals were in great force on the Plank Road . . . I determined not to press further."[86] The Secessionist onslaught ceased.

"[T]he Rebs made no attack of any consequence," Patten modestly wrote.[87] Their momentum had dissipated to where a mere show of resistance sufficed to stop them.

Three brigades of Mahone's division had routed almost seven brigades of II Corps and captured a four-gun battery. II Corps had never experienced such a disaster, which had taken less than three quarters of an hour to unfold. The question that remained was whether II Corps could salvage its honor by retaking the captured guns.

86 Mulholland, *116th Regiment Pennsylvania Volunteers*, 275. Mahone mistakenly thought that the second Federal line was falling back on Jerusalem Plank Road. Ibid.; Houghton, *Seventeenth Maine*, 208; Bloodgood, *Personal Reminiscences of the War*, 287; *OR* 40, 1:396; Horton Diary, June 22, 1864; Gove to "Dear Sister," June 23, 1864.

87 Patten to "Dear Col.," July 10, 1864. Association of Officers of the 20th Massachusetts Volunteer Infantry, "Reports, letters & papers appertaining to 20th Mass. Vol. Inf.," 234–235.

Chapter Six

"There Is No Confirmation of the Report of the Recapture of Our Guns"

IN THE II Corps sector, both sides began reorganizing. The Confederates braced to defend their gains against a Union counterstroke. The Federals prepared to retake their guns and their advanced lines.

"Boys, you have done well," Rans Wright said to the 10th Georgia Battalion. "Just hold the breastworks until the dead and wounded can be cared for."[1] Mahone's infantry turned the captured works. Each man provided himself with several captured muskets and loaded them.

Mahone ordered from the Dimmock Line the Mississippi Brigade of Brig. Gen. Nathaniel H. Harris, a Vicksburg lawyer, to support the Alabama, Georgia, and Virginia brigades. "This command left the trenches under a heavy fire from the enemy's guns," remembered Harris.[2]

Hurrying to the captured fortifications, the Mississippians deployed on the left of Mahone's line.[3] They faced roughly northward. Down a little slope in front

1 Methvin, "In the Wilderness Campaign," *CV* 23:455.

2 Letter, Nathaniel H. Harris to William Mahone, Aug. 2, 1866, in Hewett, et al., eds., *Supplement to the Official Records*, 7:318.

3 Harris wrote that he "formed line on the right of the brigades engaged." Ibid. That must be a mistake because it would have put Harris's brigade out of the path of Gibbon's counterattacks, aimed at McKnight's battery in the middle of Gibbon's front line. *OR* 40, 2:370, 376. The Confederate artillery near Mott's rear line at this time indicates that "the right of the brigades engaged" lay near the southern end of Gibbon's front line. Ibid., 441, 443. Lifelong student of the battlefield and amateur archaeologist Don Lauter recovered a Mississippi button in the area where the aforesaid maps place Harris's brigade. Email, D. R. Lauter to John E. Horn, Jan. 19, 2022; United States Geological Survey, Virginia 7.5 Minute Series, Petersburg Quadrangle.

of the Mississippians lay the densely thicketed stream that wiggled through the Federal lines and under Jerusalem Plank Road toward Blackwater Swamp.

"Our battle line was nearly at right angles with the Yankee breastworks and stretched out across an old field grown up in scrub pines and blackberry vines," Private Holt of the 16th Mississippi recalled. Holt and his comrades dug in, mainly with their bayonets and frying pans. They shared two shovels and an axe to cut roots. Each soldier got to use a shovel for five minutes before he passed it on to the next man. "We dug with frantic haste," recollected Holt.[4]

As the Mississippians entrenched, Bushrod Johnson's troops advanced southward from the Dimmock Line onto the Bailey farm, then eastward through harvested wheat tied into sheaves. The troops formed line of battle in the standing wheat and lay down. Their presence on the Bailey farm represented a Confederate insurance policy in case the Federals drove Mahone's men away.

Hill summoned to his headquarters at the Davis house the four regiments of Kirkland's North Carolina Brigade positioned near what was now near the extreme right of the Confederates in the Dimmock Line. The brigade's band received instructions to remain in position and play to deceive the Yanks about the brigade's move. The adjacent troops in the Dimmock Line stretched out to fill the space vacated.

The Ambulance Corps men tended the dead and wounded. Private Miller of the 61st Virginia returned to assist Private Wills of the 16th Virginia, but Wills had expired in the meantime. Sergeant Milton Babb of the 6th's Company E went back for Major Williams, formerly Babb's captain, and found that Williams had just died, attended by two other men of their company. One of the two had spoken to Williams, and Williams had looked at the speaker but could not reply. Babb supposed that Williams had lived "some fifteen or twenty minutes."[5]

Wilkes's section of the Jackson Flying Artillery, Clutter's battery, supported Dement's battery in its removal of the guns of McKnight's battery. Wilkes's section unlimbered its two three-inch rifles near the lunettes of McKnight's battery. Dement's battery left its position, hurried to within 100 yards of the woods from which the butternuts had driven the bluecoats, and unlimbered its guns facing Mott's rear line a short distance away. Driving the limbers into the woods, the Marylanders brought off the captured pieces of McKnight's battery with which they had dueled and turned them over to their battalion commander, who brought up teams to carry them off the field. "The guns had been spiked before being diserted, but were considered prizes nonetheless," recalled Corporal Hatton.

4 Cockrell and Ballard, eds., *A Mississippi Rebel in the Army of Northern Virginia*, 294.

5 Letter, Milton Babb to Mrs. Williams, June 24, 1864, 6th Virginia File, FNBP.

As Hatton and his comrades were standing around the captured pieces discussing the day's events, a minnie ball passed through Hatton's right hip. "I cried 'ouch,' elevated my face to the sky, fearing to look down thinking that my whole leg was gone, not having the least sensation in the limb, but putting my hand down and feeling, I found my leg was still in place," he remembered. He wondered if he could walk and tried to step out. "I had no more use of it than if it were not there at all, neither would it bear my weight, but turning very sick to my stomach I fell to the ground but did not lose consciousness," he recalled. Four men from the Ambulance Corps put him on a stretcher and hastened to the rear with him as fighting resumed. "It was evidently a flesh wound but had completely paralyzed my whole limb," remembered Hatton. "I began to recover from the fainting sensation as the blood flowing from the wound began to trickle upon the ground, marking the course we went."[6]

* * *

Birney first heard of the attack when one of Mott's staff officers reported the breaking of Barlow's line and the turning of Mott's. Lieutenant Armes returned from his ride to the front and reported that he had "discovered several regiments in full retreat." Birney sent Armes eastward across Jerusalem Plank Road to request reinforcements from Meade. On the way, Armes stopped by the Jones house and reported the situation to Hancock. "He sprang out of his bed, wild with excitement at the bad news, but, of course, the doctor would not let him go to the front, as he wished to do," remembered Armes. "[Hancock] told me to hasten to General Meade, who said we could get help from the Fifth Corps if we needed it."[7]

Riding to the right of his line, Birney learned that Gibbon had lost the 12th New York Battery. The corps commander ordered Gibbon to retake it with his division. Pierce was already reordering Gibbon's forces near the plank road. The former dentist directed Battery B, 1st New Jersey, to bring up its horses and redeploy the left section of its guns 150 yards to the rear across the plank road facing McKnight's battery. The brigadier spied the retreating officers and men of McKnight's battery, followed by portions of the 1st Minnesota and 19th Maine. Pierce halted the 1st Minnesota and 19th Maine in the timber, led them back across the road and directed them to throw skirmishers to the front. "At this time Major Hooper, of the Fifteenth Massachusetts, reported to me that the enemy came up

6 Hatton Diary and Memoir, June 22, 1864, 607.

7 Armes, *Ups and Downs of an Army Officer*, 105–106.

Byron Root Pierce
Library of Congress

in his rear and captured most of his regiment," remembered Pierce.[8]

Gibbon arrived and instructed Pierce to throw out a strong skirmish line. Pierce added the 1st Minnesota to the pickets he had already deployed. Gibbon then gave Pierce two small regiments, the 155th and 164th New York, from the Corcoran Legion in Blaisdell's brigade, to assist in the recapture of McKnight's battery. Pierce put the two regiments on the left of the 19th Maine, then pressed this thin line forward to within 100 yards of the battery. Private Benjamin F. Fairbanks of the 19th Maine's Company H remembered seeing the cook of a company officer advancing with a gun in his hands as the line prepared to charge. "He had been taking a little too much firewater and was full of fight," Fairbanks remembered. "I noticed him a little to my left and I do not think he knew which company he was in, or where he belonged."[9] A skirmisher reported to Pierce that the enemy had drawn off McKnight's guns and stood in force behind the works. Word also reached Pierce that more troops from Blaisdell's brigade were coming to his support and that he could deploy them as he saw fit. Pierce waited for their arrival.

Birney rode to the left of the II Corps line to view the situation of Barlow's division in the rear works near the Strong house. Around the same time, Barlow joined Miles's brigade in the rear works. The division commander's adjutant and two of his aides had fallen into enemy hands. Barlow wrote, "these officers, who had been sent with riders were probably gobbled by the rebs in the confusion."[10] The Red Club leader organized such men from MacDougall's, Moroney's, and Fraser's brigades as had reached the second line. Barlow posted the fugitives on the left of Miles's brigade.

8 *OR* 40, 1:370.

9 Smith, *Nineteenth Regiment of Maine Volunteer Infantry*, 213.

10 Samito, ed., *Fear Was Not in Him*, 205.

Bands of Confederates soon began arriving. "I had hardly arranged my division in the rifle-pits before the enemy made a smart attack upon one part of them, but were repulsed," Barlow recalled.[11]

The Rebels were stumbling into the extreme left of the rear II Corps line, near the Strong house. "[W]ere just in season to prevent the rebs from rushing in over," remembered Lieutenant Gove of Miles's brigade, "we opened a heavy fire on them & they retreated in confusion leaving many of their killed & wounded."[12]

Barlow's men fought off the Johnnies. Private Landis of the Irish Brigade recollected, "After the Div. reached the breastworks we immediately formed, and the rebs, I presume, were about as much surprised to find themselves upon our entrenchments, as we were to be 'outflanked' in front of them, and the[y] received in front of them about as much from our rifles as they bargained for, and were satisfied in a very few minutes to retire pretty precipitately."[13]

The rifle pits of the rear II Corps line did not afford absolute safety. "When we got back to the breastworks we found them occupied by some of our troops, and as our ranks were so entirely broken up we did not try to reform our line there, but went farther to the rear," Corporal Cushing of Fraser's brigade remembered. "As I came over the works and started on, an officer of the men in the works called to the men to stop and form a line on their left." Thinking the enemy could not drive them out of the breastworks, Cushing returned and complied. "At this time the firing was quite heavy a little farther up the line and kept coming nearer us, and soon we heard some one coming in front of us but could see no one as the bushes were so thick," he recalled. Some thought those approaching were fellow fugitives and did not want to fire. "I did not think they were, but to be sure I went out in front of the line until I could see them quite plain and found they were dressed in grey and what we called Rebs, came back and told them they were 'Rebs' and not our men," remembered Cushing. "The bushes were so thick we could not see more than four or five rods, but when they came near enough so we could see the bushes move as they made their way through them, opened fire on them." The Confederates stopped briefly, then began to yell and charged. "I had not fired more than twice and got my gun loaded when I noticed a big Reb about sixty feet away at my left," recalled Cushing. The Secessionist was standing behind a clump of tall bushes, each as thick as Cushing's wrist. "I sighted my gun for him which he noticed and jumped about to avoid my getting a good aim, but I fired, did not have time to note the effect, for just then a few bayonets were pushed over the

11 *OR* 40, 1:329.

12 Gove to "Dear Sister," June 23, 1864.

13 Landis to Father, July 2, 1864.

works near my head and as many more were behind, with the order to surrender," Cushing remembered. "They had gone around our left and come up behind us while we were engaged with those in front." A gap between II Corps' left and VI Corps' right made this Confederate maneuver possible. Commanded to lay down their guns, Cushing and his companions reluctantly complied.[14]

Despite the gap remaining between II Corps and VI Corps, Birney reported to Meade at 4:00 p.m. that II Corps' lines were reestablished in the second line of entrenchments. By this time, Griffin's and Ayres's divisions each had a brigade available to send, which Warren thought a better idea than advancing on the Confederates opposite his lines. Meade directed Warren to send the two available brigades to Birney at the Jones house. At about 4:20 p.m., the commander of the Army of the Potomac directed that the two brigades move at the double-quick. The Great Peppery also sent a member of his staff to Horatio Wright's headquarters with instructions for VI Corps to fall back to the breastworks that ran north and south on the western end of the Williams farm.

Sweitzer's brigade of Griffin's division was already in motion, led by General Griffin himself. Crossing to the west side of Jerusalem Plank Road proved hazardous. "As we filed across the road we lost many men from the shots of a battery, which were sent down it like balls in a bowling alley," remembered Capt. Edwin C. Bennett, acting assistant adjutant general of Sweitzer's brigade. "The 32nd Massachusetts Volunteers was nicked three or four times but moved steadily on."[15]

The plank road presented a terrible spectacle. "On the roadside crossed by the One Hundred and Fifty-fifth were dozens of men struck and mortally wounded, piled in the middle of the road, and crawling to the side, many shouting in their delirium of home, mothers, wives, and others appealing most piteously to the Almighty for relief," recollected Pvt. Charles F. McKenna of the 155th Pennsylvania's Company E. "The dead also strewn across the road from the same cause were very numerous."[16] After five of the 155th's men had suffered wounds from Confederate cannon fire, the 155th adjusted its crossing to avoid the fire of the Dimmock Line battery zeroing in on the plank road. Minutes later Sweitzer's brigade arrived near the Jones house.

Armes, returning to the Jones house from Meade's headquarters, went to see if Gibbon had recaptured the battery. Gibbon's troops appeared too tired and

14 Cushing, "Some Experiences of the Civil War."

15 Edwin C. Bennett, *Musket and Sword, or the Camp, March and Firing Line in the Army of the Potomac* (Boston, 1900), 282–283.

16 Charles E. McKenna, comp., *Under the Maltese Cross: Antietam to Appomattox, The Loyal Uprising in Western Pennsylvania, 1861–1865* (Pittsburgh, PA, 1910), 302.

demoralized for such a mission, and Armes conveyed this observation to Hancock. "For God's sake get a division from the Fifth Corps at once," Hancock said.

By the time Birney returned to his right, he found waiting for him in the vicinity of the Jones house Griffin with Sweitzer's brigade of the corps that wore the Maltese Cross. Griffin offered to retake McKnight's battery. "Birney seemed too proud to have it said another Corps could retake a lost battery that he had failed to take with such a force as he had engaged, and seemed to display a feeling of jealousy for fear Griffin might receive the credit he desired for himself," Armes recalled. "General Griffin seemed displeased at the refusal of General Birney to allow him to send a force from his Corps to try to recapture the battery, and so expressed himself to me."[17] Birney again ordered Gibbon to retake McKnight's guns. Sweitzer's brigade remained in position to support Gibbon.

The seven reserve companies of the 1st United States Sharpshooters lay on the ground under shellfire in front of the rear Federal line, where Birney, Griffin, and their staffs sat their horses. "[I]t was noticeable that every time a shell came over, most of the aids dodged and ducked as if they were unused to them, while the generals sat perfectly unmoved, except Gen. Griffin, who was constantly turning his head and watching where the shell exploded," Lieutenant Stevens of Company G remembered.[18] Griffin had begun the war in command of a battery.

II Corps deployed its remaining artillery in support of its infantry. The 4th New York heavies and Battery K, 4th United States Artillery, deployed in the open field near the rear line of II Corps in time to shore up the rallying position for Barlow's broken brigades. "I moved up at a trot, and just as I arrived on the line the enemy made an attack on my right," recalled 2nd Lt. John W. Roder of Battery K. He directed a subordinate "to open on them at once with the right section but with what effect I am not able to say on account of a thick wood being in my immediate front; however, the enemy left in a very short time after."[19]

The 10th Massachusetts and 6th Maine Batteries unlimbered to the left of the plank road. The 1st New Hampshire Battery dropped trail at the Jones house. Battery A, 1st Rhode Island Light Artillery, and Batteries C and K, 5th United States Artillery, went into battery along Mott's second line, the former 230 yards from the enemy. Batteries C and K engaged Dement's battery at 300 yards and after firing about fifty rounds drove it away. "During a part of the time the enemy fired canister, but did me no damage except to disable a wheel," remembered

17 Armes, *Ups and Downs of an Army Officer*, 106.

18 Stevens, *Berdan's United States Sharpshooters*, 466.

19 *OR* 40, 1:441.

Charles Griffin
Library of Congress

1st Lieutenant of Batteries C and K.[20] The 11th New York Battery moved up to deploy on the right of Jerusalem Plank Road in line with the right section of Battery B, 1st New Jersey. Battery F, 1st Pennsylvania Light Artillery, advanced preparatory to unlimbering on the right of the 6th Maine Battery. A company of engineers commenced building strong works for these two batteries.

Dushane's Maryland Brigade of Ayres's division moved out of camp en route to the support of II Corps about 5:00 p.m. Around the same time, Wright dispatched Ballier's brigade of Wheaton's division to fill the gap between the left of Barlow's division and the right of Russell's division near the Strong house. That was also approximately when the 8th New York Heavy Artillery, the Seymour Guard, which lay only about 500 yards to the rear of the lunettes of McKnight's battery, received orders to recapture the guns. When the heavies reached Pierce, he formed them into a second line, told his officers that he intended to charge and retake the works, and sent his men forward.

The Mississippians in their new line nearly perpendicular to the captured earthworks could hear the oncoming bluecoats. "The jingle of accoutrements mingled with the rustle of many men breaking through the brush like the sound of a mighty rushing wind," Private Holt recalled.

"Keep the line straight!" Yankee voices said. "Don't crowd! Steady there men, steady!"

The Mississippians kept digging, satisfied the Northerners could not keep their lines straight in the underbrush.[21]

The Union battle line burst into view 50 yards away and encountered friendly fire first. "Our line of battle . . . opened fire before my men could withdraw,

20 Ibid., 443.

21 Cockrell and Ballard, eds., *A Mississippi Rebel in the Army of Northern Virginia*, 294.

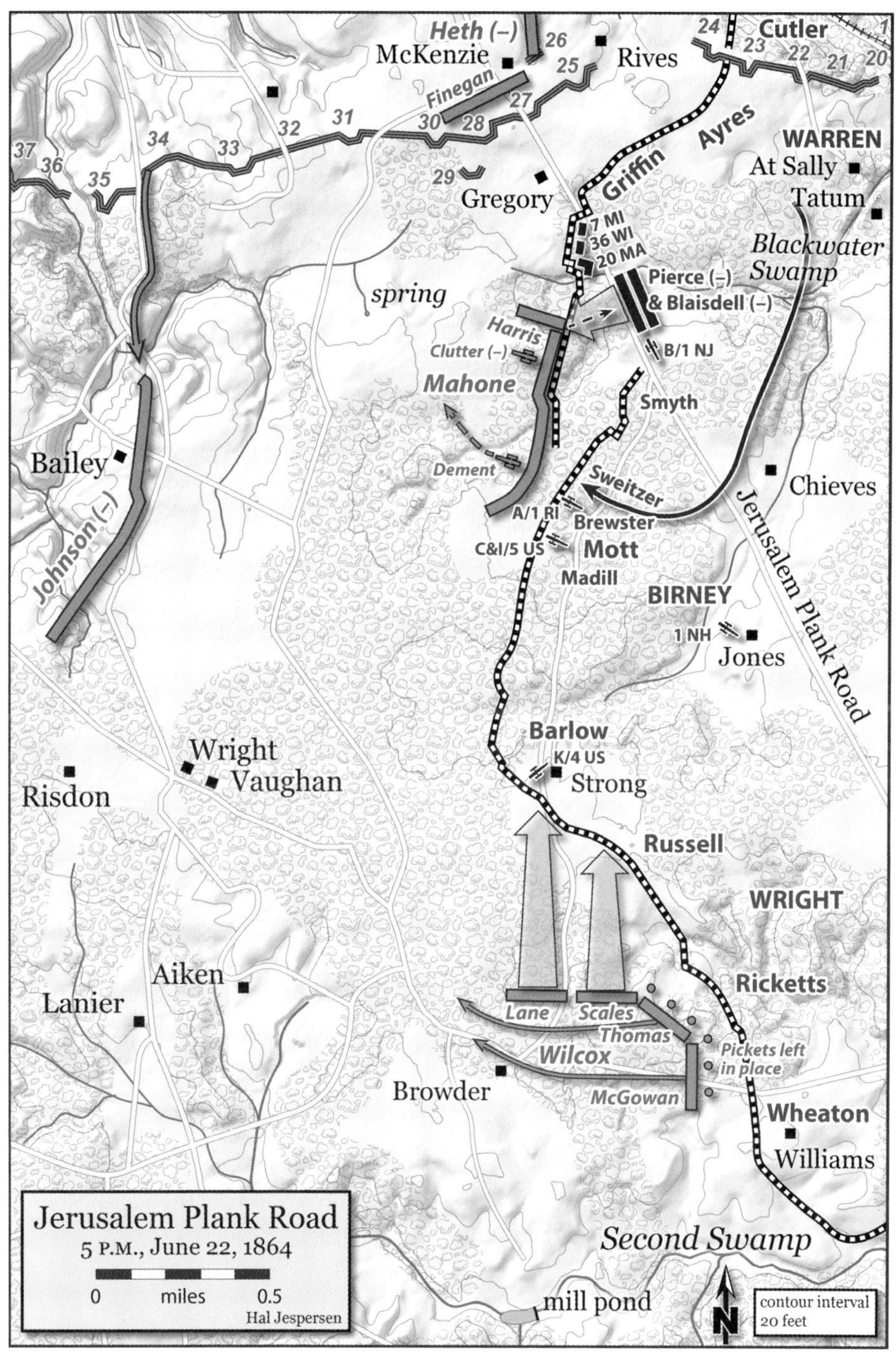

Jerusalem Plank Road
5 P.M., June 22, 1864
0 miles 0.5
Hal Jespersen

consequently some of them were disabled from the fire of our own troops," recollected Captain Farwell of the 1st Minnesota.[22]

The Confederates then unleashed a galling fire. "The colors fell three times, the bearers who successively bore them being shot dead," recalled Captain Spaulding of the 19th Maine on the right of Pierce's first line.[23]

Fairbanks saw the cook who had accompanied the line fall, mortally wounded. "In this charge a ball struck my cartridge box and a minute later one struck the barrel of my rifle," Fairbanks remembered.[24]

The Secessionist fusillade proved unendurable to the Northerners. "The first line broke, rushed through the second, carrying part of it with it, and it was by the greatest exertions of myself and staff that we stopped them," Pierce remembered. He began preparing another counterattack.

* * *

Around 5:00 p.m., Blakemore reached Wilcox at his headquarters near the Aiken house. About the same time, Wilcox remembered, "I heard heavy firing off to my left towards Petersburg and supposed it to be Mahone, this continued probably for ten minutes, it then ceased, it was heard again."[25] Wilcox ordered the skirmishers of the two brigades of the Light Division still facing VI Corps to hold the enemy until dark, falling back to the railroad and even to Petersburg if the Federals advanced. Ignoring the route to Mahone advised by Blakemore, Wilcox adhered to the course prescribed by Hill and led the bodies of the two brigades by a flank toward Petersburg.

The bursts of fire that Wilcox had heard came from Lane's and Scales's brigades bumping into the Federal rear line near the Strong house. In about half an hour of fighting, the two North Carolina brigades fired off most of their ammunition. Withdrawing from within 50 or 60 yards of the Unionist fortifications did not occur without casualties. Second Lieutenant Burwell T. Cotton of Company K, the Montgomery Boys, in the 34th North Carolina commanded, "[M]en try and fall back in good order & load and fire as you fall back," remembered Cotton's cousin 1st Sgt. William B. Coggin of the Montgomery Boys, wounded at Orange Court House in 1862. "This was the last words I heard him speak." Cotton, a former

22 *OR* 40, 1:374.

23 Ibid., 372.

24 Smith, *Nineteenth Regiment of Maine Volunteer Infantry*, 219.

25 Wilcox, Wilcox Report, "Petersburg," 2.

teacher wounded at Frayser's Farm and bruised by a grapeshot at Gettysburg, "was shot thrue the head" and "fell on his fase," recalled Coggin.

Cotton's friend Cpl. James C. Reeves of the Montgomery Boys, captured at Fredericksburg, recalled, "He was pierced through the head with a fragment of shell and instantly killed while falling back from the enemy's fortifications."[26] With his comrades withdrawing, Cotton had to lie where he fell. The dense undergrowth made pulling out in line of battle very slow. The sharpshooters of Lane's and Scales's brigades remained behind to cover the withdrawal.

Brigadier General Alfred Moore Scales, a lawyer and politician wounded at Chancellorsville and Gettysburg, enjoyed a nearly miraculous escape. "Just as we were ordered to withdraw I was struck three times with balls but thanks to a kind Providence was uninjured," he remembered. "One ball glanced from a tree & struck me on the foot laming me for a little while but did not penetrate the boot. Another struck me on the haversack but its force had been broken by some obstacle so that it only made a dent. Another passed through the skirt of my coat & went on its way."[27]

Wilcox, slogging northward with McGowan's and Thomas's brigades, met Scales's and Lane's brigades west of the Strong house around 6:00 p.m. United once again except for its sharpshooters, the Light Division floundered through the swamps and thickets toward the Bailey field. "Progress was very slow," recalled Blakemore. "Something seemed to act as a hitch every few paces."[28]

* * *

After Pierce reformed his battered attackers, Col. William Blaisdell reported with the 170th and 182nd New York, two more small regiments from the Corcoran Legion. Pierce placed one on the right and the other on the left of his second line. He was giving Blaisdell instructions for the next attack when orders arrived from Gibbon to charge the works immediately. Pierce did not comply immediately.

"As my first charge had broken from the right and left I ordered Lieutenant White, of my staff, to go to the right at once with a few men and see how near

26 Donald Hazelwood, *Tight Ranks, The Fighting Record of the 34th North Carolina in the Civil War: A History and Roster* (Ararat, VA, 2019), 220; Michael W. Taylor, ed., *The Cry is War, War, War: The Civil War Correspondence of Lts. Burwell Thomas Cotton and George Job Huntley, 34th Regiment North Carolina Troops, Pender-Scales Brigade of the Light Division, Stonewall Jackson's and A. P. Hill's Corps, Army of Northern Virginia, CSA* (Dayton, OH, 1994), 181–182.

27 Letter, Alfred M. Scales to "My own precious wife," June 29, 1864, Alfred M. Scales Papers, East Carolina University, Greeneville, NC.

28 Blakemore to Mahone, n.d., in Mahone, "A Reply to a Communication Published by Gen. C. M. Wilcox in the *New Orleans Times*, of January 1st, 1872," 20.

Alfred North Scales

Library of Congress

my right was to the Twentieth Massachusetts, which was reported as holding their position in their works," recalled Pierce. "My object was to connect with the Twentieth Massachusetts Volunteers, get a flank fire on the enemy, and fill the works in succession from the right, which I think could have been accomplished with little loss."[29] While awaiting White's report, which Pierce expected momentarily, and just as he had the assault column formed, Captain Embler arrived with an order from Gibbon placing Pierce under arrest for his tardiness and putting Blaisdell in command. Gibbon had O'Brien arrested as well.

The change of command occasioned further delay as Blaisdell familiarized himself with the situation. He also incorporated into his counterattack soldiers from O'Brien's brigade, including the 152nd New York, sent back westward across Jerusalem Plank Road under fire from the Secessionist guns in the Dimmock Line which zeroed in on the road. "When we recrossed the road, the enemy sent solid shot and shell bounding along the plank, rolling like balls on a ten pin alley, using the Yanks for pins," remembered Private Roback of the 152nd. The New Yorkers moved up the gentle wooded slope in line of battle, halting on a crest where they joined the men from the Corcoran Legion. Wilkes's section of Clutter's battery opened on the New Yorkers with grape and cannister. "We lay in that position one hour, with leaden hail showering over and around us," Roback recalled.[30]

Dushane's brigade of Ayres's division crossed the plank road around that time, too far south to furnish pins for the bowling balls hurled by the butternut artillery in the Dimmock Line. When the Marylanders reached the Jones house, Birney directed the brigade to assist Barlow's division. Dushane's brigade plodded off toward the Strong house and the Red Club Division. Barlow put the Maryland Brigade in reserve.

Around 6:00 p.m. Meade ordered an advance along his whole front for 7:00 p.m. Despite doubting the reliability of a report that McKnight's guns had

29 *OR* 40, 1:370.

30 Roback, comp., *152d N. Y. V.*, 105.

been recaptured, the commander of the Army of the Potomac forwarded it to Grant. Warren directed his division commanders to hold ready as many men as they could spare for the coming advance. Burnside, farther away and still concerned about the strength and manpower of his lines, could not act as aggressively. Horatio Wright thought his men too tired to attack and sent Lyman to inform Meade.

"Ask Gen. Wright, what am I to do tomorrow if I do not advance tonight?" said the Great Peppery when Lyman conveyed Wright's complaint.

Lyman rode back to Wright with Meade's question.

"Ah!" Wright said. "That I do not know!"[31]

* * *

Just after sundown the 10th Georgia Battalion of Rans Wright's brigade got orders for four men from each company to go out and locate the enemy in front of the lunettes of McKnight's battery. The Georgians had not gone very far when Private Methvin heard a voice.

"Halt, there!" said someone.

Immediately in front of Methvin, within 30 or 40 feet, lay two lines of soldiers. "They ordered me to 'come in,' or they would shoot me in," he remembered. Two of the soldiers aimed at a man on Methvin's right. "I raised my gun, aimed about their middle, and fired, then turned and ran for dear life, going head foremost through the embrasure where we had just captured the four-gun battery," Methvin recalled.

Just then, as it was getting dark, Blaisdell's Yankees were ordered to charge. They followed Methvin and his fellow pickets closely and received instructions to fix bayonets when within 20 steps of the Georgians. "I never heard such a rattle of bayonets before," remembered Methvin.

"Hold your fire!" his commander said. "Hold your fire!"

The Federals got closer.

"Fire!" came the order.

"I never saw such slaughter," recalled Methvin. "Our line was a blaze of fire as far as I could see."[32]

The 8th New York heavies did not falter. They "went steadily forward under a terrible fire, and succeeded in getting within fifty yards of the enemy's works," recalled Adjt. J. "Jack" R. Cooper of the 8th.[33]

31 Lowe, ed., *Meade's Army*, 223.

32 Methvin, "In the Wilderness Campaign," *CV* 23:455.

33 "Head Quarters 8th N. Y. Vol.," *Batavia* (NY) *Republican Advocate*, July 12, 1864, beyondthecrater.com. Retrieved June 15, 2024.

Then, within four rods of the captured earthworks, the regiment's commander took a bullet through the bowels. "As soon as the Col. fell the regiment halted & lay down just on the edge of a piece of woods," recalled Cpl. John J. Sherman of the 8th's Company G.[34]

The 8th threw up breastworks under heavy fire. "I lay on the ground less than two rods from the rebels for an hour with the bullets flying like hail over me," remembered the 8th's Maj. Joel B. Baker. "Then I crawled back three or four rods behind a big log where I breathed freer." Baker soon withdrew to organize his troops and under the orders of Blaisdell began building breastworks about five rods from the enemy held works. "This was hot work for the rebs kept firing upon us," recalled Baker. "We kept a steady fire upon them too which made them keep their heads down."[35]

The artillerists in Wilkes's section of Clutter's battery behind the Georgians signaled them to lie down, and they obeyed. The gunners shelled the woods in front of the Georgians and set the timber on fire. "It seemed to me that the blaze was twenty feet high," Methvin remembered. "The scene was heart-rending, and cries for help to get the wounded out of the fire were heard."[36]

A few yards in front of the 19th Maine, the pitch on a dry tree caught fire and illuminated the Mainers. "I heard some officer order a soldier to go and put out the fire, with a canteen of water," remembered Fairbanks. The soldier partially extinguished the blaze but did not return. The officer sent another man to see what had become of the first. "The second soldier found the first one dead near the tree and he himself was wounded before he got back to our lines," recalled Fairbanks.[37]

Shells overshooting Blaisdell's Federals subjected Sweitzer's brigade "to the hardest shelling we ever received," recalled 1st Sgt. David Porter Marshall of the 155th Pennsylvania's Company K. "We saw one passing through the line of a regiment . . . in front of us, instantly killing three and severely wounding four others. We saw them strike a few feet in front of us and bound over our heads. We heard them go close over our heads, and saw them strike in our rear. We saw them

34 William Russell Dunn, *Full Measure of Devotion: The Eighth New York Volunteer Heavy Artillery*, 2 vols. (Kearney, NE: Morris Publishing, 1997), 2:366.

35 Naomi B. Baker, comp., *Letters Home: Joel B. Baker, A Collection of "Letters Home" from the Civil War, written by Colonel Joel B. Baker and compiled by his great-grandaughter, Naomi B. Baker* (Lockport, NY: C. W. Baker Agency, 1996), 194–195.

36 Methvin, "In the Wilderness Campaign," *CV* 23:455.

37 Smith, *Nineteenth Regiment of Maine Volunteers*, 213.

strike nearly every place except where we were."[38] The bombardment ceased after half an hour except for an occasional shell.

The second Federal counterattack had extended to the front of the Mississippi Brigade in its works overlooking the branch. "They did not show very strong fighting spirit, and, having failed to drive us out in the second charge, they laid down in the bushes and kept up a hot fire in our direction until night," remembered Holt. "The smoke settled down among the scrub pines and made the darkness doubly so."[39] The Mississippians posted sentinels and went to sleep.

* * *

Around the same time, half a mile to the south, the reserve companies of the 1st United States Sharpshooters in front of Mott's second line advanced as skirmishers across and down a big sloping open field to within 100 yards of a thick wood, from which Confederates suddenly opened on them. The sharpshooters ducked into a ditch and briskly responded. They held their own until a brigade of Federal infantry charged down the field with fixed bayonets. "[S]ome of them were sufficiently excited to cause their pieces to discharge in a rather careless manner," recalled Stevens. Their bullets whizzed or hit all around the Green Coats.

"Stop that firing, you infernal fools," the marksmen yelled.

The firing ceased when the infantry passed and drove the Secessionists from the timber.[40]

* * *

About another half mile to the south, Birney's men charged into the woods west of the Strong farm. They encountered the sharpshooters of Lane's and Scales's brigades. "Fresh troops were moved into line," recalled Capt. John D. Young of Company C of the 34th North Carolina in the sharpshooter battalion of Scales's brigade, "the rattle of accoutrements and canteens could be heard, and the officers' words of command all indicated preparations for an early advance." Word came down the line to give the Yanks one volley and then retreat.

"Hold your fire for the line of battle!" the officers of the sharpshooters shouted.

38 D. P. Marshall, *Company "K," 155th Volunteer Pa. Zouaves, A Detailed History of the Organization and Service to the Country During the Civil War 1862 Until the Collapse of the Rebellion, Together with many incidents and reminiscences of the Camp, the March and the Battle Field, also Much of the History of the Grand Old 155th* (London, UK, 1888), 182.

39 Cockrell and Ballard, eds., *A Mississippi Rebel in the Army of Northern Virginia*, 294–295.

40 Stevens, *Berdan's United States Sharpshooters*, 466.

The Tarheel marksmen wanted nothing more.

"We gave them one volley and broke for the rear like quarter-horses," Young remembered.

The shouting of the Federals alarmed the cavalry pickets of the 3rd North Carolina Cavalry behind the fleeing sharpshooters. The horsemen, according to Young, "at once decamped, nor did they draw rein until they reached their camp."[41]

* * *

Around a mile farther south, VI Corps stormed westward. The Yanks encountered the sharpshooters of McGowan's and Thomas's brigades, who remained in the works captured by their brigades earlier. The Federals forced the marksmen back and tried to cut off and capture them after discovering their weakness. "They told me they could hear the Federals calling to one another to hurry up and cut off the rebels," Lieutenant Caldwell of McGowan's brigade recalled. "Some men said they could hear the former panting as they rushed at them."

The sharpshooters escaped. One little marksman straggled into Caldwell's line just after dark, still gasping and laughing.

"Lord God," the South Carolinian said, "you ought to see them fat Yankees run. They run arter me, a-hollerin' 'Stop, you damned rebel! Cut off the damned rebels!' I heered 'em blow. Says I to myself, 'You too fat, Yankee! You get too much to eat over your side. You don't catch me!' And you ought to 'a seed me as I slid past 'em."[42]

Having advanced half a mile, VI Corps halted a quarter mile east of the Aiken house, a mile and a half from the Weldon Railroad. First Sergeant Graham of the 10th Vermont remembered, "we went about a mile through the worst swamp I had ever seen."[43]

Disorder prevailed that night at corps headquarters at the Williams house. "The house . . . had been ransacked from top to bottom by the soldiers, carpets torn up and everything destroyed," recalled Sgt. J. Terrill Newton of the 14th New Jersey. "A splendid piano was left in the house, and as several of the men could play, dancing and singing were kept up on a rude style for several hours."[44]

41 Young, "A Campaign with Sharpshooters," 280–281.

42 Caldwell, *McGowan's South Carolina Brigade*, 164.

43 Graham Diary, June 22, 1864.

44 J. Terrill Newton, *Campaign of the Fourteenth Regiment New Jersey Volunteers* (New Brunswick, NJ, 1884), 70.

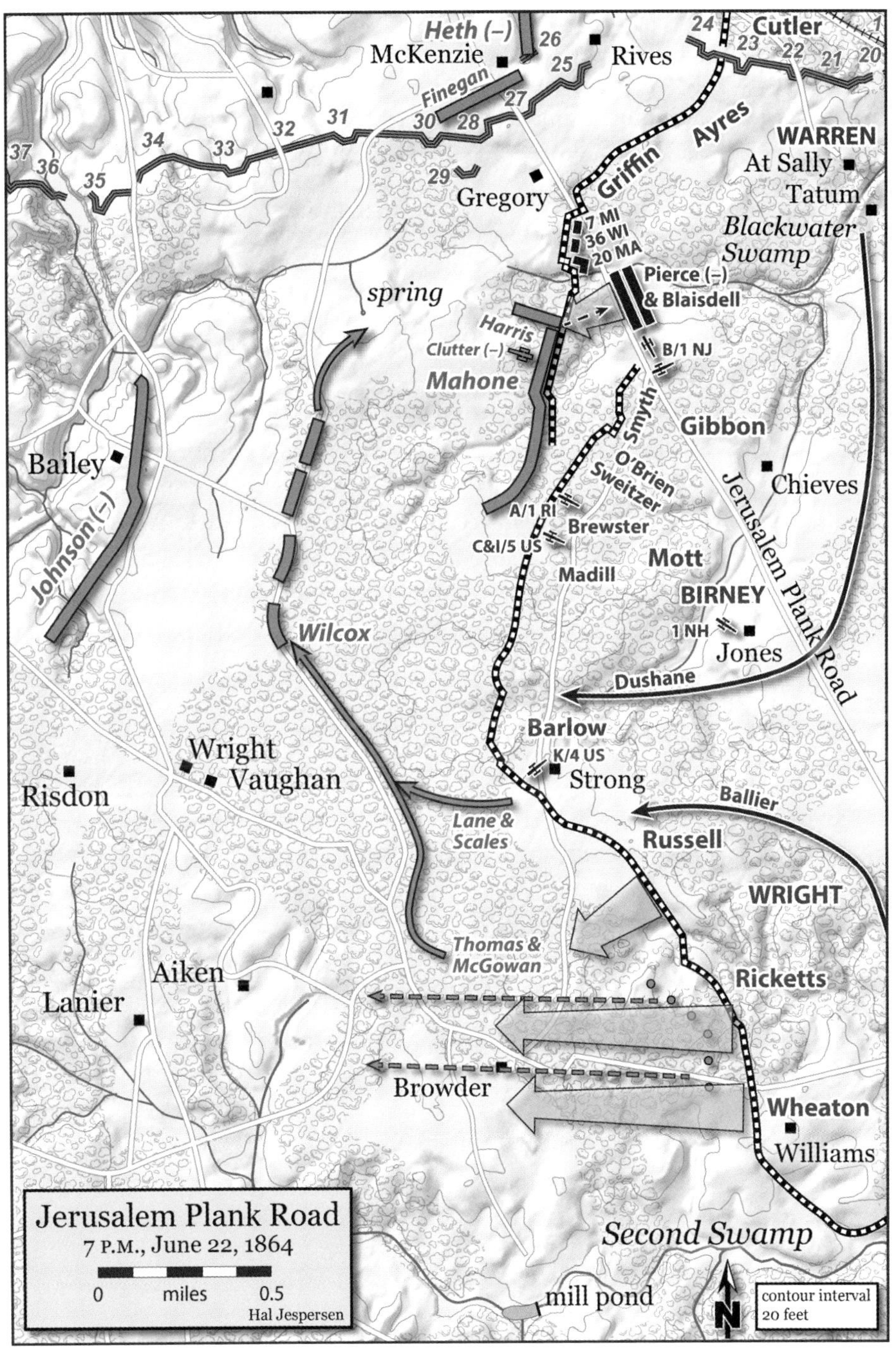
Heth (–)
McKenzie
Rives
Cutler
Finegan
Griffin
Ayres
WARREN
At Sally
Tatum
Gregory
7 MI
36 WI
20 MA
Blackwater
Swamp
Pierce (–)
& Blaisdell
spring
Harris
Clutter (–)
B/1 NJ
Mahone
Smyth
Gibbon
Bailey
O'Brien
Sweitzer
Chieves
Jerusalem Plank Road
Johnson (–)
A/1 RI
Brewster
C&I/5 US
Mott
Madill
BIRNEY
1 NH
Jones
Wilcox
Dushane
Barlow
K/4 US
Wright
Vaughan
Strong
Risdon
Ballier
Lane & Scales
Russell
WRIGHT
Thomas & McGowan
Ricketts
Aiken
Lanier
Browder
Wheaton
Williams
Second Swamp
mill pond
contour interval 20 feet
N
Jerusalem Plank Road
7 P.M., June 22, 1864
0 miles 0.5
Hal Jespersen

* * *

After the Federal counterattacks failed, Hill joined Mahone in the Bailey field and "very gracefully decline command of the field," recollected John Wesley Friend, one of Mahone's couriers.[45] Soon Wilcox's vanguard filed into the field. "It did not require any large degree of military experience to see at once that the movement was not what was expected, and that the time for this command to prove of practical use upon that occasion had passed," remembered Blakemore.[46] In response to a request from Mahone for assistance, Wilcox put Thomas's brigade in on Porte's right.

The gathering gloom helped retreat and hindered reconnaissance. "As soon as it became dark the brigade commenced to fall back & our regiment with it, all but one company," recalled Corporal Sherman of the 8th New York heavies. "There was no officer left to command our company the Capt being in command of the second Batallion & all the sergeants being absent or wounded." Sherman told his men to lie still until he found an officer to give him orders. Failing to find an officer, he returned to his company and ordered his comrades to fall back. Bringing them off in good order, he halted them and directed them to lie down. "Just as they had done this Major [Erastus M.] Spaulding & Capt [Elbridge] Sherwin came up & I turned over the command of the company to them," Sherman remembered. "I never saw men so cool under fire as they were while the company lay there."

Supposing a line of skirmishers stood between him and the captured breastworks, Sherman went toward them to reconnoiter. In the darkness he approached to within around three rods of the enemy line and stood behind a tree until he had satisfied himself that no pickets intervened between him and the Confederates. Then he retreated. "I hadent gone more than a rod or two before I met General [Gibbon], the commander of the 2nd Div. & his staff creeping along on their hands and knees while I was standing up," Sherman recalled. "They took me for a rebel & it scared them but when I told them who I was & what regt I belonged to he told me to go & have a squad of men detailed to act as skirmishers & told me to take charge of them." Returning to his company, Sherman picked out some men and stationed them where Gibbon had indicated.[47]

Establishing picket lines in darkness further obscured by the woods proved hazardous because of the proximity of the enemy. Sweitzer's brigade advanced

45 Letter, J. W. Friend to William Mahone, Feb. 1, 1872, William Mahone Papers, Duke University.

46 Mahone, "A Reply to a Communication Published by Gen. C. M. Wilcox in the *New Orleans Times*, of January 1st, 1872," 20.

47 Dunn, *Full Measure of Devotion*, 2:366. Sherman mistook Gibbon, the division commander, for Pierce, the brigadier, who was under arrest. *OR* 40, 1:370.

beyond the lines of Blaisdell's brigade and deployed as skirmishers, in some places only a few yards from the enemy. "We were in doubt about one little group which we saw ten yards from us, and challenged it, falling flat at the same time," recollected Captain Bennett of Sweitzer's brigade. "Our accent was recognized and drew its fire. We did not cultivate them any further; the hint was sufficient and we drew back."[48]

The 155th Pennsylvania's Company E included Pvt. Hugh Bayne, a former coal miner, physically hale but mentally so weak that his company commander never allowed him to carry a musket but always assigned him duty requiring an ax, shovel, or similarly peaceful implement. Private McKenna recalled:

> By some extraordinary oversight in this day's engagement, Bayne, who did not realize what danger was, accompanied the Regiment and Company. . . . Armed with a shovel, Bayne stood up . . . when all of the Regiment in response to the orders of the officers had lain down and were hugging the earth as closely as possible to avoid the enemy's shots. . . . Bayne arose, and seeing the enemy's line very distinctly, turned around to inform his comrades of the fact, when the enemy sent a minie ball through his jaw. It is said this was the only time when Bayne was ever known to look serious.[49]

At dark, Battery A, 1st Rhode Island, withdrew from its position in Mott's works, considered too near the enemy to permit occupation during the night. The 6th Maine Battery relieved Battery B, 1st New Jersey, covering Jerusalem Plank Road. The 11th New York Battery started erecting works to the right of the 6th Maine Battery, getting guns in position and sinking limbers.

Casualties filled the division's hospitals. "The wounded are coming in quite fast tonight," recalled Ryno as he worked in the hospital of Mott's division. "The Division Band played a few pieces tonight which made us think of our homes and loved ones far away."[50]

By this time, "we had eight large tents filled with wounded," remembered Private Peterson at the hospital of Gibbon's division.[51]

48 Bennett, *Musket and Sword*, 283.

49 McKenna, comp., *Under the Maltese Cross*, 303. "His wound, however, was not dangerous," remembered McKenna. "He was taken to the hospital and, after recovery, discharged for mental incapacity." Ibid.

50 Ryno Diary, June 22, 1864.

51 Peterson Diary, June 22, 1864.

Mourning the loss of his 19th Massachusetts' colors, the regiment's surgeon Major J. Franklin Dyer wrote, "the morale of [Pierce's] brigade is gone."[52]

* * *

The Southerners put most of their prisoners on an island in the Appomattox above Petersburg. There the horde of captives awaited transport to Secessionist prisons. Some still had the means to make the best of the situation. Several days earlier, the 1st Maine heavies had received whiskey rations, which a few of the men hoarded. "Sergt [Joseph A.] Burlingame and I were among those who were captured, and we had five canteens of whiskey with us at the time," recalled Pvt. Marcus M. Alley of the 1st's Company I. "Our captors took us to some small island, and that night we had a sort of consolation celebration, and got pretty happy with the aid of the liquor, in spite of surrounding circumstances."[53] Few of the other prisoners had anything with which to console themselves as they contemplated the prospect of Andersonville.

At 10:00 p.m. the Confederates in the captured works began returning to their lines. They carried with them the last spoils of their victory—the small arms they had captured. "Every man was required to carry off as many muskets as he was able to tote," recalled Lieutenant Phillips in the 12th Virginia.[54] He bore away four on his shoulders.

Meade ordered an attack to be mounted at 3:30 a.m. the following morning. "I regret to say there is no confirmation of the report of the recapture of our guns," he wrote to Grant. "It is believed the enemy drew them off."[55] Meade thought he had lost only about 100 prisoners and that his casualties were light.

* * *

During the night of June 22–23, Dushane's and Sweitzer's V Corps brigades trudged back to their camps. The troops from Bushrod Johnson's division returned to the Dimmock Line about 2:00 a.m. on June 23.

Southern sentinels from Mahone's force remained in the fortifications captured from the Federals. "These pickets were stationed some twenty or thirty yards apart, and could not plainly be seen on account of darkness, though the moon gave some

52 Michael B. Chesson, ed., *The Journal of a Civil War Surgeon* (Lincoln, NE, 2003), 175.

53 "It Was a Fearful Charge," *Charleston* (SC) *News and Courier*, July 18, 1897, p. 3 col. 1.

54 Phillips, "Sixth Corporal," 58.

55 *OR* 40, 2:304.

James Eldred Phillips

Virginia Museum of History and Culture

light," remembered the 12th Virginia's First Sergeant Whitehorne. Just before daylight, Whitehorne received orders from his company commander to go along the picket line and instruct one soldier at a time to leave his post and quietly return to the regiment. After relieving all but the last picket, Whitehorne saw a man standing behind a pine bush and walked toward him. Before Whitehorne had taken many steps toward the approaching soldier, he heard a low whistle to his right and rear and withdrew.

"You were walking right up to that Yankee," said the last sentinel. "I have been watching him all night."[56]

The two hastened back to Confederate lines.

While the Secessionist pickets withdrew from the captured breastworks, Harris's Mississippi Brigade received orders to return to those works. As the Mississippians arrived, they heard the Yanks massing for an assault. Elements of Birney's corps and Sweitzer's brigade of V Corps reinforcements advanced at 3:30 a.m. and began reoccupying the works around the Mississippians. Harris perceived the Unionists overlapping his brigade's flanks and ordered his four regiments to double-quick to the rear by companies. "Double-quick is a flexible term that can mean, fast, faster or to run like a scared rabbit," the 16th Mississippi's Private Holt clarified later. "Every company put its own interpretation on the word and acted accordingly." Those who hurried escaped. Those who took their time got to see the inside of Yankee prisons.[57]

Major Baker of the 8th New York heavies led about 25 men into the breastworks and discovered a mass of Rebels behind a little strip of trees and bushes a few yards away. "We opened fire . . . which surprised them so they skedaddled like fun," Baker recalled. "Some were so near they did not dare to run & I told them to

56 Elmore, ed., *Diary of J. E. Whitehorne*, 52.

57 Cockrell and Ballard, eds., *A Mississippi Rebel in the Army of Northern Virginia*, 295.

throw down their guns & come in or we would shoot them." Five surrendered. "For a few minutes I thought my chances for Libby Prison pretty good for if the rebs had known how few of us were there they could have taken us quite easy," Baker remembered. In a few moments reinforcements arrived and allayed Baker's worries. "We kept the rebel works all day keeping up a skirmish with the Rebs which reminded me of a squirrel hunt but it was more dangerous than interesting," he recalled.[58]

* * *

The Confederates stood in high spirits on June 23, having on the previous day routed much of a vastly superior force and captured four guns. They had killed and wounded about 647 and taken prisoner at least 1,724 from II Corps, and they had killed and wounded at least 37 and captured around 18 from VI Corps.[59]

58 Baker, comp., *Joel B. Baker, A Collection of "Letters Home" from the Civil War*, 194–195. The 91st Pennsylvania of Sweitzer's brigade lost one mortally wounded and three wounded; another man deserted. "The 91st Pennsylvania Volunteer Infantry," freepages.rootsweb.com/~pa91/military/cc46.html#19.

59 The Federals reportedly lost 142 killed, 654 wounded, and 2,166 captured or missing, for a total of 2,962. Fox, *Regimental Losses*, 547; Dyer, *Compendium*, 946. This figure includes neither II Corps casualties from June 21 nor any casualties from V Corps. Ibid. (Cos. C and D of the 1st Massachusetts Cavalry, engaged June 21, are not included in Dyer's list of participating units). Ibid., 947.

Fox and Dyer have conflated the Unionist casualties of June 22 and June 23 for II and VI corps. Bryce A. Suderow, "Confederate Casualties Near the Jerusalem Plank Road, June 21–23, 1864," *The Kepi* 3, no. 5 (Oct.–Nov. 1985): 15, n. 18. Fox and Dyer numbered the killed of the two corps at 142 and the wounded at 654. Dyer, *Compendium*, 946. At the same time, they undercounted the 2,225 Federal prisoners delivered to the Confederate provost marshal in Petersburg on June 22 and June 23. "The Fighting Around Petersburg," *Daily Richmond Examiner*, June 25, 1864, p. 2, cols. 4–5 (1,742 prisoners on June 22); "Telegraphic Reports of the Press Association," *Daily Richmond Examiner*, June 25, 1864, p. 2, col. 6 (483 captives on June 23). That does not include wounded prisoners hospitalized rather than delivered to the provost marshal.

On June 22, the 2nd Connecticut Heavy Artillery in Upton's brigade, Russell's division, VI Corps, had six killed, seven wounded, and six captured. Vaill, *Second Connecticut Volunteer Heavy Artillery*, 77. The 95th Pennsylvania lost one wounded. Bates, *History of Pennsylvania Volunteers*, 3:350.

The 93rd Pennsylvania in Ballier's brigade, Wheaton's division, lost 13 killed and wounded. Ibid., 291.

In Lewis Grant's brigade, the 4th Vermont had two captured and the 5th Vermont had one wounded. Vermont, Adjutant General, *Revised Roster of Vermont Volunteers*, 127, 140, 161.

In Keifer's brigade, Ricketts's division, the 6th Maryland had two killed, one wounded. L. Allison Wilmer, J. H. Jarrett, Geo. W. F. Vernon, *History and Roster of Maryland Volunteers, War of 1861–5, Prepared Under Authority of The General Assembly of Maryland*, 2 vols. (Baltimore, 1898), 1:226, 227, 233. The 110th Ohio lost two wounded, one of them mortally. Roster Commission, *Official Roster of the Soldiers of the State of Ohio*, 8:21, 39. The 126th Ohio had one mortally wounded and one missing. Ibid., 8:481, 482. The 9th New York Heavy Artillery lost one man wounded. Alfred Seelye Roe, *The Ninth New York Heavy Artillery, A History of Its Organization, Its Service in the Defenses of Washington, Marches, Camps, Battles and Muster-out, with Accounts of Life in a Rebel Prison, Personal Experiences, Names and Addresses of Surviving Members, Personal Sketches, And a Complete Roster of the Regiment* (Worcester, MA, 1899), 560.

In Truex's brigade, the 87th Pennsylvania had one killed, nine captured. Bates, *History of Pennsylvania Volunteers*, 3:36–63, *passim*. The 106th New York had one killed. LaForge Diary, June 23, 1864.

About 30 more killed and wounded in V Corps brought the butcher's bill to roughly 2,456.[60]

Mahone's division lost about 85 killed or mortally wounded, 315 wounded, and 19 missing, for a total of 419.[61]

I did not include among VI Corps casualties the soldiers of Russell's and Wheaton's divisions killed or wounded June 21 while they were pulling out of the trenches.

VI Corps had 37 killed and wounded and 18 captured, for a total of 55 casualties, on June 22, and had 112 killed and wounded on June 23. See Chapter Seven, n. 57, *infra*. By subtracting the missing of VI Corps on June 22 (18) from the 1,742 missing from II and VI corps on June 22, and by subtracting the killed and wounded of VI Corps on June 22 (37) and June 23 (112) from the conflated figure of 796 killed and wounded for both corps on June 22 and June 23, we find that on June 22, II Corps had 647 killed and wounded and at least 1,724 captured, for a total of at least 2,371 casualties.

60 The 22nd Massachusetts in Sweitzer's brigade of Griffin's V Corps division suffered four wounded. John Lord Parker, *Henry Wilson's Regiment: History of the Twenty-Second Massachusetts Infantry, the Second Company Sharpshooters, and the Third Light Battery in the War of the Rebellion* (Boston, 1887), 424. The 32nd Massachusetts had four wounded. Bennett, *Musket and Sword*, 284. The 4th Michigan mustered out on June 19. Jno. Robertson, Adjutant General, comp., *Michigan in the Civil War* (Lansing, 1882), 231. The soldier of the 91st wounded on June 22 probably earned his red badge on the picket line before 4 a.m. "The 91st Pennsylvania Volunteer Infantry," freepages.rootsweb.com/~pa91/military/cc46.html#19. The 155th Pennsylvania lost five wounded. McKenna, comp., *Under the Maltese Cross*, 30. The 21st Pennsylvania Cavalry (dismounted) had seven wounded. *OR* 40, 1:463.

Dushane's brigade lost one man killed in the Purnell Legion Cavalry (dismounted) when he carelessly exposed himself to enemy fire. Daniel Carroll Toomey, *The Maryland Brigade* (Baltimore, 2018), 83–84. The 7th Maryland lost one killed and one wounded, the 8th Maryland one wounded. L. Allison Wilmer, et al., *History and Roster of Maryland Volunteers, War of 1861–5*, 1:283, 318.

The V Corps casualties for June 22 are not included in Dyer's figures. Dyer, *Compendium*, 946.

61 Dement's battery lost six wounded. "List of Casualties in the First Maryland artillery," *Daily Richmond Examiner*, June 29, 1864, p. 1, col. 4.

CSRs have the Alabama Brigade losing 26 killed or mortally wounded, 97 wounded, six missing, a total of 129. Young, "Confederate Casualties in June 1864 at Petersburg." Another source reports that the brigade had 21 killed, 85 wounded, and 38 missing, a total of 144. Mahone's (Anderson's Old) Division Tabular Return of Casualties (Series II), Beineke Rare Book and Manuscript Library, Yale University, New Haven, CT. Usually, the higher number must prevail for the difficulties attendant upon Confederate statistics. Young, *Lee's Army During the Overland Campaign*, 18–21. Here the number of missing is inconsistent with the missing in the other brigades of Mahone's division, as if the missing were counted prematurely. Young, "Confederate Casualties in June 1864 at Petersburg." Sanders's brigade, according to its brigadier, lost six killed, 110 wounded. Sanders to "Dear Ma," June 28, 1864. David White counts two killed, 24 wounded, one missing in the 14th Alabama alone. David White, Study of the 14th Alabama, Private Collection of David White, Manassas, VA.

CSRs show 42 killed or dead of wounds, 147 wounded, and three missing, or a loss of 192. Young, "Confederate Casualties in June 1864 at Petersburg." Another source reports that the brigade had 32 killed, 147 wounded, and two missing, a total of 181. Mahone's (Anderson's Old) Division Tabular Return of Casualties (Series II). Wright's brigade lost 28 killed, 155 wounded, and two missing, or 185. *Augusta* (GA) *Chronicle & Sentinel*, July 21, 1864, p. 1, cols. 4–5. The 48th Georgia lost 30 killed and wounded. Folsom, *Heroes and Martyrs of Georgia*, 95. The 35th Georgia of Thomas's brigade reported three wounded, three captured. Ibid., 142. The 10th Georgia Battalion lost two killed, one mortally wounded, and 15 otherwise wounded. L. H. Carter, "For the Daily Telegraph." (Carter's recapitulation has only two killed and 15 wounded.) Ibid.

CSRs show the Virginia Brigade lost 13 killed or mortally wounded, 61 wounded, and eight missing, for a total of 92. Young, "Confederate Casualties in June 1864 at Petersburg." Another

Wilcox's division lost around 192, including 32 missing.[62]

Confederate losses thus numbered roughly 611.

Lee took heart in the results of this fight, finding confirmation of the opinion that he "had had for some time, that if we could get at our enemies we could destroy them." The results pleased Hill as well. "Mahone's three brigades have done it all," he wrote to Lee about Old Porte. "Promote him at once."[63]

"It was a beautiful fight," recalled Capt. George W. Clark of the 11th Alabama's Company B on Sanders's staff.[64] Clark had viewed the action from the picket line of Mahone's division just north of where his fellow Alabamians struck the Irish Brigade.

---

source reports that the brigade had 14 killed, 59 wounded, and eight missing, a total of 81. Mahone's (Anderson's Old) Division Tabular Return of Casualties (Series II). The 6th Virginia of the brigade lost two killed, 18 wounded, for a total of 20. Michael Cavanaugh, *6th Virginia Infantry*, (Lynchburg, VA, 1988), 76. The 12th Virginia had two wounded, three captured. George S. Bernard Diary, June 24, 1864, Alderman Library, University of Virginia, Charlottesville, VA; Henderson, *12th Virginia Infantry*, 106–167, *passim.*

CSRs reveal that the Mississippi Brigade lost four killed or dead of wounds, four wounded, and two missing. Young, "Confederate Casualties in June 1864 at Petersburg." Another source indicates the Mississippi Brigade had three wounded and two missing. Mahone's (Anderson's Old) Division Tabular Return of Casualties (Series II).

62 CSRs for McGowan's brigade show four killed or mortally wounded, eight wounded, and one missing, a total of 13 on June 22. Young, "Confederate Casualties in June 1864 at Petersburg." The brigade may have lost as many of the 38 (36 killed or wounded and two missing) of the 49 Caldwell originally reported as lost on June 22—a closer look reveals 11 of the 49 lost on surrounding dates. Caldwell, *McGowan's South Carolina Brigade*, 165–166. The surgeon of the 13th South Carolina reported the brigade's loss as "thirty or forty" and the 13th's loss as "one killed and two wounded." Spencer Glasgow Welch, *A Confederate Surgeon's Letters to His Wife* (New York, 1911), 100.

CSRs for Lane's brigade reveal nine killed or mortally wounded, 47 wounded, one wounded and captured, and 10 missing for a total of 67. Young, "Confederate Casualties in June 1864 at Petersburg." Another source indicates that the brigade lost seven killed, 50 wounded, and five captured on June 22, for a total of 62. List of Casualties in Lane's Brigade from May 5, 1864, to Oct. 1, 1864, James H. Lane Papers, Auburn University, Auburn, AL.

CSRs show that Scales's brigade lost 10 killed, 47 wounded, three wounded and captured, and 12 missing, a total of 72. Young, "Confederate Casualties in June 1864 at Petersburg." The 13th North Carolina in Scales's brigade lost seven wounded on June 22, 1864. *North Carolina Troops 1861–1865, A Roster*, Compiled by Weymouth T. Jordan, Jr. (Raleigh, NC, 1975), Vol. V, pp. 323, 339, 349, 351, 367, and 379. The 34th North Carolina in Scales's brigade lost two killed, eight wounded, and seven captured on June 22, for a total of 17. Hazelwood, *Tight Ranks*, 221.

CSRs establish that Thomas's brigade lost two killed or mortally wounded, six wounded, and seven missing, for a total of 15. Young, "Confederate Casualties in June 1864 at Petersburg." The 35th Georgia in Thomas's brigade lost three wounded and three missing. Folsom, *Heroes and Martyrs of Georgia*, 142. The 45th Georgia lost one killed, three wounded. Capt. John T. Brown, "45th Georgia," *Macon Daily Telegraph*, June 30, 1864, p. 2, col. 5.

63 Charles R. Knight, *From Arlington to Appomattox: Robert E. Lee's Civil War Day by Day, 1861–1865* (El Dorado Hills, CA, 2021), 408 n. 45.

64 George Clark, *A Glance Backward: Or Some Events in the Past History of My Life* (Houston, 1914), 55.

"We fought the 2d Corps, (Hancock's) and the prisoners state that this was the first time they had ever been whipped, and admit that it was a good one," remembered Captain Bachelor of the 48th Georgia.[65]

"It was a complete success & reflects much credit to the planer of the movement," remembered the 48th's Private Verdery.[66]

"It was the most brilliant move Mahone ever made," recalled the 16th Mississippi's Holt. "We doubled up Hancock's Corps like a jackknife."[67] Holt called the maneuver "a master move."[68]

The often-critical Sergeant Sale of the 12th Virginia wrote that of all the affairs in which his regiment had participated thus far during the campaign, this one "far outshown all the others in good management and success."[69]

The results did not please everyone. "Our brigade was in advance & did the greater part of the fighting," wrote Pvt. Alva B. Spencer of the 3rd Georgia's Company C, the Dawson Grays. "They were *supported* by other troops of our division but they are entitled to *all* the honor. The Virginia papers however, give all the praise to [Weisiger]'s brigade (Va.)."[70] Spencer, whom illness had prevented from participating on June 22, had been wounded at South Mills on April 19, 1862.

Mahone thought he would have done much more damage to the Federals if Wilcox had followed his instructions. Unaware at the time of Hill's misunderstanding, Mahone mistakenly blamed Wilcox, who justifiably complained that Hill had not fully informed him of his role in the attack.[71] Mahone and Wilcox commenced a controversy that lasted for decades.[72]

Among the Federal participants a blame game began. Meade blamed the Confederates and the landscape, writing, "The enemy resisted most persistently,

65 W. A. B., "Letter from the 48th Georgia."

66 Verdery to "Dear Father Mother & all,", June 25, 1864.

67 Cockrell and Ballard, eds., *A Mississippi Rebel in the Army of Northern Virginia*, 294.

68 Ibid., 296.

69 Letter, John F. Sale to "Dear Aunt," July 9, 1864, John F. Sale Papers.

70 Clyde G. Wiggins III, ed., *My Dear Friend: The Civil War Letters of Alva Benjamin Spencer, 3rd Georgia Regiment, Company C* (Macon, Ga., 2007), 128.

71 Wise, *The End of an Era*, 327; Gerard A. Patterson, *From Blue to Gray: The Life of Confederate General Cadmus M. Wilcox* (Mechanicsburg, PA, 2001), 81–82.

72 J. Watts De Peyster, "A Military Memoir of William Mahone, Major-General in the Confederate Army," *The Historical Magazine* 7, Second Series, no. 6 (June 1870): 390–406; C. M. Wilcox, "Military Operations Around Petersburg, the Mine, etc.," *New Orleans Times*, Jan. 1, 1872; Mahone, "A Reply to a Communication Published by Gen. C. M. Wilcox in the *New Orleans Times*, of January 1st, 1872;" Smith, *Nineteenth Regiment of Maine Volunteers*, 210 (1892 Mahone account); Mulholland, *116th Regiment Pennsylvania Volunteers*, 275 (1895 Mahone account).

Cadmus Marcellus Wilcox
Library of Congress

and several skirmishes and small affairs were had, in which, owing to the character of the country, being a dense thicket, and want of knowledge on our part of the topography, the enemy was enabled to defeat our purpose." The Army of the Potomac's commander thought Birney had "done very well."[73]

Meade's staffer Lyman initially blamed "hesitating corps commanders, exhausted troops and a dense and unknown country." The more Lyman thought about the direful affair, "the more extraordinary and disgraceful does it seem," he recalled. "At the same time, it is in the highest degree instructive as showing what a bold and well-informed enemy may accomplish in thick woods, where nobody can see more than a company front."[74]

Officially, Birney implied that Meade bore responsibility for creating the gap between II and VI Corps into which the Secessionists penetrated. The corps commander concluded, "I attribute the failure to the extraordinary losses among the commanding, staff, and other officers in this command, to the large proportion of new troops assigned to this corps to replace veterans, to the fact that the Sixth Corps did not advance simultaneously, and that in consequence my line was taken in flank, and at points even in reverse, creating a panic, and compelling a withdrawal to my line of that morning, with considerable loss." Privately, Birney blamed the army commander, writing, "It was a bold movement made contrary to my expressed views to Gen. Meade." The corps commander also blamed some of his troops. "A part of Gibbon's Division behaved badly—very badly," Birney wrote. "They were chiefly regiments whose term was up in a few days—they will not fight."[75]

Hancock blamed the officers and men who surrendered without fighting.

73 *OR* 40, 1:169; George Meade, ed., *The Life and Letters of George Gordon Meade*, 2:209.

74 Lowe, ed., *Meade's Army*, 222; Agassiz, ed., *Meade's Headquarters*, 188.

75 *OR* 40, 1:326–327; Letter, David Bell Birney to "My Dear Gross," July 4, 1864, David B. Birney Letters, AHEC.

Lieutenant Colonel Morgan blamed Meade for opening the gap into which the Rebels thrust. Lieutenant Colonel Walker blamed the losses of the corps, Meade's impatience, and credited the Southerners, writing, "Nothing but the extraordinary quickness and precision of the Confederate movements on this occasion would have made such a result possible."[76]

Armes thought Birney not up to the challenge of retaking the captured battery.

Barlow blamed the army commander for creating the gap. The division leader attributed "the loss of prisoners to the position in which we were placed by swinging forward." He also blamed some of his men. "[T]he troops engaged did not meet the attack with the vigor and determination which they would have shown at an earlier period of the campaign," Barlow wrote. "Loss of commanding and other officers, exhaustion and other causes have so affected the three concerned in these operations, Second, Third and Fourth Brigades, that they cannot just now be relied on to meet critical emergencies with much determination and spirit."[77]

Mott blamed Barlow's and Gibbon's divisions. The Diamond Division commander wrote, "the giving way of the troops of the First and Second Divisions, respectively, on my left and right, thereby allowing the enemy to get on both flanks and rear."[78]

Chaplin on the left of Mott's divisions blamed Barlow's division. McAllister on the right of Mott's division officially claimed that he did not retreat until after the left of Gibbon's division had given way. "There is no blame on me," McAllister wrote privately. "I did all that I could do, or anyone else could do."[79] Ignorant of why the left of Barlow's division rested in the air, Private Haley in the second line of Mott's division blamed Barlow.

Gibbon initially blamed the troops, writing, "It was one of those attacks in which the enemy are so often successful from their full knowledge of the country, but might have been more successfully met, but for the bad conduct of some of our troops, who are thoroughly worn out & exhausted with marching fighting & loss of sleep, and it is not much to be wondered at." Later he blamed Mott's division, writing, "The troops of the Third Division gave way in considerable confusion, exposing the left flank of my Second Brigade." Gibbon also put the blame on the losses of so many of his regimental and company officers during the Overland campaign and the June 15–18 assaults on Petersburg. He blamed O'Brien for giving way "without an attempt at resistance" and Pierce because "he was so

76 Walker, *History of the Second Army Corps*, 545.

77 *OR* 40, 1:329, 330.

78 Ibid., 388.

79 James I. Robertson Jr., ed., *The Civil War Letters of General Robert McAllister* (Baton Rouge, 1965), 449.

dilatory and allowed so long a time to elapse before moving that the enemy was enabled to organize a force to resist him." Gibbon also thought the counterattacks "rather feeble."[80]

O'Brien blamed Mott's division. Pierce blamed O'Brien's brigade.

Major Patten of the 20th Massachusetts in Pierce's brigade made excuses for the troops. "[T]he regiments on my left were completely surprised," he remembered. "It was very hot, the troops were utterly exhausted by their unparalleled hardships, and the first some of them—as I am told—knew of the matter, was waking up and finding themselves gobbled beyond escape." He laid the blame higher up the chain of command. "The most serious fault rests with some General—I don't know who—who so disposed his troops that the enemy got square in the rear of the left of Gibbon's division, unopposed," Patten remembered. "Some say it was Birney's fault and some whisper <u>Meade</u>."[81]

Patten also had Gibbon in mind as a general responsible for a share of the disaster, complaining bitterly to Lyman that Gibbon's "former gallantry was all gone, and that now he refused to expose himself, so that his conduct was a matter of comment, and the officers laid traps to get him under fire, for joke!"[82]

Unaware that Meade's orders had separated II and VI corps, Surgeon George T. Stevens of the 77th New York in Bidwell's brigade of Wheaton's division held Birney responsible.

"Commissary whiskey said to be the cause of the disaster," recalled Signal Corps Pvt. John R. Mitchell.[83]

Nobody remembered that II Corps had collapsed just as completely when flanked in the Wilderness on May 6, before most of the campaign's losses. Confederate flank attacks, not prior losses of officers and men, accounted for both the rout of May 6 and the rout of June 22.

80 John Gibbon to "My dear Maria," June 23d, 1864, US Military Academy, West Point, NY; John Gibbon, *Personal Recollections of the Civil War* (New York, 1928), 246.

81 Patten to "Dear Col.," July 10, 1864. Association of Officers of the 20th Massachusetts Volunteer Infantry, "Reports, letters & papers appertaining to 20th Mass. Vol. Inf.," 234–235.

82 Lowe, ed., *Meade's Army*, 227.

83 Greene, *A Campaign of Giants*, 1:248; Bond Diary and Memoir, June 22, 1864, 235–236.

Chapter Seven

"Don't Let 'Em Dance 'Round You, Pitch into Them"

ON THE morning of June 23, the previous day's disaster prompted Grant to reassess his plans. "The siege of Richmond bids fair to be tedious, and in consequence of the very extended lines we must have, a much larger force will be necessary than would be required in ordinary sieges against the same force that now opposes us," he wrote to his former superior Maj. Gen. Henry W. "Old Brains" Halleck, who now administered the armies of the United States for the general-in-chief.[1] Grant decided to focus Union resources on his own and Sherman's army groups and directed Halleck to dispatch XIX Corps from the Department of the Gulf to Virginia.

* * *

The Army of the Potomac's siege train began arriving at City Point that day. The bombardment of Petersburg grew still more intense. The Yankee guns swept the heart of the Cockade City. The Post Office, the Custom House, and the steeples of Tabb Street Presbyterian, St. Paul's Episcopal, and Washington Street Methodist churches furnished targets for the Federal gunners. "To persons unfamiliar with the infernal noise made by the screaming, the ricochetting, and the bursting of shells, it is impossible to describe the terror and the demoralization which was immediately created," Dr. Claiborne remembered.[2] More people fled the city including, ultimately, Mrs. Waddell.

1 *OR* 40, 2:330–331.

2 Claiborne, *Seventy-Five Years in Old Virginia*, 205.

Some hid in their houses. "All the citizens left who could, but we were unable to leave due to the fact that my brother, fifteen years of age, was ill unto death, from exposure in camp while fighting in defense of Petersburg," recalled Anne Banister Pryor, whose father had perished in the June 9 action that had kept Butler from seizing the city but cost her brother his health. Chelsea, their home, stood in the line of fire of Company I's thirty-pounder Parrotts at Battery No. 5. "For safety we were compelled to live in two large rooms in our basement," she remembered. "With hearts crushed already with sorrow, we would sit by and nurse my brother, realizing he could be saved could we only get proper food and medicine."[3] Getting proper food and medicine proved impossible; none of the town's stores remained open because of the shelling. When her brother died, the bombardment made burial in Blandford Cemetery—nearer the front lines—impracticable. The Banisters interred him in their garden.

Others dug bomb-proofs in their yards or gardens to take refuge during bombardments. "These bomb-proofs were holes dug in the ground about five or six feet deep, of dimensions commensurate with the number of persons they were supposed to accommodate, and were covered with heavy timbers, and these with earth, the door or entrance facing to the west, the direction opposite the batteries from which the shells came," Dr. Claiborne remembered. "Some of these bomb-proofs were made quite comfortable, and ladies could take a book or their sewing into them." Nowhere in the city remained secure from Federal projectiles.

One of Dr. Claiborne's subordinate physicians complained that the evacuation of the hospitals under Federal fire was going too slowly after a shell landed in one of the hospitals—fortunately a soldier had picked it up and thrown it out a window before the missile exploded. Dr. Claiborne received a message from Lee that the general "hoped it would not be necessary to order me a second time to remove the wounded from under fire." Outraged that one of his subordinates had made such a complaint, Dr. Claiborne replied to Lee that he was making every effort to comply with the general's order, "but with the limited means at hand three thousand sick and wounded men could not be removed very expeditiously and that many could not be moved without more danger to their lives than they risked from the shell." Lee rejoined that after none of his battles "were there three thousand men who could not be moved." This did not silence Dr. Claiborne. He pointed out that men wounded in battle fell in full strength and could easily bear transportation, but that heat, festering wounds, or sickness had debilitated the men who lay—some of them for months—in Petersburg's hospitals. Some would die upon the stretchers if evacuated. Two had already expired. Many had begged to take their chances with

3 Anne Banister Pryor, "A Child's Recollections Of War," *CV* XXXIX (1931), 54.

the shells. Dr. Claiborne finished by demanding that Lee send inspectors from his staff to relieve him and take charge of the evacuation.

Lee sent a pair of medical inspectors. After observing the situation, they not only declined to relieve Claiborne, but advised that Lee leave the matter to Dr. Claiborne's discretion. "I removed in a few days all that would bear transportation, and reserved the Confederate States Hospital, and the hospitals at West End Park, and the Central Pavilion, reporting that they were but little exposed to fire, and that I thought it judicious to keep these hospitals open for the desperately wounded that were now coming in daily from the lines," remembered Dr. Claiborne.[4] He heard no more about the matter.

* * *

After II Corps failed to reach the Weldon Railroad on June 22, Meade tried extending to that railway with VI Corps on June 23. The maneuvers of June 22 had left VI Corps in a curved line with the Vermont Brigade of Wheaton's division closest to the Weldon Railroad. The brigade's line faced the Aiken oat field, which had a crest in its center running north and south. Half a mile west of the Vermonters, trees along the field's far edge screened the Dunlap farm and its burnt house. A blind road ran north and south through the trees. Almost a mile farther west ran the railroad.

To the Vermont Brigade's right stretched woods, fields, swamps and thickets that made movement difficult for organized bodies of troops. Truex's brigade of Ricketts's division stretched northeastward from the right of the Vermonters. Other VI Corps soldiers extended the line until they reached the left of II Corps near the Strong house. The 87th Pennsylvania picketed the left of Truex's brigade, the 14th New Jersey the right. In the timber along the oat field's western edge, where the north-south blind road ran, about 230 soldiers from Maj. John Edward Pratt's 4th Vermont formed a skirmish line in front of the Vermont Brigade from the left of the 87th Pennsylvania to the road that ran between Dr. Gurley's house and the railroad. On the left of the 4th Vermont, facing south along Second Swamp, stood 140 pickets from Capt. Aldace Walker's battalion of the 1st Vermont Heavy Artillery under 1st Lt. Henry R. Chase of Battery E, accompanied by 2nd Lt. Merritt H. Sherman of Battery C, a graduate of Wesleyan University, and 2nd Lt. Henry E. Bedell of Battery D.

Walker congratulated himself on the position of his battalion. "We are in a clean pine wood, near a farm where we get cherries and apples, for sauce, and

4 Claiborne, *Seventy-Five Years in Old Virginia*, 207.

beets, &c., and mulberries and blackberries are plenty around," he wrote home after sending his men out on the skirmish line that morning. "We are in no danger at all, but the line is to be advanced to-day, and we follow."[5] Also known as the 11th Vermont Infantry, the 1st Vermont Heavy Artillery consisted of three battalions composed of four companies, each averaging 125 men, for a total strength of about 1,500. The 3rd Vermont extended the picket line along Second Swamp all the way eastward to Bidwell's brigade near the Williams house. It remained to be seen whether Walker was correct when he wrote that his battalion was "in no danger at all."

Meade left for Wright's headquarters at 4:30 a.m. that morning. The commander of the Army of the Potomac intended for VI Corps to pivot on II Corps and swing to face the Dimmock Line opposite the exit for the Weldon Railroad, near Battery 40 and the Lead Works. At 7:00 a.m., after imparting this to Wright, Meade departed VI Corps headquarters for the Jones house. Instructing Lyman to communicate with him by courier, Meade left Lyman with Wright.

Accompanied by Lyman, Wright rode out 25 minutes later to inspect his lines, which neither ran straight nor faced properly. Meanwhile, the Great Peppery reached the Jones house and at 7:30 a.m. informed Grant that V and IX corps must stretch beyond Jerusalem Plank Road for the Federals to invest Petersburg from the Appomattox below to the Appomattox above. IX Corps had finished strengthening its lines and had stood ready to participate in such a movement since 3:30 a.m.

At 7:40 a.m., Wright was riding out on the road past the Browder farm toward the headquarters of Ricketts's division near the Aiken house. By 8:30 a.m., the commander of VI Corps had ascertained that Ricketts's division faced roughly northwest and reports arrived that Russell's division looked westward. "That's a chronic trouble in lines in the woods," remembered Lyman. "Indeed there are several chronic troubles. The divisions have lost connection; they cannot cover the ground designated, their wing is in the air, their skirmish line has lost its direction, etc., etc." The delay tidying the lines would make Meade angry. His subordinates would respond that they were doing the best they could. "All of which is natural with a good many thousand men in position in a dense wood, which nobody knows much about," Lyman remembered. "All this while the men went to sleep or made coffee; profoundly indifferent to the perplexities of their generals; *that* was what generals were paid for." After examining the line, Wright rode to the left of VI Corps "to look at the pickets, who were taking life easy like other privates," Lyman

5 Walker to "Dear Father," June 23, 1864.

recalled. "They had put up sun-shades with shelter-tents and branches, and were taking the heat coolly."[6]

Taking the heat coolly would have struck Pvt. Wilbur Fisk of the 2nd Vermont's Company E in Grant's brigade as an extraordinary accomplishment. A self-educated former schoolteacher who corresponded with Montpelier's *Green Mountain Freeman* newspaper under the byline "Anti-Rebel," Fisk found "the intolerable heat" prevented the rest well-earned by nights of picketing, excavating earthworks, and marching. "It is of no use to try to sleep; it would be like trying to sleep in a furnace," he wrote. "It is as much as a fellow can find time to do to wipe the perspiration continually streaming from his face and body."[7]

By 10:00 a.m., Wright and Lyman had returned to VI Corps headquarters. "About this time a Vermont captain (bless his soul!) went and actually did something saucy and audacious," remembered Lyman. "With eighty sharpshooters he pushed out boldly, drove in a lot of cavalry, and went a mile and a quarter to the railroad, which he held, and came back in person to report, bringing a piece of the telegraph wire."[8]

Captain Alexander M. Beattie of the 3rd Vermont's Company F, who had earned a Medal of Honor at Cold Harbor earlier that month, led this advance just north of the lane to Dr. Gurley's house. He detailed a working party to tear up the tracks and cut the telegraph line. The initiative of another subordinate also resulted in forward motion. Around 300 troopers from the 18th Pennsylvania Cavalry brushed aside a few sentinels of the 3rd North Carolina Cavalry along the track to Dr. Gurley's house, reached the railroad near Globe Tavern, and requested special track destruction tools.

These advances prompted Wright to direct the establishment of a skirmish line linking Beattie's sharpshooters with the pickets extending from the junction of Ricketts's left and the Vermont Brigade. Shortly after 10:00 a.m., 200 men from Maj. Charles King Fleming's battalion of the 1st Vermont heavies established the skirmish line from the right of the 4th Vermont's sentinels, who picketed the right of the Vermont brigade, to the right of the sharpshooters on the railroad, along the lane from the burnt Dunlap house to the Lanier house.

They did so under the direction of Lt. Col. Samuel E. Pingree of the 3rd Vermont, the officer of the day for Wheaton's division. A lawyer who had graduated from Dartmouth College, Pingree had lost a thumb, suffered a severe hip wound, and earned a Medal of Honor at Lee's Mill on the Peninsula on April 16, 1862.

6 Agassiz, ed., *Meade's Headquarters*, 173–174.

7 Wilbur Fisk Diary, 1863–1864, Wilbur Fisk Papers, LOC, June 23, 1864.

8 Agassiz, ed., *Meade's Headquarters*, 174.

Pingree instructed Capt. James E. Eldredge of the 1st Vermont Heavy Artillery's Battery H on the right of the skirmish line along the lane from the Dunlap house to the Lanier house to "hold the line to the last minute, not to give up an inch unless . . . actually obliged to." The Vermont Brigade sent forward pioneers with tools designed for railroad destruction. "Occasionally some horsemen would come out into the oat-field in our front, but would leave on being fired upon," remembered Eldredge.[9] The special track destruction tools requested by the 18th Pennsylvania Cavalry's troopers never arrived.

Word that the Federals had reached the rails soon stirred up the Secessionists. At 11:00 a.m. a Union signal officer spotted a Confederate column a mile long with two batteries of artillery issuing from the Rebel works along the Weldon Railroad. At noon, VI Corps had still not advanced. Wright rode to Birney's headquarters at the Jones house to confer about straightening their lines. Soon Birney and Wright were joined by a frustrated Meade, "chaffing, with an eye like a rattlesnake, and a nose that seemed twice as long and sharp as usual!" recalled Lyman. Meade, Birney, and Wright then "all pow-wowed a while," Lyman remembered.[10]

The Great Peppery encouraged Wright to employ his cavalry to feel for the enemy along the roads crossing the railroad and to advance with his infantry. Wright dispatched two columns of cavalry but allowed his infantry to remain stationary. The 1st Massachusetts Cavalry discovered the approach of Mahone's division but a warning from the horsemen fell on deaf ears. The conference broke up and Wright returned to his headquarters.

At about 12:45 p.m., Meade forwarded the information about the signal officer's sighting to Wright. Around this time, the dust cloud thrown up by the approaching Southerners became visible to Pingree. He reported this to VI Corps headquarters, prompting the advance of the balance of Fleming's battalion into open timber along a low rise a couple hundred yards west of the junction of the picket lines of the 87th Pennsylvania and the 4th Vermont. The screen of woods and the crest in the oat field hid Fleming's troops from the Vermont Brigade. His detachment constructed breastworks employing newly cut fence rails piled on the ground and wood from timber piles in the trees.

About 1:20 p.m., the Rebels appeared in a corn field about a mile north of Globe Tavern, headed for the left of VI Corps. Meade soon became anxious about the Army of the Potomac's left. He feared that Lee would plunge into the army's rear and cut its communications.

9 G. G. Benedict, *Vermont in the Civil War: A History of the Part Taken by the Vermont Soldiers and Sailors in the War for the Union, 1861–1865*, 2 vols. (Burlington, VT, 1888), 2:359.

10 Lowe, ed., *Meade's Army*, 224; Agassiz, ed., *Meade's Headquarters*, 174.

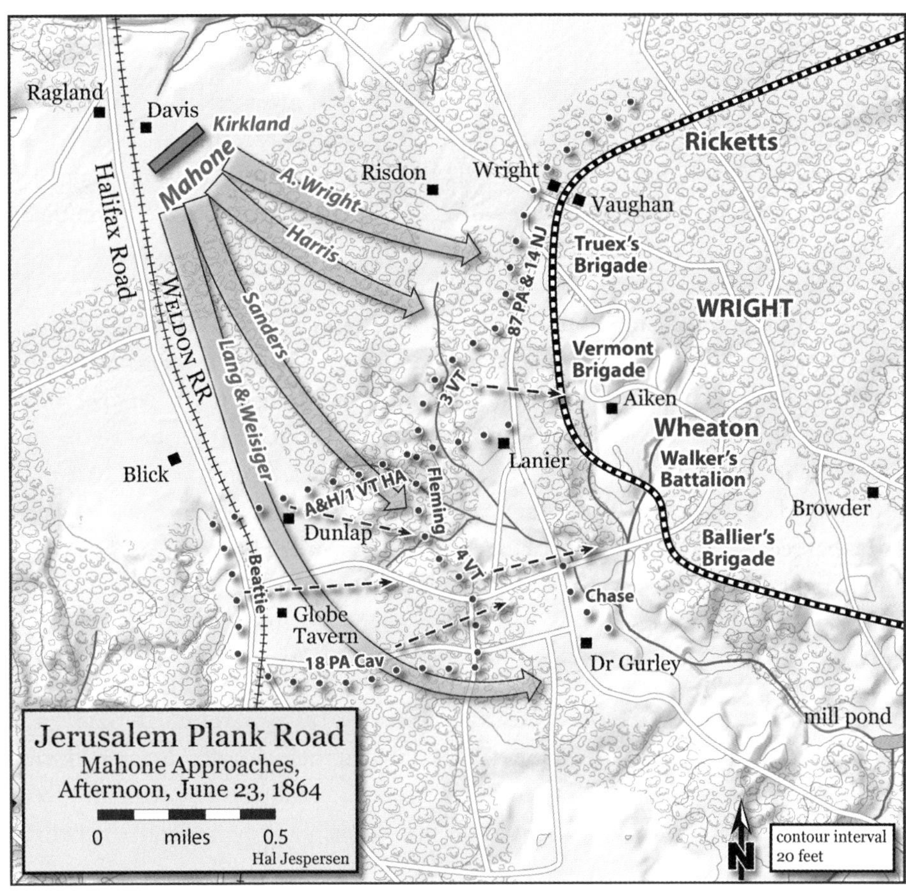

Wright arrived back at the Williams house shortly after 2:00 p.m. Around 2:15 p.m., the skirmish line of VI Corps began to advance in step with the sentinels of II Corps. Ricketts's division extended its picket line to the railroad on the right of Fleming's detachment but did not contact the Johnnies. The 4th Vermont advanced on Fleming's left. The chief scout of the Bureau of Military Information, Sgt. Milton W. Cline, was reconnoitering up to three quarters of a mile west of the tracks at this time and found no evidence of a strong force of the enemy there. He recrossed the railroad at 2:30 p.m.

"Oh, yes!" remembered Lyman, "but Rebs are not people who let you sit about all the day and do just as you like; remember that always, if nothing else." Within minutes, the men at VI Corps headquarters heard faint reports of muskets from the direction of the tracks. About 3:00 p.m. a heated sharpshooter arrived and reported, "They are advancing rapidly and have driven the working party from the railroad."

"Stop the advance," said Wright. "General Wheaton, strengthen that skirmish line and tell them to hold on."[11]

Brigadier General Frank Wheaton, who had studied civil engineering at Brown University before becoming a career army officer, strengthened the left of his skirmish line, though not the right, as he configured his division to defend the left center of VI Corps. Ballier's brigade had returned from its assignment of the previous day near the Strong house. Behind the opening picketed by the 3rd Vermont, Wheaton deployed Ballier's brigade between the right of Bidwell's brigade near the Williams house and the left of the Vermont Brigade. Ballier's brigade began building breastworks and advanced the 62nd New York, the Anderson Zouaves, as skirmishers on the left of the pickets from Walker's battalion of the 1st Vermont heavies. The 3rd Vermont returned to the Vermont Brigade. The sentinels from Walker's battalion advanced southwestward about a half mile and barricaded themselves behind fence rails, but lost touch with the New Yorkers. The fire of the skirmishers drew nearer VI Corps headquarters and became distinct.

* * *

Around 9:00 a.m., troops from Bushrod Johnson's division tramped out to the Bailey farm again and erected breastworks in case II Corps resumed its advance westward.[12] As the Syracusans had in 414 BCE when their city was threatened with landward isolation by the extension of an Athenian wall, the Confederates were blocking with a perpendicular fortification the extension of the Federal earthworks along the line of the previous day.[13]

Some of Mahone's tired men slept until 10:00 a.m. A few lucky soldiers drew passes to spend the day in Petersburg, including Captain Waddell of the 12th Virginia. "He looked worn, weary and dusty," recorded his wife, Fan.[14] She saw to it that he had a bath and some clean clothes—luxury for the captain, who had not

11 Ibid., 175.

12 Hewett, et al., eds., *Supplement to the Official Records*, 7:279; *OR* 40, 1:761, 2:376, 668–669, 678; Clark, *North Carolina Regiments*, 3:367; Elliott, *The Southern Soldier Boy*, 34; William Henry Harder Memoir, 525; Wiatt, *Confederate Chaplain*, 182; Smith Kitchens Diary, June 2–23, 1864, Winthrop University; Beckham, *Diary of Samuel Lowry*, 92. Johnson's brigade remained north of the Appomattox on the right of Pickett's division. *OR* 51, 2:1027.

13 Bennett A. Cerf, et al., eds., *The Complete Writings of Thucydides: The Peloponnesian War* (New York, 1934), 395–396, 402–404. Mahone's rout of II Corps prevented the Federals from approaching, much less attacking, the Confederate counter-wall as the Athenians attacked three Syracusan counter-walls, two of them successfully. Paul Rahe, *Sparta's Sicilian Proxy War: The Grand Strategy of Classical Sparta, 418–413 B.C.* (New York, 2023), 169–181, 208–212.

14 Mrs. Charles Waddell Diary, June 23, 1864; Charles E. Waddell Diary, Aug. 8, 1863, ACWM, Richmond, VA.

shucked his coat for a month. He had taken off his shoes only twice during that time. Mrs. Waddell provided him with breakfast, which he wolfed down.

The Norfolk Juniors and Richmond Grays of the 12th relieved part of the 6th Virginia on picket. The rest of the 12th tramped off with the remainder of Mahone's division not serving as sentinels: the Virginia Brigade, the Georgia Brigade, the Alabama Brigade, the Mississippi Brigade, and half the Florida Brigade—the 2nd, 5th, and 8th Florida. The Floridians marched under the 8th's Col. David Lang, a civil engineer educated at Georgia Military Institute and wounded at Fredericksburg and Sharpsburg. Lane's brigade of Wilcox's division had relieved Lang's Floridians. The other half of the Florida Brigade, the 9th, 10th, and 11th Florida, remained picketing the Dimmock Line under Irish-born Brig. Gen. Joseph "Barney" Finegan, a businessman. The four Napoleons of Dement's battery and the two three-inch rifles of Wilke's section from Clutter's battery accompanied the column.

Assembling his forces around noon near the Lead Works, Mahone directed his men southward down Halifax Road, parallel to and just west of the railroad, with the Georgians in the lead followed by the Mississippians, Alabamians, Virginians, and Floridians. His troops reached the Davis cornfield a mile north of Globe Tavern shortly after 2:30 p.m. and began deploying east of the tracks. The 48th Georgia, 2nd Georgia Battalion, 22nd Georgia, and 10th Georgia Battalion assembled by the right flank from left to right behind a skirmish line formed by the 3rd Georgia, then advanced. The Mississippians pushed into the oat field and pressured the Vermont skirmish line along the farm track between the Dunlap house and the Lanier house. The Alabama Brigade drove off Federal cavalry, pioneers and sharpshooters ripping up the railroad, then turned eastward into the oat field. The Virginia and Florida brigades swung around toward the left of the Vermont Brigade. As on the previous evening, the four regiments of Kirkland's North Carolina Brigade in the Dimmock Line left their band in place and proceeded to the Davis house—Hill's headquarters—where they covered the gap between the Dimmock Line and Mahone's troops. The artillery remained at the Davis house with Kirkland's brigade.

Mahone's advance boded ill for the Vermonters.

* * *

Captain Darius J. Safford of the 1st Vermont Heavy Artillery's Company L, part of Fleming's detachment, was drawing rations for his company when it hiked out to the skirmish line. As soon as he learned of the approach of the Confederates, he hurried after his men. On the way, he met the color guard coming back with the colors. He found Fleming in a hollow surrounded by breastworks Fleming's men were building. Safford urged Fleming to come up to the skirmish line, but he declined on account of illness.

"Extend the line to the left until you connect with the Fourth Vermont, and hold the line at all hazards, reporting to me every half hour," said Fleming.

Safford stretched the line as thinly as he dared but failed to find any troops on his left. "I did find a much stronger line, of the enemy, than our own, a short distance in front of us, and quite a brisk firing was kept up," he remembered. Locating the 4th Vermont behind Fleming's pickets, Safford contracted Fleming's line to strengthen it as the troops near the tracks started falling back through the line.

The cavalry withdrew to the 4th Vermont's picket line a quarter mile west of Dr. Gurley's house. The pioneers and sharpshooters retreated to the main line of VI Corps. They had destroyed a quarter mile of the railroad and a single culvert. Beattie, on his way to the rear, warned Safford.

"Captain, if you don't get out of this, you will catch hell," said Beattie.

Soon afterward Safford encountered Pingree near the left of Fleming's line, reported the situation to him, and suggested that the skirmishers fall back nearer the main line.

"The orders are to hold the line at all hazards," Pingree replied.[15]

By 3:00 p.m., Mahone had his five brigades side by side facing eastward. They confronted from their left to their right Truex's brigade screened by the 87th Pennsylvania and the 14th New Jersey, the Vermont Brigade picketed by elements of the 1st Vermont heavies and the 4th Vermont, and the right flank of Ballier's brigade screened by the 62nd New York. Porte's forces continued pressing eastward to improve their grip on the Yankees.

Horatio Wright braced for an attack on his left of the sort that had undone II Corps the previous day. While Mahone's skirmishers pushed back the pickets of the Vermont Brigade and his battle line rested nearly halfway between the tracks and the Vermonters' main line, the Green Mountain Staters in the main line received shovels to build breastworks in preparation for a frontal assault. Wright directed the troopers of the 18th Pennsylvania Cavalry, who seemed good for nothing else, into the pits with his infantry.

The commander of VI Corps asked Meade for reinforcements. At 3:50 p.m., Warren received orders to send two brigades to Wright. Ten minutes later, Meade began urging Wright to assume the offensive but left that up to his discretion, with predictable results—Wright remained on the defensive. Lyman recalled, "All the while the telegraph is going: 'Don't let 'em dance round you, pitch into

15 Benedict, *Vermont in the Civil War*, 2:360–361.

them!' suggests General Meade (not in those exact words). 'Don't know about that—very easy to say—will see about it,' replies the cautious W." About this time Pingree rode to the rear, where he said "he had got a view of the main body of the enemy . . . halted in the open, and they seemed no more than a division," Lyman remembered. "This, with their behavior, convinced me that it was not a grand movement; and, when Gen. Wright asked me, I told him I thought he ought to attack."[16] Wright did not embrace the idea. Pingree returned to his division's skirmish line.

As Meade tried in vain to prod Wright into action, the Great Peppery received a suggestion from Warren that the Army of the Potomac abandon its lines, send its wagons to Butler's Army of the James in Bermuda Hundred, and set out for the Weldon Railroad with six days' rations. Meade passed this idea along to Grant after objecting because it would invite Lee to interpose between the Army of the Potomac and the Army of the James, cutting off the former from supplies.

Grant criticized the V Corps commander's plan as insufficiently bold. "I would not think of moving the whole of your command with less than ten days' rations, and then it would be to turn the enemy's right, cross the Appomattox, and force a connection with Butler between Richmond and Petersburg," the general-in-chief wrote.[17] At the time, 3:30 p.m., Grant was still pursuing the original plan to invest Petersburg to the Appomattox above the city by directing Butler to stretch to his left and by morning relieve the right division of IX Corps.

Meanwhile, Warren acknowledged Meade's objections and the risks involved but observed that the Army of the Potomac could turn about and fight in case the Confederates interposed between it and the Army of the James. The V Corps leader urged "some decisive movement, in which, throwing all our weight into the battle, we are willing to run the risk of losing all by a failure—fight the Wilderness battle again."[18]

The risk of losing all by fighting the terrible Wilderness battle again must not have appealed to the commander of the Army of the Potomac.

* * *

The Vermont Brigade's commander, Brig. Gen. Lewis Grant, no relation to the general-in-chief, became fearful for his skirmishers. A former lawyer wounded

16 Agassiz, ed., *Meade's Headquarters*, 175; Lowe, *Meade's Army*, 224.

17 *OR* 40, 2:333–334. Grant's idea appears to have evolved from the plan reported by Dana on June 20. Ibid., 1:26.

18 Ibid., 2:346.

Lewis Grant

Library of Congress

at Fredericksburg who had earned a Medal of Honor at Salem Church, where he was also wounded, Grant according to Walker "had, by diligent study, made himself so thoroughly acquainted with the red tape of the Regulations, that he became a martinet in his disposition to require the performance of many of its absurdities, which are especially ridiculous in a field campaign." He developed a reputation for "fussiness" and "old-maidishness."[19] Lewis Grant's "bravery and . . . energy were never questioned," recalled Walker, but Grant's troops nicknamed the brigadier "Aunt Liddy" or "Aunt Lydia."[20]

Lewis Grant ordered his main line forward to the crest in the oat field, from which his infantry and artillery could protect his pickets. He asked the commanders of the brigades on either side of him to advance along with him. Wheaton directed Grant's main line back to its original position. The brigadier tried to persuade the division commander to change his mind but failed. Aunt Liddy then appealed to Wright, who rode with Grant to the crest in front of the Vermont Brigade. While stray bullets whistled around them, the brigadier showed the corps commander the vulnerability of the 4th Vermont and Fleming's command. Wright replied that Pingree had his instructions and that if the Confederates broke through on the left, the 4th and Fleming's battalion could withdraw to the right behind the skirmishers of Ricketts's division. Wright and Grant rode back to their safe position behind the crest.

Mahone's troops were rendering such a withdrawal to the north, or any withdrawal at all, impossible. The Georgia Brigade drove back the 87th Pennsylvania and 14th New Jersey upon the main line of Truex's brigade. Rans Wright instructed Lt. Col. Matthew R. Hall of the 48th Georgia to deploy his regiment and the 2nd Georgia Battalion to drive the Keystoners from an elevated point in the

19 Aldace F. Walker, *The Vermont Brigade in the Shenandoah Valley, 1864* (Burlington, VT, 1869), 18–19.

20 George S. Mahary, *Vermont Hero: Major General Lewis A. Grant* (Lincoln, NE, 2006), 21.

woods. Hall attacked and precipitated a desperate fight. Several hundred yards to the right, the 22nd Georgia and 10th Georgia Battalion attacked the 14th New Jersey. The Georgians drove the Pennsylvanians and Jerseymen into an open field and pursued them across it at the double-quick howling the rebel yell. Private Verdery of the 48th remembered, "The Yanks ran Pell-Mell strewing the ground with guns, accouterments knapsack haversack and any thing that tended to retard their progress."[21]

The Georgians nearly surrounded the 87th Pennsylvania. It was every Keystoner for himself. Private Charles Edwin Gotwalt of the 87th's Company A searched for an escape route but found that the Georgians had cut him off. He hid in the tall grass of a nearby swamp. Bullets striking the mud in front of him prevented him from digging a pit. He scrambled over to a drainage ditch and ducked down. A swishing sound came nearer and nearer. The grass parted in front of him. A Confederate officer stood before him holding the sword he had used as a scythe.

"Get out, you damn Yank," the officer shouted.

Gotwalt complied and entered captivity with 68 of his comrades.[22] The 48th Georgia captured one of the colors of the 87th Pennsylvania.[23]

The remnant of the Pennsylvanians reached the trees on the other side of the field and blasted the Georgians. Some Peach Staters perished within 10 feet of the Keystoners. Captain Llewellen G. Doughty of the 48th Georgia's Company C fell while leading the 22nd Georgia, which he had been assigned to command that day. "Captain Doughty was struck in the left cheek bone, the ball ranging upwards," remembered Private Anderson of Doughty's company, "he did not live but ten minutes after he was shot."[24]

The fire became so hot that the Georgians sought cover. Private Henry Clay Roney of the 22nd Georgia's Company H, the Gardner Volunteers, recalled, "I was making for an old tree to protect myself, but before I reached it I was shot down, through the left ankle."[25] Immediately afterward, his company assumed prone positions to fire. The remnants of the 87th Pennsylvania soon fell back on the main line of Truex's brigade, where the Georgians skirmished with them. The

21 Verdery to "Dear Father Mother & all," June 25, 1864.

22 Dennis W. Brandt, *From Home Guards to Heroes: The 87th Pennsylvania and Its Civil War Community* (Columbia, MO, 2018), 193.

23 Folsom, *Heroes and Martyrs of Georgia*, 95.

24 J. A., "From Wright's Brigade."

25 Henry Clay Roney, "Reminiscences of the Experiences of a Boy Soldier in the War Between the States," Richmond County Museum, Augusta, GA.

Peach Staters had cut off the line of retreat to the north for Fleming's detachment and the 4th Vermont.

The Mississippi Brigade of Mahone's division threw out skirmishers to push back the pickets along the lane from the burnt Dunlap house toward the Lanier house. At first the Magnolia Staters pressed against Battery A of the 1st Vermont heavies, who faced north on the left of the skirmish line. The soldiers of Battery A stood 15 paces apart across an open field, with their left near the railroad and their right near a wood. First Lieutenant Lester S. Richards commanded the soldiers of the left company. "Very soon the rebels, advancing rapidly, pressed hard on our right flank with greatly superior numbers, which caused us to fall back, after losing several in killed and wounded," he remembered. "We fell back in good order, loading and firing as fast as possible." The Vermonters withdrew across the field's crest and halted, but the Confederates soon worked their way around the Vermont flank. The Mississippians subjected the Green Mountain Staters to an enfilading fire until they retreated to the earthworks of Fleming's detachment. Richards recalled, "it was understood that we were to hold this point at all hazards."[26]

The Magnolia Staters then went to work on Battery H, farther right. Before long, remembered Eldredge, "it was evident to all on the line that we had got to fall back or we would be captured." Eldredge, whom Pingree had ordered to "hold the line to last possible minute; not to give an inch unless we were actually obliged to," sent to the rear Cpl. Edgar H. Leonard of Eldredge's company to explain the situation to Pingree. Unable to find him, Leonard talked to Fleming, who said, "Hold your line." The Mississippians advanced in line of battle on Eldredge's company and drove it back on Fleming's breastworks in the woods. "The enemy were close upon us, and there was some sharp fighting for a few minutes," Eldredge recalled.[27] The Mississippians fell back except for their left, which curled around the right of Fleming's detachment and cut the lane in its rear.

After the Confederates drove in the northern shoulder of the Federal salient and Safford became aware that the Johnnies were working around the salient's left, he reported the situation to Fleming and warned that they must choose between retreat or captivity. Fleming responded that his orders called for him to hold and that he must face captivity rather than abandon his position. He dispatched his adjutant, 1st Lt. Edward F. Griswold, to division headquarters to report the situation and request either reinforcements or permission to withdraw. The Mississippians behind Fleming's position captured Griswold. On his way to the Confederate rear, he passed several lines of Secessionist infantry.

26 Cross, *A Melancholy Affair at the Weldon Railroad*, 39.

27 Benedict, *Vermont in the Civil War*, 2:359–360.

Farther to Mahone's right, his Alabama Brigade swung eastward near Globe Tavern to push in the pickets of the 4th Vermont. Driving across the oat field, the Alabamians hit the 4th. "The enemy attacked the left of our regiment and captured it; then advanced and swung their right around the left of our regiment, at the same time attacking our front," remembered Cpl. Henry F. Silloway of the 4th's Company G on the left. "Seeing ourselves surrounded the order was given to retreat, but it was too late to do that, as we came on to their line again and had to surrender or do worse."[28]

Captain William C. Tracy of Company G, wounded in the Wilderness, found himself encircled along with the left of the 4th. He had told his brother before the beginning of the campaign "that he would never fall into the hands of the rebels alive, but if in a tight place would fight to the bitter end." While Tracy tried to cut his way through the Alabamians, one of them shot him through the neck and he died instantly.[29]

"The work of capture was begun at the extreme left of the regiment," remembered Sgt. Luther B. Harris of Company D, which belonged to the 4th's right. "One by one the men were overpowered . . . and we were prisoners of war."[30] First Lieutenant Joseph P. Aikens of Company I earned promotion and Color Sergeant James J. Drury a Medal of Honor fighting their way back to the main line from the northern half of the regiment.

The rest of the 4th retreated northward and joined Fleming's battalion, which the Mississippians continued to pressure. "In our front within shooting distance were the rebel lines and a constant exchange of shot was kept up, some of the boys using up two or three guns, using them until they became so fowl that they could not ram down another bullet, exchanging them with their comrades who were less fortunate in being able to spy out the game," recalled Cpl. Ellery H. Webster in Battery F of Fleming's battalion.[31]

Leaving the skirmishers to hold the line at all hazards, Pingree spurred his horse through a hail of bullets, succeeded in reaching the rear "and reported that [the Rebels] had broken his skirmishers and were advancing in line of battle," Lyman recollected.[32]

28 H. F. S., of Co. G, "From the Fourth Regiment," *Vermont Watchman and State Journal* (Montpelier, VT), July 8, 1864, p. 2, col. 6.

29 "Capt. Wm. C. Tracy," *Vermont Record* (Brandon, VT), July 22, 1864, page 2, col. 4.

30 Cross, *A Melancholy Affair at the Weldon Railroad*, 33.

31 E. H. Webster, "Prison Experiences," *Orleans County Monitor* (Barton, VT), Dec. 25, 1899, p. 1, col. 2.

32 Lowe, ed., *Meade's Army*, 224. Lyman mistakenly assumed that the Confederates captured the skirmishers of the Vermont Brigade at this time. Ibid., 224–225.

John E. Laughton Jr.

Virginia Museum of History and Culture

Fleming and Pratt, "instead of looking the field over and learning the situation, had a long dispute about which was the ranking officer," remembered Eldredge. "Neither of them wanted to take the responsibility."[33]

Second Lieutenant Edward B. Parker belonged to the 11th's Battery B in Fleming's detachment. "Major Fleming did not come out of his hole," recollected Parker. "He did not know what was going on out on the line."[34]

Mahone committed his Virginia Brigade along the road leading eastward from Dr. Gurley's house toward Jerusalem Plank Road. Chase's detachment faced more danger than Walker had anticipated. The sharpshooter battalion of the Virginia Brigade preceded its battle line. The marksmen met scouts from Chase's detachment on Dr. Gurley's farm. Second Lieutenant John E. Laughton Jr. of the 12th Virginia's sharpshooter company confronted Sgt. Peter Donnelly of Chase's Battery C. "I supposed him to be a scout sent out to make a reconnaissance, and as that was my business also, I ordered him to halt," Laughton recalled. "He defiantly refused the second time and he turned to leave when I fired and he fell." Laughton approached Donnelly, who could no longer speak but made signs for water. Laughton gave Donnelly water but he soon died. "I deeply regretted that I had no time to bury him," Laughton remembered.[35] A former clerk who belonged to the Petersburg Regiment's Company G, the Richmond Grays, he had been wounded at King's School House on June 25, 1862.

33 J. E. Eldredge, "The Weldon Railroad Affair," *Vermont Watchman and State Journal*, April 14, 1886, p. 5, col. 3.

34 Cross, *A Melancholy Affair at the Weldon Railroad*, 132.

35 Ibid., 35; "Local and State Items," *The Rutland* (VT) *Weekly Herald*, Oct. 12, 1865, p. 3, cols. 3–4. The newspaper quotes a letter to Donnelly's sister from Laughton, who returned Donnelly's personal effects. Ibid.

The Virginians pressed on and drove Chase's men back to their breastwork of fence rails, charging the position twice unsuccessfully before pushing into the gap between the Vermonters and the 62nd New York. Outflanked, Chase and his men skedaddled. "Chase taken prisoner," remembered Bedell. "Lieutenant Sherman shot by my side in the fore head."[36] Sherman perished "trying to reestablish the line, which was done on the old ground," recalled Walker.[37] The survivors stood where they had a few hours earlier, half a mile back from the new ground.

Having occupied the southern end of the blind road running behind Fleming's detachment, the Virginians left the Vermonters with only a narrow route for retreat. The men from the Old Dominion then drove eastward along the Gurley-Temple road south of Second Swamp and skirmished with the Federals at the Smith millpond. This generated enormous anxiety at the headquarters of VI Corps and at the Army of the Potomac's command post. Horatio Wright already had one brigade at the Williams house as well as another guarding the bridge of Jerusalem Plank Road over Second Swamp. In response to Wright's calls for reinforcements, Warren at 5:00 p.m. dispatched to Wright's left not only the two V Corps brigades sent to Birney the previous day, but artillery. Thirty minutes later, Meade sent to Wright infantry and cavalry from the provost guard. At 5:40 p.m., the Great Peppery demanded that Wright attack.

Mahone still had at least one formation available for further inroads—the elder half of his division's Florida Brigade, the 2nd, 5th, and 8th Florida regiments under Lang. His Georgia Brigade pressured the 87th Pennsylvania and 14th New Jersey, cutting off the Vermonters to the north. His Mississippi Brigade drove back the right of the Vermonters. His Alabama Brigade pinned the remnants of Fleming's battalion and the 4th Vermont. The Virginia Brigade cut off the Vermonters from escape to the left and probed the left of VI Corps. Captain Girardey, now Porte's acting assistant adjutant general because of Major Mills's capture the previous day, guided Lang's detachment of the Florida brigade northward along the blind road from Dr. Gurley's house behind the Vermonters and blocked their last escape route.

"The rebels soon came upon our right and then charged upon our left and rear with a terrible volley of musketry and their horrid yell, which I never shall forget," recalled Richards. Fleming's battalion and the 4th Vermont remnant withdrew from their breastworks to another position a few rods away and contracted their lines. "We were now in no condition for defense, as our ammunition was completely exhausted," Richards remembered. A detail sent to the rear for more

36 Lt. Henry Edson Bedell's 1864 Diary, June 23, 1864. Henry Edson Bedell Diary, The Ed Italo Collection, *Vermont in the Civil War*, vermontcivilwar.org. Retrieved Feb. 11, 2023.

37 Letter, Aldace F. Walker to "Dear Father," June 24, 1864, Aldace Freeman Walker Papers.

ammunition did not return. The Confederates began charging again. "It was a miracle we were not nearly all killed, as the bullets fell among us like hailstones," recalled Richards.[38]

* * *

At VI Corps headquarters, Wright could hear sharp skirmishing for 15 minutes. At 6:15 p.m., the Confederates advanced in greater force. Five minutes later, Wright requested two brigades from Birney. At 6:30 p.m., Meade again demanded that Wright attack. Wright replied that before attacking he must change his dispositions. "There is no time to change position, and not much for an attack if you wait much longer," responded Meade 25 minutes later. "It will be dark before anything decisive can be done."[39] At the same time, Lyman conveyed to Meade another report from the pickets of Wheaton's division that the Rebels were heading around VI Corps' left toward Jerusalem Plank Road.

At 7:00 p.m., Wright declared it impossible to attack and at the same time protect his left. He imagined the Secessionists massing all their available force on his left and requested reinforcements or authorization to withdraw. Fifteen minutes later Meade pointed out to Wright that by attacking westward he would take in the flank the Confederates he feared were flanking him. At 7:20 p.m., Meade directed Wright to attack in line of battle and threatened to hold him responsible if the Southerners interposed between him and the plank road. At 7:30 p.m., Meade ordered all his headquarters troops to Wright. The Great Peppery countermanded this order immediately upon learning that Sweitzer's and Dushane's brigades from V Corps were marching to Wright's aid.

The commander of VI Corps promised to attack with his right. "Your delay has been fatal," Meade telegraphed five minutes later. "If you do not promptly attack, or if you do, unless you meet with great success, you must withdraw after dark."[40]

* * *

After surrounding the Vermont pickets, the Confederates pressed toward the left of the main line of VI Corps. "The coolness meantime—or indifference—of the troops in line of battle was singular," Lyman recalled. "One fellow absorbed

38 Cross, *A Melancholy Affair at the Weldon Railroad*, 40.

39 *OR* 40, 2:356.

40 Ibid., 358.

his whole soul in boiling a kettle of beans!"[41] The Secessionists drove toward the Williams house. "I could hear them whooping and *ki-yi-ing,* in their peculiar way," Lyman remembered. "I felt uncomfortable, I assure you."[42] Wright, Ricketts, Lewis Grant, Lyman, and Maj. Charles A. Whittier, Wright's assistant adjutant general, came under fire from the left and front as they stood at Ricketts's headquarters in the salient of the main line.

"When the musketry begins you will get all the bullets here, sir," Whittier said to Wright.

"When we get them we will move," said Wright.[43]

Whittier lifted his brows at Lyman in reaction to the snub.

Lewis Grant walked up to Ricketts.

"Do you propose to keep your Headquarters here?" asked Grant.

"Why not?" Ricketts replied.

"Because, when the volleys begin, nothing can live here."

"Ah?" said Ricketts.

He spoke "as if someone had remarked it was a charming evening, or the like," Lyman remembered. "I felt very like addressing similar arguments to General Wright, but pride stood in the way, and I would have let a good many volleys come before I would have given my valuable advice." Wright attempted to form a column of attack as the Southern skirmishers advanced. Lyman recalled that, "the bullets began to slash among the trees most spitefully."[44] Wright led the party about 70 yards to one side, where only accidental shots flew. Dusk arrived and, by making the formation of an attack column impossible, provided Wright with another excuse for not attacking.

* * *

The end came for the surrounded Vermont pickets at dusk. "At 8 o'clock we had fallen back under cover of the woods and when almost the last ray of hope had expired we were temporarily made glad by seeing a body of men in our rear moving towards us down the hill, which we took as reinforcements of our own men," Webster recalled. The Vermonters prepared to give them three cheers. "Hardly had the first notes escaped our throats before bullets sang and snapped around our ears like hailstones in a storm," remembered Webster. "Our supposed

41 Lowe, ed., *Meade's Army*, 225.

42 Agassiz, ed., *Meade's Headquarters*, 175.

43 Lowe, ed., *Meade's Army*, 225.

44 Agassiz, ed., *Meade's Headquarters*, 175–176.

friends proved to be the enemies and they had mistook our cheer for a Yankee yell preparatory to charging bayonets."[45] Georgians and Mississippians had enveloped the right, Alabamians and Virginians the left, and Floridians had closed up the route to the rear.

The Floridians who had slipped in behind the isolated Vermonters were advancing on them. First Lieutenant Isaac McQueen Auld of the 5th Florida's Company C recalled, "We all ran up to them through the bushes more like a line of skirmishers than anything else."[46]

Lieutenant Colonel William Baya of the 8th Florida, wounded at Bristoe Station, remembered his comrades "only firing two or three shots."[47]

Called upon to surrender, the Vermonters requested and received a few minutes to consult. Fleming and Pratt held a council of war with such company commanders as could join them. All except Eldredge favored surrendering. "When at last, about sundown, [Fleming] gave me permission to see if I could find a place where I could take the command out, I personally saw the circle completed and the enemy's left and right unite in rear of our right flank," Safford recalled.[48] Eldredge unsuccessfully urged slipping away in the dark. Sergeant Lafayette Soper of Battery A overheard Eldredge, sneaked off to the right with a few other men, and saw none of the enemy on their way back to the main line.

Safford thought escape impossible for the entire force. "With 2,500—3,000 men about us, even if our flank was open, the about 400 of us would have been cut to pieces before we should have got out," he recollected.[49]

Fleming and Pratt agreed the Vermonters would lay down their arms. Some only grudgingly complied with that agreement. Second Lieutenant John S. Drenan had returned to the 1st Vermont Artillery's Company L after two wounds and had rejected the offer of going to the hospital. "[I]t made John swear some when he had to throw Down his sword," remembered his brother, Pvt. James F. Drenan of the same company, who avoided captivity but not loneliness because his comrades had "gone to Richmond and all of the officers with them."[50]

The troops tried to mitigate the damage. "As soon as we saw we were sure to be captured, most of those of Company F (and I presume others did the same) broke

45 Webster, "Prison Experiences."

46 Cross, *A Melancholy Affair at the Weldon Railroad*, 45.

47 Ibid., 44.

48 Benedict, *Vermont in the Civil War*, 2:365.

49 Cross, *A Melancholy Affair at the Weldon Railroad*, 42.

50 Jeffrey B. Marshall, ed., *A War of the People: Vermont Civil War Letters* (Lebanon, NH, 1999), 240.

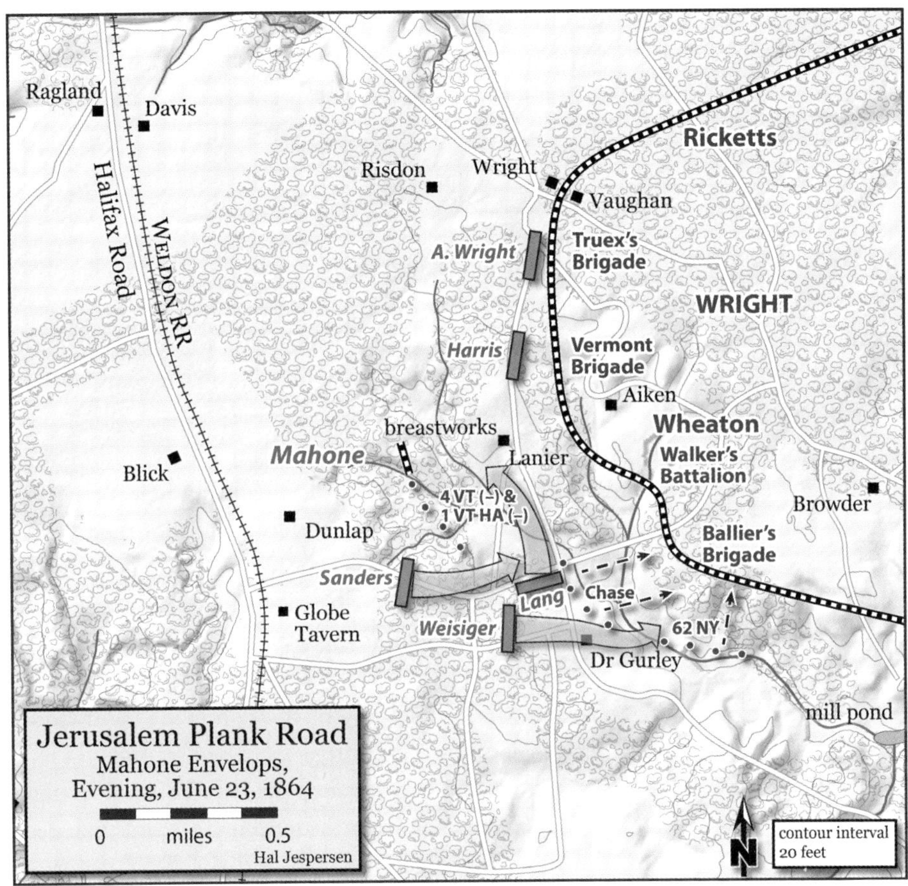

their gun stocks over tree trunks or stones, and cut their belts and straps to prevent there being of use to the enemy," remembered Webster.[51]

The Vermonters, "thinking we had a large force, surrendered, begging us not to shoot," recalled Auld, who numbered among the first to reach the Yankees.

"Are these all the men you have?" asked a bluecoat who saw the small number of Floridians.

"No sir!" said Auld. "We have a whole line of battle back there, these are only the skirmishers."

"Oh well," said the Yank, "it's no use talking, we can't help ourselves."[52]

Captain Henry Clay Simmons of the 8th Florida's Company F expressed surprise at the small number of Vermonters.

51 E. H. Webster, "Prison Experiences, No. 5," *Orleans County Monitor*, Jan. 29, 1900, p. 1, col. 1.

52 Cross, *A Melancholy Affair at the Weldon Railroad*, 44.

"Well, Captain, if we had known how few there were of you, we would have made much shorter work of it," he said to Safford.[53]

The surrender took place at nightfall, and the victors gave a shout heard by the remainder of VI Corps.

* * *

At 8:50 p.m., Wright decided to withdraw to the position his corps had held the previous night. Ten minutes later, Meade despaired of prodding Wright into action and authorized the withdrawal. As with Warren, the commander of the Army of the Potomac yielded his judgment to Wright's. Meade demanded that Wright prepare to advance in the morning.

Warren selected that moment to suggest to Meade a better way of holding their lines. The V Corps commander thought that instead of putting all their men in the trenches, the Federals should lightly hold the works and keep most of their troops in reserve. "I do not fear, all alone, an attack from any force if I have my troops concentrated, but I feel no security behind even breast-works with all in line," Warren telegraphed. "Break it once, and all go like the Second Corps yesterday and the Sixth Corps in the Wilderness."[54]

Meade ignored Warren's suggestion. The Army of the Potomac's commander directed Wright to place Sweitzer's and Dushane's brigades east of Jerusalem Plank Road when they arrived lest the Confederates advance on City Point. The night march proved miserable for the V Corps men in the scorching heat and shoe deep dust. They could not see the men in the ranks ahead and they had no water. "Drenched with perspiration, covered with thick dust, and burdened with heavy loads, I wish that I might have rushed into the house about then, and falling upon the floor, shown you a poor, panting, suffering soldier, just about 'gone up,'" remembered Pvt. Robert G. Carter of the 22nd Massachusetts.[55] Soldiers fell out by the score, many suffering from heatstroke.

Skirmishing continued long after dark and added to the butcher's bill. The lads in the battered 87th Pennsylvania had the satisfaction of capturing a Rebel around this time. A tall Confederate had lost his way in the woods after filling

53 Ibid. Safford thought he was talking to a "Captain Simons of the 6th Florida." Ibid. The Florida captain with the name closest to Simons was H. C. Simmons of the 8th Florida. Fred L. Robinson, comp., *Soldiers of Florida in the Seminole Indian, Civil and Spanish-American War* (Live Oak, FL, 1903), 198. The 6th was in Georgia. Ibid., 155.

54 *OR* 40, 2:345. Warren's idea resembles Grant's advice to Meade of June 21 to thin his lines and create reserves. Ibid., 268–269.

55 Robert Goldthwaite Carter, *Four Brothers in Blue, Or, Sunshine and Shadows of the War of Rebellion: A Story of the Great Civil War from Bull Run to Appomattox* (Norman, OK, 1999), 446.

cedar canteens for himself and his comrades. He wandered toward the 87th's entrenchments. "As he came near, the boys saw the name and number of his regiment on his hat," remembered Private Prowell.

"What regiment is that?" asked the Secessionist, who belonged to a Georgia regiment.

One of the Pennsylvanians responded with the Georgia regiment's name and number.

"All right, thought yo 'uns were Yanks," the Georgian replied, climbing over the earthworks.

"We want you and your canteens, Johnnie," a Pennsylvanian said.

"And you are Yanks, be gad," said the Georgian as he entered captivity.[56]

VI Corps lost about 595 that day, including 112 killed and wounded and 483 missing. Of these casualties, the Vermont Brigade of Wheaton's division suffered 25 killed or mortally wounded, 21 otherwise wounded, and 408 missing.[57]

56 Prowell, *Eighty-Seventh Regiment, Pennsylvania Volunteers*, 168. Prowell mistakenly reports the number of the Georgia regiment as the 8th, which belonged to Anderson's brigade of Field's division. Ibid.; see Appendix B.

57 The 2nd Vermont lost one wounded and the 3rd Vermont lost one deserter. Vermont, Adjutant General, *Revised Roster of Vermont Volunteers*, 52, 92. The 4th Vermont lost a total of 153: seven killed or mortally wounded, six otherwise wounded and 140 captured, and the 11th Vermont suffered a loss of 299: 18 killed or mortally wounded, 14 otherwise wounded and 267 captured. Cross, *A Melancholy Affair at the Weldon Railroad*, 72–73, 235.

The 62nd New York in Ballier's brigade of Wheaton's division lost five killed, seven wounded, one wounded and captured, and seven otherwise captured on June 23. museum.dmna.ny.gov/application/files/ 5715/5068/2684/62nd_Infantry_CW_Roster.pdf. Retrieved Jan. 19, 2024. About 416 of the 483 captured on June 23 thus came from Wheaton's division. "Telegraphic Reports of the Press Association," *Daily Richmond Examiner*, June 25, 1864.

The 14th New Jersey and 87th Pennsylvania of Truex's brigade in Ricketts's division had 132 killed, wounded, and missing from June 21 through June 23. Cross, *A Melancholy Affair at the Weldon Railroad*, 74; Prowell, *Eighty-Seventh Regiment, Pennsylvania Volunteers*, 164–165, 167. Of those casualties, 104 occurred in the 87th, which lost one missing on June 21, one killed and nine missing on June 22, and therefore 93 killed, wounded, and missing on June 23. Ibid., 171; Bates, *History of Pennsylvania Volunteers*, 3:36–63, *passim*. The 14th thus lost 28 from June 21 through June 23. Newton, *Campaign of the Fourteenth Regiment New Jersey Volunteers*, 70 (the 14th had "about 40 captured . . . and several killed."). Official reports underreport that the 14th lost one killed and three wounded from June 15 through June 30. *OR* 40, 1:227. Casualty lists for the 14th do not exist from mid-June through August. RG 94, Entry 652, Box 36. Nor do they exist for the 10th New Jersey or the 15th New Jersey, both of Penrose's brigade, Russell's division in VI Corps. Ibid., boxes 35 and 36. The remaining 67 VI Corps men captured on June 23 must have come from the 14th New Jersey and the 87th Pennsylvania, leaving 54 of their soldiers among the killed and wounded, for a VI Corps total of 112 killed and wounded on June 23.

VI Corps lost "about six hundred men" at the battle of Jerusalem Plank Road. Penrose G. Mark, *Red, White and Blue Badge, Pennsylvania Veteran Volunteers: A History of the 93rd Regiment, known as the "Lebanon Infantry" and "One of the 300 Fighting Regiments" from September 12th, 1861, to June 27th, 1865* (Harrisburg, PA, 1911), 277.

Though attacked "fiercely," the 18th Pennsylvania Cavalry lost none June 21–23. Theophilus F. Rodenbough, Thomas J. Grier, and William P. Seal, *History of the Eighteenth Regiment of Cavalry*

Fleming's men, including Parker, who entered captivity with Fleming, blamed Fleming for the disaster. Eldredge and Safford blamed Fleming and Pingree. Walker blamed Pingree alone. Pingree blamed Mahone's double envelopment "and the confusion sometimes occurring in such a situation."[58] Pingree did not explain why the hold at all hazards applied to his pickets but not to him.

Major George E. Chamberlin, the commander of the 11th Vermont and a graduate of Dartmouth College and Harvard Law School, blamed Wright "in not ordering supports."[59]

Major George G. Benedict, a University of Vermont graduate, newspaper editor, and staff officer in XVIII Corps who had earned a Medal of Honor at Gettysburg, also blamed the corps commander. 'The great mistake of the day was the order, for which General Wright appears to have been responsible, directing the skirmishers to hold their position at all hazards," wrote Benedict. "Such an order would have been justified if the sacrifice of the skirmish line was necessary to the safety of the corps or the division; but that was not the case."[60] Lewis Grant blamed Wheaton and Wright. Wright thought that Meade proposed attacking "without brains and without generalship."[61] Meade held Wright responsible for the fiasco.[62]

Lyman remembered:

> I look on June 22d & June 23d as the two most discreditable days to this army that I ever saw! There was everywhere, high and low, feebleness, confusion, poor judgment. The only person who kept his plans and judgment clear was Gen. Meade himself. On this particular occasion Wright showed himself totally unfit to command a corps. When he had provided a good [position] to fall back on in case of a reverse, and when he had found that there was no indication of a grand movement, he should have marched out and vigorously attacked with every man, as Meade constantly urged him to do. As it was, he allowed himself to be tied up and bullied by a force that was probably nothing but Mahone's division![63]

Pennsylvania Volunteers (163d Regiment of the Line) 1862–1865 (New York, 1909); RG 94, Entry 652, Box 62.

58 *OR* 40, 2:415.

59 Caroline C. Lutz, ed., *Letters of George E. Chamberlin, Who Fell in the Service of His Country Near Charlestown, Va., August 21st, 1864* (Springfield, IL, 1883), 340.

60 Benedict, *Vermont in the Civil War*, 2:365.

61 Charles A. Dana, *Recollections of the Civil War, With the Leaders at Washington, and in the Field in the Sixties* (New York, 1902), 227.

62 *OR* 40, 2:334.

63 Lowe, ed., *Meade's Army*, 225.

Horatio Gouverneur Wright

Library of Congress

Mahone's work pleased A. P. Hill and Lee.[64] The actions of June 22 and 23 catapulted Mahone and his division into the ranks of the Army of Northern Virginia's most renowned shock troops.[65] On June 23 against VI Corps, Mahone's force suffered around 141 casualties.[66]

64 *OR* 40, 2:685; ibid., 51, 2:1028.

65 Douglas Southall Freeman, *Lee's Lieutenants: A Study in Command*, 3 vols. (New York, 1942–1944), 3:xxxviii.

66 A tabular statement indicates that Sanders's brigade had three killed, 19 wounded, and one missing, a total of 23. Mahone's (Anderson's Old) Division Tabular Return of Casualties (Series II). A review of CSRs indicates that the brigade lost four killed, 14 wounded, one wounded and captured, and one missing, for a total of 20. Young, "Confederate Casualties during June 1864 at Petersburg." David White counts six wounded in the 14th Alabama alone. David White, Study of the 14th Alabama, Private Collection of David White, Manassas, VA.

CSRs show that Wright's brigade again bore the brunt of the fighting as on the previous day, losing 82. Young, "Confederate Casualties during June 1864 at Petersburg." CSRs reveal 12 killed or mortally wounded, 65 wounded, and five missing. Ibid. However, a newspaper indicates that the 48th Georgia had one killed or mortally wounded, and seven wounded for a total of eight rather than the six indicated by the CSRs (three wounded and three missing), suggesting a total of 84 casualties for the brigade: 13 killed or mortally wounded, 69 wounded, and two missing. *Augusta Chronicle & Sentinel*, July 6, 1864. Another source indicates that the brigade lost six killed, 70 wounded, and one missing, a total of 71. Mahone's (Anderson's Old) Division Tabular Return of Casualties (Series II). The 2nd Georgia Battalion lost a total of 31 casualties on June 22 and 23: eight killed or mortally wounded and 23 wounded, two of whom were missing. E. Saulsbury, "Casualties in 2d Georgia Battalion," *Macon Daily Telegraph*, June 30, 1864, p. 2, col. 5. The 10th Battalion had 81 killed and wounded of 200 engaged on June 22 and 23. Folsom, *Heroes and Martyrs of Georgia*, 99.

CSRs demonstrate that Weisiger's brigade incurred eight casualties: five wounded, one wounded and captured, and two missing. Young, "Confederate Casualties during June 1864 at Petersburg." Another source indicates the brigade had one killed and two wounded. Mahone's (Anderson's Old) Division Tabular Return of Casualties (Series II).

The same source shows that the Mississippi Brigade had five killed, 13 wounded, and six missing, a total of 24 casualties. Ibid. CSRs reveal that the brigade lost four killed or dead of wounds, 10 wounded, one wounded and captured, and five missing for a total loss of 20. Young, "Confederate Casualties during June 1864 at Petersburg."

CSRs establish that the portion of the Florida brigade involved incurred no casualties; the CSRs show that the one killed, six wounded, and three captured suffered by the brigade belonged to the three regiments that remained in the Petersburg lines. Ibid. Another source indicates the brigade had seven wounded and four missing. Mahone's (Anderson's Old) Division Tabular Return of Casualties (Series II).

* * *

After dark, Bushrod Johnson's division drew in its skirmish line. The division departed the breastworks it had thrown up just east of the Bailey farmhouse and hoofed it toward Rives Salient on Jerusalem Plank Road. There the division relieved Field's division, which prepared to take part in an operation scheduled for the following morning.

* * *

Though Lee had declined Beauregard's suggestion that they counterattack the vulnerable Federal left on the afternoon of June 18, by the morning of June 22 Lee was recovering his aggressiveness. He had heard "[t]he report that the Yankees did not & will not fight with spirit—some of them are said to have laid down their arms & surrendered without discharging a gun," as his adjutant, Col. Walter H. Taylor, once of the 6th Virginia, wrote.[67]

On the morning of June 23 Lee proposed his own counterattack to Beauregard—that they strike the Federal right on the Appomattox at the Junior Hare House near the northern terminus of Jerusalem Plank Road, then roll up the Yanks and recover the portion of the Dimmock Line captured by the bluecoats during the previous week's assaults on Petersburg. Later that day, encouraged by the results of Mahone's sally against II Corps, Lee inquired whether Anderson, whose troops occupied the trenches farther south, could spare a division to assist Hoke's division, which held the earthworks opposite the contemplated point of attack. At 9:00 p.m. that night, Fighting Dick promised a division of his men as well as their enthusiastic execution of their role in the plan. "You are certainly right, I think, as to the condition of the enemy's troops and as to the happy results that may be expected from following up the blow Hill has given him," Anderson wrote to Lee.[68] Anderson and Lee overlooked that the attack would begin frontally and without surprise against rested men in earthworks, whereas Mahone's blow had under cover of woods

---

Two men deserted from the four regiments of Kirkland's brigade at the Davis house. Cross, *A Melancholy Affair at the Weldon Railroad*, 78.

CSRs demonstrate that the 3rd North Carolina Cavalry, which Barringer had detached to picket the Rebel right, lost one wounded and two missing. Young, "Confederate Casualties during June 1864 at Petersburg."

The totals include the five captured by Major Baker of II Corps that morning. Baker, comp., *Joel B. Baker, A Collection of "Letters Home" from the Civil War*, 194–195.

67 R. Lockwood Tower, ed. *Lee's Adjutant: The Wartime Letters of Colonel Walter Herron Taylor, 1862–1865* (Columbia, SC, 1995), 170.

68 *OR* 51, 2:1025.

G. T. Beauregard
National Archives

surprised and flanked tired and to various degrees inebriated troops.

The army group commander delegated the details of this grandiose plan to Beauregard, who determined to attack near the house of the junior Hare on the morning of June 24. Batteries on the north side of the Appomattox would open and enfilade the enemy lines opposite Hoke's division of Beauregard's department on the river's southern bank. After half an hour, the Confederate artillery would cease fire for five minutes to signal Hoke's division to attack. To avoid endangering Secessionist troops, the guns would then resume fire against Federal batteries and soft targets. At the same time as the Rebel guns opened, the Secessionist right would begin demonstrating to keep the Yankees from reinforcing their troops near the river. Hoke's division, after seizing the enemy's works nearest the Appomattox, would wheel to face south and charge down the foe's line to retake the lines lost by the Confederates in the previous week's fighting. Field's division would place a brigade as soon as practicable in the lines captured by Hoke's division with orders to follow the advance of Hoke's division and protect its left. The rest of Field's division would fill the gap that would develop as Hoke's division proceeded southward, and attack eastward as opportunity arose to recapture Batteries 2 through 9 of the Dimmock Line. As Hoke's division uncovered Kershaw's division, Kershaw's division would wheel its left around and follow Hoke's division, acting as a reserve. Bushrod Johnson's division, having relieved Field's division the night before the attack, would pitch in to help Hoke's division in its struggle with the bluecoats opposite Johnson's division and retake Batteries 19 through 24 of the Dimmock Line. Secessionist artillery would unlimber to enfilade the Norfolk & Petersburg Railroad and Taylor's Creek behind the Federal left. Harris's Mississippi Brigade of Mahone's division drew the task of demonstrating opposite the Union left down the Weldon Railroad near the Davis house lest the Unionists draw reinforcements from that quarter.

The plan had a serious flaw. "A common superior should have been on the spot to harmonize the action of the two divisions partially engaged," recalled Brig. Gen. Johnson Hagood of Hoke's division, a graduate of South Carolina Military Academy.[69]

Hagood's division commander, Maj. Gen. Robert F. Hoke, a North Carolinian graduate of Kentucky Military Institute wounded at Chancellorsville, thought he should have had "full command of all the forces which were to participate."[70] This would not have solved the problem, because Hoke failed to grasp that his division, not Field's, had the responsibility of capturing the main Federal line.

The 11th, 21st, and 27th South Carolina of Hagood's brigade held the Confederate fortifications from the Appomattox to the City Point Railroad. Immediately in the brigade's front and parallel to it ran a ravine that formed a small branch before reaching the river. The brigade's rifle pits lay beyond the branch. About 600 level yards of oat field separated the Union and Secessionist lines.

On the night of June 23, 44 guns went into battery on the north bank of the Appomattox to enfilade the Yankee lines south of the river. Behind Hagood's brigade massed Anderson's and Benning's brigades of Field's division. Hoke received his instructions that night. He directed Hagood to prepare for an unspecified movement in the morning. Shortly after midnight, Hoke explained the plan to Hagood.

At 3:00 a.m. on June 24, the clanking of a sword coming down the line indicated to Pvt. Henry K. DuBose of the 21st South Carolina's Company B, the Wilds Rifles, the approach of an officer. DuBose and his comrades were trying to boil coffee.

"Where is Captain Wilds?" asked the officer, whom DuBose recognized by his voice as "Old Hagood."[71]

DuBose took a few steps, shook awake Capt. Samuel H. Wilds, wounded the previous July during the siege of Charleston. Dubose listened to Old Hagood explain the plan to Wilds. The three regiments between the railroad and the river would furnish about 300 skirmishers. Because of a lack of field officers, Lt. Col. P. H. Nelson from the brigade's 7th South Carolina Battalion south of the railroad would lead the skirmishers. Artillery from north of the river would enfilade the Federal line. When the bombardment ceased, Nelson would take his skirmishers and capture the enemy rifle pits. The remainder of the three regiments, about

69 Hagood, *Memoirs of the War of Secession*, 276.

70 *OR* 40, 1:798.

71 Henry Kershaw DuBose, *The History of Company B, Twenty-First Regiment (Infantry) South Carolina Volunteers, Confederate States Provisional Army* (Columbia, SC, 1909), 84.

Robert Hoke

Library of Congress

550 officers and men led by Hagood, would support Nelson's skirmishers and with them charge and seize the first line of Unionist breastworks. Anderson's Georgia Brigade would support the South Carolinians then occupy the first Federal line while Hagood brought up the rest of his brigade, formed the whole brigade facing southward, and drove down the Unionist trenches. When the supports for Anderson's brigade arrived, the Georgians would press on eastward to the second and third Federal lines. A courier from Anderson's brigade reported that formation in position. After hearing all this, DuBose resumed his coffee-making with extra urgency because he would soon advance with the rest of Nelson's skirmishers.

During the night of June 23, Cullen's New York Brigade had relieved Burnham's brigade in the trenches nearest the Appomattox's southern bank. The trenches consisted of deep and moderately wide ditches with the dirt excavated then thrown out on the side facing the enemy infantry and formed into a parapet. Inside the ditch on that side ran a wide banquette high enough for the men to stand on and fire over the parapet. Periodic traverses protected against enfilading fire. The New York Brigade gave "the greatest possible attention to the traverses," according to its commander, Col. Edgar M. Cullen of the 96th New York, a graduate of Columbia College.[72] A short distance in front of the trenches lay a string of small, detached pits a few yards apart, each holding three or four men. The pits were about 10 feet square and around three feet deep on the side facing the enemy, with the dirt excavated thrown up as a breastwork and the back open, commanded by the fire of the works in the rear. Beyond the pits stood a crop of oats high enough to afford cover within rifle range of the enemy line. Henry's brigade occupied the earthworks adjacent to the left of Cullen's brigade.

72 *OR* 40, 1:710.

Forty-four Confederate artillery pieces opened on the Federals from the north bank of the Appomattox at 7:00 a.m., enfilading the line of Stannard's division. The traverses mitigated the effects of the fire on the New York Brigade. "The men kept under cover, lay flat on the ground, never fired a gun, while the shells tore through the breastworks or exploded over their heads," remembered Col. William Kreutzer of the 98th New York, an instructor in Greek who had graduated from Genesee College. "Cullen, with drawn sword and bare head, raged and shouted, yelled and hallooed, flamed and tore along the line of his brigade." Cullen warned his men that the Secessionists would charge when the barrage ceased. "He'll think he has killed us all," Cullen said. "Then rise and stand firm."[73]

Soon stricken by sunstroke, Cullen yielded command to Lt. Col. William C. Raulston of the 81st New York, a Medal of Honor recipient who had suffered a wound on June 18. "Why the air was perfectly blue," remembered Capt. Cecil Clay of the 58th Pennsylvania, an undergraduate at the University of Pennsylvania at the war's outbreak and subsequently a Medal of Honor recipient. "There was a continuous roar, shriek, and whiz; fragments of shell flew in every direction."[74] The overshooting of the Confederate guns brought many men from the rear Federal echelon to the front and thus strengthened the main Union line.

After half an hour, the Rebel artillery shifted targets and bombarded the opposing Yankee batteries, which included the 30-pounder Parrott rifles of Company I, 1st Connecticut Artillery. Sergeant Smith was writing a letter to his Emma when the Secessionist cannon opened on his cannon, which responded immediately from its position north of the initial South Carolinian objective. "A number of rebel shells struck in our fort," Smith recalled. "One burst in the Captains tent and tore their clothes all to pieces but no one has been hurt."[75]

The Confederate barrage drew the fire of Union pieces from the South Carolina infantry, "which, as far as I could see, was the only service rendered by our guns," remembered Hoke. "Indeed I fear we were injured, more than we gained by the use of our guns, as it notified the enemy of our intended attack."[76]

73 William Kreutzer, *Notes and Observations Made during Four Years of Service with the Ninety-Eighth N. Y. Volunteers in the War of 1861* (Philadelphia, 1878), 216.

74 Cecil Clay, "Capture of Fort Harrison—How the Rebels Failed to Retake it," *National Tribune*, Nov. 26, 1881, p. 3, cols. 1–3.

75 Smith to "Dear Emma," June 24, 1864. Charles would rise to the rank of second lieutenant in Company H before the Federals took Petersburg. Connecticut, Adjutants-General, *Record of Service of Connecticut Men in the Army and Navy of the United States in the War of the Rebellion* (Hartford, CT, 1889), 153. Charles and Emma would wed on April 1, 1866. http://dunhamwilcox.net/ct/torrington_ct_marr2.htm (Torrington, Litchfield Co., CT—Marriages, *Extracted from History of Torrington, from Its First Settlement in 1737*, Rev. Samuel Orcutt, 1878).

76 *OR* 40, 1:798.

Johnson Hagood
Library of Congress

The Northerners in the main line prepared to meet the anticipated Southern onslaught. "We were expecting a charge and the men at once sprang to their feet and began peering over the parapet, while all along the line was heard the click, click, click!-click!-click! of musket locks," recalled Clay. "The rebel skirmish line came tumbling out over their works and disappearing into the oats, advanced rapidly to our skirmish pits."[77]

Hagood had intended to send his men forward at 7:35 a.m., five minutes after the Southern barrage switched targets, but confusion over the position of Anderson's brigade led Hagood to postpone his advance until Hoke peremptorily ordered the charge. At 7:42 a.m., Nelson stood on the parapet at the center of the South Carolina line between the road and the river, drew his handkerchief from his breast and held it aloft—the signal to advance. His 300 went over the top and rushed toward the Union rifle pits. The second line immediately followed at close supporting distance. "The enemy had fully prepared for us and greeted our first appearance with heavy discharges of musketry which increased in volume and deadly effect upon the skirmish line as it charged across the intervening field of oats," recalled DuBose in the first line. As Company B's 2nd Lt. T. Dargan Zimmerman cheered on his line, DuBose heard "the dull thud of a minie" hitting Zimmerman. "He spun half around before he fell." Nelson also perished during the advance.

Private James Register, the first of the Wilds Rifles to reach the Union rifle pits, met a pair of Yanks who could not speak English.

"Surrender!" said Register.

The Northerners just shook their heads. Register shouldered his musket.

The bluecoats dropped their muskets and raised their hands.

"Mein Gott!" they said.

77 Clay, "Capture of Fort Harrison—How the Rebels Failed to Retake it."

The South Carolina skirmishers seized all the pits and crouched within earshot of the main Union line. "The Federal officers could be distinctly heard imploring, and then threatening their men," DuBose remembered.[78] Instead of advancing to take the main Yankee line, Hagood's supporting line lay down in the oats about halfway to the Union trenches and awaited the advance of Field's division, which could not go forward because Hagood's men had not gotten out of the way.

Sergeant William V. Izlar of the 25th South Carolina's Company G, the Edisto Rifles, led the 25th's Company H that day. Hagood had instructed Izlar, "When the order is given cross over the breastworks and lead your company direct to the battery of the enemy you see in your front and capture it." Izlar recalled, "No one could possibly misunderstand an order as explicit as that."[79] Yet either Field or Hoke misunderstood his orders, because both expected one another's troops to break the Federal lines; and since the men of neither broke the Federal lines, neither ordered the general assault.

"There seems to have been some misunderstanding as to the part each division was to have performed," remembered General Lee, who observed from across the Appomattox.[80] At the other end of the lines, near the Davis house, Harris's brigade, instead of demonstrating, merely picketed the woods east of the railroad and observed enemy movements.[81]

Though the Federals in the pits had offered little resistance, the bluecoats in the main line, massed five lines deep, rose up behind the parapet, leveled their muskets and shouted, "Come in, Johnnie, and we won't fire."[82] Unable to retreat and afforded no protection by the Union pits, which faced only west and lay open to the rear, 130 of the Gamecocks including Dubose surrendered after a parlay.

Lee summoned his subordinates to a conference where he called off the attack after confirmation of the futility of persisting. The army group commander came down "very severe" on Hoke for his bungling of the assault, recalled Maj. William R. J. "Willy" Pegram, one of the Army of Northern Virginia's most brilliant artillerists who had been a student at the University of Virginia when the war began.[83] The remainder of the South Carolinians involved hugged the ground in the oat field until darkness allowed them to withdraw.

78 DuBose, *Company B, Twenty-First Regiment (Infantry) South Carolina Volunteers*, 86.

79 William Valmore Izlar, *A Sketch of the War Record of the Edisto Rifles, 1861–1865* (Columbia, SC, 1914), 71.

80 *OR* 40, 1:799.

81 Ibid., 805; Hewett, et al., eds., *Supplement to the Official Records*, 7:317–318.

82 Kreutzer, *Ninety-Eighth N.Y. Volunteers*, 217.

83 Peter S. C. Carmichael, *Lee's Young Artillerist: William R. J. Pegram* (Charlottesville, 1995), 125.

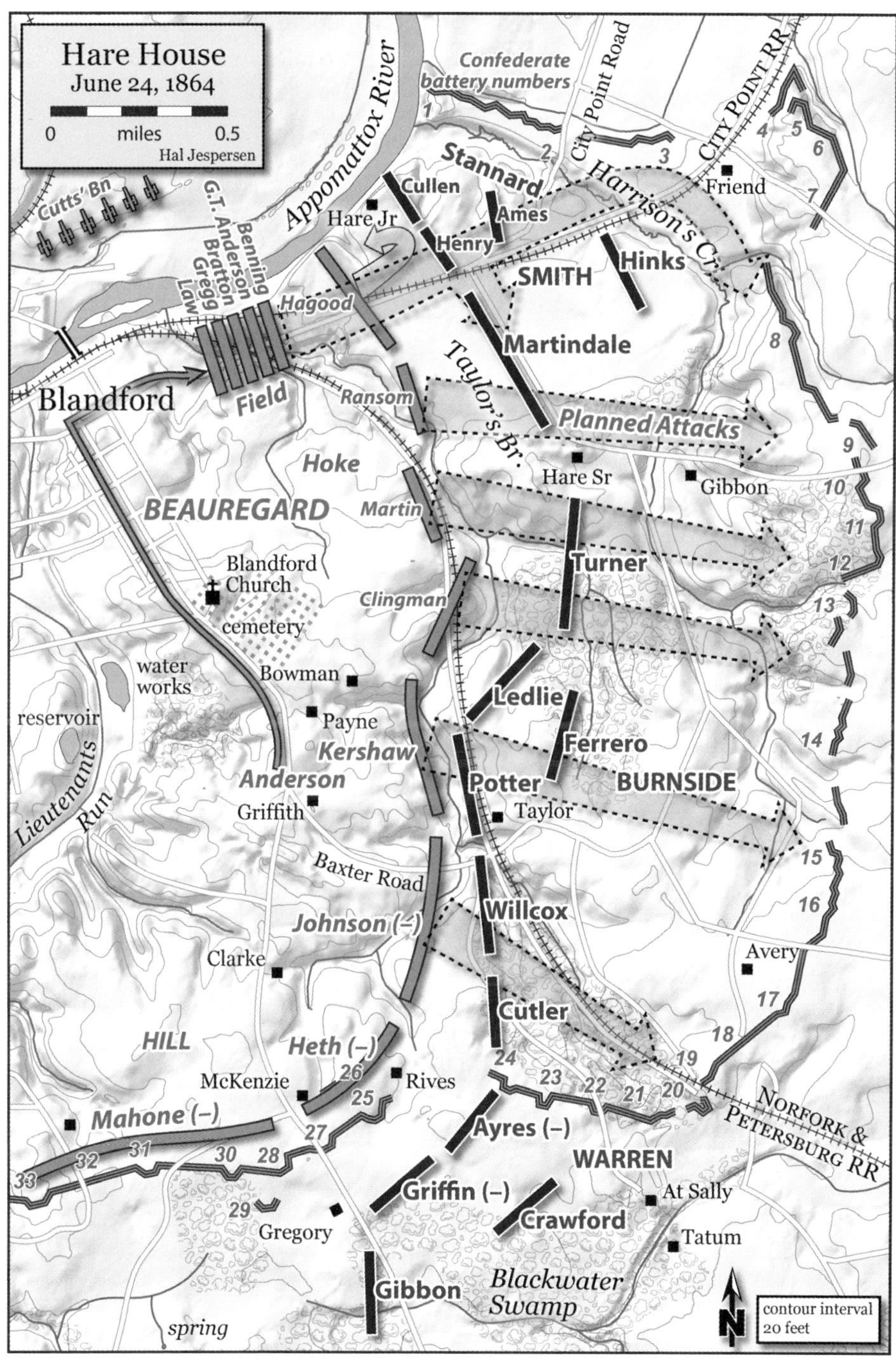
Hare House
June 24, 1864
0 miles 0.5
Hal Jespersen
Confederate battery numbers
Appomattox River
City Point Road
City Point RR
Harrison's Cr.
Taylor's Br.
Cutts' Bn
G.T. Anderson
Benning
Bratton
Gregg
Law
Hagood
Field
Blandford
Ransom
Hoke
Martin
Clingman
BEAUREGARD
Blandford Church
cemetery
water works
reservoir
Lieutenants Run
Bowman
Payne
Kershaw
Anderson
Griffith
Baxter Road
Johnson (–)
Clarke
HILL
Heth (–)
McKenzie
Rives
Mahone (–)
Gregory
spring
Hare Jr
Cullen
Stannard
Ames
Henry
SMITH
Hinks
Martindale
Planned Attacks
Hare Sr
Friend
Gibbon
Turner
Ledlie
Ferrero
Potter
BURNSIDE
Taylor
Willcox
Cutler
Avery
Ayres (–)
WARREN
Griffin (–)
Crawford
At Sally
Tatum
Gibbon
Blackwater Swamp
Norfork & Petersburg RR
contour interval 20 feet
N

The failure of Lee's counterattack ended the battle of Jerusalem Plank Road. Confederates had lost at least 306 killed, wounded, and captured, the Federals no more than 72, mostly captured pickets.[84]

* * *

To cover the Army of the Potomac's left rear, Meade shuffled his forces. XVIII Corps of Butler's army had relieved the rightmost division of IX Corps the previous night. By 3:15 a.m., Orlando Willcox's division of IX Corps had relieved Crawford's V Corps division just east of Jerusalem Plank Road, which in turn relieved Gibbon's division of II Corps just west of the plank road by 11:40 a.m. Major General Samuel W. Crawford, a former surgeon wounded at Antietam, reported Gibbon's command "in a very bad state of demoralization" deserving "special attention." Crawford thought Gibbon's position "a bad one" and sought "to remedy the confusion in the lines." Meade directed Gibbon's division away from II Corps to the Williams house, where in mid-afternoon the division relieved Sweitzer's and Dushane's brigades of V Corps on the left of VI Corps. Sweitzer's and Dushane's brigades returned to V Corps to help fill the gap between Crawford's right and Griffin's left.[85]

Grant met Meade around noon at the Army of the Potomac's headquarters across Jerusalem Plank Road from the Jones house. The general-in-chief brought with him two French officers commissioned to observe the war. Grant and Meade, after conferring about their second offensive at Petersburg, decided to abandon the operation and "give the army a few days' rest, which they now stand much in need of."[86] The two generals assumed that the Wilson-Kautz raiders would not return to the Army of the Potomac.

When Grant returned to City Point after lunch, he left the French officers with Meade's staff. "If I could have turned the class the other end to, I should have graduated at West Point, very high in French," the general-in-chief quipped about his lack of conversation with the Gauls.[87] Lyman drew the task of chaperoning them for the next three months.

84 Cullen's brigade lost 57 killed, wounded, and missing. *OR* 40, 1:711; Ibid., 51, 1:1291. Henry's brigade had no fewer than three killed and eight wounded and no more than 15 killed, wounded, and missing. Ibid., 40, 1:716; Ibid., 51, 1:1251–1252. Hagood's brigade had 25 killed, 72 wounded, and 209 missing. Ibid., 40, 1:804.

85 Ibid., 2:385, 389, 394.

86 Ibid., 373–374, 402.

87 Agassiz, ed., *Meade's Headquarters*, 178.

By 2:30 p.m. on June 24, Grant had finished reading a Richmond newspaper of the previous day. He found the rout of June 22nd much worse than he had thought. "The affair was a stampede and a surprise to both parties and ought to have been turned in our favor," he wrote to Halleck, still failing to understand that his men had experienced nearly all the surprise and that they had had little chance of turning the affair in their favor.[88] In the swamps, woods, and thickets south of Petersburg, Mahone operated in a native element that remained foreign not only to the Federals but to such compatriots as Hill and Wilcox.

Horatio Wright proceeded to demonstrate this despite a morning meeting with Meade that seemed to end with army commander and corps commander in agreement. Meade spent the day as he had the previous one, trying to prod Wright into advancing to the Weldon Railroad. Wright only made it back to the main line held the previous day by his unfortunate Vermont skirmishers, about a mile from the tracks, while part of Bryan's cavalry brigade tore up some rails near Dr. Gurley's house.

Brigadier General Robert B. Potter, a New York lawyer wounded at New Berne and Antietam, broached to his corps commander Burnside a scheme for the reduction of the enemy salient in his division's front. "Lieutenant Colonel Pleasants, of the Forty-eighth Pennsylvania Veteran Volunteers, commanding First Brigade, has called on me to express his opinion of the feasibility of mining the enemy's work in my front," wrote Potter, Pleasants's division commander. "The men themselves have been talking about it for some days, and are quite desirous, seemingly, of trying it."[89] Lieutenant Colonel Henry Clay Pleasants, a professional mining engineer born in Argentina, had in his regiment more than 100 miners.

* * *

At the same time, farther east, Sheridan was failing to occupy Hampton enough to help Wilson and Kautz.

At Samaria Church north of the James that afternoon, Hampton's cavalry corps overwhelmed Gregg's isolated division of Little Phil's horsemen in the withering heat. By evening the butternuts had driven the bluecoats through several fallback positions to within two or three miles of Charles City Court House. Gregg's troopers accomplished their mission of protecting Sheridan's wagon train, but Hampton eliminated any remaining hope that Little Phil might cross the James at Deep Bottom. Grant gave up on that crossing point and authorized Sheridan

88 *OR* 40, 2:372.

89 Ibid., 396–397.

to cross where the general-in-chief's army had crossed, from Wilson's Wharf to Fort Powhatan, about 15 miles downriver from Petersburg. Ferries would carry Sheridan's forces across the river there, a far more time-consuming procedure than a crossing on the pontoon at Deep Bottom. This would leave Hampton unoccupied and allow him to focus on Wilson and Kautz. Little Phil would also have to travel farther to come to the assistance of the raiders.

* * *

Just south of Petersburg, the Confederates were running wagons along Halifax Road to bring in forage. The picketing of the Weldon Railroad by Harris's brigade of Mahone's division served to guard the wagons as they passed the Federals near the Davis house. Farther south, the Rebels had already begun repairing Reams Station and the break there in the Weldon Railroad.[90]

West of the Cockade City the Unionists had done so little damage to the South Side Rail Road that it would require only a day or two to repair.[91] The Northerners had burned the ties but did little damage to the rails.[92]

* * *

On the morning of June 25, Grant notified Halleck of the decision to terminate the second offensive. Meade continued marching and countermarching his tired divisions in reaction to imaginary threats to his army's left rear. Sheridan commenced ferrying his trains across the James at Windmill Point. Burnside's troops began digging their mine.

Lee directed the horsemen of Hampton's division and Chambliss's brigade of W. H. F. Lee's division to proceed to the south side of the James preparatory to attacking Wilson and Kautz as they returned from their raid. Confederate morale at Petersburg improved in the wake of Mahone's lopsided victories, though Federal morale did not fall in inverse proportion.

* * *

90 George Oscar French Letter, July 6, 1864, George Oscar French Civil War Letters, VHS; Letter, Aldace F. Walker to "Dear Father," June 30, 1864, Aldace Freeman Walker Papers.

91 A. L. Rives, Col. &c, June 24, 1864, Endorsement on letter from Capt. J. M. Robinson, suggesting that a negro force could do excellent service by repairing the Danville & S.S.R.R. War Department Collection of Confederate Records, Record Group 109, NA, csa-railroads.com, retrieved June 17, 2024. "The damage to the S.S.R.R. is represented to be slight & as these laborers could hardly be there for a day or two, it is not thought judicious to send them forward without more definite information." Ibid.

92 "Raid on the Danville Railroad," *Daily Richmond Dispatch*, June 25, 1864, p. 1, col. 2.

Sheridan conferred with Grant at City Point on June 26. The general-in-chief wanted Little Phil to move in a leisurely fashion to strengthen Meade's left on Jerusalem Plank Road. Sheridan moved in a very leisurely fashion.

All remained quiet on the Petersburg front. Meade told Warren to hold his lines as he pleased. Birney arrested the officers who had allowed pickets in front of II Corps to arrange an unofficial truce with the Secessionists. He consolidated Moroney's and MacDougall's brigades of Barlow's division as well as McAllister's and Chaplin's brigades of Mott's division, dissolved a brigade of Gibbon's division, and consolidated 11 regiments.

* * *

Around 11:00 a.m., Hampton's division, along with Chambliss's Virginia Brigade of Rooney Lee's division, crossed the James on the pontoon at Drewry's Bluff and encamped at Halfway House, so-called because it stood halfway between Richmond and Petersburg. Fitzhugh Lee's cavalry division remained north of James River. That day Maj. Gen. Fitzhugh "Fitz" Lee requested and by 1:30 p.m. received permission to assist in intercepting the Wilson-Kautz raiders. Orders instructed him not to fatigue his horses but to camp that night near water. That evening Hampton dispatched Chambliss's brigade to Stony Creek Station, about ten miles south of Reams Station. This brigade encamped near Swift Creek.

The chief engineer of the Piedmont Railroad shifted laborers, teams, and tools to Staunton River Bridge and from there commenced the reconstruction of the Richmond & Danville.[93] Lee's Engineer Regiment received instructions to prepare to move to the Richmond & Danville to assist in its repair.[94] Lee kept trying to impress on the Davis administration the impracticability of holding the Weldon Railroad and the necessity of maintaining the Richmond & Danville.

By this time Early had driven Hunter back into West Virginia and turned down the Shenandoah Valley. On June 26, Early's troops reached Staunton. This was their point of no return. They could entrain and return to Lee's army at Petersburg or march northward toward Washington. A threat to the Northern capital might draw Grant's army group away from James River just as the threat Lee's army had posed to Washington in 1862 had drawn McClellan's army from the James. Lee had originally instructed Early to head northward, and Early saw no reason to deviate from the plan.

93 Eanes, *Destroy the Junction*, 165.

94 *OR* 40, 2:692.

* * *

Before 7:00 a.m. on the morning of June 27, Chambliss's Virginia Brigade moved out of Petersburg near the Lead Works heading south about half a mile west of the Weldon Railroad. Farther south, Chambliss's brigade proceeded on Halifax Road. Private John Z. H. Scott, a scout from the 10th Virginia Cavalry's Company F, had been a student at the University of Virginia at the war's beginning. He rode at the tail end of the brigade's column with another scout, Pvt. Isaac Curtis of the 9th Virginia Cavalry's Company A. General Chambliss loaned Scott and Curtis a map and told them to find Wilson after they reached Stony Creek Station. The brigade finished the day short of Stony Creek Station.

Lee directed Hampton to move his division from Halfway House across the Appomattox to Stony Creek Station. Hampton's division traveled as quickly as possible for jaded horses in the heat and dust. The division reached Lee's headquarters at Violet Bank around noon on June 27. With Hampton briefly visiting Richmond, division command devolved upon Brig. Gen. Matthew C. Butler, a South Carolina lawyer and politician who had lost a leg at First Brandy Station. Butler reported to Lee, who apprised the South Carolinian of the situation and suggested that he press on for five or six miles, then bivouac before proceeding to Stony Creek Station in the morning.

Butler led the division southward. Most of his men bypassed Petersburg to avoid the Federal bombardment of the city. The 35th Battalion Virginia Cavalry, the Comanches, traversed the city to assess the reaction to the shelling of the people who remained there. Capt. Franklin M. Myers of the Comanches' Company A remembered how the citizenry had adjusted:

> [I]t was really refreshing to see ladies pass coolly along the streets as though nothing unusual was transpiring while the 160-pound shells were howling like hawks of perdition through the smoky air and bursting in the very heart of the city, but they didn't mind it a bit; and even the children would stand and watch, at the sound of the passing shells, to see the explosion, and make funny little speeches about them, as if they had been curious birds flying over their heads. Familiarity with the danger of the bombardment had cured them of all their fears of it, and when it would be told to people on the street, as was frequently the case, that Miss or Mrs. So-and-so was killed in her house by a shell, nobody was horrified at all, but all seemed to take it as a matter of course and to care very little about it.[95]

95 Frank M. Myers, *The Comanches: A History of White's Battalion, Virginia Cavalry, Laurel Brig., Hampton Div., A.N.V., C.S.A.* (Baltimore, 1871), 309.

The division encamped about six miles south of town, at the Wyatt farm on the Weldon Railroad near Globe Tavern.

The progress of Chambliss's brigade down the Weldon Railroad had Meade more worried about a Secessionist raid on the Army of the Potomac's left rear than about the returning Wilson-Kautz raiders. The Great Peppery shifted the Colored Division of IX Corps to Prince George Court House and redeployed Gibbon's division of II Corps to the Baxter Road crossing of the Blackwater. Sheridan was just finishing crossing his trains to the south side of the James and was finally beginning to cross his troops. Meade prodded Little Phil to move to the army's left to protect it and to aid Wilson in his return. Petersburg newspapers of June 27 suggested that Wilson would proceed toward Danville and therefore toward Sherman. That very day Sherman, tired of maneuvering, launched a frontal assault on the Army of Tennessee's Kennesaw Mountain line—about as far from Atlanta as Petersburg was from Richmond. Sherman met with a costly repulse.

Grant reported to Halleck that heavy guns from the Army of the Potomac's siege train had gone into battery within 2,000 yards of Petersburg's railroad bridge. The general-in-chief expected Wilson to head for New Berne if he found his way back to the Army of the Potomac blocked. Grant did not know that Wilson had understood his orders differently. "[M]y written instructions were explicit to rejoin the army as soon as the object of my expedition was accomplished," he recollected. "My going else where was merely contingent."[96] The general-in-chief understood "blocked" to mean an enemy standing in the way. Wilson understood it to mean an enemy through whom he could not fight his way.

* * *

As of June 28, Meade had heard nothing of Wilson except from contrabands. Sheridan's troops still had not finished crossing the James. The commander of the Army of the Potomac ordered Little Phil to Jerusalem Plank Road's crossing of Warwick Swamp to assist Wilson if necessary.

Grant notified Sherman that he need no longer worry about the Army of Tennessee detaching forces to Lee. The general-in-chief thought that Lee would have difficulty supplying additional forces because of the damage the Federals had wreaked upon Secessionist supply lines.[97]

Some evidence supported Grant's view. That morning Federal scouts encountered Confederate officers' manservants provided with passes and on their

96 Wilson, *Under the Old Flag*, 1:498.

97 *OR* 40, 2:475.

way home to North Carolina. From these slaves the scouts learned "that all the negroes who could possibly be spared were being sent from the army to their homes, and . . . the want of provisions had led to this step."[98]

Other facts unknown to the general-in-chief indicated that he overestimated the damage done by the Northerners to the Southern railroads. The Confederates were repairing the break in the Weldon Railroad at Reams Station.[99] The chief engineer of the Piedmont Railroad was using that railroad's resources to rebuild the Richmond & Danville northeastward from Staunton River Bridge. Lee's Engineer Regiment was heading to the Richmond & Danville to assist in its repair. Track crews of the Virginia Central were approaching Staunton in the Shenandoah Valley as they repaired that railroad's track.[100]

While Federal troops at Petersburg rested, Grant wanted Hunter to attack Charlottesville as soon as possible, but Hunter was headed away from Charlottesville. The general-in-chief began exploring the possibility of driving a wedge westward between Petersburg and Richmond, either along the north bank of Swift Creek or between Swift Creek and the Appomattox. He was also still considering the alternative of taking ten days' rations and the Army of the Potomac, marching around Petersburg to the Appomattox above the Cockade City, and either attacking the city from there or crossing the Appomattox and attacking the Howlett Line from behind.

The army group's chief engineer, Barnard, considered either of these operations too hazardous. He favored holding with 20,000 soldiers of XVIII and IX corps the two and a half miles of line from XVIII Corps' right to the line's intersection near the Avery house with the captured portion of the Dimmock Line. This would make "60,000 or 70,000" infantry "available for extending" to the left. From that intersection with the Dimmock Line, V Corps would extend across Jerusalem Plank Road. Farther left, II and VI corps would extend to the Weldon Railroad and entrench, freeing "force available for other operations," presumably the investment of Petersburg to the Appomattox above the city.[101]

Late on June 28 Halleck notified Grant of Sherman's repulse at Kennesaw Mountain the previous day. Meade found the quiet along the Petersburg lines unusual. His fear of a Confederate attack on his army's left rear subsided. Hancock, recovered from the flare of his Gettysburg wound, resumed command of II Corps.

98 Ibid., 496.

99 George Oscar French Letter, July 6, 1864; Walker to "Dear Father," June 30, 1864.

100 *OR* 40, 2:477, 697.

101 Ibid., 478–479. This was consistent with the original plan of Grant and Meade. Ibid., 1:25–26. But II, V, and VI corps had only around 53,000 effective infantry at this point. Ibid., 2:542.

He promptly issued a general order so critical of his corps' operations on June 22 that Birney demanded a court of inquiry. Meade thought that Birney had performed well. Hancock let the matter drop.

* * *

Lee urged the Secretary of War to hasten repairs on the Richmond & Danville but cautioned him against reporting their completion. "When the repairs shall have been completed, it is of great importance that the fact should not be known to the enemy, and I trust that you will prevail upon the newspaper publishers to abstain from any reference to it, even by implication," wrote the army group commander. "If they announce that the road is again open it will only invite another expedition of the enemy against it."[102] The authorities put Brig. Gen. James A. Walker in charge of the defense of the Richmond & Danville.

Chambliss's Virginia Brigade arrived at Stony Creek Station that morning and drew rations and corn. Hampton's main body joined the Virginians there around noon, shortly before Wilson and Kautz reached the Double Bridges over the Nottoway. The South Carolinian disposed his forces to attack the raiders as well as block their retreat to Union lines. He sent scouts forward to locate the Northerners and determine which route they were pursuing. Privates Scott and Curtis had already taken some couriers and ventured forth from Chambliss's brigade on the road past Sappony Church.

At 12:30 p.m., Hampton called upon General Lee to place infantry and artillery at Reams Station. With the crossings at Reams Station and Stony Creek Station blocked, it seemed that the Federals would have to cross the Weldon Railroad at Jarratt's Station, about 10 miles south of Stony Creek Station, or at Belfield, around 10 miles south of Jarratt's Station—increasingly longer routes back to Union lines.

Beyond Sappony Church, Scott and Curtis encountered the head of Wilson's column. They sent back a courier to inform Chambliss, who in turn informed Hampton. The South Carolinian directed Chambliss's brigade to lead the way to Sappony Church and attack the Unionists as soon as they arrived. Chambliss dispatched the 10th and 13th Virginia Cavalry. The 9th Virginia Cavalry soon followed.

Hampton reported the raiders' route to his army group commander and notified him that the Confederate cavalry would attack the Federals at Sappony Church. The South Carolinian asked Lee again to send infantry and artillery to

102 Ibid., 697.

Reams Station. The army group commander complied with the request, dispatching Mahone with his Alabama and Florida brigades and two batteries of artillery. Meanwhile, Fitzhugh Lee's division of cavalry and Breathed's battery of horse artillery, the First Stuart Virginia Artillery, had crossed the James on the pontoon at Chaffin's Bluff. Fitzhugh Lee's troopers and Breathed's battery bivouacked at Port Walthall Junction between the James and the Appomattox.

The trap that the Confederates had prepared for Wilson and Kautz was ready to be sprung.

Chapter Eight

"Cavalry Must Fight or Run Away"

AS NIGHT fell on June 28, Wilson and Kautz knew that they faced Hampton's cavalry. "It is evident that all of enemy's cavalry is on this side of the James," recorded Kautz.[1] That changed the picture they thought would face them as they tried to return to the Army of the Potomac. "It was at once apparent that the prospects of penetrating their line at this place was by no means flattering and that a new route must be chosen," Wilson remembered of his predicament.[2]

The raider generals unwittingly set themselves up for another shock. Though Humphreys's assurance that Sheridan would occupy Hampton had proven hollow, Wilson and Kautz still believed Humphreys's promise that Union infantry would invest Petersburg from Jerusalem Plank Road to the Appomattox above the city. The two raider generals credited Humphreys on this point even though, as Humphreys recalled, "if we had taken the [South Side] Railroad [Wilson] would necessarily have heard of it from the people of the country, since it would have been necessary to fight a battle for its possession, an event that would have been known far and wide."[3] Wilson and Kautz had heard of no such battle, but if they considered Humphreys's line of reasoning, they did not think that failure to take the South Side railway precluded taking the Weldon Railroad. Contrabands had told Wilson that Meade occupied Reams Station.

1 Hewett, et al., eds., *Supplement to the Official Records*, 7:241.

2 *OR* 40, 1:627.

3 Humphreys, *The Virginia Campaign*, 238. Humphreys refers to the South Side Rail Road as the Lynchburg Railroad. Ibid.

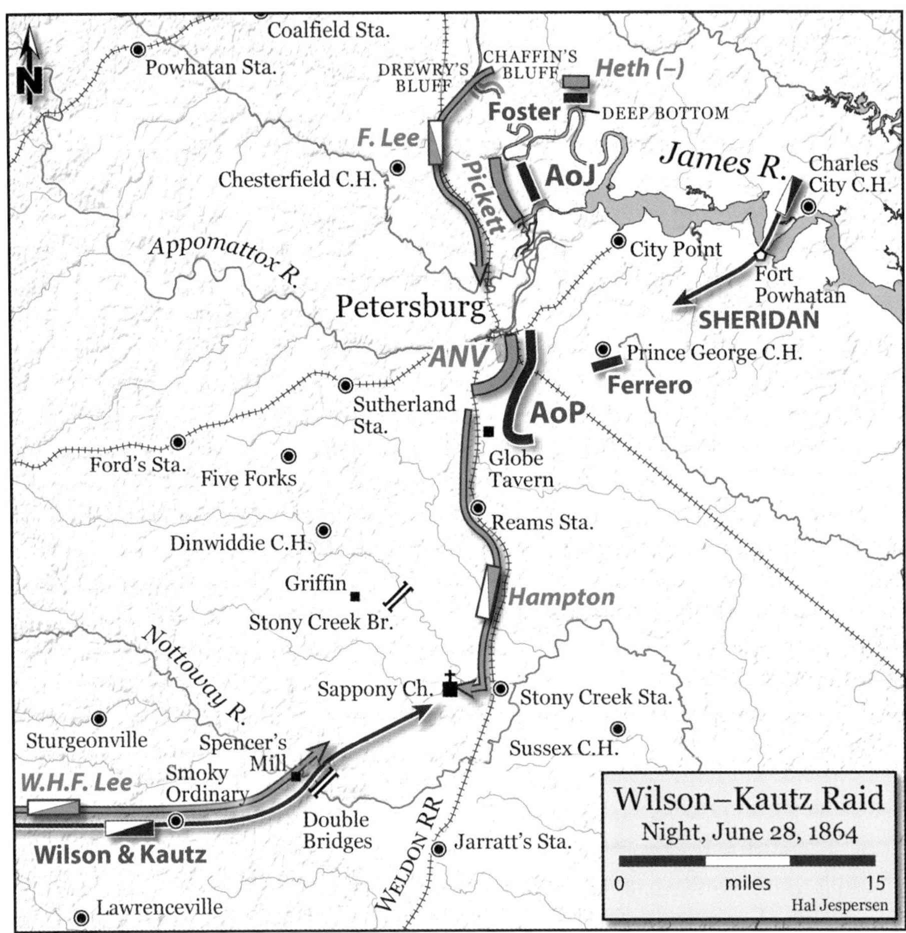

"I advised getting as near the left of the Army of the Potomac to have the support of that Army as I learn our pickets are on the railroad," noted Kautz. "Our forces must have heard our guns here."[4] Wilson examined his maps and saw that better roads and fewer streams lay to the north. Retreating to the south by way of Jarratt's Station would involve inferior roads, more streams, and lengthen his route by more than ten miles. "I determined to hold the position with my own division till the balance of the command with the train could move by the left flank through the country to the road leading to Reams Station," Wilson recalled.

4 Hewett, et al., eds., *Supplement to the Official Records*, 7:241.

"I hoped to march entirely around the cavalry at Stony Creek, and reach the left of our infantry before Hampton could discover my intention."[5]

McIntosh's brigade erected low works of fence rails for protection while its troopers blazed away from the prone position at the Secessionists to the east. "We kept up the firing as long as we could see anything that looked like a man," remembered the 2nd Ohio Cavalry's First Sergeant Chester. "After dark we could only fire at the flash of their guns and they at ours." Worn out by lack of sleep, Unionists nodded off on the firing line. "I remember several right along side of me were asleep when the carbines were being fired all about them," Chester wrote.[6]

Captain William N. McDonald, ordnance officer of the Laurel Brigade, recalled, "The battle raged furiously, and the Federals were so near the Confederate lines that their forms could be seen by the flash of the discharges, and the commands 'Forward!' 'Close up!' etc., given by their officers were distinctly heard."[7]

The fight lasted until around 10:00 p.m. Wilson strengthened his line with artillery. Battery C-E unlimbered on the Federal left and Colonel McIntosh posted it to enfilade the ground in the line's front. Battery K dropped trail near the road. In the darkness, the guns proved as dangerous to friend as to foe. About 100 yards behind the 2nd Ohio Cavalry, the gunners tried to fire over the heads of the horsemen. "One solid shot was much too low and killed a man who was asleep by my side," recalled Chester. "He never knew what happened to him."[8]

Friendly fire injured seven soldiers of the 22nd New York Cavalry. The 22nd's Private Allen remembered, "The sound of the shell going thro' the woods was very grand and a little fearful."[9]

Hampton countered by deploying all his artillery, two guns of Graham's battery. Worn out horses had prevented more cannon from keeping up with Hampton's division. Under cover of the darkness and some houses, German-born 2nd Lt. Frederick W. Fuger of Battery C-E, who had earned a Medal of Honor at Gettysburg, pushed his light 12-pounder to within 350 yards of the Confederate guns and almost silenced them.

5 *OR* 40, 1:623. Years later, Kautz decided that Wilson ought to have made this move immediately on the grounds that the entire command would have passed through Reams Station before the enemy could bar the way. Kautz, "Wilson Raid: An Expedition to Destroy the Petersburg & Lynchburg and the Richmond & Danville Railroads," in *National Tribune*, June 8, 1899, p. 1, cols. 5–7; ibid., June 15, p. 1, cols. 5-7.

6 Chester, *Recollections*, 88.

7 William N. McDonald, *A History of the Laurel Brigade; Originally the Ashby Cavalry of the Army of Northern Virginia and Chew's Battery* (Baltimore, 1907), 264.

8 Ibid.

9 Allen Diary, June 28, 1864.

Wilson directed Chapman's brigade to form a second line behind McIntosh's troops. "On we went through a piece of wood dark as Egypt, soon however coming to an open field in which the battery was firing and stray bullets passed over our heads whistling a merry tune," recalled W. H. D., a trooper in the 8th New York Cavalry of Chapman's brigade. "The order 'prepare to fight on foot!' was given and all but numbers four dismounted (they remaining to hold the horses), took their carbines, filled their pockets with cartridges and were marched to a position in rear of the 1st Brigade."[10]

Corporal Gilpin of the 3rd Indiana Cavalry recalled that "[b]oth parties threw up hasty works."[11] Chapman's brigade formed line with, from left to right, the 1st Vermont Cavalry, 8th New York Cavalry, 3rd Indiana Cavalry, and 22nd New York Cavalry. The troopers of these units erected a light breastwork of fence rails in the woods with horses waiting in a field a few rods to the rear. The 1st New Hampshire Cavalry formed a reserve.

McIntosh's brigade fell back and moved off to the left. "The enemy, however, soon found out that we were changing our line and opened a heavy fire, though owing to the darkness, it was poorly directed and did no further harm than to keep the boys awake and on the alert," W. H. D. of the 8th New York Cavalry remembered.[12]

The enemy fire in front of the 1st Vermont Cavalry proved far better directed. "An order came for thirty men to be sent over to the right of the road, and Captain Cummings with his battalion went in that direction, guided by the sound of the carbines," recalled First Sergeant Ide.[13] At the edge of the woods Cummings, captured in December 1862 and paroled the following May, took a bullet in the face and required help to get to the rear, while other Vermonters received mortal wounds. "It soon became quiet again and almost as soon most of the boys fell into a sound slumber," remembered W. H. D.[14]

Firing waxed and waned through the night as the opponents probed one another. Sergeant Eli Woodbury of Company E in the 1st Vermont Cavalry appreciated the light breastwork he and his comrades had erected, though a bullet hit the man next to him in the knee. "[M]any a time during that night the balls struck in this frail defense or in the dirt so near it as to sprinkle us with sand," Woodbury remembered.[15]

10 W. H. D., "Interesting Account of the Adventures of a Squadron of the 8th N. Y. Cavalry Cut Off from the Wilson Raiding Party," *Rochester Daily Union and Advertiser*, July 20, 1864, p. 2, col. 2.

11 Gilpin Diary, June 28, 1864.

12 W. H. D., "Interesting Account of the Adventures of a Squadron of the 8th N. Y. Cavalry."

13 Hoffman, *First Vermont Cavalry Volunteers*, 188.

14 W. H. D., "Interesting Account of the Adventures of a Squadron of the 8th N. Y. Cavalry."

15 Joseph D. Collea, Jr., *The First Vermont Cavalry in the Civil War: A History* (Jefferson, NC, 2010), 245.

The firing followed a pattern. "During the night, every once in a while, the Rebels would fall on our line, when our guns would open for half an hour," Ide recollected, "and the skirmishers would begin at one end of the line and run clear through to the other, like a row of bricks set on end so that when one was started, the rest fell one after the other."[16]

Quartermaster Sergeant Hannaford of the 2nd Ohio Cavalry was overseeing a train of pack mules. "[S]ometimes for ten or fifteen minutes not a shot would be fired, and our tired men would be all (almost) soundly sleeping, when from the rebel lines a most terrific volley would be fired, and our men springing up would return it, and then for perhaps fifteen or twenty minutes there would be kept up the most terrific musketry fire I ever heard excepting during the battle of the Wilderness," he recalled. "[T]hen it would gradually die away, to be succeeded by a [silence] that in contrast appeared oppressive and unnatural, and so it was kept up all the live long night."[17]

The Confederates experienced matters similarly. Colonel Beale of the 9th Virginia Cavalry in Chambliss's brigade remembered, "During the night, at intervals varying from fifteen minutes to an hour, there were heavy volleys of rifles exchanged."[18]

Out on the right of Chambliss's brigade, Companies C and K of the 9th involuntarily remained alert. "The night was a well-nigh sleepless one, the continuous firing on the line near us keeping us awake, and causing a constant apprehension that our own position would be assailed," recollected Lieutenant Beale of the 9th's Company C.[19]

The night's terrible beauty indelibly imprinted itself on some. "It was a grand but awful [sight] to see the long streams of fire as they shot forth from hundreds of carbines, and then the broad deep red of artillery, and bursting shell, that for an instant would light up the midnight heavens almost blindingly," Bugler Barrett remembered.[20]

Butler's brigade of Hampton's division arrived during the night on the right of Young's brigade. Private Ulysses R. Brooks of Company B in the 6th South Carolina Cavalry recalled that when Wilson's lines seemed to advance, "Up we

16 Hoffman, *First Vermont Cavalry Volunteers*, 189.

17 Eanes, *Destroy the Junction*, 124.

18 Richard L. T. Beale, *Ninth Virginia Cavalry*, 134.

19 George W. Beale, *A Lieutenant of Cavalry in Lee's Army*, 176.

20 Wickman, comp., *Letters to Vermont*, 179.

would jump . . . and pour a volley from the Enfield rifles into their ranks in the dark, which Wilson's men could not stand."[21]

Sergeant Elisha Humphries of the Phillips Georgia Legion Cavalry's Company A considered the musketry that night the heaviest he had ever encountered. "I worked harder that night than I ever did in my life trying to get us some breastworks fixed which we succeeded in doing after whipping the Yanks back twice," he remembered. "They charged us four different times that night but never got nearer than forty yards of our breastworks before we drove them back."[22]

While the Jeff Davis Legion Cavalry in Young's brigade entrenched long after dark, "a terrible fusillade from the enemy" interrupted them. "We expected every moment to see the dusky forms make their appearance," Waring recalled. "But we looked in vain." His men ceased fire after two volleys though musketry continued between the Yanks and the infantry of Holcombe's Legion on Waring's left. "The enemy's artillery poured schrapnel & canister into us, but we were secure behind our works," Waring remembered. "Soon the firing stopped."[23]

* * *

Miles away, Charles Cross reached home about midnight and informed his owner, John C. Griffin, of what had taken place at Spencer's Mill. Cross implored Griffin to hide in the woods until the enemy passed his house. Cross believed that Griffin, if captured, would die in prison because of his delicate health, which had forced him to resign his captaincy in the 3rd Virginia's Dinwiddie Greys, a company that he had raised. "I was, however, too unwell to act upon his suggestions," recalled Griffin. "I thought that it was not likely that this body of cavalry would leave the Stage Road . . . as they were near their own lines and likely to be pressed by the Confederate cavalry hanging in their rear. But, for fear they might leave the road I directed Charles to post negroes at daybreak on different approaches to the house, so that I could be informed in time to secrete myself."[24]

* * *

Wilson directed McIntosh to cover the road to Stony Creek Station while Kautz took his division and the trains back westward toward the Stage Road.

21 U. R. Brooks, *Butler and His Cavalry in the War of Secession 1861–1865* (Columbia, SC, 1909), 274.

22 Richard Coffman, *Going Back the Way They Came: The Phillips Georgia Cavalry Legion* (Macon, GA, 2011), 89.

23 Waring Diary, June 29, 1864.

24 Griffin, "Life in Dinwiddie County in the vicinity of the opposing armies," 6–7.

Kautz moved out between midnight and 1:00 a.m. The 11th Pennsylvania Cavalry of Spear's brigade led the way with its Company K as advance guard. The Pennsylvanians went a short distance then turned left and followed a narrow woods road overarched by heavy pines along Sappony Creek leading to the Stage Road. After Spear's brigade came the division's artillery. Hannaford watched from his train of pack mules pressed into the bushes on the left side of the road as staff officers galloped up and down and the guns passed, then West's brigade.

After West's brigade came the trains. The 5th Pennsylvania Cavalry protected the wagon train while the 3rd New York stood in the road. About 1:00 a.m. a staff officer ordered Hannaford to get into the road and prepare to start behind some wagons. Just as the pack mules made the left turn onto the wood road, a volley sounded followed by Rebel yells, panicking the drivers. "[S]oon one of the wagons in our front lost the road, dove in among the trees, and . . . was smashed all to pieces," Hannaford remembered. A few hundred yards farther and the trains halted, snarled in a traffic jam. Musketry and cannon fire frayed nerves. "Every one was trying to get ahead, cries of 'we are on the wrong road;' 'no we ain't, we are right;' 'I tell you we're wrong;' were constantly heard," recalled Hannaford. A staff officer volunteered to return and find out the right way. The advance of the pack train of Spear's brigade, mingled with stragglers, caught up and began pressing the rear of Hannaford's pack train. "My partner and myself planted our horses across the road and drew our Sabres, but it was impossible to keep them back;" remembered Hannaford, "they edged around our flank[s], [and] crowded up until we were wedged up in a perfect jam." Around 30 wagons were going in one direction, about 20 in the other, while still others were turning around.

The apparent approach of musketry caused another panic. The pack mules started. Hannaford and his partner struggled to remain where they belonged. The staffer returned and reported that the trains were on the right road, but the situation became worse and the drivers engaged in more swearing than before. Hannaford became separated from the brigade pack train and could not find anyone who knew its whereabouts. "[M]any of the teamsters had lighted candles, showing a scene that was perfectly indescribable," recalled Hannaford. "Every one that could, now pushed ahead . . . and although we were not certain where we were going, yet it was everybody for himself and the devil take the hindmost."[25]

Sergeant Gause was also riding among the trains. "[P]rogress was very slow, owing to the jam from thousands of men and animals rushing to a safe retreat," he remembered. "The roadside was lined with wounded men and officers, pleading for a place to ride." He heard a familiar voice.

25 Eanes, *Destroy the Junction*, 125–126.

"Is that you, Captain Pike?" Gause asked.

"Yes, I am wounded," said Capt. Henry C. Pike of the 2nd Ohio Cavalry's Company D.

Gause and his companions halted and took Pike into their vehicle. "This stopped the train behind us, for the road was so narrow that teams could not pass," Gause remembered. "Everyone in reach was furious at the delay." Shells were exploding, trees crashing down, people screaming. "As soon as he was seated we hastened to close up the gap caused by our halt, and just as the horses were checking their speed the pack-animals crowded them from the road," recalled Gause. "One wheel struck a stump and broke a hame and one horse went out of harness." Gause jumped down and by guiding the pole pulled the carriage from the road with one horse. Unable to repair the harness, he and his companies decided to abandon the carriage, saddle their horses, and ride. They soon fell to the rear of the column.[26]

Before departing for Reams Station, 1st Sgt. Horace W. Bolton of the 1st District of Columbia Cavalry's Company D requisitioned a bed from a nearby mansion for an officer badly wounded earlier in the evening. Bolton, who had previously served in the 16th Maine Infantry, intended to use the bed to carry the officer back to Union lines. "[A] soldier will never take 'no' for an answer when his comrade needs help, so we found the richest bed we ever saw, in the room off the front parlor, and, seizing it amid the barking of dogs and the threatenings of servants, we hastened to make the faithful comrade as comfortable as possible," Bolton remembered. "But alas! the ride was too much and he passed to his reward during the night, from a fine bed in a donkey cart."[27]

McIntosh's brigade followed the trains. Quartermaster Sergeant John S. Jameson of the 1st Connecticut Cavalry's Company M had not slept in 76 hours. He turned aside from his post with the mule train to catch a moment's rest and fill his canteen. The train proceeded and left him behind.

Confederates harassing the Federal rear cut Jameson off from his regiment and captured him. One harasser, Sgt. George D. Shadburne of the Jeff Davis Legion Cavalry's Company A, Hampton's chief of scouts, wended his way through the woods that night to the roads by which the disintegrating Unionist host was skedaddling, as well as the connecting lanes on which stray Federals got lost. Shadburne single-handedly captured 17 heavily armed Federals just by dashing upon them and demanding their surrender.

26 Gause, *Four Years with Five Armies*, 286–287; Roster Commission, *Official Roster of the Soldiers of the State of Ohio*, 11:69. A hame is "one of two curved supports attached to the collar of a draft horse to which the traces are fastened." merriam-webster.com. Retrieved Jan. 30, 2024.

27 H. W. Bolton, *Personal Reminiscences of the Late War* (Chicago, 1892), 84–85.

After midnight, General Matthew Butler rode down the Secessionist line to reconnoiter. As he passed the 13th Virginia Cavalry of Chambliss's brigade, the regiment's commander informed Butler that an enemy battery occupied the field of the mother of one of his men, Young Epps. Butler sent for Epps and ascertained that born and raised there, thoroughly familiar with the locality, Epps could guide a column past the swamp and behind the Federal left. Butler reported this to Hampton and promised that if given 100 picked men, he would get in the Federal rear by daylight. Hampton ordered Butler to pick his men and undertake the movement. Butler chose a force that included the Comanches from the Laurel Brigade.

"We moved off, with Young Epps by General Butler's side at the head of the column, with officers and couriers immediately at their heels, passing down the swamp as quietly as mice, protected from view by the darkness and dense thicket, we moved through a level broom sage old field, which muffled the tread of the horses and got beyond Wilson's extreme left," remembered Brooks. By this time the Federal battery had departed Mrs. Epps's field, but the Confederates could hear Yankee officers giving orders to the pickets there. Epps led the column down two dead ends too boggy to ford.

"Is there any other place we can cross?" said Butler.

"Yes sir," said Epps, "there is a better crossing lower down still."

Arriving at the third crossing, Epps again expressed reservations about its suitability.

"Now, young man, if you do not conduct this column over this swamp, I will have you tied to your horse and send you in front," said Butler.[28]

Epps then led the column across despite bogginess in some places. The Southerners dismounted, sent their horses back, and deployed in open order as far as 100 men would stretch.

While Epps led Butler and his picked men into the Federal rear, Hampton deployed Rosser's brigade to the right of Young's brigade, and Butler's brigade to the right of Rosser's brigade.

Butler's picked men initially encountered the 1st Vermont Cavalry.

"[S]everal mounted men appeared on our left, beckoned to us, and then ordered us to 'bring up those led horses,'" remembered First Sergeant Ide. "Some were about to obey this order when they were discovered to be Johnnies, and just then Company F coming up, a brisk fire was opened between the two parties."[29]

28 Brooks, *Butler and His Cavalry*, 275. "Young Epps" was probably Pvt. John W. Epps of the 13th Virginia's Company D. "Pvt John W Epps," findagrave.com. Retrieved Feb. 13, 2023.

29 Hoffman, *First Vermont Cavalry Volunteers*, 189.

Farther to the Union right stood the 8th New York Cavalry. "I had been advised by the pickets that a Confederate column was passing our left flank and forming in the rear," recalled Col. Edward M. Pope of the 8th. "It was fairly light when I went to the rear to verify the report." He had gone only a short distance when he saw the Secessionists. They challenged him and then fired upon him. "I ran back, and ordered the regiment to leave the line by the right flank," Pope remembered. "This movement was made without formation, and on a run, and most of the command escaped, for a time."[30]

Hampton, hearing Butler and his picked men open fire in the Federal left rear, loosed Butler's and Rosser's brigades on the Union left flank. Young's and Chambliss's brigades and Holcombe's Legion advanced upon the breastworks formerly occupied by McIntosh's brigade, found them empty, and proceeded to the line held by Chapman's brigade. The Confederate demonstration drew the attention of the enemy. "Steady and coolly their ranks moved up to our front," recollected the 1st Vermont Cavalry's Private Powers. "As they approached the breastworks our men took deliberate aim, and poured an effectual fire into their ranks."[31]

The Federals blasted the Rebels. "Just as we got to these another terrible fusillade began," remembered Waring in the Jeff Davis Legion Cavalry of Young's brigade.[32]

That brigade's Phillips Georgia Legion Cavalry suffered as well. "When we had advanced about half a mile, we found them behind their breastwork waiting for us and the way they did pour balls into our ranks was a sad sight," wrote Sergeant Humphries. "They were giving us fits."[33]

Holcombe's Legion suffered severely. Sergeant Ruffin led his company of Chambliss's brigade in the charge. "You may be sure that I covered myself all over with glory, or rather with dirt and mud, lying down, trying to make myself as small as possible," he recalled.[34]

The Unionist position crumbled under the concentric Confederate attack. The collapse began with the 1st Vermont Cavalry. Ide recalled that as the Secessionists

30 Edmund M. Pope, "Personal Experience—A Side Light on the Wilson Raid, June 1864," in *Glimpses of the Nation's Struggle: Papers Read before the Minnesota Commandery of the Military Order of the Loyal Legion of the United States, 1892–1897*, 6 vols. (St. Paul, MN, 1898), 4:589.

31 J. H. P., "Vermont Cavalry."

32 Waring Diary, June 29, 1864.

33 Coffman, *Going Back the Way They Came*, 89.

34 Balfour, *13th Virginia Cavalry*, 35.

charged, "the led horses began to melt away, the Rebels to press harder, and soon all the horses were on the retreat."[35]

As the mounts departed, the men had to follow. "Simultaneously with the attack upon the men, the rebels came upon the horses, and those holding them only saved them by hurrying them off by the road to the left," remembered Powers. "The rebels came down upon this road thus cutting our men off from all support, and leaving them no line of retreat."[36] About 85 men and some officers took to the woods to escape capture by the surrounding Confederate horsemen. Those who escaped included Ide and Powers.

"[T]hey got up within ten yards of us and told us to surender but I for one could not see the poin[t] and so . . . I run like the old scrach and there was four of our Co. came out," wrote Cpl. Thomas Wiswall of the 1st's Company I. "Will Hall and I wer to gather and the rebs chased us and we put to the woods and we got separated and I got to some of the led horses and got one but Will was not so lucky."[37] As Pvt. Winslow Colby of Company G lay on the ground behind the breastwork of fence rails, firing his carbine at Confederate troopers, his regiment's horses broke loose from the men holding them and ran down along the fence where his company lay. One of the horses stepped on his ankle, bruising and lacerating the flesh. Comrades got him mounted when the time came to skedaddle.

Next came the turn of the 8th New York Cavalry, on the 1st Vermont Cavalry's immediate left. After the Yanks had kept up a heavy fire for a while, the sharp crack of carbines and the "ki-yi" of the Johnnies charging the 8th's rear startled the New Yorkers.[38]

"We made a hurried and disorderly movement by the right flank, by which most of the line escaped capture, and some, fortunately finding their led horses which had been driven from our rear, mounted and wended their way to rejoin the division, while others were scattered in squads and singly, through the woods and fields," remembered Pope.[39] Separated from his troopers, he evaded the Confederates by hiding underneath a log.

The Secessionists cut off from the horses a squad of about 35 men and a few officers of the 8th with members of each of the brigade's other regiments and forced them to take to the woods to save themselves from capture by the

35 Hoffman, *First Vermont Cavalry Volunteers*, 189.

36 J. H. P., "Vermont Cavalry."

37 Jeffrey D. Marshall, ed., *A War of the People: Vermont Civil War Letters* (Lebanon, NH, 1999), 249.

38 W. H. D., "Interesting Account of the Adventures of a Squadron of the 8th N. Y. Cavalry."

39 Pope, "Personal Experience—A Side Light on the Wilson Raid, June 1864."

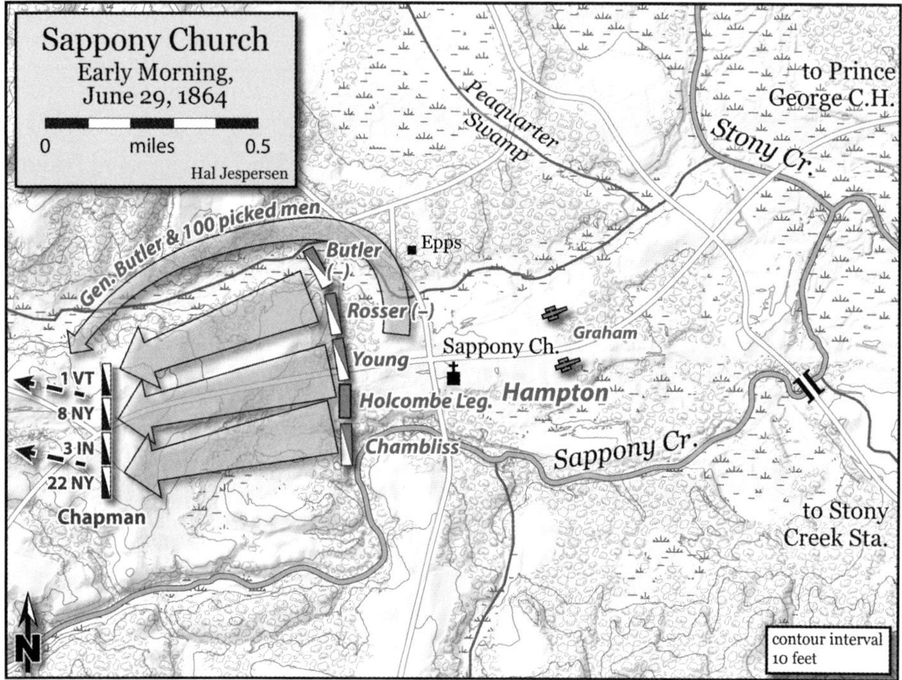

surrounding Rebels.[40] Private Henry Norton of the 8th's Company H recollected, "The most of us saved ourselves by putting spurs to our horses and scattering around the country, by running our horses and taking cross roads."[41]

Farther right, the 3rd Indiana collapsed similarly. "Daylight found our little brigade alone . . . outnumbered, flanked, surrounded, left to appease the wrath of the Confederacy for its loss in RRs, horses, jewelry, women's clothes, and silver ware," recalled Gilpin, who eluded capture.[42]

Private Allen of the 22nd New York Cavalry, still farther right, remembered, "I escaped just in time, with a small column of skedaddlers."[43]

The 1st New Hampshire Cavalry left behind only prisoners.

Private Charles M. Calhoun of the 6th South Carolina Cavalry's Company C in Butler's brigade recalled, "We soon had them routed and going in first one

40 W. H. D., "Interesting Account of the Adventures of a Squadron of the 8th N. Y. Cavalry."

41 Henry Norton, comp. and ed., *Deeds of Daring, Or History of the Eighth N. Y. Volunteer Cavalry, Containing a Complete Record of the Battles, Skirmishes, Marches, etc., that the Gallant Eighth New York Cavalry Participated in, from Its Organization in November, 1861, to the Close of the Rebellion in 1865* (Norwich, NY, 1889), 82.

42 Gilpin Diary, June 29, 1864.

43 Allen Diary, June 29, 1864.

direction and then another, some going in the direction of Ream's and some toward Jarratt's station."[44]

The flank attack of the Comanches and Butler's other picked men broke down under the weight of prisoners. "They would rush through our thin line of skirmishers in squads of twenty or thirty, decorated with all kinds of paraphernalia they had stolen from the people on their raid," remembered Brooks. "It was not uncommon for our boys to have personal encounters with them, when the butts of our rifles served a good purpose."[45]

Calhoun recalled, "The fight reminded me more of a fox chase than anything else I ever saw." He added, "We actually scoured the country, front flanks and rear, for the enemy, first making for Ream's station under a fast lope."[46]

On some occasions, the fox fought back. The Comanches, after dispatching to the rear the Northerners they had initially captured, clashed with around 200 Federals who rallied about two miles west of Sappony Church. "[I]t was found to be decidedly hot work capturing a force larger than their own, who availed themselves of every fence, house, swamp and pine forest to form a square and blaze into their pursuers a volley," recollected Captain Myers. Eventually this "batch of extremely hard-fighting Yankees" rode off mostly on the track of Wilson's column while others galloped toward Jarratt's Station by way of the Double Bridges and orders recalled their pursuers.[47]

Around 100 bluecoats were conducting a fighting retreat through heavily wooded terrain. Third Lieutenant George Baylor of the 12th Virginia Cavalry's Company B, the Baylor Light Horse which his father had raised, received orders to pursue with his squadron. Baylor had been captured in February 1862 and wounded in January 1863. His company charged as the Yanks entered a more open wood and captured most of them. In the charge, the Federals mortally wounded his horse Bonaparte. Riding "Bony," George's father had been wounded in April 1862 and George's brother killed in November 1863. Baylor mounted what he called "a flea-bitten grey" captured from the Northerners and continued the pursuit.[48]

44 C. M. Calhoun, *Liberty Dethroned: A Concise History of Some of the Most Startling Events before, during and since the Civil War* (Greenwood, SC, 1903), 134.

45 Brooks, *Butler and His Cavalry*, 276.

46 Calhoun, *Liberty Dethroned*, 134.

47 Myers, *The Comanches*, 310.

48 George Baylor, *Bull Run to Bull Run; or, Four Years in the Army of Northern Virginia, Containing a Detailed Account of the Career and Adventures of the Baylor Light Horse, Company B, Twelfth Virginia Cavalry, C.S.A., with Leaves from My Scrapbook* (Richmond, 1900), 231.

Scouts from Hampton's division pursued the Federals on the road from Stony Creek Station beyond its intersection with the Stage Road. Some Yanks galloped northeastward on the Stage Road toward Reams Station, others southward toward the Double Bridges. Scott and Curtis rode toward Reams Station. From a woman who lived at a farm along the way they learned that the Unionists had bounded by 20 minutes earlier. As they waited for the woman to bring some water, Scott and Curtis heard horses coming along the road. Unsure whether the horses carried their brigade or the enemy, the two scouts moved into a field clear of the farm building and waited to see.

A column appeared in a few minutes, "but so covered with dust and shaded by the pines immediately behind them that we could not detect whether they were 'white people' or Yankees," Scott recalled. One of several riders in an advance party sat his horse like a courier of General Chambliss. Scott thought the rider was indeed that courier and that Chambliss's brigade formed the column. The advance party looked toward Scott and Curtis and halted until the head of the column came up. One of the party beckoned toward Scott and Curtis.

"You are right," Curtis said to Scott. "That is our brigade and there is Chambliss, and he wants to let us go."

Scott and Curtis galloped toward the group. The scouts kept their eyes on the ground, rough from trampling by cattle in wet weather and then desiccating in the recent drought. They did not look up until they needed to get through the gate into the road. The column waited 40 or 50 feet away.

Scott recalled that his eyes "fell on a Yankee in full blue uniform." Curtis saw the yellow stripes of a sergeant, which clearly indicated a Northerner."

"By God, Scott, they are Yankees," said Curtis.

The Virginians reined up their horses, whirled them around and raced away.

"Halt!" cried the Unionists. "Halt!"

A volley followed. Bullets whizzed around the two Virginians but none found the mark. The scouts rode across the farm and down into a swale. A few Federals followed but stopped at the brink of the swale, then turned back and resumed their flight.

The two Virginians rode back toward Chambliss to report the encounter. On the way they encountered a group of Federals who could not keep up with their column. Curtis did what Scott called "some lofty talking" and persuaded the Northerners that they were surrounded and resistance was useless. The two scouts captured and disarmed 11 Unionists and several blacks. The Virginians took their captives into the woods where Scott guarded them while Curtis went back to the road and brought in a Yankee lieutenant. Then the group resumed its progress toward Chambliss. "En route the lieutenant last captured got away by a quick jump into a thicket while I was trying the lock of one of the captured pistols," Scott remembered. "I let him go without firing at him for fear of causing a stampede among the others." The scouts escorted the others back to Chambliss without further incident.[49]

Colonel Chapman gathered about 300 survivors from his brigade. The brigade's other survivors scattered in all directions. Wilson's division had lost 255 troopers, mostly in Chapman's brigade, during the two-day fight at Sappony Church.[50] Hampton suffered 89 casualties, mainly in Chambliss's brigade of W. H. F. Lee's division and in the Holcombe Legion infantry.[51] Sleep deprivation

49 John Zachary Holladay Scott, "John Zachary Holladay Scott, Confederate Soldier 1861–1865," 147–149, Confederate Reminiscences and Letters 1861–1865, Vol. VII, Georgia Division United Daughters of the Confederacy, 1998, GDAH. Wilson and Kautz took the Stage Road from Sappony Creek to Reams Station and later Wilson took the Stage Road from Reams Station to the Double Bridges because they would not have known the local roads and were narrowly focused on getting to and from Reams by the known route of travel. I am indebted to Greg Eanes for this insight.

50 In Chapman's brigade of Wilson's division, the 1st New Hampshire Cavalry had one wounded, six missing, and 12 captured at Sappony Creek. New Hampshire, Adjutant General, *Report of the Adjutant General of the State of New Hampshire*, 2:568–612, *passim.* The 1st Vermont Cavalry lost two killed, seven mortally wounded, six wounded and captured, three otherwise wounded, and 53 prisoners. Vermont, Adjutant General, *Revised Roster of Vermont Volunteers*, 224–262, *passim.* The 3rd Indiana Cavalry had five wounded and 10 captured. Goecker, *Hoosier Spies and Horse Marines*, 191–249, *passim.* The 8th New York Cavalry lost one killed, four wounded and missing, two otherwise wounded, and 90 missing. RG 94, Entry 652, Box 38. The 22nd New York Cavalry had one killed, one wounded, and 33 missing. Ibid., Box 39.

In McIntosh's brigade, the 1st Connecticut Cavalry lost one wounded and captured and three otherwise captured. Connecticut, Adjutants-General, *Record of Service of Connecticut Men*, 66, 85–86, 90. The 2nd Ohio Cavalry had three killed, three mortally wounded, three wounded, and three captured. Roster Commission, *Official Roster of the Soldiers of the State of Ohio*, 11:57–113, *passim.* The 2nd New York Cavalry lost one wounded. RG 94, Entry 653, Box 30, NA. The 5th New York Cavalry had one missing. Ibid., Entry 652, Boxes 38.

51 In Chambliss's brigade of W. H. F. Lee's division, CSRs show that the 9th Virginia Cavalry had one killed, one mortally wounded, 13 otherwise wounded, and one missing at Sappony Church. Young, "Confederate Casualties during June 1864 at Petersburg." Another source indicates that the 9th lost one killed and 15 wounded. James R. Richerson, "*Ninth Virginia Cavalry*," *The Sentinel* (Richmond, VA), Sept. 6, 1864, p. 3, col. 3. CSRs reveal that the *13th Virginia Cavalry* had four wounded and one missing. Young, "Confederate Casualties during June 1864 at Petersburg." The 10th Virginia Cavalry lost three killed or mortally wounded, nine otherwise wounded, and one missing. J. S. H., "The Defeat of Wilson's Raiders," *Richmond Daily Dispatch*, July 6, 1864, p. 1, col. 4. The newspaper names each of the casualties and specifies the degree of his injury. Ibid. CSRs for the 10th mark only one killed, one mortally wounded, one otherwise wounded, and one missing. Young, "Confederate Casualties during June 1864 at Petersburg."

Hampton's division had 22 casualties. *OR* 40, 1:809. These included the following from the CSRs: in Butler's brigade, one wounded in the 4th South Carolina Cavalry; in Young's brigade, one wounded in the Jeff Davis Legion Cavalry, one wounded in the 20th Georgia Cavalry Battalion, and one wounded in the 4th Alabama Cavalry Battalion; and in the Laurel Brigade, one killed, one mortally wounded, and three otherwise wounded in the 7th Virginia Cavalry, one mortally wounded and one otherwise wounded in the 11th Virginia Cavalry, four wounded in the 12th Virginia Cavalry,

had caught up with the raiders, who lost about eight prisoners for every trooper killed or wounded on the second day at Sappony Creek.

Chapman and his band followed the main column on its roundabout route toward Reams Station, and they observed further signs of disintegration. "The 1st District of Columbia Cavalry Battalion, of Kautz's command, armed with Henry rifles (16 shooters,) became badly demoralized some time during the night, as a score or more of Henry rifles, at daylight the next morning, could have been gather[ed] up through the woods and along the roads," remembered Corporal Watlington of the 3rd Indiana Cavalry.[52]

Wilson's column and the part of Chapman's brigade that followed it were riding deeper into the Confederate trap.

* * *

Rebels, not the Army of the Potomac, occupied Reams Station. The Alabama and Florida brigades of Mahone's division had arrived there after tramping south from Petersburg early that morning with the Letcher Artillery, Brander's battery, and the Purcell Artillery, Cayce's battery, of Pegram's artillery battalion. "[W]e were marched all night, until it began to get a little light in the east next morning," remembered Pvt. George H. Dorman of the 10th Florida's Company A. Near where the Depot Road joined Halifax Road, Mahone's men halted in front of Reams Station and formed line across the Depot Road facing west with the Alabamians on the left and the Floridians on the right. The Confederate batteries unlimbered behind the infantry.

Told to rest, most of the soldiers complied. "Several of the boys thought it was a good time to cook an ash-cake and fry a slice of bacon and have a little gravy for breakfast," Dorman recalled. "There were two or three little fires started by firing straw, dead weeds, etc."

A few cannon shots broke up breakfast. The Confederate artillery had opened fire prematurely when the Federals appeared. Kautz's men, alerted to danger, prepared for combat and his guns unlimbered.

"Boys, this is one time we are going to see the elephant show his works," said Pvt. Abe Register of the 10th's Company B.

and two wounded in the 35th Virginia Cavalry Battalion, "the Comanches." Young, "Confederate Casualties during June 1864 at Petersburg."

The Holcombe Legion infantry had one killed, one mortally wounded, and 31 otherwise wounded. Young, "Confederate Casualties during June 1864 at Petersburg."

52 Watlington Diary, June 29, 1864.

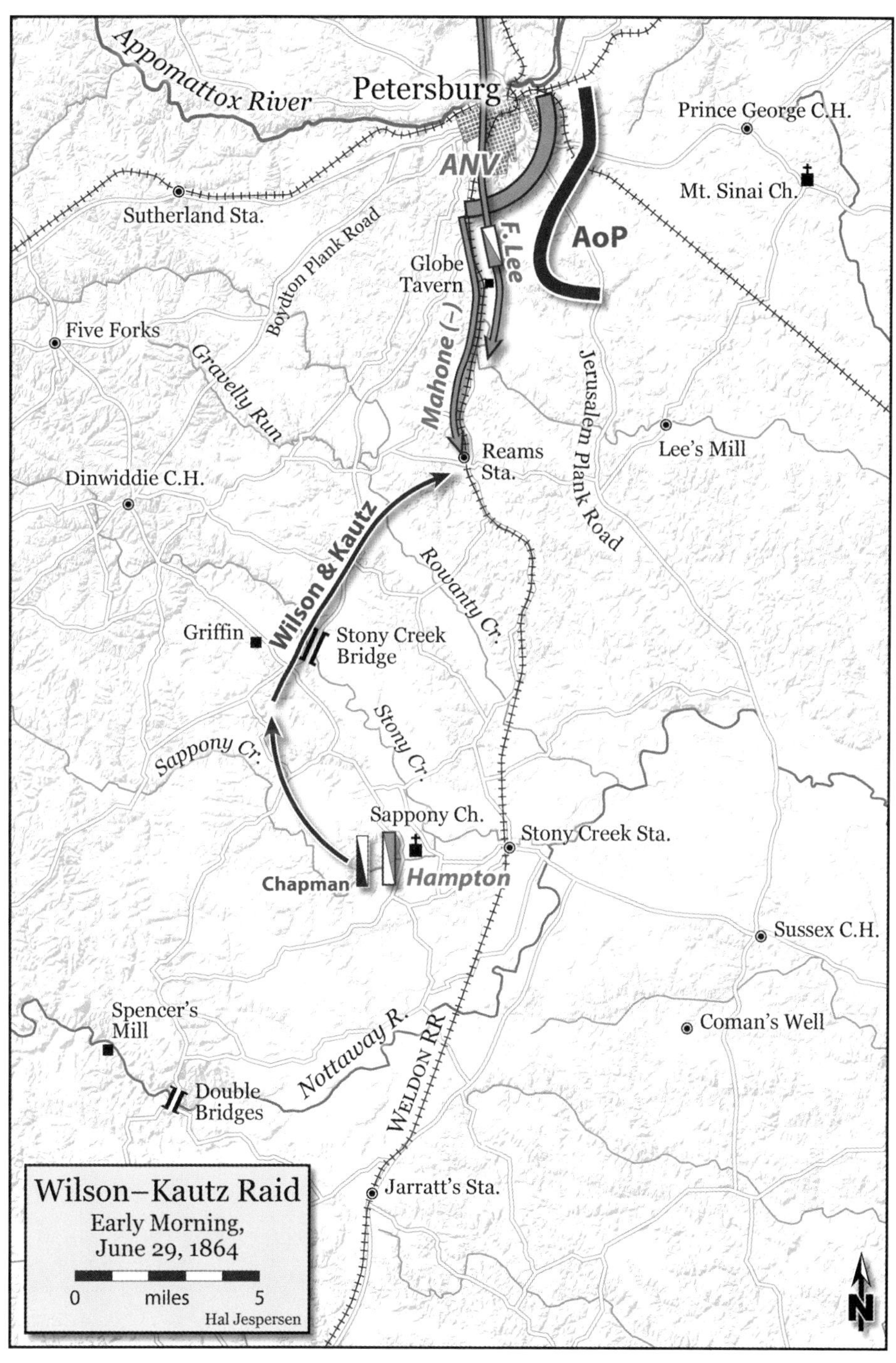
Appomattox River
Petersburg
Prince George C.H.
ANV
Mt. Sinai Ch.
Sutherland Sta.
Boydton Plank Road
F. Lee
AoP
Globe
Tavern
Five Forks
Mahone (–)
Gravelly Run
Jerusalem Plank Road
Lee's Mill
Reams
Sta.
Dinwiddie C.H.
Wilson & Kautz
Rowanty Cr.
Griffin
Stony Creek
Bridge
Stony Cr.
Sappony Cr.
Sappony Ch.
Stony Creek Sta.
Chapman
Hampton
Sussex C.H.
Spencer's
Mill
Coman's Well
Nottaway R.
WELDON RR
Double
Bridges
Jarratt's Sta.
Wilson–Kautz Raid
Early Morning,
June 29, 1864
0 miles 5
Hal Jespersen
N

The Yankee artillery made Register seem prophetic. "There came a shell from the Federal lines and killed three men—one of whom was at my side—so close that a great chunk of his flesh flew upon my pack," Dorman remembered.[53]

Captain Clark of the Alabama Brigade's staff took charge of Mahone's skirmish line of 100 men and advanced to close with the enemy.

* * *

During the night, the 1st District of Columbia Cavalry replaced the 11th Pennsylvania Cavalry at the head of Kautz's column. "[W]e proceeded along the road, riding all night, officers and men in many instances being sound asleep, and the men of various companies being intermingled, the strongest and most active horses leading the way," recollected Corporal Lunt of the 1st.[54]

Sleep spared the slumberers the anxiety that grew among the soldiers who remained awake. "Long before light men and women rushed into our presence crying as if their hearts would break, 'You's all dead; you's all dead; Massa Hill is dar with heaps of guns; you's dead. You's dead, sho,'" Bolton recalled.[55]

Having departed Reams Station on the Depot Road, Kautz's troops naturally turned off the Stage Road onto the Depot Road as they returned. Soon after daylight, most of the 1st District of Columbia Cavalry halted near the border of a plantation and received orders, "to dismount and prepare to fight on foot," Lunt remembered. "I cannot say that there was much enthusiasm among the boys, for we were hungry, weak, and exhausted."[56]

Second Lieutenant Comins replaced the hat he had lost during the ride to Reams Station, the third that he had lost during the raid. "A dirty soldier's cap taken from a negro was the best I could do," Comins recalled.[57] Dismounting to the left of the Depot Road, the 1st District of Columbia Cavalry's first battalion formed and staggered out toward the Goodwin house in its orchard on a crest in the center of an open field.

Detailed to take the advance for Kautz's division with 20 men, Bolton met an old black woman near the swamp just west of Reams Station.

"Massa, don' go down dar, for Massa Hill is dar waiting for ye," she said.

53 G. H. Dorman, *Fifty Years Ago: Reminiscences of '61–'65* (Tallahassee, 1912), 13; Robinson, comp., *Soldiers of Florida*, 223.

54 Tobie, *First Maine Cavalry*, 341.

55 Bolton, *Personal Reminiscences of the Late War*, 85.

56 Tobie, *First Maine Cavalry*, 341.

57 Comins to "My dear wife," July 13, 1864.

Bolton's orders required him to disregard her. He and his men arrived near Reams Station about 6:00 a.m. on the 29th, but instead of finding the Army of the Potomac, they found Rebels. "Go we must, and did, to be greeted with grape and canister," he remembered. "I was dismounted and many of the boys were torn to pieces."[58]

The two brigades of Mahone's infantry lay in ambush. The Secessionist guns had fired prematurely and alerted the Federals to the presence of the enemy. The shellfire surprised the 1st District of Columbia Cavalry's first battalion. The battalion's "line instantly broke," Lunt recalled, "but the boys in a few moments rallied and came back to the orchard near the house." They saw many Confederates lying behind a rail fence and hiding behind trees a few hundred yards away. Immediately opening fire, the bluecoats soon began hitting the enemy.

The Northerners perceived that the Goodwin house and its outbuildings concealed many more Southerners. Captain William S. Howe, M.D., of the 1st's Company D, led several of his men to the house's door and kicked it open, while others fired in at the windows. "As Capt. Howe kicked open the door a tall rebel levelled his musket and a bullet whistled in close proximity to his ear," Lunt recollected. Howe, though a former Baptist minister, cussed the Secessionists and emphasized his language with a round from his revolver. "Thereupon some eight or ten tall, gaunt rebels gave themselves up as prisoners, and were sent away to what we considered our rear," recalled Lunt.

Soon, reinforced by other members of the regiment, the District of Columbia troops pushed the Confederates back and lay down at the borders of the field. "Many of the men were so exhausted that they fell asleep, and it required considerable effort on the part of their officers to make them realize the dangers of their situation," Lunt remembered.[59]

The 11th Pennsylvania Cavalry encountered stiffer resistance on the right of the Depot Road. "We were in a lane with rail fences on either side of the road beyond which were cleared fences," remembered First Sergeant Cruikshank of the 11th. "A short distance to the right was another fence with a close hedgerow of bushes that ran parallel with the road." Colonel Spear ordered the fence to the left thrown down. Ten or 12 carabineers to a company dismounted and advanced as skirmishers leaving their horses held by comrades such as Cruikshank.

A volley from the hedgerow and fence to the right startled the Pennsylvanians. The 10th and 14th Alabama had advanced under cover and outflanked the Keystoners. "A broken mass of men and horses were going at full speed to the left

58 Bolton, *Personal Reminiscences of the Late War*, 85.

59 Tobie, *First Maine Cavalry*, 342.

and front," recalled Cruikshank from among the Keystoners with the led horses. The Alabamians poured over the fence and formed in the field preparatory to a charge. Cruikshank and the men with the led horses fled to the left and found shelter from the enemy's fire on lower ground.

Colonel Spear rode about among the fugitives.

"Boys, boys," he called out. "This will never do for the 11th, rally, rally!" The 11th charged back over the field.[60]

Spear advanced with the remark that, "he would ride through those d----d dismounted cavalry, or die in the attempt."[61]

Caught in the middle, Bolton and his men hugged the earth as the Keystoners charged the Alabamians. "Those horses—we seem to see them now—coming with strained nostrils, leaping and foaming, while the riders stood in the stirrups, with saber gleaming in the sunlight, and all screaming at the top of their voices," Bolton recalled.[62]

The "10th and 14th ala Regt were thrown out too far in advance of support," Private Cowan of the 9th Alabama recollected. "The yankees charged their line of Skirmishers front and flank throughout several times capturing 36 men."[63]

Private Newton J. Brooks of the 14th Alabama's Company A numbered among those who received the charge of the 11th Pennsylvania Cavalry. "They came forward toward us on their horses at full speed, but their guns being wet, failed to fire," he remembered. "Then they drew their sabers and came right on." The Alabamians fired point blank at the Pennsylvanians. "I saw a man looking right at me with his saber drawn, and by this time we were on one knee with guns sticking out in front to keep their horses jumping on us," recalled Brooks. "I raised my gun above my head just as the 'Yank' struck at me and his saber struck my gun without doing any damage." A Pennsylvanian saber partially scalped one of Brooks's friends who failed to work his gun "just right."[64] This man charged the Keystoners, shooting at them and cursing them.

"Billy Mahone now arrived and charged the aspect of officers and immediately ordered forward the balance of the Brigade also Finegan's Florida Brigade,"

60 Eanes, *Destroy the Junction*, 132.

61 "The Situation at Petersburg—Attack and Rout of the Raiders," *Daily Richmond Examiner*, July 2, 1864, p. 1, col. 3.

62 Bolton, *Personal Reminiscences of the Late War*, 86.

63 Carter, ed., *Welcome the Hour of Conflict*, 261. Kautz claimed "capturing about 50 prisoners." *OR* 40, 1:732. I did not include these Alabamian captives among the Confederate casualties because their comrades freed them by day's end. Carter, ed., *Welcome the Hour of Conflict*, 262.

64 Yeary, comp., *Reminiscences of the Boys in Gray*, 1:83.

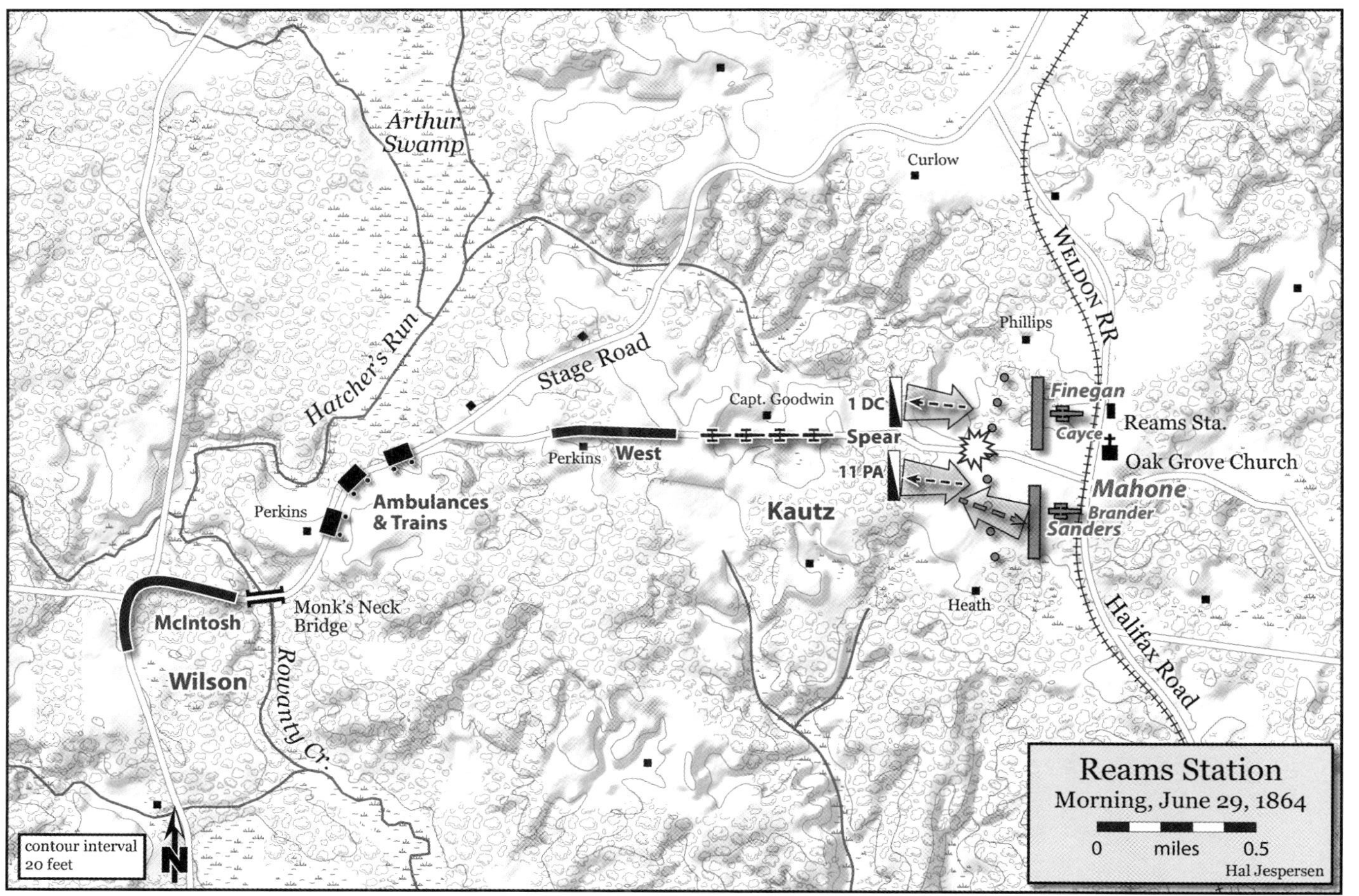

Arthur
Swamp
Curlow
Weldon RR
Phillips
Hatcher's Run
Stage Road
Capt. Goodwin
1 DC
Finegan
Reams Sta.
Cayce
Spear
Oak Grove Church
Perkins
West
11 PA
Mahone
Brander
Sanders
Perkins
Ambulances
& Trains
Kautz
Heath
Monk's Neck
Bridge
McIntosh
Halifax Road
Wilson
Rowanty Cr.
Reams Station
Morning, June 29, 1864
0
miles
0.5
Hal Jespersen
contour interval
20 feet
N

recollected Cowan. "Yankees supposing them to be dismounted cavalry presented a front, but they were soon undeceived when our old Brigade poured in one of those low deadly volleys that has sent so many yankees to their final accountability before a frowning god." The Pennsylvanians fell back leaving 32 prisoners.[65]

Kautz, learning from his captives the identity of his opposition, found "no other course left except to intrench and hold on to our position until relieved by the Army of the Potomac," he remembered.[66] Piling up rails and felling trees, his men threw up two small breastworks to protect sharpshooters who kept the enemy at bay in his front.

Barney Finegan rode up and down his line on the north side of the Depot Road, encouraging and steadying his Floridians. Clark led Mahone's reorganized skirmishers about a mile forward and ascertained that the enemy lay across a little stream awaiting attack. Clark reported this to Mahone, who ordered Clark to hold his position. Clark and his skirmishers lay on their side of the stream and awaited events. Before they moved again, several hours passed.

* * *

About daybreak, Charles Cross knocked at the door of the Griffin house and informed John Griffin that Federal cavalry "by thousands" were passing on the Stage Road. No threat appeared until around 10:00 a.m. Cross notified Griffin that some horsemen approaching the house looked "very blue." Griffin recalled:

> Believing that my premises were about to be invaded by a party from the Federal column, I told Charles that I would arm myself and go into the garden, and that if the men we saw were Yankees, I wished him to see that all doors and other places were unlocked and that these men could take what they pleased without excuse for breaking, and that, if they confined themselves to robbery, he was to make no resistance, but, if they insulted my wife, to notify me at once and I would attack them without regard to consequences.

After issuing these instructions, Griffin went into the garden armed with "two navy six-shooters, a Sharp's repeating rifle and a double barrel shot-gun loaded with buckshot."[67]

* * *

65 Carter, ed., *Welcome the Hour of Conflict*, 261.

66 *OR* 40, 1:732.

67 Griffin, "Life in Dinwiddie County in the vicinity of the opposing armies," 7.

Edward Washburn Whitaker
Library of Congress

After Kautz's division encountered resistance, the Federal column halted and began piling up. About 8:00 a.m. Wilson arrived, found his way blocked, and grasped that Humphreys's promises to keep escape routes open to Union lines had proven empty. The Illinoisan ordered Captain Whitaker and around 40 troopers of the 3rd New York's Company G to ride to Union lines requesting help. "We had been repulsed by artillery and infantry on the pike, and we could see we were in a trap prepared for our reception at 'Reams Station' where Gen. Humphreys, Meads Chief of Staff, had told me to say to Wilson, the left of the line of the Army of the Potomac would be across the Weldon R. R. on our return from the Raid," Whitaker recalled. "It was a case of desperation and I fully expected to be killed with most of my 40 men so I took them in a group and explained the situation and object of the charge and stated that whoever got through the Rebel lines must go at once to Gen. Mead and say that Wilson was surrounded and must have help for his worn out command at once." Whitaker also gave the 40 New Yorkers the opportunity to back out but none did.

The Connecticut captain led the New Yorkers to the left of the Confederate infantry on the Depot Road. Whitaker and his men passed Kautz's division about 8:30 a.m. Whitaker and the New Yorkers got as near as possible to the enemy right before charging across an open field against a cavalry outpost on the Stage Road. The Southern pickets fired and fled. "We rushed after them so hotly that that they left the road open for us, when we came plum on to an infantry reserve that were my prisoners before they could grasp their guns," Whitaker recalled. "I had their guns thrown into a pond and sent two men back to Gen. Wilson with the prisoners."

Seizing an ancient contraband, Whitaker mounted him on a dead cavalryman's horse and commanded him to guide the band straight to Meade's headquarters. Pushing through the woods to the left of the Stage Road, the group came to Halifax Road, on which a column of Fitzhugh Lee's division was hurrying toward the battle. "I had the fence pulled down and not daring to wait for the column to pass for fear of discovery, I took advantage of a gap in the column and charged across the road reaching the woods on the other side without looking back to see how many of my men were cut off."[68]

Southern horsemen and guerrillas harassed Whitaker and his men. Encountering a couple of Secessionist infantry camps, the Federals and their guide rode around them across the fields and through the woods. Eventually Whitaker led a charge through the picket lines of both armies, picking up two more prisoners and having some of his men shot out of their saddles. He arrived at Meade's headquarters at around 10:20 a.m. with 18 bloody, dirty, and exhausted troopers of the 40 who had started with him.

When Whitaker arrived at Meade's headquarters, the commander of the Army of the Potomac was absent visiting Burnside at the edge of a pine wood northeast of the Shand house. Humphreys, after debriefing Whitaker, inquired of Meade at 10:40 a.m. if he wanted an infantry force sent to Wilson's assistance. At 11:10 a.m., when the rear of Sheridan's column had just finished crossing the James near Fort Powhatan, the Great Peppery directed Gibbon's infantry division, Bryan's cavalry brigade, and Little Phil's advance to proceed on Jerusalem Plank Road south of Warwick Swamp and then head cross-country toward Reams Station. Meade instructed Wright to hold his whole corps ready to hustle to Reams at a moment's notice. Wright could hear artillery fire from the vicinity of the station at 11:50 a.m.

"Upon further reflection," at noon, Meade ordered Wright to send to Reams Station a division at once followed by the rest of his corps, while Gibbon supported the left of II Corps.[69] Getty's (formerly Wheaton's) division drew the task of tramping to Reams along with Bryan's horsemen and two batteries of artillery. Getty's division did not get going until 1:10 p.m. At 1:40 p.m., Wright received instructions to follow Getty's division with the rest of VI Corps. The last of the four brigades of Getty's division did not move until 2:25 p.m. The absence of water fit to drink along the way made the march miserable.

At 2:45 p.m., near Wind-Mill Point, Sheridan received orders issued at 12:45 p.m. to proceed toward Reams Station. At 3:45 p.m., Little Phil directed Gregg's division to head for Prince George Court House but wait there for Torbert's division, which did not move out for Prince George Court House until 5:00 p.m.

68 Angelovich, *Riding for Uncle Samuel*, 427–428. For the rest of his life, Wilson smarted from Humphreys's empty promises. Wilson, *Under the Old Flag*, 1:458, 492, 495–496, 502, 518, 520; Wilson, "The Cavalry of the Army of the Potomac," *MHSM*, 13:60–61, 64; Wilson, *The Life of John A. Rawlins*, 258–259. Grant's military secretary wrote, "The disaster was occasioned by Wilson's expectation of finding infantry in possession of the Weldon road." Adam Badeau, *Military History of Ulysses S. Grant, From April 1861 to April 1865*, 3 vols. (New York, 1882), 2:411.

69 *OR* 40, 2:494.

The head of Getty's division arrived within a mile and a half of Reams Station at 6:00 p.m., encountering only small Rebel scouting parties and no Federal cavalrymen. The division's advance reached Reams Station at 7:35 p.m. The town had recovered from the damage inflicted by Wilson's division on June 22. "When we reached Ream's station we found quite a village with a good depot, fair dwellings, work shops and well cultivated gardens and fields fenced in," wrote newly promoted Capt. Elisha Hunt Rhodes of the 2nd Rhode Island's Company D. "I made my headquarters in a house near the rail road track and procured some vegetables and ice which helped our Army rations very much."[70] Rhodes had studied at Providence's Potter & Hammond's Commercial College and after his father's death in a shipwreck had left school to support his family by working as a clerk for a mill supplier.

A citizen told the Federals that in the afternoon Wilson had engaged the Confederates until they attacked Wilson's left, and that Wilson then retired southwestward on the Stage Road. At 8:25 p.m., the Florida Brigade remained a mile west of Reams on Dinwiddie Court House Road and would soon join the column of Mahone's division returning to Petersburg by Squirrel Level Road with numerous prisoners, all of Wilson's guns, and many horses. "All the enemy's cavalry have gone after General Wilson, who, I believe, has been obliged to retire a long way," recalled Whitaker, who was accompanying Getty's division. Whitaker said he "could not devise any way to find" Wilson.[71] VI Corps entrenched at Reams Station parallel to the Weldon Railroad.[72] Sheridan's force spent the evening at Prince George Court House, about 10 miles from Reams Station.

* * *

That day the Confederates were taking up T-rails from the York River Railroad in Virginia and the Atlantic, Tennessee & Ohio in North Carolina to repair their more essential railroads, particularly the Richmond & Danville.[73] Because of short provisions caused by the depredations of Hunter, Sheridan, Wilson, and Kautz, "all the negroes who could possibly be spared were being sent from the army to

70 Robert Hunt Rhodes, ed., *All for the Union: The Civil War Diary and Letters of Elisha Hunt Rhodes* (New York, 1985), 158.

71 Ibid., 508–509.

72 Bowen, *Thirty-Seventh Massachusetts Volunteers*, 345.

73 *OR* 40, 2:701; Ibid., vol. 51, 2:1029.

their homes, and only such as were indispensably necessary were kept," according to four who belonged to officers of the 17th North Carolina.[74]

General Lee also had to provide for his horseflesh. "I have started today a train of wagons, via Dinwiddie Court House to Stony Creek Station, Petersburg and Weldon Railroad, for corn to be brought there from Weldon," he wrote to President Davis. "This, with the standing crop of clover & oats, will subsist our horses for the present."[75]

The Southerners did some railroad raiding of their own that day. Early's cavalry struck the Baltimore & Ohio and the telegraph line near Martinsburg.

* * *

Gause arrived from Sappony Creek after Whitaker's departure and dismounted in the strip of woods along Rowanty Creek where Kautz had established his field hospital. Kautz's headquarters lay well behind his battle line, which paralleled the Weldon Railroad. Artillery had unlimbered near Kautz's headquarters. Gause could see the Secessionist line constantly firing from end to end. The wounded were steadily staggering back to Kautz's field hospital. Kautz's Yanks had difficulty staying awake. "The command was so much exhausted that it was almost an impossibility to keep them from falling asleep while on the skirmish line," reported Spear.[76]

Eventually the trains appeared, filed into the woods half a mile behind Kautz's hospital, and began unloading the sick and wounded. "The refugees also poured in, and occupied the swampy ground opposite the hospital," Gause remembered. Kautz often rode into the timber for a look at the wounded. "It was easy to see how delay preyed on his mind, as it was slowly but surely thinning his faithful ranks, but he made no demonstration and spoke not a word," recalled Gause. "The constant pacing back and forth, the pallor that overspread his countenance, told the experienced soldier of the pent-up feeling that was imprisoned there."[77]

The 2nd Ohio Cavalry and 5th New York Cavalry of McIntosh's brigade came into Gause's view and turned left as if to attack the Confederates on the Stage Road, open a hole, and lead the way through to safety. The 2nd and 5th formed line northwest of the Stage Road between the strip of woods containing Kautz's field hospital and another strip of woods to the northwest. McIntosh deployed the 1st Connecticut Cavalry and 2nd New York Cavalry farther left. His horsemen had

74 Ibid., 40, 2:496.

75 Ibid., 3:38; Dowdey and Manarin, eds., *The Wartime Papers of Robert E. Lee*, 811.

76 *OR* 40, 1:740.

77 Gause, *Four Years with Five Armies*, 289.

orders to remain mounted awaiting orders from Wilson. Battery C-E unlimbered on a little knoll southeast of the Stage Road, behind the cavalrymen.

Finally, Colonel Chapman arrived with the 300 survivors of his brigade he had collected. "Our brigade was so completely broken up by our forced retreat from Stony Creek (in which the horses were driven away before the men were), that we were not put into this fight," Ide recalled. "While waiting here and sleeping, some wretch stole that bag of beans from my horse that I had carried all the way from Prince George Court House."[78]

Mahone reacted to the Federal buildup on the Stage Road by sending 650 men of Finegan's brigade to block the road. Arriving about that time, Fitzhugh Lee apprised himself of the situation. "Mahone's two brigades were very small, and he deemed himself too weak to attack," Lee recalled.[79] He learned of a blind road leading to the Union left flank and rear. After Lee personally confirmed the lane's existence, Mahone suggested that Lee begin deploying his horse soldiers across the road. Lee formed his troopers across the lane with the assistance of a local African American employed at gunpoint. Breathed's battery unlimbered near where the Stage Road crossed the Weldon Railroad. By 10:00 a.m., 20 minutes before Whitaker arrived at Meade's headquarters, Lee's pressure on the Federal left was forcing the Yanks to fall back.

By the time Hannaford reached his company, his comrades in the 2nd Ohio Cavalry were advancing and dismounting. They deployed a few paces apart about 150 yards behind the skirmish line. "Here [we] lay in the broiling sun for more than an hour," he recalled.[80] That the skirmish line faced in three directions told him that no one knew from which direction the Confederate attack would come.

While Wilson's command collected behind Kautz, the Illinoisan examined the ground and ascertained the position of the enemy. He recalled that initially, "I determined to mass the entire command on the road leading to Petersburg—artillery behind cavalry, ambulances next to the artillery, ammunition wagons last—and make a bold push to break through the enemy; having done this, to cross the railroad three miles north of Reams Station and join the left of the army."[81]

The Illinoisan asked McIntosh and Chapman what they thought of the situation, and they called it, "a little bilious." Wilson disclosed to them his inclination to try breaking through northeastward on the Stage Road. "The smile of apprehension and uncertainty that passed over the faces of these two brigade

78 Hoffman, *First Vermont Cavalry Volunteers*, 190.

79 Hewett, et al., eds., *Supplement to the Official Records*, 7:332.

80 Eanes, *Destroy the Junction*, 135.

81 *OR* 40, 1:623.

commanders at that moment was rather disheartening," recalled Wilson, who also had with him three staff officers from VI Corps familiar with Mahone's division.

"General, those fellows with a simple skirmish line could whip all the cavalry in America," said one of the staffers from VI Corps.[82]

Wilson reconnoitered with McIntosh. Hampton's cavalry at Stony Creek Station, Southern infantry in front of Reams Station and on the Stage Road, and Fitzhugh Lee's cavalry division pushing around the Federal left flank "were clear enough indications of the rebel intentions" recalled Wilson. "The Confederates intended to capture the entire command and that fact became evident to the men in the field as well as to the officers."

Wilson reconsidered and determined to flee.[83]

The Union commander ordered the issue of all the ammunition his men could carry and the firing of the wagons and caissons preparatory to retreating on the Stage Road across the Double Bridges to the south bank of the Nottoway. His troops would then cut east again by way of Jarratt's Station far to the south.

The signs of an imminent skedaddle did not escape the rank and file. "I saw arising from the place where the wagons were parked a dense black smoke . . . our wagon train and the baggage, etc., were being burnt, that being one of the items of news I had picked up while resting for I had heard the rumor that this had been determined on provided no hope of taking them through was seen," Hannaford remembered. "So now I knew things were getting into an acknowledged desperate straight, but I would not tell my comrades, well knowing they already felt quite enough disheartened and depressed." Flames, smoke, and the explosion of ammunition panicked the non-combatants, principally the refugees. "Blacker and more dense grew the smoke in our rear, and the . . . moral effect on the men was plainly visible," he recalled.[84]

Others saw the same smoke. "There was but one conclusion to be drawn from the surroundings," remembered Gause.[85] The conclusion was a grim one. "All wounded and sick who could ride were mounted," Chaplain Boudrye of the 5th New York Cavalry recalled, "all others must be left behind."[86]

82 Wilson, "The Cavalry of the Army of the Potomac," 65–66.

83 *OR* 40, 1:623. He probably had the right idea because around noon three brigades of Kershaw's division received orders to move to Reams Station "to aid Mahone and the cavalry operating against the raiders." Ibid., 761. Luckily for the raiders, they departed before the three brigades of Kershaw's division arrived, if they ever started. Ibid., 623.

84 Eanes, *Destroy the Junction*, 135.

85 Gause, *Four Years with Five Armies*, 290.

86 Boudrye, *Fifth New York Cavalry*, 149.

Around 1:00 p.m., Wilson and Kautz conferred at Wilson's headquarters. "I wanted to entrench and hold on but General Wilson decided to retreat," Kautz remembered.[87]

"Cavalry must fight or run away," said Wilson, who ordered a withdrawal by the Stage Road and directed Kautz to follow him.

Kautz suggested that they separate their commands.

"It might come to that," said Wilson.[88]

Kautz departed for his division.

Before the Federals could withdraw or entrench, Fitzhugh Lee had finished deploying dismounted across the blind road beyond the left of the 2nd Ohio Cavalry and 5th New York Cavalry. The 6th Virginia Cavalry and 15th Virginia Cavalry of Lomax's brigade under Brig. Gen. Lunsford L. Lomax, a West Point graduate, stood prepared to strike. Behind these troops the 3rd Virginia Cavalry and 4th Virginia Cavalry of Wickham's brigade stood mounted in reserve under Brig. Gen. Williams C. Wickham, a lawyer wounded at Williamsburg, captured while recovering, and wounded again at Sharpsburg. Wickham had orders to charge as soon as Lomax had shaken the Federals. The 2nd Virginia Cavalry of Lomax's brigade reported to Finegan, who posted it on his left, between the halves of his brigade. The 5th Virginia Cavalry of Lomax's brigade picketed for Mahone. The 1st Virginia Cavalry of Wickham's brigade held a road to protect the Confederate rear.

Fitzhugh Lee and Mahone attacked before Kautz had returned to his headquarters.

"I concluded that the time had come for me to look out for my command," Kautz remembered.[89]

* * *

The Confederate attack separated Wilson from Kautz.

Lomax's dismounted troopers broke in between the wings of McIntosh's line, taking the 2nd Ohio Cavalry from the west in reverse and heading for the Stage Road. "[C]rash, bang, bang came a volley from the pine woods in our left rear . . . while with an infernal yell, here came a long line of grey-backs," remembered

87 Hewett, et al., eds., *Supplement to the Official Records*, 7:241.

88 Eanes, *Destroy the Junction*, 136.

89 Ibid., 137.

Hannaford. "They were on foot running so as to cut us off from the road we had advanced on."[90]

Mahone's men and the 2nd Virginia Cavalry pushed back Kautz's eastward-facing skirmish line. Second Lieutenant Ruffin Y. Ashe of the 11th Alabama's Company D, the regiment's adjutant, who had enlisted while a medical student in 1861, fell as Sanders's brigade advanced to the left of the Floridians. "It was in this charge that Adj't Ashe was struck; the ball (a minie) entering the front and left of his neck, cut the carotid artery, thus causing his death almost instantly from hemorrhage," wrote General Sanders. "He fell as soon as he was struck, and never spoke, only uttering one sigh or groan."[91] Part of the 11th Pennsylvania Cavalry in Spear's brigade broke and ran panic-stricken toward the Stage Road where its men crashed into the 1st Connecticut Cavalry and 2nd New York Cavalry, throwing them into confusion.

Corporal Timmerman of the 3rd New York Cavalry in West's brigade had managed to replace his lost mount with a mule. He was leading the mule into the woods when what he termed "the general Skedaddle" began. "[A] shell struck him (my mule) in the side . . . and what became of him is more than I can say for I never turned around," Timmerman recalled. "I next caught a horse and mounted him . . . the shells were dropping thicker than hale amongst us and I felt some what releaved when I got out of there range."[92]

Nearly all of the 2nd Ohio Cavalry and most of the 5th New York Cavalry fell back southeastwardly, away from the 1st Connecticut Cavalry and 2nd New York Cavalry and into the ranks of Kautz's division. This widened the gap between the halves of McIntosh's brigade and exposed the trains to the Southerners.

"By fours right!" ordered Maj. Dudley Seward, who had taken charge of the 2nd Ohio when the Rebels cut off from the regiment its commander, Lt. Col. George A. Purrington.

Each battalion went into sets of fours, with the column facing right.

"Forward, march!" commanded Seward.

"[A]way we went . . . straight across the road that led to Reams and on which the rebels were swiftly advancing, sending down before them a perfect shower of minnies and which struck down several of our horses," Hannaford remembered, "but across the road . . . we were in comparative safety, sheltered by a thick pine

90 Ibid., 138.

91 "Adjutant Ruffin Y. Ashe," *Fayetteville* (NC) *Semi-Weekly Observer*, Oct. 20, 1864, p. 3, col. 3. Sanders's account came from the grave because by the time it was published, he had perished in the battle of Globe Tavern, Aug. 21, 1864. Horn, *The Battles for the Weldon Railroad, August 1864*, 191–192.

92 Eanes, *Destroy the Junction*, 141.

wood."[93] The 2nd Ohio Cavalry passed Battery C-E. The cannoneers put their guns in echelon and opened on the pursuing Rebels with grape and cannister. The butternuts halted. The battery limbered up and retired to the right and rear toward Kautz's headquarters.

Elements of the 2nd Ohio Cavalry and of the 5th New York Cavalry withdrew several hundred yards towards Reams Station and ran into Kautz's retreating pickets. Battery C-E unlimbered facing west about 400 yards southeast of its knoll, behind the east-facing batteries B and K. The gunners formed an irregular triangle with Battery B at its apex, Battery C-E at its lower left, and Battery K at its lower right. The gunners briefly held the Confederates at bay, covering the retreat of Kautz's troopers.

Gause, caught with the trains between the Confederates and the Federal artillery, had to run through friendly cannon fire to avoid capture. "The heavy line behind us compelled us to seek shelter, which could only be done by passing far enough in front of the battery so that we could pass under the storm of shell," he recalled. "We then turned to the left, dashed into the swamp, and came out near Kautz's battery," Battery B. Gause and his comrades gravitated toward their former commander and found him close by at his headquarters.

"He was a changed man from the last time we had seen him," Gause remembered. "Instead of the marble pallor, a radiant glow was on his face." Kautz directed the captain of Battery B to fire grape until his men cut the last spoke, spiked the guns, mounted the horses, and followed Kautz's column. "There was something in the last part of the order that reassured every true soldier," remembered Gause. "There was still hope."

The gunners began complying with Kautz's orders.

"Lieutenant Newton, take the advance and go that course," said Kautz, pointing 1st Lt. Warner Newton toward the right of the line, "and cross the railroad about two miles from the station, and when you get to the second road, turn to the left and join my column on the main road."

Then Kautz addressed troopers in his column from the 5th New York Cavalry and from the 2nd Ohio Cavalry.

"The Second Ohio men and Fifth New York men follow Lieutenant Newton, and ride down everything you come into contact with." Kautz directed.

Kautz led his column through a narrow neck of timber and encountered Southern pickets lined up by a ditch. The Federals charged. "The enemy gave way and gave us the advantage," remembered Gause. "The men on the outside were keeping up a regular fire that held them at bay or running for shelter." The

93 Ibid., 138.

column leapt ditches, broke down fences, and trampled thickets, putting to flight any Secessionists in the way. "There was a seething mass of men and horses rushing on like an avalanche, with a constant fusillade from its borders that must sweep everything in front of it," Gause recalled.[94]

Kautz's column turned and galloped southwestwardly into a swamp, a branch of Rowanty Creek. The swamp would have proved impassable but for the recent drought. As the troopers entered the swamp, they encountered Spear sitting with a leg thrown over his horse's neck. "He had a pocket map of Virginia spread over his knee, while in his left hand he was holding a mariner's compass, and was looking at the sun," Hannaford recalled. Purrington, reunited with the 2nd Ohio Cavalry, asked Spear what direction the Buckeyes should take.

"We must bear away south-east until we cross the R. R. and then we are completely safe," Spear said.[95]

He pointed out the course, glancing at the sun and looking at his compass.

Kautz gave a major his pocket compass and ordered him to take the advance. The general directed the major to keep a southeast course in the woods and, after crossing the railroad, to take the first road leading northeast. Swamps and woods hid the column's movement from the enemy. The Federals avoided fields and roads where they might raise dust clouds that would give away their position.

Farther back, the 2nd Virginia Cavalry swarmed around the flanks of Battery B and compelled the artillerists to spike their guns and flee. "We were advancing on a battery and when the order was given to charge it, the 2d Regiment again pushed ahead of the infantry and was in advance when we reached the battery, which we captured," recollected Maj. William F. Graves, who was leading the 2nd that day.[96] The 2nd had forged ahead of Finegan's infantry and Barney ordered the cavalrymen to halt and line up with his foot soldiers.

Battery C-E limbered up to flee but, unable to follow Kautz's troopers into the woods and swamps to the southeast, tried to rejoin Wilson's contingent. The artillerists reached the Stage Road after the Rebels had cut them off. Pistols and carbines thrown away by Federal cavalrymen littered the road. The gunners spiked and abandoned their pieces, then picked up pistols and carbines, and mounted artillery horses. With about 50 cavalrymen, the artillerists rode southeastward in Kautz's wake.

Farther right, the three remaining guns of Battery K drove off a Secessionist battery as Kautz's column and the fugitives from Battery C-E passed. Lieutenant

94 Gause, *Four Years with Five Armies*, 291.

95 Eanes, *Destroy the Junction*, 144.

96 Robert J. Driver, *2nd Virginia Cavalry* (Lynchburg, VA, 1995), 129.

Ward's two-gun section of Battery K received orders to withdraw at once through the woods to the right, gain the causeway, and catch up with Kautz's cavalry while the remaining gun covered the withdrawal. Ward then withdrew pursued by some mounted men from the 3rd and 4th Virginia Cavalry. He reached a boggy creek bottom where most of the guns of the other batteries had gotten stuck. After a slight delay to deploy some fence rails at a better spot, Ward crossed one of his guns and picked up the caissons of Battery C-E. Within a few hundred yards of the causeway, two of his gun's horses collapsed from exhaustion. "I appealed strongly to the cavalry for assistance to haul our gun—the last of Battery K—but it was of no use; it was decidedly the wrong time to swap horses," Ward recalled.[97] He spiked the gun, chopped the spokes of its wheels and abandoned his gun and the caissons. Many of the artillerists with guns stuck in the boggy creek bottom fell into Confederate hands.

As Kautz's column trotted southeastward, it shed soldiers. Hunger got the better of First Sergeant Chester. He left the column, rode to a log house nearby and asked for something to eat. A woman gave him some corn bread and cold boiled pork. "It tasted very nice and made me feel better," Chester remembered. He no sooner rejoined the column at the rear than he observed a Confederate column gaining. Chester's mule proved balky. "I got my mule headed for the woods and gave him the spurs, so that by the time the rebel Cavalry had come up I was out of sight in the woods," he recalled. "No one of the rebels followed me into the woods but all kept on after the Regiment."[98] Passing through the timber, he united with a pair of Buckeyes on the other side of an open field. A slave boy gave them directions toward Petersburg. About an hour later, the trio abandoned their mounts to wade across steep-banked Rowanty Creek. Reaching a clump of trees at sunset, they immediately lay down and went to sleep.

Kautz's column, guided by a pair of slaves, headed for the Weldon Railroad between Reams Station and Rowanty Bridge. "By-and-by we reached the edge of a deep cut, through which the Weldon Railroad was built, the sides of the cut being steep and sandy, with some twenty feet of slope," recollected Lunt.

The crossing proved challenging. "It was a wild and exciting scene to see those mounted men slide down that steep embankment to the railroad track, [and] scramble up the opposite bank," recalled Sgt. Edward Parsons Tobie Jr. of the 1st District of Columbia Cavalry's Company G, wounded and captured at First Brandy Station. Not all the mounts made it across. "Many of the horses were too weak to climb the further embankment, though the most of us succeeded in

97 Eanes, *Destroy the Junction*, 140.

98 Chester, *Recollections*, 89.

crossing and entering the thick forest beyond," Lunt remembered.[99] Compass in hand, Kautz led the way.

* * *

While Fitzhugh Lee and Mahone routed the Federals west of Reams Station, Hampton's Confederates gathered up the arms and plunder abandoned by the raiders around Sappony Church. "Over the field of flight were found shawls, silk dresses, mantles of velvet, jewelry, and every kind of light valuables to be found in the houses of well-to-do people," recalled the Laurel Brigade's McDonald.[100]

"In their flight they threw away some 50,000 cartridges and a number of other things, but unfortunately our Brigade got but little of the plunder," wrote Lt. Col. Williams Stokes of the 4th South Carolina Cavalry. "I got a nice pair of scissors (small), this paper, and a pocket comb."[101]

Sergeant Humphries re-equipped himself at the expense of Uncle Sam. "The Yanks have been very kind in furnishing me equipment since I have been out here," he wrote home. "They have furnished me with saddle, Bridle, Halter gun pistol and anything I wanted in that line."[102]

Myers remembered that "the most curious scene of all was the troops of negroes of all sizes and ages, from the three-day old baby to the gray-wooled hag of ninety, which were found hidden in the woods."[103]

After gathering up the spoils, Hampton's force reformed. Companies C and K of the 9th Virginia Cavalry awaited the rest of their regiment near Sappony Church. "I had the opportunity to inspect the bullet marks on the building, and how, in the damage inflicted, the pulpit and Bible had not escaped," recollected Lieutenant Beale. "I also saw in a near-by orchard a number of fresh graves of Wilson's men, who had fallen the evening before."[104]

Hampton's troops returned to Stony Creek Station around noon. Unapprised by Fitzhugh Lee of events at Reams Station, Hampton awaited developments while his men ate and their horses fed. Shadburne ventured back through the timber toward the roads he had raided the previous night, this time accompanied by six

99 Tobie, *First Maine Cavalry*, 337.

100 McDonald, *Laurel Brigade*, 263.

101 William Stokes and Lloyd Halliburton, *Saddle Soldiers: The Civil War Correspondence of General William Stokes of the 4th South Carolina Cavalry* (Orangeburg, SC, 1993), 153.

102 Coffman, *Going Back the Way They Came*, 89.

103 Myers, *The Comanches*, 311.

104 George W. Beale, *A Lieutenant of Cavalry in Lee's Army*, 176.

other scouts. His little band called themselves the "Iron Scouts."[105] At the edge of some trees, they captured half a dozen of Kautz's troopers. Entering a forest, Shadburne saw a much larger body of Federals approaching ahead.

"What are you going to do?" asked Scout Wallace Miller of South Carolina.

"Capture them," said Shadburne.

"My God," said Miller.

Shadburne wheeled into the edge of the road. Declaring himself a brigadier general with Mosby at his back, Shadburne bellowed a demand that the Yankees surrender. He ordered his men forward. They filed into view, one after the other.

"Ready, aim," Shadburne roared.

His men raised their weapons.

"Don't shoot, don't shoot," said the Federals. "We'll surrender."

Without halting the Northerners, Shadburne directed them to throw down their arms in the road.

"Forward, march," he said, "form fours, gallop, march."

Soon afterward he and his men delivered 80 prisoners to Hampton at Stony Creek Station.

"Shadburne, how many men did you have?" Hampton asked after being told of the Iron Scouts' exploit.

"Six, but look out, Kautz is upon us," said Shadburne.[106]

Kautz's main column was behind the Iron Scouts and their captives. Shadburne feared the Federals would escape. Hampton authorized Shadburne to gather troops quickly and pursue the Northerners. Shadburne rode to Stony Creek Station and ordered up Phillips's Georgia Legion of Young's brigade. Colonel Gilbert J. Wright, the brigade's commander, burst onto the scene. "Old Gib" threatened Shadburne with arrest if he ever again summoned Wright's men without his authorization.[107]

Hampton quickly rode up Halifax Road with Chambliss's and Butler's brigades to secure the crossings of the Weldon Railroad between Stony Creek Station and Reams Station. Butler's brigade led, followed by the 9th Virginia Cavalry, the 10th Virginia Cavalry with the artillery, and the 13th Virginia Cavalry as a rear guard. The sound of guns to their left as they rode northward informed them that Wilson

105 Joseph Frederick Waring II, "The Jeff Davis Legion," J. F. Waring Papers 1275, Chapter XXI, 1. The Railroad (pages unnumbered), Georgia Historical Society, Savannah, GA.

106 Brooks, *Butler and His Cavalry*, 281. Lt. Col. John Singleton Mosby, a partisan leader nicknamed "The Gray Ghost," conducted an intimidating campaign of raids and harassment against Union supply lines and communications in northern Virginia. "John Singleton Mosby," battlefields.org. Retrieved Jan. 30, 2024.

107 Joseph Frederick Waring II, "The Jeff Davis Legion," Chapter XXI, 1. The Railroad (pages unnumbered).

Wade Hampton
Library of Congress

and Kautz had encountered other Confederate troops at Reams Station.

When Butler's and Chambliss's brigades, except for the 13th, had crossed Rowanty Creek near the Perkins house, a big column of Union horsemen approached from the left and front of the 13th. Outnumbered, the 13th took cover in the woods to its right. The Federals attempted to cross the bridge but surrendered on demand when blocked by portions of the 9th and 10th. Butler's brigade continued on its way to Malone's crossing.

Chambliss's brigade, resuming its progress northward with the 9th in the lead, rode over a hill, covering a few hundred yards more. The 9th's men heard a volley behind them. The 10th was charging a body of bluecoats while another group of Yankees rushed eastward along a wooded lane into the 10th's left flank, entering Halifax Road near Hampton and his staff just as a cannon from Graham's battery was passing.

"Unlimber that gun," commanded Hampton.

The 9th reversed course and prepared to charge a squadron of the 11th Pennsylvania Cavalry, "a motley group of fugitive slaves," and many artillerists, including those of Batteries B and C-E, who had lost their guns and were riding artillery horses. "Calls were made to the enemy to halt and surrender; and the rattling of falling arms told that they were prisoners," remembered Colonel Beale. Another group of Federals and blacks crossed Rowanty Creek, veered right "and fled along the by-roads skirting that stream," Beale recalled.[108]

The balance of Kautz's column had already crossed the Weldon Railroad between Reams Station and Rowanty Bridge. After pausing in the woods east of the Weldon Railroad to reform while stragglers caught up, Kautz had resumed his progress. A squadron of the 9th Virginia Cavalry under Colonel Beale drew the task of pursuing Kautz's men, already a mile or two to the east. Three of the remaining squadrons of the 9th deployed west of Halifax Road on the lookout for

108 Richard L. T. Beale, *Ninth Virginia Cavalry*, 135.

further Federal fugitive bands. Another squadron guarded the prisoners. The rest of Chambliss's brigade secured the bridge over Rowanty Creek and returned to Stony Creek Station.

The men of Colonel Beale's squadron, after pounding eastward for three miles, could see the rear of the Federal column through the cloud of dust it was kicking up. As the squadron dashed toward Kautz's column, remembered Lieutenant Beale, "groups of contraband negroes, artillerymen on horses without saddles, and cavalrymen on jaded animals, were overtaken and captured."

The Virginians on the fleetest horses dashed ahead and captured more stragglers. "At one point in this exciting chase, the dust seen to our left showed that the enemy's column had rounded an angle in the road, and that we by cutting across a wide field could cut a large part of it off," Lieutenant Beale recollected. An officer and a few men crossed the field and severed the column several hundred yards from its rear. The Yanks in the rear, isolated, began throwing down their arms preparatory to surrendering. Before they finished disarming, the dust settled and the Northerners could see how few Virginians confronted them. Rallying, the bluecoats picked up their pistols and started shooting, which forced the Virginians to retreat.

Without fresh horses, the Virginians could not resume the pursuit. They could scarcely manage their prisoners. Lieutenant Beale led a detail marching the captives back. Many of the prisoners concealed on their persons articles seized from private homes. He recalled:

> An officer among them wore a handsome pair of cavalry boots, which one of our men proposed to have him exchange for his well-worn shoes; but I checked him, insisting that a prisoner's personal belongings must not be taken from him. As this officer marched back on foot, sundry women's lace collars and other articles, which had been taken from a Lunenburg house, fell to the ground from beneath his coat.

Observing this, Lieutenant Beale called the man who wanted the fine boots "and withdrew all objection to him taking them."[109]

Kautz's column reached Jerusalem Plank Road near Proctor's Tavern about 6:00 p.m. Most of the men, including their commander, were suffering from lack of rest and sustenance. Darkness ended the Secessionist pursuit. Around 9:00 p.m., Kautz and his contingent rode into the lines of the Army of the Potomac, totally fatigued. "I was asleep on horseback for several hours before reaching our lines

109 George W. Beale, *A Lieutenant of Cavalry in Lee's Army*, 177.

that night dreaming the most aggravating dreams," Kautz remembered. "The most tantalizing vision was that of marching through populous and brilliantly lighted towns; through the windows we could see the tables spread with every good thing to eat and we were not permitted to halt and partake."[110]

"Old Po'keepsie" of the 2nd Ohio Cavalry recollected, "Through swamps and deep muddy streams we took our race, and about nine o'clock that evening entered our lines a weary, worn lot of men."[111]

Second Lieutenant Comins of the 1st District Columbia Cavalry recalled, "The night before we road all night, without supper, and fought all day without breakfast or dinner, and went to bed after running away twenty miles through the woods and swamp without supper."[112]

At 9:30 p.m. Kautz telegraphed Meade of his arrival and of Wilson's probable approach by way of Jarratt's Station. Meade directed Kautz to deploy to safeguard Wilson's return, but Kautz begged off, pleading his command's exhaustion.

* * *

After Mahone's and Lomax's troops had shaken Kautz's and McIntosh's Federals, Wickham's brigade charged between the halves of McIntosh's brigade into the trains and a landscape strewn with guns, blankets, clothing, and slaves. "We moved off at a trot, passing a hundred parked wagons already set on fire, eight or ten caissons, a hospital train of fifty carriages, and a good number of carriages full of wounded from which the horses had been taken," recollected Adjt. Robert T. Hubard Jr. of the 3rd Virginia Cavalry.[113]

Chaos prevailed among the trains. "The most fearful sight which I have witnessed in the war was the confusion & terror of the poor negro women & children as we charged the Yankees through & over them," recalled Captain Watkins of the 3rd. "Little children one & two years old were strewn over the roads & fields, mounted horsemen were charging & fighting over them, the women rushing frantically about not knowing in what direction to go."[114] Pursuers in the 6th Virginia Cavalry of Wickham's brigade paused to stare at an abandoned newborn baby amid the chaos and wondered what would become of the infant.

110 Eanes, *Destroy the Junction*, 146.

111 Old Po'keepsie, "From the 2nd Ohio Cavalry."

112 Comins to "My dear wife," July 6, 1864.

113 Thomas P. Nanzig, ed., *The Civil War Memoirs of a Virginia Cavalryman, Lt. Robert T. Hubard Jr.* (Tuscaloosa, AL, 2007), 180.

114 Toalson, ed., *Send Me a Pair of Old Boots & Kiss My Little Girls*, 293.

Other Southerners viewed matters in a less sympathetic light. "Negro women were throwing their babies ruthlessly aside," remembered Maryland-born Pvt. John Gill, a courier in Fitzhugh Lee's division. "Our men became greatly enraged, and it was difficult to restrain them. It was a question of quarter or no quarter, and it was mostly no quarter."[115]

Many of the Secessionists had gone into the fight with the attitude that the blacks with the raiders had been promised "40 acres and a mule with a white man to drive the plow," recalled Gill's fellow Marylander Pvt. H. H. Matthews of Breathed's battery.[116]

Sergeant Benjamin J. Haden of the 1st Virginia Cavalry's Company E recollected, "In a short time we had captured about two acres of carriages, buggies, negroes, (men, women and children), and everything that could be picked up in their line of march."[117] The troopers of the 3rd Virginia Cavalry gathered enough pistols, sabers, and Burnside rifles to arm themselves and their comrades at home on furlough. Some recaptured silver plate stolen by the Yanks.

Mahone's infantry pushed through Kautz's pickets toward the Federal trains. "Now was seen a sight that seldom ever met even the eye of a soldier," Cowan remembered. "Yankees fleeing in dismay through the woods with Artillery, Negroes of all ages size and sex running to an froe in the wildest Confusion. Artillery would run until they would strike a tree and cut loose and, my kingdom for a horse, clucking turkeys pigs and Negroe babys strewed the country."[118]

To the right of the Alabamians, Finegan's Florida Brigade charged. Barney Finegan straddled the first gun that he reached and yelled out, "Promotion for me!"[119]

The soldiers of Wickham's two mounted regiments passed the burning park of the enemy's wagons and caissons. They captured ambulances, walking wounded, wagons, caissons, and cannon, and they liberated many of the Alabamians taken prisoner earlier. Some Confederates began gathering the spoils of their victory. Captain Watkins found one of the mules and three of the slaves the Federals had taken from his farm on the 24th, and he sent them back to his farm with two soldiers going home for fresh horses. Mahone's infantry came up and recaptured more of the Alabamians taken prisoner that morning.

115 John Gill, *Reminiscences of Four Years in the Confederate Army, 1861–1865* (Baltimore, 1904), 62, 106.

116 H. H. Matthews, "Pelham-Breathed Battery, Part XVII, Expedition of Gens. Wilson and Kautz Against the Richmond and Weldon Railroad," *St. Mary's Beacon* (Leonardtown, MD), June 15, 1905, p. 1, cols. 2–5.

117 Driver, *1st Virginia Cavalry*, 93.

118 Carter, ed., *Welcome the Hour of Conflict*, 265.

119 Dorman, *Fifty Years Ago*, 14.

Many of the wounded Federals mounted horses and tried to ride on with Wilson's column. Mortally wounded Sgt. Ichabod W. Mattocks of Company A, 1st Vermont Cavalry, who had reenlisted the previous February, started with Wilson's column but had to return. His comrades never forgot his expression of anguish and despair as he rode back to the ambulances.

"It was hard to leave the poor fellows in the ambulances to their fate," recalled Cruikshank. "As we rode by many stretched out their hands to us and bid us good-bye."[120] Cruikshank found his company's 1st Lt. John J. Barclay among the wounded in the ambulances. Intending to escape captivity, Barclay wanted a horse. Cruikshank gave up his own mount and scrounged another. Cummings rode away with his comrades in the 1st Vermont Cavalry despite his terrible wound. The 2nd Ohio Cavalry's Pike fell into enemy hands.

* * *

The withdrawal of Wilson's column took more time and covered more distance than Kautz's breakout. "Then came one of the greatest get up and get marches that was ever known," remembered Private Norton of the 8th New York Cavalry.[121] Wilson, his staff, and many stragglers barely managed to mount and flee before the Virginians seized the Illinoisan's headquarters and hospital. Wilson had to ride from his column's head to its tail before it proceeded. The column's tail then became its head. The 1st New Hampshire Cavalry led, followed by the 1st Vermont Cavalry and then the rest of the remnant of Chapman's brigade. Behind Chapman's troopers came such fugitives as had escaped the trains. The 1st Connecticut Cavalry and 2nd New York Cavalry brought up the rear.

"Soon we heard a rattling in the rear and then come our skirmishers full on a full gallop followed by Rebel cavalry," recollected Private Bradley of the 1st Connecticut Cavalry. "Then began the tallest skedaddle that has happened lately. Away went the whole division on a dead jump every man trying to get ahead for once, at any rate."[122] The column rode through six inches of dust on a hot, sultry day. Cruikshank and around 50 others from the 11th Pennsylvania Cavalry joined Wilson's column. Cruikshank lost his horse and struck out on foot. The Confederates captured the wounded Barclay despite his efforts to escape.

Up a pole cutting wires, Pvt. William J. Smith of the 2nd Ohio Cavalry's Company M slid down and with two other Buckeyes tried to rejoin their regiment.

120 Eanes, *Destroy the Junction*, 142.

121 Norton, *Deeds of Daring*, 82.

122 Angelovich, *Riding for Uncle Samuel*, 430.

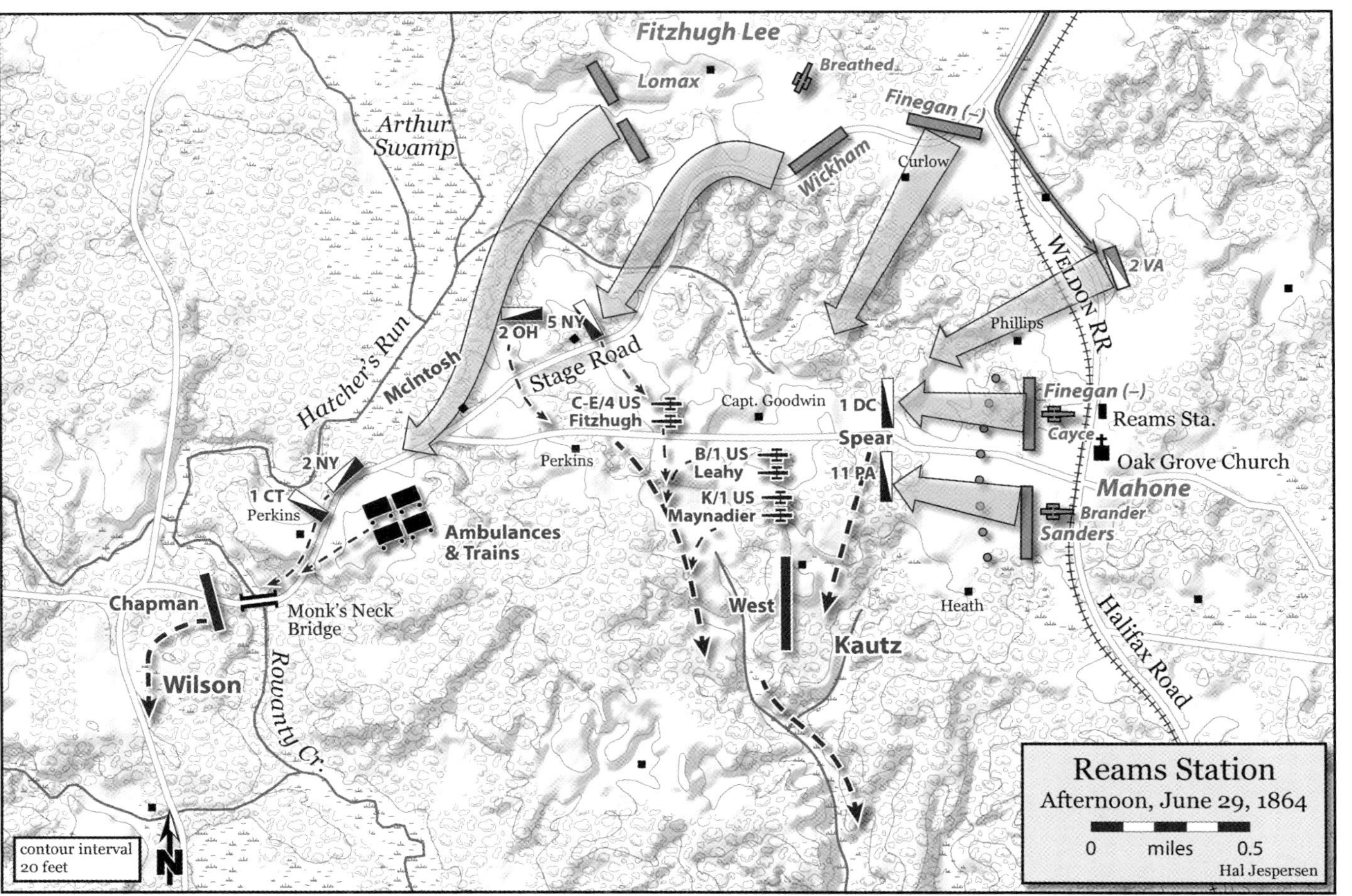
Fitzhugh Lee
Lomax
Breathed
Finegan (–)
Arthur
Swamp
Wickham
Curlow
Weldon RR
2 VA
Phillips
2 OH
5 NY
Stage Road
Hatcher's Run
McIntosh
C-E/4 US
Fitzhugh
Capt. Goodwin
1 DC
Finegan (–)
Reams Sta.
Cayce
Spear
Oak Grove Church
Perkins
B/1 US
Leahy
11 PA
Mahone
2 NY
K/1 US
Maynadier
Brander
1 CT
Perkins
Sanders
Ambulances
& Trains
Chapman
Monk's Neck
Bridge
West
Heath
Kautz
Halifax Road
Wilson
Rowanty Cr.
Reams Station
Afternoon, June 29, 1864
0
miles
0.5
Hal Jespersen
contour interval
20 feet

They found themselves isolated. "So we had to cut off in another direction, and after going through a hot place in the woods, I and one of the others got to Wilson's forces," which were "on the skedaddle and badly demoralized," Smith recollected.[123] The third man had his horse shot and took to a swamp, worked his way to the other side, swapped clothes with a slave, blacked his face with a piece of burnt wood, and sauntered as inconspicuously as possible toward Grant's lines.

At the head of the column, Chapman's band of survivors enjoyed little respite. "In the first heat of the pell mell race my horse stumbled and fell in the dust four or five inches deep," recalled Watlington. Horse and rider simultaneously got to their feet. "After remounting I moved to the side of the road and retreated at a more reasonable gait, which gave me a more favorable opportunity of observing our refugee reinforcements," he recollected. The panic-stricken contrabands were fleeing in all directions. "I several instances saw mothers leave their young babies by the road side and flee for their own safety, the old and infirm being left to care for themselves," he recalled.[124]

The Federal rear guard resisted briefly near Monk's Neck Bridge over Rowanty Creek. "They fired right sharply upon and partially checked us," remembered the 3rd Virginia Cavalry's Adjutant Hubard. The Yanks then began to withdraw in some order. "The enemy retired rather sullenly until our sabres began to nock their caps off," Hubard recollected. "They then fled precipitately exposing to view about 150 Negroes scampering across the fields, (of all sizes and sexes), with great bundles of plunder stolen from their owners' houses, upon their backs." The Virginians knocked some over and shot others. "[S]uch screaming and yelling as they sent up Pandemonium itself could scarcely beat," recalled Hubard.[125]

The Rebel advance struck the 2nd New York Cavalry behind the 1st Connecticut Cavalry after the Federals crossed Rowanty Creek. The New Yorkers "run through our column," remembered Cpl. Henry B. Parmalee of the 1st's Company B.[126]

Luck ran out for Sergeant Koempel of Parmelee's company. "Hand to hand fighting," Koempel noted. "Rebels right amongst us in dusty road. Got off my horse to help [Pvt. Giles P. Lecrenier] and found he was dead."[127] Koempel fell into the hands of four Virginians.

123 Robert W. Hatton, ed., *William James Smith's Memoirs of the 2nd Ohio Volunteer Cavalry, Company M* (Milford, OH, 2008), 23.

124 Watlington Diary, June 29, 1864.

125 Nanzig, ed., *The Civil War Memoirs of a Virginia Cavalryman*, 180–181.

126 Angelovich, *Riding for Uncle Samuel*, 429.

127 Koempel, *Phil Koempel's Diary*, June 29, 1864, 12. The diary says Koempel fell into the hands of "the Thirteenth VA Cavalry." Ibid. Adjutants General, *Record of Service of Connecticut Men in the*

The 2nd New York Cavalry's officers shouted, "Break for the woods."[128] The Empire State men and Nutmeggers left the road for the timber, soon reached an open lot, tried unsuccessfully to form, and then continued their flight.

Lomax's brigade replaced Wickham's troops in the van of the pursuit. The Secessionists followed so closely that the Clarke Cavalry, Company D of the 6th Virginia Cavalry, rode into an ambush where the Federals shot down one-color bearer after another until 1st Lt. Joseph M. Kennerly shouted, "Stand firm, men, rally to your colors!" This restored order but not until McKendree had received two disabling wounds.[129]

Breathed's battery had fired sporadically, advancing one section at a time, but had not kept up with the horse soldiers. Some of the battery's gunners mounted up and pursued with the cavalry. Major James "Jim" Breathed, a Missouri doctor born in Virginia, educated at St. James College in Maryland, and wounded at Yellow Tavern and Samaria Church, rode with the head of the 6th Virginia Cavalry. During a charge just before reaching Stony Creek, a pistol ball hit Breathed in the stomach, inflicting a wound he thought fatal. A small group from his command gathered round him as he lay on the ground.

"Boys, they have got me this time," he said as his comrades bent over trying to comfort him.

A surgeon examined Breathed and informed him that the wound was not fatal because, remembered Pvt. Edward H. O'Brien of Breathed's battery, "The ball had not penetrated the bowels, but lodged in the wall of the stomach."[130] An ambulance carried Breathed, cheered by the diagnosis, to the Malone house. Breathed's men mounted up again and headed toward Stony Creek. Farther along they found two captured cannon, which they turned on the Northerners.

The steep banks of Stony Creek hindered the retreat. Wilson, unable to cross his whole command at once over the Stage Road's narrow bridge, formed two lines of battle and attempted to reorganize on the north bank. "The men were almost completely demoralized, at least one-third either thrown away or lost their arms in the flight," remembered Chaplain Boudrye, one of those from the 5th New

Army and Navy of the United States During the War of the Rebellion (Hartford, CT, 1889), 68. The 13th Virginia Cavalry was at Stony Creek Station, not Reams Station. Balfour, *13th Virginia Cavalry*, 35.

128 Angelovich, *Riding for Uncle Samuel*, 430.

129 Michael Musick, *6th Virginia Cavalry* (Lynchburg, VA, 1990), 64; "Joseph McKendree Kennerly," findagrave.com, retrieved Feb. 13, 2023.

130 Trout, ed., *Memoirs of the Stuart Horse Artillery Battalion*, 2:139–140.

Fitzhugh Lee

Library of Congress

York Cavalry in Wilson's column.[131] Wilson did not allow dismounted men or contrabands to cross.[132]

Fitzhugh Lee dismounted his division and formed line of battle facing the reorganizing Unionists. Some of his men brought up a captured gun and forced a captured crew from the gun's battery to man the gun. The 3rd Virginia Cavalry's colonel stood by and told the crew's sergeant that "if he didn't 'point her right,'" the colonel would "cut his head off," recalled Hubard. The sergeant sighted the piece.

"Ready, aim, fire!" the sergeant commanded.

The cannonball struck among the opposing bluecoats. The sergeant became excited and forgot where he was.

"That's it, boys," he said. "Now give them another right in the same place."

A few more shots followed. Then, "our bugles blew a charge and the whole line moved enthusiastically forward with that elasticity which sure victory can give," remembered Hubard. "The enemy now crossed over the stream and fled in utter route."[133]

The panic that struck the Federals turned the crossing into a nightmare. "The rebs fired into & with Saber Cut & slashed the poor contrabands—women & children," recollected Surgeon Elias Beck of the 3rd Indiana Cavalry. "Killing most inhumanly—& such shrieks was terrible."[134] Rebel cavalrymen would leave off pursuing Yankees to shoot down black men without mercy. The Johnnies allowed women and children to surrender after knocking them senseless with the back of a saber or the butt of a gun. Hundreds of dismounted men and liberated slaves jumped into the creek. Many never emerged.

131 Boudrye, *Fifth New York Cavalry*, 150.

132 Hoffman, *First Vermont Cavalry Volunteers*, 190.

133 Hewett, et al., eds., *Supplement to the Official Records* Lee Report, 332; Nanzig, ed., *The Civil War Memoirs of a Virginia Cavalryman*, 182.

134 Goecker, *Hoosier Spies and Horse Marines*, 135.

Wilson's troopers suffered as well. "Some were pushed off the bridge, falling on others in the stream," Boudrye recalled. "Men and horses mingled in almost every conceivable shape, struggled to reach the opposite bank, while bullets whizzed among the trees, and shells screamed over their heads." Troopers urged their weary steeds down the steep banks of the creek until they fell headlong into the water. "Driving down as far as my horse would go without falling, I dismounted, and, as I knew the animal could not carry me much further on account of exhaustion and lameness, I concluded to leave him," Boudrye recalled. "Down the crevice of the rocks near the water's edge, I reached a retreat safe from falling horses and flying bullets." Having experienced captivity before, Boudrye resolved "to go forward so long as I could put one foot before the other."[135]

Federals fleeing westward ran into troopers from Barringer's brigade of Rooney Lee's division. A sergeant from the 5th North Carolina Cavalry seized a Unionist colonel and his "magnificent gray horse superbly caparisoned," recalled Captain Galloway of the 5th.[136] The horse caught Barringer's eye and he employed a combination of persuasion and authority to wheedle the horse from the sergeant.

Barringer's butternuts captured about 125 bluecoats.[137]

Once across Stony Creek, Wilson's column continued its flight. Though the Federals fired the bridge over the creek, Fitzhugh Lee's division continued the pursuit. "The poor negro women who had left their homes in the hope of obtaining their freedom remained screaming along the roads and in the forests through the night," recalled Private Gill. "As we pressed the enemy, we found the roads strewn with every description of cavalry equipment, wearing apparel, dead men and dead horses, and every variety of stolen property from a negro down to a brooch."[138]

Exhausted, some of Wilson's troopers gave up. Others passed out. Still others left the column to strike out on their own. Seventeen-year-old Pvt. William F. Clarke of the 1st Connecticut Cavalry's Company A was riding a mule at the column's rear. He had already had two horses shot out from under him and he was nursing a wound to the back of his head suffered at Sappony Church. Dozing on and off in the saddle, he let his animal set its own pace. Suddenly jolted awake, he found himself alone. He spurred his mule forward.

135 Boudrye, *Fifth New York Cavalry*, 150–151.

136 Harrell, *2nd North Carolina Cavalry*, 304; Clark, *North Carolina Regiments*, 3:539. "By a curious coincidence when General Barringer was captured in April, 1865, this Yankee Colonel was in the crowd which captured him," continued Galloway. "His first words were, 'I'll be damned, if yonder ain't my horse.'" Ibid.

137 D. B. R., "Barringer's N. C. Brigade of Cavalry."

138 Gill, *Reminiscences*, 107.

"Come in here you damned Yankee son of a bitch or we'll blow you to hell in a minute," shouted two guerrillas hidden in the bushes.

"Don't think you can frighten me, though you show me death," Clarke said, straightening up. "I've been in tight places before."

A Rebel officer stepped out, reprimanded the two guerrillas in the bushes, and took Clarke into custody.

The Confederates and their captive entered nearby woods and headed in the direction of Stony Creek. The Southerners, coming upon a road, captured a trooper from the 5th New York Cavalry and a lone African American. As darkness neared, the Rebels led their captives back into the woods and stopped a long way from the road. The two reprimanded guards shot dead the New Yorker and the unnamed black man, then aimed at Clarke. He bolted into the timber. Shots rang out and wounded Clarke. He fell to the ground. The two guards approached and fired more bullets into the Connecticut man, then left him for dead. Clarke survived despite ten bullet wounds, a broken shoulder, and a great loss of blood. He made it back to Federal lines with the help of a local Unionist farmer.[139]

* * *

Soon after Griffin entered his garden heavily armed, Cross notified him that the soldiers approaching the Griffin house were five Confederate cavalrymen. Returning from furlough, they had approached the house in search of something to eat. "Having refreshed these cavalrymen with mint juleps and the first meal they had . . . eaten in twenty-four hours, I proposed that we go down to the fighting then going on about Monk's Neck Bridge, to render such assistance as we could," Griffin recalled. He and the five cavalrymen rode to within a few hundred yards of the Stage Road crossing of Mortar Branch and dismounted. Tying their horses, the men advanced through scattered young pines toward the road. About two miles from Roberts's Bridge, they could hear "brisk approaching gunfire." After they put to flight some unidentifiable soldiers, Griffin suggested to his comrades that they go down to a big field about half a mile away that from its edge gave a "full view" of the road. The cavalrymen did not want to get that far from their horses.

Griffin decided to go to the field alone. Halfway there, as he struggled through the bushes along the bank of Mortar Branch, he saw 20 dismounted Federal

139 W. A. Croffut and John M. Morris, *The Military and Civil History of Connecticut During the War of 1861–65, Comprising a Detailed Account of the Regiments and Batteries through March, Encampment, Bivouac, and Battle; also Instances of Distinguished Personal Gallantry, and Biographical Sketches of Many Heroic Soldiers; together with a Record of the Patriotic Actions of Citizens at Home, and of the Liberal Support Furnished by the State in Its Executive and Legislative Departments* (New York, 1868), 616; Angelovich, *Riding for Uncle Samuel*, 432–433.

horsemen. At the sight of him they fled, apparently assuming that the bushes concealed more Confederates. "In a little while, the firing was over and our cavalry continued to pursue the enemy westwardly on the Stage Road," he remembered. He returned to where he had parted from his comrades and from there he headed for his house.[140] That evening Griffin arrived home to find that his cavalry friends had captured several prisoners. "These we kept under ground in a camp near the house during the night," he recalled.[141]

* * *

McIntosh assembled enough of a rearguard to ward off the butternuts pursuing Wilson's column. The rearguard included the 1st Connecticut Cavalry, the only regiment besides the 1st Vermont Cavalry that remained organized. A couple miles farther, across Sappony Creek, Corporal Parmelee "formed a line of 30 men to hold the bridge for a time but [the enemy] did not try to come," he recalled. "They threw plenty of shell and grape and canister at us all that afternoon and night. I was in the extreme rear guard with 6 or 8 men but we were not attacked."[142]

Fitzhugh Lee's troopers encamped without forage around Lloyd's Church west of the Stage Road and north of Sappony Creek. "There was, it is true, a patch of green oats near but most of the men were too tired to cut any for their horses," recollected Hubard.[143]

Parmelee and his men fired the bridge over Sappony Creek and resumed the retreat. "That night's march was the most exhausting and fearful of any of our marchings," remembered the 1st Connecticut Cavalry's Maj. George O. Marcy, wounded at Beaver Dam Station in May. "The regiment destroyed bridges in rear of the column, and put every obstruction in the way of the enemy."[144]

The men of Wilson's column pushed themselves hard. "We marched all night long sometimes halting when the advance ran on to a picket (or supposed they did) till they could form and charge them and we would follow up at a gallop for a mile or so, then walk for a mile and then another gallop," remembered Ide.[145]

Wilson, with the remainder of his command and about 500 of Kautz's men, reached the Nottoway around 10:30 p.m. His column re-formed and the

140 Griffin, "Life in Dinwiddie County in the vicinity of the opposing armies of the war," 8.

141 Ibid., 10.

142 Angelovich, *Riding for Uncle Samuel*, 430.

143 Nanzig, ed., *The Civil War Memoirs of a Virginia Cavalryman*, 182.

144 Croffut and Morris, *The Military and Civil History of Connecticut during the War of 1861–65*, 615.

145 Hoffman, *First Vermont Cavalry Volunteers*, 191.

Federals abandoned their last cannon. Wilson permitted neither contrabands nor dismounted men to cross. The 1st New Hampshire Cavalry still led the way over the Double Bridges into Greensville County, still followed by the 1st Vermont Cavalry. After completing the crossing, the bluecoats fired the bridges and headed for Jarratt's Station. The rout at Reams had cost the raiders at least 754 casualties: 44 killed or mortally wounded, 60 otherwise wounded, 12 wounded and captured, and 638 prisoners or missing.[146]

The Confederates lost about 118.[147] The raiders had more than five captured for every trooper killed or wounded.

146 In Wilson's division, the escort detachment of the 8th Illinois Cavalry had one wounded and four missing. RG 94, Entry 653, Box 30. The provost guard detachment from the 3rd New Jersey Cavalry lost seven. Ibid.

In McIntosh's brigade, the 1st Connecticut Cavalry had four killed or mortally wounded, seven wounded, and 49 captured. Angelovich, *Riding for Uncle Samuel*, 436–438. The 2nd Ohio Cavalry lost one killed and 33 captured. Roster Commission, *Official Roster of the Soldiers of the State of Ohio*, 11:53–93, *passim*. The 2nd New York Cavalry had six killed, nine wounded, and 11 missing. RG 94, Entry 652, Box 37. The 5th New York Cavalry lost 18 missing. Ibid., Box 38. Three previously wounded troopers of the 3rd Indiana in Chapman's brigade fell into enemy hands. Goecker, *Hoosier Spies and Horse Marines*, 192, 200, 255. Battery K had 38 missing. RG 94, Entry 653, Box 30 (one wounded on June 25 captured June 29); Haskin, *First Regiment of Artillery*, 205, 561; *OR* 40, 1:233. Battery C-E lost one wounded and 31 missing. Ibid.; RG 94, Entry 653, Box 30 (18 missing June 29 in Battery E); Theophilus Francis Rodenbough and William Haskin, *The Army of the US Historical Sketches of Staff and Line with Portraits of Generals-in-Chief* (New York, 1896), 363 (Battery C "lost several men wounded and eighteen captured").

In West's brigade of Kautz's division, the 3rd New York Cavalry had two killed, seven wounded, and 75 missing. museum.dmna.ny.gov/application/files/9715/4894/2594/3rdCavCW_Roster.pdf. Retrieved Jan. 19, 2024. The 5th Pennsylvania Cavalry lost two killed and 62 prisoners. Bates, *History of Pennsylvania Volunteers*, 2:578–624, *passim*. In Spear's brigade, the 1st District of Columbia Cavalry had two killed, two wounded and missing, 19 otherwise wounded, and 32 missing including five supposed killed in action. RG 94, Entry 652, Box 3; *OR* 40, 1:742. The 11th Pennsylvania Cavalry lost 21 killed or dead of wounds, seven wounded and captured, four otherwise wounded, and 46 missing. Bates, *History of Pennsylvania Volunteers*, 3:911–951, *passim*. Battery B had four wounded and 28 missing. *OR* 40, 1:.237, 733.

147 In Fitzhugh Lee's division, Lomax's brigade lost one mortally wounded, 16 otherwise wounded, and one missing. Young, "Confederate Casualties during June 1864 at Petersburg." Wickham's brigade had two killed and one wounded. Ibid. Breathed's battery had one wounded. H. H. Matthews, "Pelham-Breathed Battery, Part XVII, Expedition of Gens. Wilson and Kautz Against the Richmond and Weldon Railroad."

Mahone's division lost 92 according to CSRs: 51 in Sanders's Alabama Brigade (seven killed, three mortally wounded, one wounded and captured, 34 otherwise wounded, and six missing) and 41 in Finegan's Florida brigade (three killed, nine dead of wounds, 27 wounded, and two missing). Young, "Confederate Casualties during June 1864 at Petersburg." Another source reveals nine killed, 25 wounded, and 5 missing in the Alabama Brigade (totaling 39) and two killed, 12 wounded, five missing in the Florida brigade (totaling 19). Mahone's (Anderson's Old) Division Tabular Return of Casualties (Series II), Beineke Rare Book and Manuscript Library, Yale University, New Haven, CT.

CSRs show that in Barringer's brigade the 1st North Carolina Cavalry of Barringer's brigade lost one killed and one wounded and that the 5th North Carolina Cavalry had two wounded. Young, "Confederate Casualties during June 1864 at Petersburg."

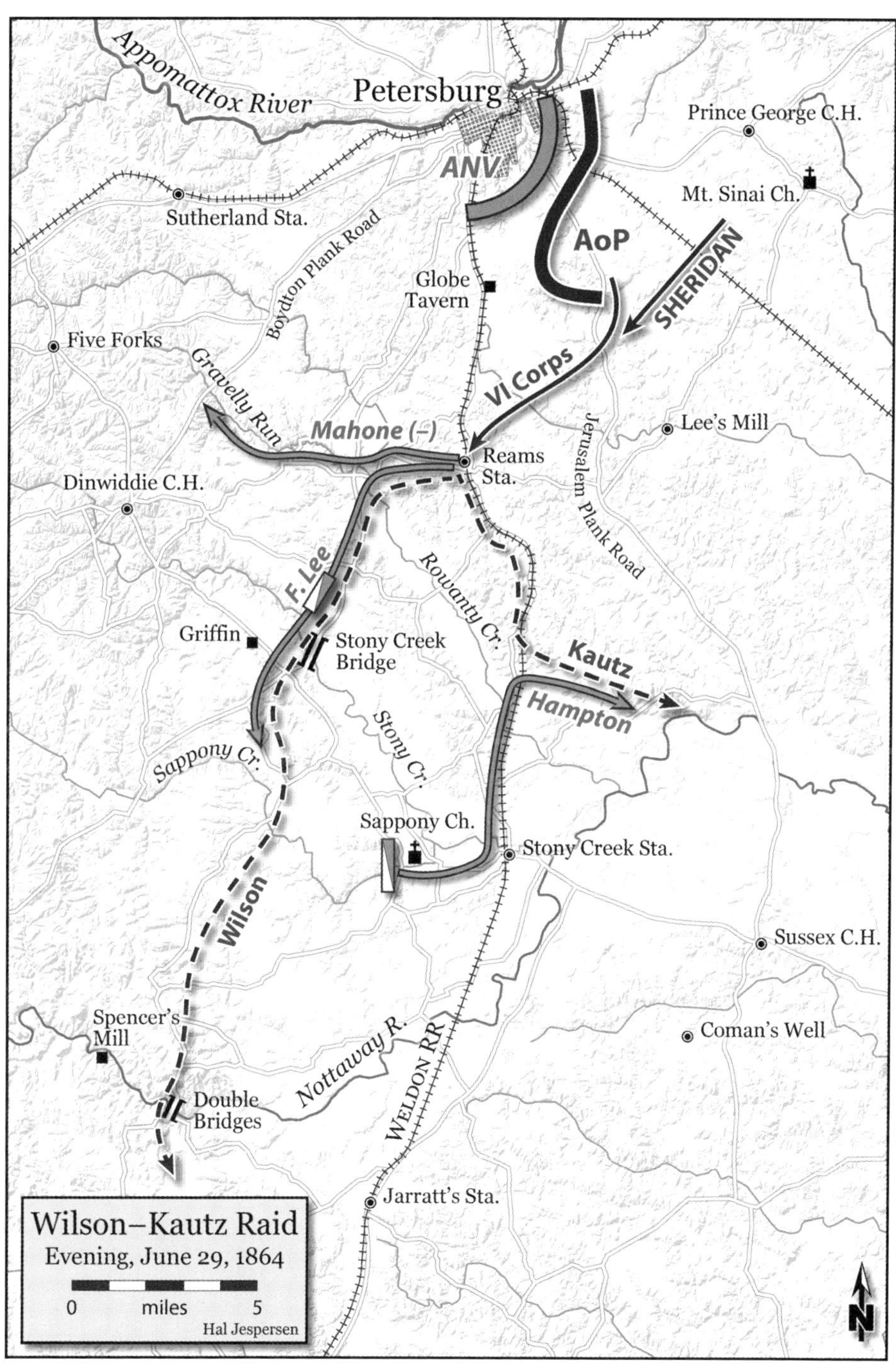

Appomattox River
Petersburg
Prince George C.H.
ANV
Mt. Sinai Ch.
Sutherland Sta.
AoP
SHERIDAN
Boydton Plank Road
Globe
Tavern
Five Forks
Gravelly Run
VI Corps
Lee's Mill
Mahone (–)
Reams
Sta.
Dinwiddie C.H.
Jerusalem Plank Road
Rowanty Cr.
F. Lee
Griffin
Stony Creek
Bridge
Kautz
Hampton
Stony Cr.
Sappony Cr.
Sappony Ch.
Stony Creek Sta.
Wilson
Sussex C.H.
Spencer's
Mill
Coman's Well
Nottaway R.
WELDON RR
Double
Bridges
Jarratt's Sta.
Wilson–Kautz Raid
Evening, June 29, 1864
0 miles 5
Hal Jespersen
N

* * *

At 1:00 a.m. on June 30, such of VI Corps as had arrived at Reams Station began to wreck the Weldon Railroad. "[I]t was a good road and hard to tear up, but by 2 o'clock we had torn it up for a good distance and piled up, ready to set on fire," recalled Sgt. Robert S. Westbrook of the 49th Pennsylvania's Company B, "then we laid down and rested till daybreak, when we got up and fired the road and heated and bent the rails, then put up a rifle pit."[148]

Units of the corps that wore the Greek Cross continued reaching Reams. Truex's brigade of Ricketts's division at the end of VI Corps' column, "having halted for an hour or two during the night," recalled Chaplain E. M. Haynes of the 10th Vermont, arrived at about 8:00 a.m.[149] At 9:00 a.m. VI Corps continued entrenching at Reams Station and kept wrecking the railroad there while awaiting Sheridan's arrival. As the corps' other divisions destroyed the railroad, Ricketts's division dug in parallel to the roadbed.[150]

The Confederates, wasting resources that Lee wanted allocated to the crucial Richmond & Danville, had repaired the Weldon Railroad at Reams Station since Wilson had passed through there on June 22. "Papers say the R.R. was 'strap iron on wooden rails' No such thing," remembered newly commissioned 2nd Lt. Oscar French of the 1st Vermont Heavy Artillery's Company C. "It was a fancy road in first best repair, and composed of 'Extension' rails, something I never saw in Vermont."[151]

Captain Walker agreed. "The railroad is in capital order, though I don't see the rolling stock," he wrote.[152]

Grant thought that "with Wright at Reams Station, Wilson south of the enemy, and Sheridan marching in that direction . . . it will be queer if the count does not turn in our favor." Grant hoped "that the enemy will be struck in the rear most disagreeably to him, and that his railroad in the meantime will be destroyed effectually as far as our troops occupy the line of it."[153] Kautz and the men of his division accompanying him were returning to the Army of the James,

148 Westbrook, *49th Pennsylvania Volunteers*, 210.

149 E. M. Haynes, *A History of the Tenth Regiment, Vt. Volunteers, with Biographical Sketches Of nearly every Officer who ever belonged to the Regiment, and many Non-commissioned Officers and Men, and A Complete Roster Of all the Officers and Men connected with it—showing all changes by Promotion, Death or Resignation, during the Military Existence of the Regiment* (Rutland, VT, 1894), 182.

150 Abbott, Personal *Recollections* and Civil War Diary, 1864, 91.

151 George Oscar French Letter, July 6, 1864.

152 Walker to "Dear Father," June 30, 1864.

153 *OR* 40, 2:516.

but the general-in-chief ordered them back to the Army of the Potomac's left to help Wilson.

Grant failed to realize that Wright's infantry could not catch Hampton's cavalry, Wilson's and Kautz's columns no longer amounted to organized fighting forces, and Sheridan was suffering from an unusual case of the slows.[154] Little Phil did not reach Jerusalem Plank Road until 12:30 p.m. on June 30. By 1:00 p.m., Kautz, who had paused at Spring Hill, informed Grant and Meade that his hungry, exhausted troops required two or three days of rest and reorganization. Meade left it up to Kautz to determine whether his men could help Wilson. Kautz's column resumed its path toward Butler's lines.

By 3:00 p.m. Sheridan had arrived at Jerusalem Plank Road's crossing of Warwick Swamp. That still left seven miles between Little Phil and Reams Station. Wright received word that Sheridan's jaded horses could not arrive at Reams until dark.[155] At 3:30 p.m., the VI Corps commander decided that no prospect of helping Wilson existed and elected to return to the Army of the Potomac. Besides ripping up several miles of track and breaking several bridges, VI Corps had wrecked Reams Station again, burning the depot and ruining a big lot of railroad iron stockpiled there. "When we left nothing remained but smoking ruins, trampled fields and a rail road useless for some days," noted Rhodes. He considered the "great destruction" inflicted by his comrades "the penalty that Virginia must pay for treason."[156]

First Sergeant Graham of the 10th Vermont remembered, "we builded fine brest works and had plenty of boards."[157] The boards came from the village's buildings.

By this time Little Phil's van had plodded a mile and a half beyond the plank road crossing of Warwick Swamp. Wright, learning of this soon afterward, suspended his departure from Reams Station to await Sheridan's arrival. The two major generals consulted and agreed that they could not assist Wilson. Little

154 "Surely it cannot be imagined that Sheridan had had enough of Hampton, or that he wanted to be 'counted out' of another 'free fight' with his old antagonist," wrote Wilson sardonically. Wilson, *Under the Old Flag*, 1:518. Sheridan attributed his slow progress to insufficiently clear orders from Meade, lack of forage, lack of preparation, and worn-out horses. Ibid., 562; Sheridan, *Memoirs* 1:440–445. The army's quartermaster contradicts Sheridan about lack of forage. *OR* 40, 2:562–563. Meade's orders directing Sheridan to Reams Station are clear, and Sheridan cannot have failed to understand them. Ibid., 493–494, 507, 510–512.

155 Sheridan's mounts, which had rested for at least three days while they waited for his trains to cross the James, could hardly have been more worn out than Hampton's. Wilson, *Under the Old Flag*, 1:488–491.

156 Rhodes, ed., *All for the Union*, 158.

157 Graham Diary, June 30, 1864. These were the breastworks expanded by II Corps at the second battle of Reams Station in August. Horn, *The Siege of Petersburg*, 220.

Phil consequently ordered his horsemen back to the Warwick Swamp crossing of the plank road and Wright commenced his withdrawal. The head of Wright's column reached Jerusalem Plank Road at 7:25 p.m. and halted while an officer reconnoitered the way to Warwick Swamp.

At 9:00 p.m., Meade instructed Sheridan to pursue Hampton and rescue Wilson. At 9:45 p.m., the commander of the Army of the Potomac directed Wright to stay put and support Little Phil. Night having fallen, Meade's subordinates left compliance with his order until the following day.

Sheridan's defeat at Trevilian Station, Hunter's fizzle at Lynchburg, the fiascoes on the Weldon Railroad, Sherman's repulse at Kennesaw Mountain, the entrapment of Wilson and Kautz at Reams Station—reverse after reverse told on Grant. He visited the Petersburg front that day unaccompanied by Rawlins, who served as the general-in-chief's guardian angel as well as his chief of staff. "I learn from one of his staff he deviated from the only path he should ever travel by taking a glass of liquor," wrote Rawlins. "It is the first time I have failed to accompany him to Petersburg, and it was with misgivings I did so. Nothing but indisposition induced me to remain behind. I shall hereafter, under no circumstances, fail to accompany him."[158]

* * *

That day Griffin's cavalry friends occupied themselves guarding their prisoners. "I concluded to go down to the Stage Road and try my hand alone at capturing other straggling Northerners who might be passing along or near this road," he remembered. Halfway to the road, he heard the "clank of sabres and carbines" and saw three bluecoats approaching on horseback on the road. Keeping an old roadside barn between himself and the riders, he ran to the barn. When the Federals reached the barn, Griffin stepped out from behind it, leveled his rifle, and demanded their surrender.

"We surrender," they said.

He ordered them to dismount and stack arms. The riders complied, asking him not to shoot them. "This, of course, I told them I would not do," he recalled. "One of them was white, the other two were very black negroes mounted on mules,

158 Wilson, *The Life of John A. Rawlins*, 239. Wilson called Rawlins the general-in-chief's "inseparable counselor and ever-vigilant guardian." Ibid. For the disputed details of Grant's drinking on this occasion, see Edward G. Longacre, *Army of Amateurs: General Benjamin F. Butler and the Army of the James, 1863–1865* (Mechanicsburg, PA, 1997), 176–181; Ron Chernow, *Grant* (New York, 2017), 422–424; Allen J. Ottens, *General John A. Rawlins, No Ordinary Man* (Bloomington, IN, 2022), 384–388.

"Kautz's Cavalry coming back to camp in Gen Butlers lines after their raid" (June 23, 1864), by William Waud. *Library of Congress*

who, although in full uniform and armed and equipped as regular soldiers, claimed to be only servants who waited on officers." Griffin marched them to his home.

"On my way home I took quite a fancy to the white prisoner," who was about 18 years old, "very intelligent and evidently a gentleman," Griffin recalled. At his house he put the black prisoners in Cross's charge and sent them to the camp where the other prisoners were under guard. Griffin took into his house the White prisoner, "gave him a drink and something to eat, for which he was very thankful." The lad, Cpl. Nelson E. Evans, belonged to the 8th New York's Company F and had resided in New York City, where his father was a merchant. After introducing Evans to Mrs. Griffin, the Virginian gave the prisoner a hat to replace the one he had lost and took him to the prisoner camp.[159]

* * *

As Early's infantry passed through New Market in the Shenandoah Valley and Bushrod Johnson's division was digging a retrenched cavalier behind Pegram's Salient at Petersburg, Finegan's and Sanders's brigades arrived at the city from

159 Griffin, "Life in Dinwiddie County in the vicinity of the opposing armies of the war," 11–12.

Reams Station. Mahone humiliated his captured foes. He made prisoners carry the infants and small children of the escaped slaves to the Provost Marshal's office in Petersburg. "I remember we had some four or five hundred negroes, men, women and children, that the enemy had collected in Southern Virginia and we had a great deal of sport that night in putting the negro babies in the arms of the Federal prisoners," wrote the Alabama Brigade's Clark.[160]

By this time, Lee had fully recovered from the funk in which he had arrived at Petersburg.[161] At 11:00 p.m., Lieutenant Phillips of the Petersburg Regiment in Weisiger's brigade finished the picket duty he had begun the previous day and returned to the Dimmock Line. He rejoined the rest of the brigade, which had spent the day guarding foragers' wagons near Globe Tavern. "Came in got orders to move at 2 o'clock next morning," Phillips noted.[162]

Ten other brigades of Southern foot soldiers had similar orders, as well as a division of Confederate cavalry. Something big was afoot.

* * *

Wilson, turning eastward, arrived within two miles of Jarratt's Station on the Weldon Railroad at 2:00 a.m. on June 30. His column stopped to rest and wait for a guide. At daylight, a strong advance guard of the 1st New Hampshire Cavalry dismounted and drove off Confederate pickets at the station. Wilson's column passed through Jarratt's Station and continued eastward along a wood road toward Peter's Bridge on the Nottoway. This route took the Federals through a country untouched by war and provided plentiful food and forage. Fitzhugh Lee's troopers resumed their pursuit but found themselves 12 miles behind the bluecoats.

At 9:00 a.m., Hampton finally received word from Fitzhugh Lee that he was pursuing the Federals across the Nottoway at Double Bridges toward Jarratt's

160 Clark, *A Glance Backward*, 56–57.

161 A note dated "June—1864" addressed from Lee possibly to A. P. Hill appears among messages of June 30 at *OR* 40, 2:702–703. The note includes the language, "The time has arrived, in my opinion, when something more is necessary than adhering to lines and defensive positions. We shall be obliged to go out and prevent the enemy from selecting such positions as he chooses. If he is allowed to continue that course we shall at last be obliged to take refuge behind the works of Richmond and stand a siege, which would be but a work of time. You must be prepared to fight him in the field." The note also appears undated between letters for May 31 and June 1 in Clifford Dowdey and Louis H. Manarin, eds., *The Wartime Papers of Robert E. Lee* (Boston, 1961), 759–760. The note refers to a message from A. P. Hill to Lee at 11:00 a.m. in June 1864 but no such note appears in *OR*. *OR* 36, 2:862–903; 51, 2:976–1029. Dowdey and Manarin have it right because the time for taking refuge behind the works of Richmond passed when Grant crossed the James; Lee had by this time taken refuge behind the works of Petersburg.

162 Phillips Diary, June 30, 1864.

Station and wanted Hampton to occupy that point. Hampton moved immediately but five miles from Jarratt's Station encountered scouts who reported that the Unionists had passed through at daylight. He attempted to intercept them by going to the road to Peter's Bridge, but when he reached that road he learned that the rear of the Yankee column had passed by two hours earlier.

Hampton gave up his pursuit about the same time as Wilson's column reached Peter's Bridge. Fitzhugh Lee, who had passed Jarratt's Station, returned to that point. He entrained his black prisoners for Hicksford and his White captives for Weldon, then encamped with his men at Jarratt's Landing, a couple miles northwest of Jarratt's Station.

Wilson found Peter's Bridge burned and used Peter's Ford. "Some of the mounted men carried double and others sent their horses back to bring over the footmen," Ide recalled.[163] While waiting for his men to ford the river, Wilson made his first diary entry since June 24.

His column resumed its trek around 6:30 p.m., now heading toward Blunt's Bridge on the Blackwater. This march, through an "unbroken forest" with "almost impenetrable underbrush," proved exceedingly trying and exasperating. "The roads were obscure and difficult to follow, and consequently our progress was slow," Wilson remembered. "The columns halted frequently and, as soon as halted, the troopers would fall asleep in their saddles, and in the blackness of the forest it was always difficult to find where the halt had occurred or to learn what caused it."[164]

* * *

Laggard individuals and groups from Kautz's column straggled into the Army of the Potomac's lines on June 30. First Sergeant Chester and his companions rode into those lines on rustled horses that afternoon.

Others did not make it. Late on the afternoon of June 30, a black man and woman arrived at the Malone house. They occupied one of the rooms. The man told Mrs. Malone in what she considered "the most insulting manner" that he was going out and wanted a meal ready when he returned.[165] Major Breathed, lying in a bed on the first floor, overheard the African American. Crawling out

163 Hoffman, *First Vermont Cavalry Volunteers*, 191.

164 Wilson, *Under the Old Flag*, 1:473.

165 H. H. Matthews, "Pelham-Breathed Battery, Part XVII, Expedition of Gens. Wilson and Kautz Against the Richmond and Weldon Railroad." For an explanation of why Breathed killed the man, see David P. Bridges, *Fighting with Jeb Stuart: Major James Breathed and the Confederate Horse Artillery* (Arlington, VA, 2006), 257–258.

of bed, the major picked up his pistol and shot the man, who fell dead at the left entrance to the porch.

The raiders lost at least another 113 troopers that day—one killed, four wounded, and 108 captured, deserted, or missing.[166]

June 30 also saw the death of George Baylor's horse Bonaparte near Stony Creek Station. The Wilson-Kautz Raid resulted in the demise of many an equine, but nobody mourned his mount as eloquently as Baylor:

> Dear Bony! How many sad memories cluster around you. You had borne my father, when he received his wound at McGaheysville. You were the companion of my brother until his life-blood was shed at Parker's Store, and now the fatal blow has fallen on you. If beyond this vail there are pleasant fields and never-failing streams for the faithful friend and companion of man, I feel assured, noble steed, thou art feeding there. The lords of creation can bow to thee! All thy years were spent for others, and thy duty was discharged with fidelity and cheerfulness. Mankind may imitate thee and desire no greater boon than to deserve the praise that is thy due.[167]

News of the fight at Reams Station reached Richmond that day. "Our people are made wild with joy to-day, upon hearing of the capture of a whole brigade of the raiders on the south side, the same that have been tearing up the Danville Road," wrote John Beauchamp Jones, a clerk in the Confederate War Department.[168]

* * *

Wilson's column reached Blunt's Bridge just after midnight on July 1. "[I]nstead of finding a passable bridge, I found the burned and blackened ruins of one, and, instead of a ford, a river apparently wide and deep enough to float the *Great Eastern*," remembered Wilson. "It was a dark and dismal scene in the midst of

166 The contingent of the 2nd Ohio Cavalry in Wilson's column had one captured. Roster Commission, *Official Roster of the Soldiers of the State of Ohio*, 11:59. The contingent of the 5th New York Cavalry lost two wounded, 67 missing. RG 94, Entry 652, Box 38. The 2nd New York Cavalry had 19 missing. Ibid., Box 37. The 1st New Hampshire Cavalry lost one wounded, seven captured, and 10 missing. New Hampshire, Adjutant General, *Report of the Adjutant General of the State of New Hampshire*, 2:564–599, *passim*. The 1st Vermont Cavalry had one captured, one missing, and one deserter. Vermont, Adjutant General, *Revised Roster of Vermont Volunteers*, 249, 251, 259. The 3rd Indiana Cavalry lost one wounded and one captured. Goecker, *Hoosier Spies and Horse Marines*, 195, 256. A contingent of the 1st District of Columbia Cavalry had one killed. RG 94, Entry 652, Box 3.

167 Baylor, *Bull Run to Bull Run*, 230–231.

168 J. B. Jones, *A Rebel War Clerk's Diary at the Confederate States Capital*, 2 vols. (Philadelphia, 1866), 2:240.

a river bottom crowded with forest trees clad with festoons of black hanging moss and resounding with the hooting of distant owls and the baying of distant dogs."[169]

Ide sat down in the road holding his horse and dozed. "I would have given $500 if I had it, for the privilege of laying down on the ground and sleeping as long as I wanted to, but this would, most likely, have resulted in a trip to Andersonville," he recalled.[170] A few Confederate cavalrymen were still trailing the column to gobble up stragglers.

Only the bridge's center trestle remained standing. Around it the Federals cobbled together in less than an hour a structure employing a pair of string pieces, one of them half burned through, four young pine trees, some fence rails, and a few pine boughs. "The column started across dismounted, each man leading his horse by the light of fence-rail fires at the ends of the bridge, but only one or two squadrons had got over when the burned stringer gave way and toppled the passing column into the river twelve or fifteen feet below," Wilson recalled, remembering that the men and horses struggled "in water as black as the Styx."[171]

An engineer, the Illinoisan oversaw the bridge's reconstruction. A trooper of the 3rd Indiana Cavalry remembered that Wilson "handled rails and timber as though he had taken lessons in the art under the 'Old Rail Splitter' Father Abe."[172] It took less than 30 minutes more to repair the structure with another tree. The column got moving again.

The bulk of Wilson's command had crossed by daylight on July 1. With the 1st Vermont Cavalry crossed Captain Cummings, who despite his wound had hitched his horse to a carriage, ridden until the carriage broke down, and taken to his horse again.

Wilson kept a rear guard on the other side of the Blackwater until after sunup on that bright, hot day to allow the passage of stragglers. "[J]ust as the enemy made his appearance at 6:15, I personally set fire to a pile of dried leaves and pine fence rails which I had got ready under the bridge while the column was crossing, and almost instantly had the pleasure of seeing the improvised structure, wrapped in a cloud of smoke, burning like a bonfire," the Illinoisan recalled.

A Secessionist officer approached the blazing bridge.

169 Wilson, *Under the Old Flag*, 1:474. The *Great Eastern* was the biggest ship ever built as of its maiden voyage in 1860 and for many years afterward. "SS Great Eastern," worldhistory.org. Retrieved Aug. 25, 2023.

170 Hoffman, *First Vermont Cavalry Volunteers*, 191.

171 Wilson, *Under the Old Flag*, 1:475.

172 Goecker, *Hoosier Spies and Horse Marines*, 136.

"Goodby, boys, I am sorry to see you safely over," he said.[173]

At 7:00 a.m. Wilson notified Meade that his cavalrymen, many of them without mounts, would come in that night. When the message reached the Great Peppery around 5:00 p.m., he recalled VI Corps and Sheridan, who had reconnoitered toward Stony Creek Station. The commander of the Army of the Potomac directed Sheridan to withdraw to Prince George Court House, reorganize, and refit after leaving a brigade to picket the Army of the Potomac's left. Wright received instructions to return to his former position on the left of the army group. Private Fisk of the 2nd Vermont remembered of that day's hike, "we only marched about five miles, but in that five miles there were several cases of sunstroke, it being so extremely warm that marching was almost impossible."[174] The commander of the Army of the Potomac shifted Gibbon's division to the left of II Corps and Ferrero's division of IX Corps to the old Norfolk road's crossing of the Blackwater.

Wilson's column, after resting at the Blackwater, reached Union lines at 1:00 p.m. on Chippokes Creek, about halfway between the Blackwater and Lighthouse Point. His troopers pitched a temporary camp at Cabin Point. Sergeant Burnham observed, "an awful worn and tiered lot of men our horses all tiered out Gen Willsons Division are a sorry looking lot of men but we have got away from the Rebs a part of us our Division badly cut up about half mising."[175] Most of those lucky enough to ride horses or mules slept as they rode, and most of those on foot limped or staggered. Those fortunate enough to have their heads covered wore everything from a slouch hat to a lady's bonnet.

The play of Federal artillery on the railroad bridges at Petersburg that day gratified Grant, who mistakenly thought Early's Corps had returned to Lee's army group. The general-in-chief sounded out Halleck on packing off Butler, not a military professional, to a department where there were "no great battles to be fought, but a dissatisfied element to control." Grant thought that "the work done by Wilson and his cavalry is of great importance" and "that it will take the enemy several weeks to repair the damage done the South Side and Danville railroads."[176]

* * *

On July 1, Early's column passed through Winchester.

173 Wilson, *Under the Old Flag*, 1:476.

174 Emil Rosenblatt, et al., eds., *Hard Marching Every Day: The Civil War Letters of Private Wilbur Fisk, 1861–1865* (Lawrence, KS, 1992), 232.

175 Burnham Diary, July 1, 1864.

176 *OR* 40, 2:559–560.

Philip H. Sheridan
Library of Congress

In front of Kennesaw Mountain in Georgia, Sherman remained stymied by rain.

Led by Hill, Kershaw's division, Mahone's division, and Scales's and Thomas's brigades of Wilcox's division marched with artillery and some of Hampton's cavalry down the Weldon Railroad before dawn, looking for trouble. "We were soon satisfied that our destination was Reem's Station where we had learned the night before that a large force of the enemy were entrenching," recorded Pvt. George S. Bernard of the 12th Virginia's Company E, the Petersburg Riflemen, a lawyer who had enlisted twice and been wounded and captured at Crampton's Gap. The foray proved a fizzle. "Arriving within 2 miles of Reems, the Cavalry who had gone forward to reconnoiter reported to us that the enemy had left the place so we were ordered back to the entrenchments," Bernard noted.[177]

Weisiger's brigade and the rest of the column had tramped at least seven miles and now had to cover the same ground again, this time in the opposite direction. "The march out was not much, but the return was dreadful, being very hot and sultry and dusty besides," recorded Sergeant Sale of the 12th Virginia, who had formed part of the same picket detail on the previous day as Lieutenant Phillips. "Numbers of men fell by the side of the road totally exhausted," among them some who had never given out on the march before.[178] Ill and exhausted, Sale had to ride back to Petersburg in an ambulance.

* * *

That morning John Griffin readied the prisoners in his farm's camp to start for Dinwiddie Court House "for delivery to the proper authorities." His cavalry friends took charge of the prisoners and handed them over.[179]

177 George S. Bernard Diary, July 2, 1864, George S. Bernard Papers, Alderman Library, University of Virginia, Charlottesville, Virginia; see *OR* 40, 2:565, 585.

178 Sale Diary, June 30, 1864.

179 Griffin, "Life in Dinwiddie County in the vicinity of the opposing armies of the war," 12.

Chaplain Louis Napoleon Boudrye

Carte de visite *by Jordan H. Abbott of Albany, NY. Ronald S. Coddington Collection, Arlington, VA*

Hundreds of Federals straggled into Grant's lines over the following days. Corporal Wiswall's comrade, Pvt. William H. Hall of the 1st Vermont Cavalry's Company I, came in after three days in the woods. Private Smith's comrade who had donned blackface arrived after three or four days. Colonel Pope came in on the morning of July 4. Chaplain Boudrye with two comrades of the 5th New York Cavalry reached Union lines on the night of July 5. Many others failed to evade capture.

During the raid, Wilson and Kautz had traveled more than 300 miles and lost a total of about 352 killed and wounded, and around 1,169 missing or prisoners, for a total of approximately 1,521.[180] The Rebels opposite the raiders captured 16 guns, 30 wagons or ambulances, and thousands of horses and small arms. The Southerners suffered about 357 casualties.[181]

Time would tell whether the damage inflicted by the raiders would justify the losses they had endured.

180 Dyer, *Compendium*, 947. Subtracting the losses at The Grove, Staunton River Bridge, Sappony Church, and along the way suggests that the Federals lost around 1,000 killed, wounded, and missing at First Reams Station and during its aftermath. Bryce A. Suderow, "Confederate Casualties During the Wilson-Kautz Raid: June 22, July 2, 1864," *The Kepi* 4, no. 1 (Spring 1986): 45–46. The Federals also lost approximately 30 bridge breakers from the Iron Brigade as well as at least 19 killed or wounded and 20 prisoners from the detachment from Gregg's division. Epperson, "A secret sidebar to the Wilson-Kautz Raid," petersburgsiege.org.; Preston, *Tenth Regiment of Cavalry New York State Volunteers*, 604. See Table 5, Casualties During Various Clashes of the Wilson-Kautz Raid, June 22–July 1, 1864, *infra.*

181 During the Wilson-Kautz Raid, among the Confederate cavalry, Fitzhugh Lee's division (including Breathed's battery) suffered 22 casualties. Hewett, et al., eds., *Supplement to the Official Records*, 7:341. Hampton's division lost 22. *OR* 40, 1:809.

In W. H. F. Lee's division, Barringer's brigade had a total of 36 killed, wounded, and missing. See Chapter Three, ns. 24 and 50, *supra*, and this chapter, n. 147, *supra*. Chambliss's brigade had 34 casualties. See this chapter, n. 51, *supra*. Dearing's brigade lost 64. See Chapter Three, n. 50, *supra*. McGregor's battery had one casualty. Ibid. Graham's battery lost six. Ibid. Among the foot soldiers, Farinholt lost 47 men. See Chapter Three, n. 129, *supra*. Holcombe's Legion infantry had 33 casualties. See this chapter, n. 51, *supra*. In Mahone's division, Finegan's brigade lost 41. See this chapter, n. 147, *supra*. Sanders's brigade lost 51. Ibid.

Chapter Nine

"I Shall Try to Give the Army a Few Days' Rest"

GRANT'S SECOND offensive at Petersburg had ended. The second phase of what would become one of the longest sieges in the history of North America consumed two weeks from the evening of June 18 through July 1, 1864. Seven additional offensives would follow until Federal infantry finally broke through to the Appomattox above Petersburg on April 2, 1865, compelling the Confederates to evacuate Petersburg and Richmond.

Like Grant's first offensive of June 15–18 against the Cockade City, his second offensive failed. Unlike the first offensive, which captured the eastern face of the Dimmock Line and established his army group in a position which threatened Lee's communications and from which Lee could not drive the Federals, the second gained little significant ground besides the Deep Bottom bridgehead. Union infantry did not permanently sever the Weldon Railroad or even reach the South Side Rail Road. Federal cavalry inflicted minor permanent damage.

The second offensive numbered among the widest-ranging and most ambitious of Grant's offensives around the city, extending from White House Landing in the northeast to Staunton River Bridge in the southwest and aiming at the capture of Petersburg and Richmond. It ranked among the longest of his offensives around Petersburg, though not among the bloodiest. The Federals lost about 4,683 soldiers, and Confederate casualties numbered around 1,461.[1] Most of the troops

1 See Table 3: Federal Casualties at Jerusalem Plank Road, June 21–24, 1864, *infra*; Table 4: Confederate Casualties at the Battle of Jerusalem Plank Road, June 21–24, 1864, *infra*; Table 5, Casualties During the Various Clashes of the Wilson-Kautz Raid, June 22–July 1, 1864, *infra*; John

in the opposing army groups remained uncommitted and the numbers lost seem relatively small, but more than 3,300 bluecoats compared to about 350 butternuts became prisoners as good as dead for the rest of the campaign of 1864, in which captives only rarely escaped or were exchanged.[2] When wounded who would never return to the ranks and the dead are included, the Northern loss for the duration of 1864's campaign approached 4,000 soldiers while the Southerners lost about 700. Grant's army group could not afford casualties in those proportions for long.

Though the second offensive failed, some of the initiatives taken during the offensive affected the entire siege of Petersburg. The size or ambition of a given initiative bore little relationship to the dividends it paid.

The United States Military Railroad did a capital job of supplying Grant's armies south of the Appomattox. The bridgehead at Deep Bottom stuck a thorn in the side of the Confederates throughout the siege. Bringing the Petersburg bridges under fire with Federal siege artillery added critical hours to the time needed for the Secessionists to transfer troops and supplies from Petersburg to the north side of the James and back. The attempt to invest Petersburg from Jerusalem Plank Road to the Appomattox above the city failed completely. Grant and Wilson exaggerated the damage done by the Wilson-Kautz Raid, which put Rebel railroads out of action more briefly than they thought, though it modestly and permanently injured Southside labor, horseflesh, and *infra*structure. Differences among Grant, Meade, and Burnside over how to exploit the mine begun by IX Corps ensured that the mine would fail to end the siege of Petersburg.

Secessionist initiatives also yielded mixed results. The reopening of Battery Dantzler on June 21, in combination with the sinking of obstructions, closed Trent's Reach to the United States Navy for the balance of the siege. Mahone's attacks on June 22 and June 23 halted the Federal attempt to invest Petersburg from Jerusalem Plank Road to the Appomattox above the city. The June 24 attack near Hare House merely added to the list of Rebel casualties. The trap Hampton planned for the Wilson-Kautz raiders failed to annihilate them but inflicted heavy casualties. Despite skimpy available resources, the Confederates organized quickly and effectively to repair their damaged railroads in Virginia.

Horn, *The Petersburg Campaign: June 1864–April 1865* (Conshohocken, PA, 1993), 44–45. Grant's first offensive accounted for more than two thirds of the casualties for June 1864.

2 More than half the prisoners taken during the battles of Grant's second offensive may have perished in captivity and many others never recovered. Cross, *A Melancholy Affair on the Weldon Railroad*, 177 (25 Vermonters killed or mortally wounded on June 23 and 407 captured, of whom 226 died as prisoners).

"City Point, Virginia. Building storehouse and railroad depot." *Library of Congress*

City Point and the United States Military Railroad

The personnel of the United States Military Railroad Construction Corps reached City Point just as Grant's first offensive at Petersburg ended. These support troops soon turned City Point into one of North America's major ports by building wharves and warehouses for the unloading and storage of supplies for Grant's army group. George Templeton Strong, now in the Sanitary Commission charged with promoting clean and healthy conditions in Union army camps, described the bustle at City Point when he debarked there around 9 a.m. on July 1:

> The water swarming with transports, hospital boats, tugs, gunboats, light steamers and all manner of river craft. Land in a scene of matchless dust confusion (apparent at least) & activity. They are repairing the R.R. Wagon trains are moving every way, gangs of contrabands following mounted leaders, who

> carry remarkably long riding whips, (*honi soit qui mal y pense*), docks are being built, officers riding about, the usual nebula of stragglers, disabled men & army followers in all pervading. Everyone desperately in earnest about something. The shore is lined three deep, yes six deep with barges, steamers are screeching, corrals of mules braying, but I can do no justice to the sights & sounds of the place.[3]

Virtually all the supplies for Grant's army group had to come from Northern ports by sea and then up James River. Preparing City Point lest the Confederates temporarily blockade the James made sense even though the Federals had sunk obstructions in Trent's Reach. Union shore batteries covered the obstructions, the US Navy usually had as many monitors on the river as the Secessionists had ironclads at Richmond, and the monitors packed much more punch than the ironclads. No blockade of City Point ever materialized, though Secessionist horse artillery would occasionally harass merchant shipping along the river.

By the end of the second offensive, the Construction Corps was well on its way to rebuilding the City Point Railroad in the combat zone as the City Point & Army Line. The corps reconstructed broken bridges, replaced rotten ties, substituted Northern T-rails for Southern U-rails and narrowed the gauge from five feet to four feet eight inches to accommodate Federal locomotives and cars. By July 5, construction crews had the railroad in running order for seven miles out of City Point. On July 7, when a convoy of 90 steamers, tugs, and barges delivered 24 locomotives and 275 cars, regular trains began operating. The well-organized transportation system and logistical apparatus established by the United States Military Railroad Construction Corps contributed significantly to Grant's ultimate victory over Lee at the siege of Petersburg.

Seizing a Bridgehead Across the James

Grant sought a bridgehead over the James to menace Richmond and thereby distract Confederate attention from the Southside. He fully achieved his goal. The bridgehead at Deep Bottom would allow the general-in-chief to attack first on the north bank of the James, drawing enemy troops there from Petersburg, then strike Southside and bring troops back from north of the James to strengthen his grip on any gains made by the Southside assault. Grant did not attempt this maneuver in his second offensive and would fail to exploit it in his third offensive in July, but in August during his fourth offensive he would employ it successfully

3 George Templeton Strong Diary, 4 vols., July 1, 1864, New York Historical Society Museum and Library, New York, NY. "*Honi soit qui mal y pense*" means "shame on him who thinks ill of it." thoughtco.com. Retrieved Jan. 30, 2024.

"Trestle Work (no. 2) on City Point & Army R.R." *Library of Congress*

to cut the Weldon Railroad permanently in his fourth offensive, and in September he would utilize it after capturing Fort Harrison north of the James to advance westward from the Weldon Railroad to Squirrel Level Road in his fifth offensive. He achieved these gains with much smaller numerical advantages over Lee than during the second offensive.[4] The territory seized by the Federals north of the James in September would help stretch Confederate lines to the breaking point on April 2, 1865.

Bringing the Bridges Over the Appomattox Under Fire

There were six Confederate bridges over the Appomattox at Petersburg. The farthest east, a pontoon bridge, spanned the river from Blandford Southside to the east side of Pocahontas on the left bank. About a quarter mile upstream, the 1863 railroad bridge crossed the river from the foot of Petersburg's 5th Street to the center of Pocahontas. Around another quarter mile westward, the Richmond

4 Grant had about 110,218 effectives at June's end (*OR* 40, 2:542, 552) and around 79,053 effectives at the beginning of August (Ibid., 3:728, 737) after the departure of the VI and XIX corps and two cavalry divisions, versus Lee's approximately 56,959 effectives at the end of June (Ibid., 2:640, 707) and roughly 50,519 effectives at August's beginning (Ibid., 3:761–762, 822) after the departure of Kershaw's and Fitzhugh Lee's divisions. Grant had around 81,629 effectives at September's end (Ibid., 42, 2:1150) versus Lee's roughly 47,522 effectives going into the late September-early October fighting (Ibid., 1243–1244, 1266–1267).

"Pontoon bridge at Deep Bottom, James River, Va." *Library of Congress*

& Petersburg Railroad used the Manchester & Petersburg Turnpike Company's Pocahontas Bridge to transport freight and passengers across the Appomattox from Petersburg's 2nd Street to the west side of Pocahontas. The Federals brought these three bridges under fire, making them too dangerous for rail traffic and negotiable by horse or on foot only at night.

Bringing the bridges over the Appomattox under fire forced the Secessionists to shift freight traffic, civilian traffic, and daytime troop traffic to two of the three bridges farther west. The first of the three, the railroad bridge to the South Side Rail Road's shops, crossed the river approximately another quarter mile westward, at Flea Island. This bridge did not help the Southerners with the displaced traffic because its tracks did not connect to or even approach any road or rail line north of the Appomattox, and without a floor beneath its ties it could not carry horse or foot traffic.

The first bridge capable of carrying the displaced traffic stood about half a mile westward, just east of Merchant's Island. Named Campbell's Bridge, it crossed from Petersburg's Fleet Street to the east side of Ettrick, where many employees of the cotton and flour mills surrounding Campbell's Bridge lived. About another half mile westward, the Battersea pontoon bridge spanned the Appomattox just west of Merchant's Island from the Cockade City's West Street to the west side of Ettrick. Campbell's Bridge and the Battersea pontoon bridge carried all the traffic the Union guns displaced from the three eastern bridges.

Crossing by way of the two bridges farthest west delayed Confederate troop and supply movements between Petersburg, the Howlett Line, Richmond, and the Confederate lines on the north bank of the James. Troops had to entrain or detrain

"Effects of shot and shell on the north side of Petersburgh, (i.e. Petersburg), Va. Bollingbrook St. View of Dunlop House." *Library of Congress*

and bulk had to be broken between Dunlop's Station about three miles north of the Appomattox and Campbell's Bridge more than three quarters of a mile to the west of the Richmond & Petersburg. This detour slowed Lee's responses to Grant's shifting of men in and out of the Deep Bottom bridgehead.

Not only the Petersburg bridges came under fire. Field artillery had been firing on the city since June 17. The shelling drove westward or entirely out of town most of Petersburg's inhabitants and installations such as hospitals. The bombardment created bitter feelings. Though Federal ordnance had hurt very few citizens as of June 26, Pvt. John R. Turner of the Petersburg Regiment's Company E wrote that day, "I hope that our Government will execute an officer (Yankee) for every citizen who is wounded by their shells."[5]

5 Letter, John R. Turner to _____, June 26, 1864, John R. Turner Letters, Duke University.

The combination of the Deep Bottom bridgehead and bringing the Appomattox bridges under fire contributed significantly to the ultimate success of the siege of Petersburg. The Union artillery's fire against the bridges ensured that on April 2, 1865, butternut reinforcements from the Howlett Line arrived Southside too late to strengthen the Confederate fortifications along Boydton Plank Road.

Investing Petersburg from River Above to River Below

The siege of Petersburg resembled the Vicksburg campaign in that both took many months. They differed in that Grant spent most of the time in the Vicksburg campaign approaching his objective to invest it, whereas during the siege of Petersburg he spent most of his time attempting to extend his investment of Petersburg to the Appomattox above the city. His biggest and most ambitious initiative in late June 1864, his attempt to invest Petersburg from Jerusalem Plank Road to the Appomattox above the city, came to practically nothing. In the shift westward of the Army of the Potomac to accomplish this goal, that army occupied the site of the future Fort Sedgwick, also known as Fort Hell, on the east side of Jerusalem Plank Road. Gaining this position did not require fighting, because Lee did not defend the plank road.

Three attempts to extend the investment of Petersburg from Jerusalem Plank Road to the Appomattox above the city failed on three successive days—June 21, 22, and 23. On June 21, Barringer's brigade ambushed and stopped the advance of Barlow's division. On June 22, Mahone with three brigades from his division routed seven brigades of the crack II Corps; with a fourth brigade, Mahone withstood a counterattack by additional Federal forces. On June 23, his division mauled a brigade of VI Corps.

The Army of the Potomac seized some ground west of the plank road within striking distance of the Weldon Railroad. That railway resumed running even before Early's July threat to Washington forced Grant to part with VI Corps, XIX Corps, and two cavalry divisions, which required him to draw his left back to Jerusalem Plank Road. This was the only time that Grant gave up ground during the siege. Lee had regarded the Weldon Railroad as indefensible as soon as he arrived at Petersburg though he defended it successfully until mid-August.

The rout of June 22 set bounds on Federal army maneuvers just as effectively as Battery Dantzler and the obstructions in Trent's Reach limited naval movements on James River. Grant and Meade would not attempt an advance westward so close to the Dimmock Line again. The Federals would move forward more than a mile farther out from the Confederate fortifications than the advance smashed on June 22. Having to cover more ground—and more difficult ground such as the toils of

Hatchers Run and its tributaries—greatly increased the difficulty of enveloping Petersburg from the Appomattox below the city to the Appomattox above.

Sending the Cavalry on a Raid

The Wilson-Kautz Raid had two purposes. One goal of the raid was to avoid another Chickamauga should the Federal infantry complete the investment of Petersburg from the river below the city to the river above.[6] After the fall of Chattanooga, the Southerners had dispatched substantial reinforcements from Lee's army. These reinforcements had detrained near the Chickamauga battlefield and contributed to a Southern victory there. The destruction of Burkeville would make it impossible for Secessionist reinforcements from the west or south to debark near the great battle that Humphreys thought would have to take place if Grant's troops cut the South Side Rail Road. The Wilson-Kautz Raid achieved this goal.

Grant also thought that cutting the railroads to the south and west of Petersburg while Hunter and Sheridan severed the Virginia Central to the northwest would force the Confederates to abandon Petersburg and Richmond for want of provisions. The Wilson-Kautz Raid failed to achieve this goal. The raid did not inflict enough damage on the railroads connecting Richmond to the Deep South.

The raiders did some damage. They destroyed three locomotives and more than 35 cars. They burned sawmills, grist mills, blacksmith shops, warehouses, water tanks, turn-tables, trestles, and miles of strap rail. They destroyed stores of grain, tobacco, and cotton. They liberated slaves and horses, hindering the harvest of ripening crops. Labor and transportation disruptions caused by the raiders and other Union forces in Virginia doubled the price of wheat in Richmond.[7] Pillaging of businesses, theft from private citizens, house robberies, and rapes terrorized the countryside.[8] Like the shelling of Petersburg, the depredations of the raiders left bitter feelings. "The War has now assumed that phase in which no mercy can be shown to the enemy," Col. Josiah Gorgas, the Pennsylvania-born, West Point-educated, Mexican War veteran who headed the Confederate ordnance department recorded on July 7. "He burns, robs, murders and ravishes, and this is to be met only by killing all."[9]

6 Grant, *Memoirs*, 2:313.

7 Mary Curtis Burgess, "A True Story," 36, Elizabeth Cocke Coles Collection, Library of the University of Virginia, Charlottesville, VA.

8 Eanes, *Destroy the Junction*, 164.

9 Frank E. Vandiver, ed., *The Civil War Diary of Josiah Gorgas* (Tuscaloosa, AL, 1947), 124.

Permanent results to the rails proved meager. Grant's Bureau of Military information knew that the Secessionists had to send away some of the surplus slave population by June 28, but full rations were generally issued throughout the brief period the railroads remained inoperable except for half rations of corn for the cavalry provided by wagon trains from Stony Creek Station.[10] Repair crews had reopened the Virginia Central to within four miles of Staunton by June 30.[11] Soldiers of VI Corps found the Weldon Railroad at Reams Station already repaired that day.

The South Side Rail Road, with ties burned but rails little damaged, was running from Burkeville to Petersburg in a limited fashion as early as July 3. Private William Henry Harris of the 18th Virginia Infantry in the Howlett Line wrote that day, "[T]he railroad has been cut but it is running again." The South Side railway announced on July 4 the limited terms on which it would accept freight.[12]

The Weldon Railroad resumed operation yet again July 9 after the damage done by VI Corps. Wagons began covering the last gap in the tracks of the Richmond & Danville July 10. On July 13, the 3rd Georgia's Private Spencer in the Dimmock Line wrote, "[T]he railroad communication is now about established." Civilians near Weldon were receiving mail from Petersburg and Richmond by July 14.[13]

The Richmond & Danville closed the gap in its tracks by July 15. Soldiers in the 16th Mississippi in the Dimmock Line were receiving letters from home dated July 1 as soon as July 19. Private Jerome B. Yates of the 16th's Company C wrote that on July 29, "[S]even trains of cars come into Petersburg loaded with blockade goods." On August 6, Spencer expressed his disgust with "cornbread and blockade bacon" because he had received a box of luxuries from Georgia.[14]

10 *OR* 40, 2:496, 3:38; Dowdey and Manarin, eds., *The Wartime Papers of Robert E. Lee*, 811.

11 *OR* 40, 2:697-698.

12 "Raid on the Danville Railroad," *Daily Richmond Dispatch*, June 25, 1864 ("We are informed that the sills were burnt, but that the rails were not much damaged."); Eanes, *Destroy the Junction*, 168, n. 22, 207 n. 22; H. D. Baird, Genl. Supt., Office, So Side R Road Co., Petersburg, July 4, 1864, War Department Collection of Confederate Records, RG 109, csa-railroads.com, retrieved June 19, 2024.

13 *OR* 40, 3:98; Quartermaster General's Letters Received Register, July 8, 1864, RG 109, csa. railroads.com, retrieved June 19, 2024; The Confederate States to Chas E Colby, July 10, 1864, RG 109 (This message disproves the report of the deserter to the Bureau of Military Information that trains were passing from Danville to Petersburg as early as July 5 [*OR* 40, 3:38]), csa-railroads.com, retrieved June 19, 2024; Wiggins, ed., *My Dear Friend*, 132; Beth Gilbert Crabtree and James W. Patton, eds., "Journal of a Secesh Lady," *The Diary of Catherine Ann Devereux Edmonston, 1860–1866* (Raleigh, 1979), 589.

14 Robert G. Evans, ed., *The 16th Mississippi Infantry: Civil War Letters and Reminiscences* (Jackson, MS, 2002), 275; Ibid., 281; Wiggins, ed., *My Dear Friend*, 133.

Passenger service resumed on the entire length of the Richmond & Danville August 9. Confederate crews had replaced the strap rail with heavy T-rails scavenged from the York River railway and from the Atlantic, Tennessee and Ohio Railroad, leaving the Richmond & Danville in better condition than before the raid. The Southerners replaced the depots burnt in the raids with temporary structures permitting the transaction of business.[15]

The Wilson-Kautz Raid ended in disaster because Union infantry failed to complete the investment of Petersburg from the Appomattox below the city to the river above and Sheridan failed to divert Hampton—conditions on which the raid was premised. The failures of the foot soldiers and Little Phil negated the modest success of the raiders.

If Humphreys had supplied Wilson with the facts available on the evening of June 21—the failure of II Corps to reach the Weldon Railroad that day and the improbability of Sheridan crossing the James at Deep Bottom, Wilson might well have decided to proceed to New Berne rather than back to the Army of the Potomac. "If we had gone on and come into our lines in N. Carolina, we should have been all right," complained Second Lieutenant Comins of the 1st District of Columbia Cavalry.[16]

Even if Wilson had decided to return to the Army of the Potomac, he might still have provided himself with a margin of safety. First, he could have tried to ride directly back to Prince George Court House through Jarratt's Station instead of through Sappony Church. Secondly, even if he attempted to proceed through Sappony Church, he might have reversed course once he found his way blocked and returned to the Army of the Potomac by way of Jarratt's Station rather than through Reams Station. Either riding straight to North Carolina, going back to the Army of the Potomac directly through Jarratt's Station, or turning back from Sappony Church and then proceeding through Jarratt's Station would probably have spared his force about a thousand casualties.

Wilson was always looking for evidence of his raid's effectiveness to mitigate its disastrous end at First Reams Station. After the war, Brig. Gen. Isaac M. St. John of the Confederate Nitre and Mining Bureau may have been humoring Wilson by telling him that the Wilson-Kautz Raid inflicted, "the heaviest blow of the kind that ever befell the Confederacy till Appomattox wiped it out forever," as Wilson

15 "Resumption of an Evening Train," *Daily Richmond Dispatch*, Aug. 9, 1864, p. 1, col. 5; *Augusta* (GA) *Daily Constitutionalist*, Aug. 11, 1864, csa-railroads.com, retrieved June 19, 2024; "The Damage to the Richmond & Danville Railroad," *Macon Daily Telegraph*, July 11, 1864, p. 2, col. 2 (The article refers to the Atlantic, Tennessee and Ohio as the "Charlotte and Statesville Road"); Eanes, *Destroy the Junction*, 165–166.

16 Letter, L. M. Comins to "My dear wife," July 1, 1864, Leander M. Comins Letters.

recalled. "[St. John] added that with all the resources at his command it was nine weeks, or sixty-three days, before a train from the south ran into Petersburg on either road."[17]

Perhaps St. John was referring to the arrival of the first Nitre and Mining Bureau train in Petersburg. Maybe he was an unintended victim of Lee's campaign to deceive the enemy about the quick recovery of the South Side and Richmond & Danville railroads. Perhaps Wilson misunderstood or exaggerated what St. John had said. Maybe St. John shrank from displeasing Wilson with the unvarnished truth—that the Weldon Railroad was running within a week of the Wilson-Kautz Raid, the South Side railway was operating within two weeks, and the Richmond & Danville was running several weeks earlier than St. John reportedly related.

Soon after the return of the raiders, Confederate newspapers complained of their depredations. Meade stirred up lasting ill-feelings within the Federal command by demanding an explanation from Wilson. The raider's response mollified the commander of the Army of the Potomac, who let the matter drop.

Dig a Mine

The second offensive also saw the beginning of a remarkable excavation that would result in one of the bloodiest actions of the Petersburg siege. The mine that culminated in the battle of the Crater began not as a Grant initiative, but as an initiative of miners in a brigade of Potter's division, Burnside's corps. Meade had doubts about the placement of the mine and vacillated in his belief about whether it would succeed. Grant knew of the mine but had not learned or did not convey to Meade and Burnside the lesson of mine warfare at Vicksburg: mining was noisy, and an alert defender would respond by countermining and constructing lines in the rear to prevent penetration beyond the crater formed by the mine's explosion[18]

At the time of Grant's second offensive, the Federals were considering three strategies for taking Petersburg: direct assault, regular approaches, and extending their investment of Petersburg to sever Lee's communications. The failure of Grant's first offensive put a hold on direct assaults until the following April. The

17 Wilson, *Under the Old Flag*, 1:462–463. In a previous book I mistakenly accepted Wilson's account of the length of time the South Side and Richmond & Danville railroads were inoperable. Horn, *The Battles for the Weldon Railroad*, August 1864, 309.

18 At Vicksburg, "the attacking Union troops easily reached the mine crater but had difficulty passing beyond it." David G. Martin, *The Great Military Campaigns of the Civil War: The Vicksburg Campaign, April, 1862–July, 1863* (New York, 1990), 149–172. Martin concludes: "One would think he would have learned more from the lesson presented by the great mine at Vicksburg." Ibid., 171.

disaster on Jerusalem Plank Road stopped until mid-August the attempt to extend the investment of Petersburg to the Appomattox above the city.

A mine represented one type of regular approach. Meade had expected as early as June 17 to employ another type—sapping. This type of regular approach consisted of the besiegers using the time-consuming and laborious process of entrenchments to draw closer to the besieged. The Federals would dig a first parallel, run forward a zigzag trench or sap, and then dig a second parallel. This would take place under cover of fire from the besieger's heavy artillery, hence Meade's concern about his army's siege train—the army's big guns. Successive parallels would enable the Federals to advance work parties and artillery until the Confederates surrendered or the Federals could assault from an advantageous position.

Grant and Meade considered employing saps and parallels on Warren's front. If the Northerners occupied the high ground overlooking Petersburg, the Southerners might not have been able to hold the city. Union engineers evaluated the matter more pessimistically; the Confederates could fortify rearward as fast as the Northerners could advance mines, saps, and parallels.

The Secessionists had already commenced a retrenched cavalier behind Pegram's Salient, but they did not have unlimited space in which to retreat. Beauregard, trained at West Point as an engineer and distinguished as such in the Mexican War, thought regular approaches along City Point Road or Jerusalem Plank Road would have produced success in "a few weeks."[19] Lee, also trained as an engineer at West Point, likewise feared Unionist use of regular approaches.

Because the general-in-chief and the Great Peppery needed success quickly, they abandoned the idea of regular approaches after Early's raid drew VI and XIX corps away to Washington and Burnside's mine failed. Before much longer, due to Meade's fears for his army's left rear, instead of constructing regular approaches, the Northerners were expending labor to protect the Army of the Potomac's left rear with fortifications and roads; Hancock and Warren complained about the negative effect on drilling and morale.[20]

In the end, regular approaches played only a small role in the siege. Extending the investment of Petersburg to sever Lee's communications prevailed as the Federal strategy. Most of the siege's fighting took place on the flanks, though direct assault achieved decisive success for the bluecoats in their ninth and last offensive in April 1865. During the periods of inaction between offensives, trench warfare

19 "Notes of Genl. Beauregard on W. J. Marrin's Acct. of the explosion of the Federal Mine at Petersburg Va. July 30th 1864," July 17, 1876, Beauregard Papers, Abraham Lincoln Presidential Library, Springfield, IL.

20 *OR* 42, 2:778, 993–994.

Ulysses S. Grant

Library of Congress

with sniping and indirect fire akin to that of World War I prevailed along the established lines.

Southern Initiatives

The Southern army-navy operation of June 20–21 seemed a fiasco to Lieutenant Parker, but it imposed further limits on the operations of the US Navy on James River than the obstructions already sunk in Trent's Reach by the Federals. Just by reestablishing Battery Dantzler west of the obstructions, the Secessionists made even the eastern portion of Trent's Reach largely uninhabitable for Union ships—wooden or ironclad.

The Army Group Commanders

Resilience remained one of Grant's principal characteristics. He bounced back immediately from the failure of his initial attempt to take Petersburg by assault. He sensibly tried to avoid further attacks against fortifications. The first steps he took were sound—establishing the Deep Bottom bridgehead, bringing Petersburg's bridges under fire, taking defensive measures against a Confederate blockade of City Point. The haste with which he and Meade improvised the movement to extend their investment of Petersburg to the Appomattox above the city contributed to the movement's collapse. The idea that damage done mostly by cavalry to the railroads around Richmond and Petersburg could compel the abandonment of those cities for want of supplies proved overly optimistic. Losing track of Early's reinforced corps threatened to cost the Federals Washington and perhaps the war.

Lee arrived in Petersburg so flummoxed by his misjudgment of Grant at Spotsylvania and during the James crossing that the Confederate army group commander uncharacteristically declined Beauregard's suggestion for an attack on the vulnerable enemy left. The Virginian presciently began prodding his government to prepare for raids against his rail communications with the rest of the South. His government and the Virginia railway companies rapidly repaired the damage done by Grant's railroad raids. Despite his doubts about the defensibility of the Weldon and South Side railways, he defended them as ferociously as if they had been the Richmond & Danville. "It is touching a tiger's cubs to get on that road!" Lyman later wrote of the most vulnerable of the three, the Weldon railway. "They will not stand it."[21]

Lee revealed in his army's June 24 attack between the City Point Railroad and the Appomattox that he had failed to grasp the advantage that earthworks and the rifled musket gave the defense. As a result of his failure to learn, his attack on Fort Stedman the following March would end in disaster. The Rebel chieftain would have done well to limit himself to counterattacks in the open field such as those of June 22 and June 23, which inflicted heavy casualties at relatively low cost.

Grant and Lee underwent attitude adjustments during the 1864 campaign. They behaved more cautiously than before they had joined battle. Grant had entered the campaign considering Lee overrated. Lee had expected to understand Grant as well as Lee had understood Grant's failed predecessors.[22]

By deceiving Lee at the Mule Shoe and during the James crossing, Grant convinced the Southern chieftain that he finally faced a foe whose movements he could not predict. Lee entered Petersburg on June 18 in such a state that he uncharacteristically declined to counterattack the Union left as Beauregard suggested, though the Virginian's aggressiveness soon returned.

By contesting almost every inch of ground from the Rapidan to the Weldon Railroad, Lee disabused the Federal general-in-chief of the idea that he might operate with impunity. During the battle of Jerusalem Plank Road, Grant declined to cut loose from the City Point bridgehead with the Army of the Potomac to sever Lee's communications as Warren suggested. Grant claimed to want to fight Lee's army outside its entrenchments, which cutting loose would compel. Meade and Barnard persuaded Grant that such an operation would be too hazardous.[23]

Sherman, criticized for lack of a killer instinct, cut loose in late August 1864 from his bridgehead over the Chattahoochee River and forced the Confederates to abandon Atlanta. Unlike Grant, Sherman did not face Robert E. Lee and did

21 Agassiz, ed., *Meade's Headquarters*, 217.

22 Theodore A. Dodge, "Grant as a Soldier," in Theodore F. Dwight, ed., *Critical Sketches of Some of the Federal and Confederate Commanders, MHSM* 10:34–35; Douglas Southall Freeman, *R. E. Lee: A Biography*, 4 vols. (New York, 1935), 2:428.

23 *OR* 40, 1:26, 2:333–334, 477–478; Dodge, "Grant as a Soldier," *MHSM* 10:43; Porter, *Campaigning with Grant*, 155; *OR* 40, 2:333, 478–479.

Robert E. Lee

National Archives

not have a corps of enemy infantry unaccounted for and possibly poised to pounce on his flank or rear.[24]

The unknown location of Early's corps justified Grant's prudence. Early's actual location proved even more problematic. Grant chose the right course in not cutting loose.

Early's approach to Washington closed the window for cutting loose by drawing off troops necessary for the operation. The window did not reopen until the troops sent in response to Early's threat to the capital returned to Petersburg, but that was after Lincoln's reelection when it was unnecessary to take the risks attendant on cutting loose.[25]

The High Command

Lincoln thoughtlessly descended upon Grant during one of the most complex maneuvers of the war. The president's visit did not affect the second offensive.

24 Albert E. Castel, *Decision in the West: The Atlanta Campaign of 1864* (Lawrence, KS, 1991), 485–486, 563–565; Richard M. McMurry, *Atlanta 1864: Last Chance for the Confederacy* (Lincoln, NE, 2001), 169–171, 182–183.

Castel wrote, "Had Sherman been the one to have gone against Lee and the Army of Northern Virginia in the spring of 1864 (Meade, when Grant visited him in March of that year, assumed that Sherman would be given command of the Army of the Potomac), in all likelihood he would have cracked beneath their terrible hammer blows." Castel, *Decision in the West*, 564. McMurry wrote, "Neither of [Sherman's] opponents was an especially able general nor received the wholehearted support of his subordinates." McMurry, *Atlanta 1864*, 182. Fuller, no partisan of Lee, wrote that Grant was "faced not by a *Pemberton* or a *Bragg*, but by *Lee*, the most renowned general of the day, and to be confronted by a task which had broken McDowell, McClellan, Pope, Burnside, and Hooker, and which had halted Meade." Fuller, *The Generalship of U. S. Grant*, 281 (emphases in original). Fuller further wrote, "As a general, *Lee* must stand or fall by his last campaign; for . . . it was the most skillful, masterful and heroic he was ever engaged in." Ibid., 381 (emphasis in original).

25 *OR* 40, 3:35–36; Ibid., 42, 3:865–867, 891–892. Sir Basil Henry Liddell Hart, the apostle of the indirect approach, who championed Sherman over Grant, would probably in principle have approved of cutting loose at some point. B. H. Liddell Hart, *Strategy* (New York, 1991), 130–133.

Grant had already issued his orders and suggestions, and he never wrote or spoke of the matter. A lesser man might well have refused to see Lincoln or blamed the president for the offensive's failure. The Railsplitter nonetheless must have sensed that he had come at an inopportune moment. The next time he visited Petersburg was in March 1865 and he came in response to an invitation from Grant.[26]

Davis and his military advisor Bragg allowed their hatred for Beauregard to lead them into bickering with him about his brilliant and successful defense of Petersburg during Grant's first offensive. Their animus toward the Louisianian blinded them from employing the successful defender of Charleston, the victor of second Drewry's Bluff, and the successful defender of Petersburg against Butler (June 9) and Grant (June 15–18) in a capacity commensurate with his demonstrated ability. Davis and Bragg might have employed Beauregard to replace Gen. Joseph E. Johnston in command of the Confederate army defending Atlanta.[27]

Army Command

Meade's putting in reserve the tired, bloodied II Corps on June 20 was a good idea. His subsequent decision to use II Corps rather than the relatively fresh, unbloodied VI Corps to lead the extension of the investment of Petersburg from Jerusalem Plank Road to the river above the city amounted to personnel mismanagement.[28] His idea of advancing II and VI corps together improved on the original plan that he and Grant had made, but circumstances intervened; VI Corps could not pull out of the trenches on the morning of June 21 under the fire of the Confederate batteries on the north bank of the Appomattox and it was too late to recall II Corps. It ought to have occurred to Meade that the departure of Wilson and Kautz would draw off much of the Secessionist cavalry in the path of the Federal infantry; substantial portions of the Rebel horsemen had followed the Yankee cavalry to Yellow Tavern in May and Trevilian Station in early June. The failure of II Corps to seize the Weldon Railroad on June 21 forfeited the element of surprise and led to disaster over the following days.

On the morning of June 22, the Confederates—now alerted to the Federal movement toward the Weldon railway—sent out first Wilcox's division and then

26 *OR* 46, 3:62.

27 On Dec. 3, 1863, Lee had recommended to Davis that Beauregard rather than Johnston lead the Army of Tennessee in the Campaign of 1864. Ibid., vol. 31, 3:779.

28 It resembled the personnel mismanagement Meade would commit during the fourth offensive in August 1864, when he employed II Corps twice and XVIII Corps not at all with the result that the tired II Corps suffered a defeat even worse than on June 22. Horn, *The Battles for the Weldon Railroad, August 1864*, 219.

Mahone's division when the fog dissipated. Meade reasonably allowed IX Corps time to strengthen its line but impatiently advanced II Corps independently of VI Corps, opening a gap between the two corps, and he failed to use the reserves available from V Corps to plug the gap. One more brigade on the left of Barlow's return on June 22 would probably have halted Mahone's attack.[29]

On June 23, Meade attempted in vain to get VI Corps moving forward. With Wright paralyzed by the prospect of getting outflanked and routed as II Corps had on the previous day, Meade—as usual—yielded to his subordinate's judgment, which allowed Mahone's division to maul the Vermont Brigade. Meade's advice to Grant not to cut loose with the Army of the Potomac was wise.

After being beaten in detail during the battle of Jerusalem Plank Road, Meade did not employ the reserves of V and IX corps to advance toward the Weldon Railroad. Instead, he used them to defend his left with the same passivity he would display on August 25 during the second battle of Reams Station. Wilson thought that at June's end Meade ought to have attacked the wagon trains the Confederates were running around the gap in the Weldon Railroad. Such attacks would have protected the Army of the Potomac's left as effectively as Meade's passive defense but would have put him in the position of a chess player taken out of the book—a situation which he disliked but one in which Grant and Lee excelled. Wilson considered Meade "somewhat lacking in aggressive temper."[30] Meade never performed so poorly as in the opening assaults on Petersburg and the battle of Jerusalem Plank Road.

In a wise move, Beauregard's men occupied the Bailey farm in case Mahone's division failed to stop II Corps on June 22 and VI Corps on June 23. On June 24, the Louisianian formulated a faulty attack plan for Anderson's and Hoke's divisions by neglecting to designate an overall commander.

Corps Command

On June 21, Birney failed to support Barlow's division in its advance toward the Weldon Railroad. As a result, a single cavalry brigade stopped the Red Club Division, but putting Barlow's and Gibbon's divisions on the railroad might have proved disastrous. With Wilcox's division approaching down the tracks and Mahone ordered to cooperate with Wilcox, Birney would have rendered Barlow's

29 Committing Bushrod Johnson's division at that point could have successfully renewed the attack, or the belated arrival of Wilcox's division could have dislodged II Corps.

30 On August 25 Meade would fail even to demonstrate against Secessionist lines at Petersburg thinned by the dispatch of eight infantry brigades which helped win Second Reams Station. Wilson, *Under the Old Flag*, 1:481, 531; Horn, *The Battles for the Weldon Railroad, August 1864*, 245.

and Gibbon's divisions vulnerable to the sort of maneuver devised by Mahone against Warren on August 19, when the Confederates inflicted about 3,000 casualties at a cost of around 600 to themselves.[31] In the absence of support from all three divisions of VI Corps, Birney probably made a fortunate choice in not supporting Barlow's division with Gibbon's.

Birney's refusal on June 22 to employ either of the two V Corps reserve brigades to retake McKnight's battery wasted Grant's wise advice to form reserves from V and IX corps to assist II and VI corps west of Jerusalem Plank Road—once Meade belatedly heeded that advice. The experience of June 22 emotionally scarred Birney. His failure to attack promptly above Fussell's Mill north of the James on August 15 stemmed in part from fear for his open flank.[32]

Warren's daring idea of cutting loose with the Army of the Potomac from City Point and Bermuda Hundred proved too bold for his superiors; it probably just added to their animus toward him, which led to his sacking the following April.

Wright's reluctance to exit the trenches on the morning of June 21 made sense. The sluggishness of his corps on the afternoon and evening of June 22 resulted from two nights without rest. His refusal to attack on June 23 and 24 supported Lyman's conclusion that on that occasion, "Wright showed himself totally unfit to command a corps."[33] That Meade did not sack Wright should have come as no surprise given that the Army of the Potomac's commander had previously yielded his judgment to Warren on multiple occasions.

Sheridan's lethargic crossing of the James and slow progress afterward toward the Army of the Potomac's left rendered Wilson and Kautz vulnerable and contributed to the disasters at Sappony Church and First Reams Station. Little Phil's excuses, both contemporaneous and postwar, ring hollow.[34]

Hampton, the *de facto* commander of Lee's Cavalry Corps, began his emergence as a pillar of Petersburg's defense. As Sheridan limped homeward after his defeat at Hampton's hands at Trevilian Station, the South Carolinian drove back Gregg's cavalry division from Samaria Church on June 24, eliminating any chance that Little Phil could cross the James closer to Richmond than Douthat's Landing. Disengaging from Sheridan, Hampton led his horsemen south of the James to block the troopers of Wilson and Kautz at Sappony Church on June 28 and overrun their rear guard there on June 29. By that time the South Carolinian had

31 Ibid., 138, 172.

32 Ibid., 52–53.

33 Lowe, ed., *Meade's Army*, 225.

34 Wilson, *Under the Old Flag*, 1:496–521.

shown that he merited elevation to command of the Army of Northern Virginia's Cavalry Corps. He would confirm the wisdom of his promotion at Second Reams Station on August 25.

Hill began experiencing difficulties in corps command almost immediately after his promotion to that level in 1863. On June 22, 1864, Hill's misunderstanding of Mahone's plan impaired the plan's execution. If Wilcox had followed Porte's instructions, the Light Division would almost certainly have inflicted substantially more casualties on II Corps, may have unhinged the rear Federal line, and could even have broken the Union grip on Jerusalem Plank Road.

Hill's mistake may also have brought down on Wilcox's innocent head the misdirected wrath of the army commander and three of the Light Division's brigadiers. General Lee may have signified displeasure with Wilcox by breaking up his division on June 25, sending Lane's and McGowan's brigades to Deep Bottom under Conner's command, and Thomas's and Scales's brigades to Swift Creek under Wilcox on July 4. The delay occasioned by Wilcox's compliance with Hill's mistaken version of Mahone's plan may have been what provoked the intent of three of Wilcox's four brigadiers to have him court-martialed for cowardice and replaced by the fourth, Brig. Gen. James H. Lane.[35]

Lee's failure to replace Hill raises questions about the army group commander's judgment. Hill's record as a corps commander had proved as dismal as that of Ewell, whom Lee replaced with Early in May when a position commensurate with Ewell's rank existed in which to put him out to pasture gracefully—the Department of Richmond. No such position existed in which to park Little Powell, and Lee did not resort to the expedient of simply sending unsatisfactory corps commanders home until the following March.[36]

Division Command

Barlow did not deserve having the fiasco of June 22 nicknamed "Barlow's Skedaddle." Nothing guaranteed that continuing the advance of Miles's brigade would have stopped Weisiger's brigade that day; when Weisiger's brigade outflanked Barlow's return, Miles's brigade had just left the breastworks near the Strong house

35 Wilcox, Wilcox Report, "Petersburg," 2–3; *OR* 40, 2:713; Ibid., vol. 42, 2:1185, 1190; (the division was reunited under Wilcox on August 24 except for Thomas's brigade, which was replaced by Anderson's brigade of Field's division; Letter, E. J. Hale, Jr. (Lane's assistant adjutant general) to James H. Lane, August 2, 1899, page 6, Series II, Box 3, Item 115, James H. Lane Papers.

36 Even after Lee stripped Early of his corps at the beginning of December, Lee left Early in command of an infantry division and two cavalry divisions in the Army of the Valley District. *OR* 43, 2:936, 938–940, 950. Lee sent Early home on March 30, 1865, after the Federals overran the district. Freeman, *Lee's Lieutenants*, 3:635.

and had at least a mile to go before it could lengthen the return. Sending Miles's brigade back to the rear line of Federal works prevented Wilcox's slow advance from wreaking even belated havoc. Like Birney, Barlow carried the scars of the June 22 debacle into the August fighting. Ordered on August 14 to leave his left unguarded, advance to Darbytown Road with two divisions, and attack there with both divisions, Barlow disobeyed orders. He deployed four of his six brigades to screen his left lest he be routed as on June 22; he attacked with only two brigades; he put them in consecutively rather than together; and he failed in his mission.[37]

Like Hampton, Mahone emerged as one of the mainstays of Petersburg's defense. The diminutive Virginian became a giant in the swamps, thickets, and woods south of the city during the campaign of 1864. On June 22, Mahone employed a ravine to overthrow II Corps. On June 23, his men advanced through woods on their left and along Second Swamp on their right to fix the Vermont pickets in a hollow near the Lanier house before advancing on a wood road in the Vermonters' rear to complete their encirclement. On June 29, he encouraged Fitzhugh Lee to use the lane that allowed Lee to outflank Kautz and separate him from Wilson. Mahone would add to his laurels with his successful counterattack at the Crater on July 30, his devastating though ultimately unsuccessful riposte on August 19, and his participation in the Burgess Mill assault on October 27, which blunted Grant's last "On to Richmond" prior to the November election.

Wheaton's failure to protect his Vermont pickets on June 23 left them in a predicament where Mahone could readily pluck them.

Hoke, who thought he should have been in command of executing Beauregard's plan for the June 24 assault, doomed the attack because he failed to understand his role in the plan. That day marked the first of a series of uncoordinated assaults by Field's and Hoke's divisions that evidenced Lee's unrealistic expectation that peers would cooperate without either being in charge.

Another instance of Lee's shortcoming in this respect occurred at the end of the Wilson-Kautz Raid. His nephew Fitzhugh Lee fought well at First Reams Station but neglected to keep Hampton informed of events there, which prevented Hampton from cutting off the escape of Wilson's column. Responsibility for the failure of Fitzhugh Lee to communicate with Hampton lay with General Lee. As Private Matthews of Breathed's battery put it, "The trouble was in this way: each division after the [May 12, 1864] death of [Maj. Gen. "Jeb"] Stuart received orders direct from Gen. R. E. Lee. . . . The consequence was there was no concerted

37 Horn, *The Battles for the Weldon Railroad, August 1864*, 29–33, 38–43.

action, because there was not a directing hand on the ground."[38] Fitzhugh Lee's cooperation with Hampton on June 29 would probably have resulted in substantially more Federal casualties.

On July 2 Lee recommended Hampton's promotion to head the Army of Northern Virginia's Cavalry Corps, which took place August 11—four days after Fitzhugh Lee's transfer to the Shenandoah had disposed of the problem.

Heth wisely declined to assault the Deep Bottom bridgehead on June 22. An attack with heavy artillery on August 13 under Pemberton failed. Even if the Confederates could eliminate the bridgehead, the Federals could establish another elsewhere at will.[39]

Simply by pursuing Wilson and Kautz, Rooney Lee limited the raiders' damage to the Weldon Railroad at Reams Station, saved High Bridge over the Appomattox on the South Side Rail Road, helped preserve Staunton River Bridge on the Richmond & Danville, and laid the foundation for the Southern victories at Sappony Church and First Reams Station. The destruction of either High Bridge or Staunton River Bridge would have hindered rail traffic far longer than the damage the raid wreaked.

Fitzhugh Lee's failure to keep Hampton informed of the events at Reams Station on June 29 cost the Confederates many captives from Wilson's retreating column.

Wilson kept at least a brigade in reserve in every one of his raid's fights until his force disintegrated under the attack of Mahone and Fitzhugh Lee at First Reams Station. Maintaining such a reserve gave up the chance of breaking through Rooney Lee's line at The Grove, destroying Staunton River Bridge, piercing Hampton's line at Sappony Church, and overrunning Mahone's line at First Reams Station; but it evidenced a very cool head in very hot circumstances and paid off at Staunton River Bridge when Rooney Lee descended upon the Federal rear.

Kautz's snap decision on June 22 to avoid an immediate clash with Confederate cavalry at Globe Tavern made the Wilson-Kautz Raid possible.

Brigadiers

Lewis Grant, the commander of the Vermont Brigade, sensibly ordered forward the body of his brigade to protect his pickets on June 23 before Wheaton, the division commander, countermanded the order. Aunt Liddy attempted unsuccessfully to change Wheaton's mind and courageously brought the matter

38 Trout, *Memoirs of the Stuart Horse Artillery Battalion*, 2:137–138.

39 *OR* 42, 2:1164; *ORN* 10:348–357; Suderow, *Target Richmond!*, 5.

to the attention of the corps commander, Wright, who also failed to support the Vermont skirmishers.

Rufus Barringer performed the best of any brigadier in either army. He began on June 21 by ambushing one of the hardest fighting divisions in the Union army with a few regiments of cavalry and a couple of guns; his Tarheel horsemen thus halted the initial thrust of II Corps toward the Weldon Railroad, the thrust with the best chance of success. Aunt Nancy's defense of that railway raises the question of whether Dearing could have saved the tracks on August 18 by defending farther forward—probably not, because Warren advanced with his whole corps, not with just a single division.

On June 23 Barringer's North Carolinians saved the day for the Confederates at The Grove, rescuing the artillery and Dearing's heavily outnumbered brigade. On June 25, the attack of Barringer's brigade on Wilson's rear guard eliminated any chance the Federals had of destroying Staunton River Bridge. By continuing to pursue Wilson and Kautz afterward, Barringer drove the bluecoats into the trap set for them at Sappony Church and Reams Station.

Field and Staff Officers

Some field officers benefited from being at the right place at the right time. Lieutenant Colonel Stewart, wrapping his 61st Virginia around the southern end of Barlow's return on June 22, touched the "critical point with a fine instrument, in exactly the right way, producing an effect seemingly altogether out of proportion to the force exerted."[40] The modest Major Patten of the Harvard Regiment halted the Mahone men as they lost their impetus that day. On June 23, Private Pryor led Rooney Lee's division to The Grove, preventing the Federals from attacking High Bridge on the South Side Rail Road. Captain Farinholt successfully defended Staunton River Bridge, the destruction of which would have severely impaired Lee's supply line.

Staff officers distinguished themselves for worse or better. By giving Wilson assurances rather than facts on the evening of June 21, Humphreys contributed to the near annihilation of the Wilson-Kautz raiders. The rosy picture painted for Wilson by the Army of the Potomac's chief of staff may well have cost Grant's army group around a thousand casualties. Captain Whitaker earned a Medal of Honor and a promotion to major by carrying Wilson's message to Meade through enemy lines and subsequently assisted in the efforts to rescue Wilson. Captain Girardey continued to engineer the record that would soon result in his remarkable

40 Walker, *History of the Second Army Corps*, 546.

promotion from captain to brigadier general.[41] Many other Federals earned Medals of Honor, and numerous Confederates won places on their Roll of Honor.

The Rank and File

The principal fighting of Grant's second offensive at Petersburg—Jerusalem Plank Road, Hare House, and the Wilson-Kautz Raid—occurred under peculiar circumstances and yielded unusual results. Surprise on June 21 enabled a Secessionist cavalry brigade to halt one of the toughest divisions in the Union army. Surprise on June 22 and fear of encountering it again on June 23 paralyzed the Federals at Jerusalem Plank Road. Gross misunderstanding and lack of coordination doomed the Confederate attack at the Hare House on June 24. Exhaustion sapped the strength of the Wilson-Kautz raiders from The Grove on June 23 through Staunton River Bridge on June 25 to Sappony Church and First Reams Station on June 28 and 29.

During the four-day battle of Jerusalem Plank Road (June 21–24), the biggest fight of the offensive, about 12,686 Secessionists whipped around 44,854 Unionists.[42] The Southerners inflicted approximately 3,162 casualties, including

41 Rans Wright wrote of Girardey's behavior at the June 25, 1862, battle of King's School House: "I was greatly assisted throughout the entire day's fight by my assistant adjutant-general Capt. V. J. B. Girardey, whose coolness, courage and daring intrepidity throughout the hottest of the fight entitle him to receive the warmest commendations of the Department." *OR* 11, 2:807. Wright wrote of Girardey's conduct during the Seven Days: "I am again called upon to acknowledge the valuable services of my assistant adjutant-general, Capt. V. J. B. Girardey, during the protracted movements of my brigade." Ibid., 2:816. Evidence exists that it was Girardey and not the brave but ailing Wright who led Wright's brigade to the top of Cemetery Ridge, possibly the high-water mark of the Confederacy, on July 2, 1863. William B. Judkins, Memoir, Sara Hightower Regional Library, Rome Floyd County Public Library, Rome, GA, 58; David L. Schultz and Scott L. Mingus Sr., *The Second Day at Gettysburg: The Attack and Defense of Cemetery Ridge, July 2, 1863* (El Dorado Hills, CA, 2016), 361. Capt. C. H. Andrews, commander of Wright's brigade at Manassas Gap on July 23, 1863, wrote of Girardey's leadership on that day: "Great credit is due Capt. V. J. B. Girardey, assistant adjutant-general, who superintended the movements of the left of the brigade, and his gallant behavior nerved the weakest soldier to a full discharge of his duty." *OR* 27, 2:627; Ezra J. Warner, *Generals in Gray: Lives of the Confederate Commanders* (Baton Rouge, 1959), 106; John Horn, "A Most Remarkable Officer," *North & South*, Series II, vol. 4, no. 1 (Dec. 2023) 29–36.

42 Mahone's (Anderson's) division numbered 5,334 present for duty on June 30, 1864, Wilcox's 5,445. *OR* 40, 2:707. To the 4,960 effectives in Mahone's division must be added the 653 effectives lost from June 21 through June 29, giving a total of 5,613 effectives on June 20. See Chapter Two, n. 68, Chapter Six, n. 61, Chapter Seven, n. 66, and Chapter Eight, n. 147, *supra*. To 4,349 effectives in the Light Division should be added the approximately 199 effectives lost June 21–22, giving a total of around 4,548 effectives on June 20. See Chapter Two, n. 86, and Chapter Six, n. 62, *supra*. Barringer's brigade had about 1,600 men, presumably effectives. See Chapter Three, n. 9, *supra*.

I assume that Hagood's brigade had one quarter or 1,327 of the 5,309 listed as present for duty in Hoke's division, hence 1,234 effectives. *OR* 40, 2:707. The attack force lost 306 and the brigade thus had 1,540 effectives. Ibid., 1:804. Only three of the five regiments in Hagood's brigade participated,

more than 2,300 captured.[43] The Northerners inflicted around 1,104 casualties, including about 284 captured.[44] Every 1,000 Rebels put out of action around 249 Yankees. This fell between the 247 Federals hit by every 1,000 Confederates at Chaffin's Farm (or Fort Harrison) on September 29–30, 1864, and the 252 bluecoats hit by every 1,000 butternuts at Shiloh on April 6–7, 1862.[45] Every 1,000 Federals at the battle of Jerusalem Plank Road put out of action around 25 of their foes. This fell between the 18 Confederates hit by every 1,000 Federals in the assault on the fortifications of Port Hudson on May 27, 1863, and the 32 Secessionists hit by every 1,000 Unionists in the assault on the fortifications of Fort Wagner on July 14, 1864.[46]

That the Southerners fought mostly on the offensive during the battle of Jerusalem Plank Road suggests that the foregoing numbers understate the Confederate performance on those days.[47] That the Army of the Potomac's losses

---

or 924 effectives assuming the brigade's regiments all had the same strength. Ibid., 803; see Appendix B, Confederate Order of Battle, *infra*. The attack's leader came from one of the brigade's regiments that did not participate, for a total of 925. *OR* 40, 1:803.

II Corps numbered 19,706 effectives on June 20, VI Corps 17,784. See Chapter Two, n. 14, *supra*. V Corps numbered 17,947 officers and men present for duty on June 30, hence 16,690 effectives. *OR* 40, 2:542. Assuming each of V Corps' 11 brigades had 1,517 effectives on June 30 and adding the 37 estimated losses on June 21–June 22 gives 3,071 effectives on June 20 for Sweitzer's and Dushane's brigades. See Appendix A, Federal Order of Battle, *infra*; Chapter Two, n. 58; Chapter Six, n. 60, *supra*.

The 18th Pennsylvania Cavalry (12 companies) and the part of the 3rd New Jersey Cavalry (likely 11 companies) in Bryan's cavalry brigade had 1,146 "men," whom I assume were effectives, and when the small detachment from the 22nd New York Cavalry (I assume one company) is considered, the brigade probably numbered about 1,200 effectives. Wilson, *Under the Old Flag*, 1:458; *OR* 40, 1:228. The two companies involved in the battle of Jerusalem Plank Road from the 1st Massachusetts Cavalry' twelve companies probably numbered around 100 troopers. Crowninshield, *First Regiment of Massachusetts Cavalry Volunteers*, viii–x.

I assume that Cullen's and Henry's brigades had two-ninths or 3,120 of the 14,042 soldiers present for duty in XVIII Corps (eight brigades of infantry and one of artillery), hence 2,901 effectives. Ibid., 552, 554–555. Adding 92 casualties yields 2,993 for the initial force. *OR* 40, 1:711, 716.

43 See Chapter Two, ns. 58, 65, 68, and 87; Chapter Six, ns. 59 and 60; and Chapter Seven, ns. 57 and 84, *supra*. See also Table 3: Federal Casualties at the Battle of Jerusalem Plank Road, June 21–24, 1864, *infra*.

44 See Chapter Two, ns. 66, 68, and 86; Chapter Six, ns. 61 and 62; and Chapter Seven, ns. 57 and 66, *supra*. See also Table 4: Confederate Casualties at the Battle of Jerusalem Plank Road, June 21–24, 1864, *infra*.

45 Livermore, *Numbers and Losses*, 140–141. Suderow's "put out of action in 1,000" is a more meaningful concept than Livermore's "hit by 1,000" in fights resulting in large numbers of prisoners. Suderow, "Confederate Casualties Near the Jerusalem Plank Road, June 21–23, 1864," 16; Livermore, *Numbers and Losses*, 63–77.

46 Ibid., 140–141.

47 T. N. Dupuy, *A Genius for War: The German Army and General Staff, 1807–1945* (London, 1977), 328–331. Dupuy adjusted his score of effectiveness downward "to reflect the known operational advantage which is conferred by defensive posture." Ibid., 328, 331.

in prisoners exceeded its killed and wounded by a ratio of more than 2.6 to one indicates significant demoralization.[48]

Comparison with aggregated statistics of World War I battles suggests that the effectiveness of the victorious Confederate attackers at the battle of Jerusalem Plank Road (5.19) exceeded that of either combatant at the battle of the Marne on September 5–10, 1914 (defeated Germans 3.86, victorious French 3.48), but fell short of the effectiveness of the victorious German attackers at the battle of the Masurian Lakes on September 9–14, 1914 (7.22), and the effectiveness of the victorious German attackers at the more famous battle of Tannenberg on August 26–29, 1914 (13.37). The effectiveness of the defeated Federals at the battle of Jerusalem Plank Road (0.51) rose to the level attained by the defeated Russians at neither the Masurian Lakes (2.44) nor Tannenberg (1.72).[49]

Wilson's force during his raid numbered about 5,500 officers and men.[50] They faced a total of around 10,311 Secessionists in the raid's major engagements—The Grove, Staunton River Bridge, Sappony Church, and First Reams Station.[51] Northern losses during the Wilson-Kautz Raid numbered about 352 killed or wounded and around 1,169 captured, a total of roughly 1,521 with a ratio of 3.32 captives to one soldier killed or wounded. Southern losses amounted to roughly 357, including very few prisoners.[52]

48 Suderow, "Confederate Casualties During the Wilson-Kautz Raid," 44.

49 See Table 6: Effectiveness, *infra*, and Dupuy, *A Genius for War*, 330–331. The battles of Tannenberg and the Masurian Lakes involved many more men on each side than the battle of Jerusalem Plank Road. Ibid.

50 *OR* 40, 1:621.

51 Suderow, "Confederate Casualties During the Wilson-Kautz Raid," 49–51. I have adjusted Suderow's figures for the initial strength of Fitzhugh Lee's division and Mahone's division to reflect the differences between Suderow's estimate of 40 casualties for Fitzhugh Lee's division (Suderow, "Confederate Casualties During the Wilson-Kautz Raid," 49, n. 12), and Lee's report of 22 casualties (Hewett, et al., eds., *Supplement to the Official Records*, 7:341), and between Suderow's estimate of 170 casualties for Mahone's division (Suderow, "Confederate Casualties During the Wilson-Kautz Raid," 50, ns. 15, 17) and CSRs showing 92 casualties (Young, "Confederate Casualties during June 1864 at Petersburg").

52 *OR* 40, 1:232–233, 237–238; Dyer, *Compendium*, 947; Epperson, "A secret sidebar to the Wilson-Kautz Raid," petersburgsiege.org. (30 bridge breakers from the Iron Brigade); Preston, *Tenth Regiment of Cavalry New York State Volunteers*, 604 (at least 19 troopers from Gregg's division killed or wounded, at least 20 captured). Confederate tallies of captive combatants exceed the Federal total. Hampton reported "806 prisoners, together with 127 negroes—slaves." *OR* 40, 1:809. Fitzhugh Lee reported "several hundred prisoners." Hewett, et al., eds., *Supplement to the Official Records*, 7:333. Petersburg newspapers reported Mahone's captures as "387, including the wounded." "Telegraphic Reports of the Press Association: From Petersburg," *Daily Richmond Examiner*, July 2, 1864, p. 1, col. 4. For Southern losses during the raid, see Chapter Eight, n. 181.

Every 1,000 butternuts put out of action about 147 bluecoats. This result neared the 150 Unionists hit by 1,000 Secessionists in the Unionist assault against Fredericksburg on December 13, 1862, though that fight took only a single day.[53] Every 1,000 Federals put out of action around 65 Confederates. This result closely approached the 66 Rebels hit by 1,000 Yankees at the battle of South Mountain on September 14, 1862, another fight that took only a single day.[54]

Comparison with aggregated statistics of World War I battles indicates that butternut effectiveness (1.22) fell short of the effectiveness of the German victors in the mobile battle of Lodz on November 11–25, 1914 (2.08). The effectiveness of the bluecoats (0.54) did not rise to the level attained by the defeated Russians (0.83) in that fight.[55]

At Reams Station the Federal ratio of prisoners to killed or wounded exceeded five prisoners for every soldier killed or wounded, which suggests extreme demoralization.[56] Exhaustion took its toll on the raiders as they encountered one group after another of Confederates, even though each of those groups was smaller than Wilson's command.

The Impact of Grant's Second Offensive at Petersburg

The position Grant established through his first offensive at Petersburg made the capture of that city and Richmond what Lee considered "but a work of time" if Grant's superiors—the secretary of war and the president—allowed the general-in-chief to stay the course.[57] In order for Grant to stay the course, he had to produce evidence of enough progress in his prosecution of the war to persuade voters to reelect the president.

Grant's second offensive at Petersburg did little to advance Lincoln's prospects of reelection. The offensive began with modest moves—the seizure of the Deep Bottom bridgehead and bringing Petersburg's bridges under the fire of heavy artillery. These moves contributed significantly to the siege of Petersburg's ultimate success, but that did not occur until long after Lincoln's reelection. Grant's second offensive ended with very ambitious moves—the Federal infantry's first attempt to reach the Appomattox above the city and the cavalry's attempt to cut the railroads

53 Livermore, *Numbers and Losses*, 140.

54 Ibid.

55 See Table 6: Effectiveness, *infra*; Dupuy, *A Genius for War*, 330–331. The battle of Lodz involved many, many more men on each side than the Wilson-Kautz Raid. Ibid.

56 Suderow, "Confederate Casualties During the Wilson-Kautz Raid," 44.

57 *OR* 40, 2:703.

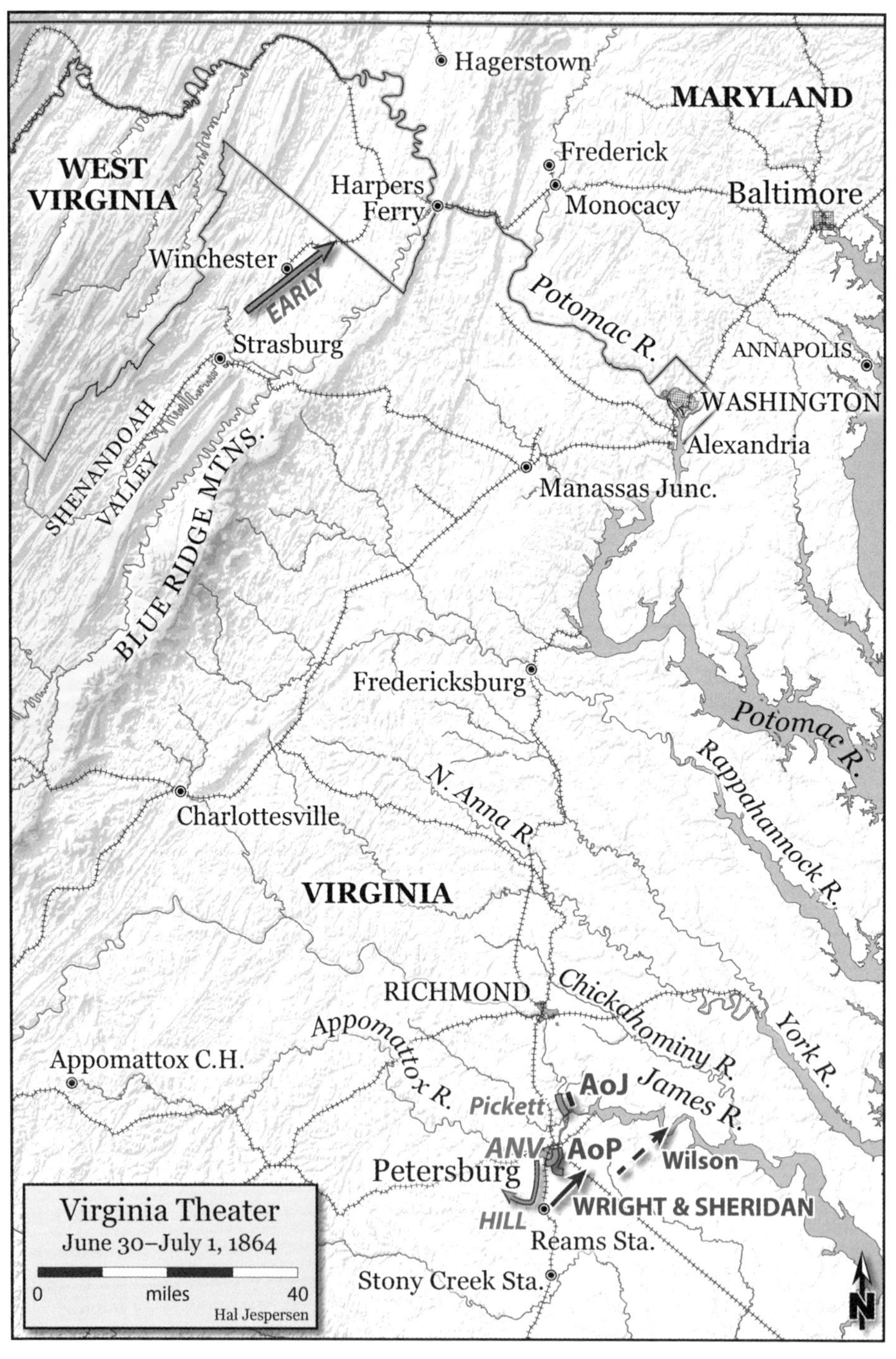
Hagerstown
MARYLAND
WEST VIRGINIA
Frederick
Harpers Ferry
Monocacy
Baltimore
Winchester
EARLY
Potomac R.
Strasburg
ANNAPOLIS
WASHINGTON
Alexandria
SHENANDOAH VALLEY
BLUE RIDGE MTNS.
Manassas Junc.
Fredericksburg
Potomac R.
Rappahannock R.
N. Anna R.
Charlottesville
VIRGINIA
RICHMOND
Chickahominy R.
York R.
Appomattox R.
Appomattox C.H.
AoJ
James R.
Pickett
ANV
AoP
Wilson
Petersburg
WRIGHT & SHERIDAN
HILL
Reams Sta.
Stony Creek Sta.
Virginia Theater
June 30–July 1, 1864
0 miles 40
Hal Jespersen
N

running to the city's south and west. Those moves contributed little beyond lengthening the casualty lists. Grant's reach exceeded his grasp, as it would often do during the remainder of the siege.

During the Virginia campaign of 1864, Grant held the initiative from the crossing of the Rapidan River through the end of his second Petersburg offensive, but even as the Federals crossed the James, Lee was reasserting himself. He unleashed Early to prevent the fall of Richmond by threatening Washington in the hope that this would prompt the Lincoln administration to withdraw Grant's army group from James River as it had withdrawn McClellan's troops from the James in 1862.

Early would soon burst like a bombshell in the North. As Early bore down on Washington, Robert G. H. Kean, a lawyer educated at the University of Virginia heading the Confederate War Department, wrote, "The rapid rise of gold in the last month is one of the most favorable indications of the time."[58] As late as August 23, Lincoln thought he would lose the November election and that as a result the North would lose the war.[59]

After Early's appearance at Washington's gates in early July, the campaign's initiative shifted to Lee, who sent more troops to northern Virginia at the beginning of August. Unlike in 1862, Lincoln did not buckle under the pressure and recall Grant from the James.

Then, as Lee dispatched still more troops northward in mid-August, Grant recaptured the initiative. His fourth offensive at Petersburg forced Lee to recall Hampton's division from its ride to northern Virginia and to cancel orders for Field's division to march to the same destination. After that, Lee stopped shifting men northward and the initiative in the siege of Petersburg remained with Grant.

Lee learned that, unlike in 1862, Lincoln had faith in his general on the James. The siege of Petersburg became indeed "but a work of time." Fortunately for the Union, Sherman's capture of Atlanta and Sheridan's victories over Early in the Shenandoah Valley gave Lincoln and Grant the time they needed to bring the siege of Petersburg to a successful close and the war to a successful end.[60]

58 Edward Younger, ed., *Inside the Confederate Government: The Diary of Robert Garlick Hill Kean* (Baton Rouge, 1993), 163.

59 Abraham Lincoln, "Blind Memorandum," Aug. 23, 1864; Grant, *Personal Memoirs*, 2:175–176.

60 Grant, *Personal Memoirs*, 2:175–176.

Appendix One: Strengths, Casualties, Effectiveness

Table 1: Federal Strength, June 30, 1864

Army of the Potomac	**Officers**	**Enlisted**	**Total**
General Headquarters	55		55
Provost Guard	85	1,214	1,299
Engineer Brigade	45	1,801	1,846
Battalion U.S. Engineers	5	306	311
Artillery	5		5
Guards and Orderlies	3	56	59
Signal Corps	16	196	212
Second Army Corps	888	16,313	17,201
Fifth Army Corps	869	17,078	17,947
Sixth Army Corps	797	17,514	18,311
Ninth Army Corps	671	15,343	16,014
Cavalry Corps	630	12,720	13,350
Present for duty total	4,069	82,541	86,610
Army of the James			
General Headquarters	26		26
Signal Corps	26	163	189
Naval Brigade	23	624	647
First New York Engineers	8	136	144
Siege Artillery	62	1,452	1,514
Unattached Troops	110	2,368	2,478
Tenth Army Corps	556	11,719	12,275
Eighteenth Army Corps	526	13,516	14,042
Cavalry Division	82	1,820	1,902
Present for duty total	1,419	31,798	33,217
Grand Total Grant's Army Group	5,488	114,339	119,827[1]

1 110,218 effectives (12,964 cavalry, 97,254 others). Livermore, *Numbers and Losses*, 67–70.

Table 2: Confederate Strength, June 30, 1864

Army of Northern Virginia, June 30	**Officers**	**Enlisted**	**Total**
Department of North Carolina and Southern Virginia			
Present for duty	891[2]	11,300	12,191
First Army Corps			
Present for duty	1,217	13,060	14,277
Third Army Corps			
Present for duty	1,335	14,328	15,633
Cavalry Corps			
Present for duty	320	7,918	8,238[3]
Artillery			
Present for duty	281	5,263	5,544[4]
Total Present for duty	4,044	51,869	55,913
Department of Richmond, June 20			
Present for duty	358	5,784	6,142
Grand Total Present for Duty	4,402	57,653	62,055[5]

2 This number includes the 12 officers excluded in the Abstract. *OR* 40, 2:707.

3 This number omits the unreported officers of Hampton's division but includes the 800 men of Dearing's brigade. Ibid.; see Chapter Three, n. 11, *supra*.

4 Only three battalions of the Second Corps artillery reported. *OR* 40, 2:707.

5 56,958 effectives (7,983 cavalry, 48,975 others). Livermore, *Numbers and Losses*, 67–70.

Table 3: Federal Casualties at the Battle of Jerusalem Plank Road: June 21–24, 1864

Formation	June 21	June 22[6]	June 23	June 24	Total
II Corps	31[7]	2,371[8]			2,402
V Corps	7[9]	30[10]			37
VI Corps	1[11]	55[12]	595[13]		651
XVIII Corps				72[14]	72
Total	39	2,456	595	72	3,162

Table 4: Confederate Casualties at the Battle of Jerusalem Plank Road: June 21–24, 1864

Formation	June 21	June 22	June 23	June 24	Total
Barringer's Brigade	35[15]		3[16]		38
Wilcox's Division	7[17]	192[18]			199
Mahone's Division	1[19]	419[20]	141[21]		561
Hagood's Brigade				306[22]	306
Total	43	611	144	306	1,104

6 Until 4:00 a.m. on June 23.

7 See Chapter Two, ns. 65 and 68, *supra*.

8 See Chapter Six, n. 59, *supra*.

9 See Chapter Two, n. 58, *supra*.

10 See Chapter Six, n. 60, *supra*.

11 See Chapter Two, n. 87, *supra*.

12 See Chapter Six, n. 59, *supra*.

13 See Chapter Seven, n. 57, *supra*.

14 See Chapter Seven, n. 84, *supra*.

15 See Chapter Two, n. 66, *supra*.

16 See Chapter Seven, n. 66, *supra*.

17 See Chapter Two, n. 86, *supra*.

18 See Chapter Six, n. 62, *supra*.

19 See Chapter Two, n. 68, *supra*.

20 See Chapter Six, n. 61, *supra*.

21 See Chapter Seven, n. 66, *supra*.

22 See Chapter Seven, n. 84, *supra*.

Table 5: Casualties During Various Clashes of the Wilson-Kautz Raid, June 22–July 1, 1864

Battle	Federal Casualties	Confederate Casualties
June 22	72[23]	7[24]
The Grove/Black's and White's/ Nottoway Court House	71[25]	96[26]
Staunton River Bridge	104[27]	47[28]
Sappony Church	255[29]	89[30]
Reams Station	754[31]	118[32]
Total Loss During the Raid	1,521[33]	357[34]

23 See Chapter Three, n. 23, *supra*.

24 See Chapter Three, n. 24, *supra*.

25 See Chapter Three, n. 51, *supra*.

26 See Chapter Three, n. 50, *supra*.

27 See Chapter Three, n. 130, *supra*.

28 See Chapter Three, n. 129, *supra*.

29 See Chapter Eight, n. 50, *supra*.

30 See Chapter Eight, n. 51, *supra*.

31 See Chapter Eight, n. 146, *supra*.

32 See Chapter Eight, n. 147, *supra*.

33 See Chapter Nine, n. 52, *supra*. This number is greater than the number of Federals lost in the individual clashes named above because other troopers were lost outside the scope of those clashes; for example, see Chapter Eight, n. 166, *supra*.

34 This number represents all known Confederate casualties incurred opposing the Wilson-Kautz Raid.

Table 6: Effectiveness

Livermore/Suderow Analysis[35]

Side	Total Engaged	Put out of action (POA)	POA in 1,000	POA by 1,000
Jerusalem Plank Road including Hare House, June 21–24, 1864				
USA	44,854	3,162	70	25
CSA	12,686	1,104	87	249
Wilson-Kautz Raid, June 22–July 1, 1864				
USA	5,500	1,521	276	65
CSA	10,311	357	35	147

Dupuy Analysis[36]

Side	Total Engaged	Losses	Losses Per Day	Percent Loss Per Day	Score Per 100	Effective Score
Jerusalem Plank Road including Hare House, June 21–24, 1864						
USA	44,854	3,162	791	1.76	0.62	0.51
CSA	12,686	1,104	276	2.18	6.23	5.19
Wilson-Kautz Raid, June 22–July 1, 1864						
USA	5,500	1,521	152	2.76	0.65	0.54
CSA	10,311	357	36	0.35	1.47	1.22

35 See Suderow, "Confederate Casualties Near the Jerusalem Plank Road, June 21–23, 1864," 16; Livermore, *Numbers and Losses*, 63–77.

36 See Dupuy, *A Genius for War*, 328–331.

Appendix Two: Orders of Battle

Federal Order of Battle

General Headquarters

Lt. Gen. Ulysses S. Grant, commanding general, United States armies

ESCORT, ETC.

5th US Cavalry, Cos. B, F, and K

4th US (joined June 22; previously with First Brigade., Second Division, V Corps)

Army of the Potomac

Maj. Gen. George G. Meade

PROVOST GUARD

Brig. Gen. Marsena R. Patrick

1st Indiana Cavalry, Cos. I and K

1st Massachusetts Cavalry, Cos. C and D (sent to II Corps June 21, then to VI Corps June 23)

80th New York (20th Militia)

3rd Pennsylvania Cavalry

68th Pennsylvania

114th Pennsylvania

ENGINEER BRIGADE

Brig. Gen. Henry W. Benham

15th New York Engineers (five cos.)

50th New York Engineers (five cos.)

BATTALION US ENGINEERS

Capt. George H. Mendell

GUARDS AND ORDERLIES

Independent Co. Oneida (New York) Cavalry

ARTILLERY

Brig. Gen. Henry J. Hunt

ARTILLERY PARK

Lt. Col. Freeman McGilvery

15th New York Heavy Artillery, Co. F

SIGNAL CORPS

Capt. Benjamin F. Fisher

II Corps

Maj. Gen. David B. Birney (June 18–27)

Maj. Gen. Winfield S. Hancock (resumed command June 27)

ESCORT

1st Vermont Cavalry, Co. M

ENGINEERS

Maj. Wesley Brainerd

50th New York Engineers (1st Battalion)

FIRST DIVISION

Brig. Gen. Francis C. Barlow

FIRST BRIGADE

Brig. Gen. Nelson A. Miles

28th Massachusetts63rd New York (six cos.)
26th Michigan
5th New Hampshire
2nd New York Heavy Artillery
61st New York
81st Pennsylvania
140th Pennsylvania
183rd Pennsylvania

SECOND BRIGADE

Capt. Richard M. Moroney

69th New York (six cos.)
88th New York (three cos.)
116th Pennsylvania

THIRD BRIGADE

Col. Clinton R. MacDougall

39th New York
52nd New York
57th New York
111th New York
125th New York
126th New York

FOURTH BRIGADE

Col. John Fraser (captured June 22)
Lt. Col. John Hastings

2nd Delaware (five cos.)
7th New York Heavy Artillery
64th New York
66th New York
53rd Pennsylvania
145th Pennsylvania
148th Pennsylvania

SECOND DIVISION

Maj. Gen. John Gibbon

PROVOST GUARD

2nd Co. Minnesota Sharpshooters

FIRST BRIGADE

Brig. Gen. Byron R. Pierce (relieved June 22)
Maj. William F. Smith
Lt. Col. Francis E. Pierce (assigned June 27)

19th Maine
19th Massachusetts
20th Massachusetts
1st Co. Andrew (Massachusetts) Sharpshooters
7th Michigan
42nd New York
59th New York (four cos.)
82nd New York (four cos.)
184th Pennsylvania
36th Wisconsin

SECOND BRIGADE

Maj. Timothy F. O'Brien

152nd New York
69th Pennsylvania
72nd Pennsylvania
106th Pennsylvania
184th Pennsylvania

THIRD BRIGADE
Col. Thomas A. Smyth

14th Connecticut
1st Delaware
12th New Jersey
10th New York (six cos.)
108th New York
4th Ohio (four cos.)
8th Ohio (mustered out June 25)
7th West Virginia (four cos.)

FOURTH BRIGADE
Col. William Blaisdell (killed June 23)
Col. James P. McIvor

8th New York Heavy Artillery
155th New York
164th New York
170th New York
182nd New York (69th New York New York National Guard Artillery)

THIRD DIVISION
Maj. Gen. Gershom Mott

FIRST BRIGADE
Col. Henry J. Madill

20th Indiana
17th Maine
40th New York
86th New York
124th New York
99th Pennsylvania
110th Pennsylvania
141st Pennsylvania
2nd US Sharpshooters

SECOND BRIGADE
Col. Robert McAllister

1st Massachusetts Heavy Artillery
5th Michigan
93rd New York
57th Pennsylvania
63rd Pennsylvania
105th Pennsylvania
1st US Sharpshooters

THIRD BRIGADE
Col. Daniel Chaplin

1st Maine Heavy Artillery
16th Massachusetts
5th New Jersey
6th New Jersey
7th New Jersey
8th New Jersey
11th New Jersey
115th Pennsylvania (attached to 110th Pennsylvania June 22)

FOURTH BRIGADE
Col. William R. Brewster

11th Massachusetts (five cos.)
71st New York
72nd New York (three cos.)
73rd New York
74th New York (six cos.)
120th New York
84th Pennsylvania

ARTILLERY BRIGADE
Col. John C. Tidball

Maine Light, 6th Battery (F)
New Hampshire Light, 1st Battery
New Jersey Light, 3rd Battery
1st New York Light, Battery G
New York Light, 12th Battery
1st Rhode Island Light, Battery A
4th US, Battery K
Massachusetts Light, 10th Battery
1st New Jersey Light, Battery B
4th New York Heavy
New York Light, 11th Battery
1st Pennsylvania Light, Battery F
1st Rhode Island Light, Battery B
5th US, Batteries C and I

V Corps

Maj. Gen. Gouverneur K. Warren

ESCORT

Lt. William H. Wheeler

1st Michigan Cavalry (detachment)

PROVOST GUARD

Capt. Henry W. Rider

5th New York (battalion)

FIRST DIVISION

Brig. Gen. Charles Griffin

FIRST BRIGADE

Col. William S. Tilton

121st Pennsylvania
142nd Pennsylvania
143rd Pennsylvania
149th Pennsylvania
150th Pennsylvania
187th Pennsylvania

SECOND BRIGADE

Col. Jacob B. Sweitzer

22nd Massachusetts (2nd Co. Massachusetts; Sharpshooters attached)
32nd Massachusetts
4th Michigan
62nd Pennsylvania
91st Pennsylvania
155th Pennsylvania
21st Pennsylvania Cavalry (dismounted)

THIRD BRIGADE

Brig. Gen. Joseph J. Bartlett

20th Maine
18th Massachusetts
1st Michigan
16th Michigan
44th New York
83rd Pennsylvania
118th Pennsylvania

SECOND DIVISION

Brig. Gen. Romeyn B. Ayres

FIRST BRIGADE

Brig. Gen. Joseph Hayes

5th New York
140th New York
146th New York
10th United States (three cos.)
11th United States (six cos.)
12th United States
14th United States
17th United States

SECOND BRIGADE[1]

Col. Nathan T. Dushane

1st Maryland
4th Maryland
7th Maryland
8th Maryland
Purnell Legion (Maryland)

1 Colonel Samuel A. Graham commanded the brigade at this time though it is referred to as "Dushane" in the official correspondence. *OR* 40 1:469, 2:410.

THIRD BRIGADE
Col. J. Howard Kitching

6th New York Heavy Artillery
15th New York Heavy Artillery

THIRD DIVISION
Brig. Gen. Samuel W. Crawford

FIRST BRIGADE
Col. Peter Lyle

16th Maine
13th Massachusetts
39th Massachusetts
104th New York
90th Pennsylvania
107th Pennsylvania

SECOND BRIGADE
Col. James L. Bates; term expired June 25
Brig. Gen. Henry Baxter

12th Massachusetts; mustered out June 24
94th New York
97th New York
11th Pennsylvania
88th Pennsylvania

THIRD BRIGADE
Col. James Carle

190th Pennsylvania (1st Veteran Reserves)
191st Pennsylvania (2nd Veteran Reserves)

FOURTH DIVISION
Brig. Gen. Lysander Cutler

PROVOST GUARD
Lt. Henry Naegely
Independent Battalion (Wisconsin)

FIRST BRIGADE
Brig. Gen. Edward S. Bragg

7th Indiana
19th Indiana
24th Michigan
1st Battalion New York Sharpshooters
6th Wisconsin
7th Wisconsin

SECOND BRIGADE
Col. J. William Hofmann

3rd Delaware
4th Delaware
76th New York
95th New York
147th New York
56th Pennsylvania
157th Pennsylvania

ARTILLERY BRIGADE
Col. Charles S. Wainwright

Massachusetts Light, 3rd Battery (C)
Massachusetts Light, 5th Battery (E)
Massachusetts Light, 9th Battery
1st New York Light, Battery B
1st New York Light, Battery C
1st New York Light, Battery D
1st New York Light, Battery E (mortars)
1st New York Light, Battery H
1st New York Light, Battery L
New York Light, 15th Battery
1st Pennsylvania Light, Battery B
5th United States, Battery D

CAVALRY DETACHMENT (ordered to II Corps June 21, then to VI Corps June 23)
Col. Timothy M. Bryan Jr.
3rd New Jersey Cavalry
22nd New York Cavalry (detachment)
18th Pennsylvania Cavalry
Detachment 1st and 2nd Cavalry Divisions

VI Corps
Maj. Gen. Horatio G. Wright

ESCORT
Capt. Charles G. Fellows
8th Pennsylvania Cavalry, Co. A

Engineers
Maj. Edmund O. Beers
50th New York Engineers (2nd Battalion)

FIRST DIVISION
Brig. Gen. David A. Russell

FIRST BRIGADE
Col. William H. Penrose

1st Delaware Cavalry (dismounted)
4th New Jersey
10th New Jersey
15th New Jersey

SECOND BRIGADE
Brig. Gen. Emory Upton

2nd Connecticut Heavy Artillery
5th Maine (mustered out June 22)
121st New York
95th Pennsylvania
96th Pennsylvania

THIRD BRIGADE
Lt. Col. Gideon Clark

6th Maine
49th Pennsylvania
119th Pennsylvania
5th Wisconsin

FOURTH BRIGADE
Col. Joseph E. Hamblin

65th New York
122nd New York
23rd Pennsylvania
82nd Pennsylvania

SECOND DIVISION
Brig. Gen. Frank Wheaton
Brig. Gen. George W. Getty (resumed command June 28)

FIRST BRIGADE
Col. John F. Ballier
Brig. Gen. Frank Wheaton
(resumed command June 28)

62nd New York
93rd Pennsylvania
98th Pennsylvania
102nd Pennsylvania
139th Pennsylvania

SECOND BRIGADE
Brig. Gen. Lewis A. Grant

2nd Vermont
3rd Vermont
4th Vermont
5th Vermont
6th Vermont
11th Vermont (1st Heavy Artillery)

THIRD BRIGADE
Col. Daniel D. Bidwell

7th Maine
43rd New York
49th New York
77th New York
61st Pennsylvania

FOURTH BRIGADE
Col. Oliver Edwards

37th Massachusetts
2nd Rhode Island (detachment)

THIRD DIVISION
Brig. Gen. James B. Ricketts

FIRST BRIGADE
Col. William S. Truex
14th New Jersey
106th New York
151st New York
87th Pennsylvania
10th Vermont

SECOND BRIGADE
Col. J. Warren Keifer[2]
6th Maryland
9th New York Heavy Artillery, 1st and 3rd Battalions
110th Ohio
122nd Ohio
126th Ohio
67th Pennsylvania[3]
138th Pennsylvania

ARTILLERY BRIGADE
Col. Charles H. Tomkins

Maine Light, 4th Battery (D)
Massachusetts Light, 1st Battery (A)
New York Light, 1st Battery
9th New York Heavy, 2nd Battalion
1st Rhode Island Light, Battery C
1st Rhode Island Light, Battery G
5th US, Battery M
Maine Light, 5th Battery (E) Keifer
1st New Jersey Light, Battery A
New York Light, 3rd Battery
1st Ohio Light, Battery H
1st Rhode Island Light, Battery E
5th US, Battery E

IX Corps
Maj. Gen. Ambrose E. Burnside

PROVOST GUARD
Capt. Milton Cogswell

8th US

FIRST DIVISION
Brig. Gen. James H. Ledlie

FIRST BRIGADE
Lt. Col. Gilbert P. Robinson

3rd Maryland
21st Massachusetts (three cos.)

SECOND BRIGADE
Lt. Col. Joseph H. Barnes

29th Massachusetts
14th New York Heavy Artillery

2 Keifer led the brigade at this time though it is listed elsewhere as under the command of Col. Benjamin F. Smith. Ibid., 1:228, 505–507.

3 Joined brigade June 28. Ibid., 506.

56th Massachusetts
57th Massachusetts
59th Massachusetts
179th New York
100th Pennsylvania
2nd Pennsylvania Provisional Heavy Artillery

ENGINEERS
35th Massachusetts

ARTILLERY
Maine Light, 2nd Battery (B)
Massachusetts Light, 14th Battery
New York Light, 27th Battery

SECOND DIVISION
Brig. Gen. Robert B. Potter

FIRST BRIGADE
Lt. Col. Henry Pleasants

36th Massachusetts
58th Massachusetts
2nd New York Mounted Rifles (dismounted)
45th Pennsylvania
48th Pennsylvania
7th Rhode Island
4th Rhode Island

SECOND BRIGADE
Brig. Gen. Simon G. Griffin

2nd Maryland
31st Maine
32nd Maine
6th New Hampshire
9th New Hampshire
11th New Hampshire
17th Vermont

ACTING ENGINEERS
51st New York

ARTILLERY
Massachusetts Light, 11th Battery
New York Light, 19th Battery

THIRD DIVISION
Brig. Gen. Orlando B. Willcox

FIRST BRIGADE
Brig. Gen. John F. Hartranft

8th Michigan
27th Michigan (1st and 2nd Cos. Michigan Sharpshooters attached)
109th New York
13th Ohio Cavalry (dismounted)
51st Pennsylvania
37th Wisconsin
38th Wisconsin

SECOND BRIGADE
Col. William Humphrey

1st Michigan Sharpshooters
2nd Michigan
20th Michigan
24th New York Cavalry (dismounted)
46th New York
60th Ohio (9th and 10th Cos. Ohio Sharpshooters attached)
50th Pennsylvania

ACTING ENGINEERS
17th Michigan

ARTILLERY
Maine Light, 7th Battery (G)
New York Light, 34th Battery

FOURTH DIVISION
Brig. Gen. Edward Ferrero

FIRST BRIGADE
Col. Joshua K. Sigfried

27th US Colored Troops
30th US Colored Troops
39th US Colored Troops
43rd US Colored Troops
31st US Colored Troops

SECOND BRIGADE
Col. Henry G. Thomas

19th US Colored Troops
23rd US Colored Troops
28th US Colored Troops
29th US Colored Troops

ARTILLERY
Pennsylvania Light, Battery D
Vermont Light, 3rd Battery

Cavalry Corps
Maj. Gen. Philip H. Sheridan

ESCORT
Capt. Ira W. Claflin

6th US Cavalry

FIRST DIVISION
Brig. Gen. Alfred T. A. Torbert

FIRST BRIGADE
Brig. Gen. George A. Custer

1st Michigan Cavalry
5th Michigan Cavalry
6th Michigan Cavalry
7th Michigan Cavalry

SECOND BRIGADE
Col. Thomas C. Devin

4th New York Cavalry
6th New York Cavalry
9th New York Cavalry
17th Pennsylvania Cavalry

RESERVE BRIGADE
Brig. Gen. Wesley Merritt

19th New York Cavalry (1st Dragoons)
6th Pennsylvania Cavalry
1st Rhode Island Cavalry (joined June 23)
1st US Cavalry
2nd US Cavalry
5th US Cavalry

SECOND DIVISION
Brig. Gen. David McM. Gregg

FIRST BRIGADE
Brig. Gen. Henry E. Davis Jr.

1st Massachusetts Cavalry
1st New Jersey Cavalry
10th New York Cavalry
6th Ohio Cavalry
1st Pennsylvania Cavalry

SECOND BRIGADE
Col. J. Irvin Gregg

1st Maine Cavalry
2nd Pennsylvania Cavalry
4th Pennsylvania Cavalry
8th Pennsylvania Cavalry
13th Pennsylvania Cavalry
16th Pennsylvania Cavalry

HORSE ARTILLERY BRIGADE
Capt. James M. Robertson

1st US, Batteries H and I
2nd US, Batteries B and L
2nd US, Battery M
2nd US, Battery A
2nd US, Battery D
3rd US, Battery C

THIRD DIVISION
Brig. Gen. James H. Wilson

ESCORT
8th Illinois Cavalry (detachment)

PROVOST GUARD
3rd New Jersey Cavalry (detachment)

FIRST BRIGADE
Col. John B. McIntosh

1st Connecticut Cavalry
2nd New York Cavalry
5th New York Cavalry
2nd Ohio Cavalry

SECOND BRIGADE
Col. George H. Chapman

3rd Indiana Cavalry (Cos. A–F)
1st New Hampshire Cavalry
8th New York Cavalry
22nd New York Cavalry
1st Vermont Cavalry

ATTACHED HORSE ARTILLERY

1st US, Battery K
4th US, Battery C-E

Army of the James
Maj. Gen. Benjamin F. Butler

X Corps
Brig. Gen. William T. H. Brooks

CAVALRY
Maj. Atherton H. Stevens Jr.
4th Massachusetts Cavalry (1st Battalion)

FIRST DIVISION
Brig. Gen. Alfred H. Terry

FIRST BRIGADE
Col. Joshua B. Howell

39th Illinois
62nd Ohio
67th Ohio
85th Pennsylvania

SECOND BRIGADE
Col. Joseph R. Hawley

6th Connecticut
7th Connecticut
3rd New Hampshire
7th New Hampshire

THIRD BRIGADE
Col. Robert S. Foster

10th Connecticut
11th Maine
1st Maryland Cavalry (dismounted)
24th Massachusetts
100th New York

ARTILLERY BRIGADE
Capt. Loomis L. Langdon

Connecticut Light, 1st Battery
New Jersey Light, 5th Battery
3rd Rhode Island Light, Battery C
1st US, Battery M

SECOND DIVISION
Brig. Gen. John R. Turner

FIRST BRIGADE
Col. N. Martin Curtis

3rd New York
112th New York
117th New York
142nd New York

SECOND BRIGADE
Col. William B. Barton

47th New York
48th New York
115th New York
76th Pennsylvania

THIRD BRIGADE
Col. Louis Bell

13th Indiana
9th Maine
4th New Hampshire
169th New York
97th Pennsylvania

ARTILLERY BRIGADE

New Jersey Light, 4th Battery
1st US, Battery D
3rd US, Battery E
4th US, Battery D

THIRD DIVISION
Brig. Gen. Orris S. Ferry

FIRST BRIGADE
Brig. Gen. Gilman Marston

133rd Ohio
143rd Ohio
148th Ohio
163rd Ohio
New York Light Artillery, 33rd Battery

SECOND BRIGADE
Col. James B. Armstrong

130th Ohio
132nd Ohio
134th Ohio
138th Ohio

NOT BRIGADED
37th US Colored Troops

XVIII Corps
Maj. Gen. William F. Smith

PROVOST GUARD

2nd New Hampshire

79th New York (one company)

FIRST DIVISION

Brig. Gen. George J. Stannard

FIRST BRIGADE

Col. Edgar M. Cullen

81st New York
96th New York
98th New York
139th New York

SECOND BRIGADE

Brig. Gen. Hiram M. Burnham

8th Connecticut
10th New Hampshire
13th New Hampshire
118th New York

THIRD BRIGADE

Col. Guy V. Henry

21st Connecticut
40th Massachusetts
92nd New York
58th Pennsylvania
188th Pennsylvania

FOURTH BRIGADE

10th New York Heavy Artillery (transferred to First Bde., Second Div. June 24)

SECOND DIVISION

Brig. Gen. John H. Martindale

FIRST BRIGADE

Col. Alexander Piper

23rd Massachusetts
25th Massachusetts
27th Massachusetts
9th New Jersey
10th New York Heavy Artillery (transferred in June 24)
89th New York (transferred to Third Bde. June 24)
55th Pennsylvania

SECOND BRIGADE

Col. Griffin A. Stedman Jr.

11th Connecticut
8th Maine
12th New Hampshire
148th New York
19th Wisconsin

THIRD BRIGADE

Brig. Gen. Adelbert Ames

5th Maryland
89th New York (transferred from First Bde. June 24)
2nd Pennsylvania Heavy Artillery

THIRD DIVISION

Brig. Gen. Edward W. Hinks

CAVALRY

Capt. Albert F. Ray

4th Massachusetts Cavalry, Cos. E and H

FIRST BRIGADE
Brig. Gen. Edward A. Wild
Col. John H. Holman (assigned June 23)

5th Massachusetts Colored Cavalry (dismounted)
1st US Colored Cavalry (dismounted)
1st US Colored Troops
10th US Colored Troops

SECOND BRIGADE
Col. Samuel A. Duncan

2nd US Colored Cavalry (dismounted)
4th US Colored Troops
5th US Colored Troops
6th US Colored Troops
22nd US Colored Troops

ARTILLERY BRIGADE

3rd New York Light, Battery E
3rd New York Light, Battery M
New York Light, 16th Battery
Wisconsin Light, 4th Battery
4th US, Battery L
2nd US Colored, Battery B
3rd New York Light, Battery K
New York Light, 7th Battery
1st Rhode Island Light, Battery F
1st US, Battery B
5th US, Battery A

NAVAL BRIGADE
Brig. Gen. Charles K. Graham

ENGINEERS
Maj. Joseph Walker
1st New York (eight cos.)

SIEGE ARTILLERY
Col. Henry L. Abbott
1st Connecticut Heavy Artillery
12th New York Heavy Artillery, Cos. A and H
3rd Pennsylvania Heavy Artillery, Co. M

CAVALRY DIVISION
Brig. Gen. August V. Kautz

FIRST BRIGADE
Col. Robert M. West

3rd New York Cavalry
5th Pennsylvania Cavalry

SECOND BRIGADE
Col. Samuel Spear

1st District of Columbia Cavalry
11th Pennsylvania Cavalry

ATTACHED HORSE ARTILLERY
1st US, Battery B

UNASSIGNED CAVALRY
4th Massachusetts Cavalry, Cos. F and G
1st New York Mounted Rifles

PONTONIERS
Capt. John Pickering Jr.
Massachusetts Heavy Artillery, 13th Company

Confederate Order of Battle[4]

Army of Northern Virginia

Gen. Robert E. Lee

PROVOST GUARD
5th Alabama Battalion
1st Virginia Battalion
48th Georgia (1 Co.)

ENGINEERS
Maj. Gen. Martin L. Smith
1st Confederate Engineers

ARTILLERY
Brig. Gen. William N. Pendleton

First Corps

Lt. Gen. Richard H. Anderson

FIELD'S DIVISION
Maj. Gen. Charles W. Field

ANDERSON'S BRIGADE
Brig. Gen. George T. Anderson
7th Georgia
8th Georgia
9th Georgia
11th Georgia
59th Georgia

JENKINS'S BRIGADE
Brig. Gen. John Bratton
1st South Carolina Infantry (Hagood's)
2nd South Carolina Rifles
5th South Carolina Infantry
6th South Carolina Infantry
Palmetto South Carolina Sharpshooters

LAW'S BRIGADE
Col. William F. Perry
4th Alabama
15th Alabama
44th Alabama
47th Alabama
48th Alabama

BENNING'S BRIGADE
Col. Dudley M. Dubose
2nd Georgia
15th Georgia
17th Georgia
20th Georgia

GREGG'S BRIGADE
Brig. Gen. John Gregg
3rd Arkansas
1st Texas
4th Texas
5th Texas

4 The Confederate batteries mentioned in the text are identified on the maps by their informal names, which are include in parentheses in this order of battle.

KERSHAW'S DIVISION
Maj. Gen. Joseph B. Kershaw

BRYAN'S BRIGADE
Col. James P. Simms

10th Georgia
50th Georgia
51st Georgia
53rd Georgia

KERSHAW'S BRIGADE
Col. John W. Henagan

2nd South Carolina
3rd South Carolina Battalion Sharpshooters
3rd South Carolina
7th South Carolina
8th South Carolina
15th South Carolina
20th South Carolina

HUMPHREYS'S BRIGADE
Brig. Gen. Benjamin G. Humphreys

13th Mississippi
17th Mississippi
18th Mississippi
21st Mississippi

WOFFORD'S BRIGADE
Brig. Gen. William T. Wofford

3rd Georgia Battalion Sharpshooters
16th Georgia
18th Georgia
24th Georgia
Cobb's Georgia Legion Infantry
Phillips's Georgia Legion Infantry

PICKETT'S DIVISION
Maj. Gen. George E. Pickett

CORSE'S BRIGADE
Brig. Gen. Montgomery D. Corse

15th Virginia Infantry
17th Virginia Infantry
29th Virginia Infantry
30th Virginia Infantry
32nd Virginia Infantry

BARTON'S BRIGADE
Col. William R. Aylett

9th Virginia Infantry
14th Virginia Infantry
38th Virginia Infantry
53rd Virginia Infantry
57th Virginia Infantry

HUNTON'S BRIGADE
Brig. Gen. Eppa Hunton

8th Virginia Infantry
18th Virginia Infantry
19th Virginia Infantry
28th Virginia Infantry
56th Virginia Infantry

KEMPER'S BRIGADE
Col. William Terry
(promoted to brig. gen. June 27)
1st Virginia Infantry
3rd Virginia Infantry
7th Virginia Infantry
11th Virginia Infantry
24th Virginia Infantry

ARTILLERY
Brig. Gen. E. Porter Alexander

13TH VIRGINIA ARTILLERY BATTALION
Maj. Wade Hampton Gibbes

Danville Ringold Virginia Artillery
Lynchburg Virginia Artillery
Richmond Otey Virginia Artillery

CABELL'S BATTALION
Col. Henry C. Cabell

Pulaski Georgia Artillery
Troup Georgia Artillery
Ellis North Carolina Artillery
1st Co., Richmond Virginia Howitzers

HASKELL'S BATTALION
Maj. John C. Haskell

Branch North Carolina Artillery
Rowan North Carolina Artillery
Palmetto South Carolina Artillery
Amherst-Nelson Virginia Artillery

HUGER'S BATTALION
Lt. Col. Frank Huger

Madison Louisiana Artillery
Brooks South Carolina Artillery
Ashland Virginia Artillery
Bath Virginia Artillery
Bedford Virginia Artillery
Richmond Parker Virginia Artillery

Third Corps
Lt. Gen. Ambrose Powell Hill

MAHONE'S DIVISION
Brig. Gen. William Mahone

FINEGAN'S BRIGADE
Brig. Gen. Joseph Finegan

2nd Florida
5th Florida
8th Florida
9th Florida
10th Florida
11th Florida
Cos. F and H, 28th Georgia Battalion Heavy Artillery

HARRIS'S BRIGADE
Brig. Gen. Nathaniel H. Harris

12th Mississippi
16th Mississippi
19th Mississippi
48th Mississippi

MAHONE'S BRIGADE
Col. David A. Weisiger

6th Virginia
12th Virginia
16th Virginia
41st Virginia
61st Virginia

SANDERS'S BRIGADE
Brig. Gen. John C. C. Sanders

8th Alabama
9th Alabama
10th Alabama
11th Alabama
14th Alabama

WRIGHT'S BRIGADE
Brig. Gen. Ambrose R. Wright
2nd Georgia Battalion
3rd Georgia
10th Georgia Battalion
22nd Georgia
48th Georgia

HETH'S DIVISION
Maj. Gen. Henry Heth

WALKER'S BRIGADE (ARCHER'S BRIGADE ATTACHED)

Brig. Gen. Birkett D. Fry (ill June 25)
Col. Robert M. Mayo (June 25)

13th Alabama

COOKE'S BRIGADE

Brig. Gen. John R. Cooke

15th North Carolina

2nd Maryland Battalion
1st Tennessee (Provisional Army)
7th Tennessee48th North Carolina
14th Tennessee
22nd Virginia Battalion
40th Virginia
47th Virginia
55th Virginia

27th North Carolina
46th North Carolina

DAVIS'S BRIGADE
Col. John M. Stone

1st Confederate Battalion
2nd Mississippi
11th Mississippi
42nd Mississippi
55th North Carolina

KIRKLAND'S BRIGADE
Col. George H. Faribault (to June 27)
Brig. Gen. William MacRae (promoted brig. gen. June 27)

11th North Carolina
26th North Carolina
44th North Carolina
47th North Carolina
52nd North Carolina

WILCOX'S DIVISION
Maj. Gen. Cadmus M. Wilcox

LANE'S BRIGADE
Col. John D. Barry

7th North Carolina
18th North Carolina
28th North Carolina
33rd North Carolina
37th North Carolina

MCGOWAN'S BRIGADE
Brig. Gen. James Conner

1st South Carolina (Provisional Army)
1st South Carolina Rifles
12th South Carolina
13th South Carolina
14th South Carolina

SCALES'S BRIGADE
Brig. Gen. Alfred M. Scales

13th North Carolina
16th North Carolina
22nd North Carolina
34th North Carolina
38th North Carolina

THOMAS'S BRIGADE
Col. Thomas J. Simmons

14th Georgia
35th Georgia
45th Georgia
49th Georgia

ARTILLERY

MCINTOSH'S BATTALION
Maj. Marmaduke Johnson

Hardaway Alabama Artillery
Chesapeake Maryland Artillery
2nd Rockbridge Virginia Artillery
Danville Virginia Artillery
Jackson Flying Virginia Artillery (Clutter's battery)

PEGRAM'S BATTALION
Maj. William R. J. Pegram

1st Maryland Artillery (Dement's battery)
Crenshaw Virginia Artillery
Fredericksburg Virginia Artillery
McQueen South Carolina Artillery
Letcher Virginia Artillery (Brander's battery)
Purcell Virginia Artillery (Cayce's battery)

POAGUE'S BATTALION
Capt. Addison W. Utterback

Madison Mississippi Artillery
Charlotte North Carolina Artillery
Albemarle Everett Virginia Artillery
Warrenton Virginia Artillery

RICHARDSON'S BATTALION
Lt. Col. Charles Richardson

Donaldson Louisiana Artillery
Norfolk Blues Virginia Artillery
Norfolk Huger Virginia Artillery
Pittsylvania Virginia Artillery

11TH (SUMTER) GEORGIA ARTILLERY BATTALION
Lt. Col. Allen A. Cutts

Company A
Company B
Company C

WASHINGTON LOUISIANA ARTILLERY BATTALION
Lt. Col. Benjamin K. Eshleman

1st Company
2nd Company
3rd Company
4th Company

Cavalry Corps
Maj. Gen. Wade Hampton

HAMPTON'S DIVISION
Brig. Gen. Matthew C. Butler

BUTLER'S BRIGADE
Col. B. Huger Rutledge

4th South Carolina Cavalry
5th South Carolina Cavalry
6th South Carolina
35th Virginia Battalion Cavalry

ROSSER'S (LAUREL) BRIGADE
Col. Richard H. Dulany

7th Virginia Cavalry
11th Virginia Cavalry
12th Virginia Cavalry

YOUNG'S BRIGADE
Col. Gilbert J. Wright

7th Georgia Cavalry
20th Georgia Battalion Cavalry
Cobb's Georgia Legion Cavalry
Phillips's Georgia Legion Cavalry (Love's 4th Alabama Battalion Cavalry attached)
Jeff Davis Mississippi Legion Cavalry

FITZHUGH LEE'S DIVISION
Maj. Gen. Fitzhugh Lee

LOMAX'S BRIGADE
Brig. Gen. Lunsford L. Lomax

1st Maryland Battalion Cavalry
5th Virginia Cavalry
6th Virginia Cavalry
15th Virginia Cavalry

WICKHAM'S BRIGADE
Col. Thomas T. Munford

1st Virginia Cavalry
2nd Virginia Cavalry
3rd Virginia Cavalry
4th Virginia Cavalry

W. H. F. LEE'S DIVISION
Maj. Gen. W. H. F. Lee

BARRINGER'S BRIGADE
Brig. Gen. Rufus C. Barringer

CHAMBLISS'S BRIGADE
Brig. Gen. John R. Chambliss Jr.

1st North Carolina Cavalry
2nd North Carolina Cavalry
3rd North Carolina Cavalry
5th North Carolina Cavalry

9th Virginia Cavalry
10th Virginia Cavalry
13th Virginia Cavalry

DEARING'S BRIGADE
Brig. Gen. James Dearing

7th Confederate States Cavalry
62nd Georgia Cavalry
4th North Carolina Cavalry

HORSE ARTILLERY
Maj. Preston R. Chew

BREATHED'S ARTILLERY BATTALION
Maj. James Breathed (wounded June 29)
Capt. Philip R. Johnston

Baltimore Maryland Artillery
Washington South Carolina Artillery (Hart's battery)
1st Stuart Virginia Artillery (Breathed's battery)
2nd Stuart Virginia Artillery (McGregor's battery)
Ashby Virginia Artillery
Lynchburg Beauregard Virginia Artillery
Petersburg Virginia Artillery (Graham's battery)

Department of North Carolina and Southern Virginia
Gen. G. T. Beauregard

JOHNSON'S DIVISION
Maj. Gen. Bushrod R. Johnson

ELLIOTT'S BRIGADE
Brig. Gen. Stephen Elliott Jr.

17th South Carolina
18th South Carolina
22nd South Carolina
23rd South Carolina
26th South Carolina

WISE'S BRIGADE
Brig. Gen. Henry A. Wise

26th Virginia
34th Virginia
46th Virginia
59th Virginia

JOHNSON'S BRIGADE
Col. John S. Fulton

17th & 23rd Tennessee
25th & 44th Tennessee
63rd Tennessee

RANSOM'S BRIGADE
Col. Paul F. Faison

24th North Carolina
25th North Carolina
35th North Carolina
49th North Carolina
56th North Carolina

GRACIE'S BRIGADE
Brig. Gen. Archibald Gracie Jr.

41st Alabama
43rd Alabama
59th Alabama
23rd Alabama Battalion

HOKE'S DIVISION
Maj. Gen. Robert F. Hoke

CLINGMAN'S BRIGADE
Brig. Gen. Thomas L. Clingman

8th North Carolina
31st North Carolina
51st North Carolina
61st North Carolina

COLQUITT'S BRIGADE
Brig. Gen. Alfred H. Colquitt

6th Georgia
19th Georgia
23rd Georgia
27th Georgia
28th Georgia

HAGOOD'S BRIGADE
Brig. Gen. Johnson Hagood

11th South Carolina
21st South Carolina
25th South Carolina
27th South Carolina

MARTIN'S BRIGADE
Brig. Gen. James G. Martin
(until June 28)
Col. Charles T. Zachry

17th North Carolina
42nd North Carolina
66th North Carolina
7th South Carolina Battalion

ARTILLERY
Col. Hilary K. Jones

COIT'S BATTALION
Maj. James C. Coit

Bradford's (Mississippi) battery
Wright's (Virginia) battery

MOSELEY'S BATTALION
Lt. Col. Edgar F. Moseley

Slaten's (Georgia) battery
Miller's (North Carolina) battery
Cumming's (North Carolina) battery
Young's (Virginia) battery
Pegram's (Virginia) battery

READ'S BATTALION
Maj. John P. W. Read

Marshall's (Virginia) battery
Dickerson's (Virginia) battery
Macon's (Virginia) battery
Sullivan's (Virginia) battery

First Military District
Brig. Gen. Henry A. Wise

South Side Appomattox
PROVOST GUARD
64th Georgia

PETERSBURG GARRISON
44th Virginia Battalion
3rd Virginia Battalion Reserves
Hood's Virginia Battalion Reserves
Hobson's Co. Second Class Virginia Militia

Vicinity of Petersburg

BOGG'S ARTILLERY BATTALION

Maj. Francis J. Boggs

Sturdivant's (Virginia) battery

Martin's (Virginia) battery

INDEPENDENT SIGNAL CORPS

Maj. James F. Milligan

Danville

4th Virginia Reserves

9th Virginia Reserves Battalion

10th Virginia Reserves Battalion

11th Virginia Reserves Battalion

Drewry's Bluff

Confederate States Marine Battalion

Chesterton Johnston Virginia Artillery (Epes's Battery)

Neblett Virginia Heavy Artillery (Coleman's Battery)

Southside Virginia Heavy Artillery (Drewry's Battery)

United Virginia Artillery (Kevill's Battery)

Fort Clifton

Wilmington North Carolina Artillery (Miller's Battery) (one section)

34th Virginia Infantry (detachment)

Hicksford

Lt. Col. Alfred Coppens

Confederate States Zouave Battalion

Co. H, 62nd Georgia (artillery)

Confederate Guards Mississippi Artillery (Bradford's Battery) (one section)

4th Virginia Reserves Battalion

High Bridge (South Side Rail Road)

Lt. Col. Robert Smith

13th Virginia Reserves Battalion

Mattoax Bridge (Richmond & Danville Railroad)

Maj. William S. Basinger

18th Georgia Battalion

7th Virginia Reserves Battalion

Vicinity of Stony Creek

Lt. Col. William J. Crawley

Holcombe South Carolina Legion

STONY CREEK (WELDON RAILROAD)

Holcombe South Carolina Legion (four cos.)

NOTTOWAY BRIDGE (WELDON RAILROAD)

Holcombe South Carolina Legion (four cos)

ROWANTY BRIDGE (WELDON RAILROAD)

Holcombe South Carolina Legion (two cos.)

Staunton River Bridge (Richmond & Danville Railroad)
Capt. Benjamin L Farinholt
Farinholt's Battalion Virginia Reserves

Burkeville (Richmond & Danville and South Side railroads)
Brig. Gen. James G. Martin (took command June 28)

Department of Richmond
Lt. Gen. Richard S. Ewell

LOCAL DEFENSE TROOPS AND RESERVES
Brig. Gen. George W. C. Lee

1st Battalion, Local Defense Troops
2nd Battalion, Local Defense Troops
3rd Battalion, Local Defense Troops
4th Battalion, Local Defense Troops
5th Battalion, Local Defense Troops
6th Battalion, Local Defense Troops
1st Regiment Reserves

CAVALRY BRIGADE
Brig. Gen. Martin W. Gary

Hampton Legion Cavalry
7th South Carolina Cavalry
24th Virginia Cavalry

NOT BRIGADED
60th Alabama
25th Virginia Battalion Infantry
1st Battalion Cavalry, Local Defense

ARTILLERY DEFENSES
Lt. Col. John C. Pemberton

FIRST DIVISION (INNER LINE)
Lt. Col. John W. Atkinson

10th Virginia Battalion Heavy Artillery
19th Virginia Battalion Heavy Artillery

SECOND DIVISION (INNER LINE)
Lt. Col. James Howard

18th Virginia Battalion Heavy Artillery
20th Virginia Battalion Heavy Artillery

LIGHT ARTILLERY
Lt. Col. Charles E. Lightfoot

Caroline (Virginia) Artillery
2nd Nelson (Virginia) Artillery
Surry (Virginia) Artillery

UNATTACHED
Capt. Charles A. Green

Louisiana Guard Artillery

Chaffin's Bluff
Lt. Col. J. M. Maury

STARK'S BATTALION, LIGHT ARTILLERY
Maj. Alexander W. Stark
Mathews (Virginia) Artillery
McComas (Virginia) Artillery

Bibliography

Primary Sources

Unpublished

Manuscripts

Abbott, Peter M. Papers. Vermont Historical Society, Barre, VT.

Allen, R. Alfred. Papers. Duke University, Durham, NC.

Beauregard, P. G. T. Papers. Abraham Lincoln Presidential Library, Springfield, IL.

Bedell, Henry Edson. Lieutenant Henry Edson Bedell's 1864 Diary. 11th Vermont Infantry (aka 1st Artillery). 11th Vermont Volunteers. The Ed Italo Collection. Vermont in the Civil War, vermontcivilwar.org.

Bernard, George S. Papers. Alderman Library, University of Virginia, Charlottesville, VA.

Bird Family Papers. Virginia Historical Society, Richmond, VA.

Birney, David Bell. Papers. United States Army Heritage and Education Center, Carlisle, PA.

Blair, James A. Papers. Georgia Department of Archives and History, Atlanta, GA.

Bond, Daniel. Diary and Memoir. Newberry Library, Chicago, IL

Burgess, Mary Curtis. "A True Story." Elizabeth Cocke Coles Collection. Library of the

University of Virginia, Charlottesville, VA.

Burnham, Philander. Civil War Diary, 1864. Vermont Historical Society, Barre, VT.

Comins, Leander M. Letters. Private Collection of Diane Fishburn. Meadow Vista, CA.

Coon, David. Papers. Library of Congress, Washington, D.C.

Cushing, L. W. "Some Experiences of the Civil War." paintedhills.org.

Dearing Family Papers. Virginia Museum of History and Culture, Richmond, VA.

Dunn, Washington L. Diary of Washington L. Dunn, Company A, 27th Georgia Infantry, May 20, 1864–February 20, 1865. Confederate Reminiscences and Letters 1861–1865, Volume XVI. Georgia Division United Daughters of the Confederacy. Georgia Department of Archives and History, Atlanta, GA.

Eighth New York Heavy Artillery Collection. Genesee County History Department, Batavia, NY.

Foard, Fred C. Papers. North Carolina Department of Archives and History, Raleigh, NC.

French, George Oscar. Civil War Letters. Vermont Historical Society, Barre, VT.

Galwey, Thomas F. Diary. Library of Congress, Washington, D.C.

Gilpin, Samuel J. B. V. Diary. E. N. Gilpin Papers. Library of Congress, Washington, D.C.

Gove, George S. Letters. Parsons Family Papers. Milne Special Collections and Archives,

University of New Hampshire, Durham, NH.

Graham, Walter. Diary. Vermont Historical Society, Barre, VT.

Griffin, John C. "Life in Dinwiddie County in the vicinity of the opposing armies during the last years of the war." The Historical Society of Western Virginia, O. Winston Link Museum, History Museum of Western Virginia, Roanoke, VA.

Harder, William Henry. Memoir. Tennessee State Library and Archives, Nashville, TN.

Hatton. J. W. F. Diary and Memoir. Library of Congress, Washington, D.C.

Henry, John Newton. Papers. Minnesota Historical Society, St. Paul, MN.

Herbert, H. A. to E. P. Alexander, August 18, 1903. Gettysburg National Military Park, Gettysburg, PA.

Horton, William M. Diary. civilwardigital.com.

Hoyle, Joseph J. Papers. Duke University, Durham, NC.

Judkins, William B. "Memoirs of a Soldier of the 22nd Georgia." Floyd County Library, Special Collections Department, Rome, GA.

Kitchens, Smith. Diary. Winthrop University, Rock Hill, SC.

LaForge, Abiel T. Letters and Diaries. Alleghany County Historical Center, Andover, NY.

Landis, Allen. Letters. Library of Congress, Washington, D.C.

Latta, James William. Diary. James William Latta Papers. Library of Congress, Washington, D.C.

Lineback, Julius. Memoir. Southern Historical Collection. University of North Carolina at Chapel Hill, Chapel Hill, NC.

Lyons, Jacob. Diary. Southern Historical Collection. University of North Carolina at Chapel Hill, Chapel Hill, NC.

Lane, James H. Papers. Auburn University, Auburn, AL.

Lincoln, Abraham. Papers. Manuscript Division. Library of Congress, Washington, D.C.

Lockhart, Samuel P. Papers. Hugh Conway Browning Papers. Duke University, Durham, NC.

Mahone, William. Papers. Preston Library. Virginia Military Institute, Lexington, VA.

_____. Papers. Library of Virginia, Richmond, VA.

_____. Papers. Duke University, Durham, NC.

Mahone's (Anderson's Old) Division Tabular Return of Casualties (Series II). Beineke Rare Book and Manuscript Library, Yale University, New Haven, CT.

McClellan, Arthur. Diary and Notebook. Series 5, Diaries, 1846–1884. George Brinton

McClellan Papers. Library of Congress, Washington, D.C.

Nichols. James M. Diary. New York State Military Museum, Saratoga, NY.

Person, Presley Carter. Papers. Duke University, Durham, NC.

Peterson, Charles H. Pocket Diary Collection. Digital Collections. Oviatt Library, California State University Northridge, Northridge, CA.

Phillips, James Eldred. Papers. Virginia Museum of History and Culture, Richmond, VA.

Poland, Charles O. Diary. Special Collections. Virginia Polytechnic Institute and State University, Blacksburg, VA.

Proctor, Wilbur Huntington. Diary. Wilbur Huntington Proctor Papers. Library of Congress, Washington, D.C.

Roebling, W. A. *Report of the Operations of the 5th Corps, A.P. in Genl. Grant's Campaign from Culpeper to Petersburg, as seen by W. A. Roebling, Maj. A. D. C. 1864*. Letterbooks Vol. 7c, Box 24. Gouverneur K. Warren Collection. Roe Archives, New York State Library, Albany, NY.

Root, Samuel H. Papers. Civil War Miscellaneous Collection. United States Army Heritage and Education Center, Carlisle, PA.

Ryno, John L. Diary. Interlaken Historical Society, Interlaken, NY.

Sale, John F. Diary. John F. Sale Papers. Library of Virginia, Richmond, VA.

Sanders, John C. C. Collection. University of Alabama, Tuscaloosa, AL.

Sanders, William Henry. Papers. Alabama Department of Archives and History, Montgomery, AL.

Scales, Alfred M. Papers. East Carolina University, Greeneville, NC.

Scott, John Zachary Holladay. "John Zachary Holladay Scott, Confederate Soldier 1861–1865."

Confederate Reminiscences and Letters 1861–1865, Volume VII. Georgia Division United Daughters of the Confederacy. Georgia Department of Archives and History, Atlanta, GA.

6th Virginia File. Fredericksburg and Spotsylvania National Battlefield Park, Fredericksburg, VA.

Strong, George Templeton. Diary. 4 vols. New York Historical Society Museum and Library, New York, NY.

Turner, John R. Papers. Duke University, Durham, NC.

Verdery, Eugene and James. Letters. Duke University, Durham, NC.

Waddell, Charles E. Diary. American Civil War Museum, Richmond, VA.

Waddell, Mrs. Charles E. Diary. Papers of Miss Georgia Hicks. Collection of the United Daughters of the Confederacy. North Carolina Division, North Carolina Department of Archives and History, Raleigh, NC.

Walker, Aldace Freeman. Papers. Vermont Historical Society, Barre, VT.

Waring, Joseph Frederick. Diary. Joseph Frederick Waring Papers. Southern Historical Collection. University of North Carolina at Chapel Hill, Chapel Hill, NC.

Waring, Joseph Frederick II. "The Jeff Davis Legion." J. F. Waring Papers 1275. Georgia Historical Society, Savannah, GA.

Watlington, William. Diary. Indiana State Library, Madison, IN.

Whitehorne, James E. Letters. James E. Whitehorne Papers. Library of Virginia, Richmond, VA.

Wilcox, Cadmus M. *Notes on the Richmond Campaign, 1864–1865* (transcribed by Noah Andre Trudeau). Cadmus M. Wilcox Papers. Library of Congress, Washington, D.C.

_____ Report. Lee Headquarters Papers. Virginia Museum of Culture and History, Richmond, VA.

Williams, Lyman. Papers. Minnesota Historical Society, St. Paul, MN.

Wilson, James Harrison. Diaries. Delaware Public Archives, Dover, DE.

Wright, Horatio. Report. Entry 160: Generals' Service Reports, 1864–1887, RG94: Records of the Adjutant General's Office, 1780's–1917.

Online Collections

archives.alabama.org

archives.gov

archives.org

babel.hathitrust.org

beyondthecrater.com

books.google.com

chroniclingamerica.com
civilwardigital.com
csa-railroads.com
digitalcollections.nyhistory.org
digitalnc.org
dmna.ny.gov
loc.gov
newspapers.com
openlibrary.org
paintedhills.org
paperlessarchives.com
petersburgproject.com
vermontcivilwar.org
vermonthistory.org

Published

Books

Abbott, Lemuel Abijah. *Personal Recollections and Civil War Diary, 1864*. Burlington, VT: Burlington Free Press Printing Co., 1908.

Adams, Henry, et al., eds., *Letters of John Hay and Extracts from Diary*. 3 vols. Washington, D.C.: n. p., 1908.

Adams, John G. B. *Reminiscences of the Nineteenth Massachusetts Regiment*. Boston: Wright, Potter Printing Company, 1890.

Agassiz, George R., ed., *Meade's Headquarters 1863–1865, Letters of Colonel Theodore Lyman, from The Wilderness to Appomattox*. Boston: Massachusetts Historical Society, 1922.

Alexander, Edward Porter. *Military Memoirs of a Confederate*. Bloomington: Indiana University Press, 1962.

Armes, George A. *Ups and Downs of an Army Officer*. Washington, D.C.: n. p., 1900.

Association of Officers of the 20th Massachusetts Volunteer Infantry, "Reports, letters & papers appertaining to 20th Mass. Vol. Inf." (Boston: Boston Public Library, 1868).

Aubery, James M. *The Thirty-Sixth Wisconsin Volunteer Infantry, 1st Brigade, 2d Division, 2d Army Corps: An Authentic Record of the Regiment from Its Organization to Its Muster Out*. Milwaukee: Evening Wisconsin Company, 1900.

Baker, Jason B. *Chicago to Appomattox: The 39th Illinois Infantry in the Civil War*. Jefferson, NC: McFarland & Company, Inc., Publishers, 2022.

Baker, L. C. *History of the United States Secret Service*. Philadelphia: L. C. Baker, 1867.

Baker, Naomi B., comp. *Letters Home: Joel B. Baker, A collection of "Letters Home" from the Civil War, written by Colonel Joel B. Baker and compiled by his great-grandaughter, Naomi B. Baker*.Lockport, NY: C. W. Baker Agency, 1996.

Banes, Charles H. *History of the Sixty-Ninth, Seventy-First, Seventh-Second, and One Hundred and Sixth Pennsylvania* Volunteers. Philadelphia: D. J. Gallagher & Co., 1876.

Baylor, George. *Bull Run to Bull Run; or, Four Years in the Army of Northern Virginia,Containing a Detailed Account of the Career and Adventures of the Baylor Light Horse,Company B, Twelfth Virginia Cavalry, C.S.A., with Leaves from My Scrapbook*. Richmond: B. F. Johnson Publishing Company, 1900.

Beale, George W. *A Lieutenant of Cavalry in Lee's Army*. Boston: The Gorham Press, 1918.

Beale, Howard K., ed. *The Diary of Edward Bates, 1859–1866*. Washington, D.C.: United States Government Printing Office, 1933.

Beale, Richard L. T. *History of the Ninth Virginia Cavalry, in the War Between the States*. Richmond: B. F. Johnson Publishing Co., 1899.

Beckham, Mickey, ed. *A Confederate Soldier's Eloquent War: The Complete Diary of Samuel Lowry, Enlistment, Hardship, Battles and Death; Yorkville to Columbia, Charleston to Kiawah, to Manassas, to Petersburg, Finally Borne Home by Servant Henry Avery*. North Charleston, SC: Book Surge, 2008.

Beecher, Herbert W. *History of the First Light Battery Connecticut Volunteers, 1861–1865, Personal Records and Reminiscences, the Story of the Battery from Its Organization to the Present Time*. 2 vols. New York: A. T. De La Mare Ptg. and Pub. Co., 1906.

Bennett, Edwin C. *Musket and Sword, or the Camp, March and Firing Line in the Army of the Potomac*. Boston: Coburn Publishing Co., 1900.

Bidwell, Frederick David, comp. *History of the Forty-Ninth New York Volunteers*. Albany, NY: J. B. Lyon Company, Printers, 1916.

Billings, John Davis. *The History of the Tenth Massachusetts Battery of Light Artillery in the War of the Rebellion: formerly of the Third Corps and afterwards of Hancock's Second Corps, Army of the Potomac, 1862–1865*. Boston: Arakelyan Press, 1909.

Bird, Kermit Molyneux, ed., *Quill of the Wild Goose: Civil War Letters and Diaries of Private Joel Molyneux, 141st Pennsylvania Volunteers*. Shippensburg, PA: Burd Street Press, 1996.

Bloodgood, John D. *Personal Reminiscences of the War*. New York: Hunton & Eaton, 1893.

Bolton, H. W. *Personal Reminiscences of the Late War*. Chicago: H. W. Bolton, 1892.

Boudrye, Louis N. *History Records of the Fifth New York Cavalry, First Ira Harris Guard: Its Organization, Marches, Raids, Scouts, Engagements, and General Services during the Rebellion of 1861-1865, with Observations of the Author by the Way, Giving Sketches of the Armies of the Potomac and Shenandoah. Also, Interesting Accounts of Prison Life and of the Secret Service*. Albany, NY: S. R. Gray, 1865.

Bowen, James L. *History of the Thirty-Seventh Regiment Mass. Volunteers in the Civil War of 1861–1865, with a Comprehensive Sketch of the Doings of Massachusetts as a State, and of the Principal Campaigns of the War*. Holyoke, MA: C. W. Bryan & Co., 1884.

Brooks, U. R. *Butler and His Cavalry in the War of Secession 1861–1865*. Columbia, SC: The State Company, 1909.

Brown, Augustus C. *The Diary of a Line Officer*. New York: n. p., 1906.

Brown, Bambi Rae, ed. *Haystacks of Limbs, The Siege of Petersburg, Virginia—1864–1865: The Civil War Diary of Anthony Gaveston Taylor, 39th Illinois Regiment—Company A—Volunteer Veteran Infantry*. Parker, CO: Outskirts Press, 2017.

Caldwell, J. F. J. Caldwell. *History of a Brigade of South Carolinians, Known First as "Gregg's" and Subsequently as "McGowan's Brigade"*. Philadelphia, PA: King & Baird, Printers, 1866.

Calhoun, C. M. *Liberty Dethroned: A Concise History of Some of the Most Startling Events before, during and since the Civil War*. Greenwood, SC: n. p., 1903.

Camper, Charles, and Kirkley, J. W., comps. *Historical Record of the First Regiment Maryland Infantry, with an Appendix containing a Register of the Officers and Enlisted Men, Biographies of Deceased Officers, Etc., War of the Rebellion, 1861–65*. Washington, D.C.: Gibson Brothers, Printers, 1871.

Carter, John C., ed., *Welcome the Hour of Conflict: William Cowan McClellan and the 9th Alabama*. Tuscaloosa: University of Alabama Press, 2007.

Carter, Robert Goldthwaite. *Four Brothers in Blue, Or, Sunshine and Shadows of the War of Rebellion: A Story of the Great Civil War from Bull Run to Appomattox*. Norman, OK: University of Oklahoma Press, 1999.

Cerf, Bennett, et al. *The Complete Writings of Thucydides: The Peloponnesian War*. New York: Random House, 1934.

Chesson, Michael B., ed. *The Journal of a Civil War Surgeon*. Lincoln, NE: University of Nebraska Press, 2003.

Chester, H. W. *Recollections of the War of the Rebellion: A Story of the 2nd Ohio Volunteer Cavalry, 1861–1865*. Wheaton, IL: Wheaton History Center, 1996.

Child, William. *A History Of The Fifth Regiment New Hampshire Volunteers in the American Civil War 1861–62*. 2 vols. Bristol, NH: R. W. Musgrove, Printer, 1893.

Claiborne, John Herbert. *Seventy-Five Years in Old Virginia: With Some Account of the Life of the Author and Some History of the People Amongst Whom His Lot was Cast—Their Character, Their Condition and Their Conduct Before the War, During the War and After the War.* New York: The Neale Publishing Company, 1904.

Clark, Charles M. *The History of the Thirty-Ninth Illinois Volunteer Veteran Infantry, (Yates Phalanx) in the War of the Rebellion, 1861–1865*. Chicago: Veteran Association of the Regiment, 1889.

Clark, George. *A Glance Backward: Or Some Events in the Past History of My Life*. Houston: Press of Rein & Sons Company, 1914.

Clark, Walter, ed. *Histories of the Several Regiments and Battalions from North Carolina in the Great War 1861–65*. 5 vols. Goldsborough, NC: Nash Brothers, Book and Job Printers, 1901.

Cockrell, Thomas D. and Ballard, Michael B., eds., *A Mississippi Rebel in the Army of Northern Virginia: The Civil War Memoirs of Private David Holt*. Baton Rouge: Louisiana State University Press, 1995.

Coco, Gregory A. *From Ball's Bluff to Gettysburg . . . and Beyond: The Civil War Letters of Private Roland E. Bowen, 15th Massachusetts Infantry 1861–1864*. Gettysburg, Pa.: Thomas Publications, 1994.

Coltrane, Daniel Branson. *The Memoirs of Daniel Branson Coltrane, Co. I, 63rd Reg., N. C. Cavalry C.S.A.* Raleigh, NC: Edwards & Broughton, 1956.

Couture, Richard T., ed. *Charlie's Letters: The Correspondence Of Charles E. DeNoon*. Collingswood, NJ: s. p., 1982.

Crabtree, Beth Gilbert, and Patton, James W., eds. *"Journal of a Secesh Lady," The Diary of*

Catherine Ann Devereux Edmonston, 1860–1866. Raleigh: Division of Archives and History, Department of Cultural Resources, 1979.

Craft, David. *History of the One Hundred Forty-First Regiment, Pennsylvania Volunteers, 1862–1865*. Towanda, PA: Reporter-Journal Printing Company, 1885.

Crowninshield, Benjamin W. *First Regiment of Massachusetts Cavalry Volunteers*. Boston: Houghton, Mifflin and Company, 1891.

Cummins, D. Duane, and Daryl Hohweiler. *An Enlisted Soldier's View of the Civil War, the Wartime Papers of Joseph R. Ward Jr., 39th Illinois Volunteer Infantry*. West Lafayette, IN: Belle Publications, 1981.

Dana, Charles A. *Recollections of the Civil War, With the Leaders at Washington, and in the Field in the Sixties.* New York: D. Appleton and Company, 1902.

De Peyster, John Watts. *The Anniversary Address Delivered before the Third Army Corps Union, 5th May 1875, The Glorious Old Fighting Third Corps As We Understand It.* New York: Atlantic Publishing and Engraving Company, 1875.

De Trobriand, Regis. *Four Years with the Army of the Potomac*. Boston: Ticknor and Company, 1889.

Dickey, Luther S. *History of the Eighty-fifth Regiment Pennsylvania Volunteer Infantry 1861–1865*. New York: J. C. & W. E. Powers, 1915.

Dodson, John L., ed. *The Civil War Journals of Col. Homer A. Plimpton 1861–1865*. Bloomington, IN: Trafford Publishing, 2012.

Dorman, G. H. *Fifty Years Ago: Reminiscences of '61–'65*. Tallahassee: T. J. Appleyard, 1912.

Dowdey, Clifford, and Manarin, Louis H., eds. *The Wartime Papers of Robert E. Lee.* Boston: Da Capo Press, 1961.

DuBose, Henry Kershaw. *The History of Company B, Twenty-First Regiment (Infantry) South Carolina Volunteers, Confederate States Provisional Army*. Columbia, SC: R. L. Bryan, 1909.

Dunlop, William S. *Lee's Sharpshooters; or, The Forefront of Battle: A Story of Southern Valor That Never Has Been Told.* Little Rock: Tunnah & Pittard, 1899.

Elliott, James Carson. *The Southern Soldier Boy: The Experiences of a Confederate Soldier of the 56th North Carolina Regiment During the American Civil War.* Driffield, UK: Echo Library, 2010.

Elmore, Fletcher L., Jr. comp. *Diary Of J. E. Whitehorne, 1st Sergt., Co. "F," 12th Va. Infantry, A. P. Hill's 3rd Corps, A. N. Va.* Utica, Ky: McDowell Publications, 1995.

Floyd, Fred. C. *History of the Fortieth (Mozart) Regiment New York Volunteers, Which Was Composed of Four Companies from New York, Four Companies from Massachusetts, and Two Companies from Pennsylvania*. Boston: F. H. Gilson Company, 1909.

Folsom, James M. *Heroes and Martyrs of Georgia, Georgia's Record in the Revolution of 1861*. Macon, GA: Burke, Boykin & Company, 1864.

Ford, Andrew E. *The Story of the Fifteenth Regiment Massachusetts Volunteer Infantry in the Civil War, 1861–1864*. Clinton, MA: Press of W. J. Coulter, 1898.

Frederick, Gilbert. *The Story of a Regiment, Being a Record of the Military Services of the Fifty-Seventh New York State Volunteer Infantry in the War of the Rebellion 1861–1865*. Chicago: C. H. Morgan Co., 1895.

Freeman, Douglas Southall, ed., *Lee's Dispatches: Unpublished Letters of General Robert E. Lee, C.S.A., to Jefferson Davis and the War Department of the Confederate States of America 1862–65*. Baton Rouge: Louisiana State University Press, 1994.

Gallagher, Gary W., ed. *Fighting for the Confederacy: The Personal Recollections of General Edward Porter Alexander*. Chapel Hill, NC: University of North Carolina Press, 1989.

Gause, Isaac. *Four Years with Five Armies: Army of the Frontier, Army of the Potomac, Army of the Missouri, Army of the Ohio, Army of the Shenandoah*. New York: The Neale Publishing Company, 1908.

Galwey, Thomas Francis. *The Valiant Hours, Narrative of "Captain Brevet," an Irish-American in the Army of the Potomac*. Harrisburg, PA: Literary Licensing, 2011.

Gibbon, John. *Personal Recollections of the Civil War*. New York: G. P. Putnam's Sons, 1928.

Gill, John. *Reminiscences of Four Years in the Confederate Army, 1861–1865*. Baltimore: Sun Printing Office, 1904.

Goldsborough, W. W. *The Maryland Line in the Confederate Army, 1861–1865*. Baltimore: Guggenheimer, Weil & Co., 1900.

Grant, Ulysses S. *Personal Memoirs of U. S. Grant*. 2 vols. New York: Charles L. Webster & Co., 1886.

Hagood, Johnson. *Memoirs of the War of Secession from the Original Manuscripts of Johnson Hagood*. Columbia, SC: The State Company, 1910.

Haines, Alanson A. *History of the Fifteenth Regiment New Jersey Volunteers*. New York: Jenkins & Thomas, Printers, 1883.

Haskin, William L., comp. *The History of the First Regiment of Artillery: From Organization in 1821 to January 1, 1876*. Portland, ME: B. Thurston and Company, 1879.

Hastings, William H., ed. *Letters from a Sharpshooter: The Civil War Letters of William B.*

Greene, Co. G, Berdan's Sharpshooters. Charlottesville: University of Virginia Press, 1994.

Hatton, Robert W., ed. *William James Smith's Memoirs of the 2nd Ohio Volunteer Cavalry, Company M*. Milford, OH: Little Miami Pub. Co., 2008.

Haynes, E. M. *A History of the Tenth Regiment Vermont Volunteers, with Biographical Sketches* of *Officers Who Fell in Battle, and a Complete Roster of All the Officers and Men Connected with It—Showing All Changes by Promotion, Death or Resignation, during the Military Existence of the Regiment*. Lewiston, ME: The Tuttle Company, Printers, 1870.

Hays, Gilbert Adams. *Under the Red Patch; Story of the Sixty-Third Regiment, Pennsylvania Volunteers, 1861–1864*. Pittsburgh: Sixty-third Pennsylvania Volunteers Regimental Association, 1908.

Hazelwood, Donald. *Tight Ranks, The Fighting Record of the 34th North Carolina in the Civil War: A History and Roster*. Ararat, VA: Laurel Hill Publishing, 2019.

Hewett, Janet B., et al., eds. *Supplement to the Official Records of the Union and Confederate Armies*. 100 vols. Wilmington, NC: Broadfoot Publishing Company, 1994–2001.

Hoffman, Elliott W. *History of the First Vermont Cavalry Volunteers in the War of the Great Rebellion*. Baltimore: Butternut & Blue, 2000.

Houghton, Edwin B. *The Campaigns of the Seventeenth Maine*. Portland, ME: Short & Loring, 1866.

Jackson, Harry F., and Thomas F. O'Donnell. *Back Home in Oneida: Hermon Clarke and his Letters*. Syracuse, NY: Syracuse University Press, 1965.

Johnson, Robert Underwood, and Buel, Clarence Clough, eds. *Battles and Leaders of the Civil War*. Vol. 4. New York: Thomas Yoseloff, 1956.

Jones, J. B. *A Rebel War Clerk's Diary at the Confederate States Capital*. 2 vols. Philadelphia: J. B. Lippincott & Co., 1866.

Kirk, Hyland C. *Heavy Guns and Light: A History of the 4th New York Heavy Artillery*. New York: Burr Printing House, 1890.

King, David H., et al. *History of the Ninety-Third Regiment, New York Volunteer Infantry, 1861–1865*. Milwaukee: Swain & Tate Co., Printers, 1895.

Koempel, Phillip. *Phil Koempel's Diary, 1861–1865*. n. p., 1923.

Kreutzer, William. *Notes and Observations Made during Four Years of Service with the Ninety-Eighth N. Y. Volunteers in the War of 1861*. Philadelphia: Grant, Faires & Rodgers, Printers, 1878.

Leeke, Jim, ed. *A Hundred Days to Richmond: Ohio's "Hundred Days" Men in the Civil* War. Bloomington, IN: Indiana University Press, 1999.

Locke, William Henry. *The Story of the Regiment*. Philadelphia: J. B. Lippincott & Co., 1868.

Lowe, David, ed. *Meade's Army: The Private Notebooks of Lt. Col. Theodore Lyman*. Kent, OH: Kent State University Press, 2007.

Lowe, Jeffrey C., and Sam Hodges, eds., *Letters to Amanda, The Civil War Letters of Marion Hill Fitzpatrick, Army of Northern Virginia*. Macon, GA: Mercer University Press, 1998.

Lutz, Caroline C., ed. *Letters of George E. Chamberlin, Who Fell in the Service of His Country Near Charlestown, Va., August 21st, 1864*. Springfield, IL: H. W. Rokker's Publishing House, 1883.

Marbaker, Thomas D. *History of the Eleventh New Jersey Volunteers, from its Organization to Appomattox, to which is Added Experiences of Prison Life and Sketches of Individual Members*. Trenton, NJ: MacCrellish & Quigley, Book and Job Printers, 1898.

Mark, Penrose G. *Red, White and Blue Badge, Pennsylvania Veteran Volunteers: A History of the 93rd Regiment, known as the "Lebanon Infantry" and "One of the 300 Fighting Regiments" from September 12th, 1861, to June 27th, 1865*. Harrisburg, PA: The Aughinbaugh Press, 1911.

Marshall, D. P. *Company "K," 155th Volunteer Pa. Zouaves, A Detailed History of the Organization and Service to the Country During the Civil War 1862 Until the Collapse of the Rebellion, Together with many incidents and reminiscences of the Camp, the March and the Battle Field, also Much of the History of the Grand Old 155th*. London: n.p., 1888.

Marshall, Jeffrey D., ed. *A War of the People: Vermont Civil War Letters*. Lebanon, NH: University Press of New England, 1999.

Marshall, Jessie Ames, ed. *Private and Official Correspondence of Gen. Benjamin F. Butler during the Period of the Civil War*. 5 vols. Norwood, MA: The Plimpton Press, 1917.

Mason, John M., Jr., ed. *Three Years in the Army or the Life and Adventures of a Rebel Soldier*. Warren, OH: n. p., 1950.

Maxfield, Albert. *The Story of One Regiment: The Eleventh Maine Infantry Volunteers in the War of the Rebellion*. New York: Press of J. J. Little & Co., 1896.

_____, and Robert Brady Jr. *Company D of the Eleventh Regiment Maine Infantry Volunteers in the War of the Rebellion*. New York: Press of Thos. Humphrey, 1890.

Meade, George, ed. *The Life and Letters of George Gordon Meade*. 2 vols. New York: Charles Scribner's Sons, 1913.

McDermott, Anthony W. *A Brief History of the 69th Regiment Pennsylvania Volunteers from Its Formation until Final Muster Out of the United States Service*. Philadelphia: D. J. Gallagher & Co., Printers and Publishers, 1895.

McDonald, William N. *A History of the Laurel Brigade; Originally the Ashby Cavalry of the Army of Northern Virginia and Chew's Battery*. Baltimore: Mrs. Kate McDonald, 1907.

Meier, Heinz K., ed. *Memoirs of a Swiss Officer in the American Civil War*. Bern: Herbert Lang, 1972.

Menge, W. Springer, and J. August Shimrak, eds. *The Civil War Notebook of Daniel Chisholm: A Chronicle of Daily Life in the Union Army, 1864–1865*. New York: Orion Books, 1989.

Merrill, Samuel H. *The Campaigns of the First Maine and the First District of Columbia Cavalry*. Portland, ME: Bailey & Noyes, 1866.

Miller, Delavan S. *Drum Taps in Dixie, Memories of a Drummer Boy, 1861–1865*. Watertown, NY: Hungerford-Holbrook Co., 1903.

Miller, Richard F. and Robert F. Mooney, eds. *The Civil War: The Nantucket Experience, Including the Memoirs of Josiah Fitch Murphey*. Nantucket, MA: Wesco Publishing, 1994.

Muffly, J. W., ed. *The Story of Our Regiment, A History of the 148th Pennsylvania Vols.* Des Moines: The Kenyon Printing & Mfg. Co., 1904.

Mulholland, St. Clair A. *The Story of the 116th Regiment Pennsylvania Volunteers in the War of the Rebellion, the Record of a Gallant Command.* Philadelphia: F. McManus, Jr. & Co., 1903.

Myers, Frank M. *The Comanches: A History of White's Battalion, Virginia Cavalry, Laurel Brig., Hampton Div., A.N.V., C.S.A.* Baltimore: Kelly, Piet & Co., 1871.

Nanzig, Thomas P., ed. *The Civil War Memoirs of a Virginia Cavalryman, Lt. Robert T. Hubard Jr.* Tuscaloosa, AL: University of Alabama Press, 2007.

Nevins, Allan, ed. *A Diary of Battle: The Personal Journals of Colonel Charles S. Wainwright, 1861–1865.* Boston: Da Capo Press, 1998.

_____, and Milton Halsey Thomas, eds. *The Diary of George Templeton Strong.* 4 vols. New York: The Macmillan Company, 1952.

Newell, Joseph Keith, ed. *"Ours." Annals of the Tenth Regiment, Massachusetts Volunteers, in the Rebellion.* Springfield, MA: C. A. Nichols & Co., 1875.

Newsome, Hampton, John Horn, and John Selby. *Civil War Talks: Further Reminiscences of George S. Bernard and His Fellow Veterans.* Charlottesville: University of Virginia Press, 2012.

Newton, J. Terrill. *Campaign of the Fourteenth Regiment New Jersey Volunteers.* New Brunswick, NJ: Daily Home News Press, 1884.

Nichols, James M. *Perry's Saints or The Fighting Parson's Regiment in the War of the Rebellion.* Boston: D. Lothrop and Company, 1886.

Norton, Henry, comp. and ed. *Deeds of Daring, Or History of the Eighth N. Y. Volunteer Cavalry, Containing a Complete Record of the Battles, Skirmishes, Marches, etc., that the Gallant Eighth New York Cavalry Participated in, from Its Organization in November, 1861, to the Close of the Rebellion in 1865.* Norwich, NY: Chenango Telegraph Printing House, 1889.

Page, Charles A. *Letters of a War Correspondent.* Boston: L. C. Page and Company, 1899.

Page, Charles D. *History of the Fourteenth Regiment, Connecticut Vol. Infantry.* Meriden, CT: The Horton Printing Co., 1906.

Parker, John Lord. *Henry Wilson's Regiment: History of the Twenty-Second Massachusetts Infantry, the Second Company Sharpshooters, and the Third Light Battery in the War of the Rebellion.* Boston: Press of Rand Avery Company, 1887.

Parker, William Harwar. *Recollections of a Naval Officer.* New York: Charles Scribner's Sons, 1883.

Pearce, T. H., and Selby A. Daniels, eds. *Diary of Captain Henry A. Chambers.* Wilmington, NC: Broadfoot Publishing Company, 1983.

Peck, Hiram T. *Army Journal: A Private Record of Life in the Federal Service during the Great Rebellion.* New Haven: n. p., 1874.

Perry, Martha Derby, comp. *Letters from a Surgeon of the Civil War.* Boston: Little, Brown, and Company, 1906.

Pickeril, W. N. *History of the Third Indiana Cavalry.* Indianapolis: Aetna Publishing Co., 1906.

Porter, Horace. *Campaigning with Grant.* New York: The Century Co., 1906.

Preston, Noble D. *History of the Tenth Regiment of Cavalry New York State Volunteers, August, 1861, to August, 1865.* New York: D. Appleton and Co., 1892.

Priest, John Michael, ed. *One Surgeon's Private War: Doctor William W. Potter of the 57th New York.* Shippensburg, Pa.: White Mane Publishing Co., 1996.

Prowell, George R. *History of the Eighty-Seventh Regiment, Pennsylvania Volunteers, Prepared from Official Records, Diaries, and Other Authentic Sources of Information.* York, PA: York Daily, 1903.

Roback, Henry, comp. *The Veteran Volunteers of Herkimer and Otsego Counties in the War of the Rebellion Being a History of the 152d N. Y. V. with Scenes, Incidents, Etc., Which Occurred in the Ranks, of the 34th N. Y, 97th N. Y., 121st N. Y, 2d N. Y. Heavy Artillery, and 1st and 2d N. Y. Mounted Rifles; also, the Active Part Performed by the Boys in Blue Who Were Associated with the 152d N. Y. V., in Gen. Hancock's Second Army Corps during Grant's Campaign from the Wilderness to the Surrender of Gen. Lee at Appomattox Court House, Va.* Little Falls, NY: Press of L. C. Childs and Son, 1888.

Robertson Jr., James I., ed. *The Civil War Letters of General Robert McAllister.* Baton Rouge: Louisiana State University Press, 1998.

Rodenbough, Theophilus F., Thomas J. Grier, and William P. Seal. *History of the Eighteenth Regiment of Cavalry Pennsylvania Volunteers (163d Regiment of the Line) 1862–1865.* New York: Wynkoop Hallenbeck Crawford Co., 1909.

Rodenbough, Theophilus Francis, and William Haskin, comps. *The Army of the US Historical Sketches of Staff and Line with Portraits of Generals-in-Chief.* New York: Maynard, Merrill & Co., 1896.

Roe, Alfred S. *The Twenty-Fourth Regiment Massachusetts Volunteers, 1861–1866, "New England Guard Regiment."* Worcester, MA: Twenty-Fourth Veteran Association, 1907.

_____. *The Ninth New York Heavy Artillery, A History of Its Organization, Its Service in the Defenses of Washington, Marches, Camps, Battles and Muster-out, with Accounts of Life in a Rebel Prison, Personal Experiences, Names and Addresses of Surviving Members, Personal Sketches, And a Complete Roster of the Regiment.* Worcester, MA: Press of F. S. Blanchard & Co., 1899.

_____, and Charles Nutt. *History of the First Regiment of Heavy Artillery, Massachusetts Volunteers, Formerly the Fourteenth Regiment of Infantry, 1861–1865.* Boston: Regimental Association, 1917.

Roe, David R. *A Civil War Soldier's Diary, Valentine C. Randolph, 39th Illinois Regiment.* DeKalb: Northern Illinois University Press, 2006.

Roper, John L., et al. *History of the Eleventh Pennsylvania Volunteer Cavalry, together with a complete roster of the regiment and regimental officers.* Philadelphia: Franklin Printing Company, 1902.

Sallada, William H. *Silver Sheaves, Gathered through Clouds and Sunshine.* Des Moines: Mills & Company, Printers and Stereotypers, 1879.

Samito, Christian G., ed. *Fear Was Not in Him, The Civil War Letters of Major General Francis C. Barlow, U.S.A.* New York: Fordham University Press, 2004.

Schneller Jr., Robert J., ed. *Under the Blue Pennant, or Notes of a Naval Officer 1863–1865, by John W. Grattan, Acting Ensign, United States Navy.* New York: John Wiley & Sons, Inc., 1999.

Scott, Kate M. *History of the One Hundred and Fifth Pennsylvania Volunteers, A Complete History of the Organization, Marches, Battles, Toils, and Dangers Participated in by the Regiment, from the Beginning to the Close of the War, 1861–1865.* Philadelphia: New-World Publishing Company, 1877.

Shaver, Lewellyn Adolphus. *A History of the Sixtieth Alabama Regiment, Gracie's Alabama Brigade: "Jucundi acti Labores."* Montgomery, AL: Barrett & Brown, Publishers, 1867.

Shaw, Horace H. *The First Maine Heavy Artillery, 1862–1865: A History of Its Part and Place in the War for the Union with an Outline of Causes of War and Its Results to Our Country.* Portland, ME: n. p., 1903.

Sheridan, Philip H. *Personal Memoirs of P. H. Sheridan, General United State Army*. 2 vols. New York: Charles L. Webster & Company, 1888.

Silliker, Ruth L., ed. *The Rebel Yell and the Yankee Hurrah: The Civil War Journal of a Maine Volunteer*. Camden, ME: Down East Books, 1985.

Simon, John Y., "The Papers of Ulysses S. Grant, Volume 11: June 1–August 15, 1864" (1984). *Volumes of The Papers of Ulysses S. Grant*. 16. Scholarshipjunction.msstate.edu/usg-volumes/16

Simons, Ezra D. *A Regimental History: The One Hundred and Twenty-Fifth New York State Volunteers*. New York: The Judson Printing Co., 1888.

Smith, John D. *The History of the Nineteenth Regiment of Maine Volunteer Infantry, 1862–1865*. Minneapolis: The Great Western Printing Company, 1909.

Sparks, David S., ed. *Inside Lincoln's Army: The Diary of Marsena Rudolph Patrick, Provost Marshal General, Army of the Potomac*. New York: Thomas Yoseloff, 1964.

Stevens, Charles A. *Berdan's United States Sharpshooters in the Army of the Potomac, 1861–1865*. St. Paul: The Price-McGill Company, 1892.

Stevens, George T. *Three Years in the Sixth Corps. A Concise Narrative of Events in the Army of the Potomac from 1861 to the Close of the Rebellion, April, 1865*. New York: D. Van Nostrand, Publisher, 1870.

Sumner, Merlin E., ed. *The Diary of Cyrus B. Comstock*. Dayton, OH: Morningside, 1987.

Stewart, William H. *A Pair of Blankets: War-Time History in Letters to the Young People of the South*. Wilmington, NC: Broadfoot Publishing Company, 1990.

Stokes, William, and Lloyd Halliburton. *Saddle Soldiers: The Civil War Correspondence of General William Stokes of the 4th South Carolina Cavalry*. Orangeburg, SC: Sandlapper Pub. Co., 1993.

Stowits, George H. *History of the One Hundredth Regiment New York Volunteers, Being a Record of its Services from its Muster in to its Muster out; its Muster in Roll, Roll of Commissions, Recruits Furnished through the Board of Trade of the City of Buffalo, and Short Sketches of Deceased and Surviving Officers*. Buffalo, NY: Printing House of Matthews & Warren, 1870.

Taylor, Michael W., ed. *The Cry is War, War, War: The Civil War Correspondence of Lts. Burwell Thomas Cotton and George Job Huntley, 34th Regiment North Carolina Troops, Pender-Scales Brigade of the Light Division, Stonewall Jackson's and A. P. Hill's Corps, Army of Northern Virginia, CSA*. Dayton, OH: Morningside, 1994.

Tenney, Frances Andrews, ed. *War Diary of Luman Harris Tenney, 1861–1865*. Cleveland: Evangelical Publishing House, 1914.

Thomas, Benjamin P., ed. *Three Years with Grant as Recalled by War Correspondent Sylvanus Cadwallader*. New York: Alfred A. Knopf, 1961.

Toalson, Jeff, ed. *Send me a Pair of Old Boots & Kiss My Little Girls: The Civil War Letters of Richard and Mary Watkins, 1861–1865*. New York: iUniverse, 2009.

Tobie, Edward P. *History of the First Maine Cavalry, 1861–1865*. Boston: Press of Emery & Hughes, 1887.

Tower, R. Lockwood, ed. *Lee's Adjutant: The Wartime Letters of Colonel Walter Herron Taylor, 1862–1865*. Columbia: University of South Carolina Press, 1995.

Turino, Kenneth C., ed. *The Civil War Diary of Lt. J. E. Hodgkins, August 1862 to July 1865*. Camden, ME: Picton Press, 1994.

Tyler, William S., ed. *Recollections of the Civil War with Many Original Entries and Letters Written from the Seat of War, and with Annotated References*. New York: G. P. Putnam's Sons, 1912.

Vaill, Theodore F. *History of the Second Connecticut Volunteer Heavy Artillery, Originally the Nineteenth Connecticut Vols.* Winsted, CT: Winsted, CT, Printing Company, 1868.

Vandiver, Frank E., ed. *The Civil War Diary of Josiah Gorgas.* Tuscaloosa, AL: University of Alabama Press, 1947.

Waitt, Ernest Linden. *History of the Nineteenth Regiment, Massachusetts Volunteer Infantry, 1865–1865.* Salem, MA: The Salem Press Co., 1906.

Walker, Aldace F. *The Vermont Brigade in the Shenandoah Valley, 1864.* Burlington, VT: The Free Press Association, 1869.

Ward, Joseph R. C. *History of the One Hundred and Sixth Regiment Pennsylvania Volunteers, 2d Brigade, 2d Division, 2d Corps, 1861–1865.* Philadelphia, F. McManus, Jr. & Co., 1906.

Welch, Spencer Glasgow. *A Confederate Surgeon's Letters to His Wife.* New York: The Neale Publishing Company, 1911.

Wells, Edward L. *Hampton and His Cavalry in '64.* Richmond: B. F. Johnson Publishing, Co., 1899.

Westbrook, Robert S. *History of the 49th Pennsylvania Volunteers: A Correctly Compiled Roll of the Members of the Regiments and Its Marches from 1861 to 1865.* Altoona, PA: Altoona Times Print, 1898.

White, Russell C., ed. *The Civil War Diary of Wyman S. White, First Sergeant of Company F, 2nd United States Sharpshooter Regiment, 1861–1865.* Baltimore: Butternut and Blue, 1993.

Wiatt, Thomas T., ed. *Rev. William E. Wiatt, The Life and Times of a Confederate Chaplain and Related Family Stories.* Morrisville, NC: Lulu Publishing Services, 2018.

Wickman, Donald H., comp. *Letters to Vermont from Her Civil War Soldier Correspondents to the Home Press.* 2 vols. Bennington, VT: Images From the Past, Inc., 1998.

Wilson, James H. *Under the Old Flag: Recollections of Military Operations in the War for the Union, the Spanish War, the Boxer Rebellion, etc.* 2 vols. New York: D. Appleton and Company, 1912.

Wiggins III, Clyde G., ed. *My Dear Friend: The Civil War Letters of Alva Benjamin Spencer, 3rd Georgia Regiment, Company C.* Macon, GA; Mercer University Press, 2007.

Williams, Edward B, ed. *Rebel Brothers: The Civil War Letters of the Truehearts.* College Station: Texas A & M Press, 1995.

Wise, John S. *The End of an Era.* Boston: Houghton, Mifflin and Company, 1899.

Wixson, Neal E., ed. *Echoes from the Boys of Company "H".* Bloomington, IN: iUniverse, 2008.

Yeary, Mamie, comp. *Reminiscences of the Boys in Gray.* 2 vols. Dallas, TX: Wilkinson Printing Company, 1912.

Younger, Edward, ed. *Inside the Confederate Government: The Diary of Robert Garlick Hill Kean.* Baton Rouge: Louisiana State University Press, 1993.

Government Documents

Bates, Samuel P. *History of Pennsylvania Volunteers, 1861–5, Prepared in Compliance with Acts of the Legislature.* 5 vols. Harrisburg: B. Singerly, State Printer, 1869–1871.

Connecticut, Adjutants-General. *Record of Service of Connecticut Men in the Army and Navy of the United States in the War of the Rebellion.* Hartford, CT: Press of the Case, Lockwood & Brainard Company, 1889.

Dyer, Elisha. *Annual Report of the Adjutant General of the State of Rhode Island and Providence Plantations, for the Year 1865.* Providence: E. L. Freeman & Son, Printers to the State, 1893.

Federal Writers Project. *Slave Narratives, A Folk History of Slavery in the United States From Interviews with Former Slaves: Typewritten Records Prepared by the Federal Writers Project 1936–1938, Assembled by the Library of Congress Project, Works Projects Administration for the District of Columbia Sponsored by the Library of Congress*. Washington, D.C., 1941.

Indiana, Adjutant General's Office. Report of the Adjutant General's Office of the State of Indiana. Vols. II (Indianapolis: W. R. Holloway, State Printer, 1865), and V (Indianapolis: Samuel M. Douglass, State Printer, 1866).

Massachusetts, Adjutant General's Office. *Massachusetts Soldiers, Sailors, and Marines in the Civil War*. 8 vols. Norwood, MA: Norwood Press, 1931.

New Hampshire, Adjutant General. *Report of the Adjutant General of the State of New Hampshire for the Year Ending May 20, 1865*. 2 vols. Concord: Amos Hadley, State Printer, 1865.

Record Group 94, Records of the Adjutant General's Office, National Archives, Washington, D.C.

Record Group 109, War Department Collection of Confederate Records, National Archives, Washington, D.C.

Robertson, Jno., Adjutant General, comp. *Michigan in the Civil War*. Lansing: W. S. George & Co., State Printers and Binders, 1882.

Roster Commission. *Official Roster of the Soldiers of the State of Ohio in the War of the Rebellion, 1861–1866*. 12 vols. Cincinnati: The Werner Co., 1886–1895.

Stryker, William S., Adjutant General. *Record of Officers and Men of New Jersey in the Civil War, 1861–1865*. 2 vols. Trenton, NJ: John L. Murphy, Steam Book and Job Printer, 1876.

United States Naval War Records Office. *Official Records of the Union and Confederate Navies in the War of the Rebellion*. 31 vols and index. Washington, D.C.: Government Printing Office, 1894–1922.

United States War Department. *War of the Rebellion: A Compilation of the Official Records of the Union and Confederate Armies*. 70 vols. in 128 parts. Washington, D.C., Government Printing Office, 1880–1901.

Vermont, Adjutant General. *Revised Roster of Vermont Volunteers and Lists of Vermonters Who Served in the Army and Navy of the United States During the War of the Rebellion, 1861–66*. Montpelier, VT: Press of the Watchman Publishing Co., Publishers and Printers, 1892.

Wilmer, L. Allison, Jarrett, J. H., and Vernon, Geo. W. F. *History and Roster of Maryland Volunteers, War of 1861–5, Prepared Under Authority of The General Assembly of Maryland*. 2 vols. Baltimore: Press of Guggenheimer, Weil & Co., 1898.

Wisconsin, Adjutant General's Office, *Roster of Wisconsin Volunteers, War of the Rebellion, 1861–1865*. 2 vols. Madison, WI: Democrat Printing Company, State Printer, 1886.

Periodical Collections

"Adjutant Ruffin Y. Ashe." *Fayetteville* (NC) *Semi-Weekly Observer*. Oct. 20, 1864.

"An Account of Wilson's Expedition." *Hartford Courant*. July 12, 1864.

Barringer, Gen. R., and Others. "Cavalry Sketches." *The Charlotte* (NC) *Democrat*. Jan. 22, 1892.

Barringer, Brigadier-General Rufus. "Ninth Regiment (First Cavalry)." In Walter Clark, *Histories of the Several Regiments and Battalions from North Carolina*. 1:416–87.

Beauregard, P. G. T. "Four Days of Battle at Petersburg." In Robert Underwood Johnson and Clarence Clough Buel, *Battles and Leaders of the Civil War*. 4 vols. New York: Thomas Yoseloff, 1884, 1888. 4:540–544.

_____. "The Battle of Petersburg, Part II." *North American Review,* Vol. 145, No. 372 (Nov., 1887), 506-515.

_____. "Letter of General G. T. Beauregard to General C. M. Wilcox, June 9, 1864. *Papers of the Military Historical Society of Massachusetts.* 5:113–117.

"Capt. Wm. C. Tracy." *Vermont Record.* July 22, 1864.

Cheek, W. H. "Additional Sketch Ninth Regiment. (First Cavalry.)" In Walter Clark, *Histories of the Several Regiments and Battalions from North Carolina.* 1:445–487.

Clay, Cecil. "Capture of Fort Harrison—How the Rebels Failed to Retake it." *National Tribune.* Nov. 26, 1881.

Coburn, Jeff L. "An Episode of the Wilson Raid: City Point to Roanoke, Va., June 21–30, 1864." *Maine Bugle.* July 1895.

Crowninshield, Benjamin W. "Cavalry in Virginia in the War of the Rebellion." *Papers of the Military Historical Society of Massachusetts.* 13: 1–32.

D. B. R. "Barringer's N. C. Cavalry Brigade." *The Daily Confederate.* Feb. 22–23, 1865.

De Peyster, J. Watts. "A Military Memoir of William Mahone, Major-General in the Confederate Army." *The Historical Magazine.* Vol. 7, Second Series, No. 6 (June 1870), 390–406.

Eason, J. T. "The Battle Of Staunton River Bridge, VA." *Confederate Veteran* II (1894), 19.

Eldredge, J. E. "The Weldon Railroad Affair." *Vermont Watchman and State Journal.* April 14, 1886,

Farinholt, B. L. "The gallant defense of Staunton river Bridge. From Richmond, Va., Times-dispatch, August 1, 1909." *Southern Historical Society Papers,* XXXVII (1909), 321–325.

_____. "The Staunton River Fight." *Southern Historical Society Papers* XIX (1891), 201–207.

Faulkner, J. B. "Farinholt's Ruse Deceived Enemy." *Richmond Times-Dispatch.* Oct. 17, 1909.

Field, Charles W. "The Campaign of 1864–1865, Narrative of C. W. Field." *Southern Historical Society Papers,* XIV (1886), 542–563.

Fortin, Maurice, ed. "Colonel Hilary A. Herbert's History of the Eighth Alabama Volunteer Regiment, C.S.A." *Alabama Historical Quarterly* 39, nos. 1–4 (1977): 5–321.

"G." to the Editor of the *Buffalo Express,* June 27, 1864. "The Loss of Capt. McKnight's Battery." dmna.ny.gov.

Galloway, John M. "Sixty-Third Regiment." In Walter Clark, *Histories of the Several Regiments and Battalions from North Carolina.* 3:528–43.

"Grant." "Defeat of Wilson's Raiders." *Macon Telegraph,* July 14, 1864. In Hewett, Janet B., et al., eds. *Supplement to the Official Records of the Union and Confederate Armies.* 100 vols. Wilmington, N.C.: Broadfoot Publishing Company, 1994–2001. 7:313.

Hall, Rowland M., and Edward G Longacre. "Would to God that War Was Rendered Impossible:" Letters of Rowland M. Hall, April–July 1864. *The Virginia Magazine of History and Biography,* Vol. 89, No. 4 (Oct. 1981).

"Head Quarters 8th N. Y. Vol.," *Batavia* (NY) *Republican Advocate,* July 12, 1864, beyondthecrater.com.

H. F. S., of Co. G. "From the Fourth Regiment." *Vermont Watchman and State Journal,* July 8, 1864.

Hill, Joshua B. "Forty-First Regiment. (Third Cavalry.)" In Walter Clark, *Histories of the Several Regiments and Battalions from North Carolina.* 2:767–787.

Hurt, William D., to T. M. R. Talcott. August 11, 1909. *Richmond Times-Dispatch.* Sept. 19, 1909.

Irish, Warren W. "How 80 of the 10th N. J. [sic] Cav. Came to be with Gen. Wilson on His Raid in June, 1864." *National Tribune*. Feb. 1, 1900.

J. H. P. "Vermont Cavalry." *Windsor* (VT) *Park*. July 16, 1864.

August V. Kautz, "Wilson Raid: An Expedition to Destroy the Petersburg & Lynchburg and the Richmond & Danville Railroads." *National Tribune*. June 1–15, 1899.

Kennedy, John T., and W. F. Parker. "Seventy-Fifth Regiment. (Seventh Cavalry.)" In Walter Clark, *Histories of the Several Regiments and Battalions from North Carolina*. 4:71–90.

Kuntz, Norbert A., ed. "A Brookfield Soldier's Report: The Civil War Recollections of Edwin C. Hall." *Vermont History*, Vol. 57, No. 4 (Fall 1989).

"Local and State Items," *The Rutland* (VT) *Weekly Herald*. Oct. 12, 1865.

Matthews, H. H. "A Maryland Confederate Matchless for Hard Fighting and Bravery, Recollections of Major James Breathed." *Southern Historical Society Papers* XXX (1902), 346–348.

_____. "Pelham-Breathed Battery, Part XVII, Expedition of Gens. Wilson and Kautz Against the Richmond and Weldon Railroad." *St. Mary's Beacon* (Leonardtown, MD). June 15, 1905.

McAlpine, Newton. "Sketch of. Company I, 61st Virginia Infantry, Mahone's Brigade, C. S. A." *Southern Historical Society Papers* XXIV (1896), 98–107.

McPhail, John B. "Another Account of the Fight." *Southern Historical Society Papers* XIX (1891), 55–56.

McPhail, Paul C. "The Battle of Staunton River Bridge, As Seen by Paul C. McPhail, Sergeant of Engineer Troops, C.S.A., Who Participated in the Engagement." *Richmond Times-Dispatch*. Sept. 19, 1909.

Means, Paul B. "Additional Sketch Sixty-Third Regiment. (Fifth Cavalry.)" In Walter Clark, *Histories of the Several Regiments and Battalions from North Carolina*, 3:545–657.

Methvin, T. V. "In the Wilderness Campaign." *Confederate Veteran* XXIII (1915), 455–456.

Old Po'keepsie. "From the 2nd Ohio Cavalry." *Painesville* (OH) *Telegraph*. July 14, 1864.

Pomfret, John E., and Fred Lockley. "Letters of Fred Lockley, Union Soldier 1864–65," *Huntington Library Quarterly*, Vol. 16, No. 1 (Nov. 1952).

Pope, Edmund M. "Personal Experience—A Side Light of the Wilson Raid, June 1864." In *Glimpses of the Nation's Struggle: Papers Read before the Minnesota Commander of the Military Order of the Loyal Legion of the United States, 1897–1897*, 4:585–604. St. Paul: H. L. Collins, 1898.

Pryor, Anne Banister. "A Child's Recollections Of War." *Confederate Veteran* XXXIX (1931), 54–55.

W. H. D. "Interesting Account of the Adventures of a Squadron of the 8th N. Y. Cavalry Cut Off from the Wilson Raiding Party." *Rochester Daily Union and Advertiser*. July 20, 1864.

Wagstaff, Henry McGilbert, ed. "Letters of Thomas Jackson Strayhorn." *North Carolina Historical Review*, vol. 13 (1936).

Webster, E. H. "Prison Experiences." *Orleans County* (VT) *Monitor*. Dec. 25, 1899.

_____. "Prison Experiences, No. 5." *Orleans County* (VT) *Monitor*. Jan. 29, 1900.

Wilcox, C. M. "Military Operations Around Petersburg, the Mine, etc." *The New Orleans Times*. Jan. 1, 1872.

Wilson, James H. "The Cavalry of the Army of the Potomac." *Papers of the Military Historical Society of Massachusetts*. 13:33–88.

Young, John D. "A Campaign with Sharpshooters." In Alexander Kelly McClure, ed., *The Annals of the War Written by Leading Participants North and South*. Philadelphia: The Times Publishing Co., 1879.

Zachry, Alfred. "Four Shots for the Cause." In *Civil War Times Illustrated.* Nov./Dec. 1994. Vol. XXXIII, No. 5.

Newspapers

Southern Watchman (Athens, GA)

Daily Constitutionalist (Augusta, GA)

Chronicle & Sentinel (Augusta, GA)

Batavia (NY) *Republican Advocate*

Buffalo Express

Charleston (SC) *News and Courier*

The Charlotte (NC) *Democrat*

Fayetteville Semi-Weekly Observer

Hartford Courant

St. Mary's Beacon (Leonardtown, MD)

Macon (GA) *Daily Confederate.*

Macon (GA) *Daily Telegraph*

Montgomery (AL) *Daily Mail*

Montgomery (AL) *Daily Advertiser*

National Tribune

The New Orleans Times

New York Herald

Orleans County Monitor (Barton, VT)

Painesville (OH) *Telegraph*

Petersburg Daily Express

The Daily Register (Petersburg, VA)

Philadelphia Inquirer

The Daily Confederate (Raleigh, NC)

The Daily Richmond Dispatch

The Daily Richmond Enquirer

Semi-Weekly Richmond Enquirer

Daily Richmond Examiner

Richmond Times-Dispatch

Rochester Daily Union and Advertiser

The Rutland (VT) Weekly *Herald*

The Caledonian (St. Johnsbury, VT)

Vermont Record (Brandon, VT)

Vermont Watchman and State Journal (Montpelier, VT)

Evening Star (Washington, D.C.)

Windsor (VT) *Park*

Secondary Sources

Unpublished

Bearss, Edwin C. "The Battle of the Jerusalem Plank Road, June 21–24, 1864." Petersburg National Battlefield Park, Petersburg, VA.

Garcia, Christopher M. "The Forgotten Sixty-Ninth: The Sixty-Ninth New York National Guard

Artillery Regiment in the Civil War." May 2012. Old Dominion University, Norfolk, VA.

Jordan, Weymouth T., Jr., comp. *North Carolina Troops 1861–1865, A Roster*. Vol. 5. Raleigh, NC: Division of Archives and History, 1975.

Lauter, D. R. "Winslow Homer Sketches The 'Piece of Shell' That Caused a Headache." Condensed from Chapter II *Winslow Homer and Friends in Prince George County and Dinwiddie County, Virginia 1864-1865*. Private Collection of John Horn, Hinsdale, IL.

Lauter, Donald Richard. Unpublished Records of Artifacts Recovered from the Battlefields of Southeastern Virginia. Private Collection of Donald Richard Lauter, Disputanta, VA.

Parker, William L. "Brigadier General James Dearing, C. S. A." August 1969. Virginia Polytechnic Institute, Blacksburg, VA.

Suderow, Bryce A. "Chapter 1: June 18–25, 1864, Operations at Petersburg." Private Collection of Bryce A Suderow, Washington, D.C.

_____. "Confederate Casualties During the Siege of Petersburg, June 13–Aug. 25, 1864." Private Collection of Bryce A. Suderow, Washington, D.C.

_____. *Target Richmond!: The Civil War North of the James, June 20–August 21, 1864*. Private Collection of Bryce A. Suderow, Washington, D.C.

Young, Alfred C., III. "Confederate Casualties during June 1864 at Petersburg." Private Collection of Alfred C. Young III, PA.

Published

Books

Angelovich, Robert B. *Riding for Uncle Samuel: The Civil War History of the 1st Connecticut Cavalry Volunteers*. Grand Rapids, MI: Inner Workings, Inc., 2014.

Armstrong, Richard L. *7th Virginia Cavalry*. Lynchburg, VA: H. E. Howard, Inc., 1993.

Badeau, Adam. *Military History of Ulysses S. Grant, From April 1861 to April 1865*. 3 vols. New York: D. Appleton and Company, 1882.

Balfour, Daniel T. *13th Virginia Cavalry*. Lynchburg, VA: H. E. Howard, Inc., 1986.

Barram, Rick. *The 72nd New York Infantry in the Civil War: A History and Roster*. Jefferson, NC: McFarland & Company, Inc., Publishers, 2014.

Barringer, Sheridan R. *Fighting for General Lee: Confederate General Rufus Barringer and the North Carolina Cavalry Brigade*. El Dorado Hills, CA: Savas Beatie, 2016.

Bearss, Edwin C., with Bryce A. Suderow. *The Petersburg Campaign*. 2 vols. El Dorado Hills, CA: Savas Beatie, 2012.

Benedict, G. G. *Vermont in the Civil War: A History of the Part Taken by the Vermont Soldiers and Sailors in the War for the Union, 1861–1865.* 2 vols. Burlington, VT: The Free Press Association, 1888.

Blake, Nelson Morehouse. *William Mahone of Virginia: Soldier and Political Insurgent.* Richmond: Garrett & Massie, Publishers, 1935.

Bonekemper, Edward H., III. *A Victor, Not a Butcher: Ulysses S. Grant's Overlooked Military Genius.* Washington, D.C.: Regnery History, 2004.

Bridges, David P. *Fighting with Jeb Stuart: Major James Breathed and the Confederate Horse Artillery.* Arlington, VA: Breathed Bridges Best, Inc., 2006.

Carmichael, Peter S. C. *Lee's Young Artillerist: William R. J. Pegram.* Charlottesville: University of Virginia Press, 1995.

_____. *The Purcell, Letcher & Crenshaw Artillery.* Lynchburg, VA: H. E. Howard, Inc., 1991.

Castel, Albert E. *Decision in the West: The Atlanta Campaign of 1864.* Lawrence, KS: University Press of Kansas, 1992.

Cavanaugh, Michael A., and William Marvel. *The Battle Of The Crater: "The Horrid Pit," June 25–August 6, 1864.* Lynchburg, VA: H. E. Howard, Inc., 1987.

Chernow, Ron. *Grant.* New York: Penguin Press, 2017.

Chick, Sean Michael. *Dreams of Victory: General P. G. T. Beauregard and the Civil War.* El Dorado Hills, CA: Savas Beatie, 2021.

Clark, Lewis H. *Military History of Wayne County, N.Y.: The County in the Civil War* (Syracuse, NY: Truair, Smith & Bruce, Printers and Binders, 1883.

Cleaves, Freeman. *Meade of Gettysburg.* Norman, OK: University of Oklahoma Press, 1960.

Coffman, Richard. *Going Back the Way Them Came: The Phillips Georgia Cavalry Legion Battalion.* Macon, GA: Mercer University Press, 2011.

Coggins, Jack. *Arms and Equipment of the Civil War.* Garden City, NY: Dover Publications, 2004.

Collea, Joseph D., Jr. *The First Vermont Cavalry in the Civil War: A History.* Jefferson, NC: McFarland & Company, Inc., Publishers, 2010.

Crew Jr., R. Thomas, and Benjamin H Trask. *Grimes' Battery, Grandy's Battery and Huger's Battery Virginia Artillery.* Lynchburg, VA: H. E. Howard, Inc., 1995.

Croffut, W. A., and John M. Morris. *The Military and Civil History of Connecticut During the War of 1861–65, Comprising a Detailed Account of the Regiments and Batteries through March, Encampment, Bivouac, and Battle; also Instances of Distinguished Personal Gallantry, and Biographical Sketches of Many Heroic Soldiers; together with a Record of the Patriotic Actions of Citizens at Home, and of the Liberal Support Furnished by the State in Its Executive and Legislative Departments.* 2 vols. New York: Ledyard Bill, 1868.

Cross, David Faris. *A Melancholy Affair at the Weldon Railroad: The Vermont Brigade, June 23, 1864.* Shippensburg, PA: White Mane Publishing Co., 2003.

Dana, Charles A., and J. H. Wilson. *The Life of Ulysses S. Grant, General of the Armies of the United States.* Springfield, MA: Gurdon, Bill & Company, 1868.

Daughtry, Mary Bandy. *Gray Cavalier: The Life and Wars of General W. H. F. "Rooney" Lee.* Boston: Da Capo Press, 2002.

Davis, Oliver Wilson. *Life of David Bell Birney, Major-General United States Volunteers.* Philadelphia: King & Baird, 1867.

Divine, John E. *35th Battalion Virginia Cavalry.* Lynchburg, VA: H. E. Howard, Inc., 1985.

Driver Jr., Robert J. *1st Virginia Cavalry*. Lynchburg, VA: H. E. Howard, Inc., 1991.

_____. *2nd Virginia Cavalry*. Lynchburg, VA: H. E. Howard, Inc., 1995.

_____. *Richmond Local Defense Troops C.S.A.* Wilmington, NC: Broadfoot Publishing Company, 2011.

Dunn, William Russell. *Full Measure of Devotion: The Eighth New York Volunteer Heavy Artillery*. 2 vols. Kearney, NE: Morris Publishing, 1997.

Dupuy, T. N. *A Genius for War: The German Army and General Staff, 1807–1945*. London: MacDonald and Jane's, 1977.

_____, et al. *Handbook on Ground Forces Attrition in Modern Warfare*. Fairfax, VA: Data Memory Systems, Inc., 1986.

Dyer, Frederick H. *A Compendium of the War of the Rebellion: Compiled and Arranged from Official Records of the Federal and Confederate Armies Reports of the Adjutant Generals of the Several States, the Army Registers and Other Reliable Documents and Sources*. Des Moines: The Dyer Publishing Company, 1908.

Eanes, Greg. *Destroy the Junction: The Wilson-Kautz Raid and the Battle for the Staunton River Bridge*. Lynchburg, VA: H. E. Howard, Inc., 1999.

Evans, Clement A., ed. *Confederate Military History, A Library of Confederate States History, In Twelve Volumes, Written by Distinguished Men of the South*. 12 vols. Atlanta: Confederate Publishing Company, 1899.

Evans, Robert G., ed. *The 16th Mississippi Infantry: Civil War Letters and Reminiscences*. Jackson, MS: The University Press of Mississippi, 2002.

Fox, John J. III. *Red Clay to Richmond: Trail of the 35th Georgia Infantry Regiment, C.S.A.* Winchester, VA: Angle Valley Press, 2005.

Fox, William F. *Regimental Losses in the American Civil War, 1861–1865*. Albany, NY: Albany Publishing Company, 1889.

Freeman, Douglas Southall. *R. E. Lee: A Biography*. 4 vols. New York: Charles Scribner's Sons, 1934–1935.

_____. *Lee's Lieutenants: A Study in Command*. 3 vols. New York: Charles Scribner's Sons, 1942–1944.

Fuller, J. F. C. *The Generalship of Ulysses S. Grant*. New York: Dodd, Mead and Company, 1929.

Girvan, Jeffrey M. *The 55th North Carolina in the Civil War, A History and Roster*. Jefferson, NC: McFarland & Company, Inc., Publishers, 2006.

Gleeson, Ed. *Erin Go Gray! An Irish Rebel Trilogy*. Carmel, IN: Guild Press of Indiana, 1997.

Goecker, James A. *Hoosier Spies and Horse Marines: A History of the Third Indiana Cavalry, East Wing*. Jefferson, NC: McFarland & Company, Inc., 2023.

Greene, A. Wilson. *A Campaign of Giants: The Battle for Petersburg*. 3 vols. Projected. Chapel Hill, NC: University of North Carolina Press, 2018.

_____. *Civil War Petersburg: Confederate City in the Crucible of War*. Charlottesville: University of Virginia Press, 2007.

_____. *The Final Battles of the Petersburg Campaign: Breaking the Back of the Rebellion*.Knoxville, TN: University of Tennessee Press, 2012.

Griffin, Ronald G. *The 11th Alabama Volunteer Regiment in the Civil War*. Jefferson, NC: McFarland & Company, Inc., Publishers, 2008.

Hardy, Michael C. *General Lee's Immortals: The Battles and Campaigns of the Branch-Lane Brigade in the Army of Northern Virginia, 1861–1865*. El Dorado Hills, CA: Savas Beatie, 2018.

Harrell, Roger H. *The 2nd North Carolina Cavalry*. Jefferson, NC: McFarland & Company, Inc., Publishers, 2004.

Hart, B. H. Liddell. *Strategy*. New York: Meridian, 1991.

Headspeth, W. Carroll. *The Battle of Staunton River Bridge*. South Boston, VA: Creative Link, 1997.

Henderson, Lillian. *Roster of the Confederate Soldiers of Georgia, 1861–1865*. 5 vols. Hapeville, GA: Longino & Porter, Inc, 1959–1964.

Henderson, William D. *Petersburg in the Civil War: War at the Door*. Lynchburg, VA: H. E. Howard, Inc., 1998.

_____. *12th Virginia Infantry*. Lynchburg, VA: H. E. Howard, Inc., 1988.

Hess, Earl J. *In the Trenches at Petersburg: Field Fortifications and Confederate Defeat.*

_____. *Into the Crater: The Mine Attack at Petersburg*. Columbia, SC: University of South Carolina Press, 2010.

Hoehling, Adolph A. *Thunder at Hampton Roads: The U.S.S. Monitor—Its Battle with the Merrimack and Its Recent Discovery.* Boston: Da Capo Press, 1993.

Horn, John. *The Petersburg Campaign: June 1864–April 1865*. Conshohocken, PA: Combined Books, 1993.

_____. *The Siege of Petersburg: The Battles for the Weldon Railroad, August 1864*. El Dorado Hills, Ca.: Savas Beatie, 2015.

_____. *The Petersburg Regiment in the Civil War: A History of the 12th Virginia Infantry from John Brown's Hanging to Appomattox, 1859–1865*. El Dorado Hills, CA: Savas Beatie, 2019.

Hudnall, William R. *Three Confederates from Kanawha County, West Virginia: The Hudnalls, Why & How They Served and The Men Who Led Them*. New Canton, VA: Kelly's Creek Publishers, 2001.

Humphreys, Andrew A. *The Virginia Campaign of '64 and '65: The Army of the Potomac and the Army of the James*. New York: Charles Scribner's Sons, 1883.

Husk, Martin W. *The 111th New York Volunteer Infantry, A Civil War History*. Jefferson, NC: McFarland & Company, Inc., Publishers, 2009.

Hyde, Thomas W. *Following the Greek Cross, Or, Memories of the Sixth Army Corps*. Boston: Houghton, Mifflin and Co., 1894.

Kautz, Lawrence G. *August Valentine Kautz, Biography of a Civil War General.* Jefferson, NC: McFarland & Company, Publishers, 2008.

Knight, Charles R. *From Arlington to Appomattox: Robert E. Lee's Civil War Day by Day, 1861–1865*. El Dorado Hills, CA: Savas Beatie, 2021.

Kotar, S. L., & J. E. Gessler, eds. *The Kepi Volume III and IV, A New Concept in Civil War Reporting*. St. Louis: Ahead of The Press Publishing, 2018.

Krick, Robert E. L. *Staff Officers in Gray: A Biographical Register of the Staff Officers in the Army of Northern Virginia*. Chapel Hill: The University of North Carolina Press, 2003.

Krick, Robert K. *9th Virginia Cavalry*. Lynchburg, VA: H. E. Howard, Inc., 1988.

Livermore, Thomas L. *Numbers and Losses in the Civil War in America 1861–1865*. Boston: Houghton, Mifflin and Company, 1900.

Longacre, Edward G. *Grant's Cavalryman: The Life and Wars of General James H. Wilson*. Mechanicsburg, PA: Stackpole Books, 1996.

_____. *Army of Amateurs: General Benjamin F. Butler and the Army of the James, 1863-1865*. Mechanicsburg, PA: Stackpole Books, 1997.

_____. *Gentleman and Soldier: A Biography of Wade Hampton III.* Lincoln, NE: University of Nebraska Press, 2003.

_____. *Fitz Lee: A Military Biography of Major General Fitzhugh Lee, C. S. A.* Cambridge, MA: Da Capo Press, 2005.

Lubrecht, Peter T. *New Jersey Butterfly Boys in the Civil War, The Hussars of the Union Army.* Charleston, SC: The History Press, 2011.

Luhrs, Kathleen, ed. *American Paintings in the Metropolitan Museum of Art.* 3 vols. Princeton, NJ: Princeton University Press, 1994.

Macrae, David. *The Americans at Home: Pen-and-Ink Sketches of American Men, Manners and Institutions.* 2 vols. Edinburgh: Edmonston and Douglas, 1870.

Mahood, Wayne, *"Written in Blood": A History of the 126th New York Infantry in the Civil War.* Hightstown, NJ: Longstreet House, 1997.

Marchall, Michael. *Gallant Creoles: A History of the Donaldson Canonniers.* Lafayette, LA: UL Press, 2013.

Martin, David G. *The Great Military Campaigns of the Civil War: The Vicksburg Campaign, April, 1862–July, 1863.* New York: Gallery Books, 1990.

McMurry, Richard M. *Atlanta 1864: Last Chance for the Confederacy.* Lincoln, NE: University of Nebraska Press, 2001.

Mesic, Harriet Bey. *Cobb's Legion Cavalry: A History and Roster of the Ninth Georgia Volunteers in the Civil War.* Jefferson, NC: McFarland & Company, Inc., Publishers, 2009.

Miller, Donald L. *Vicksburg: Grant's Campaign that Broke the Confederacy.* New York: Simon & Schuster, 2019.

Miller, Francis Trevelyan, and Robert S. Lanier. *The Photographic History of the Civil War.* 10 vols. New York: The Review of Reviews Co., 1910.

Mitchell, Wesley Clair. *A History of the Greenbacks with Special Reference to the Economic Consequences of Their Issue: 1862–1865.* Chicago: The University of Chicago Press, 1903.

Neale, Gay. *Brunswick County, Virginia 1720–1975.* Brunswick County, VA: Brunswick County, 1975.

Newsome, Hampton. *Richmond Must Fall: The Richmond-Petersburg Campaign, October 1864.* Kent, Oh.: The Kent State University Press, 2013.

Newton, Steven H. *Lost for the Cause: The Confederate Army in 1864.* Mason City, IA: Savas Publishing Company, 2000.

Ottens, Allen J. *General John A. Rawlins, No Ordinary Man.* Bloomington, IN: University of Indiana Press, 2022.

Parsons, George W. *Put the Vermonters Ahead: The First Vermont Brigade in the Civil War.* Shippensburg, PA: White Mane Publishing Company, Inc.

Patchan, Scott C. *Shenandoah Summer: The 1864 Valley Campaign.* Lincoln, NE: Bison Books, 2007.

Patterson, Gerard A. *From Blue to Gray: The Life of Confederate General Cadmus M. Wilcox.* Mechanicsburg, PA: Stackpole Books, 2001.

Phisterer, Frederick. *Statistical Record of the Armies of the United States.* New York: Charles Scribner's Sons, 1883.

_____. *New York in the War of Rebellion, 1861–1865.* 6 vols. J. B. Lyon Company, State Printers, 1912.

Porter, David D. *The Naval History of the Civil War.* New York: The Sherman Publishing Company, 1886.

Powell, David. *Failure in the Saddle: Nathan Bedford Forrest, Joseph Wheeler, and the Confederate Cavalry in the Chickamauga Campaign.* El Dorado Hills, CA: Savas Beatie, 2011.

Powell, William H. *The Fifth Army Corps (Army of the Potomac) A Record of Operations during the Civil War in the United States of America, 1861–1865.* New York: G. P. Putnam's Sons, 1896.

Rahe, Paul. *Sparta's Sicilian Proxy War: The Grand Strategy of Classical Sparta, 418–413 B.C.* New York: Encounter Books, 2023.

Rigdon, John C. *Historical Sketch and Roster of the Georgia 22nd Infantry Regiment.* Cartersville, GA: Eastern Digital Resources, 2003.

_____. *Historical Sketch and Roster of the Georgia 48th Infantry Regiment.* Cartersville, GA: Eastern Digital Resources, 2003.

Robertson, Fred L, comp. *Soldiers of Florida in the Seminole Indian, Civil, Spanish-American Wars.* Live Oak, FL: Democrat Book and Job Print, 1903.

Robertson, William Glenn. *The First Battle for Petersburg: The Attack and Defense of the Cockade City, June 9, 1864.* El Dorado Hills, CA: Savas Beatie, 2015.

Robinson, Charles M. III. *Bad Hand: A Biography of General Ranald S. Mackenzie.* Abilene, TX: State House Press, 2005.

Roman, Alfred. *The Military Operations of General Beauregard in the War Between the States 1861 to 1865 with a Brief Personal Sketch and a Narrative of His Services in the War with Mexico 1846–1848.* 2 vols. New York: Harper & Brothers, Franklin Square, 1884.

Rowland, Dunbar. *Military History of Mississippi, 1803–1898.* Spartanburg, SC: The Reprint Company, Publishers, 1988.

Schmutz, John F. *The Battle of the Crater: A Complete History.* Jefferson, NC: McFarland & Company, Inc., Publishers, 2009.

Schultz, David L., and Scott L. Mingus Sr. *The Second Day at Gettysburg: The Attack and Defense of Cemetery Ridge, July 2, 1863.* El Dorado Hills, CA: Savas Beatie, 2016.

Scott, James G., and Edward A. Wyatt. *Petersburg's Story: A History.* Petersburg, VA: Titmus Optical Co., 1960.

Sears, Stephen W. *To the Gates of Richmond: The Peninsula Campaign.* New York: Ticknor & Fields, 1992.

Sherwood, George L. *The Mathews Light Artillery; Penick's Pittsylvania Artillery; Young's Halifax Light Artillery, & Johnson's Jackson Flying Artillery.* Lynchburg, VA: H. E. Howard, Inc. 1999.

Simpson, Marc, comp. *Winslow Homer: Paintings of the Civil War.* San Francisco: Fine Arts Museum of San Francisco, 1988.

Slotkin, Richard. *No Quarter: The Battle of the Crater, 1864.* New York: Random House, 2009.

Sommers, Richard J. *Richmond Redeemed: The Siege at Petersburg, The Battles of Chaffin's Bluff and Poplar Spring Church, September 29–October 2, 1864.* El Dorado Hills, CA: Savas Beatie, 2014.

Starr, Stephen Z. *The Union Cavalry in the Civil War.* 3 vols. Baton Rouge: Louisiana State University Press, 1985.

Styles, Kenneth L. *4th Virginia Cavalry.* Lynchburg, VA: H. E. Howard, Inc., 1985.

Swinton, William. *Campaigns of the Army of the Potomac, A Critical History of Operations in Virginia, Maryland and Pennsylvania from the Commencement to the Close of the War, 1861–1865.* New York: Charles Scribner's Sons, 1882.

Symonds, Craig L. *Lincoln and His Admirals.* Oxford: Oxford University Press, 2008.

Toomey, Daniel Carroll. *The Maryland Brigade.* Baltimore: Toomey Press, 2018.

Trask, Benjamin H. *16th Virginia Infantry.* Lynchburg, VA: H. E. Howard, Inc., 1986.

Trout, Robert J. *Galloping Thunder: The Stuart Horse Artillery Battalion.* Mechanicsburg, PA: Stackpole Books, 2002.

_____, ed. *Memoirs of the Stuart Light Artillery Battalion.* 2 vols. Knoxville: The University of Tennessee Press, 2010.

Trudeau, Noah Andre. *The Last Citadel: Petersburg, June 1864–April 1865.* El Dorado Hills, CA: Savas Beatie, 2014.

Trumbull, H. Clay. *The Knightly Soldier, A Biography of Major Henry Ward Camp. Philadelphia*: John D. Wattles, Publisher, 1892.

Walker, Francis A. *Great Commanders: General Hancock.* New York: D. Appleton and Company, 1895.

_____. *History of the Second Army Corps in the Army of the Potomac.* New York: Charles Scribner's Sons, 1886.

Wallace, Lee A., Jr. *A Guide to Virginia Military Organizations 1861–1865.* Lynchburg, VA: H. E. Howard, Inc., 1986.

Walters, John. *Norfolk Blues: The Civil War Diary of the Norfolk Light Artillery Blues.* Shippensburg, PA: Burd Street Press, 1997.

Warner, Ezra J. *Generals in Blue: Lives of the Union Commanders.* Baton Rouge: Louisiana State University Press, 1964.

_____. *Generals in Gray: Lives of the Confederate Commanders.* Baton Rouge: Louisiana State University Press, 1959.

Waters, Zack C., and James D. Edmonds, *A Small but Spartan Band: The Florida Brigade in Lee's Army of Northern Virginia.* Tuscaloosa: University of Alabama Press, 2010.

Welch, Richard F. *The Boy General: The Life and Careers of Francis Channing Barlow.* Madison, NJ: Farleigh Dickinson University Press, 2003.

Wilson, James Harrison. *The Life of John A. Rawlins: Lawyer, Assistant Adjutant General, Chief of Staff, Major General of Volunteers, and Secretary of War.* New York: The Neale Publishing Company, 1916.

Wise, Jennings C. *The Long Arm of Lee, Or The History of the Artillery of the Army of Northern Virginia, With a Brief Account of the Confederate Bureau of Ordnance.* 2 vols. Lynchburg, VA: J. P. Bell Company, Inc., 1915.

Wittenberg, Eric J. *Glory Enough for All: Sheridan's Second Raid and the Battle of Trevilian Station.* Dulles, VA: Brassey's, Inc., 2001.

Young, Alfred C. III. *Lee's Army During the Overland Campaign, A Numerical Study.* Baton Rouge: Louisiana State University Press, 2013.

Articles

"35th Infantry Regiment, Army of Northern Virginia, Rosters." ranger95.com.

Brown, Russell. "Ambrose Wright." New Georgia Encyclopedia, georgiaencyclopedia.org.

Daniel, Larry. "The South Almost Won by Not Losing: A Rebuttal." *North & South*, No. 3 (Feb. 1998), 44–51.

Dodge, Theodore A. "Grant as a Soldier." In Theodore F. Dwight, ed. "Critical Sketches of Some of the Federal and Confederate Commanders." *Papers of the Military Historical Society of Massachusetts.* 10:34–35.

Epperson, Jim. "A secret sidebar to the Wilson-Kautz Raid." petersburgsiege.org.

"Georgia 49th Infantry Regiment." researchonline.net.

Horn, John. "The Army of the Potomac's proud III Corps fell victim to intra-army politics." *America's Civil War* (July 1993), 16, 20, 24, 74.

_____. "The Myth that Mahone Did Not Move on July 2, 1863." *Gettysburg Magazine*, no. 65 (July 2021), 47–57.

_____. "A Most Remarkable Officer." *North & South*, Series II, Vol. 4, No. 1 (Dec. 2023), 29–36.

_____. "Confederate Command Chaos June 22, 1864." North & South, Series II, Vol. 4, No. 3 (May 2024), 45–50.

Jussell, Paul, et al. "A Man of Maladies: Reexamining Lt. Gen. A. P. Hill's Leadership Failures at Gettysburg and Beyond." *Gettysburg Magazine*, No. 55 (July 2016), 40–57.

Lauter, Don Richard. "'*Once Upon a Time in the East* . . . ' Arabella Wharton Griffith Barlow."

In *The Journal of Women's Civil War History, From the Home Front to the Front Lines: Accounts of the Sacrifice, Achievement, and Service of American Women, 1861–1865*. Vol. 1, 8–25.

Marten, James. "A Disappointment to His Friends: 'The unknown story of the Brooks Expedition.'" *The Civil War Monitor*, Winter 2023, Vol. 13, No. 4, 46–53, 74.

Mitchell, Wesley C. "The Value of the 'Greenbacks' During the Civil War." *The Journal of Political Economy*, March 1898, 139–167.

Rhea, Gordon C. "Cold Harbor, Anatomy of a Battle." *North & South,* Vol. 5, No. 2 (Feb. 2002), 40–62.

Suderow, Bryce A. "Confederate Casualties Near the Jerusalem Plank Road: June 21–June 23, 1864." *The Kepi*, Vol. 3, No. 5 (Oct.–Nov. 1985), 6–18.

_____. "Confederate Casualties During the Wilson-Kautz Raid: June 22–July 2, 1864." *The Kepi*, Vol. 4, No. 1 (Spring 1986), 31–53.

Online sites

american-rails.com

appomattoxcountyva.gov

battlefields.org

civilwar.org

civilwarintheeast.com

cmohs.org

drillpad.net

dunhamwilcox.net

emergingcivilwar.com

findagrave.com

fold3.com

georgiaencyclopedia.org

hmdb.org

johnhorncivilwarauthor.blogspot.com

merriam-webster.com

nps.gov
odysseymagazine.com
petersburgsiege.org
ranger95.com
researchonline.net
rootsweb.com
surrycountyvahistory.org
thoughtco.com
timeanddate.com
virginia.org
virginiaplaces.org
winslowhomer.org
worldhistory.org

Maps

Campbell, Albert H. *Map of the vicinity of Petersburg*. Made under the direction of A. H. Campbell, Captn P.E. C.S.A. in charge Topl Dept D.N.V[.] Library of Congress.

_____, *Map of Dinwiddie County, Va.*: surveyed under the direction of A.H. Campbell, Capt. Engr's. P.A.C.S. in ch'ge Top'l Dep't. D.N. Va. Library of Congress.

Cowles, Calvin D., comp. *The Official Military Atlas of the Civil War*. New York: Gramercy Books, 1983.

Lauter, Donald Richard. Unpublished Maps of the Battle of Jerusalem Plank Road. Private Collection of John Horn, Hinsdale, IL.

Mahone, William. Sketch map of the Weldon Battlefield drawn by General Mahone that accompanied his letter to George G. Benedict in 1887. In David Faris Cross, *A Melancholy Affair at the Weldon Railroad: The Vermont Brigade, June 23, 1864* (Shippensburg, PA: White Mane Publishing Co., 2003), 67.

William Mahone to George G. Benedict, October 2, 1887. George G. Benedict Papers. Bailey Howe Library, University of Vermont, Burlington, VT.

Record Group 77, Maps of the area in the vicinity of Petersburg and Richmond compiled under the direction of Bvt. Brig. Gen. N. Michler, 1865–1867. National Archives, Washington, D.C.

United States Geological Survey. Virginia 7.5 Minute Series. Carson, Drewry's Bluff, Dutch Gap, Hopewell, Jarratt, Petersburg, Prince George and Stony Creek Quadrangles.

Untitled Map showing the lines of operations of the Army of the Potomac from the Rapidan River to Petersburg (Federal Engineers Map dated June 21, 1864); Virginia and the Chesapeake Bay File Unit; Civil Works Map File, 1818–1947 Series; RG 77, National Archives, Washington, D.C.

Willian, John. Map of Battle of Jerusalem Plank Road, June 22, 1864. John Willian Papers, Private Collection of John Horn, Hinsdale, IL.

Index

About the Author

Chicago native John Horn majored in English and Latin at New College (Sarasota, Florida) and has practiced law around Chicago since graduating from New York's Columbia Law School in 1976. In addition to many articles, he has written three more books about the siege of Petersburg and that city's soldiers and co-edited another. John's previous book, *The Petersburg Regiment in the Civil War: A History of the 12th Virginia Infantry from John Brown's Hanging to Appomattox, 1859–1865* (Savas Beatie) won the 2019 Army Historical Foundation's Distinguished Writing Award for Unit History. John is popular on the speaking circuit and has blogged at johnhorncivilwarauthor.blogspot.com since 2015. John's wife and law partner hails from Richmond, Virginia, and they often visit relatives there.